# Political Revolutions of the 18th, 19th, and 20th Centuries

## Timeline

### Russian Revolution

- **1905** **January 22** Petrograd demonstrations lead to "Bloody Sunday"
- **1917** **March 8** Street violence breaks out and leads to the "February Revolution"

  **March 15** Czar Nicholas abdicates his throne

  **November 6** "October Revolution" begins
- **1918** **July 17** Entire Romanov family is assassinated by Bolshevik gunmen
- **1921** Lenin announces the New Economic Policy
- **1924** Lenin dies, leaving Stalin to take power

### Iranian Revolution

- **1941** Muhammad Reza Shah rises to the throne
- **1951** Muhammad Reza Shah is challenged by Mossadeq
- **1963** Shah launches his "White Revolution"
- **1978** Anti-Shah demonstrations hit Tehran
- **1979** **January** Shah and his family leave Iran, never to return

  **April** Islamic law becomes law of the land in Iran

**1905 ·········· 1924**

**1910 ·········· 1920**

**1911 ························· 1975**

**1941 ························· 1979**

— 1900 — — 1950 —

### Mexican Revolution

- **1910** Madero leads revolution against Diaz regime
- **1912** Huerta defeats opponents to Madero's presidency
- **1913** Huerta turns on Madero, and seizes the presidency for himself
- **1914** **August** Huerta goes into exile in Spain
- **1915** Carranza rises to the presidency
- **1916** Carranza calls for constitutional convention
- **1920** Obregon establishes his own presidency

### Chinese Revolution

- **1911** Spontaneous revolution breaks out in China
- **1921** Chinese Communist Party is formed
- **1934–1935** Maoists engage in desperate "Long March"
- **1940** Communist leader Mao Zedong outlines the "New Democracy"
- **1949** Mao establishes the People's Republic of China
- **1958–1962** Mao's "Great Leap Forward"
- **1959** Mao resigns as "chairman" of the People's Republic
- **1975** Mao Zedong dies

# Political Revolutions

of the 18th, 19th, and 20th Centuries

Before the French Revolution, the Bastille prison in Paris held many political prisoners. This 1789 painting by Jean-Pierre Houel, *Storming the Bastille*, immortalizes the attack on the prison, which became a symbol of the revolution.

CHELSEA
FOUNDATION
S E R I E S

# Political Revolutions

## of the 18th, 19th, and 20th Centuries

Tim McNeese

York College

Biographies by

Samuel Willard Crompton

Holyoke Community College

Introduction by

Tim McNeese

CHELSEA HOUSE
PUBLISHERS
A Haights Cross Communications Company®

*Cover:* The demonstrations against the Shah of Iran are among the best-known examples of revolution in the twentieth century. Here, the Shah is burned in effigy while images of Ayatollah Khomeini look on.

**CHELSEA HOUSE PUBLISHERS**
VP, New Product Development  Sally Cheney
Director of Production  Kim Shinners
Creative Manager  Takeshi Takahashi
Manufacturing Manager  Diann Grasse

**Staff for POLITICAL REVOLUTIONS OF THE 18th, 19th, AND 20th CENTURIES**
Executive Editor  Lee Marcott
Editoral Assistant  Carla Greenberg
Production Editor  Noelle Nardone
Photo Editor  Sarah Bloom
Interior and Cover Design  Keith Trego
Layout  21st Century Publishing and Communications

A Haights Cross Communications ⚑ Company®

First Printing

9 8 7 6 5 4 3 2 1

Library of Congress Cataloging-in-Publication Data

McNeese, Tim.
    Political revolutions of the 18th, 19th, and 20th centuries / Tim McNeese.
    p. cm. — (Chelsea Foundation series)
Includes bibliographical references and index.
    ISBN  0-7910-8151-6  (hardcover)
1. Revolutions.   I. Title. II. Series.
JC491.M364 2005
303.6'4—dc22

                                          2004025075

# Contents
## Overview

# Contents

# Contents

# Contents

# Contents

# Contents

# Contents

# Introduction

**Nothing defines modern politics more than the phenomenon of revolution.**
Throughout the past 300 years, revolutions have risen up from one
continent to the next—from Paris to Philadelphia; Vera Cruz to
Venezuela; Madrid to Moscow. But with each revolution, history
records a thousand variations. Each group of revolutionaries has
followed its own path, revealed its own national inclinations, and
listened to the beat of a collective heart burdened by its own
destructive tyranny.

What, then, can we say of revolution and revolutionaries? Do
revolutionaries share an experience that transcends time, space, and
circumstance? Can the twentieth-century Russian peasant, heartsick
of czarist oppression, share in the frustrated will of the citizens of
1770 Boston as they chafed under the yoke of British authority? Can
those eighteenth-century bearers of the tricolor, who stormed the
Bastille in Paris, bridge the distance between themselves and those
Iranian students of the 1970s who protested the right-wing regime of
the Shah, the last purveyor of Persian power?

What do such disparate revolutions have in common, if anything? The answer may lie in the one characteristic of revolution that
is most difficult to gauge, quantify, or explain, yet is both observable
and mysterious. It is the *spirit of revolution*. This spirit takes hold of
those longing for redirection and moves them as one toward a future
that is, in part, of their own choosing. So compelling is this spirit that
it has worked its way onto the pages, not just of history, but of literature. Poets, essayists, and novelists have turned their pens into
swords, expressing emotions they could no longer keep locked away.

This emotional drive spurred the words of the great eighteenth-
century British poet and author, William Wordsworth, as he stood in
the streets of Paris in 1791 during the heady days of the French
Revolution. Twenty-one years old, his heart full of poetic dreams of
a new French world, Wordsworth reveled in the revolutionary events
he witnessed. He was in love with a woman, in love with France, in
love with the spirit of revolution. The poet expressed the joy he felt
in watching a great event unfold before his eyes: "Bliss was it in that

dawn to be alive, but to be young was very heaven. Oh, times in which the meager stale forbidden ways of custom, law, and statute took at once the attraction of a country in romance."[1]

This same spirit of revolution sprang from the words written by the nineteenth-century American essayist, Ralph Waldo Emerson, who was born too late to witness the American Revolution, but who lived in the whirlwind of change taking place in the new American republic, as well as across the continent of Europe:

> If there is any period one would desire to be born in,—is it not the age of Revolution; when the old and the new stand side by side, and admit of being compared; when the energies of all men are searched by fear and by hope; when the historic glories of the old, can be compensated by the rich possibilities of the new era? This time, like all times, is a very good one, if we but know what to do with it.[2]

This book was written with this great mysterious spirit of revolution in mind. It remained always on stage, amplifying the desire of the masses—whether American, Mexican, Russian, or Chinese—to continue fighting for their cause, their rights; their vision of a better personal and collective world, and a brighter tomorrow.

In considering these revolutions, I have found a new sense of the universal heart that beats on behalf of change. But even with that, I am reminded again of Emerson's words: "This time, like all times, is a very good one, if we but know what to do with it." Unfortunately, revolution does not always lead to a brighter future. The great British novelist Charles Dickens opened his novel, *A Tale of Two Cities*, which was set against the backdrop of the French Revolution, with the words "It was the best of times; it was the worst of times, it was the age of wisdom, it was the age of foolishness, it was the epoch of belief, it was the epoch of incredulity."[3]

Revolution has always been a double-edged sword. The sweep of revolutionary spirit may throw aside the destructive elements of control, tyranny, regime, and power madness, but serve to replace them with another form of the same. To throw off oppression is one thing; to replace it with something better often has proven difficult.

But, if the ends of revolution are impossible to control or predict, the spirit of revolution should always remain its own master. Recently, the events that began unfolding in the streets of the

In November 2004, Ukrainians gathered in Independence Square in Kiev to protest apparent election fraud.

Ukrainian capital of Kiev reminded us of the spirit of revolution. In November 2004, elections were held, pitting former prime minister, state banker, and part-time beekeeper, Viktor Yushchenko, against a former factory manager, incumbent prime minister Viktor Yanukovych. The election was only the fourth for Ukraine since it broke away from the now-defunct Soviet Union, the Communist-dominated state brought into being by the 1917 Russian Revolution.

The Ukrainian electoral process promised to offer no more than corrupt politics as usual, with reports soon surfacing of massive voter fraud in favor of Yanukovych. But this time, it would prove a different, even revolutionary election. When Yanukovych was announced the victor, Ukrainians, in the spirit of revolution, took to the streets of Kiev to express their outrage and disapproval. One witness to this massive, spontaneous uprising was a former student of mine. Lena Kozlova-Pates is a native of Ukraine who today lives outside of Washington, D.C., where she works for an international election monitoring organization. She and her team were sent to Ukraine to observe the election. As protests spread against the election of Yanukovych, Lena went into the streets of Kiev, where she saw people gathered in great throngs. In a city of three million residents, perhaps as many as one in three were in the streets. Protesters wore orange as a symbol of their solidarity. Soon, the protests were given a name: the Orange Revolution.

In the midst of this revolutionary swirl, Lena took it all in, serving as both observer and participant. Her countrymen were in protest; the future of her homeland hung in the balance. What she witnessed were the birth pangs of revolution. And what she saw, she put into words:

> The day after the election (November 22, 2004), walking around Kiev, I came eye to eye with the true Ukrainian revolutionaries. I witnessed an ocean of orange, everything from orange ribbons and scarves on outerwear to orange flags on cars and orange handouts in the streets. I quickly began to appreciate the meaning of the orange color, the color of the fall, the fall of the regime. The people filled the main square of the city, called *Maidan Nezalezhnosti*, Independence Square. They did not appear as protesters. They looked more like some happy fans of a football team that had just won a huge victory! They seemed thrilled, as if something exciting was happening. They were happy, singing, even celebrating! *There was a revolutionary spirit in the air*. And it was not only about election results. It was about choosing democracy, about getting rid of corruption; it was about saying no to the criminal regime in power. It was about the people exercising their right to express their point

of view and to defend it, if necessary. It was an incredible feeling to be standing among hundreds of thousands, perhaps even a million people of similar mind. Just standing among them, I experienced a strange and empowering feeling of strength and unity.[4]

As she walked through the excited crowds of Kievan protesters, Lena saw Ukraine's present and future altered. She shared with Wordsworth the bliss of being alive and young in a time of national redirection. She stood shoulder to shoulder with her fellow Ukrainians, sharing in the spirit of revolution—sharing that spirit with those other anxious citizens of the past, from Paris to Philadelphia; Vera Cruz to Venezuela; Madrid to Moscow.

This spirit of revolution is a constant of politics past and present. It stands ever vigilant, as it has for centuries, always on the threshold of change, regardless of cause and effect, beyond the underpinnings of ideology. It stands ready to be embraced today, as it was in the revolutions described in the pages of this book—in Samuel Adams's Boston; in Lafayette's Paris; in Madero's Mexico City; in Lenin's Moscow; in Mao's Beijing; in Lena's Kiev; and in the streets of a thousand other cities and rural villages of people around the world, waiting to partner in a new time of troubles, in anticipation of a new era of hope; ready and willing to serve as midwife to a new birth of freedom.

■     ■     ■     ■

The scope and aims of this book are dictated by the enormous volume of scholarship on the study of revolutions. It is not intended to present a comprehensive overview of all the political revolutions that have taken place in the history of the modern world. Such a text would be massive. Instead, in compiling the text, I chose to focus on seven key revolutions, beginning with the American Revolution of the 1770s and 1780s and ending with the Iranian Revolution of the 1970s and 1980s. The revolutions included in this book do not represent mere attempts to bring about sweeping social, economic, and political change; they were ultimately successful. That these revolutions happened at all caused great ripples in time and in the events that followed them. These seven revolutions, then, deserve our study and attention.

But in studying these periods of change, it is important to examine not only the events of each revolution—the rallies, protests, riots, party meetings, civil unrest, and sometimes bloody encounters—but also to examine the words of the revolutionaries themselves. To that end, the story of each revolution is told and accompanied by a selection of primary source documents that capture the words of the participants. Just as events drove each revolution, so did ideology. These words spoken and written by those who sought change and redirection for themselves and their people often served as rallying points and as mile markers defining how far a revolution had progressed and what still remained to be accomplished. Many of these documents embody the spirit of revolution.

By combining narrative history and the related historical documents, I hope to create a book that will stir and enlighten the reader as much as these events and words stirred those who participated in those revolutions.

**Tim McNeese**
**York, Nebraska**
**December 2004**

## SOURCE NOTES

1. Quoted in Eugene Weber, *The Western Tradition*, video series, episode 140: "The French Revolution." From *The Western Tradition Transcripts*, transcribed by Thomas Michael Kowalick. Alexandria, VA: PBS Adult Learning Service, 1989, p. 122.
2. Quoted in Nina Baym, ed. *The Norton Anthology of American Literature*, Volume B: American Literature, 1820–1865. New York: W.W. Norton & Company, 2003, p. 1145.
3. Quoted in Charles Dickens, *A Tale of Two Cities*. Accessible at The Online Literature Library, *http://www.literature.org/authors/dickens-charles/two-cities/book-01/chapter-01.html.*
4. Quoted in a personal interview between the author and Lena Kozlova-Pates, December 5, 2004.

# Part I:
# Introduction

**Chapter 1:** Revolutions: An Introduction

# Revolutions:
## An Introduction

**Of all the words in the political dictionary, perhaps none creates any** clearer image in a reader's mind than that of *revolution*. To the modern-day reader, the word may conjure up mental pictures of American patriots standing their ground in protest against eighteenth-century British political power as they tar and feather British tax collectors, dump taxed tea into the chilly waters of Boston Harbor, suffer through a harsh winter at Valley Forge, or zealously pen the Declaration of Independence. Others may envision overtaxed French citizens defying an absolute monarch, storming the Bastille prison (a symbol of royal tyranny), marching in protest on the king's palace, and defiantly wearing the French tricolor—the red, white, and blue symbol of their protest.

Still others may visualize Russian peasants struggling against oppression, the Czar's troops opening fire on protestors in the streets of St. Petersburg, their victims' blood spilling red in the snow, or the forced abdication of the Russian ruler, bringing an end to hundreds of years of absolute monarchy. And others might envision scenes of

The word "revolution" inspires many powerful mental images. The personification of concepts like liberty and independence has often been used to call countrymen to arms. In this illustration, Liberty herself carries the flag and sword into battle.

Muslim fundamentalists rallying by the hundreds of thousands around an aged, bearded Islamic cleric, calling for the end of the imperial reign of Iran's Shah.

Such scenes serve as touchstones of symbolism built on the actions of those who have made conscious decisions to take a stand, defy the status quo, and risk their homes, their families, and their futures, all for the sake of bringing an end to one way of life and exchanging it for another. There is often a romantic aspect to such actions, to taking one's destiny and reshaping it into something else, something better, something new, something *revolutionary*.

But such emotions may explain the nature of revolutions and revolutionary behavior only to a point. It is the purpose of this book to present seven revolutionary eras, to reveal the multilayered nature of such movements, and to provide a full picture of the circumstances that led to each revolution, including an in-depth look at those individuals who led each revolution as well as at those who followed them and those who attempted to stand in the way of significant change.

## THE NATURE OF REVOLUTION

"Revolution" is for the modern reader an overused word. Television advertisements tout products—everything from the newest car to the latest men's shaver—as "revolutionary." This use of the word as an adjective and applied to such trivial things reduces its impact as well as that of its partner, the noun "revolution," which is also applied to almost any type of change in the modern world. Thus an advertiser may proclaim its new MP3 player to be a "revolution in technology" or "the beginning of a revolution in digital convenience."

The purpose of using the word this way is to make clear to the consumer that the product in question is the latest thing, a symbol of something new, a transformation from everything that preceded it. By its nature, its use accomplishes two purposes at the same time: as a symbol, it creates a new standard even as it invalidates the very thing it is replacing. And as it is with commercials for soap, kitchen appliances, fashion, and office equipment; so it is with political change.

As applied to political change, the concept of revolution is sometimes difficult to define. What some observers of change identify as revolution is sometimes, instead, simply evolution—slow, nearly unnoticeable change that creates a new political order without any accompanying dramatic turmoil or violence. During the eighteenth and early nineteenth centuries, Europe and the United States experienced tremendous change— through advancements in technology and steam power—that historians refer to as the "Industrial Revolution." That these changes took place is clear, but the changes did not take place overnight or even in the course of one generation. The introduction of steam power, changes in manufacturing, and the development of railroads and mass production techniques required decades of adaptation, experimentation, and retooling. One could even say that the Industrial Revolution that began during the early 1700s has never come to an end, but continues to evolve even today.

By its nature, then, true revolution unfolds quickly, bringing about "sudden and radical change."[1] In the case of political revolutions, they usually result in significant change or alteration to an existing government or rule. However, not every political change is equal to a revolution. History is littered with examples of peasant uprisings, palace coups, and putsches. They number in the thousands, perhaps tens of thousands. But not every attempt to throw off the power of government, topple a leader from office, or vote out one's political opponent represents a revolution.

For example: A coup d'etat by a secret band of political radicals is unleashed, resulting in the death of a political leader. The radicals then replace the assassinated ruler with one of their own choice. Yet in the process, the government, its structures and organizations, remain intact. Such an event is not a revolution. A change in leadership at the top that does not alter the existing system of government manages to steer clear of true revolution. But when the political change results in the adoption of a completely new system of government, and in great change within the society living under that government, only then has an authentic revolution taken place.

## REVOLUTIONARY PHILOSOPHY

Revolution is a longstanding tool of political change. Instances of the violent overthrow of a government can probably be traced back as far as the first primitive tribal leader removing another from a position of power. However, the modern revolution is best exemplified in the political uprisings of the past three or four hundred years—uprisings that had their roots in the European period of the Enlightenment, which began in the early eighteenth century.

During the 1600s and 1700s, many European scientists began to look at the physical world in a different way, categorizing systems of nature based on real science that explained natural phenomena. These scientists began developing well-defined concepts of the laws of nature as well as mathematical equations to explain how their immediate world, and the universe, operated. Such revamping of scientific thought led European thinkers and scholars to begin viewing other aspects of human existence in new ways as well.

Just as scientists viewed nature as controlled by natural laws, so others searched for laws that governed human behavior. One group of thinkers were philosophers who began using reason in viewing the laws of humanity; these intellectuals were known as the *philosophes*. Their approach led to a philosophy known as the Enlightenment, which was based on the concept of an era of new, intellectual "light" that could dispel all darkness from the human mind. This "enlightenment" had the power to take away those things that made people ignorant, superstitious, and intolerant.

The philosophes used scientific method and theory as the litmus test for their views of social order, religion, and government. Religiously, the philosophes turned away from traditional Christian theology and thought, denying any direct role of God in the lives of people. Instead, their view of God became one that cast Him as a creator only, a Great Mechanic who built the world as a clockmaker would a clock, only to wind it up, and leave it to run down on its own. The philosophes' God remained aloof, never playing a role as a divine interventionist. In fact, such direct involvement—via miracles or answered prayers—would violate the very laws of nature that God had put in place. Therefore, it was up to humans to create their own answers, to develop their own means of achieving contentment, happiness, and purpose.

The seventeenth- and eighteenth-century men and women of the Enlightenment sought to achieve personal happiness and liberty by speaking out against anything they perceived was a wrong or an oppression in society. This led many of them to speak out against the absolute rule of the kings and queens of the period. During these centuries, nearly every European country was ruled by a monarch who considered himself or herself to be all-powerful, holding the well-being of all his or her subjects in hand. These monarchs were all too often oppressive and unwilling to hear any criticisms whatsoever. They were, in their minds, God's regents on earth, ruling in his name. Those who spoke out against such absolute monarchs ran the risk of persecution, arrest, imprisonment, or execution. But the times were changing.

### JOHN LOCKE, POLITICAL THINKER

One of the most brilliant philosophes of the seventeenth century was John Locke, whose ideas of how governments should operate flew directly in the face of the period's conventional wisdom that kings ruled by divine right. John Locke was an Englishman who practiced the scientific method. Through his writings, he applied the scientific method to the study of political theory.

During Locke's lifetime, Britain experienced two significant political revolutions, both resulting in the removal of the monarch of that

## John Locke

His key words were "life, liberty, and the preservation of property." Thomas Jefferson later altered the expression to "life, liberty, and the pursuit of happiness."

Born in England in 1632, Locke grew up amidst the turmoil created by the English Civil War and Oliver Cromwell's government. The bloodshed of those times gave Locke a deep aversion to spontaneous popular movements.

Locke served as recording secretary for the Carolina Proprietors, a group of seven English lords who claimed the lands between Virginia and Florida. He helped in the design and the writing of the Fundamental Orders, a constitution for Carolina. This was anything but a democratic document; the seven Lord Proprietors ruled Carolina very much as if it were a feudal fief.

During the 1680s, Locke was in Holland working on what became his two literary masterpieces. He returned to England when Prince William of Orange and Princess Mary of England overthrew her father, King James II, and became King William and Queen Mary (the university in Virginia is named for them). This Glorious Revolution — called glorious because it was free of bloodshed—was very much to John Locke's taste.

Two of Locke's books were published in 1689: *Two Treatises on Civil Government* and *An Essay Concerning Human Understanding.* Locke's great reputation among both philosophers and revolutionaries rests upon these works.

*Two Treatises* concerned itself with political matters, particularly issues related to political science. Locke was one of the day: Charles I during the 1640s and James II in the 1680s. The first revolution came about when conservative Puritans in the English Parliament rallied against the oppressive Charles, calling for his removal from the throne. When Charles refused to abandon his royal seat, the Puritans led a revolution that spilled over into civil war. Charles and his supporters lost the war, and the king was arrested, stood trial, and ordered condemned to death. In 1649, Charles was beheaded, and a civilian government took his place. After the return of the monarchy eleven years later, King James II experienced renewed

first philosophers to explicitly state that government rests upon the consent of the governed, and that a government that does not serve the people should be removed. The words "preservation of property" indicate that Locke believed in the need for occasional political revolutions but not for social ones. Indeed, he would have been horrified to know that some of his ideas would later be used by communist and socialist organizations.

Locke's *Essay Concerning Human Understanding* was, if anything, even more important. He had read the philosophy of the Frenchman Rene Descartes, but he went considerably further in his own work. Locke was one of the first writers to declare that human beings come into the world as a blank slate (tabula rasa) upon which is written the experience of their lives. He was not by any means an atheist or even an agnostic, but his thoughts were revolutionary for the time. For the next 300 years, numerous revolutionaries used Locke's words to mean that men and women are essentially malleable, and that since men and women enter the world as blank slates, and since experience determines their future, one can change the experiences and thereby change the human beings. Locke was a committed Christian who did not realize that his work would be used to justify all sorts of things in the future. Like his great contemporary, Sir Isaac Newton, Locke saw no contradiction between deeply held philosophical beliefs and belief in God.

Whether Locke would have approved of the use of his philosophy by countless revolutionary movements is debatable. He believed in orderly transitions of government, and saw England's Glorious Revolution as the best example of this. Locke's writings inspired a whole generation of American revolutionaries; Samuel Adams, John Adams, and John Hancock all knew the words of John Locke and believed him to be one of the prophets of liberty.

hostility from his subjects and was removed in 1688 through a non-violent coup called the Glorious, or Bloodless, Revolution. Both uprisings overthrew governments led by absolute monarchs.

In 1689, John Locke wrote a book about the two revolutions titled *Of Civil Government: Two Treatises*. In it, Locke attempted to explain how each revolution had occurred and what each one signified. He believed that both had occurred because the English people expected to live under some form of liberty and that they believed in the power of the people to overthrow any form of government that did not recognize their natural rights.

To Locke, the idea of absolute monarchy was unacceptable, for such harsh, repressive rule on the part of one person violated the law of nature based on the desire of human beings to live freely. He also believed this law to represent natural rights that humans are born with. Locke identified those basic, innate natural rights as the rights of "life, liberty, and property." For this English political philosopher, the only acceptable, reasonable form of government was one that not only recognized the existence of such rights but also worked to protect those rights.

Thus Locke viewed any other form of government as unacceptable, even unnatural, and that anyone living under such a government had the natural right to revolt against its leaders, since those leaders had violated the rights of his or her subjects. To Locke, the ruler had a relationship with his or her people that could be defined as a social contract: the ruler provides proper, responsive leadership for his subjects while protecting their natural rights. In his writings, Locke stressed the importance of other political ideas, including the separation of powers and the concept of popular sovereignty, or the will of the people. Rulers governed only as the people accepted their rule.

## ENLIGHTENED GOVERNMENT AND REVOLUTION

Such enlightened political thinkers as John Locke led some European monarchs of the eighteenth century to practice a style of governing that was responsive to the people under their charge. Such rulers were sometimes called "Enlightened Despots." They continued to rule by their own power, but they tried to rule justly, always working to improve the lives of their subjects. Nevertheless, a movement soon got underway in the late 1700s that steered governments away from rule by a hereditary monarch.

In the New World, the British colonies that hugged the Atlantic seaboard began to challenge the authority of the king of Great Britain to rule without input from the colonists. This movement became popular during the 1760s, and by the mid-1770s the colonies were in open rebellion and at war with the British military. The American Revolution was an exact mirror of the ideas of the European philosophes and of such influential thinkers as John Locke.

The American Revolution would serve as a catalyst for other revolutions during the next two centuries. The French Revolution that begin in earnest in 1789 sought civil liberties for the people of France and a reduction in the power of the absolute monarch, Louis XVI. It resulted in a constitutional government (as the Americans had created), eliminated the monarchy, and established personal freedoms and voting privileges for many previously disenfranchised French people. With these two events—the American and the French—the modern era of revolution began.

## THOMAS PAINE AND REVOLUTIONARY THOUGHT

Just as John Locke's political ideas provided the philosophical basis for such revolutions as the American and the French, so another political writer expressed his own views of government and dissent that inspired yet another generation of would-be political rebels. Thomas Paine, who immigrated from Great Britain to the American colonies just as the American Revolution was about to take off, wrote in support of the revolution, producing such influential political tracts as *Common Sense*. In 1792, Paine wrote another treatise, titled *Rights of Man*, in which he wrote a strong defense of popular revolution.

To Paine, all tyrannical government was morally wrong. In his mind, all forms of monarchy were the same as tyranny, since monarchy did not allow the voice of the people in selection of a state's leader. His words speak for themselves:

> All hereditary government is in its nature tyranny. An heritable crown, or an heritable throne, or by what other fanciful name such things may be called, have no other significant explanation than that mankind are heritable property. To inherit a government, is to inherit the people, as if they were flocks and herds...

When we survey the wretched condition of man under the monarchical and hereditary systems of government, dragged from his home by one power, or [driven] by another, and impoverished by taxes more than by enemies, it becomes evident that those systems are bad, and that a general revolution in the principle and construction of government is necessary.[2]

## Thomas Paine

Thomas Paine's famous words, "These are the times that try men's souls," have been echoed by one revolutionary movement after another for more than two centuries. He was no summer soldier or sunshine patriot, but rather an earnest and committed revolutionary.

Born in England in 1737, Paine tried a number of jobs and failed at most of them. In 1774 he met Benjamin Franklin in London, and the American (just about to turn into a full revolutionary) persuaded Paine to immigrate to the American colonies. Paine arrived that same year and was therefore on hand to witness the beginning of the American Revolution. From almost the first moment, he embraced the movement and wanted to become one of its spokesmen.

Everyone knows that Thomas Jefferson

wrote the Declaration of Independence and that the document became the statement of American independence. Less known is the fact that Thomas Paine's *Common Sense* was published five months before the Declaration and that it may have had an even greater effect. In this 46-page-long document, Paine laid out the case for American independence from England. He compared England to a covetous or greedy mother who would not let her adult children go free. Paine used economic arguments, saying that the colonies would soon outstrip England in population and that the maritime and commercial future belonged to them rather than to the Mother Country.

Later in 1776 Paine served in the American army under George Washington. As they endured one defeat after another

To Paine, the only justification needed for an acceptable revolution was the existence of a government led by a king and thus operating without the consent of the people of that state.

Unacceptable government leaders have provided inspiration over and over in history for their subjects to rise up and remove them from power. Such revolutions as the French, against absolute monarch Louis XVI, and the Russian, against the country's last Czar, Nicholas II, provide examples.

(Long Island, Fort Washington, White Plains), Paine wrote his next essay. *The Crisis* was published at the lowest point in the American cause, but Paine called on Americans to fight just the same. For what, he asked, is more glorious than a mighty contest well and finally won? He decried the efforts of the sometime patriot and called on Americans to stand up to this mighty test. Paine's words were vindicated by General Washington's victory at Trenton the day after Christmas of that year, and the American cause never sank so low again as it had been when Paine wrote *The Crisis*.

The rest of the war was anticlimactic for Paine. His literary fame (though not his wealth, since he took no profits from the publications) was assured, and he was seen as one of the prophets of American liberty. Ever restless, Paine went back to England in the mid-1780s, and he became intrigued by the French Revolution that began in 1789. Like many liberals, Paine welcomed the beginning of the French Revolution, and in 1790 he went to France. He published *The Rights of Man* in 1791 and 1792; he argued for the French Revolution, claiming that it was the cause of all mankind.

In 1792 Paine was elected by the French to serve as a member of the new National Convention. Much less adept a politician than a writer, Paine watched as the French Revolution drifted toward anarchy and violence. In the National Convention, Paine argued and voted against the execution of King Louis XVI: he felt this was a senseless and unnecessary act. Thereafter, Paine's own popularity dropped dramatically, and in 1794 he narrowly missed being taken to the guillotine himself. He was released only because Maximilien Robespierre, leader of the radical Jacobin party, fell from power.

Paine returned to America but did not enjoy any return to prominence. His role in the French Revolution was (unfairly) held against him, and Paine was not welcomed by any of his former friends and colleagues. He died in New Rochelle, New York, in 1809, largely forgotten by the nation to which he had helped give birth.

## SOCIALISM AND REVOLUTION

Within a generation of the American and French Revolutions, other incentives for revolution were beginning to take root. With the advent of the Industrial Revolution and the development of new techniques of production, increased reliance on steam power, and the development of factory complexes, the nature of European society and the status of the working class experienced significant and parallel changes. A new emphasis on productivity and competition for new markets and trade centers pushed the factory owners to exploit their workers in an attempt to keep production costs to a minimum. Early nineteenth-century factories and mines, in both Europe and the United States, became notorious for their poor and unsafe working conditions. Factories were dark, dirty places with little ventilation, heatless in winter, reeking with the heat of summer, and much of the equipment was unsafe, causing many worker accidents and even deaths.

Social reformers of the period began to speak out against such abuses. They not only sought better working conditions, however, but also expressed moral concerns about other social problems and ills. Some political philosophers of the early nineteenth century, especially in Europe, wrote and spoke against systems that rewarded those with power and wealth while keeping the working class in poverty. This concern led to the development of a new political and social cause, the socialist movement. (The word *socialist* was invented in 1833, and the word *socialism* came into use just six years later.)

Socialists preached that a good social order (or society) existed for the good of all its members, not just those with money and political power. It broke down the barriers and restrictions associated with class differences. While the Industrial Revolution had emphasized such social laws as individualism, competition, and laissez-faire economics, socialists argued in favor of social cooperation, planning, and control.

Great socialist thinkers of the era led the way. Such socialists as the Frenchman Louis Blanc (1811–1882) wrote that competition was the harbinger of all social problems. In casting competition negatively, he promoted the idea that government should control the economic structures within its borders. This meant the transfer of the economic and production systems from private ownership to control and ownership by the state. But Blanc's socialist ideas did not call for an end to democracy or political freedoms, just a change in economic freedoms.

His economic philosophy had a strong impact on contemporary thinkers such as Pierre Joseph Proudhon (1809–1865). Although Proudhon was born the son of a peasant, he became educated and espoused a strong concept of socialism. He decried the private ownership of property and supported sweeping social reforms. His view of socialism, however, was so extreme that he called for the dissolution of all governments, actively supporting revolution everywhere. Proudhon's concept of an ideal state focused on small communes of individuals—communities comprising those who voluntarily joined together to share everything in common.

While Proudhon, Blanc, and others defined the perimeters of early nineteenth-century socialism, no single European writer had a greater impact on the political history of Europe during the later nineteenth and twentieth centuries than the Prussian-born social thinker and theorist Karl Marx (1818–1883).

## MARXISM AND REVOLUTION

If such earlier writers as John Locke and Thomas Paine explained revolution as a natural phenomenon designed to protect one's expectation of liberty by throwing off tyranny and recreating a government of the people, Karl Marx provided new incentives and explanations that led to later revolutions as important as those of America and France. During the twentieth century, his political theories—generally termed Marxism—led to revolution in Russia in 1917 and China during the 1930s and 1940s, both of which are addressed in later chapters. Other revolutions, including the Cuban and Vietnamese, as well as several in Africa and Latin America, also took place at the hands of those who took the tenets of Marxist economic philosophy seriously.

Marx is considered, therefore, one of the most influential thinkers and writers of the nineteenth and twentieth centuries. He devoted much of his adult life to researching political and economic policy and theory, spending long hours for days on end in the archives of the British Museum. His writings helped transmit socialist theory around the world. A radical, Marx wrote for revolutionary newspapers and had membership in subversive organizations. He lived in both Germany and England, sometimes forced to flee imprisonment for his political extremism.

Marx published several works that served to explain his political theories. His *Communist Manifesto* was published in 1848, just as many radical groups called for revolution throughout Europe. A generation later, he began publishing *Capital* (*Das Kapital*), a treatise in

## Karl Marx

"**W**orkers of the world, unite! You have nothing to lose but your chains!"

These are the best-known words of Karl Marx, cowritten with fellow German socialist Friedrich Engels. Born in 1818, Marx came from a middle-class German family. He admired his father but had a painful relationship with his mother (he detested her tight-fisted, "bourgeois" values). Marx attended the university in Berlin, and in the 1840s he met Engels, the son of a wealthy manufacturer. Over the next few years, Marx and Engels worked on their collective theory on socialism, capitalism, and the future of humanity, financed by Engels's family resources. By an odd chance, their joint pamphlet on communism came out early in 1848, the very year in which most of Europe erupted in revolutionary fervor. Thus the pamphlet attracted more attention than would otherwise have been the case, and Marx and Engels became the leaders of a new intellectual movement.

For Marx and Engels, ideas were as important as concrete facts. Both men saw the previous several thousand years as a time of increasing power held by the bourgeoisie (managers, political leaders) and declining power in the hands of the proletariat (workers). As they traced it, man had been most free in the state of anarchy that had preceded civilization; once man settled into towns, cities, and corporations, he gradually lost his freedom to mayors, landlords, and taxes—hence the rallying words of their pamphlet, "Workers of the world, unite!"

Marx moved to London around 1850. He

three volumes, the first book produced in print in 1867 and the last two after his death in 1885 and 1894.

Marx spent much of his writing honing four interlocking theories that provided the foundation for his socialist thought: the materialist view of history, class warfare, dialectical change, and the theory of surplus value. Ironically, even after spending much of his life studying such matters, none of the theories were created by him.

and his family lived in very modest circumstances for the next 20 years, often helped by the generosity of Engels; even so, the academic partnership ended, and Marx was now on his own intellectually. In 1867 he published his massive and powerful *Das Kapital* (Capital), which explicitly laid out his view of the relationship between workers and their employers, and of the coming socialist revolution (Marx generally used the word "socialist" rather than "communist").

As Marx saw it, the managerial class (representing the capitalist economic system) would increasingly squeeze the workers and things would only become worse. Industrialization, which was moving very rapidly in Great Britain, would increase the power of the managers, and eventually the workers would rise up in a massive revolution and overthrow their "masters." Capitalism would then be abolished, and after a temporary "dictatorship of the proletariat," people would live in a utopia in which everyone gave according to his or her abilities and received according to his or her needs.

Marx's critics asserted that his ideas contradicted human nature, which thrives on competition and differentiation between highly skilled workers and lesser ones. Another key question was: How would the new dictatorship disappear? Might it not become a tyranny of its own?

Marx died in 1883. For the next sixty years, his ideas were seen as having great merit. The Russian revolution of 1917 and the Chinese revolution of the 1930s both seemed to validate Marx's views, but sometime in the 1940s, many Marxist writers, thinkers, and activists had second thoughts. They learned what life was truly like in Communist Russia, and they saw that the state refused to "wither and die," contrary to Marx's predictions.

Marx still has many followers in the world today, and perhaps his ideas will one day experience a renaissance. Whether the proletariat revolution will ever occur, however, is another question.

He, however, combined them into his own package of socialism. The theories are complicated and sometimes difficult to understand.

The materialist view of history argues that the events of history have been brought about as a result of material motives. Specifically, Marx focused on two aspects of the material world: economics, and the ways things are produced or made, systems referred to as the means of production. Marx's second emphasis was on historical struggles known as class warfare. Throughout history, there have been propertied classes and those without property—those with economic power and those without it. It was Marx's belief that, during any time period in history, power was held by a class of people who controlled the means of production. To help keep themselves in power, the owners of the production systems exploited or mistreated the workers.

Such an abusive relationship could only last so long, and then the working class would overthrow the controlling or ruling class, making themselves the new ruling class. Partially reflecting this view, dialectical change proposes that historical change takes place when the status quo is ultimately replaced by its opposite. Marx applied this theory to the relationship between the ruling, or "owning," class (whom he called the bourgeoisie) and the working class (known as the proletariat).

His fourth theory—surplus value—was purely an anticapitalist idea that decried the making of profit by the owners of the means of production at the expense of the workers. Marx believed that profit (surplus value) rewarded the bourgeoisie through the labors of someone else. In Marxian economics, the value of an item produced or manufactured was determined by the amount of time a workers spent producing it.

Unfortunately, many of Marx's ideas have proven untenable when put into real practice or were based on too narrow an interpretation of events and social relationships. His materialist view of history eliminates all other sources of change, including intellectual, social, and spiritual ideas. Surplus value ignored the stake the bourgeoisie had invested in the means of production, including the construction of factories, the equipment used in production, and all other benefits provided by the owners who employed the workers. Dialectical change (also known as dialectical materialism) is too narrow and deterministic. It assumes that history is little more than a series of struggles between the owners of the means of production and the workers, with the final struggle resulting in the elimination of modern capitalism and the uniting of all workers worldwide into a classless state. Yet Marx's ideas served as incentives for revolution on various fronts by the end of the nineteenth century and led to significant upheavals and political change in countries such as Russia and China, and to the establishment of international Communism in the twentieth century.

## THE CAUSES OF REVOLUTION

Before analyzing the circumstances that have led to revolution during the past few centuries, it must be understood that not all revolutions are the same in nature or scope. Some seek only limited change, while others look to sweep out every element of society, seeking "nothing less than a radical and complete change in the social, political, and moral fabric of their country."[3] One example of a limited conflict was the American Revolution. That period of political upheaval did not result in the wholesale destruction of social elements or economic realities. The colonial governments largely remained intact, the trading economies of the colonies were not destroyed, and the social order remained largely untouched. The focus of the revolution was a series of moves to bring about complete political independence for the 13 American colonies from the Mother Country, Great Britain.

On the other side of the coin, some revolutions seek the complete alteration of every part of life within a state. One of the most extraordinary examples was the French Revolution. The French revolutionary movement (or movements) aimed to alter the political order, establish a republic, write a constitution, limit the power of the monarchy, grant political rights to the people, eliminate the aristocracy, reduce the power of the Catholic Church in France, and completely revamp the tax code and legal system. In addition, more extreme leaders of the revolution later sought to destroy some elements of Christianity altogether in France, adopt the metric system, and change the calendar (including the adoption of new names for the months and a ten-day week to eliminate the old names of the seven days). Such extreme revolutions have often been accompanied by extraordinary levels of violence and domestic upheaval—and no wonder.

As for the motivations for revolution, the list is not extraordinarily long. While historians and social theorists do not agree on the most important or common cause of revolutions in history, Karl Marx did argue that when people's lives become increasingly desperate, due to poverty and elimination from the social order, they are apt to reach a point when they turn on the existing authorities and revolt. While revolutions of the poor and disenfranchised have occurred in history many times over, other revolutions appear to have taken place after a group in fact experiences economic improvement in their lives. The logic works this way: When people see "that some improvement was possible, they inevitably would yearn for more."[4] A revolution might erupt when, after a state makes some progress, it experiences a decline in the *rate* of progress or a turn-around in the trend of improvement, such as an economic depression. Those who have been experiencing the progress will not tolerate losing the improvements in their lives they may have only recently gained. In the end, this view of revolution argues that political upheavals "stem not so much from terrible suffering as from crushing disappointment."[5]

Perhaps the American Revolution serves as an example of this view of revolution. During the seventeenth and much of the eighteenth centuries, the people of the 13 British colonies of North America were able to fairly consistently improve their lives and become one of the most prosperous people in history. Decade after decade, the British government made few demands on its colonists, and many of the laws passed by Parliament—particularly those designed to control the economic activities of the colonies—were ignored by those same colonists. But, by the 1760s and 1770s, the British government began to clamp down on the colonies, creating and enforcing new taxation laws. American colonists felt put upon, their economic freedoms hampered, and many chose to turn against any form of British authority, from colonial governors to the king himself. Ultimately, at least one major goal of the American Revolution was to restore the unfettered, free economic activity that had been so commonly enjoyed in the colonies before the change in British policy.

Other historical reasons for revolution hinge on the type of government and society that exists prior to the change. Not every type of society runs the same level of risk of experiencing a revolution.

Many factors can inspire people to risk life and property in search of a change in leadership. The Russian Revolution of 1917 was born of rampant poverty and a series of costly military losses during World War I. Here, Russian soldiers and civilians parade after the downfall of the Czar.

One type of society that commonly experiences revolution is the *agrarian-bureaucratic* model. Such states are defined as "societies in which a more or less centralized bureaucracy, with the aid of locally powerful landlords, subsists on the surplus of a predominantly agricultural economy.[6] In such states, agriculture is the primary economic activity, and those who work as farmers are exploited. Sometimes they are peasants who do not own their own property, or they are overtaxed. Also, in such states economic conditions can seriously worsen during times of drought or other natural events, leading to discontent and upheaval, which may lead to revolution.

Often at the center of revolutions in such states are the landless peasants who join political movements that promise personal economic improvement through land redistribution. Another cause of revolution in such states is the fact that often those holding governmental power are drawn from the nonpeasant classes, such as aristocrats, the wealthy, and landowners, giving rise to class warfare.

Sometimes a state may experience revolution not only because of the circumstances found in that state, but because of external influences. When a state loses a major war, the result may be instability at home that leads to revolution. Both the Russian Revolutions of 1905 and 1917 were preceded by military losses for the czar and his people. The Chinese Revolution that brought the Communists to power in 1949 was partially the result of events extending from World War II. Historians count "no fewer than nineteen revolutions that followed wartime defeats in Europe alone between 1204 and 1919."[7]

Involvement in a large-scale war may increase the possibility of revolution in such a state because of the war's economic repercussions. If the armed conflict causes great upheaval, dislocation, economic loss, or significant loss of life, the people of that losing state may revolt. Also, during wartime, many more people are armed and "human life seems considerably less valuable than in peacetime."[8]

Other external influences leading to revolution may include foreign investment and influence on a state's economy. If a state's population believes another country or foreign business controls too much of their state's economy, the people may rise up and revolt against their own government because it allowed such outside influence. During the Mexican Revolution of 1910, revolutionaries were constantly critical of the government for having allowed the majority of several industries to come under the ownership of American businesses, especially oil companies. A high level of Japanese control and investment in China helped lead to the Communist revolution in that country, and many of those who called for the deposing of the Shah of Iran during the 1970s were convinced the Shah had become too friendly with American business interests—again, as in Mexico, with U.S. oil companies.

Yet another reason for revolution is the perception that a government may be too weak to stand up to extreme political turmoil. Governmental weakness is usually not tolerated by revolutionaries and, in most cases, such weakness will be exploited. During the French Revolution, as King Louis XVI wrung his hands and vacillated in his responses, his waffling was seen by revolutionary elements as weakness. They exploited the weakness and spurred protest events in France, while the king could do little more than simply react after the fact. When Louis's own military turned against him, his days as a French king were immediately numbered. Generally, when a state's military remains loyal to its government, a revolution is doomed to failure. but when the army joins the revolutionaries—as it did in the French Revolution, the Russian Revolution of 1917, and the Iranian Revolution of 1978, the upheaval is more likely to succeed.

Finally, revolutions often succeed because they have strong leaders, individuals whose personalities, actions, and words provide inspiration to the revolutionary movement. Nearly every successful revolution can be associated with a great, or at least a forceful, figure. Such examples include the American Revolution's George Washington; the French Revolution's Robespierre; the Russian Revolution's Lenin and Trotsky; various leaders of the Mexican Revolution of 1910, including Madero, Carranza, Villa, and Zapata; Mao Zedong of the Chinese Communist Revolution; and Iran's Ayatollah Khomeini. While the traits required of each revolutionary leader vary with each example, there are those qualities commonly recognized as ideal for most such charismatic figures:

> The leadership must possess the skills needed in the critical hours; the most important are the skills of agitation, violence, and administration.... The top leaders must be political and agitational. Oratory, flamboyancy, acute judgment ... and decisiveness are much in demand. The conditions of modern society demand that oratorical skills be supplemented by their kindred propagandistic skills.[9]

Such individuals, through their writing, public speeches, and political power to sway the public, serve as touchstones for revolutionary movements. They often provide the direction, the agenda, and the alternative for power once the existing power is removed.

## SEIZING THE GOVERNMENT'S SYMBOLS

Perhaps another important element of a successful revolution is the seizing of "the sacred symbols of the existing regime."[10] This may serve more of a symbolic importance than a real political or strategic one, but the value of the symbolism is significant. When, during the French Revolution, a Parisian mob captured the Bastille, an old medieval fortress believed to house countless political prisoners, it mattered little that there were almost no prisoners there at all. What was important was that the Bastille represented, in the minds of the people of Paris, the tyranny of the French monarchy. In the same way, when revolutionaries took King Louis XVI and his family as prisoners, they had seized one of the most potent symbols of French power.

Other revolutions captured their own symbols of power. During the Mexican Revolution, the military-revolutionary forces of Madero, Orozco, and Villa managed to capture the Mexican capital, Mexico City. This important symbol of Mexican power in the hands of revolutionaries indicated the inability of the existing Diaz government to even keep revolutionaries out of the city. During the Russian Revolution, rioters took control of the city of Petrograd, the seat of czarist power. When Czar Nicholas II tried to return to the city, his train was stopped by striking rail workers supporting the revolution, leaving him stranded outside the city. In the midst of the Iranian Revolution of 1978, millions of anti-Shah demonstrators gathered at the Shayyad Monument in Tehran, an architectural symbol built to honor the Shah's family dynasty. By staging their rally near the monument, the revolutionaries were sending a clear message. Such symbolic actions usually provide moral support for a revolution and help revolutionaries successfully continue their fight.

## VIOLENCE AND REVOLUTION

Violence is a hallmark of revolution. Many revolutions are accompanied by a coup d'etat (literally, a stroke of state), a violent overthrow of the recognized power or government. Generally, such coups are quick, short-lived, and over almost as soon as they begin, since the key element of a successful coup is to catch the existing authorities off their guard in an effort to bring down their government before they have an opportunity to organize a military or police response. But a coup d'etat does not necessarily equal a revolution. It serves as "part of all revolutions and exists also in a form sufficient in itself to take over the government."[11] Before most coups can succeed, however, several circumstances must generally be in place. For example, the targeted government must be weak domestically and seemingly unable to defend itself from a domestic assault. This weakness is often what convinces would-be revolutionaries to strike in the first place, since few radicals would risk losing everything in a coup against a strong government with the capacity to respond to defend itself. An example of such a weak government facing a historic coup d'etat was the czarist regime of Russia in 1917 (or, for that matter, the Kerensky government that replaced it and faced its own coup two years later).

What constitutes a weak government, one easily rattled by a coup? Essentially it begins with a lack of support on the part of the people living under the government in question. When the people do not support their government, in times of crisis (which a coup would certainly represent) the state cannot rely on the loyalty of its people to either not participate in the coup or to fight against it. Such lack of support may spring from the public perception that a government is corrupt, incompetent, poorly led, nonresponsive to the will of the people, or even oppressive.

At the same time, a coup might have a better opportunity to succeed when at least some members of the government or its military support the coup. When the members of the Third Estate of the Estates General (a part of the French government) chose to defy King Louis XVI in May 1789 and refused to obey his decision that they accept an unfair level of representation compared to the nobility and the clergy, it represented a serious challenge to the king's authority. When the king ordered his troops to force the Third Estate to accept his decision at bayonet point, the military had to decide whether to support the king or those challenging his power. When the military sided with the Third Estate, the king had little choice but to accept the group's wishes.

## REVOLUTION IN THE TWENTIETH CENTURY

While revolutions have been around since long before the 1900s, more have taken place in the twentieth century than in any other time period. Studies during the 1930s revealed that Western Europe experienced as many as 1,600 "internal disturbances" in just 11 political states during the years following World War I. Approximately 70 percent of these political upheavals involved violence.

Revolutions of the twentieth century were not only more frequent than in any other time frame, they were almost unique in their nature. Some political scientists have identified a theory behind this phenomenon that is new to more modern revolutions: that a revolution takes place as part of a "predestined future, that change in itself is both necessary and good, and that revolution paves the way to human improvement."[12] This view is mirrored in such modern-day revolutions as Hitler's dream of establishing German Nazism worldwide and his vision of the Third Reich, the founding of Marxism in Russia, the making of the People's Republic of China through the poetic guidance and ruthless leadership of Mao Zedong, and others.

The revolutionaries that guided these revolutions believed that history was already determined and that its direction was leading to each revolution in turn. They pushed a political ideology that required the complete overhaul of the state and that "recognized no limits to human potentiality, [demanding] concerted and unstinting efforts to liberate humankind from want and poverty, from material desires and social miseries."[13] But the extraordinary change sought by such revolutionaries was believed only possible when the revolution and its proponents gained total control and power over every aspect of life in their country. This explains why such revolutions produced totalitarian governments under Communist or Fascist leadership.

While these revolutions were driven by ideologies only developed during the late nineteenth century, they often took their cues, whether directly or indirectly, from a political upheaval that unfolded a century earlier—the French Revolution. That late–eighteenth century coup evolved into a complete and total revolution, one based on the goal of establishing a whole new way of life—a brave new world that required absolute social, economic, and political change.

But the comparison between the French Revolution and later total revolutions is limited. During the Russian Revolution of 1917, such radical leaders as Lenin intended to establish complete change for the Russian people. Hitler's concept of the Third Reich was to jettison everything from the past and reestablish a new modern state from top to bottom based on National Socialism. Mao Zedong recast Marxism to fit the Chinese mindset, but he pursued his revolution to establish a completely different political model. These goals were in the minds of these revolutionary leaders from day one. The French Revolution, however, changed course several times, switched leaders more than once, and ended up far afield in 1799 from where revolutionary leaders of 1789 had intended to take it. The result was that "the overall development of the French Revolution was a product of chance: that is, its most radical phase was not an obvious consequence of its initial impetus."[14]

Put simply, the French began their revolution headed in one direction and made a wrong turn along the way. The last major voice of the French Revolution was a minor one during the revolution's opening days: the French revolutionary leader Robespierre rose to political power during the revolution by sheer will through an unpredictable series of events and with lots of good fortune. During the twentieth century, such professional political figures as V.I. Lenin, Joseph Stalin, Adolf Hitler, Mao Zedong, Cuba's Fidel Castro, and Vietnam's Ho Chi Minh were able to plot out their revolutions and keep them on ideological course using such modern elements as propaganda, psychology, mass media, bureaucratic design, and modern forms of manipulation and even intimidation.

It should be noted here, however, that even charismatic leaders did not always recognize their own value to the durability of a revolution. Lenin did not believe a Communist revolution would emerge from the rallying cries of a dynamic leader, but rather from the bottom up, when the social conditions of a state were so desperate that the masses would rise up on their own. In his view, the revolutionary leaders and the radical party they formed were to serve in the role of educators—teachers to the masses—who enlightened the people, providing them with political models to replace the targeted government. However, while Lenin said he believed that the revolution's leaders should never subvert the will of the masses (the proletariat of workers), it is ironic that he saw no problem, once a revolution had succeeded, in placing a dictator in power. In his words, "The Soviet Socialist Democracy is in no way inconsistent with the rule and dictatorship of one person: ... the will of a class is at times best realized by a dictator."[15]

As Lenin put forth, all the charismatic leaders in the complicated world of politics don't count for anything if they do not rally the masses of the people behind them. This means that before a revolution can succeed, the people "must be ripe for revolution."[16] Wherever such a dissatisfied mass of people exists, revolutionary elements often merely have to organize a revolutionary organization or party and call for mass demonstrations and protests. When the

In other cases, revolutions may result from the specific policies of a leader or administration. Here, demonstrators protest a visit to the United States by the Shah of Iran. The Shah's secret police force, SAVAK, was so feared that protesters hid their faces beneath hoods to protect family members in Iran from reprisals.

gathering of support reaches its peak, the existing government will generally be forced to strike hard against the movement with extreme violence or be consumed in the tidal wave of revolution.

## SEVEN REVOLUTIONS

This book presents the subject of political revolution by focusing on seven historical models that took place during the eighteenth, nineteenth, and twentieth centuries. Although other examples could have been chosen, the seven presented here are exemplary. They reveal the different causes of modern revolution while showing how diverse those causes are. The revolutions included are: the American Revolution (1763–1783); the French Revolution (1789–1799); the series of early-nineteenth-century European revolutions (1820–1848); the Mexican Revolution (1910–1920); the Russian

Revolution (1917–1924); the Chinese Revolution (1919–1949); and the Iranian Revolution (1963–1979). The central focus of each of these sections in the book is to present the chronology of events that pushed each revolution along to its final and successful conclusion.

For each, the motivation of the revolutionaries who sought a change in government is discussed. The American Revolution was brought about by perceived repressions against the American colonies by British authorities, including King George III. A repressive monarch is at the center of the French Revolution that soon follows, as the American uprising gives inspiration to would-be French revolutionists. In turn, both the American and French models serve as catalysts for the long series of European revolutions that swept the continent, breaking out in recurring fashion, in 1820, 1830, and 1848.

This revolutionary spirit remained alive into the early twentieth century. In Mexico, the rule of strongman Porfirio Diaz and the crushing economics experienced by countless Mexican peasants led to a series of popular uprisings, each intent on improving the lives of the rural poor and bringing political freedoms long denied. The revolution produced a cast of some of the most colorful revolutionary figures in history.

The twentieth-century revolutions in Russia and China were motivated not only by harsh, centralized government control over the lives of the people, but by strong leadership driven by Marxist and Leninist ideology. The final revolution, in Iran, was the result of strong Muslim fundamentalism that rose up against yet another harsh ruler. Such Islamic extremists were also seeking the destruction of a government they considered too secular and managed to establish a militant Islamic theocracy in its place.

While some of these revolutions only replaced one repressive government with another, the revolutionary spirit often revealed itself through the same human desires to reinvent society and how states are led. In each revolution, a significant membership of each country's population reached an unspoken consensus that the existing government had failed them and that to continue living under the control, rule, and authority of a government they had lost faith in was no longer acceptable.

Whether these revolutionaries defied their government to gain personal freedom, civil rights, economic freedom, land reform, or ideological and religious redirection, in each case they represented a strong sense of the capacity of humans to take control of their own destinies; to crash through the political barriers of time and place. In doing so, countless thousands of people have sacrificed their livelihoods, their futures, and their lives so that another generation might enjoy the fruits of revolution. In doing so, they have paved the road of political change with their personal vision of a world that needed to turn differently.

## SOURCE NOTES

1. Quoted in Robert Rienow, *Introduction to Government*, 2nd Edition. New York: Alfred A. Knopf, 1956, p. 139.
2. Quoted in Thomas Paine, "The Rights of Man," in *Thomas Paine: Representative Selections*, ed. H. Clark. New York: Hill and Wang, 1967, p. 159.
3. Quoted in Thomas M. Magstadt, *Understanding Politics: Ideas, Institutions, and Issues*. New York: St. Martin's Press, 1984, p. 365.
4. Ibid., p. 360.
5. Ibid., p. 361.
6. Quoted in Ted Gurr, *Why Men Rebel*. Princeton: Princeton University Press, 1970, p. 440.
7. Quoted in Robert Hunter, *Revolutions:* *Why? How? When?* New York: Harper and Brothers, 1940, p. 126.
8. Quoted in Walter Lacquer, "Revolution," in *The International Encyclopedia of the Social Sciences*. New York: Macmillan, Free Press, 1968, p. 501.
9. Quoted in Alfred DeGrazia, *Political Behavior*. New York: Free Press, 1962, p. 283.
10. Ibid.
11. Ibid., p. 281.
12. Quoted in Magstadt, *Understanding Politics*, p. 370.
13. Ibid.
14. Ibid.
15. Ibid., p. 372.
16. Ibid., p. 370.

## BIBLIOGRAPHY

Arendt, Hannah. *On Revolution*. New York: Viking Press, 1965.
DeGrazia, Alfred. *Political Behavior*. New York: Free Press, 1962.
Ellsworth, John W., and Arthur A. Stahnke. *Politics and Political Systems: An Introduction to Political Science*. New York: McGraw-Hill Company, 1976.

George, Charles H. *Revolution: European Radicals from Hus to Lenin.* Glenview, IL: Scott, Foresman and Company, 1971.

Gurr, Ted. *Why Men Rebel.* Princeton: Princeton University Press, 1970.

Hunter, Robert. *Revolutions: Why? How? When?* New York: Harper and Brothers, 1940.

Lacquer, Walter. "Revolution," in *The International Encyclopedia of the Social Sciences.* New York: Macmillan, Free Press, 1968.

Paine, Thomas. "The Rights of Man," in *Thomas Paine: Representative Selections*, ed. H. Clark. New York: Hill and Wang, 1967.

Rienow, Robert. *Introduction to Government*, 2nd Edition. New York: Alfred A. Knopf, 1956.

Sabine, George H. *A History of Political Theory.* New York: Holt, Rinehart, and Winston, 1961.

Skocpol, Theda. *States and Social Revolutions: A Comparative Analysis of France, Russia, and China.* Cambridge: Cambridge University Press, 1979.

# Part II:
## The Revolutions

# The American Revolution

**Levi Preston served during the American Revolution as a Minuteman from** Massachusetts, a militia recruit who promised to take up arms against the British at a minute's notice. Sixty years after the revolution, the aged Preston was interviewed about his service in the cause of American liberty. He was asked to describe the British oppressions he experienced. "Oppressions?" the old man asked. "What were they? I didn't feel any." He was asked about the unpopularity of the Stamp Act. "Stamp Act?" Preston wondered. "I never saw any stamps." How about the hated tax on tea? "Well, I never drank a cup of the stuff. The boys threw it all overboard." The frustrated interviewer mentioned John Locke and his principles of liberty. "Never heard of them," said Preston. "Well, then," asked the writer, "what the dickens did you go into this fight for?" The veteran answered matter-of-factly: "Young man, what we meant was this: We always had governed ourselves, we always meant to govern ourselves. The British didn't mean for us to."[1]

For many Americans, the history books are crammed full of the causes and catalysts that contributed to the story of the American Revolution. There were real-life dramas and controversies that brought about the war, a drive toward independence, and a complete separation from control by Great Britain—issues such as the Stamp Act, the Boston Massacre, the tea tax and the Boston Tea Party, the Intolerable Acts, the first shots fired in anger on the village green in Lexington and on Concord Bridge. But behind the stage-sets of political events, street protests, and legal argumentation, there were the minds and hearts of the men and women who committed themselves first as individuals to a cause: that all people have the right to

## George III

The "king who lost America" has generally received a bad press. He was a much better man than monarch, and was more appreciated by the common people of England than by the nobility.

Born in 1738, George was the first member of the German House of Hanover to speak English as his first language (his predecessors both spoke more German than English). He came to the throne in 1760, determined to be a great king; both his mother and his tutors had encouraged him to exert the royal will in government.

For the first decade of his reign, George did quite well. He fired a prime minister he did not like (William Pitt) and brought in others who did his bidding. George III was not a tyrant, as Americans often claim, but he did wish to expand the royal power. His nemesis, as everyone knows, came from taxes and tea.

Starting in 1765, King George and his ministers tried to tax the American colonists to offset the cost of governing them. The Americans resisted the taxes, particularly George's attempt to tax their tea. The infamous "Boston Tea Party" of 1773 led to the British occupation of Boston and the battles of Lexington and Concord, which set off the American Revolutionary War.

George III did all he could to keep the

govern themselves and chart the course of their own political destiny. Each one who stood firm against the authority of Great Britain represents one link in the chain of human events that resulted in the establishment of one of the first great republics in the history of civilization. It is on that independent spirit that the true legacy of the American Revolution rests for all time.

## EARLY CONFLICTS

In 1763, British subjects everywhere were excitedly toasting their young king, 25-year-old George III. That year, the Seven Years' War

American colonies. About 50,000 British troops and perhaps 20,000 German mercenaries were sent across the Atlantic. But it was all in vain, and after the surrenders at Saratoga in 1777 and Yorktown in 1781, the British gave up the fight. American independence was recognized in the Treaty of Paris in 1783.

King George also faced revolt at home. The pro-Catholic policies of some of his ministers led to the Gordon Riots of 1780, in which homes were attacked and property destroyed. King George was probably pleased when the French Revolution of 1789 distracted attention from matters at home: Britons were united in fighting their old French adversaries.

George III started slowly to lose his mind in the 1790s. While he remained as active and as stubborn as ever, he often had sudden lapses of concentration and sometimes fell into fits (he also suffered from porphyria, a stomach disease). In addition, his several sons were a painful disappointment to him; none of them had the bluff, hearty manners of the king himself, who was called "Farmer George" by the British populace.

As the French Revolutionary wars gave way to the Napoleonic wars, King George fell further and further into insanity. He had flashes of lucidity, but all too often he was incapacitated, and the government appointed his son (the future King George IV) as regent for the monarchy.

George III died in 1820 after a 60-year rule, one of the longest reigns on record. He had lost the American colonies to one revolution, suffered revolt at home, and endured the long painful years of the French Revolution and Napoleon. One could say of George that, like his people, he had a gift for "muddling through" tough times. But his critics would claim he brought many of the tough times on himself.

had ended, with a British victory over the French. For most of a century, the troops of Great Britain and France, as well as those of several allied European nations, had been engaged in a series of wars. Each conflict had been fought to determine which powers might dominate Europe and therefore its colonial extensions abroad. The previous three such wars—known by the British and Britain's colonial subjects as King William's War (1689–97), Queen Anne's War (1702–13), and King George's War (1740–48)—had not managed to significantly change the balance of power between Great Britain and France. However, the fourth conflict, a seven-year struggle known in the American colonies as the French and Indian War (1755–1762), dramatically changed the European world of the eighteenth century.

The Treaty of Paris, signed at the conclusion of this conflict, greatly altered the map of the world. The French monarchy that had represented for many years the greatest power in Europe faced serious national losses. A significant French presence in India was lost to the British. French trading posts along the African coast fell from French control. But the greatest loss for France was in North America. For over 150 years, the French had developed a colonial power base called New France, lands which today comprise much of Canada. The economy of New France was based on extensive trade systems with Native Americans, who traded valuable furs for a wide variety of French manufactured goods, including iron cooking kettles, clothing materials, guns, knives, and decorative items. With the loss of this valuable trade territory and firm toehold in North America, the French empire overseas was nearly dismantled.

The British emerged from war owning territory in North America that included all of French Canada as well as the territory between the Mississippi River and the Appalachian Mountains. (It was a dispute between Britain and France over control of this latter territory that had led to the French and Indian War in the first place.)

While British citizens and subjects around the world celebrated the great victory of 1763, the English residents of the 13 American colonies were perhaps the most excited. British subjects up and down the Atlantic coast, from New Hampshire to Georgia, held parades and burned giant bonfires following the victory of their Mother Country over the French and her Spanish allies. At last the French challenge to British trade abroad, which included British colonial shippers and merchants, had been crippled. In addition, the evacuation of the French from Canada removed the French threat to British subjects who wanted to move west into Ohio River country.

## The 13 Colonies Before the Revolution

As the events unfolded during the 1760s and 1770s that led to the American Revolution, English colonists in America constituted a unique population. For more than 150 years, Europeans, especially immigrants from Great Britain, had made their way across the Atlantic in search of new lives in America—from the establishment of Virginia's Jamestown in 1607 to the founding of the last colony, Georgia, in the 1730s. The British colonies had become home to 2.5 million people by 1750.

They represented a diverse population. While the majority (about 60 percent) came directly or indirectly from Great Britain, other European nations provided important populations, including Scots and Scots-Irish (14 percent), Germans (9 percent), Dutch (6 percent), and Irish (4 percent). In addition, more than 500,000 colonial residents were black—the vast majority of them slaves—a number equal to 20 percent of the total non-Indian population of the 13 colonies.

In religious background, the people of the colonies were equally diverse. The largest Christian group was the Congregationalists, many of them the descendents of the Puritans who had settled New England during the early 1600s. Others were Presbyterian, Baptist, Anglican, Lutheran, German Reformed, and Catholic. One of the most unique groups in the colonies, the Quakers, did not believe in owning slaves or fighting wars. The colonies were also home to at least five Jewish synagogues.

Just as in Europe, most of the colonists were farmers, many of them occupying acreage larger than the average in Great Britain or on the European Continent. A variety of crops, including cereal grains, tobacco, rice, and indigo provided an important base for the colonial economy. Other activities included shipping, shipbuilding, ironworks, shopkeeping, printing, distilling, and a host of crafts and skills.

While colonization during the seventeenth century had proven difficult for many of the earliest European arrivals to the North American Atlantic Coast, by the eighteenth century life in the colonies was much more secure. By 1750, industrious American colonists, with few restrictions placed on them by the Mother Country, were enjoying the highest per-capita income of any European-based people in the world.

## CLOUDS ON THE HORIZON

To both British citizen and colonial subject, 1763 appeared to mark a new era for the British Empire. British subjects in the American colonies felt a new sense of pride in their Mother Country. Colonists expressed their personal happiness in living under the protection of the British Crown. One colonial leader, a Philadelphia printer named Benjamin Franklin, enthusiastically wrote: "I am a BRITON."[2] A New England minister reflected the views of many colonials when he spoke of the bright future ahead: "Now commences the Era of our quiet Enjoyment of those Liberties, which our Fathers purchased with the Toil of their whole Lives.... Here shall be the late founded Seat of Peace and Freedom. Here shall our indulgent Mother, who has most generously rescued and protected us, be served and honoured by growing Numbers, with all Duty, Love and Gratitude, till time shall be no more."[3]

However, clouds soon formed on the new international horizon. Although the British Crown had successfully won a significant victory over the French, success had come at a high cost. During the years of the French and Indian War, the British national debt soared to new heights, nearly doubling from £75 million to £137 million. Just the interest on this new staggering debt amounted to £5 million annually.

The victory over the French did not even bring an end to the British cost of maintaining colonies in America. Further debt was added soon when clashes arose between the British and the Indians of the Ohio River country who had been trade allies with the French. During the summer of 1763, the Ottawa chief, Pontiac, launched a campaign against the British. He and his followers raided and sacked eight British forts situated along the Great Lakes and laid siege to forts at Pittsburgh and Detroit. Approximately 2,000 English colonists were killed during Pontiac's Rebellion. Putting down this challenge to British authority west of the Appalachian Mountains took three years and more money from an already exhausted treasury.

To help reduce the possibility of an endless string of Indian wars in the region, the British Crown passed the Proclamation of 1763. The proclamation turned direct control of all land west of the Appalachians and east of the Mississippi River, the territory the British had wrested from France at the end of the French and Indian

War, over to the Crown. The goal of the government directive was to establish order in the oversight of these western lands by placing them in the hands of the Crown and out of the control of the 13 colonies. The proclamation recognized all previous Native American land titles west of the "proclamation line" (which followed the Appalachian Mountains) and closed all further colonial migration into the region until proper treaties might be established. The act also required "all persons whatever who have either willfully or inadvertently seated themselves" upon these western territories to "remove themselves from such settlements."[4] Thousands of British subjects had already moved west and occupied land in Ohio, Kentucky, and Tennessee. They immediately responded to the announcement by the Crown with hatred and hostility. The proclamation drove a permanent wedge between the colonists and the British government.

Some of the strongest colonial hatred was reserved for the chief minister to King George III, George Grenville, a dour and humorless man whom even the king personally disliked. He was a man who "possessed an excellent head for figures, no imagination, and extreme conceit."[5] Grenville was responsible for the Proclamation of 1763. That the act infuriated the colonists mattered little to the king's minister: he was strongly anti-American. But the proclamation was only the beginning of Grenville's antagonisms toward the British colonies.

## THE SUGAR ACT

As the chief minister studied the cost to the Crown of maintaining 10,000 British regular troops in the colonies, he estimated the force's price tag at £250,000 annually. Since the troops were supposedly assigned for the protection of the colonies, Grenville determined the colonial governments should shoulder some of the financial burden. By 1764, Grenville was intent on placing new taxes on the king's subjects in America. That April, he pushed through Parliament a bill called the Revenue Act, or more popularly, the Sugar Act.

The act had several purposes. It established a complicated list of regulations describing how ships trading with the colonies should be loaded and unloaded. This was to help British customs officials uncover the work of colonial smugglers, who were seriously undercutting British trade in the colonies. Second, the Sugar Act established trade duties, or import taxes, on a list of foreign goods commonly imported into the American colonies, such as coffee, indigo, wine, and, of course, sugar. Grenville's plan was a simple one: by his calculations, the Sugar Act might generate £100,000 for the British treasury—monies that could be used to offset the cost of maintaining British troops on colonial soil.

It was this fact alone that angered the colonists. While the colonies were accustomed to British acts that regulated their trade (even though most such acts were never enforced uniformly by British authorities), they understood the Sugar Act for what it was—a tax on the colonies to generate revenue for the Crown. Another aspect of the Sugar Act that infuriated colonists was that it allowed

## James Otis

He is little known today, but James Otis paved the way for that very American expression: No taxation without representation.

Born on Cape Cod in 1725, Otis graduated from Harvard College in 1743. He studied law and married an heiress, with whom he had three children. All this was just prelude to his revolutionary activities, however.

The British had experienced American smuggling into the colonies for decades and wanted to bring it to an end. In 1760 the British customs commissioner in Boston began to issue writs of assistance, which allowed his agents to search any home at any time. Whether or not Otis favored the illegal American trade in sugar and molasses makes no difference; he came out powerfully against the writs of assistance, which, he claimed went against centuries of British law.

"A man's house is his castle," he declared, and although Otis did not coin the expression, he used it in his legal argument against the writs of assistance in 1761. No formal record was made of that day in court, but the young John Adams, who was present, later declared it had been the beginning of the idea and the ideals of the American Revolution. Otis went on to argue that there was a "natural" or higher law that took precedence over documents such as the writs of assistance. Throughout this court proceeding, Otis used the traditions of Anglo-Saxon justice against the British customs commissioners; the case was finally decided in England in 1766, in favor of the Americans.

Otis then wrote *A Vindication of the Conduct of the House of Representatives* (1762) and *The Rights of the British Colonies Asserted and Proved* (1764). In the latter he accused smugglers to be tried outside the colonial court system, transferring cases to vice-admiralty courts, where a British judge would make a decision without a jury. (These courts were also located outside the American colonies, in Canadian Halifax.) Since the law allowed vice-admiralty judges to keep 5 percent of all allegedly smuggled cargoes, they had an additional incentive to find accused smugglers guilty.

Although the act met a strong reaction in the colonies, Grenville was not deterred. He ordered British naval ships to strongly enforce the law. As one colonial observer in Boston, home to one of America's most important ports, noted: "No vessel hardly comes in or goes out but they find some pretense to seize and detain her."[6]

used a more elegant phrase to express what later became common usage: "The very act of taxing, except over those who are represented, appears to me to be depriving them of one of their most essential rights as freemen; and if continued, seems to be in effect an entire disenfranchisement of every civil right." This was abbreviated by American patriots to the catchier phrase, "No taxation without representation!"

By 1766, Otis's ideas had caught on with many of his fellow American colonists, and he appeared ripe for a position of leadership in the coming revolution. But sadly, at the same time, his mind began to fray. There had been no warning in his earlier life, but from 1766 onward he headed further and further toward insanity. Things became so bad that his relatives asked Lieutenant Governor Thomas Hutchinson (who had long been Otis's political enemy) to remand him to their custody. He continued to appear at political meetings, and sometimes demonstrated his old lucidity, but it never lasted for long.

The Revolution brought new heartbreak. Otis's wealthy wife favored the British cause during the Revolutionary War and the family was harmed by the divergence in opinions. Otis's only son died in a British prison during the war, while one of his daughters married a British lieutenant. Otis himself struggled on during the war years, only half conscious at times. In 1783, staying at the home of a friend in Andover, Massachusetts, Otis was struck by a bolt of lightning. This dramatic exit from life in some ways mirrored his long and painful struggle with insanity. It was in the same year the colonists won their independence with the Treaty of Paris.

The passage of the Sugar Act revealed distinct differences between how the colonists saw themselves and their relationship with the Mother Country and how some British officials understood that same relationship. The colonies believed the British government should be responsible for their protection, since they existed as an extension of the British Empire. After all, British colonials were still subjects of the Crown and should enjoy the security provided by the king. Many colonists also believed they should be able to practice a certain level of independence from Great Britain. Each colony had its own assembly of representatives that made laws for that colony, whether Massachusetts, Pennsylvania, or Virginia. The colonists had also become accustomed to engaging in trade and business with little interference from the Mother Country. As early as the 1720s, Britain's first prime minister, Robert Walpole, established an official policy toward the colonies that he called "salutary neglect."[7] With greater political conflicts at home and wars to fight abroad, Walpole had believed that "if the colonial relationship wasn't broken—and British-American trade was still producing high profits for both sides—why fix it?"[8] The Sugar Act signaled a significant change from that earlier practice. The British Crown now seemed intent not only on regulating American trade, but on taxing the colonies as well.

Some colonists were prepared to speak out against an act they considered outside the scope of Parliament's power. Much of the protest was centered in the colonies of Massachusetts, Pennsylvania, and New York, home to three of the largest colonial ports—Boston, Philadelphia, and New York City. In Virginia, members of the colonial legislature, the House of Burgesses, zeroed in on the centerpiece of the developing rift between the colonies and the Mother Country: "Laws imposing taxes on the People ought not to be made without the Consent of Representatives chosen by themselves."[9] A Massachusetts lawyer, James Otis Jr., established the framework for the argument that would rage between the colonies and Great Britain for the next 15 years. In his pamphlet *The Rights of the British Colonies Asserted and Proved*, Otis wrote: "I can see no reason to doubt but that the imposition of taxes, whether on trade, or on land, or houses, or ships, on real or personal ... property, in the colonies is absolutely irreconcilable with the rights of the colonists as British subjects and as men."[10]

But overall, the colonial protest was limited, fragmented, and generally fell on deaf ears. Residents of Great Britain wondered what all the fuss in the colonies was about since they were taxed at a much higher rate than the Americans. Burdened by the second-highest tax rates in Europe, Britons paid 26 shillings per person each year while the colonists only paid between $1/2$ and $1^1/2$ shillings each annually, an amount falling between 2 and 6 percent of the British tax rate.

## THE STAMP ACT

Once in place, the Sugar Act failed to generate the income Lord Grenville had anticipated, bringing in only about £20,000 due to continued American smuggling. The disappointed British minister was forced to turn to other measures. On March 22, 1765, Parliament passed another of Grenville's revenue-generating bills— the Stamp Act.

While the Sugar Act had generally impacted only colonial merchants, the Stamp Act hit everyone—lawyers, printers, professionals of every stripe, tavern keepers—who handled paper items of any sort. It required colonists to buy special stamped paper for "newspapers, customs documents, various licenses, college diplomas, as well as legal forms used for recovering debts, buying land, and making wills."[11] (The paper in question did not actually have stamps affixed to it but was "stamped" with a watermark.) To make matters worse, the act required the stamped paper to be paid for with gold or silver coins, not paper money. Such coins were rare in the colonies, and paying with such "hard money" allowed the coinage to leave the colonies altogether.

Grenville did not anticipate the level of colonial protest to the Stamp Act, since residents of England had already been paying such a tax since 1695. But, as with the Sugar Act, protests focused on the question of Parliamentary power. Fearful of more and similar acts to follow, many colonists chose to take serious steps in opposition to the Stamp Act. Unlike earlier protests, the measures taken in the colonies against the Stamp Act were forceful and well-organized.

The Massachusetts General Court led the way. In June 1765, James Otis encouraged the colonial court (assembly) to propose an intercolonial meeting to organize protests against the Stamp Act. Nine colonies sent representatives to the convention, called the Stamp Act Congress, which met in October in New York City. This movement represented only the second time the colonies had participated in an intercolonial meeting. (The first had take place more than a decade earlier.)

## Samuel Adams and Thomas Hutchinson

The great patriot leader Thomas Jefferson once referred to Samuel Adams as "truly the man of the Revolution."[*] During the decade leading up to the outbreak of the Revolutionary War in 1775, perhaps no patriot rallied more support in opposition to British taxation and control over the colonies than did Adams. Among the British officials Adams came to despise more than any other was Thomas Hutchinson, who served as Massachusetts' lieutenant governor and later as governor. While Adams's patriotism led him to oppose men such as Hutchinson, he may also have disliked the royal official for personal reasons as well.

When Sam Adams was growing up in Boston, his father had been a prosperous malt manufacturer—so prosperous that he was able to send young Samuel to Harvard, where he hoped his son would train to become a minister. (In 1740, at the age of 18, the younger Adams graduated but had little desire to become a clergyman.) The year his son finished college, "Deacon" Samuel helped establish the Massachusetts Land Bank to help poorer citizens get loans by allowing them to put up real estate as collateral. The loans were paid by the bank in paper money.

Enter Thomas Hutchinson, then a local prosperous Massachusetts businessman and merchant. He and others like him did not like the land bank, since they did not trust the paper notes in circulation at the time as payment for debts. Hutchinson and his friends convinced the royal governor of Massachusetts to declare the bank illegal. The next year, Parliament upheld the decision. The elder Adams was financially ruined, saddled with several lawsuits, and died a few years later.

When, in 1758, Hutchinson became lieutenant governor by royal appointment, Sam Adams still blamed him for his father's reversal of fortune. Because Hutchinson and others supported various taxation acts placed on the colonies by Parliament, Adams was all too eager to rally Bostonians on a street level against the new imperial policies. To what extent Adams was motivated to lead colonial protests by his personal hatred of Hutchinson will never be known (in his later years, Adams destroyed many of his personal papers), but that he led the way in opposition to British policies he considered oppressive did succeed in making him "one of the prime movers of the ... Revolution."[**]

[*] Quoted in James Kirby Martin, *America and Its People.* New York: HarperCollins, 1993, p. 112.

[**] Ibid., p. 113.

Those present at the Stamp Act Congress wrote a petition to Parliament calling for the repeal of both the Sugar and Stamp Acts. While the petition was ignored by Parliament, the meeting was symbolic. "The Ministry never imagined we could or would so generally unite in opposition to their measures," stated a representative from Connecticut, "nor I confess till I saw the Experiment made did I."[12]

In the Virginia House of Burgesses, a young lawyer named Patrick Henry helped push through a series of proposals called the Virginia Stamp Act Resolutions. One of the strongest resolutions stated that only Virginia representatives held the power to tax the people of Virginia—a direct slap at the power of Parliament. In an incendiary speech, Henry is alleged to have stated, "Caesar had his Brutus, Charles the First had his Cromwell, and George the Third ..." (at which point the loyalist House speaker shouted, "Treason!") "... may profit by their example. If this be treason, make the most of it!"[13]

Other colonial protests were less formal and more community based. In Boston by late summer, a group of businessmen—mostly middle-class types, including shopkeepers, artisans, and distillers—led by a fiery political organizer named Samuel Adams formed a coalition called the Loyal Nine in opposition to the Stamp Act. Since the act would not take effect until November 1, the group began to organize against the act's weakest link, which stipulated that selected stamp distributors would be the only agents to be paid for watermarked papers. The Loyal Nine surmised that if those men could be intimidated, they might fail to do their jobs, and the act would never be enforced. In Boston, the appointed distributor was Andrew Oliver, a brother-in-law to the colony's lieutenant governor, Thomas Hutchinson.

## PROTEST IN THE STREETS

On the morning of August 14, 1765, public protests designed to intimidate Oliver took place. Street mobs of Bostonians hung a dummy of Oliver from an elm tree in Boston's South End. (The tree later became known as the "Liberty Tree.") When an appalled Lt. Governor Hutchinson and a local sheriff tried to remove the effigy, the gathered crowd threw rocks at them.

That evening, a crowd numbering in the thousands marched down the streets of Boston to Oliver's home, chanting "Liberty, Property, and No Stamps." The Olivers left their house before the

In an attempt to raise money to protect the western frontier of its American colonies, the British monarchy in 1765 passed the Stamp Act, which placed a tax on every piece of paper used by American colonists. Though the tax itself was minor, it drew much resentment and violent protest.

unruly crowd arrived. Once there, the protestors ransacked the home's first floor (several stole bottles from Oliver's wine cellar), then built a huge bonfire using kindling from Oliver's fence, and burned the stamp agent's effigy. Their message could not have been more clear. Frightened for his life, Andrew Oliver resigned as Boston's stamp agent the following morning.

Less than two weeks later, another Boston riot resulted in the destruction of the elegant townhouse of Thomas Hutchinson, whom many Boston residents hated. Axe-wielding rioters hacked down the front door and destroyed nearly everything inside. Hutchinson later described the aftermath of the riot: "They continued their possession until daylight; destroyed, carried away, or cast into the street everything that was in the house; demolished every part of it, except for walls, as lay in their power."[14]   Ironically, Hutchinson had never given any support to the Stamp Act.

With the successful intimidation of Andrew Oliver, other colonies organized protests to intimidate their designated stamp agents. Groups similar to the Loyal Nine formed in several colonies, calling themselves the Sons of Liberty. Such groups did not give complete support to the type of unrestricted rioting that had taken place in Boston. That riots could intimidate was clear; that mobs are difficult to control was also clear. The Sons of Liberty became so concerned that armed rioters might kill someone, even accidentally, and alienate a whole portion of the colonial populace that their leaders banned the use of weapons. If anyone was going to be killed during a protest, it was going to be one of their own. So successful were the Sons of Liberty and other colonial protest groups at intimidating stamp distributors that, by November 1, when the first stamped paper was to be made available, nearly all the distributors, royal customs officials, and court officers refused to carry out their tasks.

While paper protests, official resolutions, and street-level rioting played their roles in opposing the Stamp Act, yet another form of protest finally led the British Parliament to abandon it. On October 31, 1765, the merchants of New York City organized a boycott, called a "nonimportation agreement," of British goods to the colonies. They promised not to order "goods or merchandise of any nature, kind, or quality whatsoever, usually imported from Great Britain, ... unless the Stamp Act be repealed."[15] Within weeks, merchants in other colonial cities joined in. For two months, trade and import commerce in the colonies nearly ground to a standstill. Any business requiring the use of stamped paper ceased, including court proceedings, port of entry documents, even newspaper publication. By early 1766, commerce was reopened, and colonists ignored the

Stamp Act. In Parliament, the members responded by repealing the Stamp Act in March. (As for the highly unpopular Grenville, George III had already replaced him the previous summer with another advisor, Lord Rockingham, who was more sympathetic to the Americans.)

Even as Parliament surrendered and buried the hated Stamp Act, the British body was not admitting it did not have the right to tax the colonies. At the same time the members of Parliament threw out the Stamp Act, they also passed the Declaratory Act, which proclaimed the power of Parliament to "pass any law it wished binding the colonies and people of America."[16]

## John Hancock

Even today, a well-known expression is: "Put your John Hancock there," meaning to put your signature on a dotted line, and to thereby commit yourself to something. Hancock's signature on the Declaration of Independence is one of the most famous and recognized in American history.

Born in Boston in 1737, John Hancock was a most unlikely revolutionary. He was adopted by his uncle, Thomas Hancock, the most successful Boston merchant of the day, and grew up in something akin to luxury. He knew the feel of silk, the taste of Madeira wine, and he often rode in a stately carriage. These were hardly the normal accoutrements of a revolutionary.

Then came the Stamp Act of 1765. King George III and his ministers intended to get all they could out of American taxpayers, and wealthy John Hancock—who had inherited his uncle's estate—became one of the leaders of the resistance. In 1768, one of his merchant ships, the *Liberty*, was seized by British customs agents, who correctly suspected Hancock of smuggling. The British action won Hancock the sympathy of Bostonians and made him more committed to the revolutionary cause.

On the morning of the battles of Lexington and Concord, John Hancock and Samuel Adams, who had been staying in the area, rode to safety in a carriage: they had been alerted by the dispatch rider Paul Revere. As they headed south to Philadelphia, Hancock and Adams exulted that the great war for independence had begun.

Once they arrived in Philadelphia, Hancock was elected president of the Second Continental Congress, though there were some who whispered that due to his wealth he had bought his station (there was

## THE TOWNSHEND DUTIES

Three years had passed since the end of the French and Indian War, and the staggering British debt remained, growing larger each year. New acts designed to raise revenue in the colonies were waiting in the wings, despite the debacle created in the colonies with the Stamp Act. In 1767, the British government's money man, Chancellor of the Exchequer Charles Townshend, proposed new tariffs, or trade duties, for the American colonies. The Townshend Acts established new import duties on a long list of trade commodities, including such high-demand items as glass, lead, paints, paper, and tea. In specific terms, the Townshend duties were a form of external taxation, a duty

no truth in the rumors). Though he was not corrupt, Hancock was quite vain. He was bitterly disappointed when the Continental Congress selected George Washington and not him as the new commander-in-chief of the American army. But Hancock's best days were still to come. In the spring and early summer of 1776, the Continental Congress, presided over by Hancock, approved the document known ever since as the Declaration of Independence. Hancock was the first delegate to sign, and he did so with a flourish, saying "There! I guess King George will be able to read that."

Hancock suffered from various health ailments, and he resigned his position in 1777. He returned to Boston and was somewhat eclipsed during the second half of the Revolutionary War. But he ran for and became the first governor of the new state of Massachusetts and enjoyed great popularity.

A very astute politician, Hancock did not run for reelection in 1785, thereby managing to avoid being tainted by Shays' Rebellion in western Massachusetts in 1786. After the fracas was over, Hancock ran for governor and won yet again; he remained in office until his death in 1793.

Like George Washington, John Hancock was an ambitious man who rode the revolutionary wave. Unlike Washington, Hancock never made it to the "first tier" of the most prominent Revolutionary Americans: He remained solidly and respectably in the second tier. Most historical connections to John Hancock continue to refer to his bold signature on July 2, 1776 (though the holiday is celebrated on July 4, the signing was done two days before).

placed on goods entering colonial customhouses before they reached colonial stores, shops, and other businesses.

Like the Sugar Act, these new duties met bitter opposition in the colonies. In New England, the Massachusetts General Court once again led the protest by composing and sending to other colonies a Circular Letter, calling for new nonimportation agreements. Tired of colonial opposition to such laws, Governor Francis Bernard of Massachusetts ordered the General Court dissolved. He also sent letters to England requesting that additional British troops be dispatched to Boston, a hotbed of colonial protest. Technically, Bernard did not have the power to make such a request; only the governor's council could, but that body consisted of the upper house of the Massachusetts General Court, which Bernard had ordered dissolved.

A paper protest was also published. A wealthy Pennsylvania lawyer named John Dickinson penned an extremely popular pamphlet titled *Letters from a Farmer in Pennsylvania*, which was printed in many colonial newspapers. Disguising himself as a simple farmer, Dickinson argued that, while Parliament had the power to create duties to regulate trade, it had no constitutional authority to tax goods before they reached the open market, especially when the only goal was to raise revenue for the British treasury. However, although Dickinson did not recognize Parliament's power to create such taxes, he still encouraged colonists to "behave like dutiful children who have received unmerited blows from a beloved parent."[17] (Years later, Dickinson did not support the moves made toward independence.)

As colonial protests of the Townshend duties spread, the British government took an increasingly dim view of events across the Atlantic. Events in Boston were especially troublesome. Bostonians defied the laws, refusing to pay the duties. In June 1768, one of the richest shippers in the colonies, Boston merchant John Hancock, faced down customs agents who boarded and seized one of his sloops, the *Liberty*, for nonpayment of duties. (Hancock was a notorious smuggler.) In response, a crowd assaulted the customs officials, sending them running for their lives, some even leaving Boston altogether.

By September, street clashes between Boston citizens and British officials, including soldiers, gave rise to a town meeting in which citizens were encouraged to arm themselves. Even though no armed clashes resulted, the move led to an increase by October 1 in the number of British troops stationed in the city, including artillery regiments. One Bostonian minister lamented the arrival of so many British Redcoats—600 in all—in his city: "Good God! What can be worse to a people who have tasted the sweets of liberty! Things have come to an unhappy crisis, ... and the moment there is any bloodshed all affection will cease."[18]

## THE BOSTON MASSACRE

Such troops became hated targets of colonists over the following two years. Conflict between the two factions became common. In New York City, the Sons of Liberty erected "liberty poles" and decorated them with symbols, banners, and flags in support of their patriot causes and anti-British attitudes. British troops would follow and tear the potent symbols down. In September 1769, James Otis caused a riot when he picked a fight with British troops enjoying drinks in a local tavern. In December 1769, a clash between the Sons of Liberty and British Redcoats led to a riot involving thousands of New Yorkers carrying pistols, cutlasses, and wooden clubs. When soldiers were arrested in such riots, they were often treated harshly by colonial court judges.

While the presence of thousands of British troops was in itself troubling to colonists in Boston and elsewhere, additional flashpoints developed. British soldiers were generally poorly paid, and many of them tried to find additional work, taking jobs away from colonists. On a Friday, March 2, 1770, one such British soldier went to a Boston rope-making business looking for work. The proprietor scoffed at the off-duty Redcoat, telling him he could get a job cleaning the Bostonian's outhouse. The humiliated and angry soldier left but soon returned with several of his friends from the king's Twenty-ninth Regiment. A fight broke out that resulted in the soldiers being driven from the business.

With street tensions running high during the days that followed, a second encounter took place on the following Monday, March 5. (The weekend had witnessed additional fights between soldiers and Boston citizens.) That evening, a mob of citizens wandered down Boston's King Street to the Customs House, where a small detachment of the Twenty-ninth Regiment was stationed on guard duty.

When tensions and emotions are at their peak, anything can spark violence. The Boston Massacre of 1770 began when a British sentry struck a protestor with the butt of his musket. British soldiers soon arrived, and six colonists were killed.

Outside the Customs House, a lone British sentry, Private Hugh White, stood guard and was soon facing the mob and a variety of taunts. At one point Private White struck someone in the crowd in the face with the butt of his musket. Soon dozens more joined the mob in protest of the soldier's actions. White moved away from the crowd, fixing his bayonet on the end of his musket barrel. With snow on the ground, the rioters began tossing hard-packed snowballs and chunks of ice at the sentry, taunting him to fire on them: "Knock him down!" they shouted to the frightened soldier. "Fire, damn you, fire! You dare not fire!" The Redcoat shouted for help from his comrades, shouting, "Turn out, Main Guard!" Soon a British officer, Captain Thomas Preston, appeared with seven soldiers who were soon facing a mob that had grown to as many as 400 rioters. When Preston tried to march his men, including the hapless sentry, out of the volatile street situation, the mob blocked their path. When two of Preston's men were recognized for their involvement in the fighting at the rope business three days earlier, some of the rioters became even more antagonistic. As Preston ordered the crowd to disperse, some of the rioters began hitting the guardsmen's musket barrels with clubs. The situation had become an impossible one for anyone to control. Then, someone threw a club, striking a soldier, who fell. Private Hugh Montgomery then stood, picked up his musket and fired. Other soldiers also fired. In the aftermath of the senseless riot, three Bostonians fell dead and six others were wounded. (Two of them died later of their wounds.) Among them was a free black man named Crispus Attucks.

Immediately, the wounded and dead became heroes to the Boston patriots. As for Captain Preston and his men, he and eight others were arrested by the town sheriff an hour later. Patriot groups around the city lashed out at Governor Hutchinson, demanding that he order the removal of all British troops from the city of Boston. Within days, the troops were transferred to an island fort in Boston Harbor. The soldiers accused of murder did not stand trial until September. Ironically, one of their defense attorneys was John Adams, a well-known patriot lawyer. Adams, while having no love for the British presence in Massachusetts, believed it was more important to give the accused British soldiers a fair trial than to simply force a guilty verdict on them. On October 30, the jury returned their verdict on Captain Preston, finding him not guilty. A month later, the other eight soldiers stood trial; six were acquitted and two received brands on their right thumbs.

Once again, street violence had raised its ugly head in Boston and, unlike earlier encounters between British officials and Bostonian mobs, it had turned deadly. Some patriot leaders referred to the bloody encounter as the "Boston Massacre," and spoke of the men killed outside the Boston Customs House as martyrs to the patriot cause. Sam Adams called for March 5 to be recognized as a holiday on which the deaths of the five "patriots" would be commemorated. Others, including John Adams, saw the street demonstration as little more than rabblerousing, carried out, in his words, by "a motley rabble of saucy boys, negroes and mulattoes, Irish teagues, and outlandish jack tarrs."[19]

But regardless of the social class of those who taunted the British soldiers that wintry March evening, the Boston Massacre did have far-reaching results. British troops were removed from Boston proper. In addition, the "massacre" caused many colonists to question how far the British Crown would go to hold on to the colonies. Many also gained a greater level of mistrust of the British government and its intentions in the colonies.

## AN ARTIFICIAL CALM

On March 5, 1770, the very day of the Boston Massacre, a new British prime minister, Lord Frederick North, came before Parliament asking for the repeal of the Townshend Duties, with the exception of one—the tax on tea. Helping to push the cause of repeal along was another colonial boycott of British goods between 1768 and 1770. As for Townshend himself, he died in 1767, failing to live long enough to hear the endless complaints of the abuses brought on by his hated duties.

As prime minister, Lord North steered clear of any major confrontation with the American colonies. Too much, he believed, had been thrown at the colonists in too short a time period, causing them to respond too emotionally, too quickly, and too violently. For two years an artificial calm fell over the colonies and colonial resistance was somewhat diminished. There was one notable outbreak of violence in Rhode Island when, in June 1772, local patriots destroyed an armed British customs schooner, the *Gaspee*. The *Gaspee's* captain had gained a local reputation for his efficiency in pursuing smugglers. On the day in question, Rhode Islanders sent a small sloop out to lure the *Gaspee* into shallow waters. When the British ship ran aground, a group of locals disguised as Indians set the stranded vessel on fire, burning her to the waterline. (One of the disguised colonists fired a shotgun at Captain William Dudingston, hitting him in the buttocks.) Although British officials established a royal commission of inquiry, no one ever pointed out those responsible for the destruction of the British ship.

While the *Gaspee* incident represented a black mark on relations between Great Britain and the colonies during the early 1770s, it did not become a rallying cry against British power in the Americas. Even as a handful of patriot figures were beginning to clamor for complete separation from the Mother Country, most were convinced they should continue to protest the authority of Parliament while continuing to recognize the authority of the British monarch and pledging their allegiance to him.

## Samuel Adams

Generally considered the "rabble-rouser" of the American Revolution, Samuel Adams was actually a complex man with competing motivations.

Born in Boston in 1722, Adams was, like his cousin John Adams, from a prominent Massachusetts family. He went to Harvard College and then started his own merchant business, which eventually failed.

Early in the 1760s, Samuel Adams became one of the loudest spokesmen for intercolonial unity. He was not yet a true revolutionary; rather, he believed that the colonists needed to band together to win greater respect from King George and the British Parliament. But by the middle part of the decade, Adams was convinced that peaceful settlement of the issues was impossible, and that the colonists would eventually have to fight for their independence.

Samuel Adams's largest role in fomenting the American Revolution came in the autumn of 1773, when he and his fellow "Sons of Liberty," after Parliament's passage of the tea tax, refused to let British ships land their cargoes of tea and later boarded the three ships and heaved the tea into Boston Harbor. Not long afterward, in April 1775, the battles of Lexington and Concord marked the beginning of armed conflict. Samuel Adams's vision of the future had proved accurate.

By then both Samuel Adams and John Adams were members of the Second Continental Congress, which met in Philadelphia. Considering that he had been the firebrand who had done much to bring on the revolutionary struggle, Samuel Adams proved something of a moderate in his congressional activity; he was less active than his cousin, and drew less attention to himself.

On his return to Massachusetts and to her politics, Samuel Adams played a role in drawing up the state constitution, which was approved in 1780. He appeared destined for the "scrap heap" until he was elected lieutenant-governor in 1789. Upon the death of Governor John Hancock, Adams entered the governor's office and was reelected each time he sought the post. Even so, he retired from public service a "poor man" as he described it, but rich in years and personal satisfaction. Adams attracted little attention in his later years and was buried in a quiet ceremony at Boston's Granary Cemetery.

Adams is often misunderstood because his early career and later record are at such variance with each other. Perhaps he is best seen as a "happy warrior," one who achieved his goal of political independence, and then became more conservative as he grew older. His name remains one of those most often remembered in the public mind, helped perhaps by the well-known "Sam Adams" brand of beer. Whether the one-time failure as a merchant would have liked this representation of himself is impossible to say.

Just months after the *Gaspee* incident, events began to heat up again in the colonies as the North ministry, in the fall of 1772, began implementing the remnants of the Townshend Acts, including the provision that royal governors of the colonies (all of whom were appointed by the British Crown), as well as royally-appointed judges, be paid by collected customs revenues.

In early November 1772, patriots attending a Boston town meeting responded to the policy by establishing a Committee of Correspondence, a group designed to publicize the British move throughout Massachusetts. Boston leader Samuel Adams was appointed as the committee's head. Adams by then was 51 and still a fiery colonial voice. He was a distant cousin of John Adams and 13 years older. In fact, he was older than most of the prominent colonial patriots.

Although Adams was a man of meager means (he was little more than Boston's trash collector), he was an experienced political organizer and sometimes embodied the voice of protest in the colonies. By late November 1772, with help from James Otis and Josiah Quincy (an attorney who had helped John Adams defend the soldiers accused of murder in the Boston Massacre), Adams drafted a key statement in support of the patriot cause, titled *The Rights of the Colonists*. The pamphlet opened with a clear view of what rights the British government should recognize in the colonies:

> Among the natural rights of the colonists are these: first, a right to life; second, to liberty; third, to property; together with the right to support and define them in the best manner they can. These are evident branches of ... the duty of self-preservation, commonly called the first law of nature.[20]

Further, Adams's pamphlet complained of taxation by the Crown without representation; of the presence of British troops, as well as customs officers, on American soil; and the use of trade revenues to pay for British officials in the colonies.

Adams's words struck deep in the hearts of many patriots when he noted: "Can it be said with any color of truth and justice that this continent of 3,000 miles in length ... in which ... it is supposed there are 5,000,000 people, has the least voice, vote, or influence in the British Parliament?"[21] Through the efforts and such publications as

*The Rights of the Colonists*, the majority of Massachusetts towns and villages supported the patriot leaders in Boston.

## THE TAX ON TEA

After a period of relative calm, confrontation and violence broke out between British officials and colonial patriots in 1773. That spring, Parliament passed an act simple in purpose, yet highly offensive to many colonists. The Tea Act granted a monopoly on selling tea to the colonies to a British firm teetering on the brink of bankruptcy—the East India Company. A formerly prosperous trading firm, the East India had fallen on hard times, due in part to an abundance of tea available from India, which drove the price down, and to the recent colonial "nonimportation agreements," which had destroyed the American market for tea. Desperate for help, the directors of the East India Company had appealed to Parliament for help. Their primary request was permission to import tea directly to America (eliminating the cost of shipping first through England, as British law required, adding to the cost of doing business) and bypassing British and American middlemen. The firm also sought the right to sell its tea directly through designated colonial agents, who would function as local distributors in exchange for a 6 percent commission. Such changes would allow the ailing company to charge less for its tea and make significant profits.

That May, both king and Parliament accepted the East India Company's requests and passed the Tea Act. Tea was too important a commodity to ignore, ranking as the fourth most important British export to the American colonies. But as soon as word of the deal reached the colonies, many Americans were upset. Looking at the scope of the new arrangement, colonists understood its meaning: one company had been granted a monopoly of one commodity's trade in the colonies, but what would keep Parliament from placing monopolies on other trade goods in America? British interference in American commerce could have no limits. In addition, the arrangement between Parliament and the East India Company would allow the company to set the price on tea at a level lower than the price brought by smuggled tea, which had become an extensive and lucrative business in the colonies.

Prior to the passage of the Tea Act, English colonists in America consumed 1.2 million pounds of tea a year. Of that amount, only approximately 275,000 pounds were imported legally from England. Nearly one million pounds entered the colonies illegally, mostly through Holland. Even though the tea to be sold through the East India firm would make tea cheaper than ever before, the old Townshend duty on tea was still in effect. Buying tea from the East India Company would mean paying the hated three-pence-a-pound trade duty. Thus the Committees of Correspondence, as well as colonial newspapers, encouraged the spread of protest throughout the colonies. For many colonists, not paying the tax was a matter of principle. "Do not suffer yourself to sip the accursed, dutied STUFF," wrote one patriot. "For if you do, the devil will immediately enter into you, and you will instantly become a traitor to your country."[22]

## THE BOSTON TEA PARTY

By September 1773, the East India Company prepared to deliver 600,000 pounds of tea, worth about £60,000, to American cities. Four colonial ports—New York, Boston, Charleston, and Philadelphia—were selected to receive the first shipments. In Philadelphia, the first tea ships to arrive were turned away by royal officials, worried about a face-off with fiery patriots who had threatened to tar and feather them. In Charleston, the tea was unloaded but moved to a warehouse, where it remained unsold. The first tea ship destined for New York City finally arrived in the spring of 1774, when large crowds of New Yorkers gathered at the docks, shouting at the ship's captain. The captain raised anchor and left the harbor, refusing to face down the unruly and irate crowd. Only in Boston did the controversy over tea lead to an extensive showdown.

As they did with the Stamp Act nearly a decade earlier, Bostonians began working on tea agents in their city, trying to intimidate them into not carrying out their appointed duties. (Two of the agents were sons of Thomas Hutchinson, then the royal governor of Massachusetts.) On November 28, 1773, the first three tea ships docked at Boston Harbor, led by the *Dartmouth*. With their arrival, frightened local customs collectors fled the city. Sam Adams ordered members of the Boston Committee of Correspondence to stand guard in the harbor to make certain the controversial tea was not unloaded. An appeal to Governor Hutchinson to order the tea out of Boston was refused, and the stubborn governor called for British naval vessels to block the entrance to the harbor to ensure the tea

Angered by a tax on tea levied by the British on the American colonies, workers disguised themselves as Mohawk Indians, boarded ships in Boston Harbor, and dumped crates of imported tea overboard.

ships did not leave without first unloading their cargoes. British authority in Boston and patriot protestors were locked in a contest of wills.

Under customs law, the duty on the newly imported tea had to be paid within 20 days of the arrival of the tea ships in Boston. If the cargoes were not sold, they would be confiscated by customs officers and sold at a public auction. Hutchinson had every intention of keeping the tea ships in the harbor for three weeks, then ordering the tea sold; the Townshend duty would be paid, and all Bostonian protest would be for nothing. The target date for confiscating the tea was December 17.

Little changed throughout the weeks of wait. The tea remained

on the ships, the ships remained in the harbor, and the clock continued to tick down to a final showdown between Boston patriots and
British authorities. Then, on December 16, a Thursday morning, the
day before the cargoes of tea were to be confiscated, Samuel Adams
called a meeting of the city residents at the Old South Church. Five
thousand people gathered in and around the old meeting house.
(Since the population of Boston at that time was approximately
15,000 people, this figure represents approximately one of every
three people in the city.) At the meeting, Sam Adams chaired made

## John Adams

Born in Braintree, Mass-achusetts, in 1735, John Adams came from a distinguished New England family. He married Abigail Smith in 1764 and the couple had four children, all of whom lived to maturity.

One of Adams's early involvements in the conflict between the colonies and the British followed the Boston Massacre in 1770. Attorney Adams and a cousin represented the British soldiers at their trial—an act which can be seen as a fine example of American patriots respecting the traditions of Anglo-Saxon justice (including the right of every man to an attorney).

Like his cousin Samuel Adams, John Adams joined the American revolutionary movement. He served in both the First and Second Continental Congress, and was applauded for his strong stand against King George III and British rule. At the same time, Adams remained an admirer of the British legal system and its constitutional government, so that when he served as the first American ambassador to England's Court of Saint James (in 1785) he mixed well with the British parliamentarians.

In 1789, Adams was elected as the first vice president of the United States and served for two terms under President George Washington, but little emerges as distinctly "Adams" policy from these eight years. He lived very much in the shadow of two prominent advisors to the president: Thomas Jefferson and Alexander Hamilton. Adams's time as vice president was rewarded, however, when he won the presidential election of 1796, becoming the second president of the United States in 1797.

one final plea to Governor Hutchinson to send the offending tea ships back to England. The message was delivered to Hutchinson through one of the tea-ship captains, who traveled seven miles to the governor's country home outside the city in Milton. The governor refused.

By 6 P.M., the skies around the city darkening past twilight, the impasse remained firmly in place. Sam Adams, by a prearranged signal, announced: "I do not see what more Bostonians can do to save their country."[23] Almost immediately, a large number of patriots let

Unlike Thomas Jefferson, Adams had never been friendly toward the French revolutionaries, who overthrew King Louis XVI in the 1790s. Adams now came close to engaging in an outright war with revolutionary France, over the complicated demand for a political bribe, known in history as the "XYZ Affair" of 1798. Adams did not lead the nation into a declared war, but rather conducted a limited naval conflict with the French; the young U.S. Navy emerged as an excellent fighting force in the battles that followed.

From about 1785 onward John Adams was frequently in conflict with his fellow revolutionary, Thomas Jefferson. Adams thought Jefferson was sloppy in his thinking, while Jefferson believed Adams was too rigid. The two men had a very strained relationship for many years. In 1800, Adams lost the presidential election to his old foe. As a parting shot, Adams commissioned a number of "midnight judges" before leaving office. One of them, John Marshall, would do much to uphold Adams's idea of the Constitution as a document that backed a strong central government.

Retiring to Braintree, Adams mellowed in his later years. He and Thomas Jefferson began a correspondence around 1812 and kept it up until their deaths, both of which occurred on July 4, 1826, the fiftieth anniversary of the Declaration of Independence. Adams's last words were "Thomas Jefferson still survives."

Adams is not seen as one of the firebrand revolutionaries of 1776. Unlike Samuel Adams, he did not believe in popular movements or agitation of the crowds. Rather, it was his adherence to British constitutional law and Anglo-Saxon justice which made him a noted leader of the revolutionary movement. A rather conservative revolutionary, John Adams was still an important leader in founding the young United States.

out a loud war whoop from the church gallery. At the church door, dozens of men dressed as Indians appeared, their faces painted. Soon afterward, those in the gathered crowd began chanting: "Boston Harbor a tea-pot tonight! The Mohawks are come!"

Soon, groups of those gathered at the Old South Church began to filter out, headed straight for Boston Harbor. At Griffin's Wharf, a huge crowd gathered and watched as between fifty and sixty "Indians" boarded the three tea ships and ordered the customs officials onboard to leave. The thinly disguised patriots hauled out wooden tea crates, broke them open with axes, and shoveled the tea into Boston Harbor. From the wharf, Bostonians watched silently. Near midnight, the work of destroying the tea was finished. In less than three hours, "342 chests of blended Ceylon and Darjeeling tea worth 9,659 pounds and six shillings were methodically destroyed."[24] Nothing else on the tea ships was damaged.

One of those who stood and watched the event soon known as the "Boston Tea Party" was John Adams, who later wrote: "3 Cargoes of Bohea Tea [black Chinese tea] were emptied into the Sea.... There is a Dignity, a Majesty, Sublimity in this last Effort of the Patriots.... This destruction of the tea is so bold, so daring, so firm, so intrepid and inflexible, it must have ... important consequences ... an Epocha in History."[25]

## BRITISH PUNISHMENT

When word of the destruction of tea in Boston reached Great Britain, Lord North was stunned at the open display of defiance. Parliament was incensed. It seems that nothing the patriots had done previously had managed to unify British popular opinion against the colonies as much as the Boston Tea Party. One Englishman called the raid, "the most wanton and unprovoked insult offered to the civil power that is recorded in history."[26] Relations between the colonies and the Mother Country began to deteriorate dramatically.

Parliament immediately passed four laws intending to punish the city of Boston and redouble its control over the colonies. The bills, called the Coercive Acts, included the Boston Port Bill, which called for the immediate closing of Boston Harbor to trade and commerce, with the exception of food and firewood, until the damaged tea was paid for. Second, the Administration of Justice Act moved all criminal cases involving royal officials to England for trial. The

Massachusetts Government Act destroyed self-rule in the colony by converting most elective offices to royal appointments. Finally, Parliament augmented the 1765 Quartering Act, which required colonial families to house British troops in their homes when alternative lodging was unavailable.

A fifth act, the Quebec Act, was passed separately, transferring land in the Ohio Valley (portions of which were claimed by Massachusetts, Virginia, and Connecticut) to Canada. This final blow infuriated the colonists, who believed the act would hamper their movement west into new American frontiers.

The five laws combined were usually referred to by colonists as the Intolerable Acts. In London, prime minister Lord North understood how important the parliamentary acts were, stating: "The die is now cast, the colonies must either submit or triumph."[27] As for Governor Hutchinson, he had finally had enough of patriot protest. He requested a leave from his governorship and returned to England. Replacing him was a British general named Thomas Gage, the commander of Redcoat forces in North America.

## THE FIRST CONTINENTAL CONGRESS

Colonists saw the severe and punitive acts as part of an intentional plan by the British Crown not just to control them but to oppress them. Something had to be done in the colonies in response, something other than yet another riot and civil disobedience. In early September 1774, 12 colonies sent 56 delegates to a meeting in Philadelphia. (The governor of Georgia did not allow representatives from his colony to attend.) Among those present were Sam and John Adams, Patrick Henry, Richard Henry Lee, Thomas Jefferson, and George Washington from Virginia. Nearly all of the representatives had been selected illegally since they were chosen in colonies where the legislatures had been dissolved.

They met in Philadelphia's Carpenters Hall for the first time on September 5. As these delegates to the First Continental Congress sat down together, they understood they had three important responsibilities: (1) to create a list of American grievances against the Crown, (2) to develop an organized plan of resistance, and (3) to examine the relationship between the colonies and Great Britain and to consider the possibilities of a new relationship with the Mother Country.

For nearly two months, the delegates debated the future of their

Today famous for his revolutionary statement, "Give me liberty or give me death," Patrick Henry addresses the First Continental Congress.

colonies. As to the three responsibilities, almost everyone present agreed the Coercive Acts needed to be repealed, and they decided to resist them as they had in the past—by establishing a boycott and drawing up a petition of protest. But the third question before the delegates was much more complicated. There were conservatives present who were not interested in significantly challenging British authority and who wanted to call for the colonists to recognize Parliament's authority over them. A conciliatory proposal was presented by Joseph Galloway of Pennsylvania, who proposed the creation of an American legislature that would create laws for all the colonies but that would remain subordinate to Parliament. The delegates voted down Galloway's Plan of Union.

Overall, this Continental Congress was dominated by patriot radicals, such as Samuel Adams and Patrick Henry. During debate on the Galloway Plan, the assembly was interrupted one day by a silversmith named Paul Revere, who delivered a copy of a set of resolutions just voted on by several Massachusetts patriots in and around

Boston. The document branded the Intolerable Acts as unjustifiable and nonbinding; it called for colonial citizens to refuse to pay their taxes to the Crown and begin arming themselves.

One resolution called for a boycott of British trade goods. The Suffolk Resolves was immediately accepted by a majority of the delegates to the Congress. As for the conservative Galloway, he spoke of the resolves as "a declaration of war against Great Britain."[28] Massachusetts delegate John Adams was delighted, writing in his diary: "One of the happiest days of my life.... This day convinced me that America will support ... Massachusetts or perish with her."[29]

Two weeks before the First Continental Congress adjourned in late October 1774, the delegates passed an additional resolution. Titled the Declaration and Resolves of the Continental Congress, the bold statement was drafted by John Adams. While the document admitted the power of Parliament over the colonies, Adams limited the scope of that power:

> That the foundation of English liberty, and of all free government, is a right in the people to participate in their legislative council; and as the English colonists are not represented ... they are entitled to a free and exclusive power of legislation in their several provincial legislatures.... But, from the necessity of the case and a regard to the mutual interest of both countries, we cheerfully consent to the operation of such acts of the British Parliament as are bona fide, restrained to the regulation of our external commerce .... excluding every idea of taxation, internal or external, for raising a revenue on the subjects in America without their consent.[30]

Adams and others in the Continental Congress remained adamant about keeping Parliament's power over the colonies to a minimum. As the Congress disbanded, the delegates voted to reconvene in Philadelphia the following May, "unless the redress of grievances, which we have desired, be obtained before that time."[31] As the winter of 1774–75 approached, no one in the colonies or in the halls of power in Great Britain knew that, by spring, the collision course of conflict between patriots and Parliament would lead to the outbreak of war.

As the delegates to the First Continental Congress met that fall, the British remained intent on clamping down further on colonial agitators. With Governor Hutchinson gone and a military figure controlling Massachusetts politics, further violence seemed ready to explode at any moment. As Thomas Gage performed his duties as governor, he found he had enough men to control the streets of Boston but not enough to keep even the outlying towns in line. At one point he wrote to Lord North, informing him he would need as many as 20,000 British Regular troops to control the provincial militia in Massachusetts alone. Meanwhile, that winter Lord North declared "the New England governments are in a state of rebellion,"[32] and began establishing a strategy for crushing colonial protest and defiance once and for all. Despite the years of colonial protest, North believed the rebellion in the colonies could be smashed easily, stating, "Four or five frigates will do the business without any military force."[33]

## STEPS TOWARD WAR

Throughout the winter of 1775, many in the colonies were taking direct steps to distance themselves from the power of the Crown and of Parliament. In many colonies, committees of observation and inspection were established to keep a close watch on who in the colonies was supporting the latest boycott against British goods and who was not. In some places, these committees became the source of colonial government, working in place of colonial legislatures that had been dissolved by royal decree. In addition, by late 1774, every colony was holding popularly elected provincial conventions, which selected delegates to the Second Continental Congress, scheduled to take up business again on May 5, 1775. Just as important, these provincial conventions were organizing militia units and gathering up caches of guns, powder, and ammunition.

As events unfolded that winter, American colonists everywhere were cutting their street-level connections with the British government. Royal governors and their self-appointed councils were being ignored. Similarly, royal courts were less and less recognized, as colonists took their legal grievances elsewhere. Many of those who paid taxes paid them to convention collectors rather than to their colony's royal tax agents. Patriot militiamen began refusing to muster under orders from anyone other than their local committees of observation. Slowly, but deliberately, countless patriots were discounting any continued role for Great Britain in the American colonies.

As for Boston, it remained a thorn in the side of General Gage. The city was experiencing nearly military rule. Yet even with thousands of British Redcoats in the city, the Provincial Congress of Massachusetts met illegally across the Charles River in Cambridge, "within sight of Gage's sentries."[34] The renegade political body established the Committee of Safety and empowered it to call up all militia units in the vicinity of Boston if the ongoing conflicts turned violent. The wealthy merchant John Hancock was placed in charge of the committee, which voted that winter that "all kinds of warlike stores be purchased sufficient for an army of fifteen thousand men,"[35] and established a weapons depot at the little village of Concord outside Boston.

Tension continued to mount that winter. In early February 1775, a concerned Benjamin Franklin wrote: "I cannot but lament ... the impending Calamities Britain and her Colonies are about to suffer, from great Imprudencies on both Sides—Passion governs, and she never governs wisely—Anxiety begins to disturb my Rest."[36]

Yet even as war seemed to loom in the distance, there were still many Americans who did not want to see further conflict, much less bloodshed. American conservatives in 1774 and early 1775 published pamphlets and essays highly critical of patriot efforts, the First Continental Congress, and the committees of observation. One such essay, written by an American lawyer named Daniel Leonard, summed things up concisely: "Allegiance and protection are reciprocal. It is our highest interest to continue a part of the British Empire, and equally our duty to remain subject to the authority of Parliament."[37]

Modern historians estimate that, by 1775, approximately 20 percent of the white American population was still loyal to Great Britain and that many of these were actively working to keep the colonies under the authority of the Crown. On the other side, about 40 percent of Americans were active patriots. Another 40 percent remained neutral, including pacifist groups such as the Quakers and many of those living in the backcountry or on the frontier, away from the revolutionary politics of coastal cities such as Boston and Philadelphia.

## LEXINGTON AND CONCORD

Despite the three-way allegiances of Americans, many Britons believed the spirit of the patriots had infected the colonies and that it

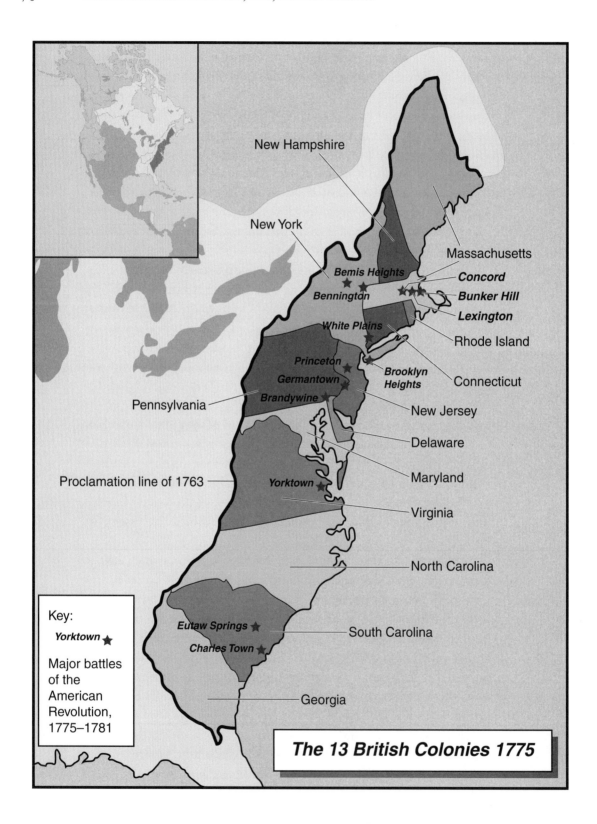

New Hampshire

New York

Massachusetts

Bemis Heights

*Concord*

Bennington

*Bunker Hill*

*Lexington*

White Plains

Rhode Island

Princeton

Germantown

Brooklyn
Heights

Connecticut

Pennsylvania

Brandywine

New Jersey

Delaware

Maryland

Proclamation line of 1763

Yorktown

Virginia

North Carolina

Key:

**Yorktown** ★

Major battles
of the
American
Revolution,
1775–1781

Eutaw Springs ★

South Carolina

Charles Town ★

Georgia

*The 13 British Colonies 1775*

had to be stopped. On January 27, 1775, Lord Dartmouth, secretary of state for America and the king's chief representative in the colonies, penned a letter to General Gage informing him that the time was right for him to take the offensive, arrest the patriot leaders around Boston, and shut down the patriot cause in the Boston region. In his missive, Dartmouth wrote: "A smaller force now, if put to the test, would be able to encounter them with greater probability of success."[38] The letter did not reach Gage until April 14.

Gage himself was eager and prepared to answer Dartmouth's request. For months, he had been preparing a strategy by which he could put down the rebellion in Massachusetts. He had 3,500 troops under his command and spies throughout the Boston vicinity informing him of patriot plans and movements. As for the rebels, their militia units had been drilling throughout the winter and had spent the winter storing weapons just outside General Gage's reach. Gage knew they had stored nearly 200 barrels of gunpowder at Concord village, and his most recent intelligence informed him that the patriot leaders he hated most, Samuel Adams and John Hancock, were themselves in Concord. Gage prepared to make his move.

On the evening of April 18, 1775, 750 British troops departed Boston under cover of darkness, headed toward Concord. Watchful eyes noted the military moves and patriot riders mounted their horses and sped off into the night to warn the townspeople and especially the Minutemen of the approaching Redcoats. The silversmith Paul Revere and a tanner named William Dawes each took different roads to the west. Both men were headed straight to Lexington, a village the British troops would reach before they arrived in Concord. It was here that Adams and Hancock were staying before heading to Philadelphia to join the Second Continental Congress.

Just before dawn on the morning of April 19, after completing a night march, an advance guard of British Redcoats under the command of Major John Pitcairn reached the common green at Lexington. Revere and Dawes had already reached the town, and the 750 residents of the sleepy Massachusetts patriot village had been awakened at 1 A.M. Immediately 130 Lexington militiamen turned out. Revere and Dawes then proceeded on to Concord.

On the Lexington green, the British Redcoats were greeted by about 70 militiamen under the orders of Captain John Parker. When the Redcoats ordered the militiamen to disperse, they refused.

Although the colonials had not gathered to fire on the British, but to warn them off the property of free British subjects, a shot was fired. (Whether by an American or a British Regular, no one knows.) British troops then began firing into the small group of militiamen, wounding several, eight of whom died of their wounds. These shots were the opening salvos of the Revolutionary War.

Following the bloody encounter, the British continued on to Concord, where they failed to turn up Adams or Hancock but found

## Men Prepared to Fight

As the first shots of the American Revolution were fired on the green at Lexington and on the North Bridge at Concord, many of the colonial militiamen who faced down British Regular troops revealed themselves to be well-trained, disciplined colonial soldiers. But such discipline had only recently been acquired.

Since the days of the French Revolution until 1774, many of the men who served in the Massachusetts militia had not taken their military roles seriously. Militia drill days often involved more drinking in taverns than actual training with their muskets. But as the political clash between the colonies and Great Britain widened, more and more militiamen began to see their roles as necessary for the protection of their colony.

At least a year before Lexington and Concord, the militiamen known as Minutemen began setting the pace for their comrades. Sworn to make themselves ready for action at a minute's notice, the Minutemen brought a new discipline to the work of local militia units. Training was serious and constant. At Concord, the Minutemen trained two and a half days weekly. At Marblehead (Massachusetts), militia units trained four times a week.

Militia drills involved intricate military maneuvers, including learning 50 different battlefield orders. The citizen soldiers practiced lining up in three-deep ranks and firing their muskets in volleys, followed by close-order reloading and refiring to the beat of a drum. Each militiaman was supposed to carry a musket, bayonet, cartridge box, and three dozen rounds of ammunition. The men armed themselves with other weapons as well, carrying tomahawks and knives. About one-third were veterans of the French and Indian War, where such "Indian" weapons were commonly used.

Whether the constant drilling helped the Minutemen in the early encounters at Lexington and Concord or not, it did instill in them at least two key elements needed for the battlefield: it gave them confidence as soldiers and helped them become accustomed to taking orders from a superior officer.

few weapons. They were met by militia forces who engaged them at the Old North Bridge. Several British soldiers were killed. The remainder of the Redcoat force fell back to Lexington, and, after meeting up with the main column of British Regulars, the Redcoats began a difficult retreat back to Boston.

Along the 20 miles back to the city, the British, numbering about 900, were fired upon from all sides. Through the night, as many as 4,000 colonial militiamen had gathered along the main road, hiding behind stone walls and the protection of large trees. The day was a miserable, violent one for the British as they experienced high casualties, including 70 men killed, 165 wounded, and several dozen missing. The lane back to Boston later became known as "the Bloody Chute." American casualties numbered near 100, including 49 killed. Despite the carnage, experts estimate that of the thousands of musket balls fired that day, only one in 300 actually hit its intended target. (The militiamen and British troops carried the same style musket, one called the "Brown Bess," a weapon that was considered extremely inaccurate.)

As the British troops staggered back into Boston, 16,000 New England militiamen had reached the outskirts of the city, besieging the British garrison. Yet even as the specter of fired shots at Lexington and Concord signaled the beginning of open rebellion and warfare, the delegates who met less than two weeks later at Philadelphia as the Second Continental Congress understood their immediate goals had been seriously altered. They were now a wartime intercolonial assembly. Although opening sessions centered on old discussions about Parliament's right to regulate imperial trade, it was not long before plans for defending the colonies took center stage. The Congress had virtually no money at its disposal and voted to print Continental money to help purchase the necessities of war. In addition, delegates set out to further friendly trade relations with European powers, including the French.

## BREED'S HILL

Even as the Congress prepared for war, it did not want to offend the British government. In mid-summer, the delegates accepted a conciliatory document titled, "Declaration of the Causes and Necessity for Taking up Arms," to be sent to the British Crown. In the missive, the Congress stressed the importance of the "union which has so long

With the seeds of revolution planted, and the first shots fired only two weeks earlier, attendees at the Second Continental Congress found themselves having to tackle the critical issues of open warfare against the British.

and so happily subsisted between us."[39] The letter assured the British that the Americans were creating an army to defend themselves and protect their private property until "hostilities shall cease on the part of the aggressors, and all danger of their being renewed shall be removed, and not before."[40]

By June 15, 1775, Congress had selected a Continental commander. George Washington, Virginia planter, member of the House of Burgesses, and a veteran of the French and Indian War, received the commission. (Washington had been "campaigning" for the job, regularly wearing his Virginia militia officer's uniform to meetings of the Second Continental Congress.) Washington wasted no time in getting to Boston, where a British force was preparing to attack the colonial troops ringing the perimeter of the city.

On June 17, 2,200 British Regulars attacked colonists entrenched on Breed's Hill and Bunker Hill over in Charlestown, just across from Boston Harbor. Forces under British Major-General William Howe attacked up the hills, maintaining the regulation straight firing lines so common in eighteenth-century European battles. Howe's men suffered many casualties (they were also severely hampered in their uphill fighting, carrying 60-pound packs and moving through tall grass), including 228 killed. The Americans were finally driven from the two hills after they ran out of ammunition, but the high casualty rate for the British caused George III to remove General Gage from command.

The war between the colonies and the British Empire quickly produced hundreds, even thousands, of casualties within just two months. But British officials were confident as they planned their war strategy under the watchful eye of Lord North, and they based their overall strategy on three assumptions: (1) the Americans would prove no match for British Regular forces, (2) the British would fight European style, including capturing American cities to bring down the colonial rebellion, and (3) a military victory on repeated battlefields would cause the Americans to surrender, which would settle, once and for all, the question of colonial acceptance of British authority and control.

## AN EXPANDING WAR

The British could not have been more wrong on all three counts. While British armies were able to capture every major American city from Boston to Savannah during the war, this success directly affected only the 5 percent of the American population that lived in those cities. Much to the surprise of the British military, the American troops—known as the Continental Army—were more disciplined and effective on the battlefield than the professional Redcoats expected. And even when patriot armies lost on the battlefield, the American government did not capitulate and surrender the patriot cause.

Little fighting took place during the winter of 1775–76, as was typically true of most of the winters during the American Revolution. In one of the few skirmishes, American forces, led by General Richard Montgomery and General Benedict Arnold, marched north and attempted to seize the Canadian city of Quebec. They failed during a predawn attack on New Year's Day.

General Washington spent that first winter of the rebellion trying to form a cohesive American fighting force. One bright spot helped to rally the American patriot cause. Washington had dispatched a Boston bookseller and self-taught artillery officer, Henry Knox, to Fort Ticonderoga in upstate New York (the British outpost had fallen in May 1775) to deliver heavy siege cannon from the fort to the hills above Boston. Knox used ox-carts and sleds to carry the cannon across the snow-covered Berkshire Mountains and frozen rivers, but succeeded. With cannon bristling in the heights overlooking Boston,

## George Washington

George Washington was a complicated figure. He led one great revolution, but wished to prevent others.

Born in Virginia in 1732, Washington as a young man aspired to join the British military; he served in the British army during the French and Indian War and was rose to the rank of major. He noticed that many regular British army officers (from the Mother Country) were suspicious of Americans, so he left the service in 1759, the same year that he married the wealthy widow, Martha Dandridge Custis. Then followed nearly 15 years out of the limelight. Washington reemerged in 1775, however, as commander-in-chief of the American Revolutionary army.

Washington as a general is less important than Washington the statesman. He guided the people and the army through the tortuous eight years of the American Revolution, and when it was over he rejected calls that he lead the country in the role of a new American kind of king. Instead, he retired to his home in Mount Vernon, content to be the most admired American and one of the most admired men around the world. Even King George III found it remarkable that Washington willingly stepped back from power.

Then came Shays' Rebellion in the winter of 1786. This farmers' uprising in western Massachusetts alarmed Washington and many of his friends, including Alexander Hamilton and Henry Knox (by contrast, Thomas Jefferson thought "a little rebellion now and then" was a good thing). At the

General Howe removed 9,000 British troops from the city on March 17, 1776, onboard 125 ships bound for Canada.

## MOVING TOWARD INDEPENDENCE

While the Continental Army experienced losses and small victories, the Second Continental Congress struggled to set the political course for the patriot cause. Throughout 1775, debate arose between those in Congress who favored independence from Great Britain (a small number of members) and a moderate faction that constituted the

urging of Knox, Hamilton, and others, Washington went to Philadelphia in 1787 to preside over the convention that wrote the new United States Constitution.

A less revolutionary document has seldom been seen. Led by Washington, the former American revolutionaries wrote a constitution that centered the power of the people in three branches of government: executive, legislature, and the courts. There was no room for spontaneous expressions of the popular will in this document. Washington did not speak much at the convention, but he was revered by his fellow delegates. When the work was complete and the Constitution was approved by the states, Washington won the first presidential election in 1789 and served until 1797.

As president, Washington veered between the liberal policies of Thomas Jefferson and the conservative ones of Alexander Hamilton. At Hamilton's urging, Washington stamped out tax resistance in the famous Whiskey Rebellion of western Pennsylvania. Washington also steered a middle course between the British and the French, who had begun their long series of conflicts known as the Revolutionary and Napoleonic wars. In 1793 Washington declared strict neutrality in this conflict, a wise choice that set the United States on a stable course. Washington retired from public life in 1797 and returned to Mount Vernon, where he died of natural causes in 1799.

At the time of his death, Washington was the most admired man in the Western world. He had kept his head and his course through difficult times, and presided over one of the most peaceful of revolutions.

Washington's contemporaries knew he was a great man; those who have come after him tend to agree with this assessment. The most frequent criticism levied against him is that Washington believed in a *political* revolution, such as the one that overthrew the rule of King George III, but not in a *social* revolution, such as the one that began in France in 1789.

majority. But by the spring of 1776, as the war spread and more colonists felt the weight of its impact, a significant number of delegates began to turn toward the option of independence. By April, Massachusetts delegate John Adams wrote: "Child Independence is

## An Inspired Voice for Independence

In 1805, no less than the patriot leader John Adams summed up the legacy of one of the great pamphleteers of the revolution:"I know not whether any man in the world has had more influence on [America's] inhabitants or affairs for the last thirty years than Tom Paine."* Paine's pamphlet, *Common Sense*, published in January 1776, put into print the thoughts of many patriots in the opening months of the American Revolution.

Paine came to America too late to experience directly the Sugar Act, Stamp Act, Boston Massacre, or Boston's famous Tea Party. He arrived in Philadelphia from England in 1774, having failed in business, and prepared to make a fresh start in the colonies. He wasted little time getting involved in patriot causes. He was a serious supporter of republicanism in America at a time when most colonials simply wanted the British Crown to tax them less.

After the outbreak of the Revolutionary War, Paine put pen to paper and supported the revolution with fiery words. In January 1776, while the members of the Second Continental Congress were debating independence, Paine anonymously published his *Common Sense*. The tract had nothing kind to say about the king of the British Empire.

To Paine, George III was "the royal brute of Great Britain," an accusation that verged on treason. He thought it ludicrous that any one man might be seen as the symbol of an entire nation and its government. In straightforward language, Paine wrote: "Of more worth is one honest man to society and in the sight of God, than all the crowned ruffians that ever lived."** Even as Paine decried the power of the British monarch, he lauded the cause of the American Revolution. "The cause of America," he wrote, "is in a great measure the cause of all mankind."***

*Common Sense* gained an astounding readership; 150,000 copies were printed during the American Revolution. Its stirring rally cries for independence from the Mother Country undoubtedly played a role in spurring tens of thousands of people to support a complete separation from Great Britain in 1776. And later, during the difficult years of the revolution, Paine's words continued to inspire, its deathless phrases ringing with hope for a future of freedom for all:"O ye that love mankind! Ye that dares oppose not only the tyranny but the tyrant, stand forth!"+

* Quoted in Weinstein, *Story of America*, p. 92.

** Quoted in Fleming, *Liberty*! p. 159.

*** Quoted in Weinstein, p. 92.

+ Ibid.

now struggling for Birth." However, he added, "It requires Time to convince the doubting and inspire the timid."[41]

On May 10, the Congress accepted John Adams's resolution calling for each colony to establish new constitutional governments. One fiery phrase later added to the resolution spoke clearly of Adams's support for independence, as he declared how "the exercise of every kind of authority under the said Crown should be totally suppressed, and all sources of government exerted under the authority of the people."[42] Some delegates protested the resolution, calling it a step toward national independence. They were right, and Adams knew it well.

Just five days later, delegates from Virginia proposed independence for the colonies and a complete separation from Great Britain. Virginian Richard Henry Lee presented a formal resolution to the Congress on June 7, one which declared "that these United Colonies are, and of right ought to be, free and independent States, that they are absolved of all allegiance to the British Crown, and that all political connection between them and the State of Great Britain is, and ought to be, totally dissolved."[43] After a two-day debate, the Congress agreed to table the issue for three weeks while a five-member committee wrote a resolution declaring American independence.

While John Adams, Benjamin Franklin, Roger Sherman, and Robert Livingston were appointed members of this committee, the lion's share of the work and wording of the document was done by the fifth member—Thomas Jefferson. Although Adams and Franklin later suggested several changes to the document, the majority of the text and its patriot spirit are Jefferson's. In early July, the history of the United States took a monumental turn when, on July 2, the Congress voted to accept the Lee resolution making the colonies "free and independent states" and then two days later voted and approved one of the most important foundational documents of America's past and present—the Declaration of Independence.

The Declaration of Independence explained to everyone—Americans, the British Crown, the nations of the world—why Americans were separating from the British Empire. At the center of Jefferson's justification was the principle that "all men are created equal, that they are endowed by their Creator with certain unalienable Rights, that among these are Life, Liberty and the pursuit of Happiness."[44] Although the document lists the grievances Americans had toward the king and Parliament, it states that the ongoing revolution and separation had always been about more than taxes or perceived mistreatments by the Crown. The revolution was about principles—important, universal concepts of the rights of the people—and how, "whenever any Form of Government becomes destructive of these ends, it is the Right of the People to alter or to abolish it, and to institute new Government."[45] Today, the principles of the American revolution continue to guide Americans as they have for more than two centuries. In creating this national document, the delegates of the Second Continental Congress were providing new inspiration to the patriot cause and to the soldiers serving in the Continental Army. For many Americans, the new nation had crossed an important threshold. Just two weeks after the Congress voted to accept the Declaration of Independence, patriot leader and elder statesman Benjamin Franklin wrote in a letter to the British admiral Lord Richard Howe: "It is impossible we should think of Submission to [the British] Government."[46]

## THE ARMY OF THE REVOLUTION

As for the Revolutionary War itself, American patriots still had to endure another five years of fighting. Often the battles did not produce American victories, and Washington lost many more battles then he won. During 1776, the British drove his army out of New York City, across New Jersey, and into Pennsylvania. The British military leadership constantly pursued a strategy based on large-scale battles against Washington's forces that they hoped would result in a British victory and an end to the war as well as to the American rebellion. However, General Washington avoided that possibility as much as possible. Accordingly, "his most practiced and useful tactic came to be the orderly retreat."[47]

By living to fight another day, Washington was able to keep his army intact. As several of Washington's officers often said: "The Army is the Revolution."[48] At year's end, Washington pulled off a brilliant but limited victory by surprising German mercenaries hired by the British at Trenton, New Jersey. (Washington's Christmas Eve assault required his men to cross the ice-choked Delaware River at night in boats.)

Through the following year (referred to by the British as "The Year of the Hangman," since the date 1777 featured three hangman's

With few funds to equip the Continental Army, and with local militias often poorly trained and armed, superior leadership was required to bring the colonists victory. In a now famous raid, George Washington led his troops across the Delaware River in a surprise attack against British forces.

gallows) the British launched a complicated strategy to cut off New England from the remainder of the colonies, a strategy based on the concept of "divide and conquer." The British general Johnny Burgoyne was to march his troops south from Canada along Lake Champlain to recapture Fort Ticonderoga, while Colonel Barry St. Leger, commanding yet another division, was to move from west to east along central New York's Mohawk River. Yet a third British force, commanded by Sir William Howe, was ordered to march his army from New York City north along the Hudson River. All three armies were to meet at Albany.

This grand British scheme (it was really Burgoyne's plan) did not come off accordingly, however. Howe did not move north, but chose instead to march south to try to capture the Congress at

Philadelphia. While Howe engaged Washington's army that fall in Pennsylvania, things did not go well for the other two British contingents. St. Leger's forces engaged American troops in battle at Oriskany, New York, on August 6, and turned away from making any further advancement. Burgoyne's march south became bogged down, requiring nearly a month just to cover 23 miles. By the time he reached Albany, he had lost all momentum and Howe and St. Leger were nowhere near. On October 17, 1777, Burgoyne was defeated by a Continental force at Saratoga, New York, under the command of General Horatio Gates. When the battle ended, Burgoyne's entire force of 6,000 men was in American hands.

The American victory at Saratoga proved a turning point on the revolutionary battlefield. Inspired by the Americans and their success in New York, the French government agreed to enter the war as America's ally, the French monarch providing much needed money, ships, troops, and weapons in support of the patriot cause. Under the Treaty of Amity and Commerce, the French recognized American independence and established trade connections with the young United States.

Throughout the final four years of the Revolutionary War, much of the fighting shifted to the southern colonies. The defeat at Saratoga caused British military strategists to concentrate on the South, since a greater percentage of that population had remained loyal to Great Britain. Two key American ports in the South were captured by the British, including Savannah in 1778 and Charleston in 1780. Early on, the British enjoyed several successes against rebel armies fighting on Southern soil, including the defeat of General Gates's army at Camden, South Carolina, in August at the hands of British general Lord Cornwallis. However, 1780 and 1781 witnessed several key British defeats, including a battle fought at King's Mountain, South Carolina (October 7, 1780), and a battle at Guilford Courthouse in North Carolina (March 15, 1781). The latter engagement, while technically a British victory, resulted in the destruction of much of General Cornwallis's army.

Severely battered, Cornwallis's army limped into Virginia (against the orders of his superiors) and took up positions at a tiny tobacco port called Yorktown. While awaiting reinforcements, General Cornwallis was unaware of an advancing rebel army to the north, one headed straight toward him. Washington's forces had remained bottled up in New Jersey for too long and he had ordered his men to move south once word of Cornwallis's actions reached his headquarters. A combined force of 5,000 Continental soldiers and an equal number of French troops (under the command of Jean de Vimeur, Comte de Rochambeau) reached the outskirts of Yorktown and joined an additional 8,000 American troops. Suddenly, victory was at hand. Cornwallis's 10,000 men were trapped on the Yorktown peninsula by a Franco-American force of nearly twice their number, with no route of escape. (Cornwallis could not escape by sea, since British ships had been turned away by French vessels blocking Chesapeake Bay.) After limited but heated fighting, Cornwallis surrendered to Washington on October 19, 1781. The American Revolutionary War was over. Back in London, after receiving the news of Cornwallis's defeat, Lord North was aghast, crying: "Oh, God! It's all over."[49] One witness described the prime minister as responding as if "he would have taken a [musket] ball in the breast."[50]

Although another two years would pass before the Americans, French, and British hammered out an official peace treaty ending the war, there was little fighting following Cornwallis's defeat at Yorktown. In fact, long before the American victory at Yorktown, the Congress had dispatched John Adams to Paris to work on a peace settlement. He was later aided by Benjamin Franklin and John Jay, of New York. Negotiations proved complicated, since the war's participants included not only the Americans, French, and British, but other allies and enemies, including Spain, Holland, Russia, Denmark, and Sweden. (The roles of these latter countries had been limited largely to conflicts in Europe.)

When the powers at the bargaining table finally completed their negotiations, the 13 colonies were recognized as a new and independent nation, with land stretching from the Atlantic seaboard to the Mississippi River. There were additional successes (and failures) for the Americans at the negotiations (for example, the Americans had wanted to gain Canada from Great Britain, but failed to do so), but the success of the American Revolution was clear: Independence-seeking patriots had prevailed on the battlefield and in the political arena. America—the new United States of America—would have the power and authority to chart the course of its own future. Those who had supported the revolution, those who had fought for their rights

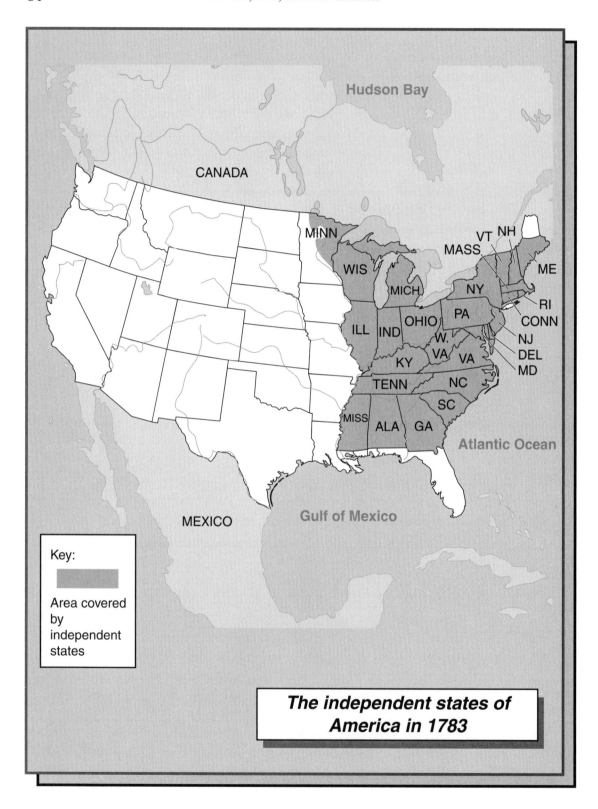

Key:

Area covered by independent states

**The independent states of America in 1783**

as a free people, could only look forward to living in a country where liberty was cherished and new ideals of self-government and individual freedoms would become a symbol for others around the world.

---

**TIMELINE**

**1755–1762** The French and Indian War results in a British victory, but the Crown emerges from the war deeply in debt, having increased its national debt by 60 million pounds.

**1763** Pontiac's War results in the deaths of 2,000 English colonists, prompting the British Crown to send additional British soldiers to the American colonies.

The Indian uprising prompts the British to establish the Proclamation of 1763, restricting the movement of American colonists west of the Appalachian Mountains.

**1764** British prime minister Lord Grenville pushes the Sugar Act through Parliament, establishing trade duties on a list of foreign goods commonly imported into the American colonies. The act prompts an American outcry.

**1765** **March** Parliament passes the revenue-generating Stamp Act, creating new taxes on the American colonies.

**June** James Otis prompts the Massachusetts General Court to propose an intercolonial meeting to protest the Stamp Act.

**August 14** A street protest in Boston results in the ransacking of a stamp agent's home.

**October 31** New York merchants suggest a boycott of British goods to the colonies as a means of protesting the Stamp Act.

**1766** Parliament repeals the Stamp Act in March, after months of colonial protest. The British body also passes the Declaratory Act, proclaiming the power of the Parliament to pass any law it wishes governing the colonies.

**1767** Parliament passes the Townshend Duties on a long list of trade commodities to the colonies, including tea.

**1770** **March 5** Rioting in Boston results in British troops firing into a street crowd, killing five protestors. The bloody encounter is dubbed "The Boston Massacre."

On the same day, British prime minister Lord North appears

before Parliament asking for the repeal of the Townshend Duties.

**1772** **June** Rhode Island residents board an armed British customs schooner, the Gaspee, after the ship runs aground and burn the vessel to the waterline.

**November** Patriots attending a Boston town meeting create the first Committee of Correspondence.

**1773** **September** East India Company delivers 600,000 pounds of tea to American cities under the Tea Act and the Townshend Duties.

**November 28** Three tea ships arrive in Boston Harbor, where locals refuse to allow the cargo to be offloaded.

**December 16** About 60 colonials dressed as Mohawk Indians board the tea ships and throw the tea overboard. The event is remembered as the "Boston Tea Party."

**1774** **September** Twelve colonies sent 56 delegates to the

**1764**
British prime minister Lord Grenville pushes the Sugar Act through Parliament. The act prompts an American outcry.

**1767**
Parliament passes the Townshend Duties on a long list of trade commodities to the colonies, including tea.

**1770**
Rioting in Boston results in British troops firing into a street crowd, killing five protestors, an encounter dubbed "The Boston Massacre." On the same day (March 5), British prime minister Lord North appears before Parliament asking for the repeal of the Townshend Duties.

# 1764

**1766**
Parliament repeals the Stamp Act in March. The British body also passes the Declaratory Act, proclaiming its power to pass any law it wishes governing the colonies.

**1765**
**March** Parliament passes the revenue-generating Stamp Act, creating new taxes on the American colonies.

**1773**
**September** East India Company delivers 600,000 pounds of tea to American cities under the Tea Act and the Townshend Duties.
**December 16** About 60 colonials dressed as Mohawk Indians board the tea ships and throw the tea overboard, an event called the "Boston Tea Party."

intercolonial meeting at Philadelphia known as the First Continental Congress.

**October**  As the First Continental Congress adjourns, the delegates pass the Declaration and Resolves of the Continental Congress, a statement declaring Parliament's restricted legislative power over the colonies. Delegates agree to meet again the following May.

**1775  January 27**  Lord Dartmouth, the king's chief representative in the colonies, sends orders to General Gage to round up colonial agitators Sam Adams and John Hancock.

**April 18**  British troops march at night out of Boston to the Massachusetts countryside to round up revolutionary leaders and confiscate patriot weapons.

**April 19**  British and American troops fire on one another on the green at Lexington and on the bridge outside Concord. The shooting war of the American Revolution opens.

---

**1775**

**January 27**  Lord Dartmouth, the king's chief representative in the colonies, sends orders to General Gage to round up colonial agitators Sam Adams and John Hancock.
**April 19**  British and American troops fire on one another on the green at Lexington and on the bridge outside Concord. The shooting war of the American Revolution opens.

**1781**
Washington defeats General Cornwallis's army near Yorktown, Virginia, on October 19, bringing about an end to the fighting.

**1781**

**1774**
**September**  Twelve colonies sent 56 delegates to the intercolonial meeting at Philadelphia known as the First Continental Congress.

**1776**
**January**  Thomas Paine publishes, anonymously, *Common Sense*.
**May 10**  Congress accepts John Adams' resolution calling for each colony to establish new constitutional governments.
**July 2**  Congress votes to accept the Lee resolution, making the colonies "free and independent states."
**July 4**  Congress votes to accept the Declaration of Independence.
**December**  Washington wins strategic victory during dawn raid on Hessian outpost at Trenton, New Jersey.

**May 5** Second Continental Congress convenes as a wartime legislature.

**June 15** Congress selects George Washington to lead the Continental Army.

**June 17** British and colonists fight the battle of Breed's Hill and Bunker Hill.

1776 **January** Thomas Paine publishes, anonymously, *Common Sense*.

**March** British troops are forced out of Boston after cannon are delivered to Washington's army from the captured British Fort Ticonderoga.

**May 10** Congress accepts John Adams's resolution calling for each colony to establish new constitutional governments.

**June 7** Virginian Richard Henry Lee presents a formal resolution to Congress, calling for independence for the newly formed states.

**June 9** Congress forms a five-man committee to draft a declaration of independence.

**July 2** Congress votes to accept the Lee resolution, making the colonies "free and independent states."

**July 4** Congress votes to accept the Declaration of Independence.

**December** Washington wins strategic victory during dawn raid on Hessian outpost at Trenton, New Jersey.

1777 American general Horatio Gates defeats General Johnny Burgoyne in the battle of Saratoga, New York, on October 17, a victory which encouraged the French to enter the Revolution on the American side.

1778 American seaport of Savannah, Georgia falls to the British.

1780 American seaport of Charleston, South Carolina, falls to the British.

1781 Washington defeats General Cornwallis's army near Yorktown, Virginia, on October 19, bringing about an end to the fighting.

## SOURCE NOTES

1. Quoted in Eugen Weber, *The Western Tradition,* video series, episode 37: "The American Revolution." From *The Western Tradition Transcripts,* transcribed by Thomas Michael Kowalick. Alexandria, VA: PBS Adult Learning Service, 1989, p. 115.
2. Quoted in John Ferling, *A Leap in the Dark: The Struggle to Create the American Republic.* New York: Oxford University Press, 2003, p. 28.
3. Ibid.
4. Quoted in *The Annals of America,* vol. 2, 1755–1783: *Resistance and Revolution.* Chicago: Encyclopaedia Britannica, 1968, p. 86.
5. Quoted in Bruce Lancaster, *History of the American Revolution.* New York: Simon and Schuster, 2003, p. 22.
6. Quoted in Paul Boyer, *The Enduring Vision: A History of the American People,* vol. 1. Lexington, MA: Houghton Mifflin Company, 2000, p. 122.
7. Quoted in Allen Weinstein and David Rubel, *The Story of America: Freedom and Crisis From Settlement to Superpower.* New York: DK Publishing, p. 76.
8. Ibid.
9. Ibid., p. 80.
10. Quoted in *Annals,* p. 107.
11. Quoted in Boyer, *Enduring Vision,* p. 123.
12. Ibid., p. 125.
13. Quoted in *Annals,* p. 148.
14. Quoted in James Kirby Martin, *America and Its People.* New York: HarperCollins, 1993, p. 124.
15. Ibid., p.126.
16. Quoted in Weinstein, *Story of America,* p. 82.
17. Quoted in John Mack Faragher, et al, *Out of Many: A History of the American People,* vol. 1. Upper Saddle River, NJ: Prentice Hall, 1997.
18. Quoted in Martin, *America,* p. 130.
19. Quoted in Weinstein, *Story of America,* p. 87.
20. Quoted in *Annals,* p. 217.
21. Ibid., p. 220.
22. Quoted in Lancaster, *History,* p. 94.
23. Quoted in Thomas Fleming, *Liberty! The American Revolution.* New York: Viking, 1997, p. 79.
24. Ibid.
25. Quoted in Bart McDowell, *The Revolutionary War: America's Fight for Freedom.* Washington, D.C.: National Geographic Society, 1967, p. 29, and Fleming, p. 80.
26. Quoted in Lancaster, *History,* p. 94.
27. Quoted in Martin, *America,* p. 139.
28. Quoted in Bernard Weisberger, ed., *The Story of America.* Pleasantville, NY: Reader's Digest Association, Inc., 1975, p. 26.
29. Ibid.
30. Quoted in *Annals,* p. 271.
31. Quoted in Martin, *America,* p. 138.
32. Quoted in Weisberger, *Story,* p. 26.
33. Ibid.
34. Quoted in Lancaster, *History,* p. 99.
35. Ibid.
36. Ibid., p. 97.
37. Quoted in *Annals,* p. 307.
38. Quoted in Fleming, *Liberty!* p. 105.
39. Quoted in Martin, *America,* p. 148.
40. Ibid.
41. Quoted in Ferling, *A Leap,* p. 163.
42. Quoted in Ferling, p. 163.
43. Quoted in Mary Beth Norton, *A People and a Nation: A History of the United States.* Boston: Houghton Mifflin Company, 1991, p. 95.
44. Quoted in John Rhodehamel, *The American Revolution: Writings from the War of Independence.* Library of America. New York: Literary Classics of the United States, 2001, p. 128.
45. Ibid.
46. Ibid., p. 156.
47. Quoted in Weinstein, *Story,* p. 98.
48. Ibid.
49. Ibid., p. 99.
50. Quoted in Martin, *America,* p. 175.

## BIBLIOGRAPHY

Annals of America. Volume 2, *1755–1783: Resistance and Revolution*.
    Chicago: Encyclopaedia Britannica, Inc., 1968.

Berkin, Carol. *Making America: A History of the United States*. Boston:
    Houghton Mifflin Company, 1995.

Boyer, Paul S. *The Enduring Vision: A History of the American People*.
    Volume I. Lexington, MA: Houghton Mifflin Company, 2000.

Dumbauld, Edward. *The Declaration of Independence and What It Means
    Today*. Norman: University of Oklahoma Press, 1950.

Faragher, John Mack, et al. *Out of Many: A History of the American People*,
    Volume I. 2nd ed. Upper Saddle River, NJ: Prentice Hall, 1997.

Ferling, John. *A Leap in the Dark: The Struggle to Create the American
    Republic*. New York: Oxford University Press, 2003.

Fleming, Thomas. *Liberty! The American Revolution*. New York: Viking,
    1997.

Higginbotham, Don. *The War of American Independence: Military Attitudes,
    Policies, and Practice, 1763–1789*. New York: Macmillan, 1971.

Lancaster, Bruce. *History of the American Revolution*. New York: Simon and
    Schuster, 2003.

Lomask, Milton. *The First American Revolution*. New York: Farrar, Straus
    and Giroux, 1974.

McDowell, Bart. *The Revolutionary War: America's Fight for Freedom*.
    Washington, D.C.: National Geographic Society, 1967.

Martin, James Kirby. *America and Its People*. New York: HarperCollins,
    1993.

Middlekauff, Robert. *The Glorious Cause: The American Revolution,
    1763–1789*. New York: Oxford University Press, 1982.

Moquin, Wayne. *Makers of America—the Firstcomers, 1536–1800*. Chicago:
    Encyclopaedia Britannica Educational Corporation, 1971.

Nash, Gary B. *The American People: Creating a Nation and a Society*.
    New York: Longman Publishing, 2003.

Rhodehamel, John. *The American Revolution: Writings from the War of
    Independence*. Library of America. New York: Literary Classics of the
    United States, 2001.

Weber, Eugen. *The Western Tradition*, video series, episode 37: "The
    American Revolution." From *The Western Tradition Transcripts*,
    transcribed by Thomas Michael Kowalick. Alexandria, VA: PBS Adult
    Learning Service, 1989.

Weisberger, Bernard, ed. *The Story of America*. Pleasantville, NY: Reader's
    Digest Association, Inc., 1975.

# The French Revolution

**Deeply embedded in thousands of personal stories is one of the most** important and far-reaching legacies of the modern world—the French Revolution. This singular stepping stone—along with the event it attempted to model, the American Revolution—set much of the course for the nineteenth and twentieth centuries of Western Civilization. Together, they created a future for democracy and helped bring down an age in which all-powerful kings and queens, emperors and empresses, and czars and czarinas forced their subjects to accept their rule and live under the typical harshness of absolute monarchies. From these revolutions, new nationalistic spirits rose around the world, from Europe to Latin America to Asia to Africa, and helped usher in new hope for common people everywhere.

To an extent, the changes brought about by these popular revolts continue to find advocates even today. Most of the countries of the world accept some level of democratic action and thought on the part of their people. Such fortunate citizens are recognized as having individual rights—including the power of the vote, the protection of a trial by jury, and representation by elected officials. Even the concept of being a "citizen" of a nation, of having an identity as an equal among, perhaps, millions of other citizens—the modern redefinition of the relationship between the people and their government—finds its modern roots in the American and French Revolutions.

Yet these two revolutions carry the weight of two extremely different histories. Only six years separated the end of the American Revolutionary War (1783) and the beginning of open rebellion against the French king Louis XVI (1789). But while both these revolutions began as expressions of the desire for all men to be free, they ended with completely different results.

In the American colonies, the revolution of George Washington, Patrick Henry, John and Samuel Adams, Thomas Jefferson, and Benjamin Franklin seemed to follow a singular track from beginning to end: the point of their uprising was to redefine the relationship between the colonies and the Mother Country. In the end, the decision was to break all ties and establish an independent people and nation.

France's, revolution, on the other hand, became extremely complicated and multidirectional. Rarely did all the elements of support within the revolution even agree with one another. It opened in 1789 with a widely accepted goal of establishing moderate reforms while leaving the French monarchy intact. It was derailed by a narrow-minded group of paranoid politicians who ran the state through intimidation and terror and ordered the executions of both King Louis XVI and the queen, Marie Antoinette. It ended with the French economy and social structure in a shambles, no constitution, and government in the hands of a poorly run, ineffective committee that relied too much on support from the military for its own good. The French Revolution was, then, "not one event but many. It failed to achieve some of the changes that were desired in 1789, and it led to many that were not foreseen."[1]

## ABSOLUTE MONARCHY

Of all the places in Europe where revolution could have taken root and blossomed during the eighteenth century, France was one that few at the time might have expected. During the late 1600s and early 1700s, France was the dominant European power, a state with a strong monarch and the largest population (more than 20 million people) of any country on the Continent. Louis XIV (1661–1715) had exemplified the figure of the true absolute monarch. However, even though he was an autocratic ruler, he was a skillful administrator, led his people into successful wars, and oversaw a French economy that was growing in international scope and proportion. Even those of the peasant class were typically better off under Louis than others of their same class in Europe. Forty percent of France's farmlands were owned by peasants.

French monarchs such as Louis XIV often held power by granting special favors to the upper class—the aristocracy—the socioeconomic group that traditionally opposed strong monarchies. In general, by the 1700s, the people of France fit into one of three important classes—the clergy (the First Estate), the aristocracy (the Second Estate), and the Third Estate, or the commoners. Such classes had been in place for hundreds of years. Most of the taxes were paid by the Third Estate, since monarchs would grant the aristocracy special favors and exempt them from paying taxes. It was the tax issue perhaps more than any other that helped drive the nation of France into revolution.

The tax structure in France was complicated, lopsided, and unfair. Two types of taxes were common—direct and indirect. Of the direct taxes, perhaps none was hated in France more than the *taille*. This tax was paid only by those who were members of France's Third Estate. The tax was not even the same from one province to another. However, it was paid "almost entirely by the rural population."[2] The *capitation*, or poll tax, and the *vingtieme*, a form of income tax, were barely paid by the nobility, if at all. (The *vingtieme* [twentieths] was originally a 5 percent tax on income, but it had been doubled during the reign of Louis XIV.) Clergy were generally exempted from taxes, paying only the *don gratuit*, a miniscule tax at best.

These direct taxes were only half the story. Indirect taxes were equally burdensome, particularly the customs duties and the *gabelle*, or salt tax. In most of the provinces, anyone over the age of eight years was required to purchase seven pounds of salt annually, on which they were forced to pay the *gabelle*. This was because the government of France held a monopoly on the sale of salt. To add to the injustice, the tax varied from province to province. In some places the salt tax was high, while in others, salt was nearly tax-free. For this reason, salt prices in one province might be 12 times higher than in another province. However, the populace was forced, by law, to buy salt only in their home provinces. It was this combination of high and unequal taxation that set many against the French government. Since most of the tax burden was placed on the backs of those least able to pay, many members of the Third Estate were desperate for some relief.

While taxes played a significant long-term role in bringing about the French Revolution, there were other, more immediate reasons that had developed during the late eighteenth century. For one, the French economy, by the 1780s, was falling apart. During the late 1770s and early 1780s, King Louis XVI (1774–1793) supported the

## Louis XVI

Misunderstood by his people and by his fellow royals, Louis XVI was definitely not "born to be a king." He was an excellent family man, a decent locksmith and mechanic, and would have been happy with a much simpler life.

Born in 1754, Prince Louis married the 14-year-old Austrian princess Marie Antoinette in 1774. She was much sharper and full of conviction than her husband. Old King Louis XV died that same year, and young Louis and Marie ascended the throne.

The locksmith and woodcrafter relied heavily on his ministers in ruling the country, and it was they who encouraged him to ally France with the American revolutionaries as a way of striking at the hated English enemy. Louis did so, and the Franco-American alliance culminated with the victory at Yorktown in 1781.

The French intervention in the American Revolution was a tactical success but a strategic error because France became mired in debt. Faced with intransigent nobles and the rising cost of staples like bread, Louis XVI summoned France's legislature, the Estates General, to meet at Versailles in the spring of 1789. By summer they had renamed themselves the National Assembly and sworn not to disband until they had given France a new constitution. Meanwhile, economic and political conditions were frustrating Parisians, a mob of whom attacked the fortress of the

American Revolution by providing troops, war material, weapons, ships—and money. Entering the war as an American ally in 1778, the French monarch was not interested in democracy or independence as much as in giving France—one of Great Britain's staunchest enemies—an opportunity to limit the power of the British monarchy. By the late 1780s, the French government was so deeply in debt that its annual interest payments were equal to half the government's annual income.

Realizing the government was facing bankruptcy, Charles-Alexandre de Calonne, the minister of finance, published a report in 1787 on the country's desperate need for money, suggesting serious

Bastille prison, killing the governor and releasing the political prisoners held there.

In October 1789, Louis, Marie, and their family were dragged from Versailles to Paris by yet another angry mob to face the demands of the people. For the next two years—1789–1791—Louis made a show of accepting a new constitution and agreeing to rule as a limited, constitutional monarch. But in 1791, he, his wife, and their son tried to flee Paris for the Netherlands, then controlled by Austria. Once across the border, they would be safe, protected by Marie Antoinette's brother, the Austrian emperor. However, Louis was recognized by a peasant; they were apprehended and taken back to Paris in shame and disgrace. The "king's flight" destroyed what little goodwill Louis still retained with his people. When the royal palace in Paris, the Tuileries, was attacked in the summer of 1792, Louis knew the French Revolution had entered a new and deadly phase.

Claiming their intent was to restore Louis and the monarchy, Austria and Prussia went to war with France. The Parisian crowd cried for the king's head and Louis was tried as an enemy of the state. He conducted himself with great dignity during the trial but was found guilty by a sizeable majority. He was sentenced to death, however, by a majority of exactly one (his cousin Philippe Egalite voted for the execution). He died by the guillotine in January 1793, an event which quickly brought Britain into the war as an ally of Austria and Prussia.

Louis's two younger brothers, the Count of Provence and the Count of Artois, later served as King Louis XVIII and King Charles X. Louis's own son, the crown prince, died in a revolutionary jail in 1795.

tax reform. But members of the nobility responded with loud opposition, and Louis XVI fired Calonne. A member of the clergy, Archbishop Lomenie de Brienne, followed Calonne as finance minister. His proposals were blocked by several of France's parlements, or law courts, which were dominated by members of the nobility. In the parlement of Paris, representing nearly two out of every five French citizens, the magistrates refused to register the tax proposals. (One of the parlement's purposes was to register all royal edicts, including those pertaining to taxes.)

As his father and his grandfather before him had done, Louis XVI banished the Paris parlement from the city in August 1787, but when the people expressed a loud protest, he called the parlement back into session in the French capital. For the next year the king engaged in a political tug-of-war with his parlements, again abolishing the Paris parlement in May 1788 only to reinstate the judiciary body in September.

### RECALLING THE ESTATES GENERAL

By that time, Brienne had been removed and Louis had appointed a replacement, Jacques Necker. As had others before him, Necker advised the king to call the Estates General back into session. (Made up of the three estates, the Estates General was a medieval institution which traditionally had held power to advise French rulers and vote on establishing new taxes.) Throughout 1787 and 1788, nearly all of the country's dozen or so parlements pressed the king to recall the Estates General, but the Estates General had not met for nearly 175 years. Through those years, French monarchs such as Louis's grandfather, Louis XIV, had become so powerful that they had relied on the Estates General less and less, until the body was ignored completely. Desperate for answers, his treasury running out of money fast, Louis finally agreed and ordered the Estates General to take up session at his palace at Versailles, outside the city of Paris, in May 1789.

By spring, the situation across France had grown almost unbearable for the average peasant farmer. With the government nearly penniless, the country was experiencing an economic depression. As one modern historian noted:

> In some ways, the timing of the great summons could hardly have
> been worse. The proclamation went out in August; the estates met

the following May. In between, one of the century's worst harvests guaranteed that the majority of French people, at one of the most critical moments in the nation's history, would be hungry.[3]

On May 2, 1789, the delegates of the Estates General met with the king in the Hall of Mirrors at Versailles, a grand salon richly decorated with marble sculpture and lit up by 14 crystal chandeliers. As the members of the three estates prepared to enter the hall and the king's presence, it became clear to the members of the Third Estate that they were considered less important. After ushering in the clergy and nobility of the other two estates, Louis XVI made the Third Estate wait three hours before they were given audience—not in the Hall of Mirrors but in a separate room and for only a short period of time.

It was one of the first clear signs to the members of the Third Estate they were going to be considered of secondary importance to the king during the confrontational days ahead. It was a station the Third Estate did not intend to accept. Prior to the May 1789 meeting at Versailles, several political pamphlets had been published and read by the members of the Third Estate. One such tract, titled *What is the Third Estate?* and written by a priest, the Abbe Emmanuel Sieyes, asked and answered several important questions directly: "What is the Third Estate?" Answer: *Everything.* "What has it been until now in the political order?" Answer: *Nothing.* "What does it want to be?" Answer: *Something.*[4]

Such works and ideas often reflected the beliefs and political theories of the eighteenth-century French philosophes, or philosophers, men such as Jean Jacques Rousseau and Voltaire. Neither philosopher accepted the idea that a royal monarch ruled by the will of God. Instead, they had argued, government should be directed by the will of the people. Rousseau had written one of the great slogans of the Enlightenment period, which spoke volumes: "Man is born free, but everywhere he is in chains."[5]

Although the Third Estate represented the masses of the peasants and poorer citizenry, it also represented the French middle class—lawyers, doctors, and professional men who did not fit into either of the old medieval institutions of the aristocracy or clergy. In fact, half of the delegates comprising the Third Estate in the Estates General in 1789 were lawyers. The Third Estate also included some priests, such as Abbe Sieyes, as well as some members of the nobility.

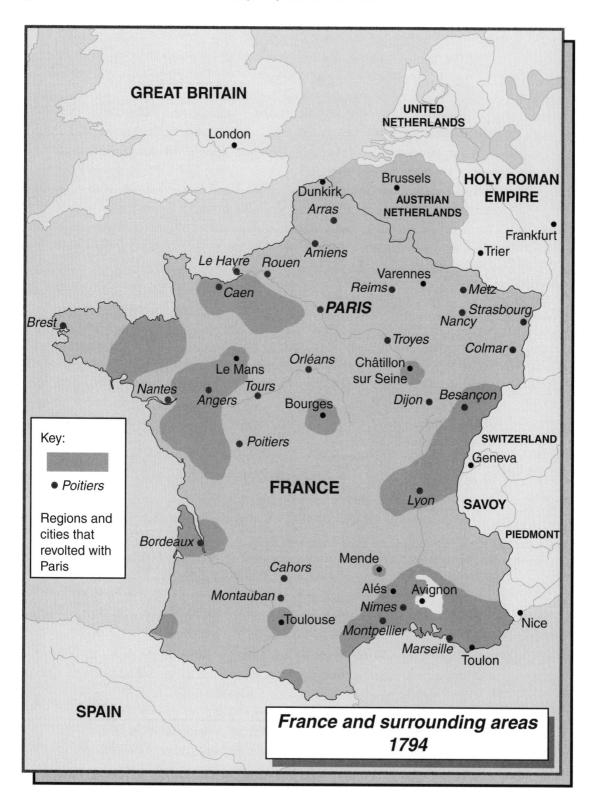

**GREAT BRITAIN**

London

**UNITED NETHERLANDS**

Brussels

**HOLY ROMAN EMPIRE**

**AUSTRIAN NETHERLANDS**

Dunkirk

Arras

Frankfurt

Amiens

Trier

Le Havre    Rouen

Varennes

Reims

Metz

Caen

**PARIS**

Strasbourg

Nancy

Brest

Troyes

Colmar

Orléans

Le Mans

Châtillon sur Seine

Nantes    Tours

Dijon    Besançon

Angers

Bourges

Poitiers

**SWITZERLAND**

Geneva

Key:

• Poitiers

**FRANCE**

Lyon

**SAVOY**

Regions and cities that revolted with Paris

**PIEDMONT**

Bordeaux

Mende

Cahors

Alès    Avignon

Montauban

Nimes

Nice

Toulouse

Montpellier

Marseille

Toulon

**SPAIN**

**France and surrounding areas 1794**

Another disappointment was how the estates were represented at Versailles. When the Paris parlement recalled the Estates General back in the fall of 1788, the court decided the estates would be equally represented with 300 delegates each, just as they had been during their last meeting in 1614. This was despite the fact that the Third Estate represented 98 percent of the country's 25 million people. The Third Estate quickly understood that the other two estates could easily vote them down on every issue, having the power of two-thirds of the vote. The king intervened, under the guidance of Jacques Necker, and doubled the number of Third Estate delegates to 600 in December 1788 in an effort to gain the support of the people. Yet even this "doubling of the Third" would not reflect the vast number of people the delegates of the Third Estate represented.

Many of the delegates of the Third Estate had arrived at Versailles unprepared to fall in line and obey the wishes of the king. They were anxious to spend their time changing the structure of the French government and were intent on expanding their power base as the true representatives of the people. When, on May 5, they were forced to listen to a three-hour-long lecture from Necker on the need for more taxes and on how the delegates must fall in line or be dismissed by the king, the Third Estate began making a psychological break from the existing French government.

## THE NATIONAL ASSEMBLY

During the weeks that followed, the delegates of the Third Estate refused to do the king's business, took no votes, listened to no debate on taxes, and generally remained in a foul mood. Their appointed leader, Jean Sylvain Bailly, a noted French astronomer, stood firm in his resolve to steer away from what was expected by the king. At one point, First Estate clergymen were sent in to convince them to change their minds and their tactics, but the Third Estate only dug in its heels. By mid-June, things were beginning to turn in a different direction. Members of the clergy, poor parish priests generally, abandoned their colleagues and began joining the Third Estate. One priest declared: "The village priests may not have the talents of Academicians but they have at least the sound common sense of villagers!"[6] Approximately half of the clergy joined the Third Estate and as many as one out of five members of the nobility also came over and began meeting with them. The enlightened tide of support was falling to the Third Estate.

Then, on June 17, the Third Estate and those who had joined its ranks took a bold step. Abbe Sieyes proposed a motion, which the delegates approved, declaring themselves a "National Assembly." By definition, this assembly saw its members as "the only representatives legally and publicly recognized ... by almost the entire nation."[7] With that one vote, the Third Estate took on the legislative power of all the estates. The delegates then formally invited anyone from the other two estates to join with them. On the June 19, the clergy voted to join with the National Assembly.

Events were now moving quickly out of the king's grasp. Faced with a decision to support the National Assembly or defy it, Louis XVI chose defiance. On the rainy morning of June 20, when the National Assembly members arrived at their meeting chamber, they found themselves locked out on the king's orders. (A note later arrived from Louis explaining the hall was being renovated.) As the delegates stood in the rain, one of their number, Dr. Joseph Guillotin, who would later invent a device for state executions, pointed to an indoor tennis court and suggested the delegates take refuge there.

The court, which had high ceilings painted black so the aristocratic sons who gathered there to play tennis could see the white ball, was soon packed with hundreds of excited and angry delegates who knew they were facing a stubborn king. President Bailly tried to call for order, but at times there were more than a hundred angry men on their feet, waving for attention and attempting to make themselves heard above the din. It was late in the afternoon before the meeting came to order. A motion was read, one amounting to a pledge among the delegates: "The National Assembly ... decrees that every member ... shall take a solemn oath not to separate ... until the constitution of the realm is established on firm foundations."[8] All but one of the assembled delegates, their clothes wet with rain, took the oath.

The challenge to the king and the monarchy's long-established authority was direct, and Louis XVI's response was immediate. He called a Royal Session of the Estates General, and, in the presence of the angry Third Estate, he vetoed the National Assembly's challenge and ordered the delegates to return to their separate meetings and take up the business for which they had been summoned—taxation. He would not tolerate any attempt to create a constitution. As the

Angered by the refusal of France's monarchy to permit representative government, deputies of the Third Estate (citizens who were neither nobles nor clergy) pledged to forge a new constitution and promised to remain convened until their goal was achieved.

king left the hall, followed by the vast majority of the gathered nobles of the Second Estate, the delegates of the Third Estate sat unmovable. They remained defiant, as one of their leaders, Comte de Mirabeau, stood and shouted to a royal official: "Tell your master that we are assembled here by the will of the people, and that we will leave only at the point of a bayonet!"[9] President Bailly added his own shouts of defiance: "The nation is assembled here, and it takes no orders."[10] A serious clash of wills was, indeed, underway.

The king soon found himself locked in a conflict that pitted old ideas of royal rule against new theories of representative government. He was uncertain how to approach the complicated situation. In the days that followed, he was counseled to use force against the

National Assembly. (One nobleman suggested that "He who wishes an omelette must not shrink from breaking eggs!")[11] But Louis XVI was, in the end, a weak-willed monarch who, on June 27, ordered the three estates to meet together, a victory the Third Estate savored. Before the end of the day, more than two out of every three members of the Estates General had joined the National Assembly. Within another two weeks, nearly all of the remaining 400 delegates had also joined. Wasting little time, the delegates at Versailles began to hammer out the details of a national constitution, the first in the long history of the French people.

### THE SPREAD OF REVOLUTION

Defiance of the French government and a strong desire for political reform was not limited that hot summer of 1789 to events centered at Versailles. A revolutionary spirit was spreading across the countryside and throughout the streets of Paris itself. During the exciting weeks that followed the creation of the National Assembly, unrest swept across the city.

By July 13, more than 15,000 foreign troops, Swiss and German mercenaries hired by the king, were stationed in and around the city. Many of the king's own guard had already thrown themselves in with the National Assembly the previous month. The French guards of the Paris garrison who had refused to take up arms against any revolutionaries had been imprisoned in their own barracks. Rumors flew across the city that the king intended to destroy the National Assembly. Such rumors were not far from the truth. Before the month was over, Paris witnessed extreme outbreaks of political violence, including street riots.

On July 14, when word reached the people of Paris that Louis had three days earlier fired Necker, the one man who had been advising the king to pursue a moderate course with the National Assembly, the city exploded. Angry crowds filled the streets, joined by the French guards, who had liberated themselves from their barracks. Everywhere they could find them, citizens seized weapons, including those from a royal storeroom in the Tuileries Palace in Paris, where rioters stole "ornamental guns and some cannon given to King Louis by the king of Siam."[12] One group of rioters engaged in a dawn raid of the Invalides, an old soldiers' hospital, where they found 30,000 muskets stored. Armed with empty weapons, the rioters went in search of powder and shot. Rumors told of a large cache of gunpowder at an old fourteenth-century medieval prison on the outskirts of the city known as the Bastille. To the people of Paris, it was a hated symbol of tyranny and was allegedly filled with political prisoners. Its defensive garrison included a few dozen Swiss guards and 82 old soldiers.

A standoff developed between the rioters and the governor of the Bastille, Marquis Bernard de Launay, who repeatedly refused to surrender the fortress. When the rioters began firing on the troops manning the 90-foot-high walls of the inner fortress of the Bastille, the defenders fired off their cannon, killing several of the besiegers. But just after noon the mob managed to open up the outer drawbridge and swarmed into the inner court.

Late in the day, as Launay watched the rioters drag up the cannon of the king of Siam, he offered to surrender the gunpowder stored inside for free passage for himself and his men. Although the leader of the riot, Lieutenant Elie of the French guard, accepted the terms, the crowd did not. When the inner drawbridge was lowered, the mob swarmed in and took the garrison prisoner. In no time, three of the Bastille's defenders were hanged on a city lamppost, while three others were hacked to death. As for Launay, his throat was cut and his head was severed and paraded around the angry streets of Paris on a pitchfork. Also among those killed in the storming of the Bastille were about one hundred of the besieging mob.

The rioters did find gunpowder stored in the Bastille, but no political prisoners. That summer, the old prison held only seven convicts, including two lunatics, four forgers, and a seventh who had been imprisoned for sex crimes.

While perhaps having little actual significance as a key event in the history of the early French Revolution, the actions taken by the rioters soon took on a symbolism of their own. Today, July 14 is celebrated as a French holiday of independence—Bastille Day.

Such events as the storming of the Bastille were difficult for the members of the National Assembly to understand. Additional acts of violence were also taking place, such as the raiding of castles, chateaus, and manor houses owned by members of the aristocracy. Outside Paris, rural peasants inspired by the fall of the Bastille attacked local symbols of authority, such as noblemen and their families. Aristocratic targets were killed and peasants tore through their victims' homes in search of the documents that identified the peasants as serfs bound to certain landowners. Such records were burned and otherwise destroyed. Across France royal authorities from Versailles to Paris to rural estates were losing their grip as revolutionary fever spread. Fearing for their lives, many members of the French aristocracy packed up their families and fled the country, including the king's own brother, who sought asylum in Holland. Historians would later refer to the abandonment of France by its aristocracy as the "Great Fear."

## THE RIGHTS OF MAN
In the meantime, Louis XVI remained uncertain of the steps he

## Marquis de Lafayette

In 1917, a group of Americans went to Paris and exclaimed, "Lafayette, we are here!" to express the debt many Americans felt to the French marquis. But few people realize that Lafayette was actually a major player in no less than three revolutions.

Born in central France in 1757, Lafayette came from a noble family; one of his ancestors had served with Joan of Arc in the Hundred Years War. His father was killed fighting the British in 1759, and the young marquis nursed a lifelong hatred of Britain.

Married and with a child on the way, Lafayette defied the wishes of King Louis XVI and went to America to join the revolution there. He became like a son to George Washington, who admired the young man's spirit. Wounded in the Battle of Brandywine, Lafayette became a hero to the Americans with whom he served.

France became an ally of the American revolutionaries in 1778. From then on Lafayette was known as the "Hero of Two Worlds." His participation in the final battle at Yorktown, Virginia, only enhanced his reputation. In 1782, he returned to France.

The next few years of Lafayette's personal life were a treasured time of peace and tranquility, mixed with international fame. Then the French Revolution began in 1789, and Lafayette was once more called into service. He became the commander of the emergency French National Guard and at one point helped save Louis XVI and Marie Antoinette from an angry mob. But by 1790 Lafayette was the leader of the Revolution, and there seemed no limit to his potential (he sent the keys to the Bastille to his friend and mentor George Washington).

But the best days were past. By 1791 Lafayette had fallen out of favor with the Parisian crowds and by 1792 he was considered should take in response to the events taking place around him. When he was awakened from sleep by one of his officials after the fall of the Bastille, Louis responded: "It is a revolt." The courtier informed him: "No, Sire, it is a revolution."[13]

On June 15, he dismissed his troops at Versailles as the National Assembly had requested. Revolutionaries convinced him to come into Paris to show his support for the revolution. The king agreed, but was so uncertain of what lay ahead for him in the city that he made out his will before leaving the palace at Versailles. The king arrived in Paris on July 17, and he accepted the tricolor, the symbol of the revolution, from the revolutionary mayor of the city, Jean Sylvain Bailly, who placed the cockade in the brim of the king's hat. (The cockade

a has-been. He served as a general in the French Revolutionary army but was taken prisoner by the Austrian enemy and spent the next five years in that country as a helpless prisoner; not even the appeals of George Washington and others could help him. Only in 1800 did Lafayette return to his beloved France, where he found that the Revolutionary ideals had been co-opted by the tyrant Napoleon Bonaparte.

Lafayette spent the next 15 years in self-imposed exile from the political arena. He and Napoleon detested one another, and Lafayette stayed away from Paris. Only the fall of Napoleon in 1814 brought Lafayette back to politics. He disliked the return of the Bourbon monarchy under the new king Louis XVIII almost as much as he had Napoleon.

In 1830, the Parisian crowds overthrew King Charles X, who had succeeded his brother Louis XVIII. This seemed the ideal opportunity for Lafayette to take a position of leadership, and many Parisians swore they would create a republic and make him their first president. But years in prison and in political exile had made Lafayette more cautious, and he turned them down. Instead, he suggested Louis-Philippe of the House of Orleans as a new constitutional monarch. Lafayette's moment had come and gone.

He died in 1834, rich in years and memories but poor in health and lacking friends. He had given his all to three different revolutionary causes and none of them, with the exception of the American Revolution of 1776, had turned out as he had hoped. Nevertheless, his name remains one of those permanently associated with liberalism and revolutionary ideals.

was a circular symbol of three colors, including white, the color of Louis's family, the Bourbons, and red and blue, the colors of Paris.)

The gathered crowd of Parisians cheered wildly. This action, plus the fact that Louis had not unleashed his mercenary troops to put down the revolution indicated the king's support for sweeping change in the French government. Perhaps, many thought, France could create a constitutional monarchy similar to Great Britain's. During the days that followed, quiet was restored to the city and the countryside, as the revolutionary National Guard fanned out across the rural areas to maintain civil order. One of the great revolutionary figures, the Marquis de Lafayette, who had served George Washington during the American Revolution, was appointed as commander of the National Guard. Throughout much of the revolution, Lafayette remained a voice of moderation.

## Thomas Jefferson: Witness to the French Revolution

Thomas Jefferson was an eyewitness to the events of 1789 in France. He arrived in Paris as a diplomatic representative of the new United States in the spring of 1788. Events were already pointing toward revolution across France. Jefferson found the city of Paris to be in a state of "high fermentation" and a "furnace of Politics."[*] By the fall of 1788, Jefferson was reporting "popular demonstrations in Paris."[**]

When Louis XVI ordered the Estates General to meet in May 1789, Jefferson was also present. He attended the May 4 opening meeting of the Estates at Versailles and became so enthralled at the exciting events there that, by June, "he went to Versailles almost every day."[***] The American diplomat did not go unnoticed. "Every body here is trying their hands at forming declarations of rights,"[+] Jefferson wrote to his friend James Madison during the winter of 1788–89. Two such declarations were sent directly to Jefferson, soliciting his opinion and direction. One of them was from his old friend, Lafayette. Jefferson wrote of Lafayette's declaration that it "contains the essential principles of ours accommodated as much as could be to the actual state of things here."[++]

The future American president also met frequently with revolutionary leaders, including Lafayette, sometimes in his own apartment in Paris, giving advice and even drafting a charter of rights of his own which he sent to Lafayette. That document was intended to be read by Louis XVI himself. Later versions of declarations were undoubtedly directly influenced by Jefferson. The version introduced to the National Assembly

National Assembly delegates labored intensely at Versailles writing a new constitution. Just weeks after the king's visit to Paris, the assembly produced a series of reforms, many voted on during the night of August 4 in a sudden and intense burst of enthusiasm. It proved a remarkable night of sweeping political change. As aristocrats within the National Assembly agreed to give up their feudal power, the assembly voted to abolish all serfdom and end special privileges for the aristocracy.

Before the end of the month, the assembly had voted to accept a document symbolizing the revolution and its developing ideals. The Declaration of the Rights of Man and the Citizen was largely the work of the Marquis de Lafayette, who patterned whole portions of the important political statement after the American Declaration of Independence. Lafayette and the author of the American document,

by Lafayette had been filtered through Jefferson.

In a letter to Jefferson, Lafayette asked his friend to "send me the Bill of Rights with Your Notes."[+++] But how much did Jefferson impact the final version of the Declaration of the Rights of Man? Historian Noble Cunningham provides a view: "It is impossible to establish Jefferson's precise influence on the declaration of rights that Lafayette presented to the National Assembly.... Only parts of the final Declaration resembled Lafayette's draft but the influence of the American Declaration of Independence on the French Declaration was evident."[#]

After the fall of the Bastille, Jefferson was ecstatic. When the king appeared in Paris a few days later and received the cockade, the American diplomat believed the revolution

was complete. He wrote of the revolutionaries: "They have prostrated the old government, and are now beginning to build one from the foundation."[##] By October 1789, Jefferson was on a ship bound for America, still convinced the French Revolution was nearly completed. On that specific point, he could not have been more wrong.

---

[*] Quoted in Noble Cunningham, *In Pursuit of Reason: The Life of Thomas Jefferson*. Baton Rouge: Louisiana State University Press, 1987, p. 121.

[**] Ibid.

[***] Ibid.

[+] Ibid., p. 123.

[++] Ibid.

[+++] Ibid., p. 127.

[#] Ibid., p. 126.

[##] Ibid., p. 125.

Thomas Jefferson, were friends, and the American patriot was in Paris during the summer of 1789.

Although the Declaration of the Rights of Man and the Citizen and the Declaration of Independence are different in many aspects, they do mirror one another in important ways. The words of Thomas Jefferson proved an inspiration to revolutionaries in Europe as well as in America. However, it appears that Jefferson's influence on the French document was not limited to merely providing an earlier document as a guide. For example, compare these two excerpts, the first from the French Declaration: "Men are born and remain free and equal in rights. The aim of every political association is the preservation of the natural rights of man. These rights are liberty, property, security, and resistance to oppression.... The source of all sovereignty is ... in the nation." The following are words from the opening of Jefferson's Declaration of Independence: "We hold these truths to be self-evident, that all men are created equal, that they are endowed by their Creator with certain unalienable Rights, that among these are Life, Liberty and the pursuit of Happiness. That to secure these rights, Governments are instituted among Men, deriving their just powers from the consent of the governed."

The French Declaration included an extensive list of each person's natural rights. The document reflected the best of Enlightened thought and would serve as the philosophical base for the constitution the National Assembly was intent on producing. It was a middle-class statement of basic liberties, including property rights and the concept of equality. No more would class rank determine a person's position in French society; each individual would stand before the law as an equal. There were guarantees of the freedom of speech, of the press, and of religious toleration. But at the core of the document was the statement that the power of the French government rested not in the hands of the monarch but with the citizens themselves.

The National Assembly voted to adopt the Declaration of the Rights of Men on August 26, 1789. Enthusiastic revolutionaries across France were soon reading the foundational document as hundreds of thousands of copies were printed.

With the passage of the Declaration and the recognition of the rights of French citizens, many people gained a renewed sense of drive and purpose regarding the revolution. However, when the king

With France's king unyielding and serious bread shortages in Paris, women took to the streets armed with pitchforks, guns, and scythes and marched to Versailles.

refused to sign the document, rumors soon spread that Louis XVI was not a true supporter of the changes enacted by the National Assembly. His words seemed to prove such suspicions, as he declared: "I will never consent to the spoliation of my clergy or my nobility and I will not sanction decrees which seek to despoil them."[14] Perhaps he was thinking of himself as well, for the Declaration clearly shifted the base of power away from the monarchy and into the hands of the people.

### THE MARCH ON VERSAILLES
Weeks passed, the king remained obstinate, the revolution's future seemed unclear, and the people of Paris were becoming more angry by the day. Making matters worse were serious bread shortages across the city that had plagued poorer Parisians for months. France had experienced several poor farming seasons, including that year's harvest. Bread riots had become common throughout the summer of 1789. On the morning of October 5, many of the bakers' shops in the slum neighborhoods had no bread for sale. Throughout the

morning, angry working women gathered and rallied in the streets, breaking into buildings and stealing muskets. In time, their numbers had swelled to seven or eight thousand.

Under a stormy sky of gray, thousands of working women, fishwives, and a few men who joined their ranks (some even joined the march dressed in women's clothing) began marching out of the city to see the king himself at Versailles. They would demand that he supply them with food. Many of those who participated in the "March of the Women to Versailles" were armed with muskets, knives, pitchforks, pikes, and hand scythes.

Many of the women knew the way to Versailles. The queen, Marie Antoinette, had made a practice of inviting the market women of Paris to her palace every August 25, the feast day of Saint-Louis. At the 1789 event, 1,200 poor women of Paris had attended, delivering bouquets of flowers to the king and queen while carrying a banner reading: "Homage to Louis XVI, the Best of Kings."[15]

After traipsing through an afternoon of rain, the women reached Versailles at around 5:30 P.M. They moved into the hall where the National Assembly was meeting, causing immediate pandemonium. Some of the women tore off their stockings and skirts and threw them over the gallery railings to dry out. The scene was chaotic, causing the delegates to halt their business: "Wet broadcloth, smelling of mud and rain, planted itself beside fastidious coats and breeches. Knives and clubs were set down on empty chairs, dripping onto papers printed with items of legislative debate."[16] The demand for bread came from every corner of the room, and the women insisted they be given an audience with Louis. When a small group was ushered in to speak to the king, their leader, a 17-year-old flower girl, lost her nerve and fainted in front of Louis. But Louis was charming, telling the women: "You know my heart. I will order all the bread in Versailles to be collected and given to you."[17]

After Louis promised bread for Paris, the crowd settled down for the night as thousands of people tried to find any place they could to lie down and recover from an eventful day. Near midnight, Lafayette belatedly arrived at Versailles along with 20,000 National Guards to provide some protection for the king and to try and keep order. Later in the night, a small group of marchers broke into the bedroom of the queen and tried to assassinate her. (The guards stationed to protect her were carrying unloaded pistols, an order issued by Louis himself. Two guards were decapitated and their heads placed on pikes, then paraded around the Versailles grounds.) Only the intervention of Lafayette and some of his guardsmen saved the royal family. The attack had awakened many around the grounds. Lafayette convinced the king and queen to go out on a balcony and greet the people. But when they did, the mob below began to chant: "To Paris, to Paris!"

## WRITING THE CONSTITUTION

The day had dawned with great change in store for the royal family. With Lafayette's assurance of protection, the king and queen agreed to leave Versailles and take up residence in the city. That day, the huge crowd at the king's palace—the Parisian women, the National Guardsmen, several of the members of the National Assembly— trudged back to Paris. Many of the women carried loaves of bread taken from the palace kitchens and wagons full of flour from the palace bins. It was a humiliating day for the royals, as many of the lower-class women shouted insults at the king and the queen, whom they hated greatly, calling the royal pair and their son, "the baker, the baker's wife, and the baker's lad."[18] The Austrian Marie Antoinette was not popular and was known as a spendthrift, wasting enormous sums on her clothing and jewelry while the French people starved. As the royals left Versailles, they could not know they would never set foot on the royal grounds ever again. The palace was boarded up, great iron locks were placed on its gates, and a handful of guards were left to keep looters out.

The chants sung by the women of Paris mocked their new relationship with the king:

[Now] we won't have to go so far
When we want to see our King
We love him with a love without equal
Since he's come to live in our Capital.[19]

That evening, October 6, the procession of thousands reached Paris and the royal family was placed in an old royal house, the Tuileries Palace, where no monarch had lived in a hundred years. The king's son summed up his feelings about his new home in a few words: "It's very ugly."[20]

With the virtual imprisonment of the king and his family, the revolution had taken a clear turn. While earlier events had been often focused on the work of the National Assembly at Versailles, the new center of the revolution was to be Paris. The National Assembly removed themselves to the city, meeting in the Manege—the grounds of a former riding school near the Tuileries, "a mere stone's throw from the palace."[21]

Yet even as the National Assembly continued its work on a constitution, many of the delegates who filled its ranks were not the same ones that had come as members of the Estates General. After the king's removal to Paris, 300 members of the Assembly panicked,

## Marie Antoinette

She is famously remembered for these infamous words, "Have they no bread? Then let them eat cake!" Whether or not she actually said this, Marie Antoinette is remembered as a person out of touch with reality, especially with that of the common people.

Born in Austria, Marie was the youngest daughter of Maria Theresa, the queen of Austria. She went to France to marry the young prince Louis, and with the untimely death of his grandfather, she was catapulted into the role of Louis's queen at an early age. It took some time for the royal couple to conceive children, but they finally did produce two. All seemed well, except for France's mounting debt.

Marie was in some ways the stronger of the two; she had a keener grasp of royal politics, though not of the plight of average people. During the 1780s, Marie exposed herself to ridicule and anger by involving herself in a swindle over a famous necklace. The necklace, which was worth a fortune, passed from one set of hands to another, and no one who possessed it seemed to fare well in his or her life. Although this was not enough to account for France's large debt (that was due to the country's participation in the American Revolution), Marie Antoinette was the object of a great deal of public anger: she was called "Madame Deficit" behind her back.

Unlike her complaisant, or perhaps

especially those loyal to the idea of continuing a monarchy. Many of them would leave France completely over the following year. From that point on, those who served in the National Assembly were members of one of three splinter groups within the revolutionary body. The largest was composed of moderates, called the Patriots and led by Lafayette, and included such men as Mirabeau and Abbe Sieyes. They wanted to see a constitution written that retained the monarchy. Another, smaller group, the Royalists or Monarchists, wanted the Revolution to come to an end and a powerful monarchy left intact, along with a reinstated nobility. The third party, the Extremists, wanted to create a democracy similar to that of the

fatalistic, husband, Marie Antoinette counseled fighting back in 1789 when the Estates General renamed themselves the National Assembly and began drawing up a constitution. She had troops brought to the royal palace at Versailles so that they might stamp out the revolt. But her action provoked public wrath, particularly that of the women of Paris, and on October 6, 1789, thousands of women, armed with pitchforks, forced Marie, her husband, and their children to go to Paris to live at the Tuileries Palace. (As they led the way, the Parisian women sang, "We're bringing the baker, the baker's wife, and the baker's little boy.)

Once at the Tuileries Palace, Marie Antoinette felt trapped. In 1791, she persuaded her husband to make a break for it; they would escape Paris and ride for the frontier with the Netherlands. But the flight was in vain, as the royals were caught just short of the border. They returned to Paris as prisoners and in January 1793, King Louis XVI was executed on the guillotine.

Marie Antoinette lived a little longer. She was tried in the summer of 1793 and found guilty of crimes against the state. She went to the guillotine with her head held high but with great anxiety over the state of her son (she did not know where he was). He died two years later in a revolutionary prison.

Marie Antoinette has always provoked conflicting feelings. She was vain and out of touch, but she was also sharper and more decisive than her royal husband. Perhaps if he had listened to her earlier, they might have put down the French Revolution in its infancy. As it turned out, she and her husband shared the fate of thousands of French men and women during that ghastly time known as the Terror, which Charles Dickens immortalized in his *Tale of Two Cities*.

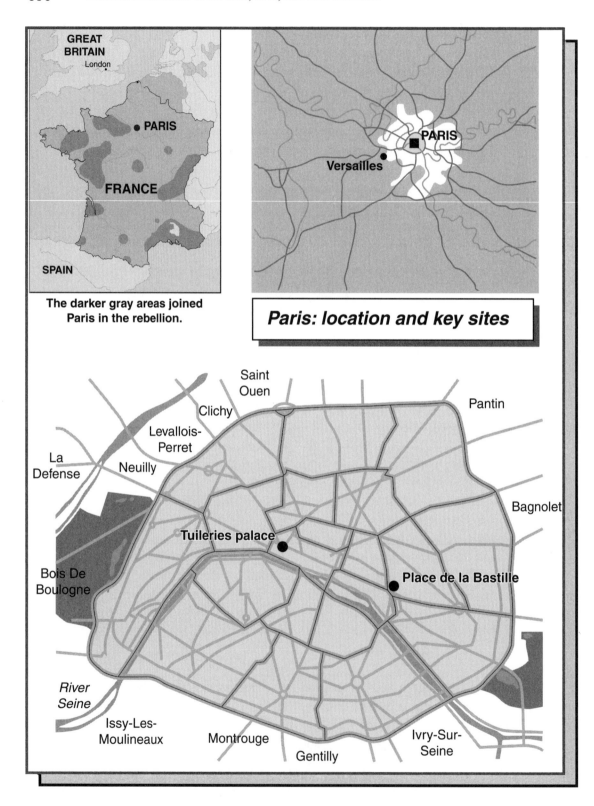

The darker gray areas joined
Paris in the rebellion.

*Paris: location and key sites*

United States, with no king or royal family. Their fiery leader was a Parisian lawyer named Maximilien Robespierre. (Since the Extremists were seated on the left and the Royalists on the right of the assembly hall at the Manege, the terms "left" and "right" remain today as words describing those who are "liberal" or "conservative.")

Over the following two years, the National Assembly remained constant in its commitment to create France's first constitution. Debates were usually emotional and many subfactions existed within the ranks of the Patriots, Monarchists, and Extremists, slowing the progress on the constitution. There were protracted debates over how much power the monarchy should be allowed; what form a new legislature should take; whether court judges should be elected or chosen; how to put the Catholic Church under state control; and how to reorganize the country into new political divisions called departments, abandoning the traditional 140 bishoprics. Church-related issues often drew great divisions between the revolutionaries, especially those who were clergymen. In the end, the constitution, when finished, was only acceptable to about half the clergy involved.

During these two heady years of political debate and change, a political organization called the Jacobin Club was gaining new power on a street level across France, often taking control of local politics. Across the land, many moderates were being pushed aside and the radicals, those who often projected the loudest voices and made the most promises to the peasants and poorer people, gained new ground daily. As the revolution appeared to take on a darker edge, the royal family became increasingly concerned about their own fates. By the early summer of 1791, Louis and Marie made a serious decision—they decided to try to escape France.

## A ROYAL ESCAPE

The escape plot was hatched by a Swedish nobleman, one loyal to the queen, named Axel Fersen. The main plan called for the royal family to sneak out of the Tuileries at night, despite the presence of hundreds of National Guardsmen patrolling the palace grounds, then move across the French countryside disguised as German noble family. On the evening of June 21, the escape unfolded. Fersen brought a coach to the palace and picked up the royal children, the king's son dressed as a young girl. The king and queen sneaked out on foot, separately to avoid suspicion, she disguised as their children's governess and Louis as a servant. At one point, Marie hid in the shadows undetected, while Lafayette passed close by, making his usual rounds. She also became "lost in the dark alleys round the Tuileries, taking half an hour before finding the carriage with its anxious passengers."[22] Once the family was free, they had only to endure a long carriage ride to the French border.

But from the beginning the escape went poorly. Despite Fersen's insistence that the family travel in a speedy, light carriage, the king insisted that they make their escape in a large, heavy, black and green coach, with bright yellow wheels, one fit for a king. This slowed their movements (they even had two carriage accidents along the way), covering only about seven miles an hour. Yet the royal party remained in good spirits, relieved they would soon be free from the control of unpredictable revolutionaries.

Despite their slow speed, the party pushed on toward the French border. But their escape had been discovered, and revolutionary riders were sending the word out across the countryside. At the frontier town of Sainte-Menehould, a local postmaster first recognized the queen from his days in the cavalry and the king by comparing his face with the one of Louis that had been printed on the new money, the assignat notes. The postmaster, Jean Baptiste Drouet, raced ahead to the town of Varennes and alerted the local revolutionary guard. At around 11 P.M., the royal entourage reached the frontier village of Varennes, where the family was finally arrested after a long day of haphazard escape. They had nearly managed to escape from the clutches of the revolution. From Varennes to the border was less than 20 miles.

The return of the royal family to Paris was a five-day humiliation. People lined the roads and jeered as the royal carriage lumbered by. Although the weather was miserably hot, the royals closed themselves inside the carriage, leaving the curtains shut. On the evening of June 25, as the entourage reached the city of Paris, there was an ominous silence as the carriage slowly rolled through the streets. Lafayette, who had been humiliated by the royals and their escape, had "enjoined [the crowd] to remain absolutely silent to show the King ... the feelings his trip had inspired."[23] Signs across Paris read: "Anyone who applauds the King will be beaten."[24] Louis and Marie reached the Tuileries against the backdrop of a gloomy silence.

Against custom and to show their disrespect to the king, the Jacobins recommended that the crowd keep their hats on and refuse to salute the monarch. Even "several scullery-boys without hats covered their heads with their dirty, filthy handkerchiefs."[25] The fates of Louis and Marie, as well as the monarchy itself, were now more uncertain than ever.

## REVOLUTIONARY PARTIES

The king soon began rebuilding support for himself. He announced his support for the new constitution, which was completed and voted on by the National Assembly on September 30, 1791. The constitution marked the singular progress the revolution had made since the spring of 1789. Hundreds of delegates had stayed the course, living up to the promise they made on the tennis court at Versailles: with the constitution in place, the National Assembly disbanded. For many, the fall of 1791 seemed to mark the completion of the revolution. The constitution was completed and royal authority had been reined in, ending hundreds of years of absolute rule. Medieval serfdom and feudalism were done away with, along with special privilege for the nobility and clergy. The people could elect their own judges, and the Catholic Church had been stripped of its special powers.

But for all these successes, the revolution was not over for many. While great strides had been made, France still faced both old and new worries. The economic problems that had led to the revolution had not been solved; in fact, they were worse. Food prices were high, bread was still in short supply, and bread riots were still plaguing the country. During the years of revolution, new paper money, called assignats, had been printed in large numbers, lowering its value. Inflation was a constant problem. In addition, the revolution had led such powers as Austria (Marie's home country) and Prussia to announce their intent to go to war against France to restore the monarchy to its full power. In late August, Austria and Prussia signed an agreement, the Declaration of Pillnitz, which included a clear statement to the French revolutionaries that both countries would "act promptly, by common consent and with such force as might be needed" to protect and preserve the French monarchy.

As the new Legislative Assembly (the body that replaced the National Assembly) met for the first time on October 1, 1791, the members faced these problems and more. Since the new constitution banned all former members of the National Assembly from holding office in the Legislative Assembly, the latter's members represented a new political group. Many were young, middle class, and untested in the fires of political leadership. Infighting and political rivalries soon overshadowed the French legislature.

While the Jacobins had been around since 1789, the political group had split into two factions, the Girondins and the Feuillants— both represented in the Legislative Assembly. The Feuillants were moderates who wanted to see the monarchy remain viable. One of their leaders was Lafayette, who had been one of the original Jacobins. The Girondins were idealists who sought a republican form of government, an end to monarchy, and the exportation of the revolution to other European countries.

There was yet another political group, one operating in the streets of Paris. This group, the Cordeliers, were urban workers, artisans, and small businessmen who did not feel the revolution had won them very much. By 1791, they were prepared to stake their claim to a portion of French political power as well.

That spring, with the constant threat posed to Marie Antoinette, Austria appeared ready for war. The Girondins were anxious to spread the revolution and succeeded in convincing King Louis to come before the Legislative Assembly and declare war on Austria (although the Jacobins, led by Robespierre, were officially opposed to war). The king's decision was a calculated political move on his part. He hoped that such a war would cause many French citizens to turn against the revolution and support him.

However, when the king made the call for war, it caused an immediate rift between the Girondins and the Jacobins. The French army performed badly in battle, and one French general was even hanged by his troops for cowardice. When things went poorly for the French troops in the field, the blame was placed on the shoulders of the Girondins, who had supported war. By midsummer of 1792, Paris was once again simmering with frustrated citizens, especially the Girondins. (Known as the "sans-culottes," the Girondins were comprised mostly of Parisian workers, who wore long pants instead of the knee breeches and stockings of the type worn by members of the aristocracy.)

The sans-culottes became furious with the king when he vetoed the Legislative Assembly's order that 20,000 *federes*, or provincial

On August 9, 1792, an angry mob demanding the removal of the French royals from power had gathered at the palace at Tuileries. Guards sympathetic to the mob refused to fight and turned their cannons away from the crowd. In the end, Louis XVI and Marie Antoinette were forced to flee.

troops, be moved to the city to protect Paris. On the night of June 10, 1792, nearly 8,000 sans-culottes marched to the Tuileries Palace, armed with pikes, swords, and pitchforks. Shouting, "Down with the veto!" the crowd broke into the Tuileries, physically jostled the king, and forced him to put on the *bonnet rouge*, "the red stocking-cap that had recently appeared as the mark of the sans-culottes."[26] They ordered Louis to drink a toast to the revolution, while the queen and their son hid in beneath a table. Yet, despite the immediate threat of the sans-culottes, the king refused to rescind his veto. The mob finally broke up and left, dissatisfied. But they would be back.

## THE REVOLUTION OF AUGUST 10

During the weeks that followed, thousands of sans-culottes began holding meetings, intent on pressing their goals for the Revolution. In Paris, they began calling themselves a revolutionary municipal assembly, and clamored for the destruction of the monarchy and the deposing of Louis. The group set a date—August 9—for the king's removal; the sans-culottes promised a counterrevolution if it did not take place. However, the king stood firm, and the Legislative Assembly made no moves to remove him.

On the hot, muggy night of August 9, 1792, the revolutionary municipal assembly illegally took control of the city government and began marching to the Tuileries. In the outer courtyard, 4,000 National Guardsmen, cannon at their sides, were on duty to protect the palace and the royal family. But these guardsmen were actually sympathetic to the citizenry and, as the mob increased in number during the night, the guards finally turned their cannon to face the Tuileries.

Inside the palace, the royal family debated whether to leave or stand firm. Louis, as usual, vacillated. Marie Antoinette wanted to stay and face the mob. There were, after all, 900 loyal Swiss guards in the Tuileries, ready to protect the king. But an adviser informed her that protection would be impossible: "Madame," he said, "all Paris is marching."[27] As the angry crowd grew to 20,000, the royal family finally fled through the palace gardens to the adjacent Manege, taking refuge in the Legislative Assembly.

This marked the second time Louis and Marie had been forced to abandon a palace, and, as with Versailles, they would never return to the Tuileries. At the Legislative Assembly, the delegates had already left the meeting hall, fearing for their lives. The majority of them never returned to their seats again. The Revolution was collapsing in just one heat-driven, passionate night.

When the mob finally attacked the Tuileries on the morning of August 10, 1792, the destruction was frenzied and bloody. The Swiss guard fought hard, but 500 of their number fell as the mob attacked with fury. Then, word came that Louis had ordered a cease-fire. But even as the Swiss soldiers stopped firing, the sans-culottes surged into the palace, killing everyone inside, including all of the royal family's servants. The bodies of the Swiss troops were mutilated, some of them even dragged through the city. The mob took from the palace what valuables they could find, destroyed the remaining furniture, then set the old royal house ablaze.

Before the end of the day, the Legislative Assembly was forced to depose the king and order the imprisonment of the royal family. Although the Girondins, who were quickly losing any power, requested the king be installed in yet another palace, the sans-culottes ordered the royals placed in a rundown, gloomy castle that had once housed an order of knights. Here, Louis, Marie and their family were still allowed 20 servants, but their surroundings were less than pleasant. Their guards often sang revolutionary songs to intimidate them, and one guard, knowing of Louis's dislike of the smell of tobacco, made a habit of blowing his pipe smoke in the king's face. As for the Legislative Assembly, it was forced to surrender to the sans-culottes, whose Insurrectionary Commune was taking over the government within Paris. The night of August 10 had changed everything for the French Revolution.

Historians recognize that the Revolution turned such a serious corner on the night of August 9–10 that the years of revolt after the attack on the Tuileries essentially comprised a second French Revolution. While these years were a continuation of earlier events, no one could have predicted the course the Revolution would follow by the fall of 1792. With the king's power removed, the French people no longer lived under a constitutional monarchy, rendering the existing constitution invalid. A new constitution had to be written, this time by delegates elected to a national convention. Since many people refused to participate in these elections or were intimidated from doing so, a minority of French delegates elected the most radical of men, including many Jacobins.

## WAR AND REVOLUTION

As the National Convention held its first meeting on September 21, 1792, the delegates faced difficult challenges. Prussia had joined France's war with Austria as an ally of the Austrians. The radical Jacobins, led by Maximilien Robespierre, called for the execution of Louis XVI, accusing him of treason. By October, the king went on trial before a Revolutionary Tribunal, which found the monarch guilty. Facing 33 counts against him, the king sat through the proceedings wearing a olive green silk coat, and answered questions succinctly and to the best of his ability. But when he heard the charge, "You have caused the blood of Frenchmen to be spilled," he immediately leaped to his feet, shouting: "No sir! I have never shed the blood of Frenchmen."[28]

However, by late January 1793, Louis was found guilty. Although the Girondins wanted Louis's life spared, the Jacobins and

## Jean Paul Marat: A Violent Voice of Revolution

While Maximilien Robespierre and Georges Danton represented a new level of radicalism for the Revolution, one of the most violent voices was that of a former physician, Jean Paul Marat.

From the Revolution's beginning, Marat was known as a proponent of extreme violence in the name of the Revolution. He became idolized by the sans-culottes, remanding the death of anyone who stood in his way and that of the Revolution. His followers became known as *enrages*, "maniacs." As one historian described him: "Marat had no politics; he was simply against anyone who held power, and it made no difference to him whether they were the ministers, the aristocrats, the royalists, the Girondists, or the courts. He flailed at them all without fear or favor."* At one point, Marat strongly suggested that more than 250,000 people be executed by guillotine.

During the transitional days of August and September of 1792, followers of Marat responded to his suggestion that mobs should "go to the Abbaye [a Revolutionary prison] ... seize priests, and especially the officers of the Swiss guards and their accomplices and run a sword through them."** On September 2, street mobs, many of them federeres from Marseilles, attacked several prisons, murdering hundreds of priests. For five days, killings took place across Paris, with victims receiving little more than a mock trial. Before the "September Massacres" were over, as many as 1,400 people had fallen victim to attacks inspired by the rabid Marat. By the spring of 1793, Marat's tactics and violent tendencies had become so extreme that he was placed on trial for sedition. But Marat proved so popular with the people, that the Girondins quickly acquitted him.

Such a virulent radical could not help but create enemies. During the summer of 1793, a Girondin supporter, a young woman named Charlotte Corday, went to visit Marat, claiming she had information about a group of opponents to the Revolution. She was invited into his home, finding the radical leader in his bathtub, where he spent much of his time treating a horrific skin disease (one he may have contracted while hiding out in the Paris sewers, evading state authorities). After giving him a list of names—to which Marat responded: "They will soon be guillotined"—Corday pulled a long steel-bladed knife from underneath her skirts and stabbed Marat in the heart. Thus Marat's violent ways had brought him to an equally violent death. The young assassin was captured and guillotined, but she kept a clear conscience, stating at her trial: "I condemned one man in order to save a hundred thousand."***

* Quoted in Dowd, pp. 92–93.

** Quoted in Corzine, p. 80.

*** Ibid., p. 92.

the sans-culottes made certain he was sentenced to death on the guillotine. On January 21, the king of France walked up the steps to the scaffold, his hands tied. He tried to deliver a speech, but the sound of military drums drowned him out. He managed only to get out the words: "People! I die innocent." He then turned to his confessor, a priest named Edgeworth, and told him: "I am innocent of that of which I am accused! I hope my blood will consolidate the happiness of all Frenchmen."[29] The gathered populace stood in stunned silence as the guillotine dropped, followed by "a terrible scream, which was choked by the knife."[30] As a guard on the scaffold picked up the severed head of Louis XVI, the crowd seemed to come alive, with shouts of "Vive la nation! Vive la republique!"

## THE RISE OF ROBESPIERRE

The news of the death of the king of France rippled through every royal palace of Europe. Other European countries—England, the Netherlands, Spain—joined with Austria and Prussia in their war against the French and their revolution. These powers were already upset with the National Convention as a result of its offer two months earlier to "extend fraternal feelings and aid to all peoples who may wish to regain their liberty."[31] It was what the other monarchs of Europe had feared might happen: the French were intent on spreading their revolution to other countries.

As the war expanded further abroad, the Girondins at home were losing influence and power. When a Girondin general defected to the Austrians after losing several battles, the days of the Girondin Club were over. Leadership of the Revolution fell squarely into the hands of the Jacobins, who ordered the arrests of several Girondin leaders by the summer of 1793. Once again, the Revolution took a decisive turn, one that would prove the bloodiest and darkest of all.

Systematically, Robespierre began to extend his control over the remaining elements of the Revolution. He gained control of the new war cabinet, the Committee of Public Safety. When members of the National Convention protested Robespierre's political power play, a mob surrounded the Manege where they were meeting, aiming cannon at the legislative hall until the offending delegates were turned over to them. Twenty-nine members were executed by guillotine. Everywhere, intimidation became the driving force of the Revolution. The Committee of Public Safety dealt harshly with anyone it perceived was less than completely loyal to the Revolution, a state of affairs that helped usher in the period of the Revolution known as the Reign of Terror.

For a time, Robespierre shared leadership of the Jacobins with a burly Parisian named Georges Danton, who had established the Insurrectionary Commune. Both men were middle-class lawyers who believed fervently in the Revolution and in the need to redirect events following the death of Louis XVI. Robespierre was intent on using the Revolution to completely reorder all of French society, government, and culture. For example, the calendar was changed. The year from September 22, 1792, to September 22, 1793, became the first year of the new French calendar. The seven-day week was replaced

## Americans and the French Revolution

As the French Revolution unfolded, perhaps no other people abroad took a greater interest in these events than the people of the United States. Having just completed their revolution against Great Britain, Americans were joyous that the spirit of 1776 had made its way to Europe, certain that the "American Revolution had inspired the reformers in France."[*] One of the leading personalities of the early Revolution was Lafayette, who had voluntarily served directly under General George Washington during the American conflict, and the French Declaration of the Rights of Man was a clear reflection of the Declaration of Independence.

The spirit of the French Revolution excited many patriotic Americans. When a French army defeated a combined force of Austrians and Prussians in December 1792, the city of Boston celebrated with a parade, followed by fireworks.

However, by 1793, the French Revolution began to turn bloody, and many American supporters turned away from its excesses. When Louis XVI was executed, no less a patriot leader than John Adams, who was serving as Washington's vice president, wrote that the French monarch's death "would lead to the destruction of discipline ... in society."[**] Alexander Hamilton, then U.S. secretary of the treasury—while not a man sympathetic with the French—described the darker side of the French Revolution as "one volcano succeeding another, the last still more dreadful than the former."[***]

Those Americans who remained loyal in spirit to the French Revolution after 1793 may have remembered how the French had aided them during the Revolutionary War. In 1778, American diplomats, including Benjamin Franklin, had signed a treaty of alliance with the French monarch, Louis XVI.

by a ten-day week (a move calculated by Robespierre to eliminate Sunday, the Christian day of worship). The months were renamed, taking on designations associated with nature, such as Floreal, the month of flowers (April 20–May 19); Thermidor, the month of heat (July 19–August 17); and Frimaire, the month of frost (November 21–December 20). When the National Convention voted in the new calendar, a Jacobin leader made its purpose clear:

> It is time, since we have arrived at the summit of the principles of a great revolution, to reveal the truth about all types of religions. All religions are but conventions. Legislators make them to suit the people they govern. It is the moral order of the Republic, of the

That treaty committed the French to providing aid to the Americans in their struggle against Great Britain. But the treaty had been a mutual one. When the French found themselves at war with England during the American Revolution, it was expected the America would ally itself with the French revolutionary government.

However, President Washington, while sympathetic to the French cause, had no intention of going to war in support of France. Although his cabinet was split on the issue (Hamilton opposed American intervention, while Jefferson supported it), Washington decided to keep the Revolution-ending treaty intact while choosing to ignore any part of the agreement which seemed to call for American involvement in the French Revolution and France's conflict with Great Britain.

As a young nation with a small treasury,

there was little the United States could actually offer the French other than psychological support. On April 22, 1793, Washington issued a proclamation of neutrality, stating that the United States would pursue "a conduct friendly and impartial towards the belligerent powers."[+] It was a position that infuriated a large number of Americans who believed the French Revolution was the continuation of greater freedom for people around the world.

---

[*] Quoted in John Ferling, *A Leap in the Dark: The Struggle to Create the American Republic*. New York: Oxford University Press, 2003, p. 357.

[**] Ibid.

[***] Ibid., p. 358.

[+] Quoted in Louis Martin Sears, *George Washington and the French Revolution*. Detroit: Wayne State University Press, 1960, p. 174.

Revolution, that we must preach now, that will make us a people of brothers, a people of philosophes.[32]

Radical leaders were intent on destroying many aspects of Christianity, associating it with the state and the clergy, many of whom had not supported the Revolution. Robespierre wanted to create a completely secularized world in which Enlightenment philosophy provided a new type of virtue. To maintain his new order, Robespierre encouraged ruthlessness, following his personal motto: "Virtue, without which terror is disastrous, and terror, without which virtue is powerless."[33]

During this phase of the Revolution, Christian institutions and beliefs were oppressed. Priests were mistreated, even executed.

## Georges-Jacques Danton

Born in 1759, Georges Danton was a brilliant lawyer who had a troubled career both in the latter days of Louis XVI and in the early days of the French Revolution.

Danton rose to prominence in the 1780s, and at the beginning of the Revolution he was one of the chief advocates for the King's Bench in Paris. The Revolution quickly made a believer out of him, and Danton played minor roles in the opening scenes, such as the fall of the Bastille, a hated prison in the center of Paris. Danton became a member of the country's National Assembly and then the Legislative Assembly.

A large man with a florid appearance, Danton was not handsome, but his oratory and wit made him many friends and allies. He was a friend of Maximilien Robespierre, at least in the early days of the Revolution. Danton and his fellow deputies from the Gironde River area soon became known as the Girondins, and they formed a majority in the Legislative Assembly.

When Louis XVI and Marie Antoinette tried to escape from France in June 1791, Danton led the calls for an end to the monarchy. His speeches helped bring about the massacre at the Champs de Mars (Field of Mars) that summer, and contributed to the general instability within Paris. About this time, many members of the higher nobility began to flee France, which was fine with Danton.

In 1793, Danton voted for the execution of Louis XVI. He had some qualms about the matter, knowing that the action would bring about hostility from other monarchical nations, but he made one of his boldest speeches, ending with "We throw them the head of a tyrant!"

Churches were rampaged by revolutionary extremists. Some were rededicated as "Temples of Reason." Sanctuaries were stripped of their valuable gold and silver artifacts, supposedly to support the French treasury. Church bells were taken, their metals melted down to make bullets and cannon for the war effort. Altars were destroyed, stained-glass windows broken, and hymnals burned. In the grand cathedral of Notre Dame in Paris, a stage was set featuring a female opera singer dressed as Liberty, bowing "to the flame of Reason and seated ... on a bank of flowers and plants."[34]

## THE REIGN OF TERROR

Robespierre and Danton continued to take the Revolution in new, yet extreme, directions. With Danton's leadership, the Committee of

War quickly commenced against England, Prussia, and Austria in 1793. While Danton was a statesman, not a soldier, he rallied the public by describing the atrocities that might befall France if she were to be conquered. The French Revolutionary army stopped the Prussians at the Battle of Valmy that September, a battle that is often seen as one of the decisive ones of world history, since the French Revolution might otherwise have been snuffed out.

On April 6, 1793, Danton was elected to the 12-member Committee of Safety. This executive body held virtually dictatorial powers in France; the population was mobilized against the enemy; and for the first time in European history a truly citizen army was created.

Fiery and fierce though he was, Danton began to lose the affection of the Parisian populace. They were now more attracted to his rival Maximilien Robespierre. Danton failed to be reelected to the Committee of Safety, and Robespierre took over as the new chief of that committee. Danton returned to the provinces, but after only a few months of rest he went back to Paris and challenged Robespierre for the leadership of the committee. As eager as he had been for the death of Louis XVI and Marie Antoinette, Danton now felt that the Revolution had gone too far in its use of the guillotine, and he vowed either to remove the guillotine from public life or to perish beneath it. He failed in the former and succeeded in the latter, and was executed on April 5, 1794. A true revolutionary, he believed in sparing no one once the Revolution was under way, but he may have regretted this stance as he came to his end.

Public Safety sought to negotiate out of the ever-expanding war, but when those efforts failed, Danton was removed from the committee during the summer of 1793. Meanwhile, Robespierre ordered the National Convention to write a second French constitution. This one was to include greater liberal goals, such as the vote for all adult males and a national system of public schools.

The redirected Revolution evoked sharp criticism, especially from the rural regions of the country. France was still plagued with food shortages as well as inflation. A new constitution was soon put

## The Fate of the King's Son

More than two centuries after the French Revolution, modern science answered one of the period's controversial mysteries: What was the fate of Louis-Charles de France, the son of Louis XVI and Marie Antoinette? In December 2000, genetic tests were done on a heart believed to be that of the royal dauphin. The DNA results cleared up the mystery once and for all.

When his father had been executed, the eight-year-old dauphin had automatically become Louis XVII. But the young boy was being held, along with his mother, in the old Templars temple in Paris to make certain no monarchists could free him and restore the royal throne. Then, on June 8, 1795, according to official records, the ten-year-old died in prison, probably succumbing to tuberculosis.

Rumors were common during the French Revolution, however, and some told of young Louis XVII's escape at the hands of supporters, who left another boy's body to be found by the temple's jailers. Complicating matters was the fact

that for decades after the Revolution, several people claimed to be Louis XVII. Had young Louis XVII actually escaped?

What was known was that a young boy had died in the temple, an autopsy had been performed, and the heart of the victim had been removed by the chief surgeon. It was that heart that would finally solve the eighteenth-century mystery using twentieth-century science.

In 2000, the heart, which had been buried in the royal crypt in the Cathedral of Saint Denis, the burial site of French monarchs, was removed. DNA tests were performed and compared with DNA samples of locks of Marie Antoinette's hair as well as with the DNA of living descendants of Marie and two of her sisters. The tests proved that the young man who had died in the Paris prison had, in fact, been the son of the French monarchs who were executed by the revolutionaries, confirming Louis-Charles as yet another royal martyr.

## The Revolutionary Calendar

As the French Revolution redefined the nation's political system, moves were made to alter the social order, as well. Personal references were changed from "monsieur" and "madame" to "citizen" and "citizeness," in an attempt to make all such designations equal. Clothing styles changed. Red, white, and blue were the patriotic colors. Old styles, including the common European tradition of wearing powdered wigs, ruffled shirts, abundant skirts, and knee britches, were replaced by straight-line, simple dresses for women and long pants for men. Hair styles were also changed to mirror the image of Roman Republicanism.

Some French revolutionaries became so obsessed with divesting all of France from Christian influences that they created a new calendar. The new months were renamed and stripped of all holy days. Even Sundays were eliminated from the days of the week.

The new calendar was a naturalistic one. It featured month names that mirrored the various seasons, temperatures, and harvests of the year:

| Old Calendar | New Month | Meaning |
| --- | --- | --- |
| September 22–October 21 | Vendemiaire | Grape Harvest |
| October 22–November 20 | Brumaire | Mist |
| November 21–December 20 | Frimaire | Frost |
| December 21–January 19 | Nivose | Snow |
| January 20–February 18 | Pluviose | Rain |
| February 19–March 20 | Ventose | Winds |
| March 21–April 19 | Germinal | Sowing |
| April 20–May 19 | Floreal | Blossom |
| May 20–June 18 | Prairial | Haymaking |
| June 19–July 18 | Messidor | Harvesting |
| July 19–August 17 | Thermidor | Heat |
| August 18–September 16 | Fructidor | Fruits |

Since each month was 30 days long, five days were left over (September 17–21). These days were named for a festival, called the *sans-culottides*.

Even though the leaders of the Revolution established punishments for those who did not abide by the new calendar of nature, nearly everyone in France, except the revolutionary officials themselves, simply ignored the strange calendar.

Just as the calendar was altered to eliminate Christian influences, several revolutionaries refused to give their newborn children Christian names, such as John, David, Mary, or Adam. Instead, they, too, turned to nature, choosing to name their offspring such things as Turnip, Cabbage, Carrot, and Dandelion. As one historian later noted, the list of the names of revolutionary children "reads rather like a seed catalog."[*]

* Quoted in Thomas Michael Kowalick, transcriber. *The Western Tradition Transcripts*. (based on videotapes featuring Professor Eugen Weber, UCLA) Alexandria, VA: PBS Adult Learning Service, 1989, p. 123.

on hold while Robespierre and his Jacobins tried to bring the counterrevolutionary rebellions under control. All critics of the Revolution were to be considered enemies of the state.

That summer, the National Convention passed the Law of Suspects, which gave the Revolutionary Tribunal broad powers to punish anyone

## Maximilien Robespierre

Robespierre "the Incorruptible" was born in Arras, in northwest France, in 1759. He studied in Paris, then returned to Arras to practice law. During the 1780s he was the star lawyer in several sensational cases; then, in 1789, he became a deputy of the Estates General (the French legislature).

The Estates General had not been called since 1613. Robespierre and other members of the Third Estate (which represented the middle class) called for greater reforms in the country, especially of the outdated tax system. By 1790, one year into the Revolution, Robespierre was one of the most outspoken critics of King Louis XVI and even of the moderate revolutionaries. Robespierre believed that nothing less than a sweep away of the old institutions would grant France a new lease on life. At an early stage in the Revolution he argued in favor of complete abolition of the death penalty (this would later be seen as the height of irony).

Robespierre fared poorly in the National Assembly (formerly the Estates General), and in the Legislative Assembly which followed. But he was a natural for the Jacobin Club in Paris. This club, which sponsored the most outlandish revolutionary measures, found something deeply appealing about the young man, who dressed like a dandy, but who spoke like the fire-breathing radical that he was. Robespierre became known as "incorruptible" because of his spartan lifestyle; aside from his handsome clothes, he kept almost nothing in the way of personal property. By 1792, he was the leader of the Jacobin faction in the new legislature, named the National Convention.

This was the year in which the Parisian crowd took matters into its own hands and stormed the Tuileries Palace, nearly killing Louis XVI and the royal family. Robespierre had been against the king and the royals all along, and the new burst of violence played right into his hands. When the king was tried in January 1793, Robespierre was among the loudest of those calling for his head. Louis XVI went to the guillotine.

The king's death plunged France into a crisis. His Austrian relatives rallied their nation against him and Britain and Prussia joined the coalition. Were it not for the fervor of the French Revolutionary armies, the Revolution might have been crushed that same year. But Robespierre and his friends had other ideas.

in opposition to the Revolution. Many innocent citizens fell victim to the guillotine. A sickening pattern soon became widespread:

> The victims were shepherded to the courtroom in the morning and, no matter how many of them there might be, their fate was

During the spring of 1793, Robespierre fought and won a struggle for control of the National Convention, defeating the Girondin deputies led by Georges Danton. By midsummer 1793, Robespierre and a handful of others, including his younger brother, effectively ran the nation. During this period the number of swift trials followed by swift executions greatly increased: Paris slipped into the period of its history known simply as the "Terror."

In the spring of 1794, Robespierre sent his former colleague Danton to the guillotine. There seemed to be no opposition left, and Robespierre felt free to carry out the drastic reforms for which he had waited. In the early summer of 1794 he changed the calendar, replacing the twelve traditional months with ten new ones. He also instituted the worship of the "Supreme Being," which (very briefly) became the institutional religion of France.

By midsummer 1794 Robespierre was on top of the world. His reforms were in place, the Prussians and Austrians had been defeated, and France lay at his feet. It is important to note that power did not lead him to seek money or pleasure: he remained the Incorruptible. But there was a resistance movement gathering, and on July 23 he was denounced by some of his foes in the National Convention. Arrested, Robespierre was soon released, but he was attacked that night by a group hired by his foes. Beaten and injured, Robespierre was sent to the guillotine the following day. He was staunch and unrepentant to the end.

settled by no later than two in the afternoon of that same day. By three o'clock their hair had been cut, their hands bound and they were in the death carts on their way to the scaffold. Execution was almost always effected on the same day the sentence was imposed.[35]

One of the Tribunal's victims was the queen herself. In October 1793, Marie Antoinette was found guilty of treason; she was executed on October 16. In all, the Reign of Terror executed approximately 40,000 people. Less than half of them—about 16,000—however, were dispatched by beheadings. Others were shot, floated out in the Seine River on barges and sunk, or left to languish in prison until they died miserable deaths.

Even as the Revolution turned more destructive and paranoid, Robespierre began to question even the loyalty of his fellow leader, Danton. That November, Danton expressed his personal disgust for the mass executions: "Perhaps the Terror once served a useful purpose, but it should not hurt innocent people. No one wanted to see a person treated as a criminal just because he happens not to have enough revolutionary enthusiasm."[36] Robespierre turned on his revolutionary comrade, and, by April 1794, Danton was guillotined along with several other Jacobin leaders. As the cart carrying Danton and seventeen others to the guillotine passed by Robespierre's rented house, the former revolutionary leader shouted, "Vile Robespierre! You will follow me. Your house will be leveled and the ground where it stood will be sowed with salt!"[37] Danton's death preceded a bloody couple of months during which nearly 1,400 people were executed as enemies of the state. (Robespierre had ordered the Revolutionary Tribunals to decide each case as either death or acquittal.)

Robespierre's excesses were slowly turning people away from the Revolution. By the end of July 1794, the Parisian leader was arrested while attending a meeting of the Convention. Others among his followers were arrested as well. In desperation, Robespierre attempted suicide the following day. (He managed only to inflict a gunshot wound to his jaw, rendering him unable to speak.) After his arrest, Robespierre was condemned by the Revolutionary Tribunal and ordered to the guillotine. At 7 P.M. on July 27—Thermidor 9, by the revolutionary calendar—he was beheaded, as his "executioner ripped the bandage from his jaw, and he shrieked with pain. Moments later, his head toppled into the basket."[38] Ironically, the law used to condemn Robespierre was one he had written himself: "Any individual who usurps the nation's sovereignty shall be immediately put to death by free men."[39]

## THE DIRECTORY

At last the horrors of the Revolution's Reign of Terror began to subside. Order and calm took over Paris as thousands of political prisoners were released from cells and holding warehouses around Paris and other cities. The Girondins were invited to join the National Convention. The Law of Suspects was suspended, the Committee of Public Safety abolished, and, by the following year, the National Convention had written a new constitution, the third penned since the French Revolution had begun in 1789.

Under this new constitution, several political gains of the Revolution were taken away, including the right of universal suffrage, allowing only people with property to vote. The government centered around a five-man committee known as the Directory, who were chosen by a two-house assembly. The Directory worked ineffectively, was unable to get the financial crisis under control, and came to rely increasingly on the power of the French military for support. During the four years of the Directory's leadership, the country continued to reel under a corrupt government. Despite some successes in dealing with the problems of inflation and a discredited currency, the Directory became a target for a military coup. On November 9, 1799, a young French general who had seen field success during France's long war seized control of the government. A military dictatorship was established, the French Revolution officially ended, and General Napoleon Bonaparte soon became a new French dictator.

## ASSESSING THE REVOLUTION

After ten years of revolution, France emerged a changed nation. But somewhere on the road to creating a new nation based on revolutionary thought, the mission had gone astray. At the end of the eighteenth century, France came under the control of not a royal dictator, but a military one. Yet a fourth constitution was written, this one with few of the republican ideals of the Revolution; instead, the vast majority of the French people supported this "new and highly authoritarian constitution."[40] Within just a few years, the general Napoleon became the Emperor Napoleon, and a new line of imperial rule was established. The irony was clear: "Throats that had yelled themselves hoarse crying the words of the old Revolutionary slogan "Liberty! Equality! Fraternity!" were now shouting "Long live the Emperor!" with just as much enthusiasm. It was as if the Bastille had never fallen, the guillotine had never existed."[41]

Where had things gone wrong? The great strides made during the summer of 1789 through 1791 may have accomplished too much

## Jean Paul Marat

Jean Paul Marat was sensational in life, but his death brought even more headlines, due to the unusual manner of his departure.

Born in Boudry, Switzerland, in 1743, Marat was part of the educated class that knew little distinction between national boundaries. He grew up in Switzerland but received his medical training in France and became a successful physician in both England and France. Marat was also something of a scientist, conducting experiments in optics and electricity. He felt snubbed by the French Academy of Science, and this may have contributed to his intense dislike for nobility, prestige, and wealth. He wrote *Chains of Slavery* to explicate the problems with the French government prior to 1789.

When the Revolution began in 1789, Marat was among the most ferocious of the journalists who reported on the scene. Time and again he called for execution of the royal family and for the creation of a temporary dictatorship—necessary, he said, for the pro-

tection of the Revolution. Marat was pursued many times, both by royalist sympathizers and by agents of the moderate revolutionary government. He evaded capture, however, and continued to publish his journal *Friends of the People* on a regular basis.

In 1792, the citizens of Paris elected him as one of their deputies to the new National Convention. This was a much more revolutionary body than either the National Assembly or the Legislative Assembly, both of which preceded it, and Marat took full advantage of the situation. He became spokesman for the "Mountain," the large body of radical Jacobin deputies who called for the death of King Louis XVI and war on the neighboring countries that also had monarchies. Marat was a brilliant speaker, but his appearance was unkempt in the extreme, and he suffered from a painful and chronic skin malady that made him look as if he were at death's door. He continued on, nonetheless.

change too quickly. Many old French political and social traditions were simply thrown aside with little thought of how deeply they were engrained in the French way of life. These early reforms—the elimination of serfdom, the guaranteeing of individual rights, the limiting of royal power, control of the Church by the state—were so extreme, they left little wriggle room for later political compromise. After 1791, much of the Revolution remained focused on holding to these reforms, causing the revolutionaries to constantly remain on the defensive.

But why did the Revolution continue to bring further change to

On one occasion Marat went too far. His fellow deputies felt themselves endangered by his ideas, and he was arrested and tried by his fellow legislators. In a brilliant self-conducted defense, he won his acquittal. Marat was now, in June 1793, at the height of his power. The king was dead, executed on the guillotine, and France was at war with England, Austria, and Prussia. This was the situation Marat had wanted, since he believed that the extremity of the times would call forth more revolutionaries and make the Revolution itself invincible.

On Saturday, July 13, which happened to be one day short of the anniversary of the fall of the Bastille, Marat welcomed a young woman from the provinces to his large apartment. She brought information concerning his enemies, the Girondins (deputies from the Gironde). Marat eagerly took information from her as he sat in his bathtub (the soak was to soothe the pain from his skin ailment). At a critical moment, when he exulted over what he would do with the information, Charlotte Corday leaned over and swiftly stabbed him in the chest. Marat died at once.

The trial that followed revealed a strong and bold young woman, convinced that Marat was a terrible danger who had to be removed:

"What was the purpose of your trip to Paris?"

"To kill Marat…

"So atrocious a deed could not have been committed by a woman your age. Someone must have incited you to it."

"I told my plans to no one. I was not killing a man, but a wild beast that was devouring the French people."

Charlotte Corday died on the guillotine—the instrument that was in full swing, due at least in part to the efforts of Marat over the previous three years. The scene of Marat in the bathtub has been immortalized by the painter Jacques-Louis David.

France even after the ratification of the constitution in 1791? Some of the blame may lie at the feet of the king, Louis XVI. Although the constitution left room for the continuation of the monarchy, many French people remained dissatisfied with Louis. His own responses to the Revolution were disappointing. His ineptitude may have cost not only his life, but the ultimate success of the Revolution of 1789. Louis's inability to provide adequate and consistent support to the Revolution caused the tide to sweep past him, resulting in the establishment of a republic in 1792 that did not need or want a king.

The final years of the Revolution fell victim to the excesses of a handful of bitter rivalries between different classes of French society. The war, also, brought on sheer paranoia and wartime hysteria that led to the Reign of Terror. But the Terror ultimately returned France to its senses once again, as the middle-class regained control of the Revolution, returning things to their center once more—at least for a while.

What, then, had the French Revolution actually accomplished? There were distinct failures and shortcomings, to be sure, but great strides had been made even if individual goals had not succeeded. As one historian summed up the Revolution's aftermath:

> The citizen of 1795 possessed freedoms that the citizen of the Old Regime could not have dreamed of. He was governed by an assembly that he had elected; he was served by courts in which justice was free and equal for all men; he could work when and where he liked; and he owed no dues and duties to the aristocrats. Although a definite class structure still existed in society, the peasant was as respectable in the eyes of the law as was the priest or the highborn. Most important, land could be bought and owned by anyone with the right price and the determination to work it.[42]

For the future of France, power was never to be centered in the hands of the aristocracy but could be claimed by those who pursued power through their talents, personal achievement, and the push and enterprise of their character and will.

The year 1799 did not mark the true end of the French Revolution. Its spirit continued to turn events in the decades that followed, not only at home, but around the world. Revolutionaries from Europe to Africa to Latin America gained inspiration from the

Revolution's loftier images—the Tennis Court Oath, the Bastille, the Declaration of the Rights of Man, the tireless work of the National Assembly—and pursued their own dreams of better government, freer society, and the power of individual choice. Above all else, the French Revolution created for its citizens, and for those who faced tyranny abroad, a lasting legacy.

---

**TIMELINE**

**Late 1600s–**

**Early 1700s** Home to 20 million people, France is the dominant power on the European continent.

**1775–1783** The War of American Independence. During the American Revolution, the French king, Louis XVI, gave support to the colonies by providing troops, war material, weapons, ships, and money.

**1787** French finance finister, Charles-Alexandre de Calonne, publishes report on France's desperate need for money, suggesting serious tax reform.

**1787–1788** Nearly all of France's dozen or so parlements (regional courts) press Louis XVI to recall the Estates General.

**December 1788** Louis XVI doubles the number of Third Estate delegates to 600.

**1789** **May 2** Delegates to the Estates General meet with Louis XVI at his Versailles palace.

**May 5** Following a three-hour-long lecture from Necker, Louis's financial advisor, delegates of the Third Estate begin psychological break from the French government.

**June 17** Third Estate abandons the Estates General and forms the National Assembly.

**June 20** Locked out of their meeting chamber at Versailles, Third Estate delegates meet in indoor tennis court and agree on the Tennis Court Oath.

**June 27** Louis XVI agrees to let all three estates meet together, a victory for the Third Estate.

**July 13** More than 15,000 foreign troops, Swiss and German mercenaries hired by Louis, are stationed in and around city of Paris.

**July 14** Riots across Paris target the Tuileries Palace, the Invalides Hospital, and the Bastille.

**July 15** Louis dismisses his troops at Versailles at the National Assembly's request.

**July 17** King pays visit to Paris as a half-hearted show of support for the Revolution.

**August 4–5** In a burst of enthusiasm, National Assembly enacts sweeping changes, including an end to serfdom.

## 1790
**June 21** Royal family attempts an escape from the Tuileries to friendly territory outside France, but the attempt fails.

## 1775–1783
The War of American Independence. During the American Revolution, the French king, Louis XVI, gave support to the colonies with troops, money, and materials.

## 1791
**September 30** National Assembly completes its work on the constitution and votes to accept the document, creating a constitutional monarchy.
**October 1** New Legislative Assembly meets, replacing National Assembly.

## 1775

## 1787
French finance minister, Charles-Alexandre de Calonne publishes a report on France's desperate need for money, suggesting serious tax reform.

## 1789
**May 2** Delegates to the Estates General meet with Louis XVI at his Versailles palace.
**June 17** Third Estate abandons the Estates General and forms the National Assembly.
**July 14** Riots across Paris target the Tuileries Palace, the Invalides Hospital, and the Bastille.
**August 4–5** In a burst of enthusiasm, National Assembly enacts sweeping changes, including an end to serfdom.
**August 26** National Assembly votes to adopt the Declaration of the Rights of Man.
**October 5–6** "March of the Women to Versailles" ends with royal family moved to Paris and installed in the Tuileries Palace.

**August 26** National Assembly votes to adopt the Declaration of the Rights of Man.

**October 5–6** "March of the Women to Versailles" ends with royal family moved to Paris and installed in the Tuileries Palace.

**1790    June 21** Royal family attempts escape from the Tuileries to friendly territory outside France, but the attempt is unsuccessful.

**1791    September 30** National Assembly completes its work on the constitution and votes to accept the document, creating a constitutional monarchy.

**1792**
**August 10** Mob action leads to Louis and Marie's removal from Tuileries. The Tuileries is fired on by revolutionary forces, and the Legislative Assembly begins to unravel. Existing constitution is abandoned.
**January 21** King Louis is executed on the guillotine.
**Summer** Control of the Revolution falls into hands of the Jacobins, led by Maximilien Robespierre. Danton is arrested as enemy of the state.
**October 16** Marie Antoinette is condemned and executed by guillotine.

**1795–1799**
France is governed by the Directory, a five-man committee.

**1799**

**1794**
**July 26–27** Robespierre is arrested during a meeting of the National Convention, is tried, convicted, and executed on the guillotine.

**1799**
**November 9** Young French general, Napoleon Bonaparte, destroys the Directory, establishes military rule, and makes himself dictator.

**1793–1794**
**Summer 1793–Summer 1794** Reign of Terror results in the executions of 40,000.

**October 1** New Legislative Assembly meets, replacing National Assembly.

**1792 Summer** Street types and middle-class revolutionaries, especially the sans-culottes, begin to turn on the constitutional government.

**June 10** Eight thousand sans-culottes march on the Tuileries, jostling the king and demanding he rescind his veto of a bill proposing thousands of troops to protect Paris from European armies.

**August 9** Revolutionary Assembly illegally takes control of Paris and marches on the Tuileries.

**August 10** Mob action leads to Louis and Marie's removal from Tuileries. The Tuileries is fired on by revolutionary forces, and the Legislative Assembly begins to unravel. Existing constitution is abandoned.

**September 21** New National Convention meets for first time to begin writing a new, second French constitution.

**September 22** First day of first year of the French Revolution's new calendar.

**October** Louis XVI goes on trial for treason.

**1793 January 21** King Louis is executed on the guillotine.

**April 22** U.S. president George Washington declares the United States to be neutral toward the French Revolution.

**Summer** Control of the Revolution falls into hands of the Jacobins, led by Maximilien Robespierre. Danton is arrested as enemy of the state.

**October 16** Marie Antoinette is condemned and executed by guillotine.

**1793–1794** Reign of Terror results in the executions of 40,000.

**1794 April** Danton is guillotined along with several other Jacobin leaders.

**July 26–27** Robespierre is arrested during a meeting of the National Convention, is tried, convicted, and executed on the guillotine.

**1795 June 8** Ten-year-old Louis-Charles, son of Louis XVI, dies in prison, probably of tuberculosis.

**1795–1799** France is governed by the Directory, a five-man committee.

**1799 November 9** Young French general, Napoleon Bonaparte, destroys the Directory, establishes military rule, and makes himself dictator.

## SOURCE NOTES

1. Quoted in Richard Tames, *The French Revolution*. St. Paul, MN: Greenhaven Press, 1980, p. 3.
2. Quoted in Georges Lefebvre, *The French Revolution From Its Origins to 1793*. New York: Columbia University Press, 1967, p. 48.
3. Quoted in Time-Life Books, *Winds of Revolution: Time Frame AD 1700–1800*. Alexandria, VA: Time-Life Books, 1990, p. 139.
4. Quoted in Emmanuel-Joseph Sieyes, *What Is the Third Estate?* London: Phaidon Press, 1964, pp. 53–54.
5. Quoted in Lefebvre, *French Revolution*, p. 66.
6. Quoted in Phyllis Corzine, *The French Revolution*. San Diego, CA: Lucent Books, 1995, p. 37.
7. Quoted in David L. Dowd, *The French Revolution*. New York: American Heritage Publishing Co., 1965, p. 23.
8. Ibid., p. 24.
9. Ibid., p. 25.
10. Quoted in Paul A. Gagnon, *France Since 1789*. New York: Harper & Row, Publishers, 1964, p. 8.
11. Ibid.
12. Quoted in Dowd, *French Revolution*, p. 32.
13. Ibid., p. 40.
14. Quoted in Corzine, *French Revolution*, p. 52.
15. Quoted in Simon Schama, *Citizens: A Chronicle of the French Revolution*. New York: Alfred A. Knopf, 1989, p. 457.
16. Ibid., p. 463.
17. Quoted in Corzine, *French Revolution*, p. 54.
18. Quoted in Schama, *Citizens*, p. 468.
19. Ibid., p. 470.
20. Quoted in Corzine, *French Revolution*, p. 55.
21. Quoted in Dowd, *French Revolution*, p. 51.
22. Quoted in Schama, *Citizens*, p. 52.
23. Quoted in Corzine, *French Revolution*, p. 65.
24. Quoted in Schama, *Citizens*, p. 558.
25. Quoted in Corzine, *French Revolution*, p. 65.
26. Quoted in Dowd, *French Revolution*, p. 82.
27. Quoted in Corzine, *French Revolution*, p. 76.
28. Quoted in Dowd, *French Revolution*, p. 99.
29. Quoted in Louis Madelin, *The French Revolution*. New York: G.P. Putnam's Sons, 1926, p. 323.
30. Ibid., pp. 323–24.
31. Quoted in Corzine, *French Revolution*, p. 83.
32. Quoted in Schama, *Citizens*, p. 776.
33. Quoted in Corzine, *French Revolution*, p. 97.
34. Quoted in Schama, *Citizens*, p. 778.
35. Quoted in Stanley Loomis, *Paris in the Terror, June 1793–July 1794*. Philadelphia: J.B. Lippincott, 1964, p. 326.
36. Quoted in Corzine, *French Revolution*, pp. 98–99.
37. Quoted in Loomis, *Paris*, p. 319.
38. Quoted in Dowd, *French Revolution*, p. 140.
39. Ibid., p. 143.
40. Quoted in Time-Life Books, *Winds*, p. 160.
41. Ibid.
42. Quoted in Dowd, *French Revolution*, p. 19.

## BIBLIOGRAPHY

Brinton, *A Decade of Revolution, 1789–1799*. New York: Harper & Row, 1934.

Corzine, Phyllis. *The French Revolution*. San Diego, CA: Lucent Books, 1995.

Cunningham, Noble. *In Pursuit of Reason: The Life of Thomas Jefferson*. Baton Rouge: Louisiana State University Press, 1987.

De La Fuye, Maurice. *The Apostle of Liberty: A Life of La Fayette*. New York: Thomas Yoseloff, 1956.

Dowd, David L. *The French Revolution*. New York: American Heritage Publishing, 1965.

Time-Life Books. *Winds of Revolution: TimeFrame AD 1700–1800*. Alexandria, VA: Time-Life Books, 1990.

Ferling, John. *A Leap in the Dark: The Struggle to Create the American Republic*. New York: Oxford University Press, 2003.

Gagnon, Paul A. *France Since 1789*. New York: Harper & Row, 1964.

Godechot, Jacques. *France and the Atlantic Revolution of the Eighteenth Century, 1770–1799*. New York: Free Press, 1965.

Hills, Ken. *The French Revolution*. New York: Marshal Cavendish, 1988.

Kowalick, Thomas Michael, transcriber. *The Western Tradition Transcripts* (videotape). Alexandria, VA: PBS Adult Learning Service, 1989, p. 123.

Lefebvre, Georges. *The French Revolution From Its Origins to 1793*. New York: Columbia University Press, 1967.

———. *The French Revolution From 1793 to 1799*. New York: Columbia University Press, 1967.

———. *The Thermidorians and the Directory*. New York: Random House, 1964.

Loomis, Stanley. *Paris in the Terror, June 1793–July 1794*. Philadelphia: J.B. Lippincott, 1964.

Madelin, Louis. *The French Revolution*. New York: G.P. Putnam's Sons, 1926.

Rude, George. *Revolutionary Europe, 1783–1815*. New York: Harper & Row, 1964.

Schama, Simon. *Citizens: A Chronicle of the French Revolution*. New York: Alfred A. Knopf, 1989.

Sears, Louis Martin. *George Washington and the French Revolution*. Detroit: Wayne State University Press, 1960.

Sieyes, Emmanuel-Joseph, *What Is the Third Estate?* London: Phaidon Press, 1964.

Tames, Richard. *The French Revolution*. St. Paul, MN: Greenhaven Press, Inc., 1980.

# 4

# The Nineteenth-Century Revolutions

**The French Revolution had opened in 1789 with hope in the hearts of** many French people, who longed for greater freedoms and self-determination. Although gains were made, including an end to serfdom in France and a flirtation with constitutionalism, the Revolution had ended, seemingly, with the rise of General Napoleon Bonaparte to power in 1799, signaling a return to authoritarian leadership. Many hopeful revolutionaries, originally spurred on by a successful revolution in America, found themselves disappointed and frustrated.

During the heady days of the French Revolution, the leaders of other European powers had watched with disgust and caution. They perceived the events taking place in France, and especially in Paris, to be a challenge to royal power abroad and centralized governments everywhere. Concerned heads of state took intense interest when the French monarch was whisked out of his royal palace at Versailles and forced to live under the watchful eye of Parisian revolutionaries. With Louis XVI held as a virtual prisoner of the state, Austria and Prussia by 1791 had joined together in a counterrevolutionary spirit and vowed,

With his army exhausted and overextended, Napoleon suffered a major defeat at the hands of the Russians and was forced into exile. A year later, he escaped and raised a new army, but was again defeated, this time by the British, in the Battle of Waterloo.

through the Declaration of Pillnitz (August 1791) that they would fight to restore the old order of France and reestablish the monarchy. The agreement was seen as a matter of "common interest to all sovereigns of Europe."[1] By the spring of 1792, these powerful European forces were at war with the French revolutionary government.

When the French Revolution collapsed under the strains brought on by the Reign of Terror (September 1793–July 1794), the war did not come to an automatic end. A coalition of European states—including Austria, Prussia, and France's perennial enemy Great Britain—fought France through 1795, only to collapse in near defeat. In 1798, Great Britain revived the coalition and fighting resumed until 1801. During the years that followed, Napoleon continued to extend the borders of his French empire until Great Britain again convinced the great powers of the Continent to take up arms in 1805. This time, the British were joined not only by the Austrians and Prussians, but by the Russians and Swedes as well. This time there would be no end to the fighting until Napoleon finally overextended himself, marching foolishly into Russia in the spring of 1812. It was to be a campaign, fought in the bitter snows of a horrific Russian winter, that witnessed the deaths of 300,000 of Napoleon's troops. It was a loss from which he, and his war-weary nation, never recovered.

After facing serious defeat in 1814, Napoleon was ordered into exile on the Mediterranean island of Elba by the victorious coalition states. The following year, after the little French general escaped, reached France, and raised yet another army, the coalition nations reluctantly returned to war and delivered their final military victory over Napoleon at Waterloo in Belgium. Napoleon was sent further into exile this time, to the tiny island of St. Helena in the south Atlantic, where he died in 1821.

With the French Revolution, the protracted Napoleonic Wars, and the final exile of Napoleon behind them, the leaders of the powerful states of Europe began to collect the shattered pieces of their continent.

Yet while the French Revolution seemed, by 1815, a series of nightmarish events that had taken place years earlier, the spirit of the Revolution remained alive. For all its failures, the Revolution that produced the assault on the Bastille, the Tennis Court Oath, and the Declaration of the Rights of Man had created a nearly mythological image in the minds of Europeans from Portugal to Russia and from Sweden to Greece. Despite its excesses, the Revolution had instilled in many neighboring Europeans a sense of new ideals:

> Its legacy is partly summed up in three key concepts: liberty, equality, and nation. Liberty meant individual rights and responsibilities, and more specifically freedom from arbitrary authority. By equality ... the revolutionaries meant the abolition of legal distinctions of rank between European men. Though their concept of equality was limited, it became a powerful mobilizing force in the nineteenth century. The most important legacy of the revolution may have been the new term *nation*.... The revolutionary concept of nationhood spread throughout Europe in response to French aggression.[2]

# The Congress of Vienna

In 1814, after years of bloody, exhausting conflict, the end of the Napoleonic Wars restored much of Europe to an artificial calm. While the French Revolution appeared over to many people, the leaders of the nations that had fought the spread of liberalism and Bonapartism feared that its spirit remained alive. (In fact, Napoleon would return from his imposed exile in 1815, only to face defeat for another—last—time at the battle of Waterloo.) As these leaders set about reestablishing a new order to post-Napoleonic Europe, they took significant steps to make certain the future would remain in their hands.

These conservatives followed two maxims for redrawing the political map of Europe: legitimacy and reaction. Napoleon had replaced several European rulers with his own supporters; several, in fact, had been his own brothers and sisters. Legitimacy called for the reestablishment of pre-Revolutionary states and ruling families across Europe. While the French Revolution had executed Louis XVI and destroyed the monarchy, now a new monarch, Louis XVIII, brother of the former monarch, was restored to the throne. In Spain, Napoleon had replaced Ferdinand VII with one of his brothers. Using legitimacy as their guide, European leaders placed Ferdinand back on his throne.

The second watchword, reaction, represented the conservatives' political response to the liberalism of the French Revolution. The intent was not only to return pre-Revolu-tionary monarchs to their rightful thrones, but for them to rule with firmness and ultimate authority. In a word, they were to rule as absolute monarchs, holding all power.

To ensure these two goals, European leaders gathered in the Austrian capital of Vienna in 1814, then again in 1815, for what they called the Congress of Vienna. These meetings were necessary for negotiating the peace treaties following the Napoleonic Wars. Key European powers played leading roles in the meetings of the Congress, including the Russian czar Alexander I and the arch-conservative Austrian diplomat Klemens von Metternich, as well as the French prince Charles Maurice Talleyrand. Alexander I spoke during the Congress in favor of liberalism and liberty, but his frightened fellow leaders were not interested, and turned even further against any ideas of revolution or liberal change. The only liberty these men were interested in was "the freedom of European states from domination by a single power,"[*] such as another Napoleon.

So intense were the efforts by those at the Congress of Vienna to push down the elements of revolution that they may have in fact helped encourage revolution. The spirit of revolution remained in the hearts and minds of many, and, despite the best efforts of Metternich and his colleagues, it had no intention of remaining quiet.

[*] Quoted in R.R. Palmer, *A History of the Modern World*. New York: McGraw-Hill, 1995, p. 446.

It was that search for nationhood, an understanding that the people of a state shared a common heritage and identity, that allowed the French Revolutionary spirit to spread like wildfire across Europe during the first half of the nineteenth century. The ideals of liberty, equality, and nationality had left the theoretical pages of revolutionary pamphlets and sloganeering and entered the minds of many on the Continent who dreamed of a better life under an elected government and who longed to be free people.

From the end of the Napoleonic Wars (1815) through the mid-nineteenth century, Europe would experience a series of revolutions. In Greece, members of a secret revolutionary society, the Heriaria Philike, rallied the people to overthrow their Turkish overlords. In czarist Russia, soldiers of Czar Alexander campaigned against him, rallying on behalf of his brother, carrying banners reading: "Constantine and Constitution." Belgians revolted against Dutch control, while such repressed German states as Saxony and Hesse-Cassel established constitutional monarchies. In Switzerland, the rulers of the cantons brought about peaceful political changes that liberalized their governments. And in France, that seedbed of European revolutionary thought and action, the workers would return once more to the streets of Paris, erecting barricades against a new monarch, reviving a spirit of revolution that had seemed lost forever.

## THE ROMANTIC REBELLION

What brought on these recurring waves of revolution that inundated the continent between 1820 and 1850? To better understand the strong desire for change through revolution in Europe during these years requires a look at a related, yet different, type of revolution taking place at the same time. Part of the revolutionary trend was rooted in a change in intellectual climate, a change in the way people thought and looked at their world. Following the era of Napoleon, a new outlook emerged in political thought, art, literature, and even religion. Historians refer to this redirection of European thinking as the Age of Romanticism. Since change was at the center of the movement, it is also referred to as the Romantic Rebellion.

It is difficult to define this intellectual, yet emotional, movement. Its effect was different from person to person, country to country.

The movement was so broad in its emphasis that it could inspire conservatives as well as liberals. Perhaps the difficulty in defining it is that its spirit tended to focus on the emotional part of humans, not their logic skills or reasoning abilities.

In part, Romanticism was a reaction to something else first—the Enlightenment. The French philosophes of the eighteenth century had written and spoken about a world that operated by set laws of nature, established by a God who was not directly involved in peoples' lives. The philosophy played down the place of God in one's life, and rejected such religious ideas as inspiration and miracles.

## Klemens von Metternich

Born in 1773, Metternich grew up in an Austria that cherished the status quo. That arrangement, cozy for the upper class at least, was severely threatened by the French Revolution of 1789. An Austrian princess, Marie Antoinette, was now queen of France, and she went to the guillotine in 1793. Metternich and his fellow Austrian nobles felt that the French revolutionaries were a great menace.

Things only got worse over the next 15 years. The ideals of the French Revolution were replaced by the thundering powers of the Napoleonic armies, and both Austria and Prussia were defeated several times by France. The worst humiliation came at the Battle of Austerlitz in 1805; soon afterward, the Austrian emperor married his daughter, Marie-Louise, to Napoleon to prevent further conflict.

Napoleon engineered his own downfall, though, by invading Russia in 1812. His retreat from Russia that winter brought the Austrians and Prussians out to join the Russians, and Metternich, along with his fellow Austrian nobles, rejoiced at the downfall of the upstart from Corsica.

At the Congress of Vienna, held in 1814 and 1815, Metternich played a leading role. He wanted to bring the monarchical powers together in a grand coalition that would fight any and all future revolutionary movements. Metternich thought Russia's Czar Alexander a little strange because of his idea of a "Holy Alliance," but Metternich managed to use this concept for his own ends. Between 1815 and 1825, Metternich was the grand statesman of Europe; he called legislative sessions in Austria; he mediated between the great powers; and he managed to prevent any further revolutionary outbreaks. People began to call Metternich the "apostle of conservatism" and his program the "Metternich system."

Things began to unravel in the late 1820s. The Greek revolutionary movement

Everything in the world was considered rational, sterile, and fixed. The philosophes were interested, as well, in dispelling false ideas, superstitions, and misinformation, and they spoke out against artificial restrictions on human behavior by governments, social norms, and religion and elevated the concept of personal freedom. (It was this emphasis that caused the Enlightenment to inspire the French Revolution as well as the American Revolution.)

In an age in which new machines powered by steam were changing how things were produced, the Enlightenment explained the world itself as a machine, like a great clock, put together by God, the

overthrew the Ottoman Turkish rule there, and Metternich was forced to watch as Europeans again became entranced with revolutionary movements. Even worse were the 1830 revolutions in Belgium and in France, but Metternich was pleased to see that both of them were followed by rather stable regimes.

Between 1830 and 1848, Metternich was the grand old man of European politics. He had outlived most of his rivals, including the French diplomat Talleyrand, and his principles of church, state, and repression were enshrined almost everywhere; Great Britain was a notable exception to the rule. But as Metternich had observed many years earlier, "When France gets a cold, all of Europe sneezes."

The late winter of 1848 saw the French overthrow King Louis-Philippe. This revolutionary success was followed by almost a dozen others. Metternich was forced to resign as prime minister and even to flee

Austria. By midsummer 1848, the revolutionary movements had succeeded almost everywhere, and it seemed as if Europe was in for a virtual bath of liberalism and nationalism.

But this was not to be. Even though Metternich was out of office and gone from the scene, his ideas and strategies were still employed. The Prussian king disbanded the parliament that had assembled; the Russians crushed the Hungarian rebellion; and Franz-Joseph, the new king of Austria, had his cannons open fire on the civilian population of Vienna to bring down the resistance. By the early part of 1849, the conservative reactions had triumphed in most parts of Europe.

Metternich died in 1859. At that time it was unclear whether Europe would continue on the path he had laid or if new revolutionary movements would sweep away his work.

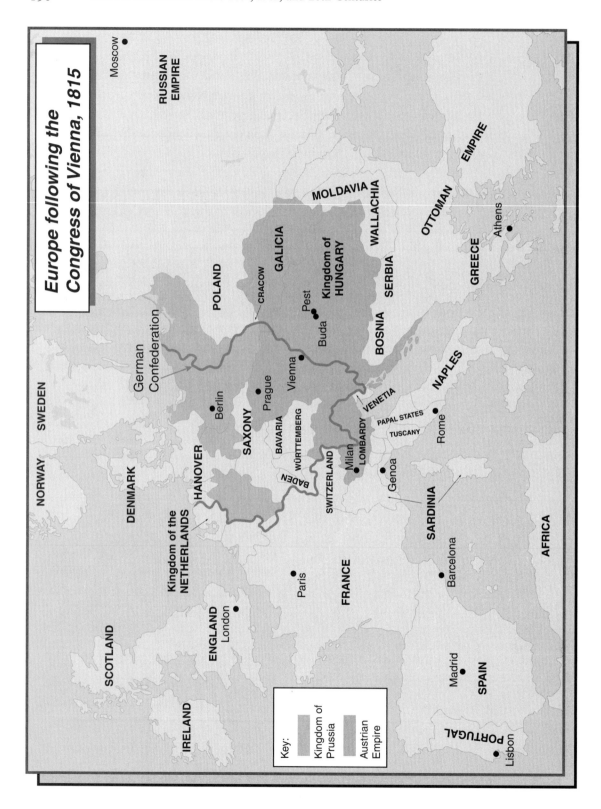

Europe following the
Congress of Vienna, 1815

Key:

Kingdom of Prussia

Austrian Empire

"First Mechanic," wound up, and then placed on a shelf to run by natural laws without further interference or intervention by Him. It was, indeed, a cold, often unemotional philosophy.

It was this coldness that the Romantic Rebellion sought to destroy. Those artists, writers, and thinkers who pushed the movement along did not completely reject reason, but they believed in a balance of elements, emphasizing feeling, emotion, and imagination. Above all else, the Romantics wanted to *feel something*. The movement encouraged painters, musicians, poets, and novelists to redefine their work. The art of the early nineteenth century, especially European and American works, presented new subjects to audiences that were sometimes not prepared for such change. The works of classical art that preceded the Romantic movement had been the product of the Enlightenment—balanced, harmonious, disciplined, formal, shrouded in reason. The new art gave emphasis to emotion, individual freedom, and sometimes revealed an artist with a vivid imagination. As one critic of the Romantic Movement noted: "Romanticism imposed itself by opposing everything that had preceded it."[3]

There were paintings of dimly lit forest scenes set against a backdrop of the ruins of a Gothic church. Exotic subjects such as violent African tiger hunts, wild-eyed horses, Turkish baths, Persian court scenes, and legends of King Arthur were thrown onto canvases, each as a lively portrait of a place that evokes emotion and fantasy. There was a Gothic element to some works, with a special emphasis on ghost stories, eerie and gloomy castles, and spooky forest dwellers. The subject of death was recurring, including the deaths of sympathetic characters in novels, poems, and paintings who commit suicide because of lost love or to maintain personal honor. These subjects were stark contrasts to the tamer topics of art that had dominated the previous age. Such painters as the Frenchman Eugene Delacroix, the Englishman Joseph Turner, and the Spaniard Francisco Goya, produced some of the most memorable paintings of the period.

The artists and writers form a who's who of early nineteenth century creativity. Writers included the American Edgar Allen Poe, whose Gothic stories and morbid poetry found an eager audience; the English author Mary Wollstonecraft Shelley, who penned the symbolic tale *Frankenstein*, and the Scottish writer Sir Walter Scott, whose story of medieval chivalry and valiant knights, *Ivanhoe*, became a benchmark of the Romantic Age.

Poets of the period included the German Johann Wolfgang von Goethe. His novel, *The Sorrows of Young Werther*, serves as a prime example of the previously taboo subject matter of Romantic works. The story's protagonist is one misunderstood by society. He leaves home and finds temporary solace in a remote cottage surrounded by nature, only to fall in love with a woman he cannot have, leaving him to end his own sorrowful existence. The novel "depicted feelings so strong that the protagonist's suicide began a vogue for melancholy young men killing themselves as Werther had, with moonlight falling across the last page of Goethe's book."[4]

For many of these and other Romantic artists, their work emphasized an understanding of nature as one based in emotion and the mysterious, rather than the reasonable and predictable. As one historian has noted: "[The Romantics] preferred freedom to order, adventure to conformity, surprise to recognition, imagination to correctness, the natural to the artificial, the irregular to the regular, individual experience to tradition."[5]

The revolutionary spirit was not limited to politics and found its way into artistic expression as well. Authors like Johann Wolfgang von Goethe pioneered a new romanticism, preferring values of creativity, emotion, and individual freedom to established order.

Any aspect of the world that revolved around such men and women could not be acceptable if it did not encourage individuality, freedom, and self-expression. Everywhere, from canvas to the written page, the Romantics devoted much of their time and talent to heroic figures, men and women of strong personality, found both in fiction and in the real world. Some of the heroes of the era were less than perfect, often flawed characters. This value is found in the pages of the French writer Victor Hugo, whose novels included *Les Miserables* and *Notre Dame de Paris*, which presented unlikely heroes such as hunchback and church bell ringer Quasimodo.

While much of the Romantic Movement had its center focused on the arts, it also had a direct impact on politics. Hugo himself defined the role that Romanticism played in helping fuel the fires of the new revolutions of the nineteenth century: "Romanticism, so often ill-defined, is only ... liberalism in literature. Liberty in Art, liberty in Society, behold the double banner that rallies the intelligence."[6] The same spirit that might inspire a Romantic painter to reject the standards of the art world of his day and paint what he felt instead could be the spirit that led a young citizen of 1830s Paris to take to the streets, man the barricades against the authorities of a new royal regime, and give his life on behalf of national liberty and personal freedom.

## A NEW ERA OF REVOLUTION

This new emphasis on change, on rejection of norms, and on escape from control and repression found its way into a new era of revolution in Europe. Even as the Old Order leaders tried desperately to reestablish the world that existed before the French Revolution and the Napoleonic Wars, newly inspired revolutionaries pushed back. During the 1820s, 1830s, and 1840s, revolution was always present, always challenging, always inspiring. These revolutions were generally liberal in nature—that is, they supported calls for greater representation, less centralized authority, more freedom for those of the middle and lower classes, and additional recognition of civil rights, such as the freedoms of speech, assembly, trial by jury, and the vote.[7]

The first of this new spate of revolutions began to unfold in Spain and the kingdom of Naples. Liberal groups, operating secretly, rallied to force their conservative kings to support elections, allow for the writing of constitutions, and establish representative government. Revolutionaries looked to the French constitution of 1791 as their example. The Spanish king, Ferdinand VII, who had been restored to his throne following the removal of one of Napoleon's brothers, struggled against this liberal reform movement. But he was already facing similar revolutions in his New World Spanish empire as Latin American colonies from Peru to Mexico to Colombia to Bolivia successfully broke free from hundreds of years of Spanish colonialism. (In doing so, these revolutionary Latin American countries took advantage of the chaos created in Europe by the wars of Napoleon and their aftermath.)

In Italy, similar popular uprisings took place in Naples, the peninsula's southern kingdom that was dominated by Austria. A secret society known as the Carbonari, "the Charcoal Burners," made plans to rally for political change in Italy. (They took their name from their practice of using charcoal to blacken their faces during secret meetings to shield their identities.) The members of the secret sect wanted government based on the vote, an end to tyranny, and the removal of Austrian control over several Italian states. In 1820, the number of Carbonari in Naples alone was 100,000.

The reactionary governments of Europe responded quickly to the revolts. In 1820, Austria, Prussia, and Russia signed an agreement, the Troppau Memorandum, to provide support to each other in the suppression of revolution. While Great Britain and France were encouraged to add their signatures, both states declined. In short order, Austrian officials began rounding up Carbonari members and shipping them off to prison. Meanwhile, in Spain, France dispatched 200,000 soldiers in 1823 to suppress the liberal movement there. The revolution was crushed, and Ferdinand's authority was again unchallenged. As hundreds of revolutionaries were rounded up, the Spanish monarch ordered many tortured and executed, a harsh response to the fledgling liberal movement.

Other revolutions exploded in other corners of Europe during the early 1820s. Portuguese revolutionaries fought for the establishment of a constitution. Revolutionaries in additional Mediterranean states, including Sicilian Palermo and the northern Italian province of Piedmont rallied behind liberal causes, only to fail. (As Austrian troops subdued such rebellions, they typically ordered the removal the right hands of captured revolutionaries.) Revolutionaries made significant gains only in Portugal, where a limited parliamentary government was established, largely due to support from Great Britain.

## REVOLUTION IN GREECE

In southeastern Europe, the Ottoman Empire faced revolution in 1821 from three states under its control: Serbia, Moldavia, and Wallachia (the latter two both Romanian provinces), and from Greece. Serbia managed to successfully throw off control by the

Turkish Ottomans, but the revolution in Greece (1821–27) raised the greatest interest among European revolutionaries in general.

Yet another secret, revolutionary society, the Herairia Philike, led the way in Greece in early 1821 and started a war against the Turks. This revolution witnessed wholesale slaughter on both sides. In time, the Greeks understood that they were no match for the Ottomans, and the Greek resistance began to unravel, jeopardizing the entire revolution. However, several powerful European governments, including France, Russia, and Great Britain, stepped in and provided support to the Greeks.

Why would these European powers lend their support to this particular revolution? For some it was about the Greeks themselves. Romantic revolutionaries saw the Greeks as the founders of Western civilization. The British Romantic poet, Percy Bysshe Shelley, explained: "We are all Greeks. Our laws, our literature, our religion, our arts, have their roots in Greece. But for Greece ... we might still have been savages and idolators."[8] A fascination in France and Great Britain with all things Greek caused a generalized support for the revolution. Another British poet, Lord Byron, a friend of Shelley's, even raised a cadre of supporters of the Greek Revolution—called the "Byron Brigade." The poet died at Missolonghi in 1824. As for the Russians, the conservative, czarist government would not give support to the Ottomans since their empire was Muslim, not Christian.

Some of the fighting during the Greek Revolution was brutal. In the spring of 1822, Greeks killed thousands of prisoners they had captured during the seizure of the island of Chios. The Turks followed this brutality with mindless massacres of their own, executing thousands (perhaps as many as 20,000) and selling another 40,000 into slavery. By 1827, British, French, and Russian naval squadrons had destroyed the combined naval forces of Turkey and Egypt in the battle of Navarino Bay.

By 1829, the Turks were forced to accept the Treaty of Adrianople, allowing Greece to become an independent kingdom. The Ottoman Empire was weakened dramatically. Serbia had already gone its own way, and even Egypt managed to gain its independence from the Ottomans in time. While earlier events resulted in a successful revolution for the Greeks, unnecessary bloodshed followed as Greek Orthodox priests called for a war to destroy Islamic populations within Greece. The result: twenty-five thousand Muslims were killed in just six weeks. The Ottoman sultan responded with a holy war of his own, which brought on the deaths of 40,000 Greeks. Even today, animosity between Greeks and Turks dates back to these horrific events of the early nineteenth century.

## THE DECEMBRIST REVOLT

Even while the Greek War of Independence was raging, still another revolution was underway, this one in czarist Russia. Rebellion there was fomented in response to the harsh rule of Czar Alexander I. He had come to the throne in 1801 at the age of 24, following the assassination of his father (a murder Alexander may have been involved

## Alexander I of Russia

He was a man of real gifts, but he failed to use them.

Born in 1777, Alexander was the grandson of Czarina Catherine the Great and the son of Czar Paul I. Alexander helped in the coup that overthrew his father in 1800. To this day it remains an open question as to whether or not Alexander was complicit in his father's murder; certainly he showed many signs of carrying a burden of guilt in later years.

Alexander appeared to be a model monarch, or czar (from "Caesar") as the Russians called him. He assembled a group of notables in St. Petersburg to write a new constitution, and he flirted with the idea of freeing the Russian serfs, but nothing came of these possibilities. Perhaps Alexander was more conservative than he himself believed, or perhaps he found Russia's systems more entrenched than he had anticipated.

In 1805, Alexander joined a coalition of nations arrayed against Napoleonic France. The Russians and their allies were soundly defeated, and Alexander came to terms with Napoleon at a place called Tilsit in East Prussia; the two monarchs met on a raft in the middle of the river and made secret agreements concerning the future of Europe. Alexander was greatly taken with Napoleon, who managed to convince the czar that he would deliver on the promises made by the French Revolution. Small chance!

In 1810, Alexander resumed Russian trade with Great Britain. Infuriated, Napoleon amassed the largest European army yet seen and invaded Russia in the summer of 1812. Alexander and his generals retreated slowly, burning houses and crops along the way. When Napoleon entered Moscow in September 1812, he found it a ghost city, and soon decided to retreat to in). As a youth, Alexander had been a "tall and handsome youth who favored skin-tight uniforms."[9] By 1815, he had become overweight, forcing him to wear corsets rather than accept wearing loose clothing. But Alexander was a brilliant leader, an intelligent regent who was possibly the most powerful autocrat in all of Europe, since Napoleon had been deposed.

For all his power, however, Alexander began to consider the need for reform in his tightly controlled state, relying on the expertise of one of his more liberal advisors, Michael Speranski, a good bureaucrat and administrator who was the son of a priest, to implement his reforms. During his fourteen years on the Russian throne, Alexander founded four new universities, doubling the number in Russia. He

France. His winter march home was deadly; perhaps half a million Frenchmen died in the invasion and subsequent retreat.

By the spring of 1813, Czar Alexander was seen as a great liberator. He led the Russian army into Western Europe, and in the spring of 1814 Napoleon abdicated his throne and was exiled to the island of Elba in the Mediterranean.

Alexander was now the master of Europe, and he promised to wear this laurel lightly. Though he had the troops and the power to occupy much of Western Europe, Alexander let himself be deluded by the idea that all the monarchical governments should swear to a Holy Alliance, one in which they would always help each other in putting down popular revolutions. Foreign diplomats snickered, but the czar's intentions were honored, at least on paper. Alexander returned home to Russia.

Over the next ten years—1815 to 1825—Alexander showed clear signs of mental instability. He gave up on his ideas for reform and showed a new autocratic tendency; it was as if the perverse tendencies of his unstable father had come to rule in him as well. Alexander died in 1825 and was honored with a magnificent state funeral. The throne was contested by his two younger brothers, Nicholas and Constantine. The former won the struggle and Russia continued on its way toward severe autocracy; serfdom continued as well.

There had always been a legend that Czar Alexander faked his own death and went to live as a humble monk in Siberia. Though no one has proved this, the theory remains intriguing, as books such as *Imperial Legend: The Mysterious Disappearance of Tsar Alexander I*, show.

allowed Poland to write a constitution and reestablish its parliament. The Finns were also allowed a constitution. Further steps led Alexander to talk of allowing a Russian constitution. He institutionalized religious toleration for Catholics, and even ordered the abolition of serfdom in parts of his empire, with an eye to eliminating it completely in the future.

Despite these changes, however, Alexander remained a strong, autocratic ruler. He continued to control the peoples of conquered states and did not allow within Russia itself "a constitution, an independent judiciary or a parliament."[10] During the later years of his reign, he became more reactionary, sending Speranski into Siberian exile and taking on a new, conservative advisor, Alexis Arakcheyev. A cruel and heartless man, Arakcheyev once "ordered a young serf flogged to death because she did a poor job at her sweeping."[11] Under his guidance, Alexander rescinded some of the reforms he had instituted. Lord Byron mocked the czar's change of heart against liberalism in a poem:

> Now half dissolving to a liberal thaw,
> But hardened back whene'er the morning's raw;
> With no objection to true liberty,
> Except that it would make the nations free.[12]

When the czar died in 1825, his empire was ripe for revolution.

Leaving no children at his death, the Russian throne was to pass to Alexander's oldest brother, Constantine, who was serving as the governor-general of Poland. But Alexander had designated another brother, Nicholas, to take his throne, a wish Constantine would not ignore.

Nicholas was unacceptable to many Russians, including the liberal officers of the czar's army. That December, a group of revolutionaries called "Decembrists" revolted. Many of these revolutionaries were from noble families and had served in the military under the czar. They wanted the usual liberal goals of the era: the abolition of the monarchy, a constitutional government, and an end to serfdom. Russian army officers held rallies to encourage their enlisted men to join with them in defiance of the czarist government.

The rebels placed much of their hope in Constantine. (They carried support signs reading, "Constantine and Constitution," but many of the illiterate common soldiers thought "Constitution" was Constantine's wife's name.) But despite their best efforts, the liberal Russian officers could not convince many of their troops to join them in their revolution, and the Decembrists were easily destroyed. Czar Nicholas ordered army officers arrested, and dealt with them harshly. Five were hanged and 121 others received severe punishments, including exile and hard labor in Siberia.

The Decembrist revolt proved an abject failure. Nicholas emerged from the challenge to his power with a hatred of liberalism. His reign became one of the most severe in Russian history. During the following 30 years of his reign over Russia, he pursued almost no liberal causes. In fact, he formed a government organization called the Third Section, which created a secret police to spy on the people and keep watch on anyone suspected of having liberal ideas. He helped create new censorship laws, restricting dissenters. The reign of Nicholas I became noted for its repressive policies and its slogan, "Autocracy! Orthodoxy! Nationality!"[13]

By the end of the 1820s, many of the revolutions of the previous ten or fifteen years had failed to produce extensive political or social change to Europe. There were successes to be sure, but overall, the conservative leaders of European nations large and small had managed to keep revolutionary change to a minimum. When the great powers of Europe—France, Britain, Russia, Austria—fought against political change, they tended to come down hard and hammer-like, further fragmenting movements that were typically fragmented to begin with. In cases where revolutionaries could play a large power against another large power, as in the Greek Revolution, the revolt and call for greater freedom might succeed. Overall, these early nineteenth-century revolutions were scattered and sporadic, often the work of secret societies or small cliques of troops who were unable to convince the masses to stand up for change.

## REVOLUTIONS OF THE 1830s

During the 1830s, however, a second wave of revolutions was more successful. One reason was that the forces of reaction were beginning to lose their grip on European politics. This new chapter of revolutionary history began where an earlier chapter had—in France. After the fall of Napoleon in 1814, the French monarchy had been reestablished as Louis XVIII, brother of Louis XVI, came to the throne.

(Louis XVI's son, Louis XVII, had died in prison in 1795 during the French Revolution.) Although Louis XVIII was, technically, an absolute monarch, he retained some of the political changes brought about by the Revolution, including limited voting to large landowners, a parliament, a narrow constitution, legal equality, the Napoleonic law codes, and the abolition of feudalism and aristocratic privilege. The king did not recognize the sovereignty of either the state or the people, however, both of which had been accepted during the Revolution. While these rights represented limited liberalism for France, the king made it obvious that they were "gifts" from him and not recognition of the "natural rights" of the people.

Louis XVIII faced little opposition to the restoration of the Bourbons to the French throne; after all, as one historian has written: "France was, above all, tired. Tired, not only by the recent catastrophes of defeat and invasion, but tired by the incessant wars of

## The Vote: An Elusive European Privilege

Even as Louis XVIII came to the throne as an "absolute ruler," he still allowed some voting privileges. But the vote during the early years of his reign was limited to 88,000 prosperous men. This number was equal to 0.3 percent of the entire population of the country, which was the largest in Europe at the time—boasting 26 million French citizens. Certainly, this figure was miniscule compared to the voting privilege allowed during the French Revolution, which amounted to nearly universal male suffrage.

As limited as the vote was in France under Louis XVIII, how did it compare to other European states of the early nineteenth century? In even the most democratic states of the Continent, such as the Scandinavian countries of Norway and Sweden, only about 10 percent of the populace held the right to vote. In Great Britain, a nation often held up as an example of political openness, the vote, in 1815, was still restricted to about 2.5 percent of adult men. In all these countries, women had no voting privileges.

Yet as limited as voting was in France under Louis XVIII, it was at a higher rate than that of several other powerful European states, including Austria, Prussia, Russia, or Spain. In addition, those countries, all ruled by a monarch, had no parliaments, unlike France. The bottom line: During the early nineteenth century, nearly all of Europe still needed to make greater strides toward democracy and toward support of greater power for the people.

Political illustrators and cartoonists have long used their art to provoke change or draw attention to important issues. Here, a French artist borrows a scene from *Gulliver's Travels* to make his point.

the Revolution and the Empire."[14] After years of chaos brought on by a bloody revolution and the destructive wars of Napoleon, many people of France were prepared to accept such compromises—at least for a while.

During the ten years of his reign, Louix XVIII and the "Compromise Constitution" he supported proved increasingly unpopular. In his last years on the throne, "tired, obese, sixty-five, and suffering from a bad case of the gout," the king turned increasingly conservative.[15] When he died in 1824, he was mourned by few. He was followed by yet another brother of Louis XVI's, the ultra-conservative Count of Artois, who was crowned King Charles X.

Throughout his life, Charles had held the French Revolution in contempt. He took the throne intent on reigning as an absolute monarch. From the beginning, he pursued policies with no less purpose "than to turn back the clock."[16] He directed the French assembly to repay aristocrats for the lands they had lost during the Revolution. He reinstated the Catholic Church once again as the directing power of French schools. These steps antagonized many French citizens, and as various elections were held, more and more liberals were added to the French Chamber of Deputies.

But in 1830, the king made several serious blunders that eventually cost him his throne. Following elections that seemed to go against Charles and his ministers, the king made decrees that would later be referred to as the "July Ordinances of 1830." It was a blatant attempt to destroy the French legislature. The ordinances (1) dissolved the newly elected parliament; (2) placed greater censorship on the press; and (3) limited the vote to members of the nobility only. Ironically, the ordinances also called for new elections.

## THE "JULY REVOLUTION"

The response to Charles's heavy-handed steps was immediate. The time was ripe for revolution in the minds of many even before Charles's misplaced ordinances. Unemployment and high prices were rampant. Poor grain harvests during the previous years had driven bread prices higher and higher. The working-class neighborhoods of Paris had been seething in hatred of Charles. The Chamber of Deputies was outraged as well, and much of Paris seemed incensed. It was time for the "July Revolution."

A liberal newspaper editor, Adolphe Thiers (he would later become a French president) announced, "The government has violated legality and we are absolved from obedience."[17] But the revolution that soon unfolded did not begin in the press rooms of Paris or the halls of the French parliament. It began in the streets of the great French city as radicals attempted to gain control of Paris. The scene was reminiscent of the summer of 1789, with some notable exceptions:

> The people of Paris took the matter into their own hands. The ordinances threw printers into the streets (and printing was the biggest single Paris industry). Other businesses shut up shop. The unemployed began to pillage the gun shops; there was no National Guard since its dissolution in 1827; the royal authority rested on a small police force and a small and ill-prepared garrison. In the

heat, the troops tried to fight their way into the swarming, narrow streets ... they failed; they wavered.[18]

Riots broke out in several corners of the city, and the windows of government buildings were smashed. Revolutionaries erected barricades along the narrow streets of the city to impede the advancement of police and soldiers. But many officers had no heart to fire on the angry crowds, and most of the army refused to attack the barricades. From July 28 to July 30, the city witnessed a whirlwind of protest that would later be called "the three glorious days." The tricolor of the Revolution of 1789 was flown from the towers of Notre Dame Cathedral once more. One revolutionary noted: "[The Bourbon flag] droops along its pole because no breath of life flutters it."[19]

Most of those who rioted in the streets and manned the barricades were unemployed workers, ideal-driven university students, along with a handful of members of the middle class, all calling for a new republic, just as many of their fathers and grandfathers had forty years earlier. With the aid of the Chamber of Deputies, Charles might have weathered the upheaval of the summer of 1830, but the Deputies stood by the revolutionaries, guaranteeing the uprising to be "not a revolt, but a revolution."[20]

Caught by a tidal wave of protest, with little support in any corner of his kingdom, Charles X abdicated his throne, but not before fleeing into exile. The unpopular king had either misread the people of his kingdom or had not considered them a threat to his power. It was as if, as one historian stated it, "In the last years of his reign, Charles X [had] moved with the confidence of a sleep-walker."[21]

While the street demonstrators rallied with dreams of a republic in mind, more moderate liberals had other ideas. France emerged from its July revolution not as a republic but as a constitutional monarchy. Charles's Bourbon cousin, Louis-Philippe, the Duke of Orleans, became the new monarch. Louis-Philippe was, in fact, a moderate liberal. He had supported the French Revolution and served in the French army until the Reign of Terror. (His father had even voted to execute his cousin, Louis XVI.) The new "Orleanist Monarchy" (it was also called the "July Monarchy") lasted from 1830 until 1848. With the king's support, France gained a liberalized constitution much like Great Britain's, which expanded the vote to approximately 200,000 people, more than double the previous number.

## REVOLUTION SPREADS ANEW

While the gains of the summer of 1830 in France were significant, many believed they did not go far enough. Nevertheless, this short-lived, liberal revolution provided inspiration to other liberals across the continent. As one European statesman noted, "When Paris catches a cold, Europe sneezes."[22] One of the first to follow the French outbreak was in the Belgian provinces of the Kingdom of the Netherlands. The 1815 Congress of Vienna had united Belgium and the Netherlands as a buffer state with France. It was an arrangement the Belgians loathed. While most Belgians were Catholic, they were suddenly ruled by a Protestant Dutch king, even though there were more Belgians than Dutch in the country. One Belgian nationalist

## Louis-Philippe

King Louis-Philippe, called the Bourgeois Monarch (and also known as the Citizen King), ruled France between 1830 and 1848. He intended his rule to be quite different from that of his Bourbon cousins, but it ended in much the same way.

Born in 1789, Louis-Philippe was a member of the House of Orleans, which was cousin to the ruling House of Bourbon. His father, known as Philippe Egalite, earned notoriety for the family by joining with the French Revolutionaries and by casting his ballot for the execution of his cousin, King Louis XVI. (Because the king was condemned by a majority of one vote, it could always be said that Philippe Egalite had done the deed.)

During the worst part of the French Revolution, young Louis-Philippe toured parts of the United States. He came back to France with an appreciation of the strength of middle-class culture, and when his opportunity came to rule, that was what he tried to install in France.

Following Napoleon Bonaparte's defeat in 1814 (and his attempted return later, which was crushed at the Battle of Waterloo), Louis-Philippe's cousin, the Count of Provence, returned from exile to become King Louis XVIII; he reigned from 1815 to 1824. He was followed by his brother, the Count of Artois, who became King Charles X and ruled from 1824 until 1830. In July 1830 Parisians rose up against Charles, and three days of bloody street fighting followed. When it was over, the king was on his way to permanent exile in London. The workers in the street celebrated and hoped to name the aged Marquis de Lafayette as the new president of a new republic. But Lafayette disappointed them, saying that France was not ready for democracy. Instead, he offered them the House of noted of the arrangement: "By what right do two million Dutchmen command four million Belgians?"[23]

By August, rioting ravaged across the city of Brussels as Dutch troops were dispatched to put down the rebellion. The revolutionary movement soon united the working class with other classes (although the middle class was slow to support the revolt until Dutch troops fired cannons against the city of Antwerp). The French monarch, Louis-Philippe, gave his tacit support to the Belgian revolt, and Great Britain did the same. By October, the Belgians established a national congress. Before the end of the year, an independent Belgium had been recognized by England, France, Austria, Russia, and Prussia. By the following year, the

Orleans in the person of Louis-Philippe. The old revolutionary (Lafayette) and the middle-aged aristocrat (Louis-Philippe) met at the Hotel de Ville in the city center, and Lafayette gave his blessing to the new so-called Bourgeois Monarchy.

In practice, Louis-Philippe turned out to be an autocrat. He made a good show of being a middle-class king: he walked the streets in civilian clothing, armed with only an umbrella, but people knew his secret police were close by. Louis-Philippe also knew how to give the upper-class French enough of what they wanted to keep his rule going, and the Bourgeois Monarchy enjoyed an outward stability that was belied by what was beneath the surface.

There were several revolts over the next 18 years, all of which were crushed. Some of the most dangerous centered around the possibility of bringing Louis-Napoleon, nephew of Napoleon, in as a new leader. To counteract this push and to placate the rebels, Louis-Philippe had Napoleon's body brought from the island of Saint Helena and interred in Paris at Les Invalides, where it remains today. By 1845, it seemed as if Louis-Philippe had succeeded in harnessing the revolutionary and Napoleonic forces and in using them for his own benefit.

But in the late winter of 1848, the Parisians rose up again. There was bloody fighting in the streets, and soon Louis-Philippe left for London, just as his cousin King Charles X had done before him. Lafayette may have been right in saying that France was not ready for democracy, but neither did it want to return to strong monarchy, disguised in the clothing of middle-class respectability.

Belgians had adopted a liberal constitution that guaranteed freedom of religion and of the press.

While successful revolutions took place in France and Belgium, liberal movements elsewhere met with great resistance and typically failure. Spain and Portugal did manage to create limited constitutional monarchies, but a bloody revolt in Poland fragmented so quickly between moderates and radicals that the movement never came together. The masses of peasants never joined either faction. In addition, the Russian government of Czar Nicholas interfered directly and repressed the movement.

## The Birth of Socialism

The revolutions that rocked the very foundations of conservative, reactionary governments across Europe during the first half of the nineteenth century were often the result of other changes sweeping the continent. The Industrial Revolution was changing manufacturing dramatically and taking thousands of people out of rural farmlife and putting them to work in dark, uncomfortable factories powered by coal. This industrial phase altered the conditions of labor for many. Factory workers were abused and exploited, working long hours in unsafe environs for little pay. The social ills brought about by the Industrial Revolution helped to spawn a social movement called *socialism*.

The word *socialist* was first coined in 1833 and the term *socialism* followed in 1839. This social philosophy promoted the idea that society exists for the good of all its members, not for those at the top of the social ladder, such as the wealthy, aristocratic, or politically powerful. While the Industrial Revolution encouraged such goals as ruthless competition and natural economic law, socialists encouraged social cooperation and a planned economy designed to provide for everyone.

The early nineteenth century produced several notable socialist thinkers. Louis Blanc (1811–1882), a French politician and journalist, believed that the kind of competition fostered by the Industrial Revolution was a social evil. He wrote that government should control the economic activities taking place within each state and that the means of production—farms, railroads, factories—should be owned by the government. This idea eliminated the concept of private property. Blanc believed government should become the protector of the lower and working classes, referring to the government as the "banker of the poor."[*] To bring about state-

## SUCCESSFUL REFORM IN GREAT BRITAIN

Great Britain managed political change without resorting to extreme revolution. England had already experienced revolution during the 1600s, which had resulted in the deposing of two kings (Charles I during the 1640s and James II in 1688). Great political change had already created a longstanding parliamentary tradition, a limited monarchy, and reliance on constitutionalism. It was another form of revolution, the Industrial Revolution, that brought on the necessity for further political change in Great Britain.

During the early nineteenth century, Great Britain was in the throes of extreme change as well as an increase in urbanization as it

supported socialism, Blanc supported universal male suffrage.

Another French socialist was Pierre Joseph Proudhon (1809–1865). Born poor, Proudhon became a noted and prolific socialist writer. He, too, decried private property ownership and even supported the destruction of all governments. He thought people should live in small communes—communities of people who joined together by choice, living and creating a small economy in which everyone shared equally. In Proudhon's mind, the basic unit of society would be the family. Proudhon's book *What Is Property?* was only one of his writings, but the work had a profound effect on those who read it, including the German socialist-intellectual Karl Marx, who is often referred to as the Father of Modern Socialism.

In England, the most notable early socialist was a manufacturer named Robert Owen (1771–1858). The owner of a textile

mill in Manchester, Owen believed he had an obligation to provide a positive working environment for his workers. He constructed a model factory town in Glasgow, Scotland, in 1800, and provided adequate housing, sanitation, even a school system for the children of workers. Owen thought the key to improving society was education.

How extensively such socialist writers and thinkers impacted the revolutions of nineteenth-century Europe is uncertain. But the political and social concept remained alive as others built on the ideas of earlier proponents. Before the end of the century, socialism had been adopted by several European governments and would provide the inspiration for later revolutions, including the communist revolts of the twentieth century.

* Quoted in Coffin, *Western Civilizations*, p. 770.

expanded its industrial base. These economic and demographic changes led British liberals to give support to the Great Reform Bill of 1832. The passing of this bill was preceded by some violence between 1830 and 1832. Revolutionary organizations, such as the Political Union of the Lower and Middle Classes of the People, engaged in bloody conflict with police and army units during the summer of 1830 (at the same time as Paris's "Three Glorious Days"). Rural violence cropped up repeatedly in the form of "Captain Swing Riots," spreading across the rural landscape of southeastern Britain. ("Captain Swing" was the name used for the wooden flail used in threshing grain by hand.) Poverty-stricken, farmers burned haystacks and destroyed the new, mechanized threshing machines they believed would put them out of work. Urban working-class riots also took place in Bristol, Derby, and Nottingham during 1831.

Such worker protests were not new to Great Britain. More than a decade earlier, 60,000 workers had gathered outside St. Peter's Field in the working-class mill and manufacturing town of Manchester, calling for political reform. The 1819 rally resulted in militia and regular British troops charging on horseback into the crowd, killing 11 protesters and injuring 400. More than one out of four injured were women. The tragic event was later dubbed "Peterloo," after Napoleon's final battlefield defeat at Waterloo.

In no mood for protest and revolution, the British Parliament reacted to the massacre by clamping down further on revolutionaries, passing the Six Acts, which outlawed revolutionary printing, allowed for easier searches of private homes, and restricted the right of free assembly.

But in just a few years, the British government began reversing its policies and restrictive laws. Of the two mainline British political parties—the conservative Tories and the more liberal Whigs—it was surprisingly the Tories who supported the reforms that included the Great Reform Bill. At the heart of the 1832 law was an expansion of voting privileges. Land ownership qualifications were made uniform from borough to borough, establishing the vote for "any male occupying a household worth ten-pounds a year."[24] Prior to the change, approximately 286,000 men could vote in Britain. Under the Reform Bill, the number moved to 800,000, a 160 percent increase.

Although a significant reform, the vote was still only available to about one out of every seven adult males. The bill also called for the redistricting of parliamentary boroughs, giving more seats to the bustling, crowded industrial towns that had sprung up over the previous century due to the Industrial Revolution. Despite these revolutionary inroads, many of the workingclass and the poor still had no access to the vote.

## ASSESSING THE REVOLUTIONS OF THE 1830s

It is clear that those revolutions centered in Western Europe were generally more successful than those taking place in Eastern Europe. This reality widened the gap between the increasingly modern states of the west and those states in the east that remained slightly medieval, aristocratic, authoritarian, and less than progressive. England and France, each a constitutional monarchy, had supported the Belgian revolution and helped facilitate its success. In the east, Austria, Prussia, and Russia each remained largely autocratic and sought to quash rebellions in Germany, Italy, and Poland.

Beyond support from such significant powers as France and Britain, western revolutions succeeded because they quickly gained support from the masses. Popular support, including that of the middle class and the urban lower class, sometimes worked hand-in-glove to keep the steam of a revolution up. However, even the successful revolutions resulted in gains for the middle class at the expense of the lower classes, who often did not even gain the right to vote.

## THE REVOLUTIONS OF 1848–1849

Because so many liberals failed to achieve their goals during the revolutions of the 1830s, the clock continued to tick toward later uprisings across Europe. That third wave of revolutions took place during the late 1840s and lasted for about a year. Many states in Europe were directly affected by this new outburst of revolutionary energy.

While they varied from east to west, the revolutions of the late 1840s had several commonalities. These similarities included the continued desire for the establishment of more democratic, liberal governments across Europe, as well as the elimination of older social and political systems, including serfdom. The revolutions of 1848, then, were an attempt to turn around the agreements made at the 1815 Congress of Vienna. Also, the 1840s uprisings were almost all based in cities, featuring middle-class leaders, including lawyers, journalists and university professors. Despite this professional leadership, much of the street fighting was done by the urban lower classes, the street-types that included artisans, market women, and other members of the working class.

There were differences between the revolutions, as well. One significant revolutionary goal in such European states as Austria, the Germanys, Hungary, and Italy was nationalism: the desire to create a national unity. In the Western European states, a primary goal of this revolutionary period was to extend political power and the vote to those outside the upper-middle class. Thus, these midnineteenth-century revolutions were, in part, about unfinished business from previous, less-than-successful revolts.

Discontent and restlessness still marked this new age in Europe. And while the discontent of the middle class, the working class, and the rural peasants might have varied from one group to another, when these three groups formed alliances, the possibility of a successful revolution against an old order were greater. But, as each sociopolitical group would discover, fighting side-by-side would prove difficult.

## THE "JULY MONARCHY" IN FRANCE

Perhaps, once again, the most important European power facing revolution in the 1840s was France. King Louis-Philippe, who had risen to the throne during the revolution of 1830, had proven to be a disappointment. His domestic policies appeared to favor the wealthy class and his foreign policy was uninspired and uninspiring. In other words, many French citizens considered the king to be dull and boring. Popular political cartoons portrayed Louis-Philippe's head in the shape of a pear—a play on words, as the French word for pear, "poire," also meant "nitwit" or "dummy."

There were other issues, of course. As were other European nations, France during the 1840s was facing difficult economic times. These years produced a series of poor harvests, partially the result of a potato blight that hit Ireland and Germany extremely hard. Food prices across Europe had doubled in just a couple of years. Bread riots, a common precursor to European revolution, became commonplace. Historians refer to the 1840s as "the Hungry Forties."[25]

During these same years, European industry faced slowdowns, resulting in large-scale unemployment. All these harsh economic realities have caused the years 1846 and 1847 to be identified as "probably the worst of the entire century in terms of want and human suffering."[26]

Louis-Philippe became so unpopular that a coalition of opposition forces began rallying against him, including liberals, the Bonapartists, and the Republicans, all holdovers from the French Revolution of the 1790s. Liberals were in support of greater voting privileges. Republicans, as always, wanted an end to monarchy and the reestablishment of a new French republic. The Bonapartists wished to destroy the monarchy of Louis-Philippe and replace him with another: Prince Louis-Napoleon, the nephew of the great French emperor and general. Louis-Napoleon promised to restore international prestige to France and to bring back some of the honor and glory of the Bonaparte years, including military expansion.

Throughout the 1830s, opposition to Louis-Philippe grew. Opposition groups held political meetings, disguising them as "banquets," since such rallies were unlawful. (During such a political banquet, those present did not offer toasts to the king but to reform, shying away from most direct references to "revolution.") In 1835, following an assassination attempt against the king, the French government ratified a new censorship law that prohibited any writings that opposed or even showed animosity toward Louis-Philippe. By 1846, things in France were at or near the breaking point as the French economy continued to spiral downward. By the summer of 1847, liberals and Republicans formed a coalition in opposition to the king. Then, on February 22, 1848, a huge banquet was held. When Louis-Philippe ordered the gathering closed, street demonstrations began almost without any formal direction. Although the king ordered the National Guard to put down the street protests, once again the military went over in support of another revolution.

On the following day, street rioters, along with members of the National Guard, were fired on by regular French troops, bringing about the deaths of 40 or 50 citizens. By February 24, with 1,500 barricades erected across Paris, Louis-Philippe understood the situation and abdicated his throne, fleeing for asylum in Great Britain. Within 24 hours, a provisional government was formed, one that declared France a republic once more. Reforms soon followed under the leadership of a Romantic poet and historian, Alphonse de Lamartine. (Lamartine had written a history of the French Revolution of 1789.)

The new liberal government set out to make significant changes, including calling for an end to slavery in French colonies, outlawing the death penalty for political offenses, and instituting extensive freedom of the press.

But even as the new National Assembly charted the course of this latest French Revolution, factions began to develop. Middle-class liberals intended to keep reform to a limited agenda, while the lower-class radicals supported such goals as universal manhood suffrage, to which the provisional government finally agreed. The revolution quickly appeared to appeal to a wide spectrum of the people. Political clubs were formed and such clubs attracted a wide following, including women. One female political revolutionary summed

## Louis-Napoleon

He was the nephew, not the son, of the great Napoleon, and he did his best to live up to the family image.

Born in 1808, Louis-Napoleon was the son of Louis Bonaparte, one of Napoleon's younger brothers. Since Napoleon had only one son, and since that son died in 1832, young Louis-Napoleon was the heir to the Napoleonic legacy.

At first he seemed to have little chance to capitalize on this. During the Bourgeois Monarchy of King Louis-Philippe, Louis-Napoleon made several attempts to stir up revolts in France, but he had no success. The Bourgeois Monarch even managed to steal some of Louis-Napoleon's thunder by having the remains of Napoleon brought back to Paris in 1840 (they remain there today, at the tomb of Les Invalides).

But in 1848, Parisians overthrew the Bourgeois Monarch in a bloody revolution, and Louis-Napoleon crossed from England, where he had lived in exile, to France. That fall there was a presidential election, the first in French history, and Louis-Napoleon won with a remarkable 5.5 million out of 8 million votes cast. The Napoleonic name was enough to overcome any hesitation concerning Louis-Napoleon's lack of political experience.

For the next two years Louis-Napoleon governed as the nation's president, but in 1851 he carried out a political coup and made himself the new Emperor Napoleon III (the "third" was out of deference to the young Napoleon who had died in 1832). Soon there was a Second French Empire and a Second French Emperor.

Unlike his famous uncle, Louis-Napoleon had no wish for war. He cultivated good relations with England, and maintained peace for a number of years. He did much to beautify up the stake women had in this new revolution: "This holy function of motherhood gives women the right to intervene not only in all acts of civil life, but also in all acts of political life."[27] However, the National Assembly denied the vote to women by a tally of 899 to 1.

Despite cooperation among the various political factions in this revolution, divisions were inevitable. After new elections were held in April 1848, the National Assembly declared its intention to pursue future political change at a slower, even cautious pace. Many of the assembly's 900 members came from the upper or middle class, while only 25 percent of its members were of the working class, so when the Assembly created a five-man executive committee whose members were nonsupporters of workers' rights, street demonstrations

Paris; the magnificent boulevards were built by an architect under his direction (and the new wider streets made it more difficult for revolutionaries to lay barriers).

Napoleon did have a taste for military adventure, but he confined it to an overseas adventure in Mexico. Starting in 1862, Louis-Napoleon installed a puppet, the Austrian archduke Maximilian, as the "emperor" of Mexico, but everyone knew that France was pulling the strings. This adventure fared well for a time, but when the United States Civil War ended in 1865, the victorious Northern states demanded that Louis-Napoleon withdraw his French troops. He did so, and poor Maximilian was caught and shot.

Napoleon had now had enough of adventure, but he was forced into another war. The diplomatic maneuvers of Otto von Bismarck, chancellor of Prussia, lured France into the Franco-Prussian War, which was a complete disaster. Louis-Napoleon himself was captured by the Prussians and forced to abdicate his throne. Like King Charles X and King Louis-Philippe before him, Louis-Napoleon went off into political exile in England.

With their (second) emperor gone, the French fought on for another six months. Under a new government, the Third Republic, France held out until the people were reduced to eating rats. When Paris finally yielded, the Franco-Prussian War ended. The downfall of Louis-Napoleon's Second Empire helped to create the second German Reich, led by Chancellor Bismarck and Emperor Wilhelm I.

The Napoleonic line and dynasty ended with Louis-Napoleon, but the mystique remains to this day. There is something about the very name "Napoleon" that conveys a sense of awe, grandeur, and fear.

were again underway by mid-May. By late June, Parisian workers once again took to the streets.

## THE "BLOODY JUNE DAYS"

What followed was known as the "Bloody June Days" (June 24–26), which pitted working-class revolutionaries against the army and the National Guard. The rioters were aided by many who joined them from outside the city. As one observer stated, "[A]ll France has joined against [the government]. The National Guard, citizens, and

## Louis Blanc

Both Karl Marx and Louis Blanc probably cribbed the expression from someone else, but Blanc got it into print in 1848. The famous words were: "Let each produce according to his aptitudes and his force; let each consume according to his need." These words, or some variation of them, have long been accepted as bywords of socialism.

Louis Blanc was born in Madrid in 1811. His father was inspector general of finances for King Joseph Bonaparte, who had been placed on his throne by his brother, Emperor Napoleon I. The Blanc family was separated during the war in Spain from 1812–1815, and though Louis Blanc and his brother eventually managed to study together in France, the family cohesion was badly damaged by the events of the war.

Blanc graduated from the Royal College at Rodez in 1830 and went to Paris. He found little work for an intellectual; these were the heady days of the July Revolution that ousted King Charles X and replaced him with King Louis-Philippe. So, in 1832, Blanc moved

to the country, settling for a while in Arras, which had been the childhood home of Maximilien Robespierre. The time spent in Arras changed Blanc, giving him a revolutionary perspective, but his ideal was of a revolution that came through social progress rather than by the force of arms.

Back in Paris by 1834, Blanc became the editor of *Bon Sense* (Common Sense). He was too socialistic for his employers, so he resigned in 1838, and in 1839 he founded the *Revue de progress politique, social et literaire* (Review of Political, Social, and Literary Progress). Blanc soon described his utopian vision to the readers.

According to Blanc, life consisted of the struggle between the haves and the have-nots. This did not obscure the fact that humans were fundamentally good, and that when exposed to wholesome philosophies, they would naturally walk away from oppression and cruelty. The trick was to bring people into these new conditions. Only political action could accomplish this and only an peasants from the remotest parts of the country have come pouring in."[28] By June 26, more than 10,000 people had been killed or wounded, an additional 12,000 arrested, with 4,000 of them convicted and deported.

These bloody days of conflict managed to break the back of most of the lower-class resistance, allowing the French middle class the opportunity to direct the future of their country. With the monarchy eliminated, the new constitution of the second French Republic established a Chamber of Deputies as the legislative house; members

eventual reconciliation between the haves and the have-nots would make society whole. Then the perfect world would emerge, in which everyone would give according to his ability and receive according to his needs.

Blanc's great opportunity came in February 1848, when King Louis-Philippe was overthrown. Frenchmen seemed ready for something truly different, and Blanc inserted himself into the provisional government, earning a cabinet post as leader of the Luxembourg Commission on Labor. He advocated the creation of national workshops that would ensure that every Frenchman was employed. This was the beginning of what would have become the first truly socialist society in modern Europe.

But Blanc and his idealistic friends were defeated by an alliance between capitalists and rural Frenchmen. City workers and the unemployed liked Louis Blanc's ideas, but rural Frenchmen saw them as anathema, and in July 1848 the provisional government used both army troops and rural militia against the workers in the national workshops. The bitter fighting known as the July Days led to the end of the socialist experiment and Louis Blanc fled to Belgium. He moved on to England in 1852.

The reign of Emperor Louis-Napoleon III was even more hostile to labor than the Bourbon monarchs had been, and Blanc remained in exile. But Louis-Napoleon was eventually defeated and captured by the Prussians in 1870, and Blanc immediately returned home after 22 years. He was elected to the Chamber of Deputies and remained a passionate voice for the unemployed, but he was too old to take up political power. Deeply depressed toward the end of his life, Blanc died without having seen a successful socialist republic. Nevertheless, his funeral was attended by about 150,000 persons and he remains one of the heroes of nineteenth-century France.

were elected through universal male suffrage. Using the example of the United States, executive power was placed in the hands of a president, who was elected by the people. The first French president—Louis Napoleon—was elected in December 1848.

Once again, the French had provided Europe with another example of revolutionary success. As one German woman noted of the French: "My heart beat with joy. The monarchy had fallen. Only a little blood had been shed for such a high stake, and the great watchwords Liberty, Equality, and Fraternity were again inscribed on the banner of the movement."[29] Other revolutions took place following this successful French model, yet nearly all of them failed to establish lasting change. The revolution in Italy failed following intervention by the Austrians. In the Germanys, revolution also proved unsuccessful.

In Austria, however, revolution met with some initial success. Student-led demonstrations in Vienna in March of 1848 led Emperor Ferdinand to promise his people constitutionalism, an elected legislature, and freedom of the press and religion. Before month's end, the Austrian government ended the last vestiges of serfdom. But the reforms did not last. After Ferdinand's abdication, his 18-year-old nephew, Francis Joseph, regained the crown and soon appealed to the Russian czar Nicholas I for help. Nicholas dispatched Russian troops to Austria and aided Francis Joseph's forces in bringing down the revolutionary government in Vienna. Hurried dismantling resulted in the disbanding of revolutionary groups, a return to censorship, and the execution by firing squad of 25 revolutionary leaders.

## FURTHER REFORM COMES TO ENGLAND

The 1840s did not deliver wholesale revolution on Great Britain's doorstep, although many people had expected a revolution there first. British liberals did give support to a middle-class movement called *Chartism*. The movement developed out of the working class's disappointment with the limits of the Reform Bill of 1832. The Chartist movement was centered in a massive effort to create a "People's Charter"—a petition calling for additional liberal reforms such as universal white male suffrage, the use of the secret ballot, the elimination of all property qualifications for membership in the House of Commons and annual elections of Commons members, and electoral redistricting.

The Chartists held large rallying campaigns during 1838 and 1839, torch-lit, outdoor events that featured revolutionary speeches. When these rallies produced a People's Charter with one million signatures, Parliament was unmoved. During the following decade, the middle-class radical Chartists joined with working-class political movements and with other European revolutionaries. Regular agitation led to the Chartist demonstrations of 1848. That spring, 50,000 protesters delivered to Parliament a giant document, called the monster petition. Its supporters claimed the document contained five, perhaps even six, million signatures (however, many of them had been falsified). Historian Simon Schama describes the event:

> On an unseasonably warm spring morning, Monday, 10 April, the Chartist crowds gathered at their four London rallying points. The atmosphere was festive, rather than threatening.... The spectators who looked at the marchers, and at the carts and cabs bearing Chartist slogans—"Live and Let Live"; "Liberty Is Worth Living and Dying For"— ... seemed quiet or gently encouraging. This was despite the authorities' advance demonology that bloodthirsty British Jacobins were out on the streets.... A glance at [a] photograph of the meeting at Kennington speaks volumes about the Chartist tradition: it shows a disciplined, Sunday-best dressed "respectable" protest by workers always anxious to give the lie to their demonization as a drunken, semi-criminal rabble.[30]

Concerned about the mass rally and possible radical violence, the British government had activated 8,000 soldiers, plus 4,000 London policemen, and "some 85,000 men [who] were sworn in as special constables."[31] But the rally never broke into street violence. Despite this peaceful demonstration, the Chartist rally did not bring about immediate change in Great Britain. (Late in the day, a heavy rain sent the giant crowd scattering.) The year 1848, in fact, marked the end of the Chartist movement. As one witness to the April Chartist rally summed it up: "From that day it was a settled matter that England was safe from revolution."[32]

But liberal goals did not die with Chartism. Over the next 20 years, liberals in Parliament and others clamored for political reforms until, in 1867, the Conservative prime minister Benjamin Disraeli pushed a new Great Reform Bill through Parliament. This

Revolutionary action does not always mean extreme violence. England's Chartist movement, while unable to change the country's leadership, did promote a climate for future liberal reforms.

Reform Bill doubled the number of eligible voters and redistributed Parliamentary seats. The bill was only a sign of things to come in Great Britain. Over the next decade, more political reforms were enacted, marking "the high point of British liberalism."[33]

## SUMMING UP THE REVOLUTIONS OF 1848

Most of the revolutionary movements of the late 1840s ended in failure. Historians have asked the question "Why?" and have noted several causes. In many movements, the revolutionary spirit lacked popular support, therefore remaining limited in scope and followers. As with earlier revolutionary movements, those of the 1840s faced strong responses from reactionary and conservative governments. In some countries, revolutionary elements were able to gain support from the lower classes during poor economic times. However, when such weak economies made serious improvements, as many did by 1848 and 1849, the revolutionaries lost a cause.

With some revolutionary groups, failure had occurred because they had been slow to take serious steps, allowing the forces and governments they wanted to challenge to prepare their own counterrevolutions. Finally, in most European countries of the 1840s, the middle class did not give much support to revolution. Those middle-class liberals typically supported more peaceful, passive change, such as reforms similar to those that eventually took place in England.

All this is not to say that the revolutions of 1848–49 were all complete failures. France did witness serious political change, including the abandonment of its monarchy (once again) for a republic administered by a president. In Italy, while the revolution appeared to fail for the moment, its leaders learned valuable political lessons that would soon bring about Italian unification and the removal of Austrian influence. As for Austria itself, serfdom was eliminated and remained so.

## THE CONTINUATION OF AN AGE

Revolution repeatedly rocked the foundations of the powerful nations of Europe during the first half of the nineteenth century. While reactionary leaders worked hard to keep the threat of such liberal challenges to a minimum, they were unable to bring about the death of the revolutionary spirit. It was, perhaps, the failures of these revolutions that kept the flame of freedom and individualism alive in Europe during these decades. Change occurred across the continent as revolutionaries achieved one goal at a time, slowly chipping away at the old regimes, making governments self-conscious of their failings and excesses.

As the century progressed, revolutionary ideas spread even further, and achieved greater success for their advocates. In time, the veneer of reaction and oppression would crack wide open. Serfdom came to an end; voting privileges were granted to more and more individuals; greater numbers of people were represented by elected officials; governments became more liberal, allowing a litany of rights, including freedom of the press, of speech, of assembly, of religion, and freedom from torture. The right to a free trial became commonplace.

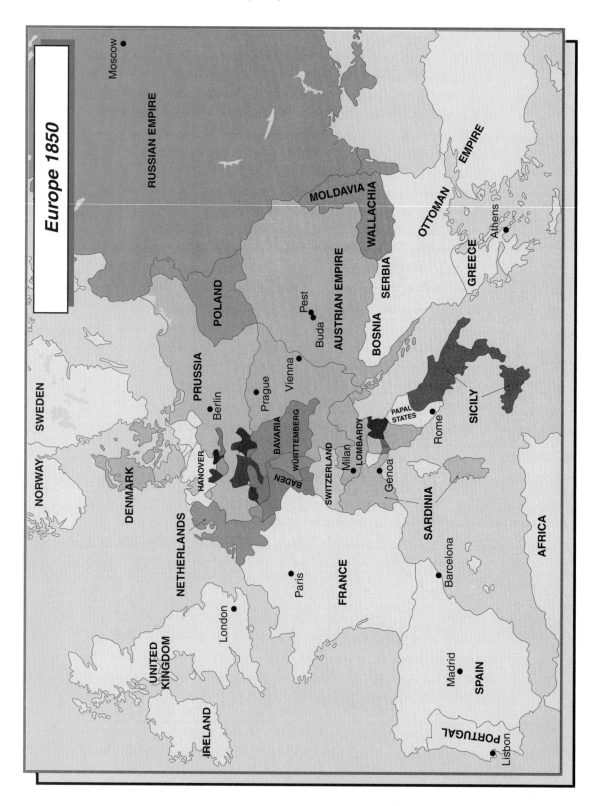

Europe 1850

Repeated cycles of revolution helped promote the liberalism that was to redefine Europe. As the historian Paul Schroeder wrote:

The light that thus began to shine in international politics in 1815 was brief, fitful, and wintry. It would be followed by a long twilight and an even longer, bitterly cold night. Let there be no mistake, however: 1815 was not a false dawn. It marked a new day, and it helps make other new days thinkable.[34]

In most countries on the continent and in Great Britain, constitutionalism was the rule of law before the end of the century; governments were elected and representative, and the medieval hierarchy of privilege for the nobility and aristocracy was drastically reduced. The future of Europe was centered on nation building, not royal dynasties. The course was set and the direction charted, as Europeans set their sights on a distant horizon where men and women were no longer expected to bow to king or queen, emperor or empress, czar or czarina, but instead were able to raise themselves up, their hearts stirred with national pride, and call themselves *citizens*.

## TIMELINE

**1799** Napoleon Bonaparte declares himself ruler of France.

**1814** Congress of Vienna establishes Louis XVIII on the French throne.

**1814–1815** Congress of Vienna provides forum for leading diplomats and rulers of Europe to reestablish traditional power following the demise of Napoleon.

**1819** British troops fire into crowd of protestors in manufacturing town of Manchester. The event is immortalized as "Peterloo."

**1820** Austria, Prussia, and Russia sign a joint agreement, the Troppau Memorandum, to provide support to each other in the suppression of revolution.

**1821** Ottoman Empire faces revolution from three states—Serbia, Moldavia, and Wallachia—as well as Greece.

**1821–1827** Greeks revolt against the Ottoman Empire.

**1823**  French government dispatches 200,000 soldiers to Spain to crush revolt.

**1824**  French monarch Louis XVIII dies, leaving the throne to his ultra-conservative brother, Charles X.

**1825**  Russian czar Alexander I dies, leaving his empire open to revolution. In December revolution takes place but is ended by military intervention called by Czar Nicholas I.

**1827**  British, French, and Russian naval squadrons destroy combined naval forces of Turkey and Egypt in battle of Navarino Bay, ensuring success of Greek Revolution.

**1821–1827**
Greeks revolt against the Ottoman Empire.

**1814–1815**
Congress of Vienna provides forum for leading diplomats and rulers of Europe to reestablish power after the demise of Napoleon.

**1825**
Russian czar Alexander I dies, leaving his empire open to revolution
**December**  Revolution takes place but is ended by military intervention called by Czar Nicholas I.

**1814**

**1821**
Ottoman Empire faces revolution from three states–Serbia, Moldavia, and Wallachia–as well as Greece.

**1830**
French king Louis XVII establishes the "July Ordinances" in an
**August**  Rioting ravages the city of Brussels as Belgians protest Dutch rule.
**October**  Belgians establish a national congress and England, France, Austria, Russia, and Prussia all recognize Belgian independence.

**1829**  Ottoman Turks forced to accept the Treaty of Adrianople, allowing Greece to become an independent kingdom.

**1830**  French king Louis XVIII establishes the "July Ordinances" in an attempt to destroy the French legislature while limiting the power of the press. That same month, revolutionaries challenge the authority and power of Charles X as they take to the streets in protest. As a result, Charles abdicates his throne.

**August** Rioting ravages the city of Brussels as Belgians protest Dutch rule.

**October** Belgians establish a national congress and England,

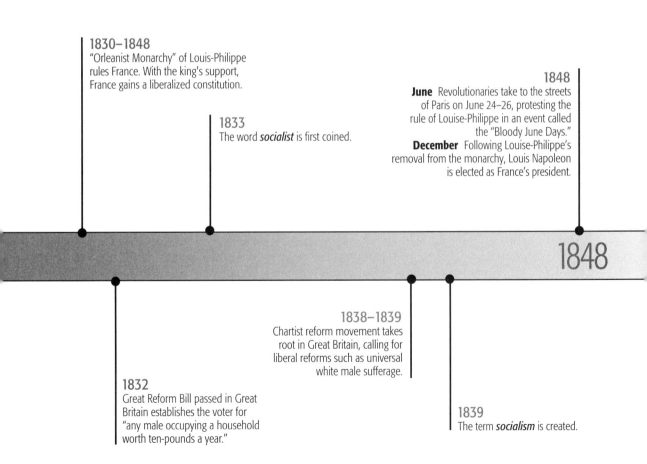

**1830–1848**
"Orleanist Monarchy" of Louis-Philippe rules France. With the king's support, France gains a liberalized constitution.

**1833**
The word *socialist* is first coined.

**1848**
**June** Revolutionaries take to the streets of Paris on June 24–26, protesting the rule of Louise-Philippe in an event called the "Bloody June Days."
**December** Following Louise-Philippe's removal from the monarchy, Louis Napoleon is elected as France's president.

1848

**1838–1839**
Chartist reform movement takes root in Great Britain, calling for liberal reforms such as universal white male sufferage.

**1832**
Great Reform Bill passed in Great Britain establishes the voter for "any male occupying a household worth ten-pounds a year."

**1839**
The term *socialism* is created.

France, Austria, Russia, and Prussia all recognize Belgian independence.

**1830–1848** "Orleanist Monarchy" of Louis-Philippe rules France. With the king's support, France gains a liberalized constitution.

**1832** Great Reform Bill passed in Great Britain. Establishes the vote for "any male occupying a household worth ten-pounds a year."

**1833** The word socialist is first coined.

**1838–1839** Chartist reform movement takes root in Great Britain, calling for liberal reforms such as universal white malesuffrage.

**1839** The term socialism is created.

**1847** French liberals and republicans form a coalition in opposition to King Louis-Philippe.

**1848** **February 24** Protesters raise barricades in the streets of Paris calling for the abdication of Louis-Philippe.

**April** French National Assembly moves slowly toward political reform.

**June** Revolutionaries take to the streets of Paris on June 24–26, protesting the rule of Louis-Philippe. The violence is remembered as the "Bloody June Days."

**December** Following Louis-Philippe's removal from the monarchy, Louis-Napoleon is elected as France's president.

**1867** Conservative British prime minister Benjamin Disraeli pushes new Great Reform Bill through Parliament, increasing the number of eligible voters and redistributing Parliamentary seats.

## SOURCE NOTES

1. Quoted in Judith G. Coffin, *Western Civilizations: Their History and Their Cultures*. New York: W.W. Norton, 2002, p. 699.
2. Ibid., p. 720.
3. Quoted in Harold Nicolson, "The Romantic Revolt," *Horizon Magazine*, May 1961, volume 3, number 5, p. 60.
4. Quoted in Steven Hause and William Maltby, *Western Civilization: A History of European Society*. Belmont, CA: West/Wadsworth, 1999, p. 684.
5. Quoted in Nicolson, *Romantic Revolt*, p. 60.
6. Quoted in Coffin, *Western Civilizations*, p. 782.
7. Quoted in William J. Duiker, *World History*. Belmont, CA: West/Wadsworth, 1998, p. 747.
8. Quoted in Coffin, *Western Civilizations*, p. 787.
9. Quoted in Hause, *Western Civilization*, p. 688.
10. Ibid.
11. Ibid.
12. Quoted in David Thomson, *Europe Since Napoleon*. New York: Alfred A. Knopf, 1963, p. 138.
13. Quoted in Hause, *Western Civilization*, p. 869.
14. Quoted in D.W. Brogan, *The French Nation From Napoleon to Petain, 1814–1940*. New York: Harper & Row, 1957, p. 4.
15. Quoted in Hause, *Western Civilization*, p. 690.
16. Quoted in Coffin, *Western Civilizations*, p. 789.
17. Quoted in Hause, *Western Civilization*, p. 690.
18. Quoted in Brogan, *French Nation*, p. 50.
19. Quoted in Coffin, *Western Civilizations*, p. 790.
20. Quoted in Brogan, *French Nation*, p. 50.
21. Ibid., p. 47.
22. Quoted in Hause, *Western Civilization*, p. 693.
23. Ibid.
24. Quoted in Thomas William Heyck, *The Peoples of the British Isles: A New History From 1688 to 1870*. Belmont, CA: Wadsworth, 1992, p. 308.
25. Quoted in Coffin, *Western Civilizations*, p. 797.
26. Ibid.
27. Quoted in Lynn Hunt, *The Challenge of the West*. Lexington, MA: D.C. Heath, 1995, p. 773.
28. Ibid., p. 775.
29. Ibid.
30. Quoted in Simon Schama, *A History of Britain: The Fate of Empire, 1776–2000*, vol. 2. New York: Hyperion Books, 2002, pp. 187–89.
31. Ibid., p. 188.
32. Quoted in Coffin, *Western Civilizations*, p. 796.
33. Ibid., p. 804.
34. Quoted in Paul W. Schroeder, *The Transformation of European Politics, 1763–1848*. Oxford: Clarendon Press, 1994, p. 804.

## BIBLIOGRAPHY

Brogan, D.W. *The French Nation From Napoleon to Petain, 1814–1940*. New York: Harper & Row, 1957.

Coffin, Judith G., *Western Civilizations: Their History and Their Cultures*. New York: W.W. Norton, 2002.

Duiker, William J. *World History*. Belmont, CA: West/Wadsworth, 1998.

Hause, Steven and William Maltby. *Western Civilization: A History of European Society*. Belmont, CA: West/Wadsworth, 1999.

Heyck, Thomas William. *The Peoples of the British Isles: A New History From 1688 to 1870*. Belmont, CA: Wadsworth, 1992.

Hunt, Lynn. *The Challenge of the West*. Lexington, MA: D.C. Heath, 1995.

Nicolson, Harold. "The Romantic Revolt," *Horizon Magazine*, vol. 3, no. 5. May 1961, 60.

Palmer, R.R., *A History of the Modern World*. New York: McGraw-Hill, 1995.

Schama, Simon. *A History of Britain: The Fate of Empire, 1776–2000*. New York: Hyperion Books, 2002.

Schroeder, Paul W. *The Transformation of European Politics, 1763–1848*. Oxford: Clarendon Press, 1994.

Thomson, David. *Europe Since Napoleon*. New York: Alfred A. Knopf, 1963.

Webster, Sir Charles. *The Congress of Vienna, 1814–1815*. New York: Barnes & Noble, 1966.

# 5

# The Mexican Revolution

**The year 1910 was one of great celebration throughout the Latin American** nation of Mexico. The year marked the one hundredth anniversary of Mexico's first revolution. The Spanish monarchy had controlled the Latin American state since nearly the days of Christopher Columbus, when it was invaded by the Spanish conquistador Hernan Cortes, whose armored and horse-bound soldiers in 1519 conquered the native empire of the Aztec. The Spanish king, Charles I, made Cortes the governor of New Spain, the colonial name for Spanish-controlled Mexico.

## MEXICO'S FIRST REVOLUTION

During 300 years of oppression since that first invasion, the Mexican people suffered under the heavy yoke of Spanish rule. They were forced to work on lands owned by Spanish officials and other powerful men. Only those colonists born in Spain—the *peninsulares*—could hold the highest offices in the government of New Spain. Locals were limited by Spanish law to lesser roles. Creoles, those

187

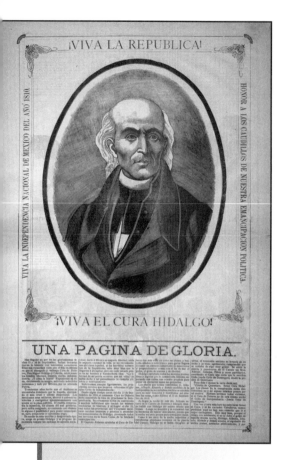

¡VIVA LA REPUBLICA!

¡VIVA EL CURA HIDALGO!

UNA PAGINA DE GLORIA.

In 1810, after over three centuries of abuses at the hands of the Spanish, the Mexican people began a revolt. Inspired by a creole priest, Father Miguel Hidalgo (seen here), they challenged the class-conscious and restrictive rule of the Spaniards.

Spanish colonists who were born in the Americas, were allowed to hold less important positions, while the original, or indigenous, people of Mexico, the Indians, lived as peasants in small villages or worked the lands of the great Spanish-owned estates and plantations. Another group, the mestizos, who were of mixed European and Indian blood, were denied the right to hold public office and were relegated to such occupations as artisans and craftsmen, farmers, and common laborers.

For hundreds of years, the Spanish forced this race-conscious, class-conscious system on the Mexican people. Then, on the night of September 15, 1810, the Mexicans began a revolt against their Spanish masters. A creole priest, Miguel Hidalgo y Costilla, called on all Indians and mestizos to rally against the Spaniards. In the early morning hours of September 16, Father Hidalgo rang a church bell, signaling his people to gather at the local church in the small village of Dolores, nearly 200 miles north of Mexico City.

Soon, the news of the revolution spread from town to town, as tens of thousands of commoners gathered under the priest's leadership, "armed only with the peasant's machete, the miner's pick, the bow and arrow, and, occasionally, a gun."[1] They were protesting their Spanish overlords, the continual Spanish practice of confiscating Indian lands, and Mexican slavery. They marched under banners bearing such slogans as "Death to the *Peninsulares*!" As Hidalgo's followers swelled in number to 80,000, the uprising became bloody and almost uncontrollable. But after just one month, the Mexican rebels had gained control of much of central Mexico. Although Hidalgo was captured by Spanish troops in 1811 and executed (Father Hidalgo's head was severed and put on display in a granary in the silver mining village of Guanajuato for nearly a decade), the revolution continued under the leadership of Father Jose Maria Morelos y Pavon.

Father Morelos and his army of ragtag followers won pitched battles and raids, taking better weapons from the Spanish troops they defeated. In 1813, Morelos marched on the city of Acapulco and declared Mexico an independent state. The new Mexican government established a liberal program of reforms that included racial and class equality and the breakup of the large estates and redistribution of land in smaller parcels to the peasants and other landless peoples. The revolutionary priest Morelos promised that, in his new Mexico, "the only thing that will distinguish one American from another is vice and virtue."[2]

But, just as the first revolution in Mexican history appeared successful, the insurrection began to unravel. Many creoles who had first supported the revolt rejected Morelos's reforms, since the fiery priest appeared intent on eliminating European influences on Mexico only to replace them with more traditional, native Mexican influences. Spanish forces loyal to their king continued to struggle against the revolution. In 1815, Father Morelos, "after a heroic campaign, was defeated, tried, officially degraded, condemned, and executed."[3] With his death, many Mexican creoles and peninsulares joined together, bonded by their common Spanish ancestry, and repledged their allegiance to the Spanish monarch, Ferdinand VII.

By 1820, Spanish forces had regained nearly all the towns, cities, and outlying territory the insurrectionists had captured. Yet far-reaching political change was in the wind and set to sweep across Mexico. A liberal movement in Spain had forced Ferdinand to accept a constitution that drastically reduced his royal powers. This alarmed conservatives in Mexico so much that they soon launched a new revolt against the Spanish monarchy. In a twist of historical irony, conservative creoles began to rally behind a royalist officer, Agustin de Iturbide. Although a mestizo by birth (Iturbide claimed he was born a creole), Iturbide had defeated Morelos on the battlefield and executed many of his followers. Under the leadership of this corrupt and greedy military leader, the creoles pushed for the establishment of a constitutional monarchy.

Soon, this new conservative-led revolution took another odd turn. After marching off to the modern-day Mexican province of Guerrero to fight Vicente Guerrero, one of the last of Father Morelos's followers, Iturbide instead met with his opponent and, on February 24, 1821, the two agreed on and signed the Plan of Iguala, which was designed to appeal to all the fighting factions in Mexico. The plan called for Mexican independence for all, regardless of race or class; the creation of a new constitutional monarchy; the establishment of Catholicism as the official state religion; and equality for all Mexicans. While the plan appealed to both conservative creoles and liberals equally, creating a free and independent Mexico, it also established Iturbide as the state's new ruler, Emperor Agustin I of Mexico.

## A SHAKY REPUBLIC

Iturbide and Guerrero, along with another of Morelos's old rebel leaders, Guadalupe Victoria, rode with their armies into Mexico City on September 27, 1821. At last Mexico was rid of Spain and a path had been laid for an independent state. But problems plagued the new Republic of Mexico from its early days. More than ten years of revolution had saddled the fledging nation with a 75-million-peso debt. Also, when Iturbide and his government replaced the peninsulares in high office with creoles and others, the wealthy peninsulares left Mexico in droves, taking their personal wealth in gold and silver out of the country. Without working capital, Mexico's mines and factories soon closed. The homes of the wealthy became targets for bandits. Unemployment was rampant. Iturbide proved unpopular and his reign lasted for less than a year.

With the removal and later execution of Iturbide, Mexico experienced further political change. A new framework of government was written—the Constitution of 1824. It established a federal republic, an office of the presidency, assured the rights of free speech and press, and brought an official end to the Indian tribute paid to the state. But eliminating a poor emperor did not guarantee Mexico would be governed by capable presidents.

From the 1820s until the 1870s, the Mexican people suffered under a variety of poor leaders, the first being Guadalupe Victoria, who proved to be "uneducated, uncontrollably jealous of rivals, and unable to inspire the republic."[4] Others proved no better. One of the strangest of Mexico's presidents was Antonio Lopez de Santa Anna, a creole born in the state of Veracruz. Between 1833 and 1855, Santa Anna presided over Mexico eleven times. Typically, he ignored the Mexican Constitution of 1824 and ruled as he pleased. His misplaced policies helped lead to a revolt in the northern province of Tejas (modern-day Texas) during the 1830s, and may have contributed to the events that led to the Mexican-American War in 1846–48, which resulted in the occupation of Mexico City by American troops and the loss of all of Mexico's northern provinces from Tejas to California. Santa Anna typically did not carry out the duties of president, but rather lived extravagantly in his hacienda in coastal Veracruz, leaving "his vice president, Valentin Gomez Farias, [to] take care of the boring day-to-day details."[5]

Santa Anna was finally driven from office for the last time in 1855 by the Liberal Party. Under the leadership of a Zapotec Indian named Benito Juarez (who is often referred to as the "Abraham Lincoln of Mexico"), Mexico experienced great change and many problems, including its conquest by the French during the 1860s. This led to new reforms, which brought about the Constitution of 1857. But even as this constitution gave further guarantees of the freedoms of speech and press as well as the freedom of education, Juarez included a law called the Ley Lerdo, which called for "all institutions, both religious and secular, to divest themselves of property not used in their normal operations."[6] The Ley Lerdo proved very unpopular with Mexican conservatives, the Catholic Church, and even Indians, since their communal lands were sold off to pay Mexican state debts. A war against these reforms followed, lasting until 1861, and ended with the defeat of the conservatives by Juarista liberals.

Following several years of French intervention in Mexico, which ended with the execution of the French-installed emperor of Mexico, Ferdinand Maximilian of Hapsburg, Mexico finally experienced a decade of relative stability, security, and peace under the leadership of President Benito Juarez. He governed as a civilian president, not as a victorious military leader. As historian Lynn Foster notes of the Juarez presidency:

Juarez's popularity in no small part helped prevent the usual military coups, but he also had to juggle many competing interests in the liberal party. To keep the hacendados behind him, Juarez granted them absolute privileges over their domains.... The middle class was pleased with the increasing number of public schools in the cities, from fewer than 2,500 in 1857 to over 8,000 in 1874. The liberals were basically satisfied with Juarez's public policies as well. Although the federalist state had become more centralist, the elections were more open than they had ever been, if not totally free of state tampering. The press was free.... The anticlerical reforms remained intact.... And congress was strengthened as a branch of government.[7]

## Benito Juarez

Often compared with Abraham Lincoln, Benito Juarez was a heroic revolutionary. Born in 1806 in the mountains of the southern state of Oaxaca, Juarez was a pure-blooded Indian. He grew up very poor, and only through extensive willpower and good fortune was he able to obtain an education and then a law degree. By the late 1840s, Juarez had become a significant member of the Mexican political establishment, and he probably could have continued to rise in comfort and ease. But he had other missions to fill.

The war with the United States between 1846 and 1848 jolted Juarez and his fellow countrymen; they saw the backwardness of their nation, and many, like Juarez, sought to change things. Many of the social liberals believed in reforming the government and the army, but only a few were as brave as Juarez, who wanted to reform the church as well.

Ever since the mid-sixteenth century, the Roman Catholic Church had been the bedrock of Mexican life. Over the centuries the church had fulfilled its duties, but it had also grown rich in the process. By the 1850s it was estimated that at least two-thirds of all land in Mexico was owned or rented by the church. Juarez set out to change this; he was instrumental in getting the 1857 constitution passed that limited the church to the amount of land it needed to perform its duties. Needless to say, such a bold and revolutionary approach earned Juarez many enemies and brought about the War of the Reform (1857–1860).

Juarez and his forces won the war in 1860 and he assumed the presidency that same year. He then made one of his few strategic mistakes, repudiating Mexico's foreign debt. In 1861, Britain, France, and Spain sent an expeditionary force to occupy Veracruz and force payment of the debts.

As one Mexican writer noted: "Until Juarez took control, Mexico never was governed."[8]

## CINCO DE MAYO

There were problems in Mexico, to be sure. Tens of thousands of soldiers were unemployed, relieved of military duty by Juarez as an expense the state could not afford. Many unemployed troops joined bandit gangs, burned villas, and terrorized the rural countryside. A half dozen rebellions broke out across Mexico, many at the hands of dissatisfied former soldiers, including General Porfirio Diaz, a

The British and Spanish soon withdrew, but the French stayed on, and in 1863 they set up an Austrian archduke, Maximilian Habsburg, as the new puppet emperor of Mexico. Defeated, Juarez and his followers went north all the way to the Rio Grande and the border with the United States (they stayed at what is now known as Ciudad Juarez, across the river from El Paso, Texas).

Maximilian and his court lived in luxury at Chapultepec Castle while Juarez and his men languished in the north. A lesser man might have crumbled under these circumstances, but Juarez was nothing if not determined. Driving about in a coach (he disdained horseback riding as too aristocratic) and wearing a black top hat, Juarez appeared to be another Lincoln, fighting for a desperate cause. In fact, the causes of the northern states of the United States and of Juarez's Reform Party were linked, because as long as the U.S. Civil War continued, the United States could

not send troops to defend the border along the Rio Grande against the French. When in 1865 the U.S. Civil War ended, troops were sent and the French began to withdraw. Maximilian foolishly remained. He was caught at Querertaro and sent to the firing squad (Juarez resisted numerous appeals for clemency in this situation).

With the War of the Reform and the French Intervention both over, Juarez was able to govern Mexico. He was less apt as a majority politician than he had been as a social revolutionary. Though he won another term in 1871, many Mexicans were eager for an end to his presidency by the time Juarez died of heart failure in 1872.

Whatever missteps he may have made, Juarez became a symbol of Mexican national unity, as important to Mexico as George Washington and Abraham Lincoln combined are to the United States.

well-known military leader considered a hero by the Mexican people. During a May 5, 1862, battle between 6,500 invading French troops at Puebla, General Diaz had routed the foreign forces. (The day became a noted Mexican holiday known as "Cinco de Mayo," meaning "The Fifth of May.")

## Porfirio Diaz

Like many successful politicians, Diaz overstayed his welcome. One might say he overstayed it by about 30 years.

Born in Oaxaca in 1830, Diaz was a *mestizo* ("mixed blood," of Spanish and native Indian stock). He spent some time in a seminary and also studied law, but his real gift was for the military. Diaz served with courage and distinction during Mexico's war with the French invaders (1861–1867) and it was his forces that liberated Mexico City in the final year of the conflict. Up to this point he had been a faithful pupil of Benito Juarez, but in 1871, Diaz ran for the presidency against Juarez and did well enough that the two men became enemies.

Juarez died of heart failure in 1872 and Diaz won the following election. He served as president of Mexico between 1872 and 1910, with one short break in 1880–1884. Even though he had campaigned against Juarez with the slogan "no reelection," Diaz

became a master at engineering his own election triumphs. His control of the machinery of state became so secure that his government was called the *Porfiriate*.

Once firmly in the presidential chair, Diaz tried to alter the tragic momentum of Mexican history. Believing that industrialization and foreign investment were the keys to success, Diaz cultivated a powerful probusiness image; he brought in Americans, Germans, and British to develop factories and to manage the nation's first oil wells. Diaz favored foreigners to the extent that Mexican citizens dreaded the law courts, which ruled time and again in favor of the outsider and against the average Mexican. But this was only the beginning of Diaz's crimes against his people.

While the ledger sheets lengthened and while Mexican bonds floated around the world, the average Mexican earned about 15 cents a day. The word *peon* entered the

In 1871, both Diaz and Juarez campaigned for the presidency. When the electorate produced no majority victor, the Mexican congress decided the election for Juarez, electing him to a fourth term. When Diaz attempted a coup, he was roundly defeated. The general's political future appeared dim for the moment, until Juarez suddenly

English language to describe the plight of the Mexican farm laborer, who owned no land and could be arrested or exiled at the whim of the hacienda owner. To enforce this rigid system, Diaz hired large groups of Mexican irregulars and made them into a cavalry force known as the *rurales*; these men were authorized to shoot on sight, and very few of the *rurales* were ever tried for their crimes. The splendid uniforms and sombreros only accentuated the hostility felt by the Mexican people, who were powerless against this militia.

As the nineteenth century yielded to the twentieth, Diaz appeared more competent and in control than ever. He regularly received letters of congratulation from foreign leaders such as Theodore Roosevelt and Kaiser Wilhelm II, both of whom applauded what Diaz had done for business and foreign interests in Mexico. But the anger underneath the facade simmered and boiled, and in 1910 Diaz faced his first real opposition in many years. Francesco Madero ran against Diaz for the presidency.

Diaz had Madero temporarily jailed and the dictator won one more election. In September 1910 Diaz celebrated the hundredth anniversary of Mexican independence from Spain; foreigners commented on the splendid uniforms, the paved streets, and the wonderful appearance of order. But everything cracked just two months later as Madero, now in the southern United States, began his revolt against Diaz.

Confident as ever, Diaz announced that if the rebels ever reached 5,000 in number he would take the field against them, despite his 80 years. For a few months the revolution was held to certain key areas, but when Madero's forces captured Ciudad Juarez in 1911, it was clear that the attempts at suppression had failed. Diaz, suffering from an abscessed tooth and a botched dental operation, announced his resignation in May 1911 and hastened to Veracruz, where a ship took him to France. He lived quietly in Paris until his death.

Some efforts have been made to rehabilitate the memory of Diaz, but none of them can alter the fact that he "sold out" his nation and his people. That he did so in the name of "law and order" cannot justify his harsh and inhumane regime.

died of a heart attack in the summer of 1872. While Juarez's vice president held the legitimate reins of government over the next four years, Diaz finally succeeded in bringing down the Mexican government in 1876. Over the next 34 years, Porfirio Diaz ruled Mexico as a virtual dictator.

Diaz, a mestizo whose mother was a Mixtec Indian, had studied law earlier in his career, but he ignored the Constitution of 1857, which called for regular terms of office and elections. After standing for reelection a second time in 1880, he dropped the pretense and held on to power into the twentieth century with a combination of treachery, cunning, sheer will, and brute force. He formed political alliances with regional governors to gain their support for his regime. He made friends with the Catholic Church by ignoring land reforms required by the Constitution, reforms which had already reduced the amount of church-controlled property. Diaz reduced the power of the Mexican congress so dramatically he eventually referred to its members as "*mi caballada*"—"my herd of tame horses."[9]

Never so popular that he did not face occasional revolts and peasant uprisings, Diaz created a ruthless police force called the *rurales*. Scattered across the rural regions of Mexico, the rurales were a law to themselves. They were authorized by Diaz to deal harshly with, and even murder, anyone suspected of disloyalty to the Diaz regime. Many of the rurales were no more than local bandits who were well paid by Diaz. The rurales arrested political agitators and broke up labor strikes. Typically, the rurales justified any of their killings with a simple legality, the *ley de fuga*: "Shot while trying to escape."[10]

For some Mexicans, Diaz brought important and productive change. He did manage to balance the national budget and pay off much of Mexico's staggering national debt. He encouraged economic growth, luring foreign investors into his country, bringing such investment, by 1910, to a total of $1.3 billion. When he took office, Mexico had fewer than 400 miles of railroads. By 1910, 15,000 miles of rail track crisscrossed his country, much of it constructed through foreign investment. This expansive rail system allowed Mexico under Diaz to further develop its industrial base. New industries producing lead, zinc, oil, copper, even steel were established, helping to double the volume of manufactured goods the newly developed Latin American nation produced.

Many Mexicans supported Diaz, including the middle class,

creoles, and the *caudillos*, local military strongmen who held power. His changes, after all, brought new prosperity to their native land. But behind the stage set of Mexico's economic expansion and growth lay one important fact: Much of the growth was made possible through the investment capital of foreign businesses. The result was predictable: "By 1900, foreign investors held some 90 percent of the incorporated value of Mexican industry; Americans held 70 percent."[11]

## THE PORFIRIATO

Under the Diaz regime—known popularly as the *Porfiriato*—most of these changes, as well as others brought by Diaz, managed to benefit the upper-class people of Mexico. Many peasants—three of every four persons living in Mexico—did not see the benefits of such changes:

> For most Mexicans, political life rarely went beyond the confines of their home village. Mexico had a long tradition of local political autonomy.... Villagers prized this independence. Effective local leadership helped villagers protect land and water rights, contest questionable taxes, and generally survive the uncertainties of a premodern agricultural economy.[12]

But Diaz made life more difficult for the rural peasants. An 1883 law created by Diaz called for a national survey and allowed anyone receiving a government surveying contract to take control of one-third of all the land he surveyed. The remaining two-thirds would come under government ownership. By the early 1890s, one out of every five acres of Mexican land came to be owned by friends loyal to Diaz, as well as foreigners—a landmass equal to more than 100 million acres. Foreign land ownership in Mexico amounted to 150 million acres, including 130 million held by Americans.

Yet even as less and less land was made available for the poor people of Mexico, their numbers were increasing steadily. Between 1877 and 1900, Mexico's population increased by 50 percent, from 10 to 15 million people. By 1910, only 10 percent of all Mexican Indians owned their own land. Many were debt-ridden, working under permanent contract to large landowners. In fact, if a peasant owed the equivalent of even one penny to a *hacendado*, the owner of an estate, that poor worker was forced by law to remain and work on estate lands perpetually.

After more than 30 years of repressive control over Mexico, the Diaz regime had reduced land ownership down to only 2 percent of the population. Without adequate land available, the peasants experienced yet another problem—food. Even as Mexico's population increased by 5 million within a few decades, the amount of maize, or corn, produced was less in 1910 than the amount raised at the beginning of Diaz's rule. While less than half as much maize was available by 1910, the price had doubled. Other crops, such as beans, had increased sixfold in price. Since wages for peasants did not increase during the Diaz regime, many found themselves starving. Rural farmers, by the last days of Diaz's rule, faced an infant mortality rate of 80 percent and a life expectancy of under 30 years. As one historian described the Diaz regime: "Don Porfirio's slogan was 'Bread and the Club': bread for the army, bread for the bureaucrats, bread for the foreigners, and even bread for the Church—and the club for the common people of Mexico and those who differed with him."[13] Gradually, but increasingly, the lower class people of Mexico were going to turn against Diaz with each passing decade of his regime.

Even as President Diaz approached his fourth decade as ruler of Mexico, by then a man in his seventies, he remained as ruthless and iron-fisted as ever. When, in 1906, the workers at a French-owned textile mill, desperate for better wages and seeking the right to unionize, went out on strike, Diaz responded by sending in troops to put down the unrest. Following the successful intervention in the dispute, Diaz commented, "Thank God I can still kill."[14]

But some saw light at the end of the tunnel during the first decade of the twentieth century. In 1908, during an interview with an American journalist writing for the popular *Pearson's Magazine*, President Diaz indicated he would not run for reelection two years later, stating that Mexico was ready for true democracy. But when the story was published in an article titled, "Thrilling Story of President Diaz, the Greatest Man on the Continent," Diaz began stepping away from his claim. In fact, he had no intention of stepping down, although he would be 80 years old in 1910. His opponents took the article at face value and convinced themselves they could "support other parties and candidates without fear of reprisals from the dictator, even if he himself ran."[15]

## THE REFORMER MADERO

One man who took Diaz's claim seriously was a creole rancher from Coahuila named Francisco Indalecio Madero, a large landowner, industrialist, and banker whose family was one of Mexico's richest. Unlike his contemporaries, Madero believed in the rights of the workers and had a strong interest in the welfare of the underclass. Although Madero had written a book titled *The Presidential Succession in 1910* in which he was kind to Diaz, the wealthy political reformer wrote in favor of a return to adherence to the Constitution of 1857, which supported free elections, an open press, and an independent court system. He established the Anti-Reelectionist Party with plans to have a direct impact on the 1910 election.

At first Diaz kept Madero at a distance, allowing him to write and speak without interference. But when Madero proved popular with the people, calling for "No Reelection," Diaz ordered the outspoken reformer put in jail until after the election. When the election was held, Diaz allowed almost no opposition. The official vote count gave the aged president more than 1 million votes, while Madero received only 200.

But Madero did not intend to allow Diaz to continue to keep Mexico under his personal control. After escaping, Madero disguised himself as a railroad worker, "with a straw sombrero pulled low on his head and a red bandanna concealing [his] pear-shaped beard,"[16] and hid in the baggage car of a northbound train to San Antonio, Texas, where he could meet with fellow members of the Anti-Reelecion Party and work out a plan of protest.

Stepping outside of a political process he considered corrupt, Madero decided to turn to revolution. By October 25, he issued a statement called the Plan de San Luis Potosi. The plan called for Mexican democracy, the right of workers to unionize, and agrarian reform. The document was a manifesto of revolutionary ideas and served as a "declaration of war on the Diaz government."[17] The small-framed, undersized Madero also declared himself the provisional president of Mexico. He called for the Mexican people to take up arms, and his paper plan gave the time and date for a unified uprising against Diaz—6 P.M., November 20, a Sunday.

As the day of rebellion approached, Madero and his immediate group of followers prepared to take to the field as armed revolutionaries.

Madero was hardly the type of leader designed for field campaigns and military campaigns. He was distinctly unfamiliar with military tactics, but he did take a serious stab at it. With a bit of irony, Madero established his headquarters in a hotel in San Antonio. (Wanting to look the part of a Mexican field revolutionary, Madero ordered a pair of yellow leather riding boots from a Texas shoe store.) On the night of November 19, he and his men slipped back across the border at Eagle Pass, but things did not go well on the first night of Madero's revolution.

## Francisco Madero

Known as the "Apostle of Democracy," Francisco Madero initiated the Mexican Revolution but did not live to see it come to fruition.

Born in 1873, Madero came from a family of wealthy landowners in northern Mexico. The Maderos were also diversified; they branched into oil, finance, and the like. On the whole, one can say that the Maderos were very unlikely, as a family, to start any type of a revolution. But there is always one different apple in the bunch, and Francisco Madero filled the bill.

During the decade of 1900–1910, Madero became a vegetarian, an ascetic, a spiritualist, and a reformer. He was convinced that the plight of the Mexican people was too much to bear. Studies conducted at the time indicated that the vast majority of the nation's wealth was held by about 1 percent of the population, and that much of even that money was in the hands of foreigners: British, American, and German financial concerns. President Porfirio Diaz and his admin-

istration lived well in Mexico City, but the people as a whole were desperate.

Madero ran for president against Diaz in 1910. When it appeared that the challenger might win, Diaz had Madero jailed and sent out thousands of militiamen to harass the voters. Diaz won the crooked election of 1910, but his actions brought upon him the anger and disgust of the public, which was finally and utterly weary of the long Diaz rule.

A popular revolution began that autumn, which was the one-hundredth anniversary of Mexican independence from Spain. Although Madero was the best-known leader, the movement took on a wild and uncoordinated aspect; dozens of militia and bandit groups roamed Mexico, each one giving its allegiance to the local strongman. Madero and his associates besieged Ciudad Juarez (held by the Diaz forces) while Americans watched from the tops of railroad cars on the other side of the Rio Grande River. The siege was hard-fought, but Madero and

His plan was to meet with one of his uncles, who had promised five hundred to eight hundred recruits for the revolution. With such a force, Madero intended to ride on to the border city of Ciudad Porfirio Diaz, seize it, then use the city's customs revenues to begin financing his revolution. However, the night of the 19th was pitch black and extremely cold. Madero and his small party of supporters became lost in the deserts of Texas, where they huddled against the cold until dawn on the 20th. They waited throughout the day, the minutes ticking toward the designated time of 6 P.M. Only late

his men won: Diaz resigned and left, and the way was paved for a new government.

In 1911, Madero won the first truly free presidential election Mexico had ever seen. He took a four-day-long train ride to Mexico City, greeted everywhere with cries of "Viva Madero! Viva Mexico!" A new day was at hand.

Once in office, Madero seemed unable to capitalize on the goodwill he had earned. He remained a deeply humane, conscientious person, but the interests and ideas of his wealthy family began to wear on him. Try as he might, Madero was not a genuine social revolutionary; he believed in law and order as much as he believed in revolutionary justice. Therefore, three guerrilla groups rose against him: the Zapatistas in the south, the Pancho Villa group in the north, and the Carranza group in the northeastern part of Mexico. Surprisingly, it was none of these three, but rather a fourth, General Huerta, who brought about Madero's downfall.

In the late winter of 1913, United States Ambassador Henry Wilson worked behind the scenes to help Huerta, who, as a tough veteran of many fights, was seen as the new potential strongman. Huerta carried out a ten-day battle for Mexico City itself, and upon success, he jailed both Madero and his vice president. A few days later, the two men were shot and killed while they were transferred from one jail to another. All the appeals that had gone out from prominent Mexicans to ask other nations, including the United States, to save Madero's life, had gone unanswered.

Madero's life and career were full of tragedy. A man of deep feeling and of great compassion, he was imprisoned by the ideas of the social class in which he grew up. If he had had the time to learn some new ways, he might have become a great Mexican leader, along the lines of Benito Juarez. Instead he is remembered as the man who launched the Revolution of 1910 and was unable to grow along with it.

## Celebrating the Centennial of a Revolution

September 16, 1910, was a date to celebrate in Mexican history. It was on that morning that Father Hidalgo, the father of Mexico's first revolution, signaled the uprising by ringing a church bell in the town of Dolores. A century later, during the last days of the rule of President Diaz, the people of Mexico witnessed a lavish celebration to mark the centennial event. It was a celebration Diaz intended everyone to remember.

Official guests gathered from around the world, representing their governments in a show of support to Diaz, who was also celebrating his 80th birthday that year. The government had spent 20 million pesos, an amount greater than the entire Mexican education budget, on elaborate ceremonies, performances, and cultural programs, all designed to honor both Mexico and Diaz.

Mexico City was decked out in all its finery, and lights were strung around the city to illuminate the centennial night sky. Special decorations festooned the city's churches and balconies, and rooftops were thick with flower arrangements. There was music everywhere, as "wooden drums throbbed, clay flutes trilled and conch shell trumpets blared."* Parades of celebrants marched down city streets, and elaborate dinners offered toasts to such 1810 heroes as Father Hidalgo and Father Morelos. Guests were treated to a host of public activities and extravagances:

> Operas were performed under a glass curtain designed by Tiffany. Plays in

French were attended by all. At one ball alone, 20 carloads of imported French champagne were consumed. With only European waiters (or European look-alikes), no one would be reminded that Mexico was the land of Moctezuma rather than Cortes. In what has been called surreal illogic, Diaz arranged for a costly exhibit of Spanish art in a building especially constructed for the purpose as part of the independence celebrations.**

The celebrations went on for a month. The night sky even offered its own tribute to Diaz, as Halley's Comet streaked across the heavens. Some, especially the peasants, however, saw the comet as a bad sign, an ill omen. Conspicuously absent from the streets of Mexico City, however, were the poor and displaced peasants. Diaz had ordered such residents of the city rounded up and removed so they could not detract from the spirit of the celebrations.

In the midst of all the gaiety of the centennial observations that fall, all designed to celebrate Mexico's glorious revolution of the past, no one could imagine that President Diaz, the public figure on historical display, would be removed from power within eight months, a victim of a new uprising—the Mexican Revolution of 1910.

* Quoted in Johnson, *Heroic Mexico*, p. 1.
** Quoted in Foster, *Brief History*, p. 154.

in the afternoon did Madero's uncle finally reach the weary group. But he did not bring hundreds of recruits; he brought only four. With a unit of Diaz soldiers on their trail, Madero, disappointed at the less-than-successful day of revolution, went back to the safety of San Antonio.

Elsewhere, revolutionary outbreaks were taking place. These early uprisings were scattered and uncoordinated, but even as Madero failed to reach his native Mexico, local guerrilla leaders, including a former cattle rustler who went by the name of Pancho Villa, were on the move. Revolutionaries from every social and political group appeared to be giving support to Madero's call for action against Diaz:

> Citizens of all kinds joined the Revolution: barefoot Indians in serapes and middle-class shopkeepers in business suits; ranchers with high-crowned sombreros and old bandits with bandoliers strapped across their chests; reformers like Madero who merely wanted to restore democracy and radicals who wanted to sweep away the old order altogether. In background, education, occupation, income and social class, and even in their goals, they were as heterogeneous a group as ever took up arms. But they were united against Diaz and in the belief that Mexico was due for change and emergence into the modern world.[18]

Although the revolutionaries had no organized plan of action, were poorly trained, and had little money to pay for guns, food, horses, or anything else, they were able to engage in a brutal and successful guerrilla war against Diaz's army. Rampaging insurrectionists burned and looted with regularity. If a state soldier was captured, he was usually executed. The Mexican army met with strong resistance largely in the northern border province of Chihuahua, where Pancho Villa and a former mule skinner, Pascual Orozco Jr., were active, and the southern state of Morelos. There, Indian villagers rallied behind an insurrectionist, Emiliano Zapata, who declared his loyalty to Madero. Zapata, a young Indian rancher, deeply hated the land grabs of the *hacendados* against Indian lands. Zapata and his force of nearly 1,000 men managed to capture a local garrison, dynamited trains, burned haciendas, and occupied whole towns with little resistance from Diaz's forces. As such revolutionists gained success, more

## Pancho Villa

Some saw him as a new Robin Hood; others believed him to be a murdering scoundrel. Pancho Villa has never lacked admirers or detractors, and the truth about his life is sometimes difficult to ascertain.

Born in the northern state of Durango, Mexico, his birth name was Doroteo Arango and he was the son of a family of sharecroppers. He wounded the local hacienda owner while defending one of his sisters' honor, and he had to flee to the mountains where he became a bandit. When his leader, Francisco Villa, was killed, young Arango took the name Pancho Villa to persuade the other band members to follow him. Villa soon became one of the most notorious bandits of northern Mexico.

The Mexican Revolution of 1910 changed Villa's life. Converted to social democratic ideals by Abraham Gonzalez, Villa became a leading member of the *maderistas* (those who followed Francisco Madero) forces in northern Mexico. Villa first met Madero in February 1911 and was deeply impressed by the older man's vision and ideals. Villa became one of the important lieutenants in Madero's army and he helped bring about the capture of Ciudad Juarez on the Rio Grande in May that year. The aged dictator Porfirio Diaz saw the handwriting on the wall, resigned the presidency, and left the country. Mexico now had a chance for a new government, the first one in almost 40 years.

Unfortunately, the Madero government was soon beleaguered by two counterrevolutionary movements, one from the right and another from the left. Villa fought on courageously, but he was hampered by his own intense rivalry with General Victoriano Huerta. The two men hated one another; Villa often lampooned Huerta for his addiction to drink, a problem from which Villa himself never suffered.

In 1913, Huerta overthrew Madero and became the new president of Mexico. Villa and a handful of other northern leaders started their own revolutionary movement. Villa led the northern division, which was equipped with artillery, the use of railroads, and even a few airplanes. His forces won three important engagements and helped bring down Huerta, who resigned in 1914 (coincidentally in the same summer that the First World War began). Villa then became the civil governor of the state of Chihuahua, where he campaigned for the creation of many new schools.

Villa met Emiliano Zapata, leader of the southern revolutionary forces, in Mexico City toward the end of 1914. This historic meeting (as symbolic as that between Garibaldi and King Victor Emmanuel in 1860) did not have notable results; Villa soon became embroiled in a new campaign against the government of President Venustiano Carranza.

By now, Villa had fought virtually every aspect of the Mexican government, but he added a new enemy: the United States. In March 1916, a group of Villa's men crossed the border and killed 18 Americans in Columbus, New Mexico. The reasons for the attack and the question of whether Villa was directly involved have never been fully resolved. But the U.S. reaction was swift and sure. American president Wilson sent General John "Black Jack" Pershing on a punitive expedition into northern Mexico. Pershing (who later was commander-in-chief of all American forces in Europe) spent months chasing Villa but never caught him. The American expedition won some applause in its homeland, but Mexicans were infuriated that the "gringos" had once again invaded Mexican soil and threatened her sovereignty.

Villa's major nemesis was Alvaro Obregon, a former schoolteacher who was as good a fighter as Villa himself. Obregon over-

Pancho Villa (center) and some of his Villistas pose for a photograph, taken around 1909.

threw Carranza in 1920, bringing ten years of revolution and civil war to an end. As part of the peace agreement, Villa received a hacienda and an annual pension.

Villa and three of his friends were shot dead in Parral, Chihuahua, in 1923 when gunmen opened fire on their automobile. Villa was mourned by many northern Mexicans who saw him as the best example of the revolutionary spirit and of social democratic ideals. Southern Mexicans remained cool toward him, and United States citizens maintain their negative view of Villa to this day. He was a complicated man, to be sure, and his image has yet to be rehabilitated.

and more men and women went to these free-roaming armies, their numbers swelling to perhaps 20,000 by April 1911.

## A SUCCESSFUL REVOLUTION

The spring of 1911 yielded extraordinary results for the revolutionaries. By February, Madero entered Mexico and joined with the forces of Orozco and Villa. Revolutionary armies sprang up in additional Mexican states and, by May 8, Orozco and Villa captured their first significant city—Ciudad Juarez. Federal forces began to melt away in the face of greater numbers of revolutionaries. By late May, facing opposition on nearly every front, Diaz resigned from his office and went into exile in Paris.

On his way to the coastal city of Veracruz, Diaz is said to have noted bitterly, "Madero has unleashed a tiger. Now let's see if he can control it."[19] Once onboard the ship bound for Europe, the discredited Diaz spoke to General Victoriano Huerta, the Indian commander of the guard train that had delivered him to Veracruz, assuring him, "Now they will be convinced, by hard experience, that the only way to govern the country well is the way I did it."[20] Although Diaz did not realize it at the time, he was offering political advice to a man who would himself one day be president of Mexico.

On the morning of June 7, 1911, Mexico City, crowded with visitors waiting for Madero's triumphal arrival, experienced an earthquake that killed hundreds of people and "cracked walls and shattered the train platform on which [Madero] was to alight."[21] Nevertheless, that afternoon, the victorious instigator of the Mexican Revolution of 1910 rode into Mexico City a hero. Some took the earthquake as a bad omen for Madero, yet that day, 200,000 people gathered in the capital streets, excitedly shouting, "Long Live Madero" and "Death to Diaz."

Despite the enthusiastic crowds in the capital city, Madero's presidency would be plagued with problems. Fighting continued in some of the rural regions of Mexico, since not all the revolutionary leaders were satisfied with Madero. Naively, the new president believed that liberation was all Mexico needed to put the country on a better course. He did little to actively solve the country's problems. By disbanding his revolutionary army, Madero left himself vulnerable to counterrevolutionaries. He made additional mistakes, including appointing his own family members to important political offices and making contracts with others. Such moves encouraged critics to accuse him of favoritism and corruption.

Holding office for only 16 months, Madero faced three major revolts and a dozen minor uprisings against his government. In towns across the country, mobs of peasants, workers, and counter-revolutionaries "sacked stores, freed prisoners from municipal jails, burned local archives ... and toppled despised municipal officials."[22] One significant threat was unsuccessfully led by a nephew of former president Diaz, Felix Diaz, who was eventually captured and thrown into a penitentiary in Mexico City. Many of the uprisings were centered in the northern provinces, a constant hotbed of revolution and counterrevolution. Madero assigned General Huerta to combat those who challenged his presidency.

Huerta was a "bullet-headed [mestizo] Indian with weak eyes and a rumbling bass voice"[23] who was known for his hard drinking. He also operated several gambling saloons and made personal profit from the army by installing his sons as suppliers of guns and uniforms. Madero did not like Huerta personally, but the mestizo general could fight. By September 1912, he had won a half dozen victories against such opponents as Pascual Orozco, an earlier ally of Madero's who had turned against him after the ousting of Diaz. While Huerta commanded regular federal troops, he also allowed irregular, guerrilla fighters to join with him, including the *guerrillero* Pancho Villa, then a Madero loyalist. When Villa and Huerta clashed in a dispute over a horse, Huerta ordered Villa executed for insubordination. Only Madero's intervention managed to save Villa.

Through Huerta's successful campaigns, challengers to Madero's government were rounded up and placed in prison in Mexico City. A harsher man than Madero would have ordered their executions as enemies of the state, but Madero could not bring himself to order the deaths of these conservatives. Then, on February 9, 1913, many of these counterrevolutionaries inexplicably escaped from prison, rallied their supporters, and began marching on the National Palace. A panicky Madero again ordered Huerta to put down this direct threat to his presidency. Brutal fighting raged across Mexico for ten days, known as the *Decena Tragica*, as pro- and anti-Madero forces fought hard, and as "the city suffered machine-gun fire and shelling, looting, and panic and hunger. Civilian casualties were in the thousands."[24]

During this bloody urban strife, Huerta turned on Madero and seized the presidency for himself. Just days following the February 1913 coup, Madero and his brother were both shot.

Although the hard-edged, hard-drinking Huerta had earlier agreed to allow for free elections, he soon made it clear he had no intention of leaving the National Palace. While Madero's presidency had not been a popular or successful one to many Mexicans of all classes, the Huerta regime would prove more disappointing and more brutal. The strong-man dissolved Congress and ordered the arrest of many of its members. During the early days of his presidency, he ordered 100 of Madero's supporters killed by

## Victoriano Huerta

Even in a time of anarchists and bandits, Victoriano Huerta stood out as one of the most audacious and ruthless of all political operators. Born in the state of Jalisco in 1854, Huerta was a mestizo who was helped along by people in his village who saw the youth's intelligence and strength. He joined the Mexican army at a young age and worked his way up the ranks to full general in the last years of Porfirio Diaz's regime. Then came the Revolution of 1910, and Huerta happily changed sides to become one of the rebel leaders.

In 1911 and 1912, Huerta bided his time. He had feuds with both Pancho Villa and Emiliano Zapata; both these men hated Huerta on a personal level but also admired his courage and feared him. In 1913, Huerta posed as the savior of the Francisco Madero government; Huerta persuaded Madero that he could reestablish order in Mexico City, and he became commander-in-chief of the national armies.

Huerta and his co-conspirator, Felix Diaz, carried out a sham ten-day fight for control of the capital city. This was done to make it seem as if Huerta was the law-and-order man, when in fact he and Diaz plotted to take the government for themselves. At the height of the disturbance, Huerta arrested President Madero and his vice president and had them assassinated as they were transferred from one prison to another.

There were a few weeks of back-and-forth pretenders to the presidential chair, but Huerta overcame all opponents and was sworn in as the new president of Mexico. The country could hardly have made a worse choice. Huerta was an excellent general and guerrilla fighter, but he knew next to nothing about orderly politics. Within months of his taking office, there were three separate revolts, all directed against Huerta. Pancho Villa led forces in the north; Alvaro Obregon led a revolt in the northwest; and Emiliano machine gun. When the governor of the Chihuahua province proved uncooperative, Huerta had him crushed beneath the wheels of a moving train.

## THE REAL MEXICAN REVOLUTION

Some historians consider the years that followed (1913–1920) as those marking the real Mexican revolution. The changes brought about during the Madero revolution and presidency had not been extensive. The revolution had not been so widespread that it had disrupted the Mexican economy. But for the next seven years, "the revolution intensified and swirled through the country like a

Zapata continued to run the tiny state of Morelas.

If events had been based solely on military ability, then Huerta might well have triumphed. But he bungled his relationship with Woodrow Wilson's administration in Washington D.C., and in the spring of 1914, the United States landed troops and marines in Veracruz. President Wilson's objective, as related to an ambassador, was to "teach the South Americans to elect good men." As appalling as Huerta's methods were, Wilson's motives and approach were almost equally bad, and many Mexicans rallied for a fight with the hated gringos.

Huerta was unable to capitalize on the anti-American sentiment. A hard drinker, Huerta spent more time at two of Mexico City's nightclubs than at the presidential palace, and he was overcome by the number of revolts against him. In 1915, Huerta resigned the presidency and went into exile, first in Spain and then the United States. He also made extensive plans for a political comeback in Mexico. He and co-conspirator Pascual Orozco were arrested in Texas on suspicion of inciting rebellion against a foreign government. Orozco managed to escape, but he was hunted down and killed by an American posse. Deeply depressed over this news, Huerta withered away in his cell at Fort Bliss, Texas. He died of cirrhosis of the liver in 1916.

There is no way to rehabilitate the reputation of Huerta; there are too many examples of his ruthlessness and cruelty. But one major biographer correctly points out that other Mexican politicians—Santa Anna for example—never suffered the same calumny for their crimes as did Huerta. Perhaps he was no worse than his times, but even that is saying a lot.

tornado."[25] Much about Mexico's economy, as well as its social structure, would be permanently altered by the political clashes that unfolded during these crucial years in Mexico's history.

Some of the most colorful names of the revolution came into greater play during these years, including Pancho Villa, Emiliano

## An American Ambassador Helps Bring Down Madero

While Madero's presidency was probably doomed to failure and brevity from its beginnings, one representative of the United States government, the American ambassador to Mexico, Henry Lane Wilson, played a significant role in helping bring down the increasingly unpopular revolutionary leader.

Wilson, "fifty-three years old ... given to nervous gestures and a quick-paced short-stepped walk,"[*] who parted his toupee down the middle of his forehead, was in Mexico City during the violence of the *Decena Tragica*. Many innocent bystanders were killed and the "rotting bodies of victims accumulated on city streets."[**] In addition, some of the street violence was a threat to the lives of Americans living in the city as well as to their property, compelling Wilson to attempt negotiating a cease-fire. However, for all of Wilson's apparently heart-felt intentions, there were other reasons for his decision to intervene in Mexico's revolutionary affairs.

Ambassador Wilson was an advocate of "dollar diplomacy," a policy which encouraged the spread of American interests abroad by supporting investment of U.S. companies and capital in foreign countries. He had powerful ties to such American businesses and consid-

ered Madero unfriendly to such U.S. firms operating in Mexico. (Madero had supported legislation, for example, calling for his government to tax production of Mexican oil, most of which was American-owned.) Wilson had spoken of Madero as "lunatic," and a man unsuitable for governing Mexico. He once described the Mexican president as "a dreamer, more of a mountebank [charlatan] than a messiah ... a disorganized brain."[***] What the American ambassador had in mind was the establishment of a new government and a president who would be friendly to American business interests, someone like Porfirio Diaz. Wilson saw General Huerta as such a man.

But the president of the United States, William Howard Taft, was opposed to any American intervention in Mexico's internal affairs, and the U.S. State Department refused to sanction Wilson's request to serve as a mediator to negotiate between the Madero loyalists and the street rebels in the Mexican capital. However, Wilson soon took matters into his own hands and opened secret negotiations with both Diaz's son Felix and Victoriana Huerta.

On February 14, Valentine's Day, Wilson took decisive steps. He called for Madero to

Zapata, Alvara Obregon, Plutarco Elias Calles, and Lazaro Cardenas. Like Huerta, and unlike Madero, these men came from the lower reaches of Mexican society. Villa was largely uneducated, having only learned to spell his own name at age 25. He had spent most of his earlier years as a bandido, teaching himself to read during several prison

begin negotiations with the rebels and threatened to call in a contingent of U.S. Marines if Madero refused. That same day, the ambassador met with the ambassadors from Great Britain, Germany, and Spain, and talked them into agreeing that Madero should resign from office. The document they drew up was called the Pact of the Embassy. Wilson then wired the State Department of the decision, stating, "The opinion of the assembled colleagues was unanimous."[+] When the Spanish ambassador delivered the message to Madero, the president angrily refused.

Three days later, Madero's brother, Gustavo, received word of a conspiracy against the president, including a list of conspirators. Gustavo ordered Huerta's arrest and presented the evidence to his brother. After questioning Huerta, President Madero was convinced the general was still loyal to him. Madero then "upbraided his brother in front of the general and personally gave Huerta back his sidearm."[++] The following day, February 18, Huerta forces raided the National Palace and arrested Madero and other government officials. Ambassador Wilson cabled the U.S. State Department of the Huerta coup two hours before it took place.

Wilson's role in the overthrow of Madero continued even after the president's arrest. Huerta and Diaz both met with the ambassador at the U.S. embassy in the capital and the three men created a new Mexican government with Huerta as president. As for Madero, even as President Huerta enjoyed a meal at the U.S. Embassy, the former president was taken to the federal penitentiary by Huerta supporters and executed, shot behind the ear. His brother, Francisco Madero, had already been killed.

Ironically, within weeks of the overthrow of Madero, the United States witnessed a new president of its own. Democrat Woodrow Wilson took office in March and immediately criticized Ambassador Wilson for interfering in Mexico's affairs of state. He also soon took a dim view of General Huerta's rule, considering the Mexican leader as nothing more than a Mexican *bandido* and usurper.

* Quoted in Johnson, *Heroic Mexico*, p. 109.

** Quoted in Gonzales, *Mexican Revolution*, p. 94.

*** Quoted in Johnson, *Heroic Mexico*, p. 110.

+ Ibid., p. 114.

++ Quoted in Gonzales, *Mexican Revolution*, p. 97.

terms. He took up arms against Huerta, as he said, "so that every Mexican child could go to school."[26]

Zapata had remained active in the field as a revolutionary in southern Mexico since the latter days of the Diaz regime. He fought as a revolutionary, he said, since the "majority of Mexicans ... own nothing more than the land they walk on."[27] Both men, one fighting in the north and the other in the south, were concerned about social reform.

## Emiliano Zapata

Emiliano Zapata is the most admired, even adored, hero of the Mexican Revolution. Though his story is complicated, his motivation was essentially simple. Until the day he was murdered, he fought for social justice.

Zapata was born in the small state of Morelos in 1879, the ninth of twelve children. Of mostly Indian blood, the family had a small ranch and was better off than its neighbors, most of whom were tenants and sharecroppers. The Zapata family suffered tragedies of its own: eight of the twelve children died before reaching adulthood. Even though he was the ninth out of twelve, young Emiliano inherited the property when his parents died. He was just fifteen.

In his twenties, Zapata was known as a good horseman, a horse trainer, and some-

thing of a dandy about town: he favored tight-fitting clothes and an enormous sombrero. But in 1909 he was elected president of the village council and in 1911 he married the daughter of a nearby livestock owner; both actions made him quickly into a mature adult. In 1910, the year lodged between these two events, the Mexican Revolution broke out, and there was a need for charismatic men to lead the way in creating a new Mexico.

Zapata and Pancho Villa (far to the north) both created guerrilla groups and helped to bring down the government of Porfirio Diaz. Zapata and Villa then agreed to disband their groups, but changed their minds when they saw that the new Madero government was essentially a middle-class

The others all came from similar, improverished backgrounds: Obregon was a mechanic and small rancher from Sonora; Calles was a poor teacher who never wore shoes until the age of 16; and Cardenas, who had joined the revolution during his teens, was the sole breadwinner of a poverty-stricken family.

Although each of these revolutionary figures fought against the Huerta regime for their own reasons, they all led their followers under a common banner: *"Tierra y libertad!*—Land and liberty!"[28]

revolutionary movement, not one for the peasants and workers. Zapata put together the Plan of Ayala in 1911, designed to foster redistribution of land throughout the nation.

Zapata went on to become general of the Liberation Army of the South. He, Pancho Villa, Obregon, and Carranza all fought against the new dictatorial government of Huerta, established in 1913. Huerta was defeated in 1914 and the fight changed to a new one, with Carranza and Obregon matched against Zapata and Villa. At one point the forces of both Zapata and Villa converged on the capital and occupied it for a brief time. A famous photograph shows Villa in the presidential chair and Zapata on his left. The two men had much in common in attitude, but they did not take to each other. One bright spot of the occupation was that the city people, who had feared a bloodbath, were astonished at the mild and gentle attitude of their conquerors. Zapata even more than Villa genuinely believed in a revolution of peasants and workers, and he did not wish to antagonize the people of Mexico City.

General Obregon defeated Pancho Villa in an epic battle in 1915. This reduced the fight to Zapata against Carranza; the latter tried to defeat Zapata in his native Morelos, but found the people of that area staunchly in favor of their leader. Through treachery and deceit, Carranza had one of his colonels lure Zapata into a meeting during which two men emptied their guns into the Mexican revolutionary. He died on the spot, and his body was brought to the capital of Morelos to demonstrate that the rebel was well and truly dead. Even so, stories soon spread of people seeing Zapata riding an elegant white horse at night.

Zapata did not live to see the fruits of his work, but the long revolution ended in 1920. Carranza was gone, a new president was elected by the people, and some of the basic reforms were enacted. The plight of many people in rural Mexico continued to be a major issue, and whenever issues of land, liberty, and social justice are brought up, one is sure to hear the name of Emiliano Zapata.

These men fought not solely against the illegitimacy of the Huerta presidency, but for a long list of social, agrarian, and political reforms. Of them all, perhaps Zapata was the most selflessly motivated. A strong advocate of Mexican Indians, his men wore distinctive uniforms of white pants and white shirts, the kind typically worn by field peasants. As Zapata raided the larger estates, he took control of the land and distributed it to poor families among his supporters.

Villa was a natural-born fighter. In a newspaper interview, he stated his belief that "God brought me into the world to battle."[29] He had been born Doroteo Arango, but his career as a bandit before the revolution had caused him to change it to "avoid detection by the police."[30] His followers, known as the Division of the North, constantly menaced federal outposts, carrying out hit-and-run raids against military and government positions. His men, numbering in the thousands, regularly plundered federal army transport trains carrying cattle, which he stole, then drove the animals into New Mexico, where he sold them to pay for weapons. In time, Villa's forces carried their own artillery and commandeered a 60-car federal train the northern revolutionaries used as a hospital facility for his wounded troops.

Although most of Villa's 20,000 followers were men, his army also included *soldaderas*, women soldiers, who marched along "slinging a rifle over one shoulder, a child on the other."[31] (In fact, *soldaderas* were a part of nearly every revolutionary force during this period; they were also part of the federal armies, as well.) Often such women also served as laundresses and cooks, preparing meals of beef and tortillas by the thousands. When Zapata's army began to lose too many men through battle deaths, captures, and deportations, he recruited from among the women of Morelos, resulting in some of the most colorful fighting of the revolution:

> In Puente de Ixtla the widows, wives, daughters, sisters of rebels formed their own battalion and revolted "to avenge the dead." Under the command of a husky ex-tortilla maker called La China, they raided wildly through Tetecala district. Some in rags, some in plundered finery, wearing silk stockings and dresses, sandals, straw hats, and gun belts, these women became the terrors of the region.[32]

Alvaro Obregon, a middle-class creole who fought in his native Sonora, came late to the revolution, but would become one of the revolution's greatest generals. He moved in the field with Indians as his followers, fighters early on supplied only with bows and arrows. But as his men carried out successful raids against federal troop and supply trains, their revolutionary arsenal was supplemented by "huge quantities of artillery, guns, ammunition and other stores from federal troops."[33]

Despite the popularity of Obregon and Villa among the common people in the northern provinces, they both served under the leadership of the governor of the state of Coahuila, Venustiano Carranza. While not as popular as such folk heroes as Villa and Zapata, Carranza was still an imposing political figure. Unlike his contemporaries, his family had been wealthy landowners, and the governor "had elegant tastes; he enjoyed good food and travelled in his own private three-carriage train."[34] A strong advocate of the Juarez Constitution of 1857, Carranza, along with Villa and Obregon, became known as the Constitutionalists. (Carranza's father had supported Benito Juarez.) It was predetermined that, once this Mexican triumvirate was successful in bring down Huerta, Carranza would stand for the presidency.

To meet the challenge of these revolutionaries in the field, President Huerta tried to raise an army of 250,000 federal forces and another 50,000 rurales. He also ordered the owners of loyal haciendas to raise their own private armies. However, he never managed to meet even half that quota. He risked further unpopularity by instructing government officials to enlist convicts from their local jails and kidnap recruits at gunpoint. On one occasion, during a bullfight in Mexico City, soldiers grabbed up 700 men and forced them into uniform. The result of such ruthless tactics by Huerta was an army of untrained and disloyal recruits who often deserted, many going over to the side of the revolutionaries.

It was the field success of Pancho Villa that may have proven the most effective against the Huerta regime. As his well-equipped and resolute men moved undetected from one village to another, Huerta's men suffered repeated defeats. Across the northern provinces, chaos reigned as "mines shut down, and the crops went unharvested."[35] The cost of the campaigns against the likes of Villa, Obregon, and others soon began to bankrupt the country. With federal currency losing its value, other entities—including Mexican provinces, private banks, even revolutionary armies—began printing their own currencies. By early 1914, there were at least 25 different forms of paper money in circulation in Mexico, and nearly all of them were worthless. Only the army of Zapata was able to create a valued currency, casting their own coins by melting stolen silver ingots.

By 1914, extreme pressure was coming to bear on Huerta and his unpopular regime. The American president Wilson had already cut off all arms sales to the Huerta government in September 1913. In April 1914, Wilson, who had criticized his ambassador a

## Alvaro Obregon

Like Pancho Villa and Emiliano Zapata, Alvaro Obregon was a leader of revolutionaries. Unlike Villa and Zapata, Obregon also had what it took to be a president of Mexico.

Born in the northwest province of Sonora, Obregon was the youngest of 18 children, born to working-class parents. On his father's side he claimed descent from an Irishman who had been special bodyguard to the last of the Spanish viceroys of Mexico. Obregon's father died when he was very young; his mother proved a constant source of inspiration. After a hard struggle, Obregon prospered as a farmer and was raising chickpeas when the revolution began in 1910. He stayed out of this first phase of the revolution because his children were young. Once there was a new fight to bring down the regime of Victoriano Huerta, Obregon joined the revolutionary ranks with great enthusiasm.

Like other revolutionary chieftains, Obregon was noted for swift decisive action, but unlike his colleagues, Obregon purposely drew advice from all members of his revolutionary band. This use of consensus-based decision making was unique among the Mexican revolutionary leaders. Famed for his extensive memory, Obregon never forgot either a face or the lay of the land in a particular area. These talents were of great use to him in the mountain and desert fighting that occupied much of his career.

In 1913, Obregon joined with Pancho Villa and Emiliano Zapata to fight the new regime of Victoriano Huerta. Obregon was, of all the revolutionary chiefs, most distant from the capital city, but he played a major role in bringing about the ouster of Huerta. Toward the end of 1914, Obregon broke with Pancho Villa and allied himself with Venustiano Carranza, who controlled much of northeast Mexico. Since Obregon held northwest Mexico, Villa was caught between the two of them, and Obregon won a decisive series of engagements in the spring of 1915. He did year earlier for meddling in Mexico's internal affairs, dispatched American gunboats to the port city of Veracruz, where they blockaded the harbor, cutting off Mexico's customs duties, a key income for the Huerta government. The American presence also "interrupted delivery of 200 machine guns and 15 million rounds of ammunition aboard a German vessel."[36] (However, as American Marines occupied the port, it nearly united all of Mexico behind Huerta.)

By early summer, Villa's forces fought a field battle near the northern mining town of Zacatecas, a pitched battle involving

this mainly through his use of modern tactics, complete with machine guns and artillery. By contrast, Villa generally staked everything on mad cavalry charges, which worked against many foes but failed against Obregon. Even so, Obregon's career nearly ended in the battles. His arm was blown off by a grenade, and in agony Obregon tried to kill himself. He failed and lived on.

Obregon then served as the number-one military leader in Carranza's new government. Also, Obregon's northwest section of the Sonoran Desert did not suffer the type of rampages or U.S. military intervention that plagued Pancho Villa's area. Then, in 1919, Obregon turned against his former chief and helped force Carranza out of office. When Carranza died, shot by his own men, Obregon became the new president of Mexico in 1920.

Obregon was as skillful an administrator as a general. He assembled a cabinet of talented individuals and set to work on Mexico's many troubles. As dedicated as he and his team were, they found that Mexico was nearly shattered by ten years of revolution and warfare, and the population had shrunk from about 15 million to 12 million.

Obregon served well during his term, then stepped down; he did not want to repeat the mistakes of former President Porfirio Diaz. But popular acclaim persuaded Obregon to run for the presidency again in 1928. The former general won handily and appeared ready to lead the nation once more. However, shortly before he was to take office, Obregon was shot in the face and killed by a fanatical Roman Catholic who believed Obregon's presidency would be the downfall of the Church in Mexico.

Less known than Pancho Villa or Emiliano Zapata, Obregon was nonetheless one of the most important and successful of the Mexican revolutionaries.

23,000 *Villistas* and half as many *federalis*. There, Villa's victory meant death for 6,000 of Huerta's troops and the capture of nearly 6,000 more. When General Obregon soon followed up this revolutionary victory by capturing Guadalajara, Huerta's days were numbered. By August 12, 1914, Obregon met with federal officials and

## Venustiano Carranza

Born in the northern state of Coahuila in 1859, Venustiano Carranza was an unlikely revolutionary. Unlike Zapata and Villa, both of whom came from the peasantry, Carranza was from a solid, middle-class background. He became a mayor, a state deputy, and then a federal senator from Coahuila, but when he ran for governor in 1909, he lost as a result of interference from the dictator Porfirio Diaz. That was enough to push Carranza into an alliance with Francisco Madero at the beginning of the Revolution of 1910.

From the beginning, Carranza was the most conservative of the major revolutionary leaders. He stayed in the United States during some of the crucial early battles, and, once elected as governor of Coahuila—under the Madero presidency—Carranza built up a separate state military. He wanted to be prepared for the next outbreak of violence, which came, predictably enough, in 1913. When Victoriano Huerta overthrew Madero, Carranza entered into serious negotiations with Huerta, which, if successful, would have made the two men partners. The talks failed due to Huerta's stubbornness, and Carranza became the leader of the second revolution, that of 1913–1915.

Carranza called himself "First Chief" of the constitutionalist group opposing Huerta. Pancho Villa, Alvaro Obregon, and Emiliano Zapata all had reasons to distrust Carranza, but they accepted his leadership during the fight against Huerta, which succeeded in 1914. Carranza then became the unofficial leader of Mexico; he was not actually sworn in and inaugurated until 1917.

In the spring of 1915, Carranza and Obregon allied with each other to oppose Villa and Zapata. Carranza was not much of a military man (he left that to Obregon) but he was a fine organizer and a fierce defender of Mexican sovereignty. Time and again he rebuffed United States demands for concessions in return for American help to the Carranza government.

Villa was defeated in the spring of 1915, and Zapata retreated to his nucleus area around the state of Morelos. Carranza now became the de facto president of Mexico. He secured recognition of his government from the United States, but, determined not to be an American patsy, he also flirted with Kaiser Wilhelm II's German government. Early in 1917, a German diplomat named Zimmermann sent his famous telegram, signed an armistice. Two days later, his men marched into Mexico City. General Huerta had left the city several weeks earlier and was on the German battle cruiser *Dresden* by July 20. He left Mexico, remaining in exile in Spain the rest of his life.

asking Mexico to join the war, fight the United States, and in turn receive the lands which had been taken by the Americans in 1848: New Mexico, Arizona, and Texas. Carranza rejected the offer, but the news of the telegram was enough to push many Americans into support for United States entry into the war against Germany. However obliquely, Carranza had helped to shape the great conflict known as the First World War.

In 1917, under Carranza's direction, the Mexican Congress drafted and approved a new constitution and reinforced that the country would still be governed by the document's provisions. The Constitution of 1917 was more radical than Carranza really wanted, but he had to throw some "bones" to the radicals who had helped him overthrow Huerta and defeat Villa and Zapata. One of the provisions of the constitution was that no one could be reelected to the presidency, so 1920 would be Carranza's last year in office.

In 1920, Carranza promoted a chosen successor, Ignacio Bonillas, in the presidential election. Alvaro Obregon appeared a stronger candidate, however, and Carranza had to flee Mexico City as Obregon's troops appeared from the northwest Sonoran Desert. Carranza's railway train was intercepted and a gunfight ensued. He and a few followers escaped the train, but Carranza died a day or two later (whether he was killed by his own men or committed suicide remains open to question).

Carranza was essentially a middle-class revolutionary with limited goals in mind. He provided an important transition between the lawlessness of Victoriano Huerta and the tough reforms of Alvaro Obregon.

### NO END IN SIGHT FOR THE REVOLUTION

Even with the removal of Huerta from power, the leaders of the revolution were unable to establish a new government by cooperation. As Obregon entered the capital, he ordered federal forces to hold their positions south of Mexico City to hold off advancing Zapatistas moving north from Morelos. Villa was kept out of the city by Carranza, who feared the northern revolutionary as a rival. Governor Carranza withheld coal supplies from Villa, stalling the Chihuahuan general's movements, allowing Obregon to reach Mexico City first. Carranza soon joined Obregon in the city, where the two revolutionaries began establishing a provisional government.

Soon, Zapata and Villa were fighting new enemies—Obregon and Carranza. Zapata and Villa had made a constant practice of handing out land to local peasants after capturing the extensive estates of the wealthy. It was a gesture of social change Carranza did not support. Carranza was driven by a fervor for free elections, for political reforms. Such things were not top priorities for men such as Villa and Zapata. In addition, most of Villa and Zapata's followers were among those displaced by the Mexican government—Indians, peasants, miners, sugar plantation workers, sharecroppers, lumberjacks, railroad laborers, and *vaqueros*, or Mexican cowboys. Most of Carranza's support came from the Mexican middle class. For Villa, however, it was most important that he had the best field army. He had brought about victories which had helped bring down Huerta, and he saw Carranza's supporters as "men who have always slept on soft pillows. How could they ever be friends of the people, who have spent their whole lives in nothing but suffering."[37]

The following October, representatives of the various revolutionary factions and armies sat down together in Mexico City at a meeting called the Convention of Aguascalientes, with the intent of hammering out the selection of a provisional president. (Villa, Zapata, and Carranza did not themselves attend the meeting. As for Villa, his army was closest to the meeting site, "a menacing presence only a short train ride away.")[38]

When the talks made it clear that the delegates would not accept Carranza as the new president, his representatives rejected the ultimate authority of any decisions the convention might reach. At one point, the delegates requested Carranza's resignation as interim president. Carranza sent word to the convention he would do so only if

Zapata and Villa would not be elected and that they disband their armies. The convention then "removed Carranza as first chief and rescinded Villa's military command."[39] Although Carranza refused to accept the decision, Villa did. Villa even boldly suggested that he and Carranza both be executed for the good of the revolution. Of course, Carranza would not agree to this suggestion either.

Furious and frustrated at the lack of progress made during the convention, Villa finally sent his forces into Mexico City, where Villistas began to remove Carranza officials from their offices. The removal of Huerta and his government was beginning to result in chaos and possible anarchy, as the factions of revolution turned on one another. As historian Michael Gonzales writes:

> Villa and Carranza were on a collision course. Villa did not need Obregon's allegiance to win battles, but Carranza certainly did. Obregon hated Villa for nearly executing him on two occasions, while Obregon merely disliked and distrusted Carranza for his underhanded political machinations. Obregon, whose mother came from the Sonoran elite, may have also felt closer social ties with the first chief. Carranza, moreover, could also offer Obregon something Villa could not: control over his home state of Sonora. On November 19, 1914, Obregon announced in the Mexico City press a formal declaration of war against Villa.[40]

## NEW HOSTILITIES ARE OPENED

The year 1915 witnessed a new phase in the Mexican Revolution of 1910. In late November 1914, the American military forces occupying Veracruz were packing up and leaving, but not until they handed over captured weapons caches to the Constitutionalist troops, including:

> 12,000 rifles and carbines, 3,375,000 rounds of ammunition ... artillery, machine guns, 632 rolls of barbed wire, armorers' tables, cars, trucks, shortwave radios, sabers, uniforms, and 1,250 boxes of sodium cyanide (which forms a poison gas when combined with nitric or sulfuric acid). The Constitutionalist commander in Veracruz was Candido Aguilar, Carranza's son-in-law.[41]

With such weaponry reaching the battlefields of Mexico, 1915 was, perhaps, the bloodiest year in Mexican history, at least the bloodiest since the Spanish conquest of the Aztec empire four hundred years earlier.

Most of the fighting during 1915 unfolded between Villa and Obregon, whose Constitutionalist army was fighting for Carranza. Early in the year, Obregon's forces drove Villa out of Mexico City, and chased the northern general's men into the state of Guanajuato. As military fighting became more intense than ever that year, General Obregon used tactics similar to those being implemented simultaneously on European battlefields. During the summer of 1914, Great Britain, France, and Russia had gone to war with Germany, Austria, and the Ottoman Empire. This massive conflict—known later as World War I—included armies living in trenches protected by barbed wire and machine gun emplacements.

Obregon employed those early-twentieth-century methods of fighting. Fighting in defensive positions, Obregon's forces mowed down the advancing armies of Villa, putting their machine guns to deadly use. During two battles fought just days apart in April 1915, Villa lost "at least 6,000 men, a quarter of his army, and possibly more than twice that."[42] During the fighting, Villa was plagued by a shortage of artillery pieces and his shells were largely defective. Hundreds of his officers were captured and rounded up in a corral at Celaya and executed by machine gun, their bodies then doused in gasoline and ignited.

In later fighting outside the city of Leon, Villistas and Carranzistas fought for 40 days, both sides relying on trench works and barbed wire. New weapons such as hand grenades were added to the violence. (An airplane was also used, flying low over the battlefield, but it was shot down by rifle fire.) Villa rallied his forces so extensively they nearly overran Obregon's men. During the fighting, General Obregon was seriously wounded, his right arm destroyed by an exploding shell. Delirious with pain, Obregon even tried to commit suicide, but his handgun was unloaded. Never again would General Obregon seriously threaten the existing Mexican government. As for his arm, the limb was removed in the field by a surgeon and preserved in a jar of alcohol. It was displayed years later in a monument to Obregon erected in Mexico City.

## CARRANZA IN CONTROL

With the threat of Villa reduced, and many of Zapata's men having returned to their lands where they took up farming, Carranza was able to extend his power base as president. President Wilson recognized Carranza as Mexico's legitimate leader, a move that angered Pancho Villa so intensely that he turned on American interests in the region. His men murdered 16 American mining engineers and even crossed over into New Mexico, where they raided the American border town of Columbus, shouting "Death to the gringos!"[43] Here, they killed another 18 innocent victims. Wilson responded to the Villa raid by dispatching American troops under the command of General John J. Pershing. While U.S. forces searched high and low for Villa and his main force, the seasoned Mexican campaigner remained at large.

Having gained the upper hand politically, Carranza called for a constitutional convention in December 1916 to legitimize his government and ratify his election as president. While 200 delegates attended the sessions held in Queretaro, no Villistas or Zapatistas were allowed to participate, and anyone related to Madero by blood was also denied involvement. Four out of every five delegates, in fact, came from the Mexican middle class.

Despite having stacked the political deck, the delegates at the convention went against Carranza's expectations and hammered out a document containing significant social changes. The new constitution's Article 27 gave the Mexican government all rights to the country's natural resources, thus effectively nationalizing them. The document also limited the size of the haciendas, called for land redistribution, and nearly banned all foreign ownership of Mexican properties. Even church properties were to be confiscated by the state. Another portion of the constitution, Article 123, ended all debt peonage of the poor and called for protections for workers. Before the delegates were finished, they legalized collective bargaining for labor unions, created a minimum wage law, introduced education reforms, and limited the hours of the average work week. Freedom of religion was also included, despite the wishes of the long-powerful Catholic Church. When completed, the Constitution of 1917 "provided a legal framework for the government that, though amended, continues to this day."[44] So far-reaching in its political, social, and economic reforms, it would take nearly the next twenty years to fully implement it.

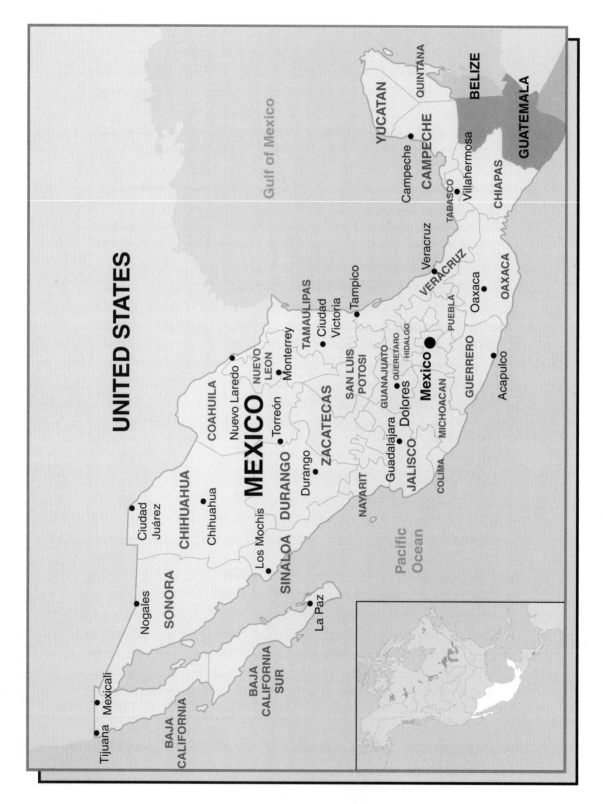

Ironically, just as the government began implementing these significant and revolutionary reforms, much of the revolutionary wind had died out across Mexico. The newly legitimized Carranza led poorly; his administration became quite corrupt and its leadership stagnant. Even Obregon became disenchanted, referring to Carranza as "a great man for little things and a small man for great ones."[45] Carranza ignored most of the reforms delineated by the Constitution of 1917, a policy that drew extensive criticism.

One of the most outspoken critics was the tireless revolutionary leader from Morelos, Emiliano Zapata. In a letter written to Carranza in March 1919, Zapata (through another writer) expressed his strong feelings toward the Mexican leader:

> From the time when you first had the idea of revolution ... and named yourself ... chief of a movement which you maliciously called "constitutionalist" ... you proceeded to turn the struggle to the advantage of yourself and the friends and allies who helped you climb and then shared in the booty—riches, honors, business, banquets, sumptuous fiestas, bachanals of pleasure, orgies of satiation, of ambition, power and of blood. It never occurred to you that the Revolution was fought for the benefit of the great masses, for the legions of the oppressed whom you stirred up with your harangues.... You took justice in your own hands and created a dictatorship which you gave the name of "revolutionary" ... you have given or rented our haciendas to your favorites ... and the people are mocked in their hopes."[46]

Zapata's relentless campaigns against Carranza made him one of the state's most fierce enemies, and Carranza went to great lengths to destroy his influence. A month following the publication of his open letter to Carranza, Zapata and ten of his closest companions were ambushed by government forces outside a hacienda in San Juan Chinameca. As government rifles blasted away at the famous revolutionary leader, "Zapata turned his horse, his pearl-handled pistol still in its holster. He stood in the stirrups with his arms outthrust and then crashed to the ground. His companions fell with him."[47]

Government soldiers then took Zapata's body, his white peasant shirt red with blood, "tied [it] to a horse like a sack of corn"[48] and took it to the municipal palace of a nearby city to be put on display, proof to those who doubted, that the brave and idealistic revolutionary was, in fact, no longer alive. At his death, Zapata was only 39 years old.

Despite the death of Zapata, Carranza's rule was soon brought to an end. Armed opponents sprang up against him, and whole provinces declared their independence. When Carranza failed to support Obregon as a candidate for the presidency, his old ally turned on him and marched his forces into Mexico City in May 1920. Carranza escaped, along with 20 rail cars filled with the state treasury of Mexico. However, he was gunned down on his way to Veracruz, shot in bed by a former ally.

## A DECADE OF REVOLUTION

Ten years had passed since the November 20 march of 1910 that removed President Diaz from power. Mexico was generally tired of revolution and, as Obregon attempted to establish his own government, the few revolutionaries remaining in the field seemed more than ready for compromise and cooperation. Even Pancho Villa accepted an offer from Obregon of a 50,000-acre estate as his personal property in the state of Durango. But Villa's retirement lasted only three years. In July 1923, unidentified gunmen, perhaps former colleagues of Villa who were upset he had abandoned the revolution, ambushed the old guerrilla fighter in his Dodge touring car, one popularly referred to as "La Cucharacha,"—the cockroach. His body was cut down and riddled with 13 bullets. (There was confusion later about the number of gunshots. When photographs of Villa's dead body later began to appear across Mexico, they were captioned "the forty-seven wounds of Pancho Villa.") Even in the confusion of gunfire, Villa was able to draw his own handgun and kill one of his rifle-toting assailants.

Obregon did make serious efforts to implement the tenets of the Constitution of 1917. He returned land to Indians that had been confiscated during the revolution. He appointed former followers of both Villa and Zapata to his government. Those generals who would not cooperate with his government, he usually paid off, as he had done with Villa. Labor unions gained membership and legitimacy. Schools were established. But Obregon had old enemies, and after his reelection to the presidency in 1928, he, too, was gunned down, by a zealous Catholic fanatic. His assassin was an artist as well, and had just finished a sketch of Obregon in a restaurant near Obregon's residence. When the young man tried to hand the picture to the Mexican president, he reached in his jacket pocket, produced a pistol, and shot Obregon in the face.

With Obregon's death, a new era of stability in Mexico followed. A new political party—the Partido Nacional Revolucionario, the National Revolutionary Party—was founded the following year, and its membership included nearly every revolutionary faction in Mexico. In a distinct break from the past, future change was to come to Mexico through peaceful means, not warfare, violence, and assassination.

The Mexican Revolution of 1910 finally ended, having made great strides in political, economic, and social change. It had been a bloody, factional process. All the great fighters, organizers, and political minds—Madero, Carranza, Villa, Zapata, Obregon—had lost their lives, but each had fought for his concept of what a revolution should be about. Perhaps it was their differences that helped fragment the very revolution they fought for. Perhaps it was true, as one Mexican writer later penned, that "All the men of the Mexican Revolution were, without a single exception, inferior to its demands."[49] Each man represented his own followers, formed his own piece of the puzzle of the revolution. In the end, the factionalism of the revolution helped to create not only a new theory of government for Mexico, but perhaps a completely new Mexico; no longer a state torn apart by a diversity of interests and age-old prejudices, but a single nation, its citizens bound by their hope in a future that held great promise.

## TIMELINE

**1519**   Spanish conquistador Hernan Cortes defeats the Aztec empire. He is selected as the first Spanish governor of New Spain (modern-day Mexico).

**1519–1810**   Mexican people live as colonial subjects of the Spanish.

**1810**   Mexicans launch a revolt on September 15 to overthrow their

Spanish colonial masters. After a month, the Mexican rebels control much of central Mexico.

1813    Mexican priest, Father Morelos, marches on city of Acapulco and declares Mexico an independent state.

1820    Spanish forces regain nearly all towns and territory captured by the revolutionaries.

1821    After another revolutionary movement challenges Spanish authority over Mexico, both sides agree to Plan of Iguala, which calls for Mexican independence.

1862
**May 5**   Mexican general, Porfirio Diaz, defeats invading French troops at Puebla. The day becomes a noted Mexican holiday—Cinco de Mayo.

1810
Mexicans launch a revolt on September 15 to overthrow their Spanish colonial masters and after a month's control, much of central Mexico.

1913
Huerta turns on Madero, seizing the presidency. Madero is assassinated. Several key Mexican revolutionary leaders, including Villa, Zapata, Obregon, and Carranza challenge Huerta's regime.

1910
Madero leads revolution against Diaz regime.

1810

1876
General Diaz seizes power over Mexico.

1912
Huerta defeats revolutionary opponents to Madero's presidency.

1824
New Mexican government writes Constitution of 1824, establishing a federal republic of Mexico.

1914
**August**   Obregon leads his troops into Mexico City. Huerta goes into exile in Spain.
**October**   Representatives of various factions and armies meet at the Convention of Aguascalientes to select a new president.

**September** Rebel leaders succeed in ousting the Spanish colonizers, creating an independent Mexico.

**1824** New Mexican government writes Constitution of 1824, establishing a federal republic of Mexico.

**1833–1855** During this period, military dictator Santa Anna rules over Mexico eleven times.

**1855** Santa Anna finally driven from office by Liberal Party. Benito Juarez provides leadership for Mexico.

**1857** New reforms in Mexico lead to Constitution of 1857, which allows greater freedoms of speech and press.

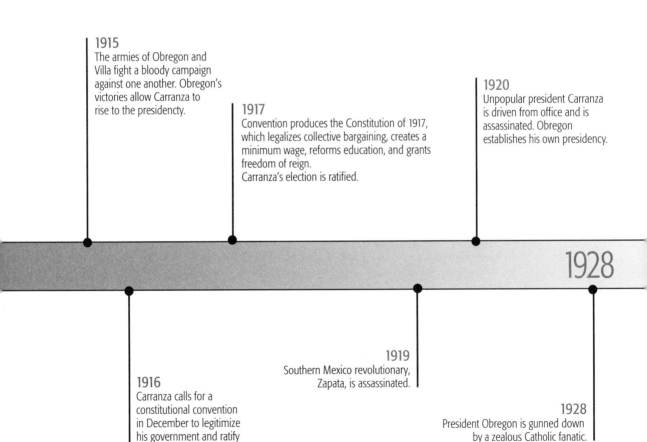

**1915**
The armies of Obregon and Villa fight a bloody campaign against one another. Obregon's victories allow Carranza to rise to the presidency.

**1917**
Convention produces the Constitution of 1917, which legalizes collective bargaining, creates a minimum wage, reforms education, and grants freedom of reign.
Carranza's election is ratified.

**1920**
Unpopular president Carranza is driven from office and is assassinated. Obregon establishes his own presidency.

**1928**

**1916**
Carranza calls for a constitutional convention in December to legitimize his government and ratify his election as president.

**1919**
Southern Mexico revolutionary, Zapata, is assassinated.

**1928**
President Obregon is gunned down by a zealous Catholic fanatic.

**1862**  **May 5**  Mexican general, Porfirio Diaz, defeats invading French troops at Puebla. The day becomes a noted Mexican holiday—Cinco de Mayo.

**1876**  General Diaz seizes power over Mexico.

**1876–1910**  Diaz rules Mexico with an iron fist through his Porfiriato.

**1900**  Foreign investors hold 90 percent of the invorporated value of Mexican industry; Americans hold 70 percent.

**1910**  Madero leads revolution against Diaz regime.

**1911**  Madero enters Mexico City in triumph as Diaz resigns from office and goes into exile in Europe.

**1912**  Huerta defeats revolutionary opponents to Madero's presidency.

**1913**  Huerta turns on Madero, and seizes the presidency for himself. Madero is assassinated after governing Mexico for 16 months. Several key Mexican revolutionary leaders, including Villa, Zapata, Obregon, and Carranza challenge the Huerta regime.

**1913**  U.S. President Woodrow Wilson cuts off all American arms sales to Huerta in September.

**1914**  **August**  Obregon leads his troops into Mexico City. Huerta goes into exile in Spain.

**October**  Representatives of various revolutionary factions and armies sit down in Mexico at the Convention of Aguascalientes, to select a new president.

**1915**  The armies of Obregon and Villa fight a bloody campaign against one another.

With Obregon's victories, Carranza is able to rise to the presidency.

**1916**  Carranza calls for constitutional convention in December to legitimize his government and ratify his election as president.

**1917**  Convention produces the Constitution of 1917, which legalizes collective bargaining, creates a minimum wage, reforms education, and grants freedom of religion. Carranza's election is ratified.

**1919**  Southern Mexico revolutionary, Emiliano Zapata, is assassinated.

**1920**  Unpopular president Carranza is driven from office and is assassinated on his way to Veracruz with the state treasury of Mexico. Obregon establishes his own presidency.

**1923**  Pancho Villa is assassinated.

**1928**  President Obregon is gunned down by a zealous Catholic fanatic.

## SOURCE NOTES

1. Quoted in Lynn V. Foster, *A Brief History of Mexico*. New York: Facts on File, 1997, p. 108.
2. Ibid., p. 110.
3. Quoted in William Weber Johnson, *Heroic Mexico: The Violent Emergence of a Modern Nation*. Garden City, NY: Doubleday, 1968, p. 13.
4. Quoted in Foster, *Brief History*, p. 115.
5. Ibid., p. 117.
6. Ibid., p. 129.
7. Ibid., p. 135.
8. Ibid., p. 134.
9. Quoted in Time-Life Books, *Mexico*. Amsterdam: Time-Life Books, 1985, p. 108.
10. Quoted in Foster, *Brief History*, p. 140.
11. Quoted in John Mason Hart, "The Mexican Revolution, 1910–1920," in Michael C. Meyer and William H. Beezley, *The Oxford History of Mexico*. New York: Oxford University Press, 2000, p. 436.
12. Quoted in Michael J. Gonzales, *The Mexican Revolution, 1910–1940*. Albuquerque: University of New Mexico Press, 2002, p. 13.
13. Quoted in Lesley Byrd Simpson, *Many Mexicos*. Berkeley: University of California Press, 1962, p. 258.
14. Quoted in Gonzales, *Mexican Revolution*, p. 64.
15. Quoted in Foster, *Brief History*, p. 153.
16. Quoted in Johnson, *Heroic Mexico*, p. 46.
17. Ibid.
18. Quoted in Time-Life Books, *Mexico*, p. 109.
19. Ibid., p. 110.
20. Quoted in Johnson, *Heroic Mexico*, p. 69.
21. Quoted in Time-Life Books, *Mexico*, p. 110.
22. Quoted in Gonzales, *Mexican Revolution*, p. 82.
23. Quoted in Johnson, *Heroic Mexico*, p. 69.
24. Quoted in Foster, *Brief History*, p. 159.
25. Ibid., p. 160.
26. Quoted in Martin Luis Guzman. *Memoirs of Pancho Villa*. Translated by V.H. Taylor. Austin: University of Texas Press, 1965, p. 393.
27. Quoted in Michael Meyer and William Sherman. *The Course of Mexican History*, 5th Edition. New York: Oxford University Press, 1995, p. 515.
28. Quoted in Time-Life Books, *Mexico*, p. 111.
29. Ibid.
30. Quoted in Gonzales, *Mexican Revolution*, p. 126.
31. Quoted in Foster, *Brief History*, p. 163.
32. Quoted in John Womack Jr. *Zapata and the Mexican Revolution*. New York: Vintage Books, 1968, p. 170.
33. Quoted in Time-Life Books, *Mexico*, p. 111.
34. Ibid., p. 112.
35. Ibid.
36. Ibid.
37. Quoted in Robert E. Quirk. *The Mexican Revolution, 1914–15: The Convention of Aguascalientes*. New York: Citadel Press, 1963, p. 135.
38. Quoted in Gonzales, *Mexican Revolution*, p. 135.
39. Ibid., p. 137.
40. Ibid., p. 138.
41. Quoted in Meyer, *Mexican History*, p. 453.
42. Quoted in Time-Life Books, *Mexico*, p. 114.
43. Quoted in Foster, *Brief History*, p. 166.
44. Ibid., p. 167.
45. Quoted in Time-Life Books, *Mexico*, p. 114.
46. Quoted in Johnson, *Heroic Mexico*, p. 331–332, and Meyer and Sherman, *Mexican History*, p. 548.
47. Quoted in Johnson, *Heroic Mexico*, p. 336.
48. Ibid.
49. Ibid., p. 338.

## BIBLIOGRAPHY

Time-Life Books, *Mexico*. Amsterdam: Time-Life Books, 1985.

Foster, Lynn V. *A Brief History of Mexico*. New York: Facts on File, 1997.

Gonzales, Michael J. *The Mexican Revolution, 1910–1940*. Albuquerque: University of New Mexico Press, 2002.

Guzman, Martin Luis. *Memoirs of Pancho Villa*. Translated by V.H. Taylor. Austin: University of Texas Press, 1965.

Haynes, Keen. *A History of Latin America*. Boston: Houghton Mifflin, 2000.

Hart, John Mason. "The Mexican Revolution, 1910–1920," in Michael C. Meyer, *The Oxford History of Mexico*. New York: Oxford University Press, 2000.

Johnson, William Weber. *Heroic Mexico: The Violent Emergence of a Modern Nation*. Garden City, NY: Doubleday & Company, 1968.

Knight, Alan. *The Mexican Revolution, 1910–1920*, 2 vols. Cambridge: Cambridge University Press, 1986.

Meyer, Michael and William Sherman. *The Course of Mexican History*, 5th ed. New York: Oxford University Press, 1995.

Quirk, Robert E. *The Mexican Revolution, 1914–15: The Convention of Aguascalientes*. New York: Citadel Press, 1963.

Ross, Stanley. Francisco I. *Madero: Apostle of Mexican Democracy*. New York: Columbia University Press, 1955.

Simpson, Lesley Byrd. *Many Mexicos*. Berkeley: University of California Press, 1962.

Womack, John. *Zapata and the Mexican Revolution*. New York: Vintage Books, 1968.

# 6

# The Russian Revolution

## THE EMPIRE OF CZARS

**Early in the twentieth century, the largest empire in the world, Imperial** Russia, stood on the brink of revolution. For hundreds of years, autocratic, hereditary rulers known as czars (the word derives from the title caesar, the same given to emperors of the later Roman Empire) had led the Russian people with a tightfisted approach to politics and economic growth. Such strong, singular rule held back their giant land and its multi-ethnic population from enjoying the progress taking place in other countries across Europe. Even after making attempts to modernize their empire, the Russian czars always ruled over a state that produced too little economically; whose people enjoyed few freedoms or opportunities; and whose laws, customs, and public practices forced Russia to remain a largely medieval state long after the Middle Ages had come to an end.

Perhaps it was the vastness of Russia that made it such a difficult place to rule and improve, or perhaps it was its diversity. Unlike other European states whose populations consisted of one or two

233

major nationalities, Russia was home to dozens of European and Asian ethnic groups, including Armenians, Balts, Caucasians, Finns, Germans, Jews, Kazakhs, Mongols, Poles, Tatars, Ukrainians, and Uzbeks. These peoples looked different from one another; they dressed differently and practiced different customs and even different religions. While the official religion in Russia was the Russian Orthodox Church, many people were members of other Christian bodies, such as the Roman Catholic Church. There were many Muslims and Buddhists, as well. As an early-twentieth-century minister of finance observed of his unique country: "The outside world should not be surprised that we have an imperfect government, but that we have any government at all. With many nationalities, many languages, and a nation largely illiterate, the marvel is that the country can be held together even by autocratic means."[1]

Although the Russian people had become a widely diverse population by the nineteenth century, many of them had at least one thing in common—they lived hard-scrabble lives as poor peasants. At the beginning of the twentieth century, 90 percent of the population of Russia were peasants, living on the vast rural lands of their underdeveloped country. Many worked on the immense, wheat-producing estates of the wealthy aristocrats, while others farmed tiny plots of land on which they barely produced enough food to eat. Much of the land that was not owned by the wealthy was in the hands of the Russian state or the Russian Orthodox Church.

For hundreds of years, Russian peasants had lived as serfs, obligated to work the land owned by someone else. They were viewed by the aristocracy as little more than animals, creatures almost impossible to mistreat. They were sometimes actually used as beasts of burden, carrying heavy loads along Russia's poor system of roads where carts and wagons often broke down.

One of the great symbols of peasant abuse can be seen in the practice of harnessing serfs together in gangs, with heavy leather straps tied around their torsos, the hapless workers then forced to pull barges and other boats along the Volga River. These gangs were a common sight along the Volga, including gangs of peasant women. To drive such workers along, drivers used a whip called the knout, "a braided leather whip six and a half feet long that could break a person's back with one blow, [which] became a potent symbol of czarist power."[2] When any one member of the hauling gang fell from

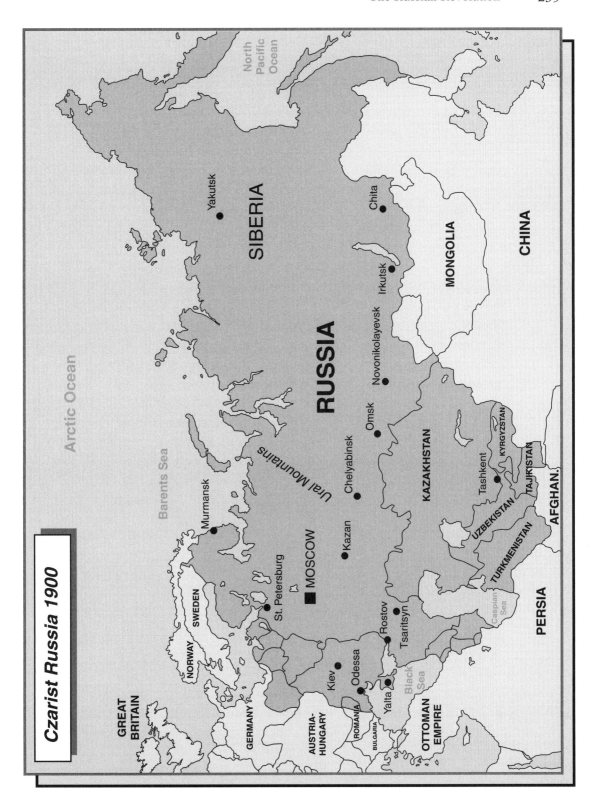

Czarist Russia 1900

exhaustion or illness along the river, he or she was paid a small fee and abandoned.

Serfdom had come to an official end during the spring of 1861, with an emancipation decree signed by Czar Alexander allowing a small proportion of serfs the opportunity to buy their own land. The great majority, however, became even poorer, as there was not enough land to be distributed among them. Typically, these peasants received land allotments equal to half the land they had been cultivating previously as serfs. During that first year of "freedom," Russian peasants organized nearly 500 major riots, protesting their living and work conditions. Many of these riots were put down by the Russian military, resulting in the deaths of hundreds.

Life for many peasants became increasingly burdensome and challenging. As the Russian peasant population continued to rise, the poorer classes experienced higher rents on the property they worked, as well as food shortages, even famines. Taxes increased, such as the national sales tax, which was set especially high on alcohol, "the peasants' principal solace."[3] The tax on liquor became, by 1900, the greatest source of revenue for the Russian government.

There were some successes for peasants after their emancipation from serfdom, however. By 1883, the government formed the Peasants' Land Bank, which provided loan money to peasants, allowing them to buy small plots of property. A significant shift in land ownership occurred, so that, by 1905, two-thirds of all Russian land suitable for farming was owned by peasants. Only one-fifth of the land was owned by the nobility, their holdings having been reduced by one-third during the previous 30 years.

Many peasants remained little more than serfs in practice, however, while others faced a new kind of misery as laborers in the few factories being built in Russia during the late nineteenth century. Such workplaces were as harsh to the peasants as their earlier lives had been, where they were bound to work lands they had not owned. Working conditions were primitive, the equipment unsafe, and the working environments unhealthy.

The typical Russian industrial workday was eleven or twelve hours. More than one of every three factory workers were women who worked the same number of hours as men and were given no time off or special accommodations if they were pregnant.

Many of these Russian factories were located in the larger cities, such as Moscow and St. Petersburg. Those who worked in the industrial centers lived in poor housing in crowded slums, and their long hours of labor produced low wages. Sometimes these urban working communities became strongholds of labor unrest and worker organizations, such as labor unions, as well as more revolutionary groups.

Assisting this expansion in the industrial sector in Russia during the late nineteenth century was the Russian government. Sergei Yulievitch Witte was appointed as minister of finance in 1892, and he worked hard to develop an extensive industrial program for the czar. The former railway administrator raised investment and expansion capital through heavy taxation and by taking out large loans from foreign investors. Many of his taxes were levied on the peasant class. Often, Russian industrialists, railroad builders, and other businessmen received extraordinary cooperation from the Russian government in support of the expansion and growth they delivered to the country's economy.

To some in Russia, this collaboration between the state and capitalism laid the seeds of discontent and distrust. Revolutionaries later blamed these capitalist influences for the poor lot of the peasant class that had developed by the early twentieth century.

## THE SEEDS OF REVOLUTION

But dissatisfied peasants were never going to provide the leadership for any revolutionary movement in Russia. It would fall to another social group, a broad-based collection of younger Russians, many of them educated abroad in other European cities, and conscious of the harshness of Russia's czarist government. This group included many professionals, such as university professors, lawyers, doctors, even businessmen who favored serious change from the old rule pattern of czarist leaders. These dissidents favored the formation of political parties in Russia, as well as free elections and a parliamentary legislature with genuine power. They looked to Western Europe through much of the nineteenth century for the best examples of revolution bringing down kings and other autocratic rulers to be replaced by various elements of democracy and representative government.

While these would-be reformers agreed on their dislike for czarist rule and their disgust with the backwardness of the Russian economy and society, they often did not agree on how to solve such problems. Some wanted gradual reform through peaceful means; others were led by revolutionary thought and popular writings that encouraged the immediate overthrow of the Russian leadership, beginning with the czar.

The ruler of Russia during the late nineteenth and early twentieth centuries was part of a long-standing ruling family, the Romanovs, who had ruled Russia since the early 1600s. Traditionally, the Romanovs were absolute autocrats who believed in the authority given to them by God—the divine right of kings. Many European monarchs ruled by this authority, and the Russian family of czars was no different. Many czars were known for their harsh application of authority, which often made them unpopular with the people. Secret societies were formed to challenge the government. As the number of such dissidents, political radicals, and intense revolutionary thinkers increased dramatically across Russia during the second half of the nineteenth century, they were able to occasionally bring down the czars themselves through assassination. In 1881,

## A History of Harsh Rule in Russia

While Czar Nicholas II was an unpopular Russian leader, he was the descendent of a long line of czars, one stretching back into the mists of 300 years of Russian history. Russia had only been united as a single state for just over a century when the first of the Romanovs came to power. Earlier, Ivan III (1462–1505), Grand Duke of Muscovy, had led a revolt that brought an end to 240 years of rule over Russia by the Tartars, a Mongolian people from central Asia. Known as "Ivan the Terrible" for his harsh rule and uncontrollable temper (he killed his oldest son by striking him during a violent outburst), he was followed by Ivan IV, his grandson.

Ivan IV managed to centralize his government and created a new nobility of government officials and the first Russian assembly, although it was not a representative body. After his death, Russia experienced decades of chaos and civil war. During those years, the Russian government forced its peasants into serfdom in a desperate attempt to control its poor economy and make the Russian nobles happy. By the early 1600s, a grandnephew of Ivan III, Michael Romanov (1613–45) became the Russian leader and established the Romanov dynasty, which continued to rule their empire until 1917.

Czar Alexander II was killed when two terrorists, members of a secret society known as the People's Will, succeeded in tossing a bomb beneath the czar's carriage. At least six previous attempts to kill Alexander II had failed, prompting the confused czar to wonder: "What have these wretches got against me? Why do they hunt me down like a wild beast?"[4] Although Alexander had ordered the end of serfdom twenty years earlier, his rule had become "more rigid ... more repressive."[5]

While Alexander II had never been a true political liberal, he introduced some reforms to Russia. His successor, Alexander III (1881–1894), was intent on breaking the back of all dissident movements within his empire. He cracked down hard on any political agitation, establishing special security measures and relying on a new, secret police force, the Okhrana, to ferret out any and all revolutionary elements. Their methods were extreme:

> Without police permission, a Russian could not become a student; ... individuals could not travel either abroad or within the empire; citizens could be exiled by administrative decrees and their property could be partially confiscated. All sorts of civil disqualifications were forced on suspected revolutionaries.... One police chief, General Zubatov, established the first central photographic and fingerprinting files of revolutionaries.[6]

Such extreme controls placed on the general populace of Russia did not manage to seriously hamper the movements of revolutionary groups. They did, however, cause many people to turn further against the leadership of Alexander III.

## A NEW CZAR

When Alexander died suddenly in the fall of 1894, his son, Nicholas II (1894–1917), succeeded his father's throne. Nicholas soon proved that he was different from his father in several ways, while identical in others. He had been raised by a demanding father, yet Nicholas "loved and revered his father. He wanted to be like his father in everything."[7] However, while Alexander III had been a tough-acting, tough-minded autocrat, Nicholas was "slight, gentle and quiet."[8] The younger czar was shy in public, yet he could be quite charming. He was stubborn as well as secretive. But above all, he did not look forward to ruling an unruly Russia. When his father died, Nicholas wrote that his accession to the throne "was the worst thing that could have happened to me."[9]

As his father lay dying, Nicholas had become engaged to a woman named Alexandra. The two had married a month after the old czar's death. Alexandra was a daughter of the German Grand Duke of Hesse-Darmstadt and the granddaughter of England's Queen Victoria. (Since her mother had died when Alexandra was only six, the young girl was raised in Victoria's household.)

## Czar Nicholas II

The last czar of imperial Russia was a handsome, warm, and caring individual. Those personal qualities were not enough for him to ride out the terrible storm of revolution.

Nicholas succeeded his father, Czar Alexander III, in 1894. Nicholas and his wife Alexandra (who was a granddaughter of Queen Victoria) were an attractive couple, but they were soon tormented by the discovery that their oldest son was a hemophiliac: His blood did not clot properly, and he could easily die from a small wound. Because of the prince's vulnerability, a strange figure named Rasputin came to the fore. Rasputin was able to calm the prince with his words, and stop the bleeding. The uneducated self-ordained monk from Siberia soon gained a degree of control over the royal family.

Even worse, Czar Nicholas became involved in two international upheavals—first, the disastrous Russo-Japanese War of 1904–1905, and then the First World War. The results of the first were bad enough; the results of the second were devastating.

Something like three million young Russians died on the fronts that faced Germany and Austria; the Russians were poorly equipped and many of the soldiers ran out of bullets as well as shoes. Nicholas, who was conservative and traditional by nature, could not think of a political or military solution, and was forced to abdicate his throne while Russia drifted toward complete anarchy.

There had for a long time been a revolutionary aspect to Russian society—revolutionary groups had assassinated Czar Alexander II and had often threatened the life of Czar Alexander III. But by 1917, things were worse, because a new, more severe type of revolution emerged: one led by the Bolsheviks.

Bolsheviks (the word means "majority") had taken over the budding Communist Party by 1905. Led by Vladimir Ilyich Ulyanov (better known as Lenin), the Bolsheviks were certain that an industrial proletariat (members of the working class) would overthrow the czar and then proceed to liberate the

Alexandra embodied the stereotype of the Victorian aristocrat and was described as "blue-eyed, fair-haired, complexioned like a rose and delicate and beautiful in all her features except just possibly her chin, which had rather a determined mold."[10] She was extremely religious, shy, modest, and a born romantic. She had first met Nicholas, four years her elder, during a visit to Petrograd at the age of seventeen. The two had a brief fling, but Nicholas broke it off, convinced she was too beautiful for him. But events drew them back together, and, five years later, they married. Nicholas was

workers of the rest of the industrial world. Necessary first, though, was revolution.

In February 1917, soldiers, bureaucrats, and street people united behind the Social Democrats, led by Alexander Kerensky. He was a careful, middle-of-the-road politician who accepted Czar Nicholas's abdication. The czar and his family were put under house arrest while Kerensky and his followers established the beginning of a constitutional government.

Russian involvement in the First World War dragged Kerensky down as effectively as it had the czar. The Russians continued to take pounding losses on the German and Austrian fronts, and in October 1917 Lenin led the Bolsheviks in a second revolution. This, the "October Revolution," was chronicled by an American observer in *Ten Days that Shook the World*. Kerensky was defeated and had to flee the country. Lenin and the Bolsheviks took over; their red flags were soon seen as the symbol of the "Red" Communist Revolution of 1917.

Czar Nicholas, Czarina Alexandra, and their children were taken to Tobolsk, in eastern Siberia. The few pictures that remain of the royal family from this period show a still-handsome and apparently calm ex-czar using a hatchet to chop wood. He had never been much interested in politics anyway, and had always cared more about home and family than the nation.

This period of relative tranquility was brief. In the fall of 1918, Lenin sent orders east. The former czar, his wife, and the royal children were taken outside and shot. Their bodies were not located or properly identified until much later, and for some time there were a number of imposters, usually claiming to be the Princess Anastasia.

Like Louis XVI of France, Nicholas II of Russia was a good, kind human being. He had the misfortune to live at a time when a new revolutionary movement called for the heads of former leaders; nothing, it was believed, should stand in the way of the workers' revolution.

Russia's Czar Nicholas II inherited a nation on the verge of climactic change. The harsh conditions of the industrial age increased dissatisfaction among workers. A war with Japan and another brewing in Europe would impose further hardships on the Russian people and would ultimately help to end czarist rule.

twenty-six; Alexandra twenty-two. In the first ten years of their marriage, the Romanovs had five children, four girls and a boy: the grand duchesses Tatiana, Marie, Anastasia, and Olga, and the czarevitch, Alexis, the heir to the Romanov throne.

While Nicholas's marriage and family brought him great comfort and happiness, his role as czar proved difficult and exasperating. He understood few things about the general state of Russia, the living conditions of his people, or how to truly lead. He spent much of his time away from court life, living with his family outside of St. Petersburg at the family estate of Tsarskoye Selo. He was often "out of touch with courtier and commoner alike."[11] He never took seriously the liberal goal of allowing a constitutional monarchy, as other European state leaders already had. All through his years of rule, he was autocratic, as his father had been, and relied on the power of his military and his secret police to hold on to his throne. But even then he was often out of touch with the people, relying too often on advice from family and friends as well as on the Russian secret police. It was his remoteness, as well as his refusal to adequately lead his empire directly, that helped open the door to revolutionaries intent on bringing his government to its knees.

Such revolutionaries were becoming significant in number in Russia by the turn of the century. The intellectuals spoke at rallies and in secret meetings against the czar and his government. They went from town to town, recruiting peasants to their various revolutionary causes. This practice led to success in the towns, especially among the urban poor and the working class.

By 1900, two major anticzarist movements were underway in Russia—the Socialist Revolutionaries (the SRs) and the Social Democrats. The SRs preached a revolutionary gospel based on appealing to the peasantry, which constituted the vast majority of Russia's people, and suggested that the key to political reform lay in changing the traditional village structure to that of a commune, where all things were owned in common, individual property rights were abolished, and all decisions within a group of citizens was done through collective and cooperative agreements between all peoples. The SRs were intent on establishing a social state in Russia.

Social Democrats pursued other strategies for Russia's future. These political creatures followed the ideas of Marxism, which, by the 1880s, were becoming known across Russia. Marx had been a German philosopher who lived for much of his life in London, where he studied and wrote, developing a unique theory of socialist thought. Marx believed in the inevitability of historical warfare between the classes. Through his studies he was convinced that the modern world would experience three stages of economic and social development: feudalism, capitalism, and, finally, socialism. Marx's vision of the final class conflict anticipated the rallying of the world's working-class people—those he always referred to as the "proletariat"—against the forces of capitalism. After sweeping capitalism aside, socialism would create the perfect classless society in which the means of production would be in the hands of the workers and everyone would live equally, in harmony, in a socialistic state based on communism.

In such a state, the workers would hold all in common, allowing no private ownership of property. All government would become purposeless, Marx taught, and all political states would eventually "wither away."[12] Although Marx died several years before Nicholas rose to the throne, his ideas laid a groundwork for Russian revolutionaries. Ironically, Marx himself never considered Russia a viable testing ground for his economic theories. He became convinced they did not apply to Russia's political situation, observing on one occasion how "the Russians ... always snatch at the most extreme things the West offers."[13]

## THE ARCHITECT OF REVOLUTION

While Marx's ideas of class warfare and his theory of the workers creating a classless world were riddled with logical holes and misapplications of history, Marxism was taken seriously by many Russian revolutionaries. Doggedly, such revolutionaries became relentless in their pursuit of a worker revolt in Russia, campaigning among the rural peasants and the urban working poor. Among the most influential revolutionaries in Russia was a fiery and brilliant political agitator named Vladimir Ilyich Ulyanov, who became popularly known as Lenin.

Lenin was born in 1870 in the village of Simbirsk (modern-day Ulyanovsk), situated on the banks of the Volga River. His father was a middle-class teacher, and Lenin grew up in a well-to-do, bourgeois home. His older brother proved to be the first revolutionary in the family when he was implicated in a plot to assassinate Czar Alexander and was hanged by the state in 1887. The death of his brother left Lenin bitter and traumatized, pushing him into a secret revolutionary society at the university he attended. At about the same time, Lenin was introduced to one of Marx's books, titled *Das Kapital* ("Capital"), which profoundly impacted Lenin's ideas about economics and politics. (Marx had died five years earlier.)

Through his late teens and his twenties, Lenin worked actively with several revolutionary organizations. His writings were extensive, and he produced a multitude of pamphlets, political tracts, and socialist essays—the beginnings of at least 10 million words he would put to paper during his adult political career. When Lenin married, his wife, Krupskaya, proved as fiery a Marxist as he. She once wrote how her husband was a master of hiding his works and his activities from the state police: "He knew all the through courtyards. He taught us how to write in books with invisible ink, or by the dot method, how to mark secret signs, and thought out all manner of aliases."[14]

Lenin did not have an inspiring appearance. He was a thin man, prematurely balding, with a reddish goatee. His contemporaries saw him as a highly intelligent man, one driven by a singular purpose. His political activities finally caught up with him in 1895, when he was arrested while working on a socialist newspaper. Sent into exile in Siberia, he was released four years later, and left Russia to live on the border of neighboring Estonia, out from under the prying eyes of the czar's secret police. There he worked on the Social Democrats' news-paper, *Iskra* (*The Spark*). It was during this period, the early 1900s, that he took on the name "Lenin," after the Lena River, the longest in Russia.

The paper proved highly popular with several underground revolutionary groups in Russia and elsewhere. It became Lenin's primary tool for converting divergent elements of the Social Democrats to his view of Marxism. Simultaneously, Lenin produced a pamphlet titled *What Is to Be Done?* through which he presented his goals for revolution in Russia. He believed the key to bringing down the Russian government lay in the formation of a core revolutionary group consisting of "a tightly organized body, staffed by dedicated professional revolutionaries who should lead the working class and not be dragged by it."[15] Other revolutions had failed because of a lack of centralized leadership. Lenin, by 1902, had set himself up as the leader of such an organization and assumed to establish the direction of any approaching revolution. He wrote: "Give us an organization of revolutionaries and we shall overturn the whole of Russia."[16] Lenin proved so forceful in his views that he caused a permanent split between two groups operating within the Social Democrat organization: the Bolsheviks (the men of the majority) and the Mensheviks (the men of the minority). The Mensheviks remained intent on working side by side with other revolutionary groups in Russia, while Lenin continued to hammer away in support of a small cadre of professional revolutionaries calling all the shots. Menshevik leaders separated from Lenin in the process.

## THE RUSSO-JAPANESE WAR

Even as the split was taking place within the ranks of the Social Democrats, war broke out between Russia and its Far Eastern neighbor, Japan. The two powers had long disagreed on the ownership of some Asian territory, including Korea, which finally led the Japanese to attack a Russian naval base at Port Arthur in Manchuria. The attack was swift, sudden, and successful, and a complete surprise to Czar Nicholas. An 18-month war followed.

Although the czar had 100,000 Russian troops in the Far East when the war began (one-tenth of his entire army), the Japanese army numbered 330,000. The typical Japanese soldier "was hardy, well-trained, and well-equipped, and he considered it an honor to die for his Emperor."[17] The Russian military proved inept, suffering from poor leadership by its field officers. When Russia's Baltic Sea Fleet reached Asian waters, the Japanese Navy destroyed it in the Battle of Tsushima Straits on May 27, 1905. This Japanese victory brought an effective end to the war.

The following autumn, diplomats representing both sides met at Portsmouth, New Hampshire, to negotiate a peace treaty. They were there at the invitation of the American president, Theodore Roosevelt, who had offered to arbitrate negotiations. When the Russians and Japanese finally negotiated an end to the war, the Japanese extracted territorial gains from the czar, including dominance over Manchuria and Sakhalin Island, as well as the right to maintain "a zone of influence" over Korea.[18] The defeat was

## Georgi Appollonovich Gapon

Born in 1870, Georgi Gapon grew up in Russia at a time of increasing resentment and repression. The czarist government employed secret police to put down incipient revolutionary movements, yet those movements grew in strength even though their major efforts were thwarted.

By 1904, Gapon, now a Russian Orthodox priest, had become the leader of a workers' association in St. Petersburg. Surprisingly, Gapon actually had the assistance of the city police; they believed that with a priest in charge, this movement would not endanger the state. Then came the Russo-Japanese War.

In 1904, Imperial Japan carried out a preemptive strike (or what might be called a sucker punch) against the Russians at Port Arthur on Russia's east coast. This attack seemed like folly since Russia was so much larger in size and industrial strength, but the Japanese had chosen their moment well. Czar Nicholas II had no choice but to enter the Russo-Japanese War, even though he was aware that most of his nation's military and industrial strength was located on its western rather than eastern borders.

The war swiftly became a disaster. Russia struggled under the immense price (in blood and treasure) of fighting this far-away war, while workers and peasants continued to suffer at home. Seeing how desperate the situation had become, Father Gapon organized a major petition to the czar, signed by thousands of Russians. They asked for redress of grievances and a new form of constitutional government. At the same time, there was no bitterness expressed against the czar, since Russian tradition had long embraced the idea that counselors and ministers might be humiliating for Nicholas, and the Russian people turned against him even more.

## BLOODY SUNDAY

During this war, events at home were setting a new course for the Russian revolutionary movement and the future of Czar Nicholas's rule. As 1905 opened, the city of St. Petersburg was in the throes of a general strike. Additional demonstrations were taking place in other parts of Russia, as well. Dissatisfaction seemed everywhere, and nearly all of it was aimed at Czar Nicholas. While the upper classes and the middle-class bourgeoisie were restless as usual, the workers were extremely miserable. They continued to suffer in harsh working environments and primitive living conditions. Czar

evil, but the czar himself was the father of his people. Following this belief, Father Gapon led thousands of Russians into the streets of St. Petersburg, headed for the Winter Palace on January 22, 1905, carrying signs that said "God save the czar."

Alerted to the situation, Czar Nicholas and the royal family were out of the city, safe in the countryside. The czar left orders that his troops should fire if the crowd appeared to threaten the royal residence. Even though the protestors carried the czar-friendly signs, the soldiers opened fire and hundreds of men and women were killed. This terrible day, known ever since as "Bloody Sunday," was the beginning of the Revolution of 1905 in Russia.

Father Gapon escaped the slaughter of Bloody Sunday and went into exile in neighboring Finland. He was used as a symbol by the Russian revolutionaries of 1905, who won their cause through a series of strikes and battles with police. By the end of 1905, Czar Nicholas had agreed to a new constitution and a legislature (the Duma) to be elected by the people. These were substantial changes, but they did not come quickly enough or in enough force to prevent a second revolution, in 1917.

Father Gapon was murdered by social revolutionaries in Finland in 1906. He ceased to be an important symbol because the demands of 1905 were met, and because the Revolution of 1917 would be led by much more radical men, among them Lenin and Trotksy. Father Gapon's brief time on the world stage served to indicate the brutal and out-of-touch beliefs that governed the czar and his inner council.

Nicholas continued to appear unwilling to improve the lot of the lower classes, and he had taken no steps to release his tight grip on his empire. He continued to live by a maxim he stated when he had ascended the throne more than ten years earlier, in which he had vowed to "maintain the principle of autocracy just as firmly and unflinchingly as it was preserved by my unforgettable dead father."[19]

On January 22, a priest named Father Georgi Gapon organized a peaceful march on the czar's Winter Palace in St. Petersburg. Gapon, a "charismatic Orthodox priest,"[20] was certainly no revolutionary or radical. Over the previous year, he had helped organize the Assembly of Russian Factory Workers in an effort to lure workers away from radical groups. The Russian police had even provided financial support for Father Gapon's program, which had attracted thousands of poor, urban laborers. In an effort to present worker grievances and demands to the czar, Gapon organized the march:

> At the appointed time on January 22, some 200,000 men, women and children gathered on the snowbound streets, carrying ikons and pictures of the Czar, and with Father Gapon at their head converging on the Winter Palace. They sang "God Save the Czar" as they moved along. Gapon carried in his hand their petition for an eight-hour day, a minimum wage of one ruble a day (about fifty cents), no overtime, and a constituent assembly—and this he hoped to hand personally to the Czar while the crowd waited in the snow outside the palace.[21]

In all, 135,000 people had signed the petition. Many in the march, including Father Gapon, were hopeful their meeting with the czar would yield significant results. They did not blame him personally for their problems, but felt he had the power and will to hear them out, then promise to alleviate their suffering. As one worker stated in a speech before his fellow laborers:

> You know why we are going. We are going to the Czar for the Truth. Our life is beyond endurance.... Now we must save Russia from the bureaucrats under whose weight we suffer. They squeeze the sweat and blood out of us. You know our workers' life. We live ten families to the room. Do I speak the truth? And so we go to the Czar. If he is our Czar, if he loves his people he must listen to

us ... We go to him with open hearts. I am going ahead in the first rank and if we fall the second rank will come after us. But it cannot be that he would open fire on us."[22]

The vocal worker was, however, sadly mistaken. On the eve of the planned march, Nicholas took his family from the Winter Palace to Tsarskoye Selo, located several miles outside of the city. It would remain for the military and the city police to deal directly with the mass of hundreds of thousands of demonstrators. Two days before the planned march, 3,000 Russian troops were stationed in St. Petersburg. By January 21, 1905, there were more than 10,000, plus thousands of police, all ready to meet the demonstration head-on.

As the massive group of workers arrived at the Winter Palace, they were met by more than 2,000 troops, including a squadron of Cossacks, their sabers already drawn as a warning. As the demonstrators moved in closer, a military officer shouted at the crowd:

In 1905 working conditions in Russia's factories were at a new low. A young priest named Georgi Gapon sought to take the grievances of the workers to the Czar himself. But when they arrived at the Czar's palace, Gapon and his followers were met by soldiers. Many workers were killed and injured in a massacre that came to be known as "Bloody Sunday."

"Disperse or we'll shoot!" From the crowd, someone shouted a response: "Shoot! We've come in search of the truth."[23] Then, under orders from a Colonel Delsal, the palace guards deliberately opened fire on the crowd. At a distance of less than twenty yards, the crowd faced a withering fire. Panic ensued, screams broke the winter air, and the thronging mass of the working poor witnessed the slaughter as hundreds fell to their deaths. Perhaps as many as 500 were killed and 3,000 wounded in the aftermath of the assault. Among those who witnessed the massacre, perhaps the most vivid memory "was the red blood on the snow."[24] As the crowd dispersed that day, the peaceful event was to forever bear the name of "Bloody Sunday."

The massacre outside the Winter Palace represented the first significant violence between the czar's government and the Russian people in the new twentieth century. Little would be the same afterward. Nearly everyone who had maintained a faith that Czar Nicholas would one day right all of Russia's wrongs lost such hopes. After the massacre at the Winter Palace, Lenin summed up its impact: "The prestige of the Czarist name has been ruined forever."[25]

The revolutionaries, of course, were delighted that the government had played its hand so heavily. They believed the massacre would signal the revolution they had been calling for for years. One revolutionary voice, that of Leon Trotsky, spoke the minds of many Russian socialists: "The Revolution has come! One move of hers has lifted the people over scores of steps up which in times of peace we would have had to drag ourselves with hardship and fatigue."[26]

As for Father Gapon, he escaped death and arrest by leaving Russia and taking up residence in Finland. The peaceful priest soon turned radical revolutionary, blaming Nicholas for the government's heavy-handed response. In a letter he wrote to the czar, he included harsh words: "The innocent blood of workers, their wives and children, lies forever between thee, oh soul destroyer, and the Russian people. Moral connection between thee and them may never more be ... Let all the blood that has to be shed, hangman, fall upon thee and thy kindred!"[27]

## THE REVOLUTION OF 1905

While 1905 would witness extraordinary unrest across Russia throughout the year, the revolution of Lenin and Trotsky did not take place. The czar's initial reaction to the Bloody Sunday massacre was emotional and heartfelt. Writing in his diary, he penned: "January 22, Sunday. A painful day! There have been serious disorders in Petersburg because workmen wanted to come up to the Winter Palace. Troops had to open fire in several places in the city; there were many killed and wounded. God, how painful and sad!"[28] But his official response was issued on March 3 in a declaration reaffirming his rule as autocratic and immovable, and he called on all Russians to give support to his leadership. The people would not prove cooperative.

Strikes, demonstrations, even assassinations followed. Within a week of the massacre, 400,000 workers went out on strike, and the number rose to 2.5 million within months. Such striking workers demanded a constitution for Russia. Organized and unorganized protests and rallies convulsed cities and towns, and the rural poor "went plundering and pillaging and looting the property of their masters."[29] In June, the crew on board the battleship *Potemkin* mutinied, then sailed the czar's ship into the Black Sea, where they bombarded coastal towns. By August, peasants had formed their first political organization, the Peasants' Union. The more radical groups staged demonstrations and riots. The Socialist Revolutionaries carried out planned assassinations. An uncle to Nicholas, the commander of the Moscow military region, was killed. The governor of Moscow was murdered outside the Kremlin compound. Before the end of 1905, 1,500 government officials had been killed.

Also before year's end, the radical elements began forming their first soviets in several of the larger Russian cities. The soviets were "councils of workers' deputies elected to give a central direction" to striking workers.[30] But these soviets soon became accepted as the alternate representatives of the workers in those same cities. One of the most powerful soviets was St. Petersburg's, which included 500 delegates representing a quarter of a million workers. The president of the St. Petersburg soviet was a longtime revolutionary, Leon Trotsky. Trotsky had been a radical since 1898, when, at the age of 19, he was first arrested for socialist agitation. Throughout the seven years leading up to 1905, he spent almost all his time either in prison or in exile in Siberia. While originally allied with Lenin, he had broken away to join the Mensheviks. After the Bloody Sunday massacre, he returned to Russia and became a significant radical voice.

But Trotsky and the Mensheviks did not believe in a significant role for the workers as they planned their next steps toward full-scale revolution. They taught that the bourgeoisie middle class would lead the way. Lenin, of course, did not agree and sought to direct a second revolutionary movement, one in which the workers would be admonished to take up violence against the Russian government. He went to libraries to study tactics to use in street demonstrations and fighting as well as methods used in fighting a guerrilla campaign. At one point he was furious that his worker cells had not taken up arms: "It horrifies me ... to find that there has been talk about bombs for over six months, yet not one has been made.... Form fighting squads at once everywhere."[31] He encouraged the accumulation of a vast assortment of revolutionary weapons, including "rifles, revolvers, bombs, knives, knuckle-dusters, clubs, rags soaked in oil for starting fires, ropes or rope ladders, shovels for building barricades, dynamite cartridges, barbed wire, tacks against cavalry ..."[32]

But just as Lenin and his closest associates arrived in St. Petersburg in November 1905, Czar Nicholas finally began to surrender to the pressure of constant violence and upheaval that had nearly brought his government to a standstill. On October 30, he reluctantly signed the "October Manifesto," a liberal-minded document that appeared to establish a constitutional monarchy in Russia while granting civil rights and other liberties to the Russian people. In addition, there was to be a national legislative assembly, called the Duma, with its representatives elected by the will of the people.

The declaration excited revolutionaries of every stripe as well as moderates. While nearly every other European power had long abandoned the rule of absolute monarchy, Russia, under the leadership of Nicholas, appeared about to turn a significant political corner. With extraordinary support for the czar's manifesto, "workers began to drift back to the factories, the Saint Petersburg soviet was forcibly dissolved by troops, and Trotsky was arrested and ... exiled to Siberia."[33] The Revolution of 1905 seemed to have ended successfully for millions of Russians.

## A PERIOD OF REPRIEVE

For the next 11 years, the Russian people lived in a limited parliamentary democracy. Elections were held during the spring of 1906, as every male, 25 years and older, was allowed to vote. However, only landowners with estates of at least 400 acres were granted the direct vote. The peasants and city dwellers had the indirect vote. This restriction gave the landowners 31 percent of the votes, the peasants 42 percent, and the urbanites just 27 percent. Since most of the radicals with membership in the Socialist Revolutionaries or the Social Democrats were urban, they refused to participate in these early elections. This move allowed the liberals to form the Constitutional

Democratic Party and gain the largest percentage of seats in the Duma.

The reforms promised by Nicholas might have changed Russia forever and allowed its people to bypass wholesale revolution, but it was not to be. Within six months of announcing his "October Manifesto," Nicholas II issued a public statement making it clear that "the Emperor of All Russia has supreme autocratic power. It is ordained by God himself that his authority should be submitted to...."[34] The Duma's powers were to be limited. The czar retained control over the military, the Orthodox Church, and could dissolve the Duma at any time. Such reversals ensured that the political reforms of the czar would be hollow, thus dooming the true nature of the Revolution of 1905.

Despite these disappointments and restrictions, many Russians refused to take up arms again or even strike against the government. The violence of the revolution had frightened many who were unwilling to repeat the experience. Many workers simply could not afford to go out on strike in the name of revolution. While three million workers participated in strikes in 1905, by 1910, fewer than 50,000 walked off their jobs. That same year, membership in revolutionary groups in Russia had dropped to approximately 10,000, perhaps a tenth of its 1905 number.

Czar Nicholas received additional support through the efforts of his prime minister, Pyotr Stolypin, who served in this important government post from June 1906, until September 1911. In an attempt to win the approval and loyalty of the vast number of peasants, Stolypin enacted land reforms that allowed many peasants to establish independent farms, having gained the right to buy and sell property. In his words, such agrarian reforms were the key to his government's "resisting revolution."[35]

The Stolypin program proved successful. By 1916, more than 6 million peasant families owned their own property, a number equal to three out of every four. The following year, when the Bolsheviks tried to rally the rural poor with the slogan, "All Land to the Peasants," the radical tag line seemed a little late in coming. Stolypin became one of Russia's greatest prime ministers, and the czar was able to write in a letter to his mother, "I cannot tell you how much I have come to like and respect this man."[36]

But by 1911, Stolypin's reforms were having some negative

repercussions. His land reforms did nothing for the urban middle class, which began to return to some of its old revolutionary ways. Radical group membership began to increase again, and a government report that year noted how "the strike movement is definitely growing to threatening dimensions, more and more taking on a political coloring."[37] Then, on September 14, 1911, while attending a performance with the czar of Rimsky-Korsakov's *Tsar Saltan* at the Kiev Opera House, Stolypin was gunned down by a radical named Dmitri Bogrov during the program's intermission. Nicholas later wrote about what he saw and heard that night:

## Pyotr Stolypin

Pyotr Stolypin was both the first and the last real prime minister of czarist Russia. However, the Russian adaptation to constitutional monarchy came too little, too late.

Born in Dresden, Germany, Stolypin was a member of the old-line Russian aristocracy—those who were derided by the playwright Chekhov in numerous plays. Stolypin was a country squire in the province of Kovno, and was marshal of the nobility of that province from 1887 until 1902. He therefore was able to witness the Russian nobility at a time when its world was beginning to collapse. But Stolypin was not the type of man to give up; he became one of the last, fierce fighters for Russia's old regime.

Named governor of the province of Grodno in 1902, Stolypin was transferred to a similar post in Saratov, on the Volga River, in 1903. This was a perilous time for the Russian social system; peasant disturbances were almost equaled by worker strikes in the cities, and the country seemed listless, with-

out direction. At this time, Czar Nicholas II allowed himself to be dragged into a fruitless war with Imperial Japan. The two powers seemed so mismatched that people called it the contest between the bear and the fish. But to everyone's surprise, the more technologically advanced Japanese defeated the Russians in battle after battle, with the climactic victory coming in the naval contest at Tshushima Straits. The czarist navy was practically destroyed, and Czar Nicholas had to submit to the Treaty of Portsmouth (New Hampshire), which was mediated by American president Theodore Roosevelt.

Stolypin emerged as one of the few provincial governors able to quell uprisings. Many peasants and workers went on strike toward the end of the Russo-Japanese War, and Stolypin was able to subdue them in his region through massive use of force. When contrasted with the activities of other governors, Stolypin's seemed stellar, and in May 1906, the czar appointed him minister of the

[W]e heard two sounds as if something had been dropped.... Women were shrieking and, directly in front of me in the stalls, Stolypin was standing.... Only then did I notice that he was very pale and that his right hand and uniform were bloodstained. He slowly sank into his chair and began to unbutton his tunic.... People were trying to lynch the assassin."[38]

While Stolypin's replacement was far from incompetent, he was not Stolypin. There were serious attempts to maintain policies, but the revolutionary movement was already afoot. By 1912, strikes

interior. This was followed by his appointment as premier (prime minister) in July of that same year.

Stolypin certainly had a tough row to hoe. Russia had never before had a constitutional government, and this new one, which included the Duma (legislature), had been forced on Czar Nicholas by the revolutionaries of 1905. Stolypin made it clear that he had two goals: law and order first, followed by agricultural reforms. He believed that Russia's greatest weakness was the disparity in land ownership between the noble and peasant classes. Between 1906 and 1911 he worked feverishly to increase the number of peasant landowners.

The reforms met with considerable success. In just six years Stolypin laid the basis for what became a prosperous class of peasant farmers (they would perish under the later regime of Joseph Stalin). Stolypin matched his earnest reforms with ferocious repression; his machine-gun squads and secret police became infamous during his tenure as prime minister.

Czar Nicholas II did not truly wish to be a constitutional monarch; he accepted Stolypin and the Duma as the price he had to pay to keep his throne. However, the czar was not sad when Stolypin was attacked by an assassin in Kiev on September 1, 1911. He died four days later. With him perished the last chance for real reform under the czarist system.

Questions remain: Would Stolypin have taken Russia into the First World War? Might his agricultural reforms have succeeded and thereby prevented a communist revolution? Most of the questions cannot be fully answered, since each imponderable stacks up on the heels of others. We can say, however, that Stolypin was more useful to czarist Russia than the czar himself knew. Without Stolypin, Russia teetered and tottered to the calamities that awaited it: the First World War, the influence of Rasputin, and the twin revolutions of 1917.

were becoming commonplace once again. A half million workers went out on strike before the year's end; within two more years, the number had doubled. That year, 1914, would prove extremely difficult for the czar.

## A CATASTROPHIC WAR

Even after the assassination of Prime Minister Stolypin, Russia enjoyed a few more years of peace and prosperity. But in 1914, the empire of Czar Nicholas II was plunged into a catastrophic war that eventually engulfed the whole of Europe. The war emerged out of the Balkan states, where Russia had sided with several breakaway Slavic states, such as Serbia, against the power of the Ottoman Empire. Russian foreign policy had helped to reduce the power of the Turkish empire while allowing Russia to take control of the sea lanes between the Black Sea and the Mediterranean. When war broke out during the summer of 1914 between Serbia and the Austria-Hungarian empire, following the assassination of Archduke Franz Ferdinand by a Serbian terrorist group, the heir to the Austrian throne, Russia sided with Serbia. Through a diplomatic and military house of cards, all Europe was soon plunged into war. The primary alliances included Germany and Austria-Hungary facing the three-way military agreement between Great Britain, France, and Russia. (Interestingly, Czarina Alexandra had been a German princess, and Nicholas was a cousin to the German emperor, Kaiser Wilhelm II.)

As Russians marched off to war in August 1914 (Germany declared war on Russia officially on August 1), it would prove to be "the last day of peace" for the empire of the czar.[39] But the war also united the Russians as nothing else could. In a symbolic move, the name of the city of St. Petersburg was changed to Petrograd, which sounded considerably less "German." With the war on, Russian revolutionaries toned down their rhetoric, while many people supported the czar and their country in their struggle against the German and Austrian empires

Since the Bolsheviks had opposed Russia's entrance into the European conflict, the radical group soon became the object of scorn by patriotic Russians. During the early days of the conflict, the czar's rule seemed revitalized as many of his subjects focused their attention on other enemies. As one British diplomat observed: "Russia seemed to have been completely transformed.... Instead of provoking a revolution, the war forged a new bond between sovereign and people."[40]

However, the early euphoria and patriotic zeal of the Russians did not last long. The war proved devastating. During the first two and a half years of the conflict, the Russian army racked up more than 5 million casualties, 80 percent of them during the first year of the war alone. The logistical system of the Russian military completely collapsed, leaving Russian troops in the field without adequate equipment, including enough firearms and the ammunition required. The fighting men of Russia went into the field "without boots, without proper clothing, and sometimes even without rifles."[41] Such shortages led one Russian soldier to write home: "We go about in ragged uniforms, and without books. I have to go practically barefoot, just in my socks."[42]

So severe was the shortage of artillery ammunition that some units were rationed to five shells a day. Meanwhile, back home, the Russian people experienced shortages and bread lines, as well as wholesale bread riots and the constant threat of domestic strikes. The czar's government appeared extremely incompetent. Representatives to the Duma, many of whom had supported Russia's entrance into the war, were beginning to turn against the czar by early 1915, the war barely six months old.

By the summer of 1915, the war was proving disastrous for the Russians. Enemy prisoner-of-war facilities held 1.5 million Russian officers and men. The Germans had managed to take control of large tracts of Imperial Russia's territory. Panic seized the Russian people as they began to witness not only obvious shortages, but the return of soldiers from the fighting fronts whose stories spoke of poor leadership, lost battles, and low morale. In addition, Russian refugees, displaced by the war, told countless stories of German victories. In June alone, 80,000 workers went out on strike. At a textile mill in Kostroma, striking workers were attacked by police. Labor unrest in August resulted in the czar's troops firing into worker crowds. By September, 200,000 workers engaged in protest strikes. The revolutionary spirit was winning out over an earlier war enthusiasm that was quickly dying.

Desperate to turn the lackluster Russian war effort around, Czar Nicholas took personal command of the Russian military during the fall of 1915. It was a crucial misstep for the czar, who knew little

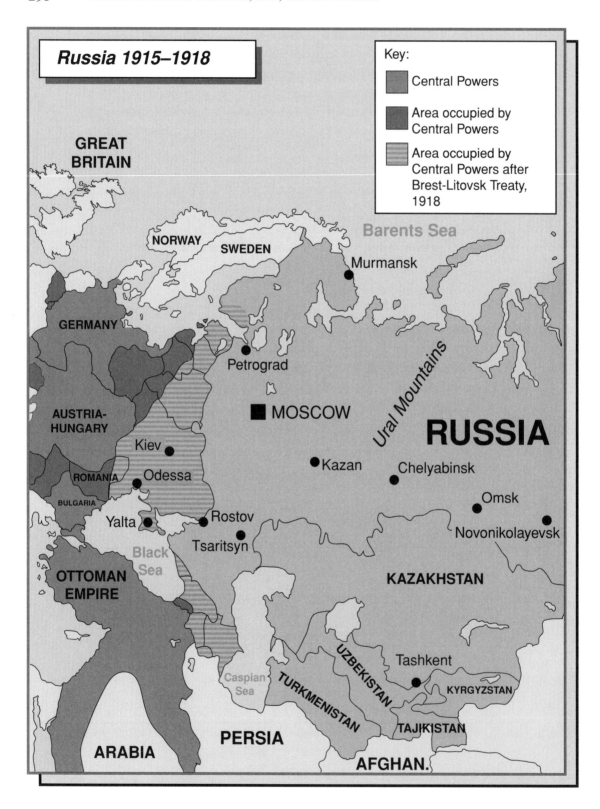

**Russia 1915–1918**

Key:

Central Powers

Area occupied by Central Powers

Area occupied by Central Powers after Brest-Litovsk Treaty, 1918

GREAT BRITAIN

NORWAY

SWEDEN

Barents Sea

Murmansk

GERMANY

Petrograd

■ MOSCOW

Ural Mountains

RUSSIA

AUSTRIA-HUNGARY

Kiev

Kazan

Chelyabinsk

ROMANIA

Odessa

Omsk

BULGARIA

Novonikolayevsk

Yalta

Rostov

Black Sea

Tsaritsyn

KAZAKHSTAN

OTTOMAN EMPIRE

Caspian Sea

TURKMENISTAN

UZBEKISTAN

Tashkent

KYRGYZSTAN

TAJIKISTAN

PERSIA

ARABIA

AFGHAN.

about military strategy or tactics. As director of the war, Nicholas also made a second serious mistake. He placed his wife, Czarina Alexandra, in charge of Russia's domestic affairs. The czarina, even before the war, had become an unpopular figure in Russia. Following the birth of her only son, Alexis, in 1904, the czarina had withdrawn increasingly from public life, rarely appearing at court events. With Germany fighting Russia, her German heritage made her loyalty to Russia suspect to many. Most such concerns were groundless, for Alexandra had lived in Russia as the wife of Nicholas for more than twenty years, and she had shown an "almost fanatical devotion to her adopted homeland."[43]

But another dark cloud hung over the czarina. For years, Alexandra, a deeply religious woman, had sought spiritual direction from a mysterious monk named Grigory Rasputin. Her hemophiliac son, Czarevich Alexis, was weak and sickly, but Rasputin was able to revive him through hypnosis, a technique the czarina interpreted as miraculous healing. Rasputin, in time, held such sway over Alexandra that many observers began to gossip about their relationship. At the center of the controversy was the perception that the czarina was gullible and easily led by a dirty, unwashed monk of dubious motives:

> The hatred surrounding this couple—the pious, German-born princess and the grotesque monk—had developed almost into hysteria in Petrograd, and it possessed the aristocracy quite as much as anybody else.... In Petrograd society the Empress was universally referred to as "The German,"... As for the monk Rasputin, even the most vocal of the politicians and the nobles were finding it difficult to choose words to express their loathing and contempt...Under the protection of the palace he proceeded serenely on his course, dismissing the ministers he did not like, dropping a word to the Czar on how to conduct the war, and using his hypnotic powers to stir up the addlepated, superstitious mind of the Empress to the point where she hardly knew what she was doing any more.[44]

Aristocratic hatred and suspicion of Rasputin became so intense that, on the icy night of December 30, 1916, a conspiracy of young noblemen, as well as members of the Duma, arranged for the murder of the Siberian monk. Rasputin was lured to the private residence of Prince Felix Yusupov in Petrograd. The assassins justified their actions, by the words of one of their members, "so that the Monarchy can be saved."[45]

## THE REVOLUTION OF 1917 BEGINS

Indeed, a new revolution was about to engulf Russia. Rasputin's murder had solved nothing in reality. The war continued to bring serious losses, the Russian military was experiencing extremely low morale, food was scarce, and the cities were beginning to ignite with protests. More strikes took place during the first six weeks of 1917 than had occurred through all of 1916. The Bolsheviks planned a

## Grigory Efimovich Rasputin

Few figures in history conjure up darker, more sinister responses than the strange monk, Grigory Efimovich Rasputin.

Rasputin was raised in the backwoods of Siberia, the son of a coachman and sometime horse thief. He was married, with two daughters and a son. Around 1900, he left his family and became a monk. The theology he developed was an especially strange and suspect one. Rasputin believed one received forgiveness from God only after committing serious sins. He claimed to have the power to save sinners, especially women, but they first had to be "united with him both in soul and body."* Using his personal magnetism, including his hypnotic eyes, Rasputin lured countless women to his bed, poor peasant and aristocrat alike.

There was little about Rasputin's physical appearance that would attract anyone. The historian Harrison Salisbury describes the repulsive, yet mystifying figure:

He was a strong man of medium height with sharp gray eyes which had penetrating qualities. He wore his hair long over his shoulders and looked like a saint or at least a monk. His chestnut hair was heavy ... and greased. His beard was tangled and thick.... He had no table manners. Or rather he had the manners of an animal. He ate with his fingers, plunging his hands into the platters on the table and plucking tasty heads and fillets out of his *ukha* (fish soup).... He had a powerful body odor. The higher the society, the more coarse and vulgar his language.**

He arrived in St. Petersburg in 1903, having recently returned from a pilgrimage to Jerusalem. In the capital, he drew the attention of several religious leaders, including a massive demonstration for January 22 to mark the anniversary of the Father Gapon–led Revolution of 1905, but before they could print the leaflets calling for a street demonstration, Petrograd police had raided the radical group's print shop.

Events finally broke on March 8, 1917, when a group of female workers began demonstrating in the streets of Petrograd against poor living conditions in the city while "calling for bread and peace and singing the 'Marseillaise,' the anthem of the French Revolution."[46] Thousands of workers soon joined, creating a mass of street protests. Over the next two days, more street demonstrations led to violence as protesting workers and revolutionaries from across the city stormed government buildings, including police stations. The District

bishop with connections to the royal family. After a pair of duchesses told the czar and czarina of an early meeting they had had with the strange monk, Rasputin was soon invited to the royal palace on November 1, 1905. Over time, he ingratiated himself to the Russian leaders, becoming a favorite of the czarina.

Rumors of Rasputin's sexual activities both inside the royal palace and out began to circulate. When Rasputin began seducing those inside the royal household, including the czarevich's nurse, Czarina Alexandra refused to listen, claiming such stories were only jealous lies.

Above all his other qualities, Rasputin had one which Czarina Alexandra treasured more than any other—his claim to the power of healing. The Romanovs' son, Alexis, was sickly, a hemophiliac who would bleed at the slightest cut or bruise. More than once, Rasputin claimed to have healed the boy of various ailments. His mesmerizing words did appear to have a calming and potent effect on the czarevitch. As for the czarina, she came to believe only Rasputin could keep her son alive. While it is extremely unlikely that Alexandra and the mystical monk ever had a sexual affair, she remained entirely devoted to him, sewing him silk shirts by her own hand, and referring to him as "my beloved unforgettable teacher, redeemer and mentor! My soul is quiet and I relax only when you, my teacher, are sitting beside me."***

That this unwashed, drunken, peasant monk should have such power over the royal family eventually became more than the Russian aristocracy could stand. A plot developed to assassinate the odd, religious figure.

---

&ast; Quoted in Moorehead, *Russian Revolution*, p. 71.

&ast;&ast; Quoted in Salisbury, *Black Night*, p. 206.

&ast;&ast;&ast; Quoted in Moorehead, *Russian Revolution*, p. 72.

# The Monk Who Would Not Die

Throughout 1916, a conspiracy developed in the city of Petrograd with one goal in mind: To rid Russia of the filthy, yet influential, Siberian monk, Grigory Rasputin. Russian aristocrats despised the peasant "holy man," a commoner who wielded an extraordinary power over the czarina. Russian nobles became so obsessed with him that the murder "of Rasputin [became] a favorite subject in Petrograd drawing rooms."*

The plan to kill Rasputin was to be a simple one. Prince Felix Yusupov was to invite Rasputin to his palace to meet his beautiful wife, Irena, toward whom Rasputin had shown some interest. (Yusupov's wife was actually visiting her parents in the Crimea.) Conspirators were to drive the monk to Yusupov's in a chauffeured automobile. Specially prepared almond and chocolate cakes were to be served at Yusupov's home, laced with the poison potassium cyanide. Rasputin would be served poisoned wine as well. (The conspirators chose poison as their weapon, rather than handguns, since Yusupov's home sat across the street from a police station.) Once Rasputin succumbed to the poison, fellow assassins were to take his body to a local river, tie the corpse up with weights, and sink it into the river. To throw off police later, a call was to be made to one of Rasputin's favorite night clubs, the caller to ask if Rasputin had arrived yet. Although the plan was as simple and straightforward as possible, it involved the collaboration of several conspirators, including members of the military and those in the imperial household.

But the plan did not come off quite as simply. When Rasputin arrived at the prince's palace, Yusupov escorted him to a basement room which had been specially decorated for the assassination, including a "bearskin rug on the floor, armchairs, a labyrinth cupboard full of mirrors on which stood a crucifix."** As the prince entertained the monk, co-conspirators waited upstairs, making noise as though Princess Irena was entertaining female guests. (The conspirators included a phonograph as part of their charade, but had only brought along one record, which forced them to play "Yankee Doodle" over and over.)

Down in the basement, Yusupov sat nervously, trying to entertain the hated monk. At first, Rasputin refused all offers of food or drink, but finally he ate two poisoned cakes and began drinking wine. He did not die immediately. Rasputin began to insist that Yusupov play the guitar and sing for him. The prince performed song after song, but Rasputin remained alive, becoming increasingly drunk. Yusupov finally excused himself, went upstairs, and frantically discussed matters with his co-conspirators. One exasperated conspirator, a member of the Duma named Vladimir Purishkevich, offered to shoot Rasputin with a handgun he had brought along. But Yusupov was determined to kill the monk himself. He took a Browning automatic from a desk drawer, and returned to his victim.

The drunken Rasputin took more wine, then stood to take a closer look at the crucifix Yusupov had put on display in a wall cabinet. His eyes fixed on the cross, the prince moved behind him, gun in hand, and spoke: "You'd far better look at the crucifix and say a prayer."*** With those words, he shot Rasputin. Yusupov's fellow conspirators rushed downstairs at the sound of the gun and the thud of a falling body. As they began removing the body, they discovered that Rasputin, filled with poisoned cakes and wine, and now shot, was still not quite dead. Then, the hated monk opened one eye, struggled to his feet and moved toward Yusupov and the cellar door. The astonished prince shouted for help, since his fellow assassins had left the room. By the time they responded, Rasputin had staggered out the front entrance of the palace into the court, mumbling: "I'll tell it all to the Czarina."+

Before he could reach the street, a second armed conspirator fired repeated shots at Rasputin until the fourth round felled the dying monk. The shots alerted two soldiers passing by, but once they were informed of the victim's identity, they joyously kissed the assassin and helped drag the body back into the palace. Uncertain whether their victim was dead or alive, Yusupov grabbed a two-pound, steel-and-leather billy club and began to beat Rasputin on the head.

The assassins then wrapped and tied Rasputin's body in a blue curtain and drove to a bridge over the Neva River, where they tossed the dying monk. When his body was discovered the following morning, by one account Rasputin had managed to untie the ropes binding his body and had only died after drowning in the river, the police discovering his lungs full of water. While few Russians mourned the death of Rasputin, the czarina was crushed at the news. She had become so reliant on the hypnotic monk and his claim of healing powers, she could not imagine life without him at her side. She wrote in a letter: "I cannot & won't believe He has been killed."++ Still others saw Rasputin's death as a turning point in Russian history. As one monk who despised the excesses of Rasputin's life predicted: "Don't they know that the bullet directed at Rasputin will strike the Czar's family and that with this shot has begun the Revolution?"+++

---

    * Quoted in Salisbury, *Black Nights*, p. 296.

   ** Quoted in Moorehead, *Russian Revolution*, p. 108.

  *** Quoted in Salisbury, *Black Nights*, p. 304.

    + Ibid., p. 305.

   ++ Ibid., p. 308.

 +++ Ibid.

By March of 1917, with working conditions poor and troop morale low, Russia stood on the verge of collapse. Widespread strikes all but shut down the country's economy. A well-organized Bolshevik opposition had formed. Protest marches quickly degraded into violence, and revolution soon followed.

Court building was set ablaze. Perhaps as many as 300,000 workers went out on strike, a figure equivalent to more than one out of every ten of Petrograd's 2.5 million people. The city was soon at a standstill, as "no trams ran. No cabs ran. Not an industrial plant operated. Only the most essential services such as gas, electricity, and water were maintained."[47] By March 10, many districts of Petrograd were under the control of the workers.

Late on March 10, Czar Nicholas, stationed at the Russian army headquarters in Mogilev, sent a telegram to the commandant of the Petrograd garrison, ordering him to use his troops to put down the street demonstrations and strikes. But the czar soon found that most of the troops were sympathetic to the workers and would not fire on street demonstrators. Many, in fact, of the 170,000-man garrison joined with the street radicals. With no military means to quell the events besieging Petrograd, the czar began to lose control of events. Many of his cabinet ministers fled the city in a panic.

Like a house of cards, the czar's leadership began to crumble. Even as Nicholas attempted to return to Petrograd, his train was stopped by striking rail workers, leaving him stranded in the countryside. Party leaders in the Duma stepped in to fill the void of leadership caused by the resignations of Nicholas's ministers, resulting in the formation of an emergency committee on March 12 to restore order to the city. On March 15, this committee was re-formed into a provisional government under the direction of a liberal aristocrat, Prince Georgy Lvov.

Two representatives of the Duma were dispatched to meet with the czar to discuss his abdication. The March 15 meeting was extremely productive, considering that Nicholas had ordered the dismissal of the Duma's representatives the day before. As the political leaders talked, it became clear that the czar was prepared to accept the idea of his resignation. The Duma delegates suggested Nicholas name Czarevitch Alexis as his immediate successor. The czar balked, thinking the 12-year-old Alexis too young and frail, and suggested the throne be handed to his brother, Grand Duke Michael. When Michael refused to accept leadership, Nicholas became the last czar of Russia. With his abdication, "the 1,000-year-old Russian monarchy came to an end."[48] As the representatives of the Duma prepared to leave the czar, one spoke to Nicholas in a voice of emotion: "Your Majesty, if you had done all this earlier, even as late as the last summoning of the Duma, perhaps all that ..." As he stopped himself in midsentence, Nicholas asked innocently, "Do you think it might have been avoided?"[49]

Several days later, the czarevich was informed by his tutor, a Mr. Gibbes, that his father had abdicated and was no longer the leader of Russia. Confused, the boy asked simply, "But who's going to be czar, then?"

The tutor answered as straightforwardly as he could: "I don't know. Perhaps nobody now."[50]

## A NEW REVOLUTION

With little opposition from Nicholas, the monarchy of Russia had suddenly collapsed, then evaporated. The street demonstrations and worker clashes had resulted in 1,500 casualties, with only 200 people killed. As the Bolshevik leader Leon Trotsky later noted, the spring revolution had taken place almost entirely on the streets of Petrograd. In the meantime, the new provisional government tried to get control of Russia's immediate future. The war with Germany and Austria was

## Lenin (Vladimir Ilyich Ulyanov)

Vladimir Ilyich Ulyanov (known more familiarly as Lenin) was born in 1870 and grew up in Simbirsk, Russia. As a young person Lenin was faintly aware of Alexander Kerensky, an older citizen of the same city, whose path would intersect later with his own.

Lenin's older brother was part of an anarchist movement that tried to kill Czar Alexander III. There were many such movements in the 1880s; one of them had succeeded in killing Czar Alexander II in 1881. This older brother was tried and executed, and Lenin committed himself henceforth to a life dedicated to revolutionary principles.

Sometime in the 1890s, Lenin read the works of Karl Marx. Deeply impressed with Marx's vision for the future, Lenin began to add his own thoughts to those of the deceased Marx, making for what was later called Marxist-Leninist theory. Unlike Marx, however, Lenin believed that the great worker's revolution must happen soon. Marx believed that all one had to do was observe the dialectical process in action and that one day the oppressions of the capitalist would naturally produce a revolution by the workers. By contrast, Lenin believed that one had

to work to bring about this revolution—to speed up its timing.

In 1902, Lenin was a prominent member of the socialist convention that debated revolutionary theory. Lenin's group, the Bolsheviks, won the debate and therefore the votes and henceforth considered themselves the majority representative of socialist views. Their opponents became known as the Mensheviks, or "minority."

By the time the First World War began in 1914, Lenin was in neutral Switzerland. He went there to escape the persecution of the czarist police and to write in relative safety. The start of the war seemed a godsend to Lenin, since he believed the suffering of the workers would only intensify, thereby bringing on the great revolution even earlier.

Lenin was half right. The sufferings of average people, particularly in England, France, Germany, Austria, and Russia did intensify, and there was a considerable increase in revolutionary activity. But it came to a boil in none other than Lenin's native Russia, and this he did not expect. Having read Marx, Lenin always believed that it would be the urban workers who would ignite and carry out the revolution; instead, it was begun by some still active, and the provisional leaders were intent on continuing the war effort. But, despite the ease with which this new government had swept aside the monarchy, it was soon challenged by its own political opponents. It became clear that the real power of government lay in the hands of the Petrograd Soviet of Workers' and Soldiers' Deputies.

Russian workers and carried out by millions of illiterate Russian peasants.

Lenin was too practical a person to let this opportunity slip. He made his way to St. Petersburg in the spring of 1917 and found the city and nation run by Kerensky. Lenin let Kerensky dig his own grave by continuing Russian involvement in the World War; by the autumn of 1917, the people were more desperate than ever. Lenin led his Bolsheviks, a few thousand strong, in a takeover of St. Petersburg in the October Revolution of 1917. Kerensky fled the country, and Lenin and fellow socialist Leon Trotsky, his right-hand man, became the two new leaders of Russia.

Lenin took Russia out of the World War by signing the Treaty of Brest-Litovsk with the Germans. The price was high; Russia yielded a great deal of valuable land. But at least the treaty allowed Lenin and Trotsky to begin the serious business of unifying the nation under Bolshevik principles, and to start the transfer of power to the people.

This begs the question: Was Lenin a genuine communist? Did he really want the state to wither away? The answers remain obscure. Faced with civil war by former czarists, with famine in the countryside, and with strikes in the cities, Lenin reacted as fiercely as any czar had: He put the country under martial law, stamped out the rebellions, and brought the urban workers to heel. All this was done in the name of Marxist-Leninist theory.

Lenin also introduced some new economic reforms that seemed to indicate a small slide toward capitalism. He died in Moscow in 1924, uncertain about the future and predicting that his fellow revolutionary Joseph Stalin would become a dangerous new dictator. Much as Lenin's name is revered by many revolutionaries around the world, one can certainly argue that he did a lot of damage, perhaps even paving the way (however unintentionally) for Stalin's brutal regime.

Most of this urban soviet's leaders were revolutionaries, including Mensheviks and SRs. As the new Russian minister of war, Alexander Guchkov, noted: "One can flatly say the provisional government exists only so long as it is permitted by the soviet."[51] Initially, the leaders of the Petrograd soviet were prepared to give their support to the provisional government. In addition, Bolsheviks also supported the provisional government's power, including such important radicals as Joseph Stalin. But Lenin rejected the leadership of the rovisional authorities, arguing, as he had in 1905, that Russia's workers should lead the country.

When the street demonstrations of March 1917 broke out across Petrograd, Lenin was in exile in Switzerland. In the weeks that followed the abdication of the czar, Lenin, as well as other exiled revolutionaries, were desperate to return to their homeland. Traveling through German-held territory might have proven difficult for these Russian radicals, except that the German government had been supporting such anticzarist elements during the war and wanted them to play a role in bringing down the Russian government. German officials provided free passage.

On April 9, Lenin and some compatriots boarded a special car on a train bound for Petrograd and traveled "in a locked and guarded carriage on a train specially provided for them by German authorities."[52] Bound for Russia, a colleague convinced Lenin to buy a new pair of shoes before reaching Petrograd, so he could better look the part of a leader. Lenin arrived in Petrograd on April 16. During the secret train trip home, Lenin faced personal concerns about his reception in Petrograd, thinking he and his fellow radicals might be arrested by Russian authorities. But, upon arriving in Petrograd's Finland station, he was "thronged with supporters who greeted Lenin like a returning hero," and he was carried from the train platform on the shoulders of his supporters while a band played the "Marseillaise."[53] He soon met with the Menshevik leader of the Petrograd soviet, Nikolay Chkheidze, who called for the Bolsheviks and Mensheviks to join together in opposition to the provisional government. It was a proposal that Lenin immediately rejected.

Through secret meetings and public speeches, Lenin soon made it clear he believed the true revolution had not yet taken place. The provisional government was intent on establishing a parliamentary republic. Lenin, on the other hand, "advocated a soviet republic, which would nationalize the land and the banks, take over the production and distribution of goods, and replace the existing police force, army, and bureaucracy with proletarian [worker-led] institutions."[54]

By late spring, Lenin had established himself and his plan for Russia's future as a rallying post for Bolsheviks, the workers, and the people of Russia. His slogans—"Peace, Land, and Bread" and "All Power to the Soviets"—proved extremely popular. Then, on July 16, Bolshevik-backed rioting again hit the streets of Petrograd, and the provisional government reacted harshly, raiding the Bolshevik headquarters and arresting their leaders. The government also published articles intent on smearing Lenin, claiming he was a German spy. Fearing for his life, Lenin went into hiding, disguised himself as a worker, shaved off his beard, and again left Russia, this time going into exile in Finland.

That summer, the Bolsheviks attempted to gain control of the provisional government. An attempt in July failed. Then, in August, a conservative general, Lavr Kornilov, attempted a military takeover of Russia. The provisional government met the challenge head-on, arming the workers of the Petrograd soviet and forming the "Red Guards." Twenty-five thousand of them, mostly men from the city's factories and military barracks, established barricades in the streets of Petrograd. Socialist groups who had jockeyed against one another for power and influence now banded together and fought alongside the government to eliminate the military threat. Resistance against Kornilov included telegraphers who would not transmit his war messages and rail workers who stopped his trains.

The coup attempt was quashed by September, and the Bolsheviks emerged dominant, gaining control over the soviets in both Petrograd and Moscow. With a new sense of mission and authority, the Bolsheviks pressed on to seize control of the government. From his exile in Finland, Lenin wrote to his comrades: "History will not forgive us if we do not seize power now."[55] In the midst of these political events unfolding during the fall of 1917, the provisional government sent Nicholas, Alexandra, and their children into exile in Siberia.

Lenin arrived back in Petrograd in late October, and soon he convinced the Bolshevik Central Committee to launch a full-scale political coup of its own. Planning the military details of the coup fell to Leon Trotsky, the leader of the newly-formed Military Revolutionary

Committee (MRC). Trotsky had just returned to Russia the previous spring. He had escaped from Siberian exile ten years earlier and had spent time in Europe and the United States. That spring, he had

## Leon Trotsky

History records few men or women as energetic and self-sacrificing as Leon Trotsky (formal name: Lev Davidovitch Bronstein). He brought about a gigantic revolution and saved it from counterrevolution, and his reward was to be assassinated in exile.

Born in southern Ukraine in 1879, Trotsky was the son of prosperous Jewish farmers. He felt neglected emotionally and was attracted at an early age to the revolutionary movements that wanted to topple Czar Nicholas II. Trotsky was arrested in Odessa, sent to Russia, and then deported to Siberia. Just before being sent, he married Alexandra Sokolovskaya, and later the couple had two daughters.

Trotksy left his wife and infant children in 1902, escaped Siberia, and made his way to London. He and Lenin (Vladimir Ilyich Ulyanov) agreed on many things, including the necessity for bringing about a workers' revolution in Russia. Trotsky played a leading role in the Russian Revolution of 1905, which failed to dislodge the czarist government: Trotsky went to Siberia again, this time for a short duration.

For the next ten years Trotsky lived in exile, either in Britain, Austria, or Switzerland. He met a second woman, Natalya Sedova,

who became important in his life. The couple never married, and Trotsky never divorced his first wife, but he and Natalya had two sons.

Trotsky, Natalya, and their sons were in New York City when the February 1917 revolution broke out in Russia. The Trotsky family made its way to St. Petersburg by freighter, and Trotsky immediately became the number-two man in the movement, second only to Lenin.

Trotsky organized the nuts and bolts of the November revolution of 1917, which overthrew the moderate government of Alexander Kerensky and started Russia on the path toward true socialism. But there was little time to celebrate, for the "White," or czarist, forces rallied against the revolution even though the czar and his family had been become the leader of the Mensheviks, who had subsequently sided with Lenin's Bolsheviks. The date was set for the Bolshevik-led revolution: November 6, 1917.

exiled during the revolution. Trotsky then embarked on the most legendary aspect of his long career: organizing and motivating the Red Army.

For three years Trotsky traveled the length and breadth of Russia in a train, writing, publishing, revising, and constantly giving speeches to Red Army units. Lenin later admitted that Trotsky was the indispensable man in the long and vicious civil war of 1918–1921: Without Trotsky's efforts the revolution would have been crushed.

Victory came in 1921, none too soon for the exhausted Trotsky. He hoped to retire to a more private way of life and enjoy his beloved family, but events conspired against him. Lenin died in 1924 and leadership of the Communist Party fell into the hands of Joseph Stalin, Trotsky's archenemy. Trotsky mistakenly believed that Stalin was a weak man; he soon found out otherwise. After a series of power struggles between the two men, Stalin prevailed, and Trotsky was sent to Siberia for the third time in his life. The greatest hero of the revolution went to a concentration camp.

Stalin allowed Trotsky to leave the country and for several years Trotsky and his family floated between Turkey, France, and Norway. But pressure from Stalin's government fol-

lowed the Trotskys wherever they went, and Trotsky was happy to receive an invitation from the Mexican artist Diego Rivera in 1937 to come to Mexico. (Rivera painted huge murals, many of which commemorated revolutionary and socialist causes.)

By the time he went to Mexico, Trotsky had written his major work, *The Permanent Revolution,* in which he argued that it was not enough for socialists to prevail in Russia, or indeed in any single country. They must, he argued, carry the revolution to all other nations so that socialism could not be nipped in the bud by capitalism. Trotsky's thesis was countered by Stalin's own publication, *Socialism in One Country.*

Even Mexico was less than a safe haven. Trotsky broke with Diego Rivera in 1939, and the Trotsky family purchased their own villa in one of the suburbs of Mexico City. Trotsky was assassinated in October 1940.

A man of tremendous intellect, compassion, and will, Trotsky was the single best salesman for the Russian revolutionary movement. With Lenin dead, Trotsky assassinated, and Stalin in power, the Russian Communist government began to resemble that of the czars as much as it did the ideals of a socialist state.

Three days earlier, the revolutionaries were assured the Petrograd garrison would declare its loyalty to the Petrograd soviet, and two days later, 100,000 rifles were transferred from the Saint Peter and Paul Fortress to the Petrograd soviet. The following morning—November 6—the provisional government, under the leadership of its war minister, Alexander Kerensky, who had replaced Lvov during the July riots, announced his government to be in a state of insurrection and issued warrants for the arrests of Bolshevik leaders, including Trotsky. At the Smolny Institute, an all-female academy established more than a century earlier by Czarina Catherine the Great, where the Bolsheviks had established their headquarters, the government cut off telephone service. Lenin, who was just outside the city, had no way of knowing what was happening in the streets. He set out on foot for the Smolny, wearing a wig and a facial bandage as a disguise, arriving around midnight to meet with Trotsky. Two hours later, Trotsky glanced as his watch and told Lenin: "It's begun."

Lenin, overly excited, responded: "From being on the run to supreme power—that's too much. It makes me dizzy."[56]

The Bolshevik Revolution of 1917 was in motion. The day happened to be Trotsky's thirty-eighth birthday.

Over the following 48 hours, government forces and revolutionaries battled across the urban landscape of Petrograd. There was little opposition mounted by the government, however. The only significant holdout was at the Winter Palace, where military cadets and a group called the Amazons, "patriot women who had sworn to fight to the death against the Germans and other enemies of the state,"[57] held out throughout the day until the building was shelled by cannon at the Peter and Paul Fortress. When all the smoke cleared, the city was held by the revolutionaries, and Kerensky had left Petrograd in an automobile given to him by the U.S. ambassador. It had been an unexpectedly quick revolution. Trotsky seemed disappointed, as he described it all later: "The final act of the revolution seems, after all this, too brief, too dry, too businesslike—somehow out of correspondence with the historic scope of the events."[58]

On the evening of November 8, the All-Russian Congress of Soviets met. Lenin, the new chairman of the Council of People's Commissars—equivalent to a Bolshevik cabinet—stood to address his fellow revolutionaries. The American left-wing journalist John Reed was present and described the scene:

> It was just 8:40 [p.m.] when a thundering wave of cheers announced the entrance of the presidum, with Lenin—great Lenin—among them. A short stocky, figure, with a big head set down on his shoulders, bald and bulging ... Dressed in shabby clothes, his trousers much too long for him. Unimpressive, to be the idol of a mob, loved and revered as perhaps few leaders in history have been. A strange popular leader—a leader purely by virtue of intellect; colorless, humorless, uncompromising and detached ... but with the power of explaining profound ideas in simple terms, of analyzing a concrete situation, and combined with shrewdness, the greatest intellectual audacity.[59]

During his speech, Lenin read his Decree on Land, which called for the abolition of all private property. Under this directive, the Bolsheviks eventually placed more than half a million acres of land in the hands of the poor and middle-class peasants. The owners of large estates, the aristocracy, and the Orthodox Church were collectively stripped of more than 400,000 acres of property. That evening, the Congress ratified a constitution for a "provisional workers' and peasants' government, the Council of People's Commissars."[60]

Through the remaining weeks of 1917, the Council of People's Commissars met daily, hammering out a new structure of government. While membership in the Bolshevik Party numbered approximately 350,000, the party's true strength and base of support lay in the millions of Russians who supported the various "soviets, the trade unions, the factory committees, and the soldiers' and peasants' committees."[61] All industry, banks, land, and merchant ships became the property of the people and the new government. The revolutionaries declared men and women equal under law, allowing them to receive equal pay. But the coalition of revolutionary groups did not remain intact, and many of the Mensheviks and Socialist Revolutionaries walked out of the meetings.

The Bolsheviks soon found themselves wrestling a wide variety of problems as the new national power. There was the ongoing war with Germany, which Lenin had never supported. He called for an immediate and "just and democratic peace."[62] By December, Trotsky was dispatched to negotiate with the Germans.

In the meantime, the Russian military was in shambles, and the revolutionaries were unmotivated to continue the war. German armies were busy grabbing up ever larger tracts of Russian territory, making negotiations difficult. Finally, on March 3, 1918, the Russians signed a peace treaty with the Central Powers, including Germany, Austria, and Turkey, in the town of Brest Litovsk (the modern-day Russian city of Brest). It was a costly way out of the war, as the Germans claimed large amounts of Russian soil, including land in the Baltic, Poland, Ukraine, and the Caucasus. This territorial loss included one-third of Russia's farmlands, one out of four of its rail systems, one of every three industrial plants, and 80 percent of the former empire's coal mines. In addition, the Germans extracted war damages amounting to 6 billion marks.

## REVOLUTION LEADS TO CIVIL WAR

But even as the Bolsheviks severed Russia's stake in the Great War, within months of the Treaty of Brest Litovsk a new war, a civil war, broke out. Anti-Bolsheviks, known popularly as the Whites, led by dissatisfied former military leaders loyal to Nicholas, organized offensives against Bolshevik power. The Bolshevik "Red Army" was expanded to meet the challenge to their revolutionary causes, with Trotsky as their leader. By the summer of 1918, the Whites had captured much of eastern Russia, and their army was approaching the city of Moscow, the newly chosen Russian capital. Desperate, Trotsky conscripted many anti-Bolsheviks into the Red Army, mostly from the ranks of the former czar's office corps. To ensure their cooperation, Trotsky coerced them by threatening the lives of their family members. To keep a close watch on such officers, the Bolsheviks appointed military commissars, Bolsheviks who shadowed the army commanders at all times. Trotsky proved ruthless in his military campaigns, tolerating no losses on the battlefield. Commanders who failed were shot, as well as every tenth man in his ranks.

The Bolsheviks continued to face other political challenges, including the assassinations of their leaders. Socialist Revolutionaries killed several. Even Lenin was wounded in an assault by a female assassin in August 1918. (It was not the first attempt on Lenin's life that year. In January, someone had fired three shots at him as he rode in a car, the bullet missing only after a comrade pushed Lenin out of view.) Under both military and political siege, the Bolshevik leadership turned paranoid, ordering the deaths of anyone suspected of opposing the radical leadership. Thousands were executed by the new police force, the Cheka.

As the Bolshevik Revolution took a dark and bloody turn, the Romanovs were caught in the cross-fire. Having been shipped out to Siberia a year earlier by the provisional government, Nicholas, Alexandra, and their five children were being held under house arrest at the home of a wealthy merchant in the Ural Mountains mining town of Ekaterinburg. The family had been reduced to only two servants, and the Romanovs had few privileges. Nicholas even helped cut firewood to keep his family warm. On July 16, 1918, the family was escorted into the cellar, the former czar having to carry his weak, sickly son. There, they were read a sentence of execution, and a group of armed gunmen shot them. Nicholas was dispatched with a shot to the head. An assassin emptied his entire pistol into Alexis. The youngest Romanov daughter, Anastasia, shot but still breathing, was stabbed with a bayonet. The family dog, a spaniel, was also killed, with a rifle butt to the skull. The bodies were then taken to a local mine shaft and burned with gasoline and sulfuric acid, their charred remains then dropped down into the abandoned mine.

The war between the Reds and the Whites took a decided turn following November in 1918. After the Allied Powers defeated Germany and the Central Powers, they then turned their attention to the Soviet government. Fourteen nations sent troops to give assistance to the Whites, hoping to stave off an ultimate Bolshevik victory. But direct Allied intervention into Russia was never particularly extensive or well-coordinated. The British and French sent few forces, and only the Japanese dispatched a significant number of soldiers—approximately 70,000—into Russia's Far Eastern provinces, but only to protect Japanese interests. In fact, much of the equipment and ammunition delivered by the Allies to the Whites ended up in Bolshevik hands, including tanks and airplanes, after White armies abandoned them on various battlefields. For two more years, the Bolsheviks fought on. Consistently, they won field engagements due to the superior training of the Red Army. The fighting produced millions of casualties, including civilian victims. By the end of 1920, the Bolsheviks emerged victorious.

## REVOLUTION LEADS TO DICTATORSHIP

Through this victory, Lenin was able to guide the revolution and establish his version of Marxist doctrine, banding the workers and the peasants together, creating a classless state where personal property was outlawed. The war and his devastating economic policies nearly destroyed the country, however:

# Joseph Stalin
# (Joseph Vissarionovich Dzhugashvili)

For most people, the name "Hitler" takes precedence over "Stalin" in conjuring up a specter of evil, but the two were actually equals in violence, brutality, and hatred.

Stalin was born in a mountain town of Georgia (part of the Russian empire) in 1879. His tyrannical father beat him frequently while his mother read to him and nurtured his interest in books. Stalin entered a seminary of the Russian Orthodox Church but soon left it, and by 1900 he was a revolutionary, committed to bringing down the government of Czar Nicholas II.

Stalin met Lenin and Trotsky in 1902 and 1903. He greatly admired Lenin but found Trotsky too much of an intellectual; Stalin nursed a long and deep hatred for those who cherished ideas over practicalities, because they reminded him of the seminary priests. Stalin became a member of Lenin's group, the Bolsheviks (meaning "majority"), but he was not a significant leader until the twin revolutions of 1917.

The February revolution of that year ousted Czar Nicholas II. Then Stalin, Lenin, and Trotsky worked together in pulling off the October revolution that ousted the social democratic government and replaced it with the Bolsheviks. From that day on, Stalin began to rise in importance. He was neither the deep thinker that Lenin was nor a great man of action like Trotsky; rather, Stalin was a methodical thinker and planner. He worked his way up the ranks of the Communist Party, quietly removing those who opposed him from the party leadership. At the time of his death in 1924, Lenin was convinced that Stalin intended to seize dictatorial powers.

With Lenin gone, Stalin and Trotsky fought a series of power struggles. Stalin prevailed each time because he had arranged for the party leadership to support him and

The country over which the Bolsheviks now presided ... was in a state of virtual collapse. The towns were hungry and half-empty, the railways were breaking down, and industry was almost at a standstill, with industrial production less than one-third of its 1913 level. The shortage of goods, plus the government's propensity to print more and more money, caused chronic inflation....

his ideas. Trotsky was exiled in 1927 and assassinated in 1940, probably on Stalin's order.

With Trotsky gone, Stalin implemented his idea of "Socialism in One Country." He labored to make Soviet Russia an industrial powerhouse, and he succeeded, though at the cost of countless lives: Many Russians died in industrial accidents and "forced removals." Stalin also purged both the military and the Communist Party leadership in the late 1930s, removing anyone who opposed him. These purges were carried out by means of "show trials," which began to convince many liberals outside the Soviet Union that the Russian Communist experiment had failed.

In 1939, Stalin made a cynical "Non-Aggression Pact" with Nazi Germany. Stalin moved against Poland that year and took one-third of that nation. But in the summer of 1941, Hitler turned on his former partner and invaded Russia, thereby starting what was probably the most vicious and destructive war of all human history. About 20 million Russians were killed, wounded, injured, or displaced during the war.

Stalin won the titanic struggle of wills with Hitler, and the Red Army occupied Berlin in the spring of 1945. Russian victory was complete, but Stalin, echoing past Russian leaders, decided that Russia needed a buffer zone for the future. He therefore annexed much of Eastern Europe to the Soviet Union, and set the stage for the Cold War between the United States and the Soviet Union. Stalin also had the satisfaction of seeing his country develop the world's second successful atomic bomb, in the fall of 1949.

By about 1950 Stalin was the world's most powerful and most dangerous man. One could argue that the American president Harry S. Truman commanded an even stronger economy and military, but Truman did not have the dictatorial power of Stalin, who was feared around the world. Millions of people breathed a great sigh of relief when Stalin died in 1953.

Despite his numerous violations of human rights, Stalin deserves some acknowledgment as a strong national leader, but as a revolutionary, he was an abject failure. He failed to implement the ideals of either Karl Marx or Lenin and he drove out the true idealistic leader of the Russian Revolution, Leon Trotsky.

Deaths from hunger and disease in 1921 and 1922 were to total some five million—more than the combined military casualties for the Great War and the civil war.... [T]here were armed uprisings in the Ukraine, the northern Causasus, and western Siberia.[63]

Conditions proved so desperate that Lenin, the architect of Russia's communistic revolution, ordered the adoption of extreme measures called the New Economic Policy, or NEP. Under this emergency system, capitalism was restored to the country, as industrial plants were placed in the hands of private owners and peasants were allowed to sell their agricultural produce for personal profit. The measures seemed to work, bringing about "the rapid increase in agricultural and industrial production."[64] All of Russia's economic woes did not vanish, however. Through the mid-1920s, food rationing continued, and unemployment was a constant problem.

Even as Lenin took the hard edge off of Marxism and allowed capitalism to guide his country's economy, he entrenched in other arenas. The Bolsheviks, who renamed themselves the Communist Party, cracked down on organized religion, denying clergymen the vote, placing high taxes on them, and shutting down religious schools. These moves were often paralleled by violence, as churches were ransacked, even destroyed, and priests were arrested and killed. As early as 1921, more than 1,000 Orthodox clergymen, including more than two dozen bishops, had been jailed or executed.

Even within the Communist Party, Lenin engaged in hard-line policies. He banned all opposition political parties and cut out half of the membership of his party in an attempt to weed out those he perceived as disloyal to him. The party's central committee came to hold nearly full power, and Lenin was the committee's center. The Bolshevik Revolution was becoming an obvious irony: "Under the autocracy of the czars, the Russian people had been told what to do; now, under the virtual dictatorship of Lenin, they were increasingly being told what to think. Russia was on the road to becoming a totalitarian state."[65]

But Lenin would not live to see his dream of a Russian state based on a pure Marxist model. At the age of 51, Lenin, after years of hard work, exile, political agitation, and civil war, suffered a debilitating stroke in May 1921. Although he continued on as the head of the government's Central Committee, his paralysis kept him from performing to his former capacity. Others began to move into position to take control of events and the direction of the ongoing revolution. Trotsky was among them. Another was Joseph Stalin, who held the position of general secretary of the Communist Party.

Stalin was a single-minded, iron-fisted party member, whose true abilities lay in administration. Lenin had always served as the brains of the revolution, the thinker who understood Marxism inside and out. Trotsky's expertise lay in military organization and battle plans. Stalin was the armchair bureaucrat, a skilled organizer of men and government power. (His nickname among his colleagues was "Comrade Card-Index.")   It was through Stalin's influence that regional minority states, those formerly held by the czar's imperial power, lost their newly won independence and were forced to join with Russia into a federation of Communist states known as the Union of Soviet Socialist Republics (U.S.S.R.).

For a time, these three men—Lenin, Trotsky, and Stalin—shared power over the party and the Russian people. But Lenin suffered additional strokes, which paralyzed him so severely he lost his capacity to write. Even as his influence was fading, Lenin was concerned for the future of the revolution, fearful Stalin was the wrong man to lead Russia: "He saw that the state had become a mass of red tape and incompetence; furthermore, the increased centralization had robbed regional and representative bodies of their power. He reserved his strongest criticism for Stalin ... urging the party to remove him from office."[66] But the influential voice of Lenin was dying out. On March 10, 1923, he suffered yet another stroke, losing his capacity for speech. Pushed aside by Stalin and other party officials, Lenin died on January 21, 1924.

Over the next five years, Stalin pathologically and ruthlessly retooled the Communist Party and the U.S.S.R. into his own personal empire. He purged the party of all opposition and brought an end to the New Economic Policy. He installed by force across the Soviet Union a system of state-owned factories and mines. Any private property was again taken away and farms were transformed into collectives, where farming peasants were given state-mandated quotas and kept in virtual poverty. As for Trotsky, Stalin maneuvered the party to force his expulsion and ultimate exile from Russia in 1929. (Trotsky was murdered later, in 1940, by Stalinist agents in Mexico City.) Until his death in 1953, Stalin ruthlessly ruled the

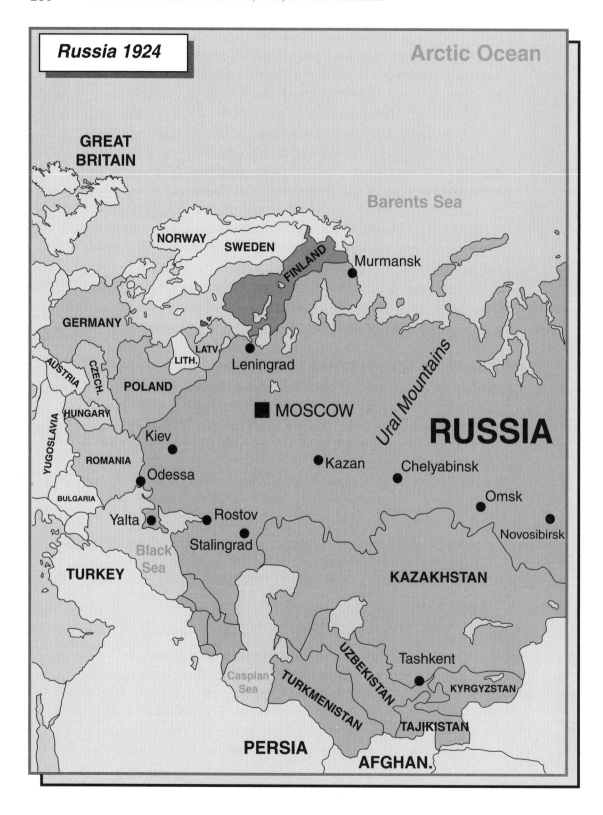

**Russia 1924**

Arctic Ocean

GREAT
BRITAIN

Barents Sea

NORWAY
SWEDEN
FINLAND
Murmansk

GERMANY

LATV.
LITH.
Leningrad

Ural Mountains

RUSSIA

AUSTRIA
CZECH.
POLAND

MOSCOW

HUNGARY

YUGOSLAVIA

Kiev

Kazan

Chelyabinsk

ROMANIA

Odessa

Omsk

BULGARIA

Yalta

Rostov

Novosibirsk

Stalingrad

Black
Sea

TURKEY

KAZAKHSTAN

UZBEKISTAN
Tashkent

Caspian
Sea

TURKMENISTAN

KYRGYZSTAN

TAJIKISTAN

PERSIA

AFGHAN.

Soviet state, killing millions in repeated purges. While he did manage to drag Russia into the modern world, "the cost in human suffering would surpass the harshest excesses of the czars."[67]

[Author's Note: Until February 1, 1918, Russia's Julian Calendar and Western Europe's Gregorian Calendar differed by 13 days. The dates presented in this chapter are based on Russia's adoption of the Gregorian Calendar after February 1, 1918. This change moved the "February Revolution of 1917" into March and the "October Revolution," into November.]

## TIMELINE

**1613** Michael Romanov becomes the first Romanov czar. The Romanovs would rule Russia for the next 300 years.

**1881** Assassination of Czar Alexander II at the hands of a terrorist organization called the People's Will.

**1881–1894** During the reign of Alexander III, the state attempts to destroy all dissident movements within the Russian Empire.

**1887** Socialist radical Lenin's brother is hanged for his involvement in the death of Czar Alexander II.

**1892** Sergei Witte is appointed Russia's minister of finance and works to develop an extensive industrial program for Czar Alexander III.

**1894** Czar Nicholas ascends to the Russian Imperial throne following the assassination of his father, Czar Alexander III.

**1897** Lenin is exiled to Siberia.

**1900** Two major anticzarist movements underway in Russia—the Socialist Revolutionaries (the SRs) and the Social Democrats. Lenin goes into voluntary exile abroad.

**1904–05** Russo-Japanese War results in humiliating defeat for the Russians.

**1905** **January 22** Street demonstrations outside the czar's winter palace in Petrograd are fired on by government troops, resulting in "Bloody Sunday."

Russian Revolution that year fails, but pressured Czar Nicholas issues the liberal-minded document, the "October Manifesto." Before year's end, the monk Rasputin is invited to the royal palace and soon becomes a favorite of the czarina.

**1906**   Prime Minister Pyotr Stolypin replaces Witte. His economic reforms prove extremely popular in Russia.

**1911**   Stolypin is assassinated by a radical.

**1914–17**   Russia engages in World War I with disastrous results.

**1916**   **December 30**   A conspiracy of Russian noblemen and Duma members assassinates Rasputin.

**1917**   **March 8**   Street violence breaks out and leads to the "February Revolution."

**March 14**   Duma forms a provisional government under Prince Georgy Lvov.

**1894**
Czar Nicholas ascends to the Russian Imperial throne following the assassination of his father.

**1914–1917**
Russia engages in World War I with disastrous results.

**1905**
**January 22**   Street demonstrations outside the czar's winter palace in Petrograd are fired on by government troups, resulting in "Bloody Sunday."

**1894**

**1900**
Two major anticzarist movements underway in Russia—Socialist Revolutionaries (the SRs) and Social Democrats. Lenin goes into voluntary exile abroad.

**1905**
Russian Revolution fails, but Czar Nicholas issues the liberal-minded document, the "October Manifesto." Before year's end, Rasputin is invited to the royal palace and becomes a favorite of the czarina.

**March 15**  Czar Nicholas abdicates his throne.

**April 16**  Lenin arrives in Petrograd.

**July 16–18**  The "July Days" Bolshevik uprising fails.

**November 6**  "October Revolution" begins.

**November 8**  Revolutionaries seize the czar's Winter Palace.

**December 20**  New Russian secret police, the Cheka, is established.

1918  **March 3**  Treaty of Brest Litovsk is signed, taking Russia out of World War I.

**March 10**  Lenin moves the seat of government from Petrograd to Moscow.

1917
**March 8**  Street violence breaks out and leads to the "February Revolution."
**March 14**  Duma forms a provisional government under Prince Gregory Lvov.
**March 15**  Czar Nicholas abdicates his throne.
**November 6**  "October Revolution" begins.
**November 8**  Revolutionaries seize the czar's Winter Palace.

1924
Lenin dies, leaving Stalin to accrue power to himself while bringing about the ouster of Trotsky, his chief rival.

1924

1921
Desperate to salvage Russia's economy, Lenin announces the New Economic Policy.

1918
**March 10**  Lenin moves the seat of government from Petrograd to Moscow.
**July 17**  Entire Romanov family is assassinated by Bolshevik gunman.

**June**  Russian Civil War begins.

**July 17**  Entire Romanov family is assassinated by Bolshevik gunmen.

**August 30**  Female assassin makes an attempt on Lenin's life.

**1919**  White armies threaten Bolsheviks in Petrograd and Moscow.

**1920**  By November, the Bolsheviks have defeated the Whites in the civil war.

**1921**  Desperate to salvage Russia's economy, Lenin announces the New Economic Policy.

**1922**  Lenin suffers first stroke.

**1924**  Lenin dies, leaving Stalin to collect power around himself while bringing about the expulsion of Trotsky, his chief rival.

## SOURCE NOTES

1. Quoted in Time-Life Books, *TimeFrame AD 1900–1925: The World in Arms.* Alexandria, VA: Time-Life Books, 1989, p. 50.
2. Ibid., p. 51.
3. Ibid., p. 54.
4. Ibid., p. 52.
5. Quoted in Harrison E. Salisbury, *Black Night, White Snow: Russia's Revolutions, 1905–1917.* Garden City, NY: Doubleday, 1978, p. 11.
6. Quoted in John Bradley, *The Russian Revolution.* New York: Bison Books, 1988, p. 12.
7. Quoted in Alan Moorehead, *The Russian Revolution.* New York: Harper & Brothers, 1958, p. 17.
8. Ibid.
9. Quoted in Time-Life Books, *Timeframe,* p. 53.
10. Quoted in Moorehead, *Russian Revolution,* p. 18.
11. Quoted in Time-Life Books, *Timeframe,* p. 53.
12. Quoted in Philip Clark, *Wars That Changed the World: The Russian Revolution.* New York: Marshall Cavendish, 1988, p. 9.
13. Ibid.
14. Quoted in Time-Life Books, *Timeframe,* p. 55.
15. Quoted in Bradley, *Russian Revolution,* p. 21.
16. Ibid.
17. Quoted in J.N. Westwood, "The Russo-Japanese War," in A.J.P. Taylor, ed., *The 20th Century, Volume I.* Milwaukee: Purnell Reference Books, 1979, p. 101.
18. Quoted in Moorehead, *Russian Revolution,* p. 27.
19. Quoted in Time-Life Books, *Timeframe,* p. 57.
20. Quoted in Reginald E. Zenik, "Revolutionary Russia, 1890–1914," in Gregory L. Freeze, ed., *Russia: A History.* New York: Oxford University Press, 1997, p. 214.
21. Quoted in Moorehead, *Russian Revolution,* p. 55.
22. Quoted in Salisbury, *Black Night,* p. 121.
23. Ibid., p. 125.
24. Quoted in Moorehead, *Russian Revolution,* p. 55.
25. Quoted in Clark, *Wars,* p. 10.
26. Quoted in Zenik, *Revolutionary Russia,* p. 108.

27. Quoted in Moorehead, *Russian Revolution*, p. 55.
28. Quoted in David Floyd, *Russia in Revolt, 1905: The First Crack in Tsarist Power*, London: MacDonald & Co., 1969, p. 109.
29. Ibid.
30. Quoted in Time-Life Books, *Timeframe*, p. 58.
31. Ibid., p. 59.
32. Ibid.
33. Ibid., p. 60.
34. Quoted in Floyd, p. 111.
35. Ibid., p. 112.
36. Quoted in Moorehead, *Russian Revolution*, p. 67.
37. Quoted in Time-Life Books, *Timeframe*, p. 60.
38. Quoted in Moorehead, *Russian Revolution*, p. 74.
39. Quoted in Alexander Grunt, "Russia at War," in A.J.P. Taylor, ed., *The 20th Century, Volume 5*. Milwaukee: Purnell Reference Books, 1979, p. 674.
40. Quoted in Time-Life Books, *Timeframe*, p. 60.
41. Ibid., p. 61.
42. Quoted in Grunt, "Russia at War," p. 677.
43. Quoted in Time-Life Books, *Timeframe*, p. 61.
44. Quoted in Moorehead, *Russian Revolution*, pp. 5–6.
45. Quoted in Bradley, *Russian Revolution*, p. 42.
46. Quoted in Time-Life Books, *Timeframe*, p. 63.
47. Quoted in Salisbury, *Black Nights*, p. 342.
48. Quoted in Time-Life Books, *Timeframe*, p. 63.
49. Quoted in Moorehead, *Russian Revolution*, p. 156.
50. Quoted in Salisbury, *Black Nights*, p. 392.
51. Quoted in Time-Life Books, *Timeframe*, p. 63.
52. Ibid., p. 64.
53. Ibid.
54. Ibid., p. 65.
55. Ibid., p. 66.
56. Ibid., p. 67.
57. Ibid.
58. Ibid.
59. Ibid., p. 68.
60. Quoted in Y.N. Gorodetsky, "The Bolshevik Revolution," in A.J.P. Taylor, ed., *The 20th Century, Volume 6*. Milwaukee: Purnell Reference Books, 1979, p. 760.
61. Ibid., p. 766.
62. Quoted in Time-Life Books, *Timeframe*, p. 68.
63. Ibid., p. 73.
64. Ibid.
65. Ibid., p. 74.
66. Ibid., p. 75.
67. Ibid.

## BIBLIOGRAPHY

Bradley, John. *The Russian Revolution*. New York: Bison Books, 1988.

Clark, Philip. *Wars That Changed the World: The Russian Revolution*. New York: Marshall Cavendish, 1988.

George, Charles H. *Revolution: European Radicals from Hus to Lenin*. Glenview, IL: Scott, Foresman, 1971.

Gorodetsky, Y.N. "The Bolshevik Revolution," in A.J.P. Taylor, ed., *The 20th Century, Volume 6*. Milwaukee: Purnell Reference Books, 1979.

Grunt, Alexander. "Russia At War," in A.J.P. Taylor, ed., *The 20th Century, Volume 5*. Milwaukee: Purnell Reference Books, 1979.

Killingray, David. *The Russian Revolution*. St. Paul, MN: Greenhaven Press, 1980.

Mazlish, Bruce, *Revolution: A Reader*. New York: Macmillan, 1971.

Moorehead, Alan. *The Russian Revolution*. New York: Harper & Brothers, 1958.

Salisbury, Harrison E. *Black Night, White Snow: Russia's Revolutions, 1905–1917*. Garden City, NY: Doubleday, 1978.

Time-Life Books, *TimeFrame AD 1900–1925: The World in Arms*. Alexandria, VA: Time-Life Books, 1989.

Westwood, J. N. "The Russo-Japanese War," in A.J.P. Taylor, ed., *The 20th Century, Volume I*. Milwaukee: Purnell Reference Books, 1979.

Zenik, Reginald E. "Revolutionary Russia, 1890–1914," in Gregory L. Freeze, Ed., *Russia: A History*. New York: Oxford University Press, 1997.

# 7

# The Chinese Revolution

## AN ACCIDENTAL REVOLUTION

**Although revolutionaries had worked for years quietly, underground, to** bring about the fall of the Manchu leaders of China, when the revolution opened up suddenly in October 1911, it was purely by accident. On October 9, as insurgents manufactured a bomb, the device suddenly exploded. The incident led police in the central Chinese town of Hankow to raid the headquarters of republican insurgents, arresting several leaders, collecting weapons, and seizing a stash of propaganda material calling for the deposing of the Manchu monarchy. A regional search for additional revolutionaries was ordered. Fearing their movement would collapse in the face of a government crackdown and manhunt, the leftist revolutionaries were forced into making a fateful decision: revolutionaries stationed at the military fortress at Hankow revolted on October 10, "tearing down the yellow dragon flags of the Manchu Dynasty."[1]

Soon, other enclaves of political resistance revolted, including those in the industrial cities of Hanyang and Wuchang. Before the month's end, nearly all of southern China was in rebellion. The tidal wave of protest and violent defiance caught Manchu officials unprepared and off-guard. Hankow, Hanyang, and Wuchang all fell to the revolutionaries. Then, the revolution spread to the city of Shanghai. By February 12, 1912, Prince Chun (Ch'un), then just six years old, abdicated his throne. Suddenly, more than two and a half centuries of rule by the Manchus, invaders from Manchuria who had conquered China in 1644, came to an end. Perhaps more important, the end of the Manchu dynasty marked the culmination of 2,500 years of imperial rule over the vast regions of China.

For many in China, the collapse of the Manchus had not come soon enough. Since the seventeenth century, the Manchus had dominated China as unpopular rulers. By the nineteenth century, their imperial governments had become increasingly corrupt and ineffective, failing to correct such domestic problems as repeatedly poor economies. The vast millions of rural peasants continued to live under the strain of incessant poverty and military oppression.

To hold on to power, the Manchus, throughout the last 50 years of the 1800s, had allowed foreigners into their empire, giving European leaders trading rights and granted special status for businessmen, diplomats, and missionaries, which caused a decline in China's sovereignty.

By 1900, China's major cities—Shanghai, Guangzhou (Canton), Nanjing (Nanking), and Xianggang (Hong Kong)—had become outposts for European merchants and shippers. At the same time, the Chinese people watched helplessly as their Asian neighbor, Japan, kept foreign influence and investment to a minimum, modernized its government and its economy, and began challenging China's control of Korea. The 1894 Sino-Japanese War ended in an absolute and humiliating defeat for China, resulting in Korean independence and the loss of the island of Formosa to the aggressive Japanese.

### THE "THREE PRINCIPLES OF THE PEOPLE"

The spontaneous 1911 revolution did not bring the changes many Chinese had hoped for. The initial success of the revolution and the rise of Dr. Sun Zhongshan (known by Westerners as Sun Yat-sen) did give many revolutionaries a new sense of hope about China's immediate future. Dr. Sun had become a potent voice for change, modernization, and democracy in China. Born in 1866, in southern China, he had formed the revolutionary China Renaissance Society in Hawaii in 1894. (Dr. Sun had a wealthy brother living in Honolulu at the time.) The following year, he had led a minor revolt in Guangzhou (Canton) against the Manchu government. The uprising failed, and Sun was forced to flee China, living first in London, then settling in Tokyo. There, he founded another revolutionary organization, the Alliance Society, whose single-minded aim was to remove the Manchus from power, remove foreign influences, establish a democratic republic, and carry out land reform by allowing peasants their own property. Although many Chinese disliked Japan, Sun saw the island nation as an example of a modernized, Westernized nation.

By 1905, Dr. Sun had been chosen as the leader of a coalition of various Chinese dissident groups operating out of Tokyo. The newly formed Revolutionary Alliance became the frontrunner for a later revolutionary organization, the Guomindang (Kuomintang). At the center of Dr. Sun's political reform plans for China was his "Three Principles of the People," a program based on nationalism, democracy, and aid to the peasants, which Sun referred to as "the people's livelihood."[2] He became such an expressive and popular voice of dissent against the Manchu government that Chinese authorities placed pressure on the Japanese to expel Dr. Sun in 1907.

For the next several years, Sun Zhongshan toured the world, including visits to Indochina, Europe, and the United States, raising money and gaining support as he spoke to sympathetic audiences, including thousands of Chinese students studying abroad, or "drinking foreign ink," as the contemporary saying went.[3] As many of those students returned to China, they became revolutionaries in the cause of Dr. Sun and the Revolutionary Alliance. Between 1907 and 1911, these educated rebels organized uprisings across southern China. In 1909 alone, there were three major attempts to overthrow the Manchus.

When the "accidental" revolution broke out in the fall of 1911, Sun was abroad in the United States. He first read of the rebellion in a Denver newspaper. Receiving news of the scattered uprisings, he began making plans to return to China as soon as possible. But two crucial months passed before Dr. Sun was able to reach Chinese soil, arriving at Shanghai on Christmas Day, where he was enthusiastically greeted. He was soon elected as the provisional president of a new Chinese republic, the first in the ancient nation's history.

But Dr. Sun's election was a stage set. At the outbreak of rebellion in October, the Manchu leadership had turned to one of their generals, Yuan Shikai, who had served as the Qing regime's minister of war. Yuan, a crafty old warhorse, agreed to march against the rebellion in southern China, Dr. Sun's stronghold region, but only on the condition he be named both commander-in-chief and prime minister of the empire. After retaking Hankow and Hanyang, however, General Yuan called for a cease-fire and began negotiating with the

## Sun Zhongshan

Late in life, Sun Zhongshan (Sun Yat-Sen) confided to a journalist: "I am a coolie and the son of a coolie." The rough translation of coolie is "bitter labor." This word entered the American lexicon because of Chinese immigrants who came to Hawaii and California. One of them was Sun Zhongshan.

He was born in a small village about 80 miles from Canton (now Guangzhou), China. When he was 12, he went to Hawaii to visit his older brother who had gone there and was making a successful life for himself in the islands. Sun Zhongshan spent only three years in Hawaii, but they clearly changed his outlook on China, his family, and life as a whole. Though he had grown up in a conservative, tradition-bound family, he now embraced change and development as his new way of life.

On returning to China, Sun Zhongshan felt profoundly dissatisfied with the village in which he had grown up. He moved to Hong Kong, earned a medical degree, and married.

Sometime around 1894 he gave up the practice of medicine and became a full-time revolutionary. Like many Chinese he hated the Manchu government which had run China since about 1644; unlike many of his fellows Chinese, he intended to do something about it.

For 15 long years, from 1896 to 1911, Sun Zhongshan was away from China. He traveled to London, the Continent, and the United States, but time and again his exile led him to Japan, just off mainland China. There he read Karl Marx and Friedrich Engels and became an ardent Marxist. He happened to be on a trip to the United States when the Chinese Revolution of 1911 began: he learned the news in Denver, Colorado.

Making a fast trip home, Sun Zhongshan arrived in China at the end of 1911, and he was acclaimed as the genius of the new revolution. Totally sincere in his beliefs and fairly naive in his methods, he allowed himself to be outmaneuvered by General Yuan, who rebels. Yuan struck a deal, promising he would convince the Manchu emperor to resign his rule if Yuan were recognized as China's new republican president. The revolutionaries, with little choice, agreed, but not before they convinced Yuan to first allow Dr. Sun to be named president, then resign. All parties agreed.

In additional to living with this devil's bargain, Dr. Sun faced an uphill battle for legitimacy and acceptance as China's new leader. Many in China did not support revolutionary politics, and Europeans in China knew he was hostile to their continued presence. The military was squarely against him as well. After fewer than seven

intended to bring back the Manchu system of government with himself as the new emperor. Sun Zhongshan broke with Yuan and found himself exiled yet again, to, of all places, Japan. He spent several years there before returning to China and setting up his own Guomindang (Chinese Nationalist) government in south China.

In the early 1920s, he articulated a set of beliefs which he admitted he borrowed from the American hero Abraham Lincoln. Where Lincoln spoke of "government of the people, by the people, and for the people," Sun spoke of *Min yu* (the people to have); *Min chih* (the people to govern); and *Min hsiang* (the people to enjoy). These Three Principles of the People became his platform, and by about 1923 he had won over most of south China to his cause.

In that same year, he opened warm relations with the new Communist government of Russia; Russians went to Guangzhou and served as his close advisers. Sun Zhongshan went north and arrived in Beijing at the end of 1924; he died the following March of cancer.

It is difficult to classify Sun. Was he a nationalist? A communist? A socialist? He fits no easy pattern. This much we can say; he was a remarkably selfless patriot and he remains the most admired Chinese leader of the entire twentieth century.

weeks as China's first president, Sun resigned his post and handed power over to General Yuan on February 13, 1912. The move proved disastrous for China and the revolutionary cause. Yuan initially appeared supportive of revolutionary goals, agreeing to accept a republican constitution. He also accepted a call for parliamentary elections before the end of 1912. When the new legislature was formed, Yuan supporters vastly outnumbered Sun's newly-formed Guomindang (Chinese Nationalist Party), and the ambitious general began making plans to eliminate not only Sun's power, but the whole experiment with Chinese republicanism.

In November 1913, Yuan cracked down, banning the Guomindang and dissolving parliament. With the army already under his control, General Yuan had little opposition as he assumed full dictatorial powers over China. Dr. Sun and members of his revolutionary organization had little choice but to flee the country, taking asylum in Tokyo. Until his death in 1916, General Yuan controlled China with an iron fist. In 1915, he announced his intention to declare himself emperor, but the move proved unpopular with his various regional military governors, who forced him to step down as ruler of China on March 22, 1916.

To some extent, Yuan never actually gained full power over China's vast countryside. He had remained reliant on these cooperative governors, who were often no more than powerful warlords. Just three months after his humiliating resignation, General Yuan died. His funeral was as grand and elaborate as that fitting a Chinese emperor.

## A NEW ERA OF POLITICAL CHAOS

With the collapse of General Yuan's rule, China was soon plunged into political turmoil and a series of power struggles. As had been true of the Yuan years, real political power in post-Manchu China was held by a dozen or so local warlords, known as *tuchuns*. Many such local powers were former military officers. Others were a "mixed assortment of able administrators, land-hungry soldiers of fortune, and ambitious ex-bandits."[4] For much of the decade following the collapse of the Yuan presidency, centralized power in China was nonexistent. The warlords set high taxes for everyone, including the peasants, making life miserable for many. This "Era of the Warlords" generally dominated Chinese politics between the years 1916 and 1928. But as such regional rulers kept China politically fragmented, events outside of China were also setting the course for the country's political future.

During the summer of 1914, much of Europe was plunged into a protracted conflict known as the Great War, later known as World War I (1914–1918). (The Chinese referred to it as the European Civil War.) Serving as an ally of the British, French, and Russians, the Japanese used the war to take advantage of China's weakness, and, in 1915, it took control of Germany's trade interests in Shandong. In addition, the Japanese government presented General Yuan's administration with a preposterous list, called the Twenty-One Demands. These were designed to give Japan nearly complete wartime control over China. His back against the wall, the increasingly unpopular Yuan agreed to allow Japanese influence over the region of Manchuria. But as Japan extended its influence over China, it infuriated the country's middle class as well as its young revolutionaries—men and women who were extremely nationalistic.

Under pressure from Japan, China broke off diplomatic relations with Germany by late March 1917 and declared war on the Germans on August 14. But China's contribution to the war was extremely limited, dispatching labor battalions to France, the Middle East, and Africa. At the war's end, the Chinese soon realized that, although Japan had entered the war on the winning side, it intended to use the victory as an opportunity to further its sphere of influence over China. During the peace negotiations held at Versailles, France, in 1919, the victorious European powers, along with the United States, confirmed Japan's control over Shandong.

## THE MAY FOURTH MOVEMENT

This turn of events caused many Chinese to rally in a strong showing of nationalist support for their country. Led by a group of young students and other intellectuals, a political revolt called the May Fourth Movement took place. It began as a series of demonstrations on May 4 in Beijing by 3,000 students who called for extraordinary change in Chinese politics, culture, and social order. During their demonstrations, the rioters burned several homes of Chinese officials who had supported Japanese efforts to control China. Many ran in the streets shouting such slogans as "Down with the Traitors!" and "Return Shandong!"[5] Other rallies followed "in towns and on the new university campuses" where "students, teachers, intellectuals, and business men were translating feeling into action."[6]

The aim of the rioting was to clearly express Chinese nationalism. As one rebel stated: "China's territory may be conquered, but it cannot be given away. The Chinese people may be massacred, but they will not surrender. Our country is about to be annihilated. Rise up, brethren!"[7] Chinese officials in Beijing took serious steps against the political demonstrations, jailing as many as one of every three rioters. But the weak government could do little else, and it freed those students they arrested a few weeks later. In the meantime, pro-Japanese officials were removed from their bureaucratic offices.

The May Fourth Movement spread strong feelings of nationalism

## "The Three Principles" of Dr. Sun

Dr. Sun served during his political career not only as a revolutionary organizer, but as a planner and a philosopher who hammered out an agenda based on three principles, or tenets, he considered necessary as the building blocks of reform for his native China. He referred to these important political thoughts as the "San Min Chu I," or the "Three Principles of the People." Although he delivered these ideas publicly in a series of speeches to members of the Guomindang in 1924, they represented views he had held generally as early as 1905.

In their simplest form, the principles were identified by Dr. Sun as "nationalism, democracy, and the livelihood of the people." Yet, despite their seeming simplicity, Dr. Sun had developed a highly involved interpretation and definition of each of the principles. The first principle was *Min zu*, which translates as the "People's Nationhood."

When Sun first considered this political principle, its focus was the assertion of Chinese nationalism, which would require the removal of the Manchus from power. But after the 1911 revolution that ended Manchu rule, Sun began to redefine his principle, defining nationalism as the unification of all peoples living in China. His nation could not be home for just one ethnic group, but a state based on the unity of everyone—Chinese, Mongols, Tibetans, even Manchus, as well as lesser peoples. How, exactly, Dr. Sun intended to bring about this difficult goal was never spelled out. Some of his followers believed it would be fairly implemented through a federated state in which, for example, "Mongols and Tibetans were to have the standing of majorities within their own territories."* Sun did partially blame China's lack of national solidarity on the significant influence of outsiders, especially Europeans. This across several regions of China. It helped to rekindle the revolutionary movement as well, but it was a movement without any clear leadership or significant personalities to which revolutionaries could attach their loyalties. There was the continuing influence of Dr. Sun Zhongshan, who, although he had held no office in China's government after his short tenure as its first president, had never completely abandoned Chinese politics. But he never held real power in office either. He tried at least twice to establish revolutionary governments in Canton, but this required the backing of local warlords. All along, he continued to appeal to the Western democracies, including the United States, for support. But these powers never gave their full support to Sun, given his insistence that in any China he might govern,

meant "his First Principle was frankly anti-imperialistic."**

Sun's second principle was *Min chuan*, which translates as the "People's Power." In 1905, he promoted democracy as the alternative to a monarchy such as Manchu imperial rule. By 1924, his concept of democracy was formed by four influences, three of which were foreign. They included: (1) the Western example of republican government, (2) the Swiss political system, which allowed such political reforms as the initiative, referendum, recall, and open elections, (3) the Russian soviet model of centralized government, and (4) the historical Chinese concept of government "examination and control." In Sun's mind, Min chuan included a government based on the existence of an executive, legislative, and judicial branch, as well as historical models of Chinese political education and centralized control.

His third principle, *Min sheng* (meaning the "People's Livelihood") addressed the concept of social reform. His theory of government included socialism but not the hard-line Marxist model. (Dr. Sun was not an advocate of Marxist doctrine.) Instead, his economic ideas included such socialist ideals as eliminating extreme wealth in the hands of a few, and redistributing capital. He also favored the idea of the government providing support and capital to increase manufacturing output and production. To protect Chinese industry, Sun advocated the use of protective tariffs.

* Quoted in Paul Clyde, *The Far East: A History of the Western Impact and the Eastern Response.* Englewood Cliffs, NJ: Prentice-Hall, 1971, p. 314.

** Ibid., p. 315.

foreign influences would be kept to a minimum. He became so desperate that in February 1923, the Chinese nationalist proposed that the United States "lead an international occupation force with authority over the Chinese army and police [with] the right to appoint key administrators."[8] The offer was turned down. By 1923, then, Dr. Sun became convinced that his nationalist movement needed to alter its strategy. He no longer looked to such western powers as Great Britain, France, or the United States for help, but came to believe that "the only country that [shows] signs of helping us is Soviet Russia."[9]

### ENTER CHINESE COMMUNISM

Many Chinese had become disillusioned with the relatively ineffective democracy of their republic. They watched enviously in 1917 as the Russian people organized a street-level revolution that brought the proponents of Marxism to power. Some Chinese intellectuals began introducing communist thought into their country during 1917. The 1919 May Fourth demonstrations further encouraged Marxist thinkers, and more and more revolutionaries turned to communism as the answer to their country's political problems. By the following year, Soviet officials sent Communist agents to China to assist them in the organization of a Chinese Communist Party (CCP). That party was formed in the summer of 1921 by a dozen Chinese members as well as a Dutch and a Soviet Communist who officially represented the Communist International organization (Comintern).

Dr. Sun had already made contact with Soviet officials in November 1917. After the formation of the Chinese Communist Party, he met with party officials, and came to believe that Soviet Communists and his party, the Guomindang, should unite forces. He opened up membership in the Guomindang to Communists. The Soviets, in a good faith effort, promised military support against the Chinese warlords, as well as backing for Dr. Sun's return to a position of power in Canton. The Soviets forced the CCP to accept the leadership of the Guomindang, primarily because the Chinese Communist Party was small, with fewer than 500 members in the summer of 1923, while Sun's party claimed several hundred thousand followers.

By the fall of the year, Dr. Sun's alliance uniting the Guomindang and the CCP was producing results. The Russians sent a party official, a Latvian named Mikhail Borodin, who had earlier operated a language training school in Chicago, to restructure the party as a centralized Communist organization. Among Borodin's goals: Form a capable fighting force of revolutionaries to match the armies of both the Chinese government and any of the warlords that might stand in their way. A military academy was established on the Cantonese island of Huang Pu and its director was a Chinese military man of great resolve and sobriety, a veteran of a Japanese military school—the gray-eyed Jiang Jieshi (Chiang Kai-shek).

Jiang had been involved in revolutionary activities for years. In 1911, he had led a regiment of insurgents in the name of Dr. Sun, although the military unit was backed by a Japanese secret society. Although Jiang's activities resulted in his fleeing China for the safety of Japan, the two men had become friends.

## JIANG JIESHI TAKES CENTER STAGE

Jiang Jieshi did not fit the mold of a Chinese insurrectionist. He was wealthy, having made a fortune speculating in the Shanghai stock market. He also had connections with organized criminals in Shanghai, including the Green Gang, a crime syndicate that owned much of Shanghai's illegal activity, including gambling, prostitution, extortion, and the opium smuggling trade. In 1927, he became even more wealthy when he married Soong Mei Ling, whose brother was an influential and extremely wealthy Chinese banker. Soong's sister, Soong Jing Ling, was married to Dr. Sun. (Soong Mei Ling, known as Madame Jiang Jieshi, outlived nearly everyone who provided leadership for the Chinese Revolution, dying in 2003 at the age of 105 in her apartment in New York City.)

Not only was such wealth rare for Chinese revolutionaries, but Jiang had a personal and professional dislike for Communists. Nevertheless, he was prepared to work on behalf of Dr. Sun, whom he considered a mentor. China's national independence was an important incentive for a man like Jiang. He would use the CCP and the Soviets to achieve his goals, which included personal power over events guiding the future of China. Once he took power and gained control of his country's customs revenues, he would modernize China and "crush his Communist colleagues."[10]

Jiang set out to establish a network of support to achieve his personal aims. He attached himself to Dr. Sun and treated him as though he was a father figure. He courted the Russians, who provided military support that he could use as leverage against Japan, who still controlled much of Manchuria. He bargained with the Japanese from whom he received financial support in exchange for his promise to keep Soviet influence in China to a minimum. His business connections, both legitimate and illegitimate, supported him while he promised to eliminate Communist influences from labor unions in China's industrial cities. As for those in real power in China, the troublesome warlords, General Jiang offered to buy them out if they gave him their loyalty and support.

With the alliance between the Guomindang and the Chinese

## Jiang Jieshi

A great hero to Nationalist China, Jiang Jieshi (Chiang Kai-shek) is a villain to Communist China. His legacy continues today, in the division between mainland China, which is communist, and the island of Taiwan (Formosa), which is capitalist.

Born in 1887, Jiang Jieshi was from the village of Chikow in the province of Chekiang. His father and grandfather had both prospered as salt merchants, but his father died when he was young. Jiang had to make his way in the world, and he chose the military, serving first on the Chinese mainland and then going to Japan, where he studied at an advanced military academy. Sometime in 1910 he heard a speech by the political exile Sun Zhongshan; the speech changed Jiang forever, making him into a National Chinese patriot.

The Chinese Revolution began in 1911 and the Manchu emperor was forced to abdicate, even though he lived in the Forbidden City for several more years. Jiang resigned his army commission, went home, and became an organizer of the 1911 revolution. Like many Chinese, he felt betrayed by the double-cross performed by General Yuan and was greatly disappointed that Sun Zhongshan did not remain as the new president of China. For the next several years Jiang lived either in Japan or in Shanghai, and he returned to the political scene only in 1918, when he joined Sun's government in Guangzhou.

In 1923, Jiang led a Chinese group to Moscow, where they saw the Russian communist experiment firsthand. This was the

Communist Party, there were other important figures who soon became part of the revolutionary movement. One of Jiang's fellow military advisers at Huang Pu was a young man named Zhou Enlai (Chou En-lai), who helped found the CCP. For the next half century, Zhou would become one of the leading figures in the establishment of the Communist-led People's Republic of China. Another important player in the alliance was a 30-year-old member of the Guomindang's Central Committee, a former peasant from Hunan province named Mao Zedong.

beginning of the serious communist movement in China, and, on his return, Jiang seemed willing to allow Communists into the Nationalist government. But the death of Sun in 1925 made Jiang the new leader of the Nationalist movement, and he turned against the Communists. In 1927 he carried out a series of attacks that killed about 50,000 out of a total of 60,000. From then on it was open war between the Nationalists and the Communists.

Several times Jiang appeared on the brink of a complete victory, but the Communists outwitted him with their heroic "Long March" of 1934–1935, and by 1937 he was on the defensive. Things only became worse when Japan invaded China in that year; both the Nationalists and the Communists fought Japan while continuing to fight each other.

Jiang hit the peak of success in 1943. World War II had brought both recognition and applause for his government and he was invited to the Cairo Conference with Franklin Roosevelt and Winston Churchill. Both these men very much preferred Jiang and his government to the Communist alternative, and he won some important concessions, including the abrogation of some earlier treaties which had been humiliating to China. But this high point did not last.

The Second World War ended in 1945, and a major diplomatic effort by the United States (which included sending George Marshall to China) failed to reconcile the two sides. Jiang fought on until January 1949, when he resigned the Nationalist presidency. Just a year later he resumed the presidency, but he did so from the island of Formosa (Taiwan) just off of mainland China.

For the next 25 years, Jiang stood as a symbol of the new Chinese Nationalist Republic and of the resistance to Chinese Communism. He was elected and reelected to the presidency, serving a total of five terms in office. He died in 1975, just one year earlier than his hated rival, Mao Zedong.

## MAO ZEDONG LEADS THE REVOLUTION

Mao was born in 1893, the son of a Guizhou (Hunan) peasant. During Mao's childhood, however, his father speculated shrewdly in the rice market and became relatively prosperous. Mao despised his father, a strict disciplinarian, calling him "the dictator."[11] The young

## Mao Zedong

When Mao Zedong (Mao Tse-tung) was born in 1893, there were about 400 million Chinese. By the turn of the millennium in 2000, there were about 1.3 billion. Given these numbers, there is no disputing China's place among the great world nations and no disputing the importance of the man who made China a communist country.

Mao was born in the village of Shoshan in central China. He enjoyed no advantages growing up; indeed, he had to rebel against his father in order to obtain a secondary school education. Mao witnessed the Revolution of 1911 that overthrew the Ching dynasty and he, like many Chinese, welcomed the new Chinese republic. But over the next eight years he and other Chinese saw little improvement, and when he came across a Chinese translation of Karl Marx's *Communist Manifesto*, Mao was converted to classic Marxist philosophy.

One could argue that Marx never had an agrarian country like China in mind; he had always written that the great communist revolution would occur in cities and be carried out by industrial workers. But Mao took Marx's ideas and converted them to the reality of China in the 1920s and 1930s. He became the leader of the small Chinese Communist movement.

During the 1930s, Mao had to fight both the National Chinese forces, led by Jiang Jieshi (Chiang Kai-shek), and the Japanese, who invaded China in 1937. Mao and his core band of followers undertook the "Long March" up the west side of China, crossing ravines, gorges, and numerous mountains in order to surprise and attack their National Chinese foes. By about 1940, Mao held most of rural China.

Mao was a bright student, and his father sent him to school, where Mao hated his teacher with equal intensity because the teacher forced him to study Confucian classics, which he disliked. Defiant of authorities and established conventions, he imagined himself as a Chinese Robin Hood, striking against the rich and helping the poor.

The final struggle between the Communist and Nationalist Chinese was postponed until 1945, when the Second World War ended. Mao and Jiang then went at each other with hammer and tongs, and Mao emerged the victor. In September 1949, he led his men into the central part of Beijing and announced the start of a truly Communist state. This event (coupled with that of the Russian explosion of an atom bomb) frightened many Americans and helped contribute to the scandalous accusations of Senator Joseph R. McCarthy against American citizens he believed to be Communist in what was called America's "Red Scare."

Mao ruled China and its vast population from 1949 until his death in 1976. During that time the Chinese population almost doubled, in spite of the fact that Mao carried out purges of those who had "counterrevolutionary" principles. The so-called Cultural Revolution of the 1960s involved many young Chinese accusing their elders of being counterrevolutionaries, with disastrous results for both groups.

Despite the importance of his ideas and philosophy, Mao the practical man left the deepest imprint on China. Knowing that birds feed on precious grain, he hired millions of young Chinese to hunt and kill birds, with the attendant ecological results. Mao also divided China into thousands of small agricultural areas and made the peasants greatly increase their crop yields. Sometimes this was done through the introduction of new fertilizers, but often it was accomplished by driving the people even harder than before. Mao had some success in developing surpluses and in feeding the huge population, but he did so at great environmental and ecological cost.

Mao died in the fall of 1976. The world was stunned by the news, since he had come to represent China so completely in the minds of millions of Westerners. His ideas were carried on by his successors for about a decade and appeared to triumph when student uprisings were squashed in Tiananmen Square in 1989. But China's leaders strayed from Mao's pattern in the 1990s, and by 2000, China was well on the way to developing a marketplace based on supply and demand rather than on the "command" economy of the past.

Had there been no Karl Marx and Lenin, he would have been a rebel in the traditional sense.[12]

Trained as a university librarian in Beijing, Mao became a serious student of Marxism, a political writer in his own right, and a poet. He drew as much inspiration from the works of ancient Chinese writers as he did from modern communist theory. As the son of a peasant, Mao had a unique insight into the mind of the Chinese peasant class that was difficult for others in the revolutionary movement to match. In a 1927 writing, Mao described the peasants in allegorical terms:

> The force of the peasantry is like that of the raging winds and driving rain. It is rapidly increasing in violence. No force can stand in its way. The peasantry will tear apart all nets which bind it and hasten along the road to liberation. They will bury beneath them all forces of imperialism, militarism, corrupt officialdom, village bosses and evil gentry. Every revolutionary party, every revolutionary comrade will be subjected to their scrutiny and be accepted or rejected by them.[13]

Both a poet and a student of politics, Mao's "combination of romantic idealism and practical knowledge would prove vital to the Communists' survival in the years after the death of Sun Zhongshan."[14]

By June 5, 1925, Jiang was named as the commander in chief of the National Revolutionary Army (the NRA). Throughout the later 1920s, General Jiang carried out military campaigns across China. Dr. Sun did not survive to return to true power or even to witness Jiang's military success; he contracted terminal cancer in 1924 and died in Beijing in March 1925. With the death of the influential Sun, who failed to pick a successor, the alliance between the Guomindang and the CCP nearly collapsed, held together by Jiang's sheer will. Thoughout 1926, he won military incursions against several warlords and, by January 1927, was in control of central and southern China, including the manufacturing cities of Hankow, Hanyang, and Wuchang. With each field success, the Guomindang gained new members, as did the CCP, whose membership skyrocketed to 70,000 by early 1927. By the spring, Jiang's forces were in control of seven southern provinces and nearly half of China's population and

Nanchang (Nanking) and Shanghai had been captured. At that point, a confident Jiang turned on his Communist allies.

Perhaps he had good reason. Already, Communists had abandoned the Guomindang-CCP alliance and established a new Chinese capital at Wuhan, a central province where leftists were a majority in number. (Jiang intended to establish a new capital at Nanchang.) Shanghai was the logical city for the businessman in Jiang, since the city was "China's window on the world, and ... the best place to demonstrate to foreign powers that the kind of Guomindang government he envisaged posed no threat to [business] interests."[15] In the city, Jiang made contact with his associates in the local crime syndicate, the Green Gang, whose members, on April 12, began raiding leftist enclaves including labor union halls, killing Communist loyalists. Over a weeklong period, the Green Gang killed perhaps as many as 5,000 leftists, often beheading them, "their dripping heads displayed on bamboo poles or platters."[16] Zhou Enlai, the chief organizer of revolutionary activities in Shanghai, barely escaped with his life.

General Jiang's purges were launched in additional cities, sometimes resulting in fierce street battles between Guomindang members and Communist holdouts. By week's end, the general attended a party banquet with Soviet Communist advisors present, raised his wine glass, and called for his supporters to join him in a toast: "Down with the Communist party."[17] The Soviets soon left for Moscow. But Chinese Communist forces remained in the field, unprepared to bow to the pressure exerted by a powerful Jiang and his successful Guomindang party. CCP members led revolts against Jiang in several provinces and southern Chinese cities. Mao Zedong led one himself in Chang Sha, the capital of the Hunan province. He was badly defeated, as were many other leftist insurgents, and the future leader of the People's Republic of China abandoned his urban campaigns and began taking refuge in the mountains along the border of the Hunan and Jiangxi provinces. By early 1928, General Jiang was powerful enough to have himself declared the head of the Nationalist government at Nanchang. Less than six months later, his forces entered the city of Beijing, the ultimate goal of Jiang and his military campaigns.

## THE CHALLENGE OF THE CCP

With business-friendly General Jiang in charge, foreign nations watching from a distance gave him their full backing. In a good faith effort, the British abandoned two of their Chinese treaty port cities. The United States was also supportive of Jiang, in part because he represented strong business interests, but also because there were many American-supported Christians in China during the 1920s, and Jiang had earlier converted to Methodism, his wife's religious preference. As for the Japanese, their influence over some Chinese cities and provinces remained intact. But a new day had dawned for the Chinese people, reflected in the words of one Guomindang leader: "Something new has come to China: The birth of patriotism and public spirit."[18]

As Jiang attempted to systematically dismantle and destroy the presence and influence of the Communists in China, CCP leaders remained organized, developing a strategy to meet the right-wing general's measures head-on. At the forefront, Mao Zedong provided the inspirational leadership of words. The political poet spoke clearly to his fellow Communists: "Arise! Overthrow those who have oppressed you and who have benefited at your expense!"[19] But the challenge that Jiang represented required a military response as well. In 1927, a Nationalist military leader named Zhu De (Chu The) defected from Jiang and joined with Mao and his followers, establishing the military force the Communists so desperately needed—the Red Army. Within two years, Zhu's troops numbered more than 10,000 men. Mao was often unimpressed with their military might, once referring to the Red Army as a ragtag force carrying no more than "spears and old fowling pieces [out-of-date muskets]."[20] While sometimes lacking proper equipment and training, the Red Army made up for such deficiencies with a determined sense of spirit and drive.

Through the late 1920s and early 1930s, China continued to face extraordinary problems as the various political forces battled for power. The warlords had wielded their control for personal gain, accomplishing little for the sake of the Chinese people. Political and military struggles simply made the lives of the peasants even more miserable. With little direction or assistance from the Chinese government, six million Chinese died during a famine brought on by bad harvests. Even as Jiang ruled, his focus remained on the endless challenge of the Chinese Communist Party. Although he attempted to curb corruption during his early rule, he soon became disenchanted

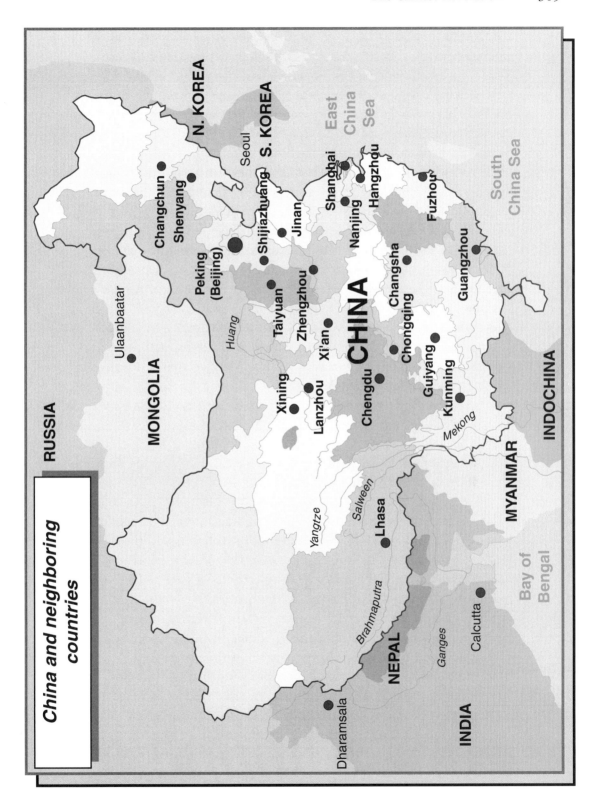

*China and neighboring countries*

with democracy and began to systematically establish himself as an all-powerful dictator. He organized his supporters into a nearly fascist order he called the Blue Shirts. (The fascist party in Italy was called the Black Shirts, and Hitler's Nazi Party members were the Brown Shirts.) In the meantime, the widow of Dr. Sun, disappointed in Jiang's leadership, left China, calling the Guomindang "a tool for the rich to get still richer and suck the blood of the starving millions."[21]

Yet as Jiang fretted about the Communists, they were growing to even greater numbers. Mao's leadership was crucial to the movement's survival, even though much of the military training was left to Zhu De and a fellow Red Army officer, Lin Biao, who, in 1930, was only 23 years old. Mao was most capable as a Communist philosopher and sloganeer. He wrote short, pithy sayings, easily remembered by the most illiterate party member or Red Army troop. After the manner of Dr. Sun, the party established "Three Principles" for its revolutionaries: "Obey orders at all times; do not take even a needle or a piece of thread from the people; turn in all confiscated property to headquarters."[22] As for field tactics, Mao created a four-line rhyming poem for the Red Army:

> When the enemy advances, we retreat.
> When he escapes, we harass.
> When he retreats, we pursue.
> When he is tired, we attack.[23]

But, despite his poetic heart, Mao Zedong was a pragmatic political figure, one who understood the nature of revolution and the difficulties inherent in challenging the authority of any government, including General Jiang's. In a political report written in 1927, he defined the difficulties of fighting a Marxist revolt:

> A revolution is not a dinner party, or writing an essay, or painting a picture, or doing embroidery; it cannot be so refined, so leisurely and gentle, so temperate, kind, courteous, restrained and magnanimous. A revolution is an insurrection, an act of violence by which one class overthrows another.[24]

To fight this violent struggle, Mao had collected an army of 30,000 by 1930.

## CAMPAIGNS OF ANNIHILATION

That year, Jiang struck hard against the Communists, ordering the "First Annihilation Campaign." (It was sometimes called the "Bandit Extermination Campaign.") Amassing 100,000 men armed with rifles and machine guns, with most of the troops supplied by the regional warlords, Jiang sent them into the provinces of Guizhou (Hunan) and Jiangxi (Kiangsi), where Communist-inspired peasant revolts had recently taken place. (The Communists controlled the region generally, governing through a Communist committee.) Although heavily outnumbered, the Red Army led Nationalist troops into the craggy hills of Jiangxi, where they attacked them while confined in long narrow valleys, picking them off in separated units. The forces of Mao were completely successful, taking nearly 10,000 of Jiang's forces prisoner and nearly as many weapons, which were desperately needed. (Perhaps even more important was the capture of a pair of field radios that "greatly improved the Communist army's communications.")[25]

But Jiang was not deterred by his 1930 losses. Between December 1930 and June 1932, the Nationalists carried out three additional military campaigns against the Red Army. All ended in failure. Maoists used their limited advantages—field mobility, familiar terrain, peasant support—to pull off successful defensive measures. A frustrated Nationalist commander lamented: "Wherever we go we are in darkness; wherever the Reds go they are in light."[26] General Jiang's primary strategy was to amass a superior number of Nationalist forces, augmented with fighters loyal to various warlords. But, in time, the warlords became less cooperative with Jiang, believing correctly "that their forces were being used as cannon fodder while the generalissimo [Jiang] kept the Nationalist Army intact."[27]

Adding to Jiang's difficulties was a 1931 invasion by Japanese troops of several Chinese coastal cities in Manchuria. Japan had fallen under the domination of its own warlords, who were intent on extending Japanese military and political influence throughout Asia. Manchuria was China's richest industrial province, and the Japanese occupation put it out of China's reach. Immediately, the Chinese Communists declared war on Japan. General Jiang, however, did nothing. The presence of Japanese troops in China was problematic for Jiang. After all, he was receiving aid from Japan, and he understood his Nationalist forces were no match for the highly trained, highly aggressive Japanese troops. When the Japanese occupied Shanghai in 1932, Jiang's government angrily appealed to the League of Nations in protest, but did little else. After the Japanese established their own puppet government in Manchuria, followed by their invasion into the northern province of Jehol in 1933, many Chinese were bitterly angered, blaming Japan's success on Jiang's inaction. For his part, Jiang believed the Japanese were not interested in conquering China but in establishing a war with the Soviet Union. The Japanese represented a "disease of the skin," Jiang explained to his critics, while the Communists remained "a disease of the heart."[28]

Convinced that the Communist threat was greater to his country than the presence of Japanese troops, Jiang remained committed to the eradication of the CCP and the Red Army. His state policy became "first pacification, then resistance."[29] In October 1933, General Jiang dispatched 700,000 Nationalist troops into the south-central Jiangxi region where, under the advisement of German military strategists, he planned to surround the Red Army. Jiang's troops moved with methodical intent. A string of blockhouses were erected connected by elaborate systems of barbed wire. The blockhouses were erected along every road and trail leading into the encircled region. To eliminate food resources, the Nationalists created a "fiery wall," burning villages and fields of crops ready for harvest. Hundreds of thousands of additional troops were sent into the region, augmenting Jiang's original force and boosting Nationalists forces to nearly one million.

The Red Army soon found itself outnumbered by more than five to one. But the Communist forces had become increasingly better equipped, better armed, "backed up with armor, artillery, and air-craft, and directed by a purposeful central command with good communications."[30] Such weaponry was crucial to Communist strength in the region. It was as Mao himself noted: "Power grows from the barrel of a gun."[31]

After only a few months, Jiang's encirclement of the Red Army appeared to be working. The blockade proved so effective that Mao's forces were soon suffering dramatically from shortages of food, clothing, medicines, and, perhaps most important, salt. Salt prices had skyrocketed, so that "salt alone cost a Communist nearly 10 cents a day ... whereas ... six years earlier he had had to spend only

5 cents a day on his meals except for the rice."[32] But with Jiang's besieging army, the point was not the cost but the availability. In time, "the lack of an adequate supply of salt had become so serious that the peasant soldiers were simply too weak physically to continue the fight."[33]

Locked into a geographic prison, Mao and Zhu De called for the Red Army to organize a full-scale breakout and scatter in small bands to fight another day. But other Communist party leaders refused to allow such a defeatist strategy. Despite Mao's wishes, party officials encouraged "their troops with the slogan: 'Don't give up an inch of Soviet territory.'"[34]

Through the winter of 1933–34, the Red Army struggled help-lessly against the iron-clad encirclement of General Jiang. After launching an offensive in April 1934, Communist forces were repulsed, their losses including 4,000 men killed and 20,000 wounded. Desertions became common, representing, as one Communist publication summed up, "an enemy more fearful than Jiang Jieshi."[35] By the summer of 1934, Mao was desperately dis-patching special Red Army corps to break the blockade, but with no success. With few options remaining, by the fall of 1934, Mao and Zhou Enlai were finally able to convince party leaders that the Jiangxi soviet must be abandoned. Surrender was still not an option, however. The Red Army would attempt to punch its way out of Jiang's encirclement and retreat to the Shaanxi (Shensi) Province to the north. The decision was climactic, but desperate. Shaanxi was thousands of miles away. The soldiers of the Red Army had been reduced to running for their lives.

## THE LONG MARCH

Against long odds, harsh prewinter weather, and a formidable land-scape, between 85,000 and 100,000 Red Army troops began aban-doning their long-held positions in the Jiangxi soviet. Among their number were hundreds of women, including Mao's wife, He Zizhen, who was unfortunately suffering through an advanced pregnancy. On the night of October 18, 1934, the main units of the Red Army broke out of the town of Yudu straight into the portion of Jiang's perimeter they considered the weakest. That evening began a year-long migration of Chinese revolutionaries that would one day be called the "Long March." After successfully breaking through, the

Red Army split up into smaller units and headed west into the mountainous and rugged region of Guangdong (Kwangtung), Hunan, and Guangxi (Kwangsi) Provinces.

The movements of the Red Army were constantly hampered by the terrain and the baggage the army carried, including food, printing presses, and the wounded on stretchers. Alongside the soldiers were the noncombatants, "a mass of peasants with carrying-poles (their Service of Supply)."[36] Even as the Communists began their march, they left behind more than 25,000 people, including many of the sick and dying—those incapable of being moved.

## An Army Constantly on the Move

The Red Army's "Long March" proved to be a nightmarish experience of survival. Nearly every day, the Communist forces faced challenges at every turn. For each member of the Mao-led march, the experiences were different only in the details.

Once the Reds reached the highlands of Guizhou during the early weeks of their march, they abandoned everything but the essentials, dumping their printing presses and other political equipment. Everyone was ordered to carry only food, ammunition, and their personal weapons. There were few beasts of burden, so all military supplies, tools, and additional equipment had to be carried by the men and women of the Red Army.

Food was always in short supply. Each Red Army member was to carry "a rice ration of about four and one-half pounds"* in a sack slung over the shoulder on a pole. But such quantities were not always available. Making matters worse, Mao had ordered his follow-ers to restrain from taking any peasant's property, including any food. (The property of all landowners could be confiscated, however.) One marcher recalled a troop of hungry marchers passing a field of fruit trees, the fruit ripe for the picking. But since the leaders did not know whether the fruit trees were those of a peasant or a landlord, the fruit remained on the trees until a local woman revealed herself as the owner and sold the fruit to the famished followers of Mao Zedong.

For the women on the march, life was especially difficult. Approximately 2,000 women participated in the Long March and a constant problem was how to cope with menstruation, or what one female marcher called "women's special suffering."** According to one woman: "When women started menstruating, it was miserable. We didn't have any place to dry our pants in the sun. We had to wear the wet ones and let them dry with the heat of our bodies, so it

Yet the Red Army pushed on. When they reached the Xiang (Hsiang) River, however, they were met by a formidable force of Nationalist troops. The fighting along the river spread out over a week, resulting in 30,000 casualties, but the Communists were able to cross the river and reach Mao's home province, Hunan. For weeks, the Red Army units marched in zigzag fashion through the mountains, desperately searching for a breakout site to take them beyond Guomindang forces. Heavy fog and low cloud cover hid them from Nationalist planes searching for them from the air, and the Red Army reached the next western province, Guizhou

was easy for us to get sick."[***] For many, pregnancy was their greatest challenge. Some women had to abandon their newborns so as not to slow down the marchers. One marcher, Liao Siguang, later talked of giving birth to a premature baby and abandoning it:

> What a lovable child! ... What were we to do? At that time, our first aim was to keep alive in order to accomplish the revolution. After the birth, I was very weak and had to be carried on a stretcher. If I had brought along the baby, it would have added considerably to the burden of the soldiers. So I made the decision and endured the pain of leaving the child behind.[+]

Mao's wife, He Zizhen, was pregnant and gave birth early in the march. Even she had to give up her baby girl to a local mountain family.

For everyone on the march, there were the rugged mountains that wore shoes out in days; cold weather and rain; and the constant tension of facing such challenges for endless days. There were, however, inspirational moments which helped to rekindle the spirit of revolution in thousands of weary marchers, as one of Mao's engineers later recalled:

> Night marching is wonderful if there is a moon and a gentle wind blowing. When no enemy troops were near, whole companies would sing and others would answer. If it was a black night and the enemy was far away, we made torches from pine branches or frayed bamboo, and then it was truly beautiful. When at the foot of a mountain, we could look up and see a long column of lights coiling like a fiery dragon up the mountainside.[++]

* Quoted in Time-Life Books, *Timeframe*, p. 151.
** Quoted in Helen Praeger Young, *Choosing Revolution: Chinese Women Soldiers on the Long March*. Urbana: University of Illinois Press, 2001, p. 203.
*** Ibid.
+ Ibid., p. 197.
++ Quoted in Time-Life Books, *Timeframe*, p. 152.

Facing overwhelming opposition from Chinese troops, Mao Zedong faced the uneasy decision of abandoning his encircled stronghold, and leading his Red Army into the northern and western mountains. The difficult, year-long journey claimed many lives and is referred to as the "Long March."

(Kweichow). Here, the army abandoned all items considered unnecessary and continued their march toward the Yangzi (Yangtze) River.

Along the opposite banks of the Yangzi, Nationalist troops had gathered by the thousands, ready to halt the progress of the Red Army. Nationalist forces destroyed bridges across the river into Sichuan (Szechwan) Province, floated all ferries to the northern side of the river, and established positions along all mountain passes. For months, the Red Army searched for a way across the river, until the Communists turned south and crossed at Zhou Ping Fort into the rugged and remote Yunnan Province.

## HEROICS AT LUDING BRIDGE

Soon, Red Army forces faced a serious obstacle to their advance. When troops reached the Luding Bridge near the Suchuan (Szechuan) border, they found the bridge damaged by Nationalist forces. The Luding Bridge had been built in 1701 by Emperor Kang Xi, and the ancient bridge spanned the river as it ran through a deep canyon at a distance of 100 yards. The bridge included 13 large iron chains, their ends attached to the canyon sides, and wooden planking serving as the walkway. The Nationalists had removed the planks on the southern side of the bridge, leaving only the chains. Across the river, two regiments waited, entrenched for a fight. Faced with a hopeless situation, 22 of Mao's fighters volunteered to try and cross the remains of the bridge. With death-defying courage, the volunteers began to cross the bridge, swinging "hand over hand across the gorge until they reached the middle,"[37] taking heavy enemy fire. Three of the men were hit and fell into the river far below. A Red Army regimental leader later wrote about the suicide crossing:

> The attack began at four in the afternoon. The buglers of the regiment gathered together to sound the charge, and we opened up with every weapon we had. The noise ... reverberated through the valley. The twenty-two heroes ... climbed the swaying bridge in the teeth of intense enemy fire. Each man carried a tommygun, a broad sword and twelve hand grenades.[38]

Amazingly, most of the men reached the remaining planking. But opposition forces had already poured kerosene on the bridge planking, which exploded into flames. As some of the Red Army volunteers hesitated, a platoon political leader "sprang down on the flooring before the flames reached his feet, calling the men to follow."[39] The others bravely followed, storming across the bridge while tossing hand grenades, as the Nationalist forces abandoned their posts and fled. Having successfully reached the opposite side of the river, the daring volunteers replaced the removed planks, allowing their comrades to cross the bridge. The event would become one of the most potent legends of the "Long March" and of the Maoist revolution.

## THE MARCH CONTINUES

But greater challenges lay ahead. Once across the river, Mao and his forces were only 100 miles in a straight line away from their fellow troops in the province of Sichuan. The true distance was much greater, however, following winding paths across seven separate mountain chains. After resting for more than a month, the Communist troops began their frozen trek. The greatest of the seven ranges was the first they encountered, the Great Snow Mountains. Reaching an elevation greater than 16,000 feet, the Red troops suffered from icy winds, freezing temperatures, and altitude sickness. Soldiers dropped out, succumbing to the cold. One marcher described a recurring scene: "All along the route we kept reaching down to pull men to their feet only to find that they were already dead."[40]

Coming down from the last of the summits, Mao's troops rendezvoused with the Sichuan Red Army. Even after such a grueling march, the leaders of the two groups could not agree on strategy and decided to separate just as they had come together. The Sichuan forces pushed further west into Tibet, while Mao led his army even further north into the Shaanxi (Shensi) region "in the shadow of the Great Wall, close to possible Russian aid."[41]  Ahead lay yet another forbidding stretch of landscape, the Grasslands, an endless, pathless wilderness of tall grasses that hid many swamps and bogs. For ten days, the Red Army slogged through the rain-swept Grasslands, finding little food and no shelter. With no place to lie down flat, marchers slept with their backs against one another. The tall, thick grasses hid the marchers from each other and several became disoriented and lost, and died. If one fell ill, he or she was abandoned, since the grasses were too thick to allow for stretchers. When Mao and his comrades finally emerged from the Grasslands, nearly one out of three had perished.

The Grasslands were followed by another six weeks of marching, as they marked the passage of a full year since they had broken out of General Jiang's stranglehold. Finally, on October 20, 1935, they reached the relative safety of northern Shaanxi Province. The marchers had crossed dangerous rivers; struggled along narrow, rocky trails; conquered giant, icy mountains; and blindly maneuvered through thick grasslands, but they had managed to complete their Herculean march of 6,000 miles. The cost, however, had been extraordinarily high. Of the 100,000 followers of Mao who began the march, only 7,000 survived. (Another 15,000 completed the march, but they had been recruited along the way.) While the loss of life impacted every one of Mao's marchers, those who completed the challenging journey emerged with a renewed sense of commitment to the Communist cause.

The Long March remains a historic event with no parallel. The historian Jerome Chen sums up the accomplishment's place in the history of human endeavor:

> One may compare the Long March with Hannibal's journey across the Alps and say smugly that the Chinese did better, or with Napoleon's retreat from Moscow and say coldly that the Chinese did worse. But it must be admitted that man has never seen the equal of it before or since. It was a flight in panic; yet it was also an epic of human endurance. In 370 days from 16 October 1934

to 20 October 1935 the 1st Front Army under Mao [Zedong] walked on and on, to cover a distance of 6,000 miles.[42]

No one understood the significance of the Long March more than the marchers' leader, Mao Zedong. While his party members and Red Army soldiers emerged from the ordeal damaged and dramatically reduced in number, the yearlong trial produced followers for Mao who were extraordinarily disciplined and sacrificial in the cause of social and political change for their native China. Just two months after the completion of the historic march, Mao reflected on the previous year and its relative success against long odds:

> For twelve months we were under daily reconnaissance and bombing from the skies by scores of planes, while on land we were encircled and pursued, obstructed and intercepted by a huge force of several hundred thousand men, and we encountered untold difficulties and dangers on the way; yet by using our two legs we swept across a distance of more than twenty thousand li [about 6,000 miles] through the length and breadth of eleven provinces. Let us ask, has history ever known a long march to equal ours? No, never. The Long March ... has proclaimed to the world that the Red Army is an army of heroes.... The Long March ... has announced to some 200 million people in eleven provinces that the road of the Red Army is their only road to liberation.... In the eleven provinces [the Long March] has sown many seeds which will sprout, leaf, blossom and bear fruit, and will yield a harvest in the future. In a word, the Long March has ended with victory for us and defeat for the enemy.[43]

From the success of the Long March, the army of Mao gained a legendary reputation for invincibility. Mao would become the unrivaled leader of Chinese Communism. At the same time, the Communist movement in China would remain a rural fight. For generations of Chinese then unborn, the legacy of the Long March remained a touchstone of the Communist rise to power.

## THE JAPANESE INVASION

As for General Jiang, he remained undaunted, still intent on destroying all elements of communism in his country. Yet the specter of

Japanese imperialism also continued to cast a shadow over his country. Many in China, including Mao and his followers, believed the Japanese posed a greater threat to China than Jiang did to them. There were calls from several factions within China for the Nationalists and the Maoists to join forces in opposition to the Japanese threat. In December 1936, while visiting the Shaanxi Province, Jiang was kidnapped by a local warlord who forced the generalissimo to make peace with the Communists so that both political powers could pool their resources and fight Japanese aggression. Zhou Enlai intervened, calling for Jiang to be placed on trial, but when the Russian leader, Joseph Stalin, stepped in, he pressured the

## Zhou Enlai

No one save Henry Kissinger traveled so many miles and met so many foreign leaders as Zhou Enlai (Chou En-lai). At the same time, Zhou holds the record for longevity in office during the twentieth century. Put together, these accomplishments place him right at the top of the heavyweights of his time.

Born in 1898 in Kiangsu province, Zhou Enlai grew up in a happy family. His father died when he was young and Zhou was therefore raised by an uncle; it is said that his remarkable diplomatic ability began at this early age, when he had to adapt to new circumstances. By the time the Chinese Revolution of 1911 began, Zhou was a moderate revolutionary who wanted to remove the Manchu regime but keep many of China's old and respected institutions.

After some time spent in Japan, where he became a more radical revolutionary, Zhou joined with Mao Zedong in the leadership of the new Chinese Communist Party.

The relationship between the two men remains a source of fascination for China scholars to this day: Was Mao as dominant as he seemed? Was Zhou as amicable as he appeared? Truly it is impossible to know the answer to these questions, because Mao and Zhou both believed in subordinating personalities to party leadership. This is in keeping with an ancient Chinese tradition that exalts the movement or the results and not the particular leader.

Zhou was with Mao on every step of the grueling "Long March" of 1934–1935. This dramatic event made the Communists more appealing than before, and Mao and Zhou capitalized on their newfound success. There was even a brief time when it appeared that the two men might undergo a reconciliation with Jiang Jieshi, but this possibility evaporated.

World War II ended in 1945 and the Chinese Revolution ended in 1949 with

Communists and the warlords to release Jiang. When the Russians then made a strong request for the Nationalist leader to ally with Mao, Jiang reluctantly agreed. Soon, the Russians were delivering 1,000 planes and 2,000 pilots to China.

The year 1937 proved difficult for the Chinese in their stand against Japan. That summer, Japanese troops fought near Beijing, taking control of the city in July. Before the year's end, Shanghai and Nanjing also fell. In an effort to psychologically bring the Chinese Nationalist government to its knees, the Japanese spent two months on a killing spree in the streets of Nanjing. Before the Japanese were finished, their troops had slaughtered more than 200,000 men. The

complete success for Mao, Zhou, and the Communist cause. Mao became the head of state, but Zhou became the premier, a position he would hold for most of the rest of his life. Unlike Mao, who delighted in provoking capitalistic nations and teasing their leaders, Zhou was a born diplomat, able to see two sides to a matter, and eager to find some common ground with China's capitalistic foes. His only major diplomatic defeat was in the area of American-Chinese relations; Zhou was unable to obtain recognition, or even civility, from United States leaders. A story is told of how U.S. secretary of state John Foster Dulles snubbed Zhou at a chance meeting in Geneva in 1954: The hurt remained with Zhou for many years.

Zhou played less important a role during the "Cultural Revolution" of the 1960s. Perhaps he feared he might be seen as one of the "old" and "out of touch" leaders who were continually denounced by China's young Red Guards. In any case, Zhou steered away from this as much as he could and saved his energies for one last diplomatic triumph: the visit of President Richard Nixon to Beijing.

In 1971, American secretary of state Henry Kissinger arrived in China for secret talks with Zhou. The two men drew up plans for an American presidential visit in the following year, and Nixon did descend from an airplane in February 1972. This visit, heralded in the newspapers of all nations, showed a change in U.S. policy and allowed China to become a third "major player" in geopolitics.

Zhou died at the end of 1974. His long and fruitful career had witnessed great changes, and none were so spectacular as the transformation of China from a weak and divided nation into a powerful, Communist one.

extermination was systematic and cold-blooded. One eyewitness described how Chinese men were captured, lined up, then executed:

> Those in the first row were beheaded, those in the second row were forced to dump the severed bodies into the river before they themselves were beheaded. The killing went on non-stop, from morning until night, but they were only able to kill 2,000 persons in this way. The next day, tired of killing in this fashion, they set up machine guns. Two of them raked a cross-fire at the lined-up prisoners. Rat-tat-tat-tat. Triggers were pulled. The prisoners fled into the water, but no one was able to make it to the other shore.[44]

In addition, 20,000 women were raped, then killed, because, as one Japanese soldier stated matter-of-factly: "[D]ead bodies don't talk."[45] Many of the female victims of the Japanese were mutilated and dismembered by soldiers.

Jiang's government soon went on the run, fleeing west toward the region of Wuhan. As his army moved, the generalissimo ordered dikes along the Huang Ho (Yellow) River destroyed, which caused wholesale flooding across the Chinese landscape. The move halted temporarily the advance of the Japanese, but the flood waters killed hundreds of thousands of innocent Chinese peasants. As the Japanese extended their influence across China, there were few military victories for Jiang and his Nationalist forces. Despite a singular victory over the Japanese in the spring of 1938 at Taierzhuang in Shandong Province, which ended in more than 15,000 Japanese deaths, the Jiang government remained in search of a safe haven.

By late October, Jiang had removed himself to the Sichuan town of Chongqing (Chungking), behind the natural barrier of the Sichuan mountains. Before year's end, the Japanese were in control of the majority of Chinese territory, and the Nationalist government remained paralyzed. Yet even as events disintegrated his state into a Japanese colony, General Jiang refused to surrender. His only remaining hope was that the United States would go to war with Japan and help rescue his government. But such a possibility still seemed remote in 1938.

Jiang's inactivity was unacceptable to many of the Chinese people. They saw his government as inert, one endlessly stuck in a defensive mode. And Guomindang officials became notorious for their corruption. Although Jiang generally remained personally uncorrupted, others in his party apparatus did not. As the Nationalists lost state income from the Japanese control of Chinese trade and customs monies, they began wildly printing great quantities of paper money that soon became worthless. (The Jiang government had "nationalized" all Chinese silver in 1935, requiring everyone to hand their silver over to the government, forcing the use of paper money in all legal transactions.) Between 1942 and 1944 alone, China witnessed near hyperinflation as prices skyrocketed. Additional taxes were placed on regional populations by cash-strapped Guomindang governors. Such taxes as the "contribute-straw-sandals-to-recruits" tax were created alongside the "train-antiaircraft-cadres" tax. The Nationalists were not only losing vast territories to the Japanese, they were also losing the battle for control of the minds and hearts of the people of China.

Still living in northern China after their "Long March," the Communists remained in the field, fighting the Japanese through hit-and-run guerrilla tactics. Since the Japanese military relied on their control of various Chinese railroads, the Maoists attacked these transportation lines and the blockhouse complex that connected the parts of each line. The Communists proved so bothersome that the Japanese increased the number of their troops in China and ushered in a new strategy, the Three All's: "Kill all, loot all, burn all."[46]

Such a heavy-handed response to the Communist threat caused Chinese peasants to flock to join the party of Mao Zedong. They were encouraged to join the fight to protect their country alongside patriotic Communist loyalists. Mao was also able to attract new party members and lure an increased number of peasants to his party by calling for various socialist reforms. In a 1940 speech, Mao outlined his program for China's future, which he labeled the "New Democracy." He claimed to embrace Sun Zhongshan's Three Principles. As for any Chinese economy under his control, important industries and banks would be government owned, but a great amount of capitalist production would remain in private hands, as long as it would not "dominate the livelihood of the people."[47] Local warlords agreed with his demand to lower land rents required of peasants, as well as reductions in taxes. He also called for immediate land reform and managed some success. He ordered his followers to "devote 70 percent of their energy to Communist expansion and 20 percent to 'coping with' the [Guomindang], leaving 10 percent to be used against Japan."[48]

Mao's followers, the farmer-worker-soldiers of the Red Army, were fighting two revolutions at once—one military, one social—and he was gaining more followers with each passing day. By 1940, Mao's supporters numbered around 400,000. Even as Jiang sat immobile in a remote corner of China, the Communists were increasing around their own rallying post—Chairman Mao.

## ENTER THE UNITED STATES

In the United States, President Franklin Roosevelt was intent on giving aid to the Chinese, sending financial support in 1939. (Neutrality laws restrained the U.S. government from supplying arms and other military equipment.) Roosevelt was alarmed by the creation of a Japanese-controlled puppet government headed by a former Jiang military leader who had defected to the Japanese. Regional governors and warlords were also making deals with the Japanese. But even as Jiang received aid from the United States, he remained reluctant to use it, trying to save his resources for the struggle between his government and the Communists.

Then, Jiang's hope for a war between the United States and Japan opened up in December 1941, following the Japanese attack against U.S. military forces in Hawaii. With America and the Japanese empire at war, the United States was free to deliver large quantities of weapons, military vehicles, and other war materiel to Jiang's beleaguered government through its Lend-Lease Program. Much of this war arsenal was delivered through Burma along the winding, twisting mountain-pass highway called the Burma Road. An American general, Joseph Stilwell, the commander of the U.S.-China-Burma-India theater, was dispatched to Jiang to serve as his chief of staff. An American volunteer air force called the Flying Tigers, was formed to help meet the challenge of superior Japanese air power over China.

As for both the Communists and the Nationalists, "both sides acted as if the war against Japan had already been won, and they began to think in terms of a postwar struggle between themselves."[49] Mao and Jiang believed the United States would eliminate the threat of Japan. As for the American military, it still considered Jiang responsible for protecting his own country, with aid provided by the United States.

Yet Jiang remained immovable, refusing to use his increased military power against the Japanese, leaving much of the fighting for his country to other Allied powers, including the United States. As Stilwell prodded the Chinese leader to move his forces, Jiang stated he would not commit any Chinese divisions to the fighting until they outnumbered Japanese forces five to one, a completely unrealistic goal. In his diary, the American general wrote of Jiang's demands: "What a directive. What a mess."[50] Stilwell and Jiang did not get along under such circumstances, and Jiang asked for General Stilwell's removal by 1944. The U.S. government could do nothing but recall Stilwell to Washington.

Jiang's number one objective was to face down the threat of the Chinese Communists. But by June 1944, the United States government had reached out to the Maoists and made its first direct contact with the Communists. When American officials reached the region of China then controlled by the Maoists, largely the north and central provinces, they were surprised. One member of the American party noted: "We have come into a different country and are meeting a different people."[51] While Jiang had remained obstinate, uncooperative, and immovable, the Communist army appeared "loyal, well-disciplined, respectful of civilian rights, and highly motivated."[52] The Maoists appeared in control of more than 300,000 square miles of Chinese territory and were keeping the Japanese at bay.

While American foreign policy had expected to provide support to the Jiang government, some Americans were already questioning the legitimacy of the Nationalist regime. But President Roosevelt remained loyal to Jiang throughout the war. Largely through the influence of his ambassador to China, Patrick Hurley, FDR never gave consideration to the significance of the Communists or their threat to the stability of a postwar China. Hurley did organize a meeting between Nationalist and Communist leaders; in late August 1945, after the surrender of the Japanese government following the dropping of two American atomic bombs over two Japanese industrial cities, Mao Zedong made a trip to Chongqing where he met with Jiang and the Americans through six weeks of diplomatic sessions. Nothing of substance emerged from the joint negotiations.

Although FDR had died the previous April, the failure of the autumn meetings between Mao and Jiang ensured that American support under President Harry Truman would remain with the Nationalists. Truman was a staunch anti-Communist who did not personally like Jiang but felt the Nationalist government was the only legal regime in China. Thus, in the postwar world, Mao found himself with few friends. By 1945, he had made a break from the Soviet Union and its leader, Joseph Stalin. He had determined that his brand of Communism would not match the Soviet model, publicly stating that there "was no place for doctrinaire Marxists in China."[53]

Jiang remained firmly in power, with support from both the United States and the Soviet Union. Stalin considered Mao a traitor to the Marxist cause, calling Chinese Communism nothing more than "two peasants wearing the same pair of pants."[54] Stalin expressed the same sentiment to Ambassador Hurley during a visit by the American diplomat in Moscow. He told Hurley he considered Mao's followers to be "radish Communists—red on the outside, white inside."[55]

Despite the failure of the 1945 meetings between Mao and Jiang, President Truman took additional steps. He dispatched U.S. Army general George C. Marshall to China as a special ambassador to bring the two sides together. Another conference was called for 1946. Both sides again attended; again, nothing important was agreed upon. Marshall emerged from the experience frustrated: "The greatest obstacle to peace has been the complete, almost overwhelming suspicion with which the CCP and the Guomindang regard each other."[56]

Jiang had few incentives to compromise with Mao. He enjoyed American support; China, at the insistence of the United States, had been granted status as one of the "Big Five" nations that emerged victorious from World War II, along with the United States, Britain, France, and the Soviet Union. As such a key player, Jiang's China had been honored with permanent membership status on the new United Nations' Security Council. He had a 1,000-plane American air force at his disposal and an army of more than 3 million men, now highly trained and supplied with British and American equipment. (By comparison, Mao's troops—his Red Army had been renamed the People's Liberation Army (PLA)—numbered fewer than 1 million.) Jiang's government had survived the war, and everything indicated that, whatever his political future, he would not face the challenge of the Maoists alone.

## JIANG'S FINAL CAMPAIGNS

In the face of such opposition from the Jiang government, plus the power symbolized by Jiang's allies—Great Britian, America, the Soviets—Mao began to hedge slightly, indicating he might accept a limited role in a Jiang-dominated government. But Mao's olive branch was met by Jiang's use of military might against him. During the summer of 1946, Jiang's troops made moves against Mao's PLA. Outnumbered and outgunned, the PLA lost their hold over vast regions of China, and, by late 1947, Guomindang forces "controlled every provincial capital, most other important cities, and China's major transportation routes."[57]

But even as Jiang used his military against the threat of Communism, it was clear that his political power had always been based only on the threat of military might. After ruling China for more than a decade, Jiang had never implemented Dr. Sun's Three Principles, his countrymen did not live under the freedoms of true democracy, and his Nationalist officials had often been and continued to be corrupt, drawn to General Jiang for personal gain. In addition, Jiang's hard-edged, sometimes paranoid policies, including his harsh economic programs, had resulted in a loss of middle-class support. This active class of businessmen, urban professionals, merchants, shippers, bankers, and traders "found itself living under an authoritarian military dictatorship that used force to stifle even the mildest demands for reform."[58]

In addition, the money system in China was falling apart. In 1937, the rate of exchange between Chinese and American dollars was a reasonable three to one. In early 1946, the exchange rate was a lopsided 2,020 to one, followed by a precipitous fall in the value of Chinese dollars to a rate of 73,000 to one by year's end. By 1948, "to print a paper bill cost more than the face value it bore, and the government lost money every time a piece of paper money came off the printing press."[59]

The cities were turning against Jiang, driven by rampant inflation that, by the summer of 1947, had driven the price of a pound of rice to a quarter million Chinese dollars. As food prices soared, thousands of people died of starvation. Foodless Nationalist troops abandoned General Chiang and joined the PLA. Since the Communists lived in the rural places, outside the money economy, they did not experience the same food problems. Maoist socialism was already demanding that everyone in Mao's classless cadre of followers be supplied the same.

By the fall of 1947, the Communists were on the offensive again, led by forces commanded by Lin Biao. Most of the fighting was centered in Manchuria. Through brilliant campaigns, Lin brought victories. His troops gained control of the Manchurian railway system by year's end. Nationalist forces, fed up with Chiang's regime, defected by the thousands. Three out of every four Nationalists who were captured by the Communists did so by simple surrender. A year after Lin Biao's campaign went offensive, the Communists emerged stronger then Jiang's Nationalists.

## Lin Piao

The Chinese Communists won the war with the Chinese Nationalists because of men like Lin Piao.

Born in Wuhan in the province of Hubei, he was the son of a landowner and small factory owner. His father lost the business and became a customs official on the Yangtze River. Lin Piao joined the Chinese Communist Party in 1925 or 1926 and soon became a shooting star in the Communist military. After attending China's Whampoa Military Academy, Lin Piao participated in the struggles of 1927 between National and Communist groups on the latter's side, and he became one of the small handful of leaders trusted by Mao Zedong and Zhou Enlai. Lin Piao was also with these men on the Long March of 1934–1935.

The Sino-Japanese War began in 1937, and for a time the National and Communist groups stopped fighting each other. Early in the Sino-Japanese War, Lin Piao won an important victory in the mountains, routing a crack division of Japanese troops. At a time when neither the Communist Chinese nor the National Chinese had much to celebrate, his victory took on an added meaning: he was the first Chinese leader to win a significant battle in the long war.

The Sino-Japanese War ended in 1945 and was followed by the life-or-death struggle between the National and Communist Chinese. By 1946, Lin Piao was in command of 250,000 Communist troops, and in January 1949 he was the first Communist general to enter Beijing: By then he commanded 800,000 men. What distinguished Lin Paio from his brother officers was his use of varying tactics; he did not become tagged as either a guerrilla fighter or a regular army fighter. A complete pragmatist, Lin Piao used whatever worked at the time.

When the struggle ended, Lin Paio was held in high regard. But Mao Zedong became

Jiang's last stand was a battle for control of the city of Nanjing. The fight was large-scale, involving a million combatants, equally divided between the Communists and the Nationalists. The fighting continued for more than nine weeks, but Maoist forces systematically destroyed the enemy divisions, each falling as if they were so many dominoes. Following the urban struggle, an embattled General Jiang resigned as the president of China and turned his government over to an underling, who then began offering to negotiate with Mao. But Mao took a hard line and "demanded virtually unconditional surrender and the punishment of 'war criminals' headed by [Jiang Jieshi]."[60] After a diplomatic lull in the fighting, the

envious of his general, and Lin Piao was accorded less attention over the next decade. Although he rose to become minister of defense, this did not happen until 1959, and there was no special celebration of his special talents. Therefore it took the Cultural Revolution of 1966 to bring Lin Piao to the forefront.

What happened in China during the Cultural Revolution remains somewhat mysterious. It seems clear, however, that Mao pitted the young against the old, and the urban against the country dwellers. His tactics worked, and Mao emerged more powerful than ever. Such a man needs a designated heir and successor, and Lin Piao received this honor at the Chinese Communist Party Congress of 1969. He had reached the summit of fame and honor.

Just two years later, in September 1971, Lin Piao was killed when his plane was shot down over the People's Republic of Mongolia. What happened that autumn was even more mysterious than the Cultural Revolution. Did Lin Piao try to carry out a coup? Was he shot down while trying to escape to Communist Russia? The answers have not been forthcoming. Many scholars doubt that Lin Piao would have turned against the leader he had served for so long, and believe rather than Mao's wife used a pretext to have Lin killed so she could assume his place as the number-two person in the Chinese Communist hierarchy.

A terrific soldier and a loyal Communist Party member, Lin Piao is little remembered today. But then, China throughout her history has emphasized the movement and the actions of groups and sought to downplay those of individuals (Chairman Mao being a prominent exception to the general rule).

Communists returned to their offensive in April 1949. Mao ordered his fighters to cross the Yangzi River to seize control of Jiang's capital, which fell before the month's end. Jiang fled mainland China for the island of Taiwan (Formosa), off the Chinese coast. Considering his exile temporary, Jiang promised to return to the fighting and restore his control over China, but he never did.

After more than two decades of fighting to bring revolutionary change to China, Mao Zedong stood at the helm of leadership. On October 1, 1949, he stood at a podium erected at the age-old Gate of Heavenly Peace in Beijing and announced a new government—indeed, a new state: the People's Republic of China. Mao had proven himself a forceful leader, one who inspired his followers with his poetry, his politics, and his sheer will to survive in the face of extraordinary adversity. He had survived the political massacres of 1927, had endured the difficulties of the Long March, had outreached the long arm of General Jiang's Guomindang and the armies of Japan. He had known death and destruction, war and civil war, hunger and privation, discouragement and disillusionment, but he had successfully led his followers to power. From 1949 until his death in 1976, Mao Zedong would remain the powerful figure of leadership, the deathless symbol of a revolution that continued to redefine itself with each passing decade.

Why had Jiang failed? After years of holding extraordinary power, of commanding millions of loyal Nationalist troops, of receiving support from the greatest powers in the West, including the United States, he had failed to hold on to the one thing that meant the most to him—power. Historian C.P. FitzGerald sums up some of the reasons why Jiang, despite his advantages and international support, lost the revolution of wills and ideologies to determine China's future:

> The Nationalists lost the war because they were badly led, followed wrong strategy, were corrupt, and lost the support of the people, including that of their own ill-treated conscripts. The Communists won because they had a disciplined and dedicated army, were accepted as liberators by the peasantry, conceived their strategy on sound principles, and executed their operations with brilliant tactics. They had no air cover or any air force at all; the Nationalist superiority in equipment and American-supplied

weapons remained intact until the end, as did their command of the air. It availed them nothing.[61]

## A CONTINUING REVOLUTION

Just as the American Revolution had its George Washington, the French Revolution its Lafayette, and the Russian Revolution its Lenin, so the Chinese Revolution had Mao Zedong. Mao, from the early years of the campaign to liberate China, was the perceived leader, referred to by some revolutionaries as "the Great Helmsman."[62] He held the chairmanship of the CCP as well as the leadership of the People's Republic of China. He remained a leader greatly adored by his people, one who thrived on their adoration and reworked it to provide support for his political strategies both during the revolution and after 1949.

During the 27 years that followed, Mao continued to provide leadership for the various socialist programs he established to improve the lives of the Chinese people. As a Communist leader, he called for dramatic change. All land was taken away from the landlords and redistributed. Under his programs of land reform, 43 percent of Chinese land was handed off to 60 percent of the population, many of them peasants.

Chairman Mao enacted sweeping social reforms, introducing the Marriage Law in 1950 to recognize equal rights for women, to ban child and arranged marriages, and to end prostitution and concubinage, or the practice of having more than one wife.

He sought public health programs for the Chinese people, encouraging his followers to practice regular hygiene and cleanliness. Hygiene workers plastered posters in every city calling for the eradication of four common pests—bedbugs, flies, mosquitoes, and rats. Young Chinese students brought "boxes of dead insects" to show their teachers, as they made their own small contribution to the cause of national health.[63]

There were literacy campaigns under Mao and a dramatic increase in the number of schools, which children of all ages attended, regardless of their class or social standing.

As a Marxist, Mao believed in government ownership of private property. During the early years following 1949, Mao allowed many Chinese cities to retain private enterprise, which was monitored

Mao did much to inspire the respect and adoration of his followers and has been referred to as "the Great Helmsman." Here, a large group of Red Army soldiers and officers gather in Mongolia for a lecture on the political situation.

closely by the state. But by 1952, Mao's revolutionary government was confiscating private lands, businesses, shipping firms, factories—the entire means of production.

In time, Mao's revolution called for government control of many aspects of life in China. Nearly all farms were forced to become state-owned cooperatives, while factories were turned into state-run industries. Yet such changes did not manage to solve all or even most of China's greater problems. Although food production rose dramatically through the early 1950s in China, by 1958 Mao perceived such gains had not been enough. He ordered the widespread establishment of communes across the country. These vast economic and social systems forced millions of people to live in collective communities, where their lives were controlled and structured by the government—all part of the chairman's "Great Leap Forward":

> Twenty-four thousand communes were set up in the first two months of 1958 alone.... In them, all aspects of people's lives were effectively "collectivized" and regimented. Communal nurseries freed the women from looking after their children and communal dining halls fed their families, so they could devote all their time and energy to working under strict discipline. Instead of money, residents of the rural "people's communes" were provided with six community services absolutely free: education, food, funerals, haircuts, health care, and movies.[64]

But Mao's "Great Leap Forward" resulted in a general failure. As Mao had encouraged more and more peasants to abandon food production for industrial output, especially in steel production, food shortages resulted, bringing about the deaths of an estimated 20 million people by starvation between 1959 and 1962. In 1959, Mao resigned as "chairman" of the People's Republic. (He did retain his position as chairman of the Communist Party.) The elderly Mao, 69 years old in 1962, became the target of harsh criticism within his own party.

Mao did not remain on his nation's sidelines for long, however. Throughout the 1960s and early 1970s, he continued to direct and redirect the revolution that he always considered a work in progress. During the 1960s, he launched a new program, one designed to revitalize China as well as his leadership. "The Great Cultural Revolution" was intended to "reassert an ideological and cultural revolutionary spirit."[65] Mao's supporters printed hundreds of millions of copies of a book containing the words of the elderly revolutionary, titled *Quotations from Chairman Mao*. The "little red book" was intended as an inspiration to a new generation to follow the teachings of Mao Zedong.

Mao's "Cultural Revolution" targeted any element of Chinese life that appeared to be in opposition to the spirit of the revolution. Books were burned, theaters were closed, artists and performers who did not include revolutionary themes in their work were persecuted, even executed. Mao used the program to target any and all critics and eliminate political rivals. As one critic observed: "Anyone in power became a target, whether they were right or wrong."[66] Those caught without a copy of Mao's "little red book" were persecuted. Thousands of innocent Chinese people were killed by Mao's Red Guards. China nearly became a victim of its own revolutionary excesses.

By the late 1960s, the Great Cultural Revolution had run its bitter course, leaving many Chinese people completely disenchanted with Mao and the revolution, although he continued to wield power until his death in 1976. Zhou Enlai, Mao's old revolutionary comrade, died the same year. Today, the People's Republic of China continues to struggle with ever-changing concepts of the revolution of Mao Zedong. While China is still governed by Communist leaders who deal harshly with those who oppose them ideologically, the country is in the midst of great change. The hard-line elements of socialism are softening, and elements of capitalism are allowed greater inroads by a government struggling with its twentieth-century heritage of revolution yet experiencing a twenty-first century in which the future of socialism and Communist control seem less and less a part of China's great historical destiny. Perhaps Mao's own words may signal a message to the next generation of Chinese youth as they consider the possibilities ahead for their own political, social, and cultural future: "The world is yours, as well as ours, but in the last analysis, it is yours.... Our hope is placed on you.... The world belongs to you. China's future belongs to you.[67]

[Author's Note: The Chinese place names and surnames referred to in this chapter are derived from the Chinese Pinyin system of romanizing Chinese ideographic characters based on phonetics. The Pinyin system was created in the mid-twentieth century as a replacement for the nineteenth-century Wade-Giles system. Because the Wade-Giles spelling is still commonly used, most Pinyin names are followed by the Wade-Giles version placed in parentheses. For example: Jiang Jieshi (Chiang Kai-shek).]

## TIMELINE

**1644**  Rule of China by foreign invaders, known as the Manchus, begins.

**1905**  Dr. Sun Zhongshan chosen as leader of a coalition of various Chinese dissident groups.

**1907–1911**  Chinese rebels organize periodic uprisings across southern China. None manages to topple the Manchu regime.

**1911**  **October 9**  Spontaneous revolution breaks out in China after insurgent bomb accidentally explodes.

**1912**  **February 12**  Chinese ruler, Prince Chun, abdicates his throne.

**February 13**  Dr. Sun turns over presidential post to General Yuan.

**1913**  **November**  General Yuan cracks down on Chinese dissidents, including Dr. Sun's Guomindang (Nationalist Party), establishing dictatorial rule.

**1916**  **March 22**  General Yuan is forced to step down by various regional military governors. Yuan dies three months later.

**1916–1928**  "Era of the Warlords".

**1917**  **August 14**  China is forced by Japan to declare war on Germany.

**1919**  **May 4**  May Fourth Movement is launched as a grassroots revolutionary movement.

**1921**  Chinese Communist Party is formed by a dozen Chinese members.

**1923**  Dr. Sun's Guomindang allies itself with the Soviet Union.

**1925**  **June 5**  General Jiang is named as the commander in chief of the National Revolutionary Army (NRA).

**1930**  **December–June 1932**  General Jiang launches "First Annihilation Campaign" with intention of destroying the Chinese Communist Party (CCP).

**1930**  Nationalists carry out three additional military campaigns against the Communists' Red Army.

**1931**  Japanese troops attack several Chinese coastal cities in Manchuria.

**1933**  **October**  General Jiang dispatches 700,000 Nationalist troops into the Jiangxi region, intent on surrounding and crushing the CCP enclave.

**1934**  **October–October 1935**  Maoists engage in desperate "Long

March" in an attempt to escape the ring of steel Jiang has estabished around CCP forces.

**1936**  **December**  Jiang is kidnapped by Shaanxi Province warlord to force Jiang to make peace with the Communists. Pressure exerted by Soviet leader, Joseph Stalin, secures release of Jiang.

**1939**  American government begins sending financial support to the Jiang government to aid in campaign against the Japanese.

**1940**  Communist leader Mao Zedong outlines program for China's future, called the "New Democracy."

**1941**  United States and Japan declare war on one another, allowing United States to supply Jiang through Lend-Lease program.

**1944**  Jiang orders recall of American commander General Stilwell from China.

1911

**1911**
**October 9**  Spontaneous revolution breaks out in China after insurgent bomb accidentally expodes.

**1921**
Chinese Communist Party is formed by a dozen Chinese members.

**1934**
**October 1934–October 1935**
Maoists engage in desperate "Long March" in an attempt to escape the ring of steel Jiang has established around CCP forces.

**1919**
**May 4**  May Fourth Movement is launched as a grassroots revolutionary movement.

**1925**
**June 5**  General Jiang is named as the commander in chief of the National Revolutionary Army (NRA).

**1930**
**December 1930–June 1932**
Nationalist carry out three additional military campaigns against the Communists' Red Army.

**1936**
**December**  Jiang is kidnapped by Shaanxi Providence warlord to force him to make peace with the Communists. Pressure exerted by Soviet leader, Joseph Stalin, secures release of Jiang.

**1945**  **August**  Japanese surrender. Maoist and Nationalist forces renew their long-term struggle for power in China.

**1945**  Mao breaks with Soviet Union's Joseph Stalin; is determined that his brand of Communism will not mirror the Soviet model. Mao and Jiang meet at U.S.-backed conference, but come to no agreement.

**1946**  Another conference between the Nationalists and the Communists ends in failure.

**1946–1947**  Jiang's Nationalist forces launch effective campaign against Communists, taking control of every provincial capital.

**1947**  Inflation and food shortages cause many Nationalists to defect to Communists, resulting in successful Maoist offensives against Jiang.

**1948**  Jiang resigns as president of China.

1940
Communist leader Mao Zedong outlines program for China's future, called the "New Democracy."

1945
Mao breaks with Soviet Union's Stalin determined that his Chinese Communism will not mirror the Soviet model. Mao and Jiang meet at U.S.-backed conference, but come to no agreement.
**August**  Japanese surrender. Maoist and Nationalist forces renew their long-term struggle for power in China.

1958–1962
Mao's "Great Leap Forward" program designed to modernize China ends in failure.

1975

1975
Mao Zedong and his old Communist comrade, Zhou Enlai, die.

1949
**October 1**  Mao establishes the People's Republic of China.

1959
Mao resigns as "chairman" of the People's Republic.

1941
United States and Japan declare war, allowing the United States to supply Jiang through Lend-Lease program.

**1949**    Jiang flees mainland China for sanctuary on island of Taiwan.

**October 1**  Mao establishes the People's Republic of China.

**1958–1962**  Mao's "Great Leap Forward" program designed to modernize China ends in failure.

**1959**    Mao resigns as "chairman" of the People's Republic.

**Mid-1960s**  Mao pushes a new program, "The Great Cultural Revolution," and attempts to purge China of all opposition to his government and the revolution. Program devolves into near anarchy.

**1975**    Mao Zedong and his old Communist comrade, Zhou Enlai, die.

---

## SOURCE NOTES

1. Quoted in Richard Marshall, ed., *Great Events of the 20th Century: How They Changed Our Lives.* Pleasantville, NY: Reader's Digest Association, 1977, p. 66.
2. Quoted in Time-Life Books, *Timeframe AD 1925–50: Shadow of the Dictators.* Alexandria, VA: Time-Life Books, 1989, p. 137.
3. Quoted in C.P. FitzGerald, "The 1911 Revolution," in A.J.P. Taylor, ed., *The 20th Century*, vol. 3. Milwaukee: Purnell Reference Books, 1979, p. 301.
4. Quoted in Marshall, *Great Events*, p. 68.
5. Ibid., p. 69.
6. Quoted in Ronald Iain Heiferman, "The Triumph of the Kuomintang." in A.J.P. Taylor, ed., *The 20th Century*, vol. 10. Milwaukee: Purnell Reference Books, 1979, p. 1347.
7. Quoted in Time-Life Books, *Timeframe*, p. 138.
8. Ibid., p. 139.
9. Ibid.
10. Ibid., p. 141.
11. Quoted in Dun J. Li, *The Ageless Chinese: A History.* New York: Charles Scribner's Sons, 1965, p. 478.
12. Ibid.
13. Quoted in B.I. Schwartz, *Chinese Communism and the Rise of Mao.*

Cambridge, MA: Harvard University Press, 1951, p. 74.
14. Quoted in Time-Life Books, *Timeframe*, p. 140.
15. Ibid., p. 143.
16. Ibid.
17. Ibid.
18. Ibid.
19. Quoted in Marshall, *Great Events*, p. 251.
20. Ibid., p. 252.
21. Quoted in Time-Life Books, *Timeframe*, p. 145.
22. Ibid., pp. 145, 148.
23. Ibid., p. 148.
24. Quoted in Mao Zedong, "Report on an Investigation of the Peasant Movement in Hunan" (March 1927), in *Selected Works, Volume I*, Beijing: Foreign Languages Press, 1967, p. 28.
25. Quoted in Time-Life Books, *Timeframe*, p. 148.
26. Ibid.
27. Ibid.
28. Quoted in Dun J. Li, *Ageless Chinese*, p. 484.
29. Quoted in Marshall, *Great Events*, p. 254.
30. Quoted in Time-Life Books, *Timeframe*, p. 149.
31. Quoted in Heiferman, *Triumph*, p. 1352.

32. Quoted in Jerome Ch'en. *Mao and the Chinese Revolution*. New York: Oxford University Press, 1965, p. 179.
33. Quoted in Dun J. Li, *Ageless Chinese*, p. 480.
34. Quoted in Time-Life Books, *Timeframe*, p. 150.
35. Ibid.
36. Quoted in O. Edmund Clubb, *20th Century China*. New York: Columbia University Press, 1964, p. 202.
37. Quoted in Marshall, *Great Events*, p. 253.
38. Ibid., p. 251.
39. Quoted in Time-Life Books, *Timeframe*, p. 154.
40. Ibid., p. 155.
41. Ibid.
42. Quoted in Ch'en, *Mao*, p. 185
43. Quoted in Mao, *Quotations*, p. 160.
44. Quoted in Iris Chang, *The Rape of Nanking: The Forgotten Holocaust of World War II*. New York: Basic Books, 1997, p. 48.
45. Ibid., p. 49.
46. Quoted in Time-Life Books, *Timeframe*, p. 156.
47. Quoted in Li, *Ageless Chinese*, p. 495.
48. Ibid.
49. Ibid., p. 494.
50. Quoted in Time-Life Books, *Timeframe*, p. 159.
51. Ibid.
52. Ibid.
53. Quoted in Li, *Ageless Chinese*, p. 495.
54. Quoted in Time-Life Books, *Timeframe*, p. 160.
55. Ibid.
56. Ibid.
57. Ibid., p. 162.
58. Ibid.
59. Quoted in Li, *Ageless Chinese*, p. 504.
60. Ibid., pp. 499–500.
61. Quoted in C. P. FitzGerald, "China: Communist Victory," in A.J.P. Taylor, ed., *The 20th Century*, vol. 15. Milwaukee: Purnell Reference Books, 1979, p. 2090.
62. Quoted in Godfrey Hodgson, *People's Century: From the Dawn of the Century to the Eve of the Millennium*. New York: Times Books, 1995, p. 466.
63. Ibid., p. 467.
64. Ibid., p. 470.
65. Ibid., p. 475.
66. Ibid., p. 476.
67. Quoted in Mao Zedong, *Quotations From Chairman Mao Tse-Tung*. New York: Bantam Books, 1967, p. 165.

## BIBLIOGRAPHY

Chang, Iris. *The Rape of Nanking: The Forgotten Holocaust of World War II*. New York: Basic Books, 1997.

Ch'en, Jerome. *Mao and the Chinese Revolution*. New York: Oxford University Press, 1965.

Clubb, O. Edmund. *20th Century China*. New York: Columbia University Press, 1964.

Clyde, Paul. *The Far East: A History of the Western Impact and the Eastern Response*. Englewood Cliffs, NJ: Prentice-Hall, 1971.

Dirlik, Arif. *Anarchism in the Chinese Revolution*. Berkeley: University of California Press, 1991.

Fitzgerald, C.P. "China: Communist Victory," in A.J.P. Taylor, ed., *The 20th Century*, vol. 15. Milwaukee: Purnell Reference Books, 1979.

———. "The 1911 Revolution," in A.J.P. Taylor, ed., *The 20th Century*, vol. 3. Milwaukee: Purnell Reference Books, 1979.

Heiferman, Ronald Iain. "The Triumph of the Kuomintang." in A.J.P. Taylor, ed., *The 20th Century*, vol. 15, Milwaukee: Purnell Reference Books, 1979.

Hodgson, Godfrey. *People's Century: From the Dawn of the Century to the Eve of the Millennium*. New York: Times Books, 1995.

Isaacs, Harold R. *The Tragedy of the Chinese Revolution*. Stanford, CA: Stanford University Press, 1961.

Latourette, Kenneth Scott. *The Chinese: Their History and Culture*. New York Macmillan, 1962.

Lazzerini, Edward J. *The Chinese Revolution*. Westport, CT: Greenwood Press, 1999.

Li, Dun J. *The Ageless Chinese: A History*. New York: Charles Scribner's Sons, 1965.

Marshall, Richard, ed. *Great Events of the 20th Century: How They Changed Our Lives*. Pleasantville, NY: Reader's Digest Association, 1977.

Rue, John E. *Mao Tse-tung in Opposition, 1927–1935*. Stanford, CA: Stanford University Press, 1966.

Schiffrin, Harold Z. *Sun Yat-sen and the Origins of the Chinese Revolution*. Berkeley: University of California Press, 1968.

Schwartz, B.I. *Chinese Communism and the Rise of Mao*. Cambridge, MA: Harvard University Press, 1951.

Short, Philip. *Mao, A Life*. New York: Henry Holt, 1999.

Spence, Jonathan D. *The Gate of Heavenly Peace: The Chinese and Their Revolution, 1895-1980*.New York: The Viking Press, 1981.

Time-Life Books. *Timeframe AD 1800–1850: The Pulse of Enterprise*. Alexandria, VA: Time-Life Books, 1989.

———. *Timeframe AD 1925–50: Shadow of the Dictators*. Alexandria, VA: Time-Life Books, 1989.

Young, Helen Praeger. *Choosing Revolution: Chinese Women Soldiers on the Long March*. Urbana: University of Illinois Press, 2001.

Zedong, Mao. *On Guerrilla Warfare*. New York: Frederick A. Praeger, 1961.

———. *Quotations From Chairman Mao Tse-Tung*. New York: Bantam Books, 1967.

———. *Selected Works of Mao Tse-tung, Volume 1*. Beijing: Foreign Languages Press, 1967.

# 8

# The Iranian Revolution

**By the mid-1970s, the dynastic ruler of the Middle Eastern nation of Iran** had occupied his legendary Peacock Throne for more than a third of a century. To everyone who knew him and his centralized style of governing his kingdom, Muhammad Reza Shah Pahlavi appeared indomitable. His rule was absolute, "so entrenched that not many, even among the Shah's opponents, dared to speculate about his possible overthrow, at least in the near future."[1]

He enjoyed the backing of a loyal military machine and domestic security forces. Many conservative elements in Iran—the landholders, businessmen, and government bureaucrats—provided support from the country's upper and middle classes. The Shah rested in the knowledge that his country was wealthy in oil and that its markets were international. The United States was among his closest allies, a great provider of sophisticated military hardware.

The Shah's eye was always riveted on the future of his country, this inheritor of one of the great civilizations of the ancient world, the mighty Persian Empire. His country was one of the most progressive

337

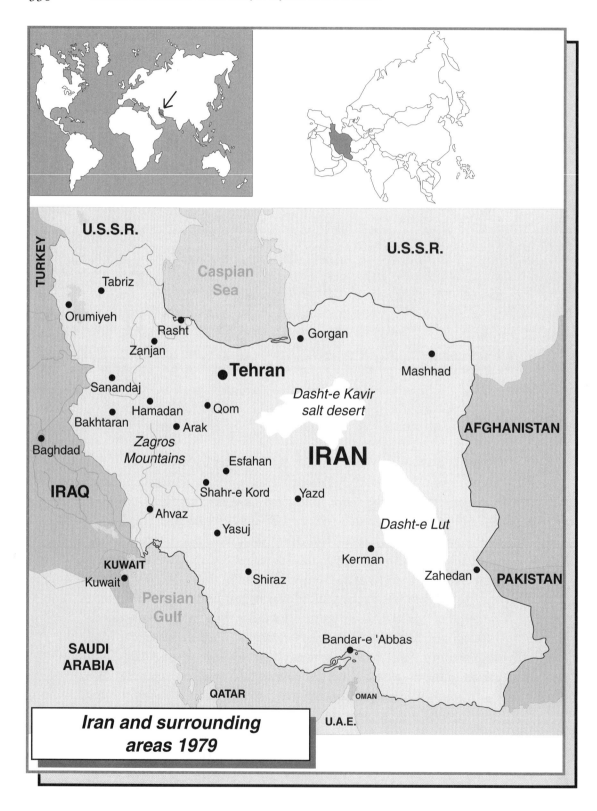

**Iran and surrounding areas 1979**

and Westernized of any in the Middle East. But of all these certainties, the primary one was that Muhammad Reza Pahlavi believed his rule was one chosen by God, the Muslim Allah, and that he was Allah's agent on earth, honored and armed by the Divine with a "spiritual vision that he was being instructed ... to lead his predominantly Shia Muslim people."[2] Few kingdoms in the history of the world seemed as safe as that of the Shah of Iran.

Yet, in January 1979, the Shah; his wife, the Shahbanou; and their family boarded a plane at the Mehrabad Airport in the Iranian capital of Tehran and flew into exile, leaving their native land and their Pahlavi dynasty for the last time. Before the year's end, "an ample-bearded, humorless Muslim cleric,"[3] the Ayatollah Ruhollah Khomeini, declared himself to be the de facto leader of a new Iran, whose government would be transformed into an Islamic theocracy. Ecstatic Shiite Muslims greeted the Ayatollah Khomeini with great enthusiasm, wildly excited about his dream of establishing Iran's first "government by God."[4]

How had such a dramatic turn of events transpired in a kingdom considered by many as unassailable? How had a scattered, unorganized revolution of Muslim extremists managed to topple the Shah of Iran? To many Westerners, it was a revolution of mysterious proportions and mystical fanaticism. To the majority of Islamic fundamentalists, it had been a simple matter of carrying out the will of Allah.

## THE LONG HISTORY OF PERSIA

In 1971, the Shah of Iran presided over elaborate celebrations marking the 2,500th anniversary of the founding of the great Persian Empire by its ruler, Cyrus the Great. But the ancient land of the Persians, modern-day Iran, had been occupied thousands of years prior to the establishment of its imperial heritage during the 300s B.C. Although archaeologists date the first humans in Iran back 100,000 years, the first recorded culture was established by the Elamites in around 3000 B.C.

By 1000 B.C., just as the Bronze Age was giving way to the new Iron Age, two Aryan peoples, known throughout history as the Medes and the Persians, reached Iran from the north, passing through the Caucasus Mountains. The Medes reached the region first, establishing their kingdom in the north, while the Persians settled in the south. Although the Medes dominated their Persian neighbors first, the tables were turned when, in 550 B.C., the Persian king, Cyrus the Great, married into the royal house of Medes, conquered his neighbors in battle, and absorbed Media into his Persian state. The result was a new Persian Empire.

Although it began as a smallish kingdom, the Persian kingdom "needed only about 30 years to burst from obscurity and create the first world empire."[5] In a few short years, the Persians had established their dominance over a vast region stretching from Asia Minor in the west to the Indus River Valley, more than 1,600 miles away.

But the Persian Empire had expanded so quickly, it was susceptible to challenge. After the death of Cyrus the Great, his successors faced serious revolts that shook the foundations of the empire. Led by the Ionian Greeks of western Asia Minor (modern-day Turkey), the Persians fought two wars against the Greeks during the 480s B.C. that resulted in the defeat of the empire. Although these battlefield losses did not result in the collapse of the Persian Empire, it did bring about independence for many of the Greek colonies that had been held under the thumb of Persian authority. Then, during the 330s B.C., the Persian world was conquered by one of the great generals of the Ancient Near East, a Macedonian named Alexander the Great.

As Alexander established his Hellenistic (Greek-like) empire throughout the lands he had conquered, including the Persian Empire, the Persians were introduced to new ideas, philosophies, and social customs. Alexander educated tens of thousands of young Persian noblemen in the ways of the Greeks. While the world of Alexander held together for a few years, after his death in 323 B.C., his empire was divided between his generals, one of whom, General Seleucus, who had married a Persian princess, was granted the region that included the Persian Empire. The Seleucids ruled over Persia for two centuries, but, by the 100s B.C., a nomadic people from the eastern state of Parthia took control of the kingdom of Seleucus under King Mithradates II.

For the next four centuries, the Parthians administered the old Persian Empire, adopting Greek culture yet making allowances for the reestablishment of ancient Persian customs, religious ideas, and traditions.

Far to the west, the Romans were busy establishing an empire of their own, but the Parthians were able to keep them at bay and even extended their own empire east to India and to the southwest into Egypt. Then, in 224 A.D., a regional Parthian leader named Ardashir (he had ruled over lands that are today part of Iran's western neighbor, Iraq) conquered the last Parthian monarch. His people, the Sasanians, ruled over Persia from the early 200s until the 600s. It was during this period of Sasanian rule that the Persian religion of Zoroastrianism helped to unify the people of Persia in their loyalty to the Sasanians. In turn, the Sasanians declared Zoroastrianism as the state religion.

Over hundreds of years of rule, the Sasanians became increasingly unpopular with their Persian subjects. Royal corruption, a line of ineffectual kings, repeated wars, and a domestic system that included the enslavement of millions of Persian subjects led to the collapse of Sasanian rule. The weakened empire was seen as easy prey for a new militant, religious force, born on the Arabian peninsula to the west: Islamic Arabs. In 642, with the arrival of Arab armies, the Persian Empire finally came to an end. As one Muslim poet wrote of the empire's demise: "O men, do you not see how Persia has been ruined and its inhabitants humiliated? They have become slaves who pasture your sheep, as if their kingdom was a dream."[6]

As the Arabs established their dominance over the Persians, they forced their new subjects to convert to the Islamic faith. Islam was a relatively new religion, only established during the early 600s by a mystical Arabian trader named Muhammad. Although Zoroastrianism had been firmly entrenched in Persia for more than a thousand years, the Arabs destroyed much of the old religion and installed Islam as the new national faith. While Zoroastrianism survived in a few places, Persia, and thus modern-day Iran, was destined to be a Muslim state.

However, the followers of Islam had split after the death of their religion's founder, Muhammad, in 632. Two significant Islamic sects had developed, the Sunnis and the Shiites. While they were different in other ways, their primary disagreement focused on Islamic leadership. The Sunnis believed each new Islamic leader had to be selected by practicing Muslims, while the Shiites taught that only the descendents of Muhammad could direct the Islamic faithful.

The majority of Persians adhered to the Shiite tradition; however, the region of Persia was dominated by the Sunni Umayyad caliphate (a territory under Muslim control, with power held by a *khalifa*, or caliph, a title meaning "successor or deputy of Allah"). With their superior numbers, the Shiites led a rebellion against Sunni domination in 750 that brought the first Abbasid caliph, a direct descendent of Muhammed. But the Abbasid rulers were often weak and proved unable to hold their Islamic state together. By the ninth and tenth centuries, Persia had split into smaller, independent kingdoms, including Tahirid and Samanid.

Yet Persia remained an unstable region. Such smaller kingdoms did not last long, and, by the eleventh century, the nomadic Seljuk Turks entered, another invading peoples from central Asia. Seljuk dominance of Persia lasted only a few generations, until they were driven from power by the Mongols under the leadership of the infamous Asian conqueror, Genghis Khan. It was a difficult time for the people of Persia as the barbarous Mongols attacked and destroyed Persian cities and towns, executing thousands of innocent victims. For an entire generation, from 1220 to 1258, the native Persian population declined by 25 percent. Remaining in power until the 1400s, the Mongol leaders (the *khans*) were removed by a Turkoman sect called the Al-Quoyunlu, a name which literally translates as "possessing white sheep."[7]   Persia was again in the hands of foreign invaders and ruled by a sub-group of the Al-Quoyunlu, the Safavids, who had migrated from modern-day Azerbaijan.

The Safavid shahs proved highly competent, and Persia prospered. They declared Shi'ism as the state religion once again. These early shahs of Persia often did not keep themselves at a distance from their subjects, but were reported to "show great familiarity to strangers and even to their own subjects, eating and drinking with them pretty freely."[8] Perhaps none was greater than the fifth Safavid shah, Abbas I (1587–1629), who completely unified the kingdom of Persia during the late sixteenth and early seventeenth centuries. As shah, Abbas I, known as Abbas the Great, moved the Persian capital from Qazvin to Isfahan in 1598. He made diplomatic deals with neighboring powers, including the Ottoman Turks, to keep his borders intact. He reordered his military and his governmental bureaucracy so they would remain personally loyal.

Abbas I even introduced a renaissance in the Persian arts. His kingdom became famous for its rich textiles, including the famed Persian carpets. The literary arts flourished, as Persian books, with their elaborate illustrations and ornate calligraphy, were prized and highly sought after. But Abbas I also took bold steps outside of his corner of the Muslim world of the Middle East. He "opened his court to Westerners, making a treaty with Britain that gave it the sole right to trade Persian silks."[9] This direct trade alliance with the British would serve as the beginning of interest in Persia on the part of the young British Empire.

With his death in 1629, Abbas I was followed on the throne by several weak Safavid rulers. By 1722, Afghans had taken control of much of the Persian countryside and captured Isfahan, ultimately removing Shah Sultan Husayn from his throne. The Safavid dynasty came crashing down. But Afghan rule only lasted a decade, as an energetic military leader, Nader Qoli, led his Persian forces to victory against the Afghans. Having vanquished the occupiers of his land, Nader declared himself the shah of Persia. He then turned to the offensive and marched his men east where they conquered Afghanistan, not stopping until they reached Delhi, India. Nader returned with many treasures from the East including a special throne, one destined for legend, the golden, bejeweled Peacock Throne, on which the twentieth-century shah, Muhammad Reza Pahlavi, would one day sit.

Shah Nader's rule proved burdensome to the Persians, who suffered under high taxes, and he was assassinated by one of his own palace guards after only a few years in power. He was followed by another shah, Karim Khan Zand Muhammad, who ruled for a quarter century, restoring his kingdom to tranquility and peace. Yet, in a repeat of history, his reign was followed by poor Persian leaders, opening up a weakened state to foreign invasion. Again, the Turks returned, this time as the Qajars, led by Agha Muhammad Khan, Armenian descendants of one of the last of the former Mongol Khans. After taking control of Persia in 1787, the Qajars established yet another capital, this time at Tehran, where they ruled for a century and a half.

Yet during these decades of Qajar rule, additional influences were gaining a voice over Persian affairs. The Qajars were wily negotiators, making diplomatic agreements with other regional powers, including the British and the Russians, who were, by the early 1800s, powerful enough to challenge Qajar rule. Both powers were interested in acquiring Persian markets for their domestic goods. They also considered Persia part of a general regional buffer zone that included Afghanistan, Turkestan, and Transcaspia that kept the two powers from direct contact. The Turks at first played the two European powerhouses off of one another by making separate treaties. But when the Qajars attempted a regional power grab against Afghanistan in 1856, the British turned on them, driving the Turkish Qajars out of Afghanistan permanently. The resulting Treaty of Paris (1857) marked a new era of Afghanistan independence and signaled further losses of Persian territory to Afghanistan.

For the remainder of the nineteenth century, the British and the Russians were involved in a "quest for respective spheres of influence within the country [of Persia]."[10] A weakened Qajar kingdom was increasingly forced to accept compromises and concessions. (In part, the Qajars allied themselves with the British and Russians as an insurance against losing power. The regime was often unpopular with Shi'ite forces, especially when various shahs attempted to modernize Persia.) Both European powers collaborated and established the eastern border of Persia in 1893. Meanwhile, the Qajars were too weak to make any serious move in response. Nearly bankrupt at the end of the nineteenth century, the Qajars accepted large monetary loans from the Russians, while granting Britain the right to establish the Imperial Bank of Persia, to help finance British exploration for Persian oil deposits. Both moves significantly hamstrung the Qajars, who were suddenly economically dependent on these two aggressive European powers.

By 1906, such foreign pressures on Persia were creating a backlash among the people. Such groups as "merchants, members of the Islamic clergy, and political reformists"[11] began to exert extreme pressure on the shah to allow a constitution fashioned after Western models. The political reforms also included the establishment of a Persian national assembly, the Majlis. Much of the leadership of this small-scale but vocal revolution came from the Shi'ite religious leaders, who managed to rally supporters among both rural peasants and urban merchants. In several of its elements, the 1906 uprising would mirror some of the events that would comprise the 1979 Iranian Revolution.

Despite the political changes within Persia, foreign aggression continued. The following year—1907—Britain and Russia established a zone of influence within Persia, the Russians controlling the northern third, while the British took virtual possession of Persia's southeast corner, with an outlet to the Arabian Sea. These territorial grabs gave the Russians complete control of the Caspian Sea while providing the British with territory adjacent to British-controlled India.

The following year, the British Burmah Oil Company discovered significant deposits of oil in the foothills of the Zagros Mountains, located about 150 miles from the coast of the Persian Gulf. Within months, the British government established the Anglo-Persian (later known as the Anglo-Iranian) Oil Company. By 1913, the British Admiralty acquired a controlling interest in the company at Persia's expense.

When World War I erupted, even though Persia declared its neutrality, its territory was crossed by Russian, British, and German armies. At the end of the war, diplomats attending the peace conference held at Versailles, outside Paris, agreed to allow Britain power over Persia's future. In a panic, the Qajars made a new treaty with new Russian leaders, the Bolsheviks, who had taken control of Russia during their revolution in 1917. Under this agreement, the Russians were allowed access to Persian ports in exchange for canceling Persia's debts to Russia.

However, the future of Persia was about to change significantly. In 1921, before the new treaty went into effect, a general commanding the Persian Cossack Brigade, Reza Khan, led a successful coup against the Qajar regime. Within two years, Reza Khan was named as Persia's prime minister, the last Qajar shah was ousted, and, in 1926, the leader of the Persian revolt was crowned as a true Persian ruler over a true Persian dynasty, the first in centuries. Khan was renamed Reza Shah Pahlavi.

## REZA SHAH'S CAMPAIGN TO MODERNIZE

The rise of Reza Shah Pahlavi to the Peacock Throne of Persia changed his country's history forever. Although he had removed the Qajars through military action, his power was created by a vote of the Majlis, the Persian representative body, and a change in the Persian constitution. He proved effective in turning the Persian ship of state around and refashioning it to his demands. The Russians were experiencing much domestic turmoil as their revolution continued, and the British considered the new Shah of Persia friendly ("many even saw him as a British agent").[12] Reza Shah, however, was a strident nationalist, wanting Persia for Persians. He was extremely interested in establishing pro-Western reforms in his country, wasting no time in turning around Persia's traditions of economic underdevelopment.

During the years of his reign (1926–1941), Reza Shah introduced many reforms in Iran. One was the name of his country. In 1935, the Shah changed the name Persia to Iran, deriving the word from *Aryan*, a reference to some of the earliest, ancient people in the region, and symbolizing his plan to restore the historical greatness of

## Reza Shah Pahlavi

Born into humble circumstances, Reza Shah Pahlavi made a remarkable rise to power. Confronted by superpower politics, however, he had to make a swift withdrawal and died in obscurity.

Savad Kuh was born in the Persian province of Mazandaran, near the Caspian Sea, in 1878. Both his father and grandfather were cavalry officers and Savad Kuh followed in their footprints. He joined the Persian Cossack brigade at fourteen and displayed considerable courage and ability. Like many of his fellow Persians, Savad Kuh disliked his commanding officers, most of whom were Russians. In 1920, in the aftermath of the Communist Revolution in Russia, some of those officers were called to their homeland. Savad Kuh carried out a coup against the remainder and in short order he became commander of the Persian Cossacks.

One year later, in 1921, Savad Kuh led a daring coup against the Persian government in the capital of Tehran. He succeeded, and though he shared power with a journalist for the first six months, it became apparent that Savad Kuh could be neither second nor equal to anyone: He had an insatiable drive for power (and money).

In 1925, a grateful Persian government made Savad Kuh the new monarch. He took the title *Shahinshah*, meaning king of kings, and he was properly known as Reza Shah Pahlavi from then on.

One might think that a cavalry officer without an education would make a poor monarch, but not in this case. Not only was Reza Shah fierce and determined, but he had a vision for the future of Persia; he wanted the nation to resume its place among the great powers of the world. Westerners tend to forget that the empire of Cyrus the Great (another Persian cavalryman) had been the world's greatest power about five hundred years before the birth of Christ. Reza Shah had not forgotten; neither had his people.

his country. To promote Iranian nationalism, he ordered Arabic and Turkish words removed from the Persian language. Iranian men were encouraged to dress in Western-style business suits and drop their practice of wearing robes and turbans. Anyone wearing traditional dress in public was subject to a prison term.

Many new laws were instituted aimed at women, including ordering them to move about in public without wearing the traditional veils—a change that proved extremely upsetting to the fundamentalist Muslim clergy. In the 1990s, an Iranian woman remembered how upsetting the Shah's new policies regarding dress

In 1935, Reza Shah changed the country's name to Iran. He sought to modernize his nation, encouraged Iranian women to abandon their use of the veil, changed the calendar from the lunar Muslim one to a solar-based one, and subdued the rebellious tribes that had been a thorn in the side of the government for decades.

In 1931, Reza Shah negotiated a new financial agreement with the Anglo-Iranian Oil Company (AIOC). This company had run Iran's oil refineries since about 1901, and most of the profits had gone to private citizens in Britain. Though the new agreement did not end all disputes, there is no doubt that Reza Shah gained more for his people than had his predecessors.

Unfortunately, Reza Shah also intended to profit for himself. He became the largest landowner in Iran and amassed a great fortune. This in itself was not enough to bring him down; World War II was required for that to happen. In 1939, when the war began,

Reza Shah announced Iranian neutrality. Both Britain and Russia suspected that Reza Shah had strong Nazi sympathies, however, and given the extent to which British and Russian concerns had infiltrated his country over the decades, it may have been the case. But his link with Hitler, however tenuous, was the reason for his fall.

In August 1941, British forces invaded from the south and Russian forces invaded from the north. The two nations—recently allied because of Hitler's invasion of Russia—wanted to secure both the oil and the supply routes. The Iranian army put up only a token resistance, and Reza Shah was taken into British custody. He abdicated his throne in favor of his eldest son and went into exile. He died in South Africa three years later.

If he were not tainted by his distant association with Hitler, Reza Shah would be hailed as one of the great leaders of his time. He brought Persia into the twentieth century.

had been to her mother, who expressed her disapproval: "He is trying to destroy religion. He doesn't fear God, this evil Shah—may God curse him for it!"[13] Khadija Saqafi, the wife of one Muslim cleric—the future Ayatollah Khomeini, who would provide leadership for the fundamentalist revolution of the 1970s—was so opposed to the Shah's order to abandon traditional dress that she "went without a bath for a year rather than venture to the public bathhouse unveiled."[14]

In transportation, the Shah was intent on bringing Iran into the twentieth century. He ordered the construction of modern, paved highways across his country and financed the building of the Trans-Iranian Railway, which ran from the Persian Gulf to the Caspian Sea. An Iranian airline was established. Oil revenues provided the monies for such large-scale building projects.

In the cities, the Shah called for the destruction of urban slums and inferior housing and erected new apartment buildings, businesses, and factories. Reza Shah believed that Iran must build its own future or it would remain at the mercy of foreign, especially European, interference. Yet such changes required an infusion of foreign expertise. Rather than rely on just British and Russian experts, the Shah invited engineers, planners, and architects from other countries, including the United States, China, France, Germany, and Austria, to participate in the modernization.

His reforms introduced new standards of medical practice and the building of modern hospitals. There were new schools and the opening of the University of Tehran. To reduce the power of the Muslim clerics, the Shah eliminated many holy days from the Iranian calendar. Although the Shah intended to completely secularize his state, many of his reforms angered Muslim fundamentalists, causing riots in 1935 that led to the burning of the Majlis government building.

Although the Shah's policies were often controversial, calling for a complete refitting of Iranian society as well as massive changes in the structure of its economy, none of his decisions proved as unpopular as the positions he took during World War II. Through the late 1930s, Hitler's Germany had courted the Shah, encouraging trade and offering technical assistance through German experts. By 1940, more than 600 German experts were in Iran providing assistance in such fields as industry, education, and commercial businesses. Trade greatly expanded during these years between Iran and Germany, and, by 1939, more than 40 percent of Iran's foreign trade was with Germany.

Reza Shah's reasoning for fostering a close relationship with Nazi Germany was in part historical. After decades of bullying from Great Britain and Russia, the Shah believed his best bet for the future was to become a supporter of Germany. Watching these events and alliances unfold from London, Winston Churchill, who was elected Britain's prime minister in 1940, observed that "German prestige stood high" with the Iranians and their Shah.[15]

Once Germany invaded the Soviet Union in 1941, the British and the Soviets became intent on reducing the political and economic ties between Iran and Germany. Iranian oil fields could not be allowed to fall into the hands of the Nazis. Before year's end, military forces from both countries invaded Iran, occupied the Middle Eastern nation, drove the Germans out, and ousted Reza Shah from his Peacock Throne.

Generally, the invading Allies, with help from the United States, occupied the northern and southern zones of influence they had established in Iran in 1906–07. When Reza Shah was removed from power, he went into exile in South Africa, where he died in 1944 before the war's end. The throne remained in the family, however, as Reza Shah's son, Muhammad Reza Shah, a mere 20 years old, followed his father's rule, although his real power was drastically reduced.

Even so, Iran played a key role during the war. Allied supplies of American lend-lease materials to the Soviet Union were routed through Iran, often delivered along the highway system implemented by Reza Shah. The Allies did attempt to eliminate some of the animosity of Iranians by signing a treaty in January 1942 that stated the Allies intention "to safeguard the economic existence of the Iranian people against the deprivaton and difficulties arising as a result of the present war."[16] To the Americans, Iran, as late as 1940, was of little interest diplomatically. However, by the early 1940s, tens of thousands of American troops were temporarily stationed there, and, by early 1944, the U.S. State Department declared diplomatic relations with Iran.

In 1943, the three primary Allied leaders—Joseph Stalin, Winston Churchill, and Franklin Roosevelt—met at a wartime leaders' conference in Tehran. The "Big Three" signed the Tehran Declaration, which "pledged respect for the sovereignty and integrity of Iran."[17]

The symbolic document also called for the withdrawal of all Allied troops from Iran by 1946. A serious problem developed, however, when the Soviets, who had troops stationed in the province of East Azerbaijan, announced their refusal to leave and their intention to continue giving support to rebels in Azerbaijan and Kurdistan. After Iran appealed for help from the newly formed United Nations,

## Muhammad Mossadeq

Muhammad Mossadeq was one of the first great heralds of twentieth-century nationalism. A fierce anticolonialist, he did his best to get foreigners and foreign business out of his native Iran. His personal demeanor detracted from his message and through no fault of his own, nationalistic movements won a bad name for the next 20 years.

Born in Tehran in 1879, Mossadeq came from the Persian upper class (the country name was changed to Iran in 1935). He spent ten years in the Persian finance industry, then traveled to Europe for his legal education. He studied in Paris, Belgium, and Switzerland, and came home a highly educated and sophisticated man. His years in Europe had not made him fond of the West, however.

Once home, the new lawyer tried to become the nemesis of the Anglo-Iranian Oil Company (AIOC). This company had gained a special concession from the Persian government in 1901, and most of the profits from oil-rich Iran went to private contractors living in England. Mossadeq entered the government of the new Reza Shah Pahlavi in 1921, and as minister of foreign affairs he tried to bring about reforms that would cast the foreigners out. Though many Persians liked the idea, Mossadeq was seen as too radical and dangerous, and Reza Shah confined him first to prison and then to a long period of house arrest.

The abdication of Reza Shah in 1941 was like a doorway opening to the ambitions of Mossadeq. He had long since overcome any the Iranians were able to remove the presence of Soviet troops from their soil. However, support from the United States was crucial to the success of Iran's anti-Soviet policies.

## POSTWAR IRAN AND THE POLITICS OF OIL

Just as oil had become the most important commodity in the Iranian economy before World War II, the same was true after the war. Yet the young shah did not want his country to remain dependent on oil deals with any foreign power. Many British and Soviet requests to

personal desire for money or fame; he burned with a desire to have "Iran for the Iranians" (now formally the country's name). Mossadeq won election to the Iranian Parliament, where he soon squashed ideas that he was "soft" on Russian Communism. He was above all an Iranian nationalist, and, unlike other Iranian leaders, he did not want to play one foreign government off against another. He wanted to eject all of them from Iran.

In 1951, Mossadeq led the committee that introduced the Oil Nationalization Bill, which intended to seize all oil refineries for the government (compensation would be offered to foreign governments). He was very popular in Parliament and with the people, but Shah Muhammad Reza was against the nationalization movement. The bill passed, however, and went into law.

Mossadeq had some personal weaknesses that played into the hands of his foes. A highly emotional man, he wept in public on many occasions, sometimes from relief

and sometimes out of anxiety. This behavior, coupled with his frequent public appearances in what appeared to be bathrobe-type clothing worked against him; in this way, Mossadeq was just the opposite of another Iranian nationalist, the Ayatollah Khomeini, whose appearance worked very much in his favor.

In 1952, Mossadeq and the Shah went head-to-head on other issues regarding the constitutionality of the Shah's government. The Shah briefly fled the country, but he returned after just two weeks, backed by the United States, the Central Intelligence Agency, and British spy operatives. Money was spread around Tehran, seeking to destabilize Mossadeq's government, and in 1953 he was arrested on charges of conspiring against the state.

Sentenced to three years in prison, Mossadeq served his time and then went into exile. He died in 1967.

expand drilling on Iranian soil were largely rejected by the Shah and his prime minister, Muhammad Mossadeq, the leader of Iran's National Front Party (the Jebhe-ye Melli). The National Front Party was a new coalition formed from several conservative, nationalistic groups, including the highly charged religious fanatics called the Devotees of Islam. As part of Mossadeq's plan to bolster Iranian nationalism, he advocated the complete nationalization, or state takeover, of the British oil industry in his country. The representative body, the Majlis, supported Mossadeq in these steps.

For Mossadeq, as well as many Iranians, national control of domestic oil production, sales, and distribution would be the key to Iran's future. In a June 1951 message, the Iranian prime minister made his goals clear:

> Our long years of negotiations with foreign countries concerning the legitimacy of our claims to ownership of the [oil] industry, which no power in the world can deny us, have yielded no results this far. With the oil revenues we could meet our entire budget and combat poverty, disease, and backwardness among our people. Another important consideration is that by the elimination of the power of the British company, we would also eliminate corruption and intrigue, by means of which the internal affairs of our country have been influenced. Once this tutelage has ceased, Iran will have achieved its economic and political independence.[18]

Mossadeq was a long-standing, important voice for Iranian politics. During the late 1920s until 1944, he had held no public office but was constantly critical of Reza Shah Pahlavi's policies. In 1944, he was elected to the Majlis, where he served until 1953. He and Muhammad Reza Pahlavi did not agree on key issues, so, in the spring of 1951, the Shah supported another candidate as the new prime minister, General Ali Razmara. However, the Majlis rejected Razmara, who was subsequently assassinated by an Iranian terrorist organization, the Fed'iyan-e Islam (Devotees of Islam). The same group also threatened to kill the Shah. In the midst of this political turmoil, the Majlis voted Mossadeq as prime minister in late April 1951. The following day, Prime Minister Mossadeq began nationalizing British oil interests in Iran.

During much of the next two years, Mossadeq wielded a heavy

hand in Iranian politics. By 1953, the Shah was reduced to a secondary role, as Mossadeq attempted to take control of "the constitutional position of the Shah as commander-in-chief by a referendum, and bypass the responsibility of the Majlis."[19] During the ensuing power struggle, Mossadeq appeared to have successfully seized control of the Iranian government by August. The Shah, driven from his position of power, left Iran for Rome, but his exile lasted only a week.

Mossadeq's nationalist policies had created economic chaos in Iran. Intent on removing British oil interests, he drove out the last British oil advisers, and Britain withdrew all its assets from Iran, even as it withdrew Iran's privileges with the Bank of England. Mossadeq's stubborn policies pushed the British to "double their production [of oil] in Saudi Arabia, Kuwait, and Iraq"[20] helping them make up for their Iranian losses. However, for Mossadeq, the move was devastating. Under the British-led economic lockout of Iran, the country's oil production dropped precipitously, from nearly 250 million barrels in 1950 to just above 10 million barrels through 1952. In just a matter of months, the Mossadeq-led Iranian government was facing economic disaster.

During these economically unstable years, Iran's northern neighbor, the Soviet Union, watched with anticipation, believing an unstable Iran would be vulnerable to a Communist takeover. By January 1953, Mossadeq desperately turned to the United States for economic support.

That month, a new American president took office. President Eisenhower was soon advised by State Department officials that the best scenario for the future of Iran was the return of the Shah. There was a strong belief that "a reliable alternative to Mossadeq's administration would be a government headed by the anticommunist but pro-Western monarchy."[21] As U.S. government officials watched the Shah being driven into exile in late summer, U.S. Central Intelligence Agency operatives began secretly rallying pro-Shah supporters across Iran, sometimes paying such supporters with American tax dollars. At the center of the American-led operation were CIA director Allen Dulles, the American ambassador to Iran Loy Henderson, and General Norman Schwarzkopf, a CIA military specialist who had helped train the Shah's security forces during World War II. (Schwarzkopf had organized the New Jersey State

Police force during the 1930s.) That fall, Mossadeq was toppled from power and placed in jail. For the next 14 years, Mossadeq was either held in prison or under house arrest until his death in 1967.

The Shah returned to power through the CIA-backed coup and condemned Mossadeq's policies of absolute nationalism. Such strong policies had driven away European economic support and resulted in the country's near bankruptcy. Shah Pahlavi announced a new approach, "positive nationalism," and set out to reestablish positive relations with oil companies to redirect their efforts in Iran. But he did not make the request entirely to the British. Instead, grateful for assistance in his return to power, the Shah granted new oil concessions to

## Muhammad Reza Shah

Muhammad Reza Shah intended to Westernize Iran, but his actions brought about a fundamentalist revolution.

Born in Tehran in 1919, Reza was the oldest son of Reza Shah Pahlavi. When his father went into exile in 1941, the British occupiers looked for someone to use as a puppet king. They settled on the 22-year-old prince because he seemed to be something of a playboy, without serious political interests. They couldn't have been more wrong.

Muhammad Reza steered his way adroitly between the British and the Russians during the Second World War. When he met the first American diplomats in Iran, the Shah became convinced that the United States would be a better geopolitical partner than either London or Moscow, and by 1950 he had steered his country in the direction of Washington D.C. In 1951, the Shah faced the first serious uprising, led by his prime minister Mossadeq.

The prime minister wanted to nationalize all the oil refineries and, if necessary, to kick out the American, British, and German oil concerns. The Shah distrusted Mossadeq and the nationalism for which he stood, so he allowed the Americans to help engineer a coup that brought Mossadeq down and confirmed the Shah in his place. From that day forward there was complete understanding between Tehran and Washington D.C.: The Shah would promote the flow of oil to the West, and the United States would help him with money, advisers, and military equipment.

Iran managed to stay clear of the long Arab-Israeli conflict that began in 1948, and during the 1950s and 1960s, Iran appeared (with the exception of Lebanon) to be the most stable nation in the Arab world. But the Shah was standing on dynamite, both materially and spiritually. He repressed the Shi'ite clerics in Iran and used the secret police to

American oil firms. In 1954, his government signed agreements with eight oil companies, including six American firms—Standard Oil of New Jersey, Standard Oil of California, Texaco, Mobil, Gulf, and Shell. (British Petroleum and a French oil company were also included.)

Such moves permanently changed the future of his country, as well as his personal future:

> This resulted in three major developments: Iran's growing dependence on the United States and alliance with the West in the 1950s; Iran's assumption of outright opposition to communism;

hold down domestic dissent. Only a perceptive eye could have seen how stern the repression was and how much the Shah had to work to keep the country together.

Iran has always straddled the line between Persian and Arab values and between Sunni and Shi'ite beliefs. The Shah believed that the refining and sale of oil would keep his throne intact, but he failed to recognize the beliefs of the influential Shi'ite clerics. One of them, exiled in the 1960s, came back to haunt the Shah in the 1970s. This was the Ayatollah Khomeini.

Early in 1978, strikes began against the Shah and his government. In the past the Shah had generally been able to maintain order, but this time things were different. The strikers and protestors called for an end to

Empress Farah and Muhammad Reza Shah

the secret police and for the return of the Shi'ite clerics—Khomeini in particular. The Western world watched with fascination as the Shah continued to lose ground throughout 1978, and early in 1979 he left the country, headed to exile in Mexico. The Shah died in Egypt in 1980 after suffering from cancer for some time.

In the 1950s, the United States formed a strong alliance with Iran's leader, Shah Reza Pahlavi. Seen as a buffer against Communism in the Middle East, the Shah received a great deal of financial and military aid from the United States. Soon, the Shah used his newfound might to consolidate his power—eliminating any political opposition and creating a feared secret police force known as SAVAK. Here, the Shah meets with President John F. Kennedy.

and the transformation of the traditional Anglo-Russian rivalry into American-Soviet rivalry; from then on the United States, not Britain, was the major protagonist in Iran and the world against the Soviet Union.[22]

## THE SHAH TAKES FULL POWER

Even as the United States welcomed the opportunity for American oil companies to invest in Iran's oil program, it left the distribution of political power in Iran to the Shah. With no power rival in his country, and with the force of American support, Shah Pahlavi set out on a course of consolidating his power through the 1950s. He centralized his rule and eliminated some of the power of the Majlis. The United States turned a blind eye to such policies, since the Shah held a strong opposition to the Soviet Union and Communism. With Iran receiving 50 percent of all oil profits earned by the eight Western companies, the Shah's Iran was soon recovering financially, and the country was revitalized.

By the late 1950s, the Shah was one of America's most loyal allies in the Middle Eastern region. Between 1953 and 1957, the United States loaned Iran more than a third of a billion dollars in aid. In addition, the Shah's military was supplied with $500 million in direct American support. By 1960, in just seven years, Reza Pahlavi had increased his army from 100,000 to nearly 200,000. The CIA also trained the Shah's secret police force. During the late 1950s, Pahlavi established SAVAK (Sazman-e Ettela'at Va Amniyat-e Keshvar), the Iranian State Intelligence and Security Organization. SAVAK was seen by the United States as an effective and necessary tool in the fight against Communism in the region. However, the Shah also used SAVAK as a means of repressing political dissent in his country. The organization sometimes even carried out purges of the Iranian military. One such purge resulted in the arrest and trial of 600 Iranian military officers, many of whom were imprisoned or executed. SAVAK agents regularly tortured and killed dissidents, creating a high level of antigovernment anger among several Iranian groups. The Shah's harsh policies were exacting a heavy price:

> Despite its claim to great achievements, by the end of the 1950s, it was clear that the Shah's regime had consolidated its position in a way that was very costly for Iran and for the future of the regime itself. The regime had failed to bring about a marked improvement in the social or economic conditions of an overwhelming majority of Iranians. In spite of the country's oil riches, a majority of its people were still among the poorest in the world; they lacked basic civil liberties, and lived virtually under a reign of terror. The masses were generally dissatisfied with the regime, and the Shah's domestic power base remained dangerously narrow. Neither the Shah nor Washington could have much confidence in the future of his monarchic rule.[23]

## THE "WHITE" REVOLUTION

In the early 1960s, Muhammad Reza Pahlavi initiated a series of agrarian, political, foreign policy, and social reforms in Iran, known as the "White" Revolution—meaning a "bloodless" revolution. The Shah was intent on changing the fundamental ways his country was governed and its people lived. While he had relied for years on general repression and intimidation to hold onto power, by the late 1950s Reza Pahlavi had come to understand "he could not rely on a policy of repression, a narrow domestic power base, and American support forever."[24] In a public statement, the Shah had stated that his "country cannot be ruled by the force of the bayonet and secret police.... Only a majority can rule a society."[25] Through the White Revolution, Reza Pahlavi hoped to lead Iran down a new path.

The changes were intended to bring Iran further along on its path of progress and twentieth-century change. The Shah also hoped he could gain additional support from several Iranian domestic groups, which would increase his popularity. In the United States, the administration of President John Kennedy was extremely supportive of the Shah's moves to modernize his country, seeing Reza Pahlavi's base of support as limited and fragile. In 1962, Reza Pahlavi put his agrarian reforms into place. Under this plan, large landowners were stripped of some of their land holdings and the designated lands were redistributed to Iran's poorer rural element under government supervision. Such poor farmers represented 70 percent of Iran's population.

There were additional political and social reforms, as well. Women were granted the right to vote for the first time in Iran's history. More schools were opened, and a general campaign to fight Iranian illiteracy was launched. The Shah attempted to raise health consciousness among his people as health standards were improved. Such moves were often popular, especially with those Iranians who longed for their country to modernize. These same moves also antagonized others. The land reforms angered traditional landowners, since they lost the rents from confiscated property. But the primary element of opposition to the Shah's bold steps to improve Iran came from the Islamic fundamentalists.

Often at the center of the religious opposition to the Shah's changes was an elderly Islamic leader, the Ayatollah Ruhollah Khomeini. (The term *ayatollah* was an important title of respect typically granted to significant scholars and teachers of the Shi'ite sect of the Muslim religion.) Khomeini was a respected scholar who lived in the holy city of Qum. He had been an outspoken critic of the Pahlavi dynasty since the 1930s, and had first criticized Reza Shah Pahlavi. Khomeini became a more public critic by 1961, speaking out against the Shah's harsh rule as well as his reform measures. In general, the Ayatollah was opposed to any Westernization efforts. He did not, for example, believe in the emancipation of Iranian women. In fact, all the Shah's efforts to modernize in the manner of the Western powers were unacceptable to Ayatollah Khomeini.

His campaign against the Shah led to his arrest by SAVAK in 1962, but no formal charges were filed against the Islamic leader. Following his release, Khomeini led opposition elements in the "June Uprisings" of 1963, a series of protests that led to bloody confrontations between his followers and Iranian troops. The Ayatollah was again arrested by SAVAK the following October, after he called for a boycott of that year's Majlis elections. (Typically, the members of the Majlis did not oppose the Shah, choosing instead to cooperate with the royal leader, who sometimes threatened to dissolve the Iranian parliament.)

Before the year's end, the Shah ordered government raids on Khomeini's headquarters in Qum. With the arrest of Khomeini, violent protests took place in the streets of several Iranian cities, including the capital of Tehran. Public pressure forced the Shah to release the Ayatollah by 1964, but the Islamic leader was ordered out of the country. As a religious and political exile, Khomeini moved to Turkey and then to Iraq, until he finally landed in France in 1978. Yet, in spite of his official exile, the Ayatollah would return to Iran in triumph during the 1979 revolution.

Although Iran's conservative Muslim population remained critical of the Shah's modernization program during the 1960s, for many others it signaled Reza Pahlavi's intent to improve the lives of his people. An Iranian journalist noted the changes with a positive view:

> When the shah started his program, Iran was a backward country. Land reform, granting voting rights to women, bringing women up to the level of men in our society, literacy drives, bringing new ideas and technology to the villages. Iran was being covered with new factories and public buildings. And everywhere the pace of change was frantic. Iran was really being transformed.[26]

Such changes required the establishment of greater connections with the West and the arrival of a new generation of Europeans, Asians, and Americans with the technical skills Iran needed to modernize. Not only did the Shah's moves toward progress introduce key economic, political, and agrarian reforms, it also allowed the importation of completely new lifestyles for many Iranians.

In the Shah's Iran of the 1960s and 1970s, Western entertainment such as movie theaters, nightclubs, bars, and discotheques were opened in the cities, especially in the sprawling urban landscape of Tehran. Such activities were completely acceptable to many Iranians who frequented such establishments and media in search of a good time. As one secularly-minded Iranian male admitted: "We used to go to cafes, we used to enjoy ourselves, we gave parties and we went to parties. We drank if we wanted to."[27] The nightlife in Iran became similar to that of any European or American city, but for some Iranians, again the conservative Muslim fundamentalists, these forms of entertainment and social practice were unacceptable. They believed that Western films, music, and nightlife "encouraged immorality and blasphemy."[28]

Even with the exile of the Ayatollah Khomeini, there were still millions of Muslim fundamentalists who spoke out against these Western influences. Many Iranians were Shi'ites who believed these unacceptable social customs and art forms were dangerous and an affront to the followers of Islam. Such conservatives were among the country's poorer residents, those who lived in the towns and cities as common laborers, where they were exposed to the corrupted art forms. Many of these urban poor did not personally experience the new wealth the Shah's changes were bringing to their country, making it easy for them to be critical of the Shah and his opening of Iranian society.

During the 1960s and 1970s, the Shah's reign over his country took on ironic overtones. His attempts to modernize the backward elements of Iran met with measurable success. His country's economy was expanding, bringing in greater wealth through extensive trade with the Western world. Oil sales remained the centerpiece of Iran's economic base while limiting the diversification of Iran's economy. However, overall, his agrarian policies had proven popular. Also, many women enjoyed new freedoms, including their use of the vote, for the first time, in 1963.

The Shah called for a referendum of the people to determine their support for his ongoing reforms. Overwhelmingly, the Iranian people supported his policies. He continued to enjoy the support of the American government, which continued to deliver modern weapons, diplomatic connections, and regular infusions of cash through loans. The Ayatollah Khomeini was out of the country, exiled, and out of sight. A January 1963 *New York Times* editorial expressed what appeared to be the obvious: "The great mass of the Iranian people are doubtless behind the Shah in his bold new reform efforts."[29]

Yet all was not well within the Shah's ever-modernizing Iran. The Shah still ruled with a strong hand. Behind his one-man rule of Iran was a consistent justification: Iran must be protected from Communist infiltration delivered from the Soviet Union, its aggressive neighbor to the north. It was a general hatred of Communism that led the Shah to develop such close relations with the United States, beginning in the late 1940s. And Reza Pahlavi's centralized power in Iran did not lessen with the passage of time. By 1975, he destroyed the limited two-party system in Iran, banning all other political opposition groups.

The 1970s brought a new level of criticism among many Iranians toward the Shah. His policies had hardened and his reforms continued; such moves, including his ties to the West, especially the United States, had given rise to a bitter opposition to his regime among some in the population, particularly young people. Iranian students attending universities were taught by instructors and professors who spoke out against the Shah. Many considered the United States little more than a supporter of his repressive rule. Critics of the relationship between the United States and Iran could reasonably accuse the United States of providing the weapons the Shah needed to remain in power and keep opposition to a minimum. Between 1950 and 1970 Iran had received $1.8 billion in United States military-grant aid. In the following six years, American arms sales totaled $12.1 billion, of which 80 percent was for equipment. By comparison, 80 percent of the dollar value of United States sales to Saudi Arabia during the same period went for construction and support services.[30] American diplomats seemed more aware of this increasing trend than did Iran's leader, but the Shah believed he had his people and events in his country under control.

However, despite massive oil sales and continuing American support, the Shah's Iran, by the 1970s, was still a poor nation. Many people were still peasants, and three of every four rural families lived on less than $66 each month. Inflation caused prices to rise rapidly. Between 1961 and 1971, food prices in Iran rose by more than 10 percent. By the mid-1970s, the inflation rate had doubled. As the nation had modernized, many poorer Iranians had moved to the

## A Historic Celebration Brings Criticism

During the turbulent and progressive reign of the Muhammad Reza Pahlavi, Iran achieved a monumental historical milestone few nations have ever experienced—or ever will. In 1971, the Persian monarchy marked a unique achievement, a celebration of the passing of two and a half millennia since the founding of the Persian monarchy. It was Persia's birthday party, and it was not an event the Shah intended to let go by without notice and an extraordinary amount of fanfare.

That year the celebrations planned by the Shah included a massive public ceremony held in the ruined city of Persepolis, the ancient capital of Persia. The Shah's guest list included hundreds of foreign dignitaries and celebrities, all flown in from 69 different countries. In the remote region of Iran, the invited guests of the Shah were treated much like Persian royalty themselves. The Shah housed them in temporary yet well-appointed tents, each featuring several rooms and running water, including two bathrooms.

While the celebrations were to take place amid the ruins of an ancient city, those in attendance were wined and dined in luxury. The Shah spared no expense, and his guests "drank the finest champagne from crystal goblets and ate food flown in from Maxim's in Paris."* Such an elaborate celebration carried a monstrous price tag, perhaps as high as $200 million. Marking the historical event in such style might help hundreds of the Shah's guests remember Iran's significant contribution to ancient history, but for many Iranian people, the amount of money spent was unnecessary and even obscene.

One Iranian critic of the Shah's overblown historical event saw it all as too much being spent on too few: "I saw that billions of dollars needed by our poor country—with no water, no electricity, no hospitals, no roads—was being spent on ceremonies for kings."** For many Iranians, the grand celebration represented another sign of the misplaced values of their leader, the latest to occupy the throne of a monarchy thousands of years old.

* Quoted in Hodgson, *People's Century*, p. 560.
** Ibid.

cities to find work, but there were never enough jobs. Between 1962 and 1971, Iran's gross national product doubled, yet the country experienced an increase of less than 25 percent in employment. Despite the Shah's promises and seemingly endless resources, "there were simply not enough teachers and schools to implement the projected free education, not enough facilities for improved health care; there was not even enough milk for a school milk program."[31] By 1974, Iran's economy was experiencing serious cracks, including inflationary strains, bureaucratic mismanagement, slippage in oil markets overseas, and a general slowdown in Iran's rate of development.

As for the wealthy, oil profits made their lives increasingly comfortable. They were able to afford foreign luxuries, and they could afford "to buy food abroad rather than produce it at home with Iranian labor."[32] The city of Tehran, long touted by the Shah as the shining example of his successful efforts to modernize his country, became a symbol of failure to the Shah's critics. By the early 1970s, Tehran "consumed 50 percent of the country's available services and products, though it held only 10 percent of the population."[33] The city's residents lacked adequate housing, causing rents to double between 1970 and 1973. The city was riddled with government corruption, and the urban poor were increasingly turning to alcohol and drug abuse.

Tehran represented two urban populations: the wealthy who lived in the highly Westernized northern and central neighborhoods and the rest of the city where the poor suffered. As one city official noted:

> North Tehran's problem is having flowers along highways and high-rise parking lots, while South Tehran's problem is having a drinking water tank and drying North Tehran's sewage. Whereas North Tehran can be compared with the best of the world's cities, South Tehran has problems which, at times, do not even exist in the most backward Iranian villages.[34]

When the revolution erupted in 1978, many of the demonstrators against the Shah's government came out of the slums of South Tehran.

The city was home to "islands of prosperity in a sea of poverty."[35]

The royal family's lifestyle was a constant reminder of the gap in Iran between the "haves" and the "have-nots." In February 1976, the Iranian government was forced to announce to the public a $2.4 billion budget deficit for the next year, while the previous day, the Shah's wife, "Empress Farah [returned] from Europe with a planeload of three tons of French rose marble for the royal family's new swimming pool."[36]

Such inconsistencies between the upper and lower classes in Iran were causing the level of unrest to skyrocket. It was as one Iranian newspaper editor stated: "What does this Westernize-or-bust program give us?: Western banks, Western guns, Western secret police, Western buildings. They are supposed to solve our problems, but do they? I don't think so."[37] Iranian revolutionaries were beginning to form opposition groups across Iran, as well as outside its borders. From his exile, the Ayatollah Khomeini kept close contact with his supporters in Iran, the Muslim conservatives, who hated reforms, hated modernization, hated the Shah, and hated the United States. The seed bed for the oncoming revolution was the various Muslim extremist groups. One such Iranian Muslim explained his radical view for revolution in his country:

> We had a great goal. It was to liberate Iran from a regime that was associated with foreigners.... We believed we must be independent, and independence meant we must struggle against the shah's regime. The best way to make the masses aware was to revolt against the shah. Religion and politics are the same thing.[38]

Such religious opponents of the Shah used the country's many mosques as their base of support and operation. In this opportunistic combination of politics and religion, the mosques were gathering places for radical Muslims. Following regular prayers, radicals could spend time talking with their fellow revolutionaries. As one *mullah* (a religious title meaning "master") explained: "Young people and intellectuals came to the mosque, and it would turn into an ideological meeting, and this would be recorded. The courtyard and all the alleys leading to the mosque would be full of people. Some of them would bring pieces of carpet to sit on, and people would bring tape recorders."[39] Revolutionary publications were handed out at the mosques, which would then be posted around the common gathering places of the cities, "on the walls of the mosques, at bazaars, in shops and alleys."[40]

As late as 1978, despite underground elements in Iran whose singular goal was to remove the Shah from power, Reza Pahlavi appeared "more popular than he had ever been before."[41] SAVAK kept political opposition to a minimum, and, outside the Muslim extremist community, there was no observable anti-Shah effort. Even as American officials in Tehran noted an increase in dissent, the government seemed unconcerned. Some Americans believed in the Shah's powers of survival. When a U.S. diplomat put the question of whether the future of the Shah's regime was in jeopardy to the director of the State Department's Office of Iranian Affairs, the questioned official "waved his hand at a row of pictures showing the shah meeting every United States president from Roosevelt on. 'Well,' he replied drily. 'He's been there this long.'"[42] But the clock was winding down for Muhammad Reza Pahlavi.

In 1977, dissatisfied elements of the people of Iran began to make public displays of anti-Shah sentiment, while giving their support to the exiled Ayatollah Khomeini. Many of the would-be revolutionaries were young university students who were followers of Khomeini. These defiant students took to the streets, participated in demonstrations, and even burned some government buildings. These efforts were the small but sudden steps that marked the early revolution. The Shah chose to crack down hard on these demonstrations, but his efforts did not bring them to an end. Iranian prisons were beginning to fill with political dissidents.

Then, on January 9, 1978, just days after an important visit to Iran by the American president, Jimmy Carter, a single event occurred that, for many, would later be remembered as the revolution's true beginning. Students angered by a government-published article critical of the Ayatollah Khomeini rioted in the streets of Qum, Khomeini's former hometown. Police responded, firing into the street mobs, killing several rioters. Weeks later, on February 18, the city of Tabriz witnessed two days of riots that resulted in the deaths of hundreds of demonstrators at the hands of the police and security forces. Then, on March 29, Tabriz erupted a second time in riots. On May 11, the rioting struck in Tehran, where demonstrators marched in the capital streets shouting such slogans as "Down with the Shah!" The local Muslim clerics gave their support to the demonstrations and called for a citywide strike. After several weeks, rioting again took place in Tehran, as 2,500 students marched on the campus of Tehran University. Throughout the summer, rioting and demonstrations took place in other Iranian cities, including Meshed, Isfahan, Shiraz, and Ahvaz. Despite these protests involving thousands of demonstrators, the Shah remained defiant and confident, stating publicly: "Nobody can overthrow me. I have the support of 700,000 troops, all the workers, and most of the people. I have the power."[43]

The year 1978 brought new forms of protest beyond street demonstrations. Throughout the year, fundamentalists burned movie theaters in Iran, including a cinema in Abadan where an August 20 fire killed 377 people. The fires were set to keep theaters from showing "immoral" films. Against this violent backdrop, the Shah tried to appear responsive. Even three weeks before the Abadan fire, the Shah made pubic statements intended to calm dissident actions, including a promise to establish open, parliamentary elections by 1979.

Yet despite such significant promises in the face of expanding protests, the Shah generally remained uncertain of the steps he should take in response to such demonstrations. He sometimes saw the riots as nothing more than the work of criminal street gangs having nothing to do with politics. Even when he interpreted demonstrations as political in nature, he still regularly discounted their importance. In late August 1978, Reza Pahlavi commented in an interview: "There are people everywhere who are easily instigated. They hear a few words and immediately they are electrified and stop thinking."[44] That fall, uncertain of what steps to take, the Shah declared Iran to be under military rule.

## "BLACK FRIDAY"

Martial law did not stop the Iranian fundamentalists and others from continuing their street demonstrations. The Ayatollah Khomeini regularly sent messages to his followers, encouraging them to continue their protests. Then, on September 8, 1978, events came to a head. During the final days of Ramadan, the holy Muslim month of fasting, Khomeini was able to call for a general protest in Tehran. The event was attended by perhaps as many as 750,000 demonstrators. At 6 A.M., marchers began converging on Tehran's central Jaleh

Square. Government forces gathered in the face of the demonstrators. One revolutionary witness described the scene: "There were many soldiers, many commandos. They had anti-riot gear, they had clubs; they were prepared to beat people and kill people."[45]

The Shah's troops ordered the demonstrators to disperse. When they refused and began to toss rocks and bricks at the troops, they were fired upon. The number of those killed during the morning demonstrations has been placed between 700 and 2,000.

After receiving word of the Jaleh Square shootings, Khomeini was pleased, calling the September 8 massacre a "victory of blood over the sword."[46] For the Ayatollah, such deaths were necessary. He had already stated his view on such losses: "Our movement is but a fragile plant. It needs the blood of martyrs to help it grow into a towering tree."[47] As for the Shah, his orders to his troops to fire on the crowd that day would help lead to his ultimate downfall. Despite the bloodshed, President Carter, in the midst of negotiations with the Israeli prime minister and the Egyptian president over other Middle Eastern issues, telephoned the Shah and gave him his continued support. When that statement was subsequently broadcast over the government-owned media, Radio Tehran, many anti-Shah proponents saw the United States as an opponent. Some even blamed the Jaleh Square massacre on American agents working for the Central Intelligence Agency. Anti-Shah activities soon included anti-American protests, as well.

## THE PROTESTS CONTINUE

Through the month of September, revolutionary events accelerated. There were constant riots and protests. Strikes emerged everywhere, including in such industries as public transit, railroads, the postal service, airline services, factories, and media outlets. Even government bureaucrats and minor officials appeared ready to protest the policies of the Shah. The economy, already in dire straits, began to seriously tumble. Panic hit as millions of people began to buy up large supplies of food and other items, uncertain about the future. By the end of the year, the wealthy citizens of Iran were quietly wiring a half billion dollars of assets from their bank accounts to financial institutions overseas.

Khomeini, who had been living in neighboring Iraq, was forced out. He moved to Paris where "he would have access to the Western

After failed attempts to both appease protesters and to crack down on uprisings, Iran's Shah found himself on the verge of disaster. Islamic fundamentalists loyal to religious leader Ayatollah Khomeini eventually ousted the Shah in an armed uprising, forcing the leader to flee the country.

media."[48] From the French capital, Khomeini encouraged the street demonstrations, his words telephoned to his followers, and distributed "to people in the mosques through the various mullahs."[49] On the walls of his small, bungalow located in a Parisian suburb, Khomeini hung posters, including one that read "35 million Muslims have said 'no' to the shah," and another that depicted the dead killed during the Jaleh Square massacre.

Besieged with the obvious signs of revolution, the Shah still attempted to hold the line on his policies and pretended he was facing little more than an extensive series of uprisings. He tried to convince himself that the civil disturbances were only the work of minority factions, the "black and red reaction"[50] of Muslim extremists and Communists. To placate some groups, he gave wage increases to striking workers and ordered the closings of several theaters, nightclubs, and casinos. He banned public drinking and pornography. His prime minister, Sharif-Emami, eliminated the government position of women's affairs minister. He even announced the return to Iran of the Muslim calendar. But these steps were ineffective, and the protests continued. So did the government crackdown, and thousands of demonstrators continued to be killed. Security forces and police "were using tear gas and bullets without any consideration for women or children. [The] streets were battlefronts."[51] Even the Majlis assembly, typically working under the control and direction of the Shah, began to protest the street killings.

Desperate for a way out of the difficult circumstances of protest at every turn, the Shah was in a quandary. By mid-October, he considered stronger measures, a more violent approach he called the "iron fist."[52] But he had already gone as far as he could with his government hard line. At his political core, Reza Pahlavi was not a man of violence or a leader who was nothing more than a "bloodthirsty villain."[53] He had his limits. As historian Barry Rubin later wrote:

> He genuinely felt responsibility as a symbol of the national identity and, in his own words, as head of the Iranian family. His reign had been based on a nationalistic goal of building Iran into a mighty and respected nation. Such sentiments forbade him from setting off a public bloodbath in his own country, among his own people.[54]

By December, the demonstrations were taking on a life of their own. For many revolutionaries, the protests indicated that the "people were very united—the whole nation. It was like a miracle, all the young and the old. People were working for the triumph of the revolution."[55] For Muslim extremists, the Shah and the government represented only the final target. There were smaller victories during the course of these difficult months in Iran. Through the winter months of 1978–79, Islamic radicals destroyed such sinful targets as movie houses and taverns and liquor stores. Women caught in the streets without veils were attacked and beaten.

Before the year's end, the Shah was facing opposition on an unprecedented scale, not only from extremists, but from moderates as well. Striking oil workers, called off their jobs by Khomeini, nearly shut down the production and shipment of Iran's single most important commodity. Iranian wells that had produced six million barrels of oil a day at the opening of 1978 were producing almost nothing by year's end. Everything across the country was shutting down, and the Shah remained powerless. When he finally placed Iran under complete military rule, he had few, if any, cards left to play.

## How the Shah Fell from Power

During 1978, as revolutionary events threw Iran into a tailspin of disruption and protest against the Shah, few political observers believed there was any possibility that Reza Pahlavi might lose his power and be removed from his office as the leader of his country. Yet after only months of street demonstrations and general unrest, the Shah became the last Persian monarch, marking the end of 2,500 years of royal rule. How had the Shah, whose power was undisputed at the year's opening, lose power so quickly? What were the prevailing reasons for the demise of the strong royal ruler of one of the Middle East's fastest-modernizing nations?

The end of the Shah's monarchy by 1979 was preceded by other attempts to remove the Shah from power. All previous attempts had either failed initially or had only succeeded for a short period of time. As historians wrestle with the question, dozens of answers have been considered. Some played a greater role than others, but the fact is that few inside or outside of Iran should have been surprised when the Shah's royal house of cards collapsed in the face of serious challenge and protest. Much of the power of the Shah rested on intimidation and fear. Once the Shah was revealed as vulnerable, the revolutionaries of the late 1970s were only too willing to work to remove him from power.

Among the most important reasons was the role played by religion. Conservative Muslims believed there were close links between religion and "secular politics," a connection which the Shah constantly played down. As the Shah attempted to further Westernize his country, which included allowing Western practices and morals, strict Muslims saw such change as a violation of the laws of Muhammad and the *Qur'an*. The Shah became a great symbol of the secularization of Iran that drove hundreds of thousands of Muslim fundamentalists to turn against his reign.

In the same light, the Iranian religious conservatives, as well as other elements in Iran, believed their country was becoming too Westernized and was too vulnerable to the will of European and American leaders. The Shah's strong ties of alliance and trade with such countries as the United States was interpreted by Iranian extremists as a series of international relationships that left Iran weak and dependent on foreigners, a circumstance unacceptable to many Iranians.

Even officials in the United States were convinced the Shah should step down and make way for a peaceful transition of power.

Despite the Ayatollah's influence, many moderates in Iran favored a "Muslim but democratic Iran with political freedoms and civil liberties."[56] Muslim fundamentalists wanted an Islamic state, ruled by the word of the *Qur'an*, the holy book of their religion. Still

During his reign, the Shah also strengthened and revitalized the Iranian monarchy, centralizing the state around himself. The Majlis was often hamstrung by the Shah, the people were denied civil rights and personal freedoms, and there were even times when any challenge aimed at the Shah was considered treason.

Another explanation for the Shah's removal from power was that the Iranian economy was, by the late 1970s, on shaky ground. The Shah's constant programs calling for economic reform and increased trade with the West had not produced the level of affluence the Iranian leader had expected. His 1960s "White Revolution" never fully translated into a greater economic status for Iran's lower classes. In effect, the much touted economic reforms brought on by the Shah were never actually as profitable as the Iranian leader had hoped, leaving Iran's urban middle class, its merchants and professional elites dissatisfied with the level of benefits the White Revolution was supposed to create. Also, the Shah may well have spent far too much of his nation's income on increasing his military, a move which caused him to rely increasingly on the United States as his chief ally. During the 1970s, those who developed an opposition to the Shah believed the United States wielded too much influence on their leader.

There were additional reasons: Much of the Shah's repression, including the activities of SAVAK, targeted the urban populations of Iran, where the Shah's base of support usually existed. By creating enemies among Iran's urban middle class, the very group that was supposed to provide the backbone of support for the Shah ultimately turned against him. In addition, the Shah's illness may have had a direct effect on the Iranian leader's ability to respond to the revolution adequately and with a personal force of will.

Of course, in the end, the sheer will and image of the Ayatollah Khomeini must be included in the discussion. Revolutions typically require a mouthpiece, a spokesperson with a broad base of appeal. The Ayatollah provided such a voice, one which was joined by millions of his fellow countrymen and women. It was a voice powered by a great will of the people of Iran; a voice which could effectively call for the end of Muhammad Reza Shah Pahlavi's reign of 37 years.

others sought a Marxist government with socialism at its center. The poor who marched against the Shah were driven by the desire for political rights and a greater stake in their country's oil wealth. But regardless of the fragmentation found among the opponents of the Shah in the fall and winter of 1979, the revolutionary movement "maintained and strengthened its anti-Shah unity over time despite heavy human and material losses."[57]

On December 11, the scope of the revolution intent on bringing an end to 37 years of rule by Reza Pahlavi became clear when several million opponents gathered in Tehran at the Shayyad Monument, which had been erected by the Shah in honor of his family's dynasty.

## Shahpur Bakhtiar

Born in 1915, Shahpur Bakhtiar came from a distinguished family; his grandfather twice served as prime minister of Iran. Bakhtiar went to France to complete his education; he earned his doctorate at the University of Paris in 1940. This was the same year that Hitler's Nazis invaded France and Bakhtiar served as a resistance fighter against the Germans.

Back in Iran by 1946, Bakhtiar served in the ministry of labor, then joined the Iran Party and the National Front, led by Muhammad Mossadeq. Bakhtiar admired the secular program and nationalist ideals of Mossadeq and he became the deputy minister of labor in the Mossadeq administration. The government fell in 1953, prompted by CIA funds and operatives, and Bakhtiar resumed the private practice of law. He remained fairly controversial in this retirement from public life, and was investigated by SAVAK (the Iranian secret police).

Not until 1977 did Bakhtiar come back to politics.

Working with Karim Sanjabi, a fellow lawyer, Bakhtiar brought the National Front back to life. During 1978, Muhammad Reza Shah was unable to quiet unrest on the streets; striking workers and university students led the opposition in the streets. Panicking, the Shah asked Bakhtiar to become premier and form a temporary coalition government with the understanding that the Shah would leave Iran for a time, and later return to serve as a constitutional monarch. Seeing the fulfillment of all he had hoped and worked for, Bakhtiar rapidly agreed. The Shah left Iran on January 14, 1979.

Left behind as the nation's new leader, Bakhtiar never had a chance to build a new government. His actions were immediately labeled as suspect due to his cooperation with the departed Shah, and attention

At Shayyad, the gigantic throng of revolutionary supporters, prompted by the Muslim central clergy council, shouted "Death to the Shah!" Although the country was under military rule, the Shah did not respond by ordering in massive numbers of well-armed troops or assault tanks. He did not have the heart. He had always believed himself to be a servant of the people of Persia. There was little left to do but surrender his seat of power, the ancient Peacock Throne, to another leader.

The American government, on the following day, was in agreement. President Carter, who had supported the Shah through a challenging year, expressed his desire for the Shah to relinquish power

shifted to focus on the Ayatollah Khomeini, a religious leader who had been in exile for many years. Bakhtiar did his best to prevent the return of Khomeini, even closing the Tehran airport for a time, but the demand from the streets became overwhelming, and Khomeini came back on January 31, 1979. Bakhtiar's government lasted just two weeks longer; he was brought down by a coup that combined students, workers, and religious hard-liners.

Bakhtiar went into exile in France. He made arrangements for a possible coup in July 1980, but the attempt failed, bringing further discredit down on Bakhtiar and his fellow exiles. In 1981, Bakhtiar worked with Iraqi President Saddam Hussein, helping the latter to plan his invasion of Iran: This started the seven-year-long Iran–Iraq War.

Despite his past rebellions against the Shah and the government of the 1950s and 1960s, Bakhtiar became convinced that the Ayatollah Khomeini and his religious coleaders were a greater danger than the Shah had ever been. Bakhtiar founded the National Resistance Movement in 1982 and developed warm relations with Reza Cyrus Pahlavi, heir to the Peacock Throne. None of these efforts succeeded, however, and Bakhtiar was hunted down by Iranian assassins and killed in a suburb of Paris in 1991.

Like many middle-class revolutionaries, Bakhtiar wanted to win greater freedoms and rights for the common people. In the 1950s he adroitly combined this desire with the strong nationalism of Muhammad Mossadeq, and the two might have created a new Iran. But failing in this, Bakhtiar became just another opponent of the Shah and his regime, and, given only about five weeks in which to organize his own 1979 government, Bakhtiar fell victim to the combined religious-nationalist movement of the Ayatollah Khomeini.

and establish a civilian government. The Shah began organizing a new government through moderate political figures. He appealed to Dr. Shahpur Bakhtiar, the deputy leader of the National Front who had long opposed the Shah's regime. It was agreed the Shah would not only abandon his throne, but that he would leave Iran and promise never to return with the intent to rule again.

On January 16, 1979, Shah Reza Pahlavi left the land of his family's heritage, taking his immediate family to the Tehran airport and flying out "for a holiday abroad."[58] He was bound for Egypt. All of Iran remained close to their televisions and radios as the history of

## The Last Days of the Shah

With his removal from power after 37 years on the Peacock Throne, the former Shah of Iran was literally a man without a country. Unwelcome at home, he was allowed refuge in Egypt. But his future was in doubt in more ways than one. Even before the revolution had succeeded in toppling Reza Pahlavi from power, the Shah was already wrestling with another enemy—a life-threatening bout with lymphatic cancer.

As early as the mid-1970s, the Shah began experiencing serious illness, but the cancer went undiagnosed. By early 1978, French doctors informed him he was dying of the disease, one that would require irrigation of the brain. He was warned that such treatments "could slow his reactions and decision-making ability."[*] The news that he was suffering from terminal cancer was kept from the public.

As the events that developed into the Iranian Revolution of 1978 and 1979 unfolded, the Shah was well aware he was

dying. Nevertheless, he never considered stepping down from power, assuming to the end that he would weather the storm of revolt even if he was facing certain and inevitable death. How much the disease impaired his judgment during these challenging months as his regime faced dissent can never be fully known. Historian Barry Rubin noted a connection between the Shah's declining health and his inability to face down his opponents: "The shah's illness and personal paralysis made it impossible for his regime to respond to the challenges of 1978. To some extent, this was due to his personality and in part to the effects of his cancer."[**]

Once the Shah stepped down from power on January 16, 1979, his primary focus became receiving the proper treatment to combat the disease that was slowly killing him. Unable to remain in Egypt due to political pressures, the Shah requested asylum in the United States, where his cancer could be

Iran took a decisive turn toward a new future. One Iranian listener described his response: "The radio announced that the shah had left the country. People were clapping, they jumped up and down in the streets.... That day I bought a lot of sweets and distributed them."[59]

At the airport, before boarding his plane, the Shah reminded Bakhtiar that he had been removed from power once before, in 1953, only to return a week later to reclaim his throne. He told the new leader of Iran that the revolution would produce such negative results that he would be called back out of his exile a second time. But he would never return to Iran. With the Shah's departure, Iran

best treated. But, again, political pressures kept the Carter administration from allowing the Shah permanent entrance.

For a time, Reza Pahlavi went to Mexico for medical care, but on October 20, it was revealed the Shah needed a gallbladder operation and specialized cancer treatment allegedly not available in Mexico. Two days later, the U.S. State Department agreed to allow the Shah to enter the country for medical and humanitarian reasons. The Shah entered the New York Hospital–Cornell Medical Center for the treatments he desperately needed.

President Carter's acceptance of the Shah sparked new protests in Iran with dire consequences for the United States. Just weeks following the Shah's arrival in America, pro-Khomeini students took control of the American Embassy in Tehran in protest of the supportive U.S. policy toward the Shah. Fifty-five American personnel were taken hostage, their release dependent on the United States

government handing over the Shah to the Iranian Revolutionary Council for trial on charges of treason. Carter refused to negotiate with the Iranians concerning any trade of the former Iranian ruler for American hostages. The hostage crisis continued through the remainder of President Carter's term in office.

In the meantime, the Shah's life was running out. After treatment, the Shah left America for Panama in December, then returned to Egypt in March 1980. It was there the deposed Shah finally died in July, 18 months after he had been removed from power, a bitter end to years clouded by the dual tragedies of revolution and disease. As for the American hostages, they were not released for another six months.

&ast; Quoted in Rubin, *Paved*, p. 204.
&ast;&ast; Ibid., p. 271.

exploded with enthusiastic celebration. People crowed into the streets of Tehran, carrying "banknotes with the shah's portrait cut out of them."[60] After 2,500 years, the monarchy of ancient Persia and modern-day Iran had come to a dramatic close.

The revolution would change course, however. The Bakhtiar government was never given an opportunity to succeed or fail on its own merit. Within two weeks of the Shah's departure, the Ayatollah Khomeini returned aboard a chartered Air France plane, arriving at the same airport from which the Shah had left, where he was received by a crowd of hundreds of thousands of his fundamentalist followers. At the airport, Iran's most important mullahs greeted their colleague. Verses from the *Qur'an* were recited, and the Ayatollah gave a returning speech. One eyewitness described his reaction to seeing the Ayatollah at the airport: "My father had gone on a trip and was now returning. The shah was darkness to us; it is a Koranic verse—from darkness, we take you into light."[61]

With the Ayatollah back on Iranian soil, Bakhtiar faced grim odds of his government surviving. Yet the new leader kept an optimistic, public appearance. The day following the arrival of Khomeini, Bakhtiar assured his supporters that he had the backing of the military, stating: "For 50 years, never has the army been so obedient to a prime minister."[62] But even this hopeful assurance proved misplaced as thousands of Iranian soldiers deserted in support of the Ayatollah. The Shah's old security force, SAVAK, was collapsing, agents abandoning their field posts. The prime minister attempted to gain as much favor from the revolutionary elements as he could, cutting many ties between Iran and the United States, including canceling billions of dollars in weapons contracts. But none of his efforts to desperately hold onto power swayed the masses. There were more demonstrations and strikes than had taken place under the Shah. The Majlis refused to cooperate.

Given the popularity of the Ayatollah, Bakhtiar knew he would have to negotiate with the aged cleric for his government to have any legitimacy with many Iranians. But there would be no negotiations. Khomeini announced his rejection of Bakhtiar's leadership, and the first government to follow that of the Shah's long reign over Iran fell after only a month. On February 11, after the army refused to back him, officially declaring its neutrality, Bakhtiar slipped out of Tehran on a helicopter and went into hiding. As he left his government building, "machine-gun fire began to open up all around the prime ministerial office."[63] He soon surfaced at the Mehrebad Airport, boarded a commercial plane, and went into exile in France. In a matter of a few short weeks, Bakhtiar and Khomeini had effectively traded places internationally.

With the removal of Bakhtiar, the Ayatollah Khomeini was in a position to set the course for Iran's future. The destruction of the Iranian monarchy was of utmost importance to the Islamic leader. "It is the kings of Iran that have constantly ordered massacres of their own people and had pyramids built with their skulls," the Ayatollah claimed. "Islam came in order to destroy these palaces of tyranny. Monarchy is one of the most shameful and disgraceful reactionary manifestations."[64]

For decades, the aged cleric had dreamed a new vision for his country. Iran would not be governed in the style of a Western democracy, nor would he allow the establishment of a socialist or Communist state. Instead, he intended to establish a complete Islamic nation, its society formed around the tenets of the *Qur'an*. An Iran administered by the Ayatollah and his ideas of moral and religious leadership would also include a new isolation for his country. His aim was to eliminate foreign influences on Iran: "Let them erect a wall around Iran and confine us inside this wall. We prefer this to the doors being open and plunderers pouring into our country."[65]

The followers of the Ayatollah explained to themselves and the outside world that "the Shah was not bad because he was ruthless and repressive but because he performed these deeds for a bad cause, for unacceptable goals."[66] He had attempted to alter his country into a Western-style state, where Western values were promoted, and where the voice of Islam was only one voice among many. One of the Ayatollah's advisors, Abol-Hassan Bani-Sadr, explained how a new Iran would succeed as a Muslim theocracy where "monotheism means that we should guide the community toward one identity and give it one heart, one tongue, one instinct and one conscience."[67] Just as dissent had been limited by the Shah's repressive rule, so Iranians under an Islamic government would be encouraged to limit their dissent, since any voice of opposition represented a challenge to the will of the Islamic faithful and revealed the dissenter as one who could not possibly be a true believer and follower of the Prophet Muhammad.

In the wake of Bakhtiar's resignation, the Ayatollah's Revolutionary Council, a group of followers, many with previous political experience, took control of the country. They formed an Islamic republic and wrote a new constitution for Iran. On April 1, 1979, Islamic law—known as the *sharia*—became the law of the land, controlling and determining every aspect of life for Iranians. The country's national anthem was abandoned, and Iranian

## Ayatollah Ruhollah Khomeini

Rome had its Hannibal, Britain had Napoleon, and so, it might be said, the United States had the Ayatollah Khomeini. Few leaders have been so adroit at "twisting the lion's tail" as the thickly bearded religious leader from Iran.

Born in the village of Khomeini (from which he took his name), he was the son and grandson of religious leaders. Khomeini was born in 1902, when the area was still called Persia. A large majority of Iranians are Shi'ite Muslims, which means they believe in a direct line of succession from the Prophet Muhammad (many other nations in the region have a majority of Sunni believers). Khomeini grew up in a land and a time when religious persuasion was very important, but he saw it weaken during the middle years of his life.

Reza Shah Pahlavi took the throne in 1925 and abdicated in 1941. He was succeeded by his son, Muhammad Reza Shah, who continued the path of modernization and Westernization. Khomeini was appalled to see that the Pahlavi dynasty encouraged women to give up the veil and discouraged

pious Muslims from the call to prayer (five times daily).

Living in the city of Qum, Khomeini became the focus of popular discontent with the Shah. In 1963, major riots took place and Khomeini was blamed. He may not have actually fomented the disturbance, but he was happy to take credit, and as a result he was first jailed and then exiled. In 1965, Khomeini left for neighboring Iraq. He took up residence in the holy city of Najaf, where many Shi'ite leaders and martyrs are buried. Over the next decade he kept up an unrelenting criticism of the Shah and the schoolchildren recited from the *Qur'an* instead. A new conservative theocracy took over the ancient state of Iran, one which continues to rule over the lives of its people after a quarter of a century, resulting in more change than the Shah's attempts to Westernize his country had ever accomplished. Even as much of the rest of the world has continued to modernize, many elements inside Iran continue to draw their country ceaselessly into the past.

Westernization process in Iran. The criticism was smuggled into Iran on tape recordings, and the Shah became so furious that he pressured Iraq to send Khomeini into exile. The religious leader went to Paris, where his voice found more listeners than before. At the beginning of 1979, the Shah was overthrown, and Khomeini returned to Iran on February first of that year.

He was welcomed as a great hero. Iranians loved their fierce and forbidding new leader. He called a spade a spade, and he was merciless when it came to the United States. America was the "Great Satan," and its people were robbers, according to Khomeini. Though he did not plan it, he was pleased when a large group of Iranian students took over the U.S. Embassy in Tehran. Fifty-three Americans were held as hostages for the next 444 days; the evening news in the United States showed blindfolded and helpless prisoners, and Khomeini appeared to have humiliated the Americans more than any other twentieth-century leader.

In January 1981, Khomeini freed the hostages, just as Ronald Reagan became the new U.S. president. Iranian-American relations remained poisoned for some time to come; Americans could not forget the images of the hostages or of the implacable Ayatollah who condemned the West in general and the United States in particular. But Khomeini soon found a new enemy, Saddam Hussein, the leader of Iraq.

Hussein began the Iran–Iraq War in 1981. The Iraqis had better equipment, but the Iranians, inspired by Khomeini, fought with a vengeance. The war dragged on and on, and probably caused a million casualties on each side. Finally, in 1988, a cease-fire was arranged.

Khomeini died in June 1989, in the same week that Chinese revolutionaries were crushed in Beijing's Tiananmen Square; there was no connection between the two events, but newscasters had to shift between them. Khomeini's funeral was probably the largest of modern history; as many as three million people filled the streets as the coffin was handed back and forth, and wept over. Few leaders from any part of the world have inspired so much love, fear, and dread.

## TIMELINE

**500s B.C.** Cyrus the Great establishes the kingdom that becomes the Persian Empire.

**642 A.D.** Arabs invade the lands of Persia, bringing the Persian Empire to an end.

**1000s** The Seljuk Turks begin domination of the Persians that lasts only for a few generations.

**1200s–1400s** Persia is dominated by the Mongol Khans.

**1941**
British and Russian troops invade Iran and oust Reza Shah from his throne. Reza Shah goes into exile and his son, Muhammad Reza Shah, rises to the throne. United States declares diplomatic relations with Iran.

**1926**
Reza Khan is crowned as Persian ruler over the first true Persian dynasty in centuries. Khan renamed Reza Shah Pahlavi.

**1950s**
Shah develops a growing dependence on the United States and alliance with the West.

## 1926

**1951**
Muhammad Reza Shah is challenged by Mossadeq, who is chosen as prime minister by the Majlis.

**1926–1941**
Reza Shah Pahlavi rules over Persia, establishing pro-Western reforms in his country.

**1962**
Muslim cleric and critic of the Shah, Ayatollah Khomeini, is arrested by SAVAK and later released.

1730s   Energetic Persian military figure, Nader Qoli, leads Persian forces that oust Afghan rule. Nader becomes Shah of Persia, introduces the Peacock Throne to Persia.

1787    Qajars take control of Persia and establish their capital at Tehran.

1893    Great Britain, Russia collaborate to establish eastern border of Persia.

1906    Reforms lead to establishment of Persian national assembly, the Majlis.

1907    Great Britain and Russia establish separate zones of influence in Persia.

## 1963
**January** Shah launches his "White Revolution," designed to further Westernize his country.
Women allowed to vote for the first time in Iran's history.
**August** "June Uprisings" include a series of protests that lead to bloody confrontations between Muslim extremists and Iranian troops.

## 1979
**January 16** Shah and family leave Iran for "a holiday abroad" never to return to Iran.
A new government is formed under leadership of Shahpur Bakhtiar, deputy leader of the National Front.
**April 1** Islamic law becomes law of the land in Iran, paving the way for the creation of an Islamic republic for Iran.

## 1979

## 1977
Dissatisfied elements in Iran begin to make public displays of anti-Shah sentiment, while giving their support to the exiled Ayatollah Khomeini.

## 1978
**February 18–19** City of Tabriz witnesses two days of anti-Shah rioting.
**May 11** Anti-Shah demonstrations hit Tehran, as Muslim clerics call for a city-wide strike.
**September 8** Hundreds of thousands of anti-Shah demonstrators converge on Jaleh Square in Tehra. Troops open fire, killing thousands.
**December 11** Several million demonstrators gather at Shayyad Monument during massive anti-Shah rally.

1913    British Admiralty acquires controlling interest in Anglo-Persian Oil Company.

1921    Commander of Persian Cossack Brigade, Reza Khan, leads successful coup against Qajar regime.

1923    Reza Khan is named as Persia's prime minister.

1926    Reza Khan is crowned as a true Persian ruler over a true Persian dynasty, the first in centuries. Khan renamed Reza Shah Pahlavi.

1926–1941    Reza Shah Pahlavi rules over Persia, establishing pro-Western reforms in his country.

1935    Reza Shah changes Persia's name to Iran, deriving the word from "Aryan." Muslim fundamentalists riot and burn Majlis building.

1939    Reza Shah is important ally to German leader, Adolf Hitler.

1941    British and Russian troops invade Iran and oust Reza Shah from his throne, sending him into exile to South Africa. Reza Shah's son, Muhammad Reza Shah, rises to the throne. United States declares diplomatic relations with Iran.

1944    Reza Shah dies in exile.

1951    Muhammad Reza Shah is challenged by Mossadeq, who is chosen as prime minister by the Majlis.

1953    Mossadeq drives Shah from power, but only for a week. In the meantime, the U.S. Central Intelligence Agency topples Mossadeq from power and supports return of Shah to power.

1954    Shah signs agreements with eight oil companies, including six American firms.

1950s    Shah develops a growing dependence on the United States and alliance with the West.

1961    Shah launches a land reform program in Iran.

1962    Muslim cleric and critic of the Shah, Ayatollah Khomeini, is arrested by SAVAK and later released.

1963    **January**  Shah launches his "White Revolution," designed to further Westernize his country. Women allowed to vote for the first time in Iran's history.

**June**  "June Uprisings" include a series of protests that lead to bloody confrontations between Muslim extremists and Iranian troops.

**October**  Khomeini is arrested again by SAVAK.

1964    Khomeini is ordered into exile and forced to leave Iran.

**1960s–1970s** Shah continues Westernization of Iran. United States becomes one of Shah's closest allies and primary weapons supplier.

**1971** Shah presides over elaborate celebrations marking the 2,500th anniversary of the founding of the great Persian Empire by Cyrus the Great.

**1974** Iran's economy experiences serious problems, including inflationary strains, slippage in oil markets overseas, and slow down in Iran's rate of development.

**1975** Shah destroys limited two-party system in Iran, banning all other political opposition groups.

**1976** Iranian government announces $2.4 billion budget deficit for following year.

**1977** Dissatisfied elements in Iran begin to make public displays of anti-Shah sentiment, while giving their support to the exiled Ayatollah Khomeini.

**1978** **January 9** Anti-Shah student rioting hits the streets of Qum, hometown of the Ayatollah.

**February 18–19** City of Tabriz witnesses two days of anti-Shah protests and rioting.

**May 11** Anti-Shah demonstrations hit Tehran, as Muslim clerics call for a city-wide strike.

**September 8** Massive demonstration of hundreds of thousands of anti-Shah opponents converge on Jaleh Square in Tehran. Troops open fire, killing thousands.

**October** Shah considers strong measures against protestors—his "iron fist" strategy—but ultimately refuses to implement them.

**December 11** Several million demonstrators gather at Shayyad Monument during massive anti-Shah rally.

**1979** **January 16** Shah and his family leave Iran "for a holiday abroad." They never return to Iran, effectively ending 2,500 years of Persian monarchy. A new government is formed under leadership of Shahpur Bakhtiar, deputy leader of the National Front.

**February 11** Bakhtiar government collapses.

**April 1** Islamic law becomes law of the land in Iran, paving the way for the creation of an Islamic republic for Iran.

## SOURCE NOTES

1. Quoted in Amin Saikal, *The Rise and Fall of the Shah*. Princeton: Princeton University Press, 1980, xi.
2. Ibid., p. 71.
3. Quoted in Peter Jennings and Todd Brewster. *The Century*. New York: Doubleday, 1998, p. 459.
4. Ibid.
5. Quoted in Jim Hicks, *The Persians*. Nederland, B.V.: Time-Life International, 1979, p. 9.
6. Quoted in Francis Robinson, ed., *The Cambridge Illustrated History of the Islamic World*. London: Cambridge University Press, 1996, p. 11.
7. Quoted in Gretchen Bratvold, *Iran in Pictures*. Minneapolis: Lerener Publications, 1988.
8. Quoted in William Duiker and Jackson J. Spielvogel. *World History*. Belmont, CA: West/Wadsworth, 1998, p. 585.
9. Quoted in Bratvold, *Iran*, p. 28.
10. Quoted in Saikal, *Rise and Fall*, p. 12.
11. Quoted in Bratvold, *Iran*, p. 29.
12. Quoted in Saikal, *Rise and Fall*, p. 20.
13. Sciolino, Elaine. *Persian Mirrors: The Elusive Face of Iran*. New York: Free Press, 2000, p. 134.
14. Ibid.
15. Quoted in Saikal, *Rise and Fall*, p. 24.
16. Ibid., p. 28.
17. Quoted in Bratvold, *Iran*, p. 31.
18. Quoted in Saikal, *Rise and Fall*, p. 40.
19. Ibid., p. 43.
20. Ibid., p. 41.
21. Ibid., p. 44.
22. Ibid., p. 45.
23. Ibid., p. 71.
24. Ibid., p. 78.
25. Ibid.
26. Hodgson, Godfrey. *The People's Century, 1900–1999: The Ordinary Men and Women Who Made the Twentieth Century*. New York: Times Books, 1996, p. 558.
27. Ibid.
28. Ibid.
29. Rubin, Barry. *Paved With Good Intentions: The American Experience and Iran*. New York: Oxford University Press, 1980, p. 110.
30. Ibid., p. 128.
31. Ibid., p. 145.
32. Ibid., p. 143.
33. Ibid., p. 144.
34. Ibid., p. 211.
35. Ibid., p. 144.
36. Ibid., p. 156.
37. Quoted in Jennings, *The Century*, p. 460.
38. Quoted in Hodgson, *People's Century*, p. 561.
39. Ibid.
40. Ibid.
41. Quoted in Rubin, *Paved*, p. 149.
42. Ibid.
43. Ibid., p. 206.
44. Ibid., p. 212.
45. Quoted in Hodgson, *People's Century*, p. 563.
46. Quoted in Sciolino, *Persian Mirrors*, p. 174.
47. Ibid.
48. Quoted in Hodgson, *People's Century*, p. 563.
49. Ibid.
50. Quoted in Saikal, *Rise and Fall*, p. 194.
51. Quoted in Hodgson, *People's Century*, p. 563.
52. Quoted in Rubin, *Paved*, p. 219.
53. Ibid.
54. Ibid.
55. Quoted in Hodgson, *People's Century*, p. 564.
56. Quoted in Saikal, *Rise and Fall*, p. 194.
57. Ibid.
58. Ibid., p. 197.
59. Quoted in Hodgson, *People's Century*, p. 564.
60. Quoted in Rubin, *Paved*, p. 243.
61. Quoted in Hodgson, *People's Century*, p. 566.
62. Quoted in Rubin, *Paved*, pp. 249–50.
63. Ibid., p. 251.
64. Quoted in Sciolino, *Persian Mirrors*, pp. 162–63.
65. Quoted in Rubin, *Paved*, p. 273.
66. Ibid., p. 274.
67. Ibid.

## BIBLIOGRAPHY

Avery, Peter. *Modern Iran*. New York: Frederick A. Praeger, 1965.

Bratvold, Gretchen, ed. *Iran in Pictures*. Minneapolis: Lerner Publications, 1988.

Burrell, R.M., and Alvin J. Cottrell. *Iran, the Arabian Peninsula, and the Indian Ocean*. New York: National Strategy Information Center, 1972.

Clark, Charles. *Islam*. San Diego: Lucent Books, 2002.

Duiker, William J., and Jackson J. Spielvogel. *World History*. Belmont, CA: West/Wadsworth, 1998.

Frye, Richard N. *The Heritage of Persia*. Cleveland: World Publishing, 1963.

Hicks, Jim. *The Persians*. Nederland, B.V.: Time-Life International, 1979.

Hodgson, Godfrey. *The People's Century, 1900–1999: The Ordinary Men and Women Who Made the Twentieth Century*. New York: Times Books, 1996.

Jennings, Peter, and Todd Brewster. *The Century*. New York: Doubleday, 1998.

Mannetti, Lisa. *Iran and Iraq: Nations at War*. New York: Franklin Watts, 1986.

Miller, John, and Aaron Kenedi. *Inside Islam: The Faith, the People, and the Conflicts of the World's Fastest-Growing Religion*. New York: Marlowe & Company, 2002.

Omstead, A.T. *History of the Persian Empire*. Chicago: University of Chicago Press, 1966.

Ramazani, Rouhollah. *The Foreign Policy of Iran: A Developing Nation in World Affairs, 1500–1941*. Charlottesville: University of Virginia, 1966.

Robinson, Francis, ed. *The Cambridge Illustrated History of the Islamic World*. London: Cambridge University Press, 1996.

Rubin, Barry. *Paved With Good Intentions: The American Experience and Iran*. New York: Oxford University Press, 1980.

Saikal, Amin. *The Rise and Fall of the Shah*. Princeton: Princeton University Press, 1980.

Sciolino, Elaine. *Persian Mirrors: The Elusive Face of Iran*. New York: Free Press, 2000.

Time-Life Books. *Persians: Masters of Empire*. Alexandria, VA: Time-Life Books, 1995.

Zeinert, Karen. *The Persian Empire*. New York: Benchmark Books, 1996.

# 9

# Epilogue:
## The Future
## of Revolution

**Today, the world has only just begun to experience the twenty-first century.** Nation–states still dominate the various regions and geopolitical spheres of influence as they have for millennia. Politics still direct those governments that preside over the hundreds of countries that dot a half-dozen continents. The role played by revolution has been crucial in the formation of several of those governments, both large and small. Leading states, such as the United States, France, Russia, China, Great Britain, and others, can trace the types of government they have to revolution.

While the causes of modern revolutions have varied, it is possible to summarize the major incentives that lead to their occurrence. This book has focused on seven major revolutions that have unfolded over the past two centuries, revealing a wide spectrum of causes. The American, French, early-nineteenth-century, and Mexican revolutions were each generally guided by powerful elements intent on establishing greater liberties and freedoms for the people. By contrast, later twentieth-century upheavals, such as the

Chinese and Russian revolutions, were the result of applying an ideology—Marxism—to the political realities of those two states in an attempt to give greater economic freedom to the people. In those revolutions, the state was considered the answer to the myriad problems the Chinese and Russian peoples were experiencing prior to the political uprisings they fostered.

But these revolutions, important as they are, represent only the tip of the revolutionary iceberg. The twentieth century witnessed repeated revolutionary movements in Asia, Africa, Latin America, even Europe. Third World revolutions, such as those in Cuba and Nicaragua, provided great transformational changes for their populations. Toward the end of the century, the whole of eastern Europe, including the former Soviet Union, turned against decades of Communism and created a raft of independent, democratic states. The century also introduced new reasons for revolution, including anticolonialism, as in Algeria, Vietnam, and southern Africa. Sometimes the changes brought by revolution have been broad-based, cutting across the grain of every element of a country's society, economy, and political reality, such as those in Mexico, China, Cuba, Iran, Nicaragua, Algeria, Vietnam, and the African countries of Zimbabwe, Angola, and Mozambique. And sometimes the government and society created by that revolution no longer exists, such as in Russia, which today is a struggling democracy. Slowly, China continues to toss aside the rigid economics of Marxism, replacing them with a vibrant, nearly rampant, capitalism. In other states, initial revolutionary success was short-lived, and revolutions in Guatemala, Bolivia, Chile, and Grenada were turned around almost before they were completed.

While revolution has been a defining element for government and political power throughout the past 200 years, modern political scientists can only speculate where revolution will strike next in the twenty-first century. That revolution will occur is clear. Pinpointing where is a less-than-exact science. However, by looking at the factors that often lead to revolution—limited political and personal freedoms, economic hardship, strong political conviction, the perceived need for reform, the opportunity to seize power—it is possible to speculate (guess might be a better word) where the next significant revolutions might unfold.

## THE MIDDLE EAST: A REGION IN TRANSITION

With the incursion of the United States military into Iraq in the spring of 2003, the people of the Middle East may well witness the establishment of a democracy in their region. Such a development represents a significant shift for the Arab world. Of the 22 Arab governments in the Middle East and North Africa, none is a democracy. They are governed by either royal families, military rulers, or religious extremists. Many of these governments and their ruling agents will not be lured easily toward democracy. To do so would require them to surrender at least a portion of their individual power:

> Arab countries such as Saudi Arabia, Jordan, Kuwait, and Egypt will not welcome the United States in carrying out so-called democratization in the region: Even if their political, cultural, and historical traditions, as well as religious beliefs, are not totally incompatible with Western democratic values, they can be described as cars traveling on different roads. Hence, it is by no means easy to promote Western democracy in the Middle East and the Arab world.[1]

With a democratic Iraq in place as a model, the possibility for further unrest in the Middle East is strong. There are revolutionary elements in the Arab world, those seeking greater civil liberties, political freedoms, and economic change, who are willing to rally on behalf of democracy in their own nations. One such nation in the region (not an Arab nation, but a Middle Eastern country nevertheless) is Iran. The potential for a new revolution in the Islamic Republic of Iran is not only a strong possibility for the immediate future, but is, say critics of the conservative fundamentalist regime, possibly already underway.

A generation ago, the Shah of Iran was forced from power by militant Islamics, who were offended by decades of Westernization encouraged by Reza Pahlavi. Because the Shah ruled with an iron hand, keeping civil liberties and freedoms out of reach of Iran's citizens, he became increasingly unpopular. When Iran's economy began to fail during the late 1970s, even the middle class turned on their long-standing ruler. The revolution that ousted the Shah from power also resulted in the establishment of a theocratic government led by Muslim extremists. This movement swept out the Shah's Western reforms and progress and replaced them with a fundamentalist state that worshiped the *Qur'an* as the foundation document for governing.

Now, that same fundamentalist regime is under steady fire from some of the same elements that helped give rise to the movement a generation ago. Although the Ayatollah Khomeini, who served as the rallying post of the Iranian Revolution of 1978–79, died ten years after the revolution drove the Shah from power, conservative Islamic clerics—the mullahs—have continued to hold the Iranian people to an impossible moral standard while claiming to govern over a republican democracy. Iranians are tired and disappointed with the Muslim conservatives that run their country, and protest is becoming more and more common.

It is clear to the majority of Iranians that they do not live in a democracy, as the government insists they do. The government may be able to legitimately claim that the harsh edge of Khomeini's theocratic state has been removed, that the current president, Mohammed Khatami, is a reformer, and that Iranian women have more political freedoms than those of many other Middle Eastern countries. But "Iran's democracy is a sham."[2] In an editorial written by an Iranian in an American news magazine, the writer explains why so many in Iran are fed up with their government, including its leader, who was elected in 1997:

> The president, Mohammed Khatami, is a figurehead, allowed to give high-minded speeches and do little else.... [H]e has accomplished virtually nothing by way of political reform. In some ways Iran is more closed today than it was when he was elected in 1997. For example, more than 80 reformist newspapers have been shut down in the last few years.[3]

Today in Iran, the legacy of the Ayatollah Khomeini is no longer held sacred by every part of Iranian society. Although his revolution sought to bring economic liberation to the dispossessed, there are many goals of the revolution that were lost in the emphasis placed for two decades on creating a state based on religious piety. Now, fifteen years after his death, "Khomeini's cult [has] faded."[4] A new generation of Iranian youth know little about the Ayatollah, are vague on the circumstances of the 1978–79 revolution, and are not inspired

by Khomeini's legacy. An Iranian in his late twenties reveals his feelings toward the Ayatollah in an interview with a journalist:
"Khomeini means nothing to me or my life.... The mullahs promise;
they don't deliver. There is no country here." Instead, the young man
expresses his desires for himself and his family. They have little to do
with a conservative Islamic faith, and everything to do with the eternal dream of prosperity: "I want a house of my own. I want a car, a
good car to take trips in."[5]

The voices of such disenchanted Iranian youths will probably
chart the way toward yet another revolutionary era for the Middle
Eastern country. Iran's future lies in its youth. Since the Iranian
Revolution, the country's population has doubled. Two out of every
three Iranians are under the age of 25. Sixty percent of the country's
70 million people are under the age of 30. (Ironically, it was
Khomeini who encouraged Iranians a generation ago to have as
many children as possible, especially during the early 1980s, when
Iran was at war with Iraq.) Now, those same young people are keenly
aware of just how much their nation is out of step with the rest of
the world, especially the West. While their fathers and mothers
fought against the Westernization of their country and the Shah's
progressive reforms, Iran's young people are eager to take on
Western ways:

> Their fathers and uncles were sacrificed to Iraqi missiles and mines
> in the eight year Iran-Iraq war, which claimed more than 300,000
> Iranian lives. They have inherited bitter memories and unrelenting
> strictures, and now the boys want girlfriends with whom they can
> hold hands and socialize freely, and the girls want to wear color-
> ful head scarves rather than the black, tentlike veil known as the
> chador. They see only one way they can get those freedoms. "We
> want to change the nature of the state," says Abdollah Momeni, a
> student leader. "We want more democracy, human rights."[6]

In a delightful twist of irony, the young people of Iran are not
anti-American, as many of their fathers and mothers were. When the
Shah was toppled from power, it was seen as a defeat for the United
States, since many Iranians believed America had wielded far too
much influence over the Shah during much of his 37 years in power.
But no more. Today's Iranian youth are entranced, even "openly

enthusiastic about the American way of life."[7] Even though the Iranian government regularly broadcasts anti-American messages and slogans to its people, many young people have access nightly to at least four different radio stations out of Los Angeles. These satellite broadcasts "have become manna for information-starved Iranians."[8] But those radio programs do not base their appeal through political messages. Instead, they present American "news, entertainment, fashion."[9] The strong religious sentiment against the "sinful" nature of American movies, dress, and behavior may have served as rallying points for the Iranian Revolution of the 1970s, today the lure of American culture may prove the catalyst for the next revolution in Iran.

But a love of all things American does not make for a revolution in Iran. That a new generation of Iranian university students appears disgusted with the theocratic regime and are willing to protest in

The Islamic fundamentalists that ousted the Shah from power now face challenges of their own. A new generation of young Iranians is demanding that government be accountable not only to Allah, but to the people as well.

the streets of Tehran as they have periodically, especially since 1999, is not enough to immediately bring down the mullahs that hold much of the political power. However, the clerics running Iran are currently facing a long list of problems that are making life difficult and unsatisfactory for many, not just the young. Unemployment is rampant. The Iranian economy is "marked by isolation, underinvestment, unpredictable regulations, corruption, inefficiency, and overdependence on oil."[10] (For those who remember the elements that helped bring down the Shah, the list seems eerily familiar.)

Those dissatisfied with Muslim fundamentalism as a way of life in Iran have at least one advantage that the ruling mullahs can not take away from them: time. The young of Iran are a ticking bomb, and they vote. They turned out in large numbers to cast their limited ballots in 1997 and again in 2000 and 2003. With a minimum voting age in Iran of sixteen, it may well be the patience and the voting patterns of Iran's young people that will eventually bring about yet a second revolution. Iranian writer Amir Jahanchahi has expressed a confidence that such change will one day soon sweep across his country:

> We need not ask ourselves now whether it is possible to overthrow the regime. Its fate is sealed.... But victory lies at the end of the road. Victory for freedom: freedom of thought, freedom of movement, freedom to choose one's own future. Freedom plus the responsibility of my generation, mobilized to lay the foundations of a different kind of Iran. An Iran that will no longer be an international outcast ... A proud and modern Iran.[11]

## LATIN AMERICA: THE CONSTANT PRESENCE OF REVOLUTION

The Caribbean island nation of Cuba may be standing at a political crossroads. Cuba experienced its own major revolution during the 1950s when revolutionary leader Fidel Castro and his followers successfully overthrew the harsh dictatorship of Fulgencio Batista, who had seized power during the 1930s. After six years of jungle fighting, Castro succeed in taking power in January 1959. Since then, the revolutionary leader has overseen a Marxist government that regularly received support from the Soviet Union in the form of weapons and money until the collapse of that Communist state in the early 1990s.

Since then, Castro's Cuba has struggled to survive despite losing Soviet support. For more than forty years, the fiery Castro has fought a war of words to maintain his island as a Marxist state, despite an embargo placed on trade between the United States and Cuba, a policy that the American government put into place in the early days of Castro's regime. It is a policy strongly supported by the Cuban-American community, many of whom escaped the repression of Castro's regime decades ago.

Through the decades, Castro's Marxist policies have reduced the

Cuban economy to one of desperate proportions. When Castro took power in the late 1950s, the Cuban economy ranked fourth among its Latin American counterparts. Today, its economy is in a shambles, ranking several dozen rungs from the top. In 2003, the aging revolutionary turned 77 years old, making him the "world's longest ruling head of government and leader of only four remaining socialist countries in the world."[12] Critics of Castro's regime believe that Cuba will turn away from its forced socialism after his death, but the old Cuban leader has insisted otherwise.

In a speech delivered in December 2003, President Castro assured the world, including his supporters and his critics, that "This revolution does not depend on one individual, or two, or three."[13] The lifelong revolutionary added that his country has survived for decades and that, despite American foreign policy against him, his "country has resisted 45 years of blockade."[14] However, there can be no question that Castro represents for Cubans the embodiment of the revolution. Whether the people of Cuba, impoverished by more than four decades of harsh socialism, will continue to support socialism and the revolutionary spirit in their country after the death of Castro remains one of the significant questions regarding the future of Caribbean politics.

## VENEZUELA: A DEMOCRACY OF TYRANNY

Throughout the past two centuries, South America has witnessed repeated revolutions. Since the late 1990s, the nation of Venezuela has been in the throes of revolutionary change. But that revolution has taken, and continues to take, decisive turns politically, leaving the people of Venezuela confused about their government, their leaders, and their political and economic future.

For 40 years, Venezuelans lived under a civilian government that came to power in 1958 following the ouster of dictator Marcos Perez Jimenez. Throughout the 1960s, 1970s, and 1980s, Venezuela remained a democracy, at times one of the few in South America. Its economy spurred by oil production, the country prospered. Two political parties vied for power and each supported extensive social programs for their country's people.

But, by the early 1990s, falling oil prices led to serious downturns in the economies of many oil-producing countries, including Venezuela. Dissatisfaction with government scandals involving

Venezuela has long been one of the few stable democracies in South America. Since 1998, under the leadership of former paratrooper and general, Hugo Chavez, the country's fortunes have risen and fallen, as has Chavez's popularity. His administration has been plagued by strikes and charges of corruption. Here, an anti-Chavez protestor waves a banner.

corruption, fraud, and embezzlement led to violent protests and street demonstrations in several urban centers, including the capital of Caracas. In 1992, a military leader, Colonel Hugo Chavez, led a coup attempt that failed. Although his paratrooper unit managed to surround the parliament building, the mass of Venezuela's military did not support the coup. Chavez lost his rank and spent two years in prison. He remained, nevertheless, a popular figure in Venezuela and, by 1998, won election to the presidency. Almost immediately, Chavez began to preside over his country with an iron hand as an authoritarian dictator. By the following year, he renamed the country Bolivarian Republic of Venezuela. In 2000, he was re-elected.

Following these elections, Chavez promised to completely alter the Venezuelan framework of government. He announced his intention to move his country's economy away from privatization and develop a more open economy. At the same time, Chavez stated he would "clean up politics by setting up a popular assembly to draw up a new national constitution."[15] "The constitution and with it the ill-fated political system to which it gave birth 40 years ago has to die," Chavez stated in a speech following his election. "There will be no backtracking in the political revolution upon which we are embarking."[16]

Chavez's base of support derived from the mass of poor people in his country who saw the political leader as one responsive to their needs. Yet over the following four years, Chavez continued to reveal himself increasingly not as a true reformer of Venezuela's government and its flagging economy, but a political leader seemingly intent on establishing himself as dictator. His policies did not improve the Venezuelan economy and, in 2003, Venezuela experienced its worst economy in decades. Factories and industrial plants closed. Unemployment continued to inch higher, as oil prices languished. The year produced significant rioting and protests, as well as extensive strikes. In February 2003, a general strike was held, calling for the ouster of the leftist Venezuelan president. Chavez responded with harsh reprisals, ordering his secret police to round up the strike's leaders, including the head of Venezuela's national business chamber, Carlos Fernandez. The strike's organizers were "tumors we have to remove," announced Chavez, "coup mongers, saboteurs, fascists, assassins."[17]

Throughout 2003, Chavez led his country in dictatorial fashion, becoming increasingly unpopular with his people. Venezuelan democracy became little more than a hollow shell, as Chavez cracked down on dissent and took more power for himself. For many observers, the Venezuelan leader not only became more autocratic, but unstable, as well. Some opposition leaders even called for Chavez's ouster from power under a constitutional article due to his "mental incapacity." By year's end, the political future of South America's oldest democracy remained uncertain. In May, 2004, Chavez's support was still strong enough for him to win a referendum designed to remove him from power. The "election" was heavily monitored and declared fair by the Organization of American States and the Carter Center. Whether counterrevolutionary elements will successfully organize in the future against the repressive rule of Chavez and remove the leftist leader remains to be seen.

## CHINA: COMMUNISM AND CAPITALISM

Although the People's Republic of China remains, officially, the most populous (1.2 billion people) Communist country in the world, the legacy of Chairman Mao is in the midst of extraordinary change. What the future holds for the massive Asian power and Mao's revolution of more than a half century ago is one of the most significant political questions of the early twenty-first century. Modern China "is undergoing ... revolutionary change along every dimension of national power: economic, political, military, technological, and social."[18]

Today, the Asian giant is a powerhouse of economic growth, as the nation and its people continue to industrialize and further their trade extensions overseas. Politically, change is also taking place, but, because it is China, the pace of change is sometimes glacial. Any consideration of the possibilities for political revolution in China, from Communism to some type of democracy, must take into account that even China's earlier revolution required two or three generations of change before Mao and his followers gained complete power over Jiang Jieshi's strongman control of Chinese far flung provinces. Yet progress toward both a Western-style capitalism and an Asian style democracy are unfolding little by little.

China's moves toward democracy and away from the arbitrary, harsh rule of Communist government have been a painfully slow process. Following the death of Mao in 1976, the new Chinese Communist Party leader, Deng Ziaoping, was critical of several of Mao's programs. While he did not actively encourage extreme democratic tendencies, he did allow for some limited dissent. Deng "encouraged the Chinese people to speak out aginst earlier excesses, particularly in the late 1970s when ordinary citizens pasted [posters] criticizing the abuses of the past on the so-called Democracy Wall near Tiananmen Square in downtown Beijing."[19] But allowing criticism of past leaders and policies that had seemingly failed was one thing; criticizing and challenging the existing governmental leaders was another. Also, Deng and his cohorts did not allow for any direct criticism of the Communist Party or of Marxism in general. Those who called for democracy in China were typically suppressed, and many were tried and thrown into prison.

Yet such oppression at the hands of the CCP did not bring an end to dissent. One noted dissident, Fang Lizhi (Fang Li-chih), became one of the loudest voices in opposition to Communism during the 1980s. In speeches, Fang spoke out against the Chinese government and its leaders, whom he considered corrupt. "China will not be able to modernize," said Fang in a speech, "if it does not break the shackles of Maoist and Stalinist-style socialism."[20]

Events came to a head in Beijing when, in May 1989, thousands of young Chinese students protested Communist rule by demonstrating in Tiananmen Square. As the Chinese economy had begun to dramatically improve during the early 1980s, such economic success drove many in China to call for other improvements, such as "better living conditions, relaxed restrictions on study abroad, and increased freedom"[21] The Tiananmen Square demonstrations included 150,000 protestors, most of them students, carrying signs bearing slogans such as "Give Me Liberty or Give Me Death!" The demonstrations marked the seventieth anniversary of the May Fourth Movement. Although the protests caused serious division between Communist leaders over an official governmental response, the CCP officials ultimately chose to send tanks and troops into the streets of Beijing to quash the student movement and arrest its leaders.

Although the government remained harsh in its treatment of dissent in the immediate aftermath of the Tiananmen Square demonstrations, for some, including Deng Ziaoping, the handwriting was on the wall: The future of the Chinese Communist Party and its harsh rule was shaky. Deng brought in new leadership to direct the party and the country. Following Tiananmen Square, Deng appointed Jiang Zemin, a party chief from Shanghai, to power.

During the 13 years that followed, Jiang guided his country and its enormous population into new political and economic waters, charting a new path for his party into the twenty-first century. At the heart of Jiang's new policies was the continuation of the economic growth that had already begun a decade earlier. Through the 1990s, China's economy went skyward, doubling in a decade, with an average annual growth rate of more than 9 percent. By the late 1990s, China oversaw the peaceful transition of British-controlled Hong Kong, one of Asia's most prosperous and capitalist cities, back under Chinese control. Jiang's home city, Shanghai, experienced dramatic growth, and new skyscrapers went up across the urban landscape. By 2003, one out of every six high-rise building cranes were at work on construction projects in Shanghai. Across the city, "Communist Party slogans compete for space with ads for Coke, Pepsi, Pizza Hut, and McDonalds."[22] The new economic watchword for China was capitalism. And China's new government slogan reflected the shifting times: "One Country, Two Systems." Although the Communist Party continued to lead the country politically, Jiang allowed for greater elements of capitalism into his country with each passing year.

By the end of 2002, the 76-year-old Jiang Zemin announced the end of his leadership of the Communist Party at the party's sixteenth National Congress. He handed power off to Vice President Hu Jintao, age 59. As Jiang gave up his seat of power, he was able to convince party officials to approve his "call for a 'well-off society' that embraces the private sector, entrepreneurs, and their wealth."[23] In thrusting capitalism into the lap of China's future, Jiang may have "pulled off the political conjuring trick of the century by burying Communism while saving the Chinese Communist Party."[24]

Yet even as China's enjoys the fruits of nearly a generation-long fling with capitalism, the Communist Party continues to rule, limiting the political freedoms of its people. While no one expects an abrupt revolution, such as the underorganized Tiananmen Square protests, to bring down the party ultimately, China's history may soon witness the end of the party that brought Mao to power in 1949. If one remembers that change in China always takes place slowly—as evolution, not revolution—then one may expect Communism to eventually become an element of China's past.

## CENTRAL ASIA: THE STANS AND BEYOND

Since the collapse of the Soviet Union in 1991, the Central Asian region remains a volatile place, where civil wars and various political uprisings can be common. Even Russia itself has struggled with the transition from autocratic Communist control to a more open society and economy. The Russian economy continues to underproduce, and many in Russia are dissatisfied with the lack of jobs, financial security, and adequate housing. Elements within Russia still clamor for another revolution, one designed to turn the struggling country back to its Communist legacy. But such elements remain limited in their reach. Nevertheless, a revolution in Russia is no less likely today than it has been during the past dozen or so years since the fall of Communism.

In other states in the region—Georgia, Azerbaijan, Tajikistan, Uzbekistan, Kyrgyzstan, and others—many governments remain unstable even as they continue to expand their post-Communist economies. Social pressures continue to threaten the outbreak of violence and revolution. Ethnic pressures keep groups within these states from cooperating with one another, while the threat of militant Islamism remains constant. Also, strongman rule is not uncommon. Such "sultanistic regimes" include that of President Akaev of Kyrgyzstan, an autocratic ruler who came to power when the Soviet Union collapsed. In Turkmenistan, President Niyazov continues to lead a repressive regime. Although he has promised to step down in

2010, there are those who believe he may simply pass the throne on to his son. If that takes place, his opponents have promised to rally against him and deliver a coup to his doorstep. In Uzbekistan, President Islam Karimov also keeps opposition parties out, limits freedom of the press, and heavily controls the activities in his country's mosques, where Islamic militants sometimes gather to talk politics. Although his term will continue to 2009, revolutionary challenge to his harsh rule remains a possibility.

Until 2003, another Central Asian autocratic leader was Eduard Shevardnadze of Georgia, age 73, whose government was extremely corrupt. In the face of declining support and mounting political opposition, the elderly leader had stated he would not run for office again in 2005. But promise and patience did not match-up. By the fall of 2003, the Georgian public took to the streets, including outside the parliament building in Tbilisi, the capital. Rather than stand against a torrent of protest, Shevardnadze chose to step down. The public was ecstatic, as were Shevardnadze's political opponents. On September 23, as Shevardnadze left office, opposition leader, Mikhail Saakashvili announced the meaning of the bloodless ouster that was already gaining the name, the "Velvet Revolution:" "Today is the greatest day in the history of Georgia. This is the day of our dignity, the birth of a new Georgia,"[25]

But the political future of Georgia remains in question, as does much of the political future of the rest of the region. Whether the region witnesses any significant revolutionary movements in the coming years may depend on whether the perceived needs of the people of these states are met. With the hope of democracy and capitalism, Central Asians have rising expectations. They are aware of their place in the world, of their lack of opportunity and security, and the inequality of living in Third World countries. If the existing political systems cannot meet the expectations of their people, then revolution may follow.

## THE WINDS OF POLITICAL CHANGE

In the end, any speculation concerning where the next major revolution might take place around the world is anyone's guess. As the Danish physicist Neils Bohr, a 1922 Nobel Prize recipient, noted nearly a century ago: "Prediction is very difficult, especially about the future."[26] The continent of Africa is still a volatile powder keg of

It is difficult to predict where the next revolutions will strike. A common ingredient of most revolutions seems to be an economically polarized society—extreme poverty and poor working conditions for the many, with wealth and power for the few. Here Mexican teachers protest economic changes proposed by Mexican President Vicente Fox.

revolution as coups remain commonplace. The West African nation of Liberia, in 2003, overthrew its strongman ruler, Charles Taylor. In the Democratic Republic of Congo (DRC) two revolutionary factions—the Congolese Rally for Democracy (RCD) and the Congolese Liberation Movement (MLC) agreed in the spring of 2003 to share power in a transitional government. But revolutionary violence continues to erupt in the Congo. At the heart of the continuing revolutionary movements in the Congo is the basic question that must be asked of all revolutionary movements that bring change: "Have the factors that led them to take up arms and go into the forests to stage rebellions now suddenly been eliminated?"[27] Uprisings and government transitions; poor economies and joblessness; tribal clashes and the rampant spread of the AIDS virus continue to plague African states helping to keep the African continent unstable.

In Mexico, the government of Vicente Fox came to power through elections in 2001, marking "the first peaceful handover of power to the political opposition in 179 years since independence and the end of 71 years of [Institutional Revolutionary Party] rule."[28] Fox's campaigned for the Mexican presidency promising a revolution: "After seven decades of PRI dominance, the country is shackled with the remains of a rusted-out authoritarian system in which a privileged minority divided up the spoils and flouted the laws."[29]

While his election as a right-of-center politico of the National Action Party broke the revolutionary pattern of Mexico's past two centuries of governance, Fox faces revolutionary elements in opposition to his government. In the Mexican state of Chiapas, a province located so far south it borders the Central American country of Guatemala, revolutionaries known as the Zapatistas have struggled for the past decade to bring change to Mexico. The indigenous Indian movement began in 1994 with hundreds of members. Now, its membership counts in the tens of thousands. The Zapatistas remain primarily interested in expanding rights for Mexican Indian peoples. To that end, they favor a change in the nature of Mexican democracy, calling for a dramatic increase in local rule and autonomy. Their watchword slogan: "Liberty! Justice! Democracy!"[30] Taking their cue from the Mexican revolutionary of a century ago, Emiliano Zapata, the revolutionary Indian movement remains a loud voice in Mexico. While the Fox presidency has been responsive to the Zapatistas and their political and social agenda, the revolutionary group continues to campaign for their view of democracy.

What, then, is the future of revolution on planet earth? Perhaps your guess is as good as mine. Where revolution will ignite and how bright the fires of protest will burn remains a mystery waiting for the twenty-first century to reveal. That revolution will take place is a certainty. For, today, as well as hundreds of years ago, the spirit of revolution is ever-present on the political horizon. Just as American colonists and French subjects rose up against perceived tyranny; as the people of Europe took to the streets of their cities, erected barricades, and rallied for political freedoms; as the people of Mexico fought for liberty, land, and labor; as the fiery ideologues Lenin and

Mao reformed the words of Marx and brought down overly confident governments; as the people of Iran struggled out from under the oppression of strongman rule, so the twenty-first century will continue to witness the flames of revolution fanned by the winds of political change.

## SOURCE NOTES

1. Quoted in Li Xuejiang, "Democracy and the Middle East," *World Press Review*, July 2003, p. 7.
2. Quoted in Fareed Zakaria, "Time to Expose the Mullahs," *Newsweek*, December 23, 2002, p. 45.
3. Ibid.
4. Quoted in Elaine Sciolino, *Persian Mirrors: The Elusive Face of Iran*. New York: Free Press, 2000, p. 65.
5. Ibid.
6. Quoted in Tim McGirk, "Sending a Message to the Ayatullahs," *Time*, June 23, 2003, p. 8.
7. Ibid.
8. Quoted in Zakaria, *Time to Expose*, p. 45.
9. Ibid.
10. Quoted in Sciolino, *Persian Mirrors*, p. 284.
11. Quoted in Amir Jahanchahi, "The Regime Is Already Dead!" *World Press Review*, September 2003, p. 32.
12. Quoted in Jose Goitia, "Castro: Socialism Will Survive in Cuba." *USAToday*, December 5, 2003. Website: www.usatoday.com/news/world/2003-12-05-castro-elian_x.htm
13. Ibid.
14. Ibid.
15. Quoted in Nick Caistor, "Venezuela's Democratic Record." *BBC News*, December 7, 1998. Website: www.news.bbb.co.uk/a/hi/world/americas/228321.stm
16. Ibid.
17. Quoted in Tim Padgett, "Crackdown in Caracas." *Time Online Edition*, February 23, 2003. Website: www.time.com/tim/nation/printout/0,8816,425841,00.html.

18. Quoted in Zalmay Khalilzad, *Sources of Conflict in the 21st Century: Regional Futures and U.S. Strategy*. RAND's Project Air Force. Rand Distribution Services. (MR-897-AF), 1998, p. 74.
19. Quoted in William J. Duiker and Jackson J. Spielvogel. *World History*. Belmont, CA: West / Wadsworth, 1998, p. 1050.
20. Ibid., p. 1051.
21. Ibid.
22. Quoted in Brodie Fenlon, "Leashing the Economic Dragon," *World Press Review*, February 2003, p. 18.
23. Ibid.
24. Quoted in Catherine Armitage, "China: Better Rich Than Red," *World Press Review*, February 2003, p. 14.
25. Quoted in "Georgians Party as President Steps Down." (November 23, 2003) Website: www.cnn.com/2003/WORLD/europe/11/23/georgia.protests/.
26. Quoted in Tim McNeese, *American Timeline: Future Problems and Alternatives*. St. Louis: Milliken Publishing Company, 1986, p. 1.
27. Quoted in Steven Kyomo, "Can the Rebels Be Trusted?" *World Press Review*, August 2003, p. 13.
28. Quoted in Tim McGirk, "Newsmakers of 2000: Vicente Fox Quesada. *Time Europe*, December 25, 2000. Website: www.time.com/time/europe/magazine/2001/1225/poy_fox.html.
29. Ibid.
30. Quoted in "A Brief History of the Zapatistas." University of Texas Website: www.studentorgs.utexas.edu/nave/zaps.html.

## BIBLIOGRAPHY

Armitage, Catherine. "China: Better Rich Than Red," *World Press Review*, February 2003.

"A Brief History of the Zapatistas." University of Texas Website: www.studentorgs.utexas.edu/nave/zaps.html.

Caistor, Nick. "Venezuela's Democratic Record." *BBC News*, December 7, 1998. Web site: www.news.bbb.co.uk/a/hi/world/americas/228321.stm

Duiker, William J., and Jackson J. Spielvogel. *World History*. Belmont, CA: West / Wadsworth, 1998.

Fenlon, Brodie. "Leashing the Economic Dragon," *World Press Review*, February 2003.

Goitia, Jose. "Castro: Socialism Will Survive in Cuba." *USAToday*, December 5, 2003. Website: www.usatoday.com/news/world/2003-12-05-castro-elian_x.htm.

Jahanchahi, Amir. "The Regime Is Already Dead!" *World Press Review*, September 2003.

Kyomo, Steven. "Can the Rebels Be Trusted?" *World Press Review*, August 2003.

Li Xuejiang, "Democracy and the Middle East," *World Press Review*, July 2003.

McGirk, Tim. "Sending a Message to the Ayatullahs," *Time*, June 23, 2003

Padgett, Tim. "Crackdown in Caracas." *Time Online Edition*, February 23, 2003. Website: www.time.com/tim/nation/printout/0,8816,425841,00.html.

Khalilzad, Zalmay. *Sources of Conflict in the 21st Century: Regional Futures and U.S. Strategy*. RAND's Project Air Force. Rand Distribution Services. (MR-897-AF), 1998.

McGirk, Tim. "Newsmakers of 2000: Vicente Fox Quesada. *Time Europe*, December 25, 2000. Website: www.time.com/time/europe/magazine/2001/1225/poy_ fox.html.

McNeese, Tim. *American Timeline: Future Problems and Alternatives*. St. Louis: Milliken Publishing Company, 1986.

Oliker, Olga, and Thomas Szayna, eds. *Faultlines of Conflict in Central Asia and the South Caucasus: Implications for the U.S. Army*. Rand Distribution Services. (Mr-1598-A), 2003.

Sciolino, Elaine. *Persian Mirrors: The Elusive Face of Iran*. New York: Free Press, 2000.

Zakaria, Fareed. "Time to Expose the Mullahs," *Newsweek*, December 23, 2002.

# Part III:
## Primary Source Documents

# John Locke, *Two Treatises of Government*, (1680–1690)

*Locke's most influential works were the two treatises in Of Civil Government. Locke's second treatise dealt with Locke's own justification for government and his ideals for its operation. This treatise introduced the "Lockean proviso" which says that one should not simply take whatever one wants, but should instead take the common good into consideration. In fact he was a firm advocate of salus populi suprema lex est (the welfare of the people is the supreme law).*

## CHAPTER II: OF THE STATE OF NATURE

**SECT. 4.** To understand political power right, and derive it from its original, we must consider, what state all men are naturally in, and that is, a state of perfect freedom to order their actions, and dispose of their possessions and persons, as they think fit, within the bounds of the law of nature, without asking leave, or depending upon the will of any other man.

A state also of equality, wherein all the power and jurisdiction is reciprocal, no one having more than another; there being nothing more evident, than that creatures of the same species and rank, promiscuously born to all the same advantages of nature, and the use of the same faculties, should also be equal one amongst another without subordination or subjection, unless the lord and master of them all should, by any manifest declaration of his will, set one above another, and confer on him, by an evident and clear appointment, an undoubted right to dominion and sovereignty.

**SECT. 5.** This equality of men by nature, the judicious Hooker looks upon as so evident in itself, and beyond all question, that he makes it the foundation of that obligation to mutual love amongst men, on which he builds the duties they owe one another, and from whence he derives the great maxims of justice and charity. His words are:

"The like natural inducement hath brought men to know that it is no less their duty, to love others than themselves; for seeing those things which are equal, must needs all have one measure; if I cannot but wish to receive good, even as much at every man's hands, as any man can wish unto his own soul, how should I look to have any part of my desire herein satisfied, unless myself be careful to satisfy the like desire, which is undoubtedly in other men, being of one and the same nature? To have any thing offered them repugnant to this desire, must needs in all respects grieve them as much as me; so that if I do harm, I must look to suffer, there being no reason that others should shew greater measure of love to me, than they have by me shewed unto them: my desire therefore to be loved of my equals in nature as much as possible may be, imposeth upon me a natural duty of bearing to them-ward fully the like affection; from which relation of equality between ourselves and them that are as ourselves, what several rules and canons natural reason hath drawn, for direction of life, no man is ignorant." Eccl. Pol. Lib. 1.

**SECT. 6.** But though this be a state of liberty, yet it is not a state of licence: though man in that state have an uncontroulable liberty to dispose of his person or possessions, yet he has not liberty to destroy himself, or so much as any creature in his possession, but where some nobler use than its bare preservation calls for it. The state of nature has a law of nature to govern it, which obliges every one: and reason, which is that law, teaches all mankind, who will but consult it, that being all equal and independent, no one ought to harm another in his life, health, liberty, or possessions: for men being all the workmanship of one omnipotent, and infinitely wise maker; all the servants of one sovereign master, sent into the world by his order, and about his business; they are his property, whose workmanship they are, made to last during his, not one another's pleasure: and being furnished with like faculties, sharing all in one community of nature, there cannot be supposed any such subordination among us, that may authorize us to destroy one another, as if we were made for one another's uses, as the inferior ranks of creatures are for our's. Every one, as he is bound to preserve himself, and not to quit his station wilfully, so by the like reason, when his own preservation comes not in competition, ought he, as much as he can, to preserve the rest of mankind, and may not, unless it be to do justice on an offender, take away, or impair the life, or what tends to the preservation of the life, the liberty, health, limb, or goods of another.

**SECT. 7.** And that all men may be restrained from invading others rights, and from doing hurt to one another, and the law of nature be observed, which willeth the peace and preservation of all mankind, the execution of the law of nature is, in that state, put into every man's hands, whereby every one has a right to punish the transgressors of that law to such a degree, as may hinder its violation: for the law of nature would, as all other laws that concern men in this world 'be in vain, if there were no body that in the state of nature had a power to execute that law, and thereby preserve the innocent and restrain offenders. And if any one in the state of nature may punish another for any evil he has done, every one may do so: for in that state of perfect equality, where naturally there is no superiority or jurisdiction of one over another, what any may do in prosecution of that law, every one must needs have a right to do.

**SECT. 8.** And thus, in the state of nature, one man comes by a power over another; but yet no absolute or arbitrary power, to use a criminal, when he has got him in his hands, according to the passionate heats, or boundless extravagancy of his own will; but only to retribute to him, so far as calm reason and conscience dictate, what is proportionate to his transgression, which is so much as may serve for reparation and restraint: for these two are the only reasons, why one man may lawfully do harm to another, which is that we call punishment. In transgressing the law of nature, the offender declares himself to live by another rule than that of reason and common equity, which is that measure God has set to the actions of men, for their mutual security; and so he becomes dangerous to mankind, the tye, which is to secure them from injury and violence, being slighted and broken by him. Which being a trespass against the whole species, and the peace and safety of it, provided for by the law of nature, every man upon this score, by the right he hath to preserve mankind in general, may restrain, or where it is necessary, destroy things noxious to them, and so may bring such evil on any one, who hath transgressed that law, as may make him repent the doing of it, and thereby deter him, and by his example others, from doing the like mischief. And in the case, and upon this ground, EVERY MAN HATH A RIGHT TO PUNISH THE OFFENDER, AND BE EXECUTIONER OF THE LAW OF NATURE.

**SECT. 9.** 1 doubt not but this will seem a very strange doctrine to some men: but before they condemn it, I desire them to resolve me, by what right any prince or state can put to death, or punish an alien, for any crime he commits in their country. It is certain their laws, by virtue of any sanction they receive from the promulgated will of the legislative, reach not a stranger: they speak not to him, nor, if they did, is he bound to hearken to them. The legislative authority, by which they are in force over the subjects of that commonwealth, hath no power over him. Those who have the supreme power of making laws in England, France or Holland, are to an Indian, but like the rest of the world, men without authority: and therefore, if by the law of nature every man hath not a power to punish offences against it, as he soberly judges the case to require, I see not how the magistrates of any community can punish an alien of another country; since, in reference to him, they can have no more power than what every man naturally may have over another.

**SECT, 10.** Besides the crime which consists in violating the law, and varying from the right rule of reason, whereby a man so far becomes degenerate, and declares himself to quit the principles of human nature, and to be a noxious creature, there is commonly injury done to some person or other, and some other man receives damage by his transgression: in which case he who hath received any damage, has, besides the right of punishment common to him with other men, a particular right to seek reparation from him that has done it: and any other person, who finds it just, may also join with him that is injured, and assist him in recovering from the offender so much as may make satisfaction for the harm he has suffered.

**SECT. 11.** From these two distinct rights, the one of punishing the crime for restraint, and preventing the like offence, which right of punishing is in every body; the other of taking reparation, which belongs only to the injured party, comes it to pass that the magistrate, who by being magistrate hath the common right of punishing put into his hands, can often, where the public good demands not the execution of the law, remit the punishment of criminal offences by his own authority, but yet cannot remit the satisfaction due to any private man for the damage he has received. That, he who has suffered the damage has a right to demand in his own name, and he alone can remit: the damnified person has this power of appropriating to himself the goods or service of the offender, by right of self-preservation, as every man has a power to punish the crime, to prevent its being committed again, by the right he has of preserving all mankind, and doing all reasonable things he can in order to that end: and thus it is, that every man, in the state of nature, has a power to kill a murderer, both to deter others from doing the like injury, which no reparation can compensate, by the example of the punishment that attends it from every body, and also to secure men from the attempts of a criminal, who having renounced reason, the common rule and measure God hath given to mankind, hath, by the unjust violence and slaughter he hath committed upon one, declared war against all mankind, and therefore may be destroyed as a lion or a tyger, one of those wild savage beasts, with whom men can have no society nor security: and upon this is grounded that great law of nature, Whoso sheddeth man's blood, by man shall his blood be shed. And Cain was so fully convinced, that every one had a right to destroy such a criminal, that after the murder of his brother, he cries out, Every one that findeth me, shall slay me; so plain was it writ in the hearts of all mankind.

**SECT. 12.** By the same reason may a man in the state of nature punish the lesser breaches of that law. It will perhaps be demanded, with death? I answer, each transgression may be punished to that degree, and with so much severity, as will suffice to make it an ill bargain to the offender, give him cause to repent, and terrify others from doing the like. Every offence, that can be committed in the state of nature, may in the state of nature be also punished equally, and as far forth as it may, in a commonwealth: for though it would be besides my present purpose, to enter here into the particulars of the law of nature, or its measures of punishment; yet, it is certain there is such a law, and that too, as intelligible and plain to a rational creature, and a studier of that law, as the positive laws of commonwealths; nay, possibly plainer; as much as reason is easier to be understood, than the fancies and intricate contrivances of men, following contrary and hidden interests put into words; for so truly are a great part of the municipal laws of countries, which are only so far right, as they are founded on the law of nature, by which they are to be regulated and interpreted.

**SECT. 13.** To this strange doctrine, viz. That in the state of nature every one has the executive power of the law of nature, I doubt not but it will be objected, that it is unreasonable for men to be judges in their own cases, that self- love will make men partial to themselves and their friends: and on the other side, that ill nature, passion and revenge will carry them too far in punishing others; and hence nothing but confusion and disorder will follow, and that therefore God hath certainly appointed government to restrain the partiality and violence of men. I easily grant, that civil government is the proper remedy for the inconveniencies of the state of nature, which must certainly be great, where men may be judges in their own case, since it is easy to be imagined, that he who was so unjust as to do his brother an injury, will scarce be so just as to condemn himself for it: but I shall desire those who make this objection, to remember, that absolute monarchs are but men; and if government is to be the remedy of those evils, which necessarily follow from men's being judges in their own cases, and the state of nature is therefore not to be endured, I desire to know what kind of government that is, and how much better it is than the state of nature, where one man, commanding a multitude, has the liberty to be judge in his own case, and may do to all his subjects whatever he pleases, without the least liberty to any one to question or

control those who execute his pleasure, and in whatsoever he cloth, whether led by reason, mistake or passion, must be submitted to, much better it is in the state of nature, wherein men are not bound to submit to the unjust will of another: and if he that judges, judges amiss in his own, or any other case, he is answerable for it to the rest of mankind.

**SECT. 14.** It is often asked as a mighty objection, where are, or ever were there any men in such a state of nature? To which it may suffice as an answer at present, that since all princes and rulers of independent governments all through the world, are in a state of nature, it is plain the world never was, nor ever will be, without numbers of men in that state. I have named all governors of independent communities, whether they are, or are not, in league with others: for it is not every compact that puts an end to the state of nature between men, but only this one of agreeing together mutually to enter into one community, and make one body politic; other promises, and compacts, men may make one with another, and yet still be in the state of nature. The promises and bargains for truck, &c. between the two men in the desert island, mentioned by Garcilasso de la Vega, in his history of Peru; or between a Swiss and an Indian, in the woods of America, are binding to them, though they are perfectly in a state of nature, in reference to one another: for truth and keeping of faith belongs to men, as men, and not as members of society.

**SECT. 15.** To those that say, there were never any men in the state of nature, I will not only oppose the authority of the judicious Hooker, Eccl. Pol. lib. i. sect. 10, where he says, The laws which have been hitherto mentioned, i.e. the laws of nature, do bind men absolutely, even as they are men, although they have never any settled fellowship, never any solemn agreement amongst themselves what to do, or not to do: but forasmuch as we are not by ourselves sufficient to furnish ourselves with competent store of things, needful for such a life as our nature doth desire, a life fit for the dignity of man; therefore to supply those defects and imperfections which are in us, as living single and solely by ourselves, we are naturally induced to seek communion and fellowship with others: this was the cause of men's uniting themselves at first in politic societies. But I moreover affirm, that all men are naturally in that state, and remain so, till by their own consents they make themselves members of some politic society; and I doubt not in the sequel of this discourse, to make it very clear.

---

## SOURCE

*Two Treatises of Government by John Locke* (1690) [At Hanover].

The text of this document can be found at:
http://www.fordham.edu/halsall/mod/1690locke-sel.html.

# Thomas Paine, *The Rights of Man* (1792)

*Between March 1791 and February 1792 Thomas Paine published numerous editions of* The Rights of Man. *The book was written in response to Edmund Burke's* Reflections on the Revolution in France, *which questions the motives of those involved in the Revolution. Paine uses the theory of the social contract as the basis for his views, and justifies revolution partly on the grounds that no generation can bind its successors, and partly by the argument that the social contract must be embodied in a formal constitution. According to Paine, when these conditions did not exist, an unjust tyranny prevailed. He was entirely opposed to Burke's ideas. To criticize the faults of the existing state of things was easy and obvious; but Paine expounded, including also a radical constructive policy of parliamentary reform, old age pensions, and a progressive income tax.*

## CHAPTER III: OF THE OLD AND NEW SYSTEMS OF GOVERNMENT

Nothing can appear more contradictory than the principles on which the old governments began, and the condition to which society, civilisation and commerce are capable of carrying mankind. Government, on the old system, is an assumption of power, for the aggrandisement of itself; on the new, a delegation of power for the common benefit of society. The former supports itself by keeping up a system of war; the latter promotes a system of peace, as the true means of enriching a nation. The one encourages national prejudices; the other promotes universal society, as the means of universal commerce. The one measures its prosperity, by the quantity of revenue it extorts; the other proves its excellence, by the small quantity of taxes it requires.

Mr. Burke has talked of old and new whigs. If he can amuse himself with childish names and distinctions, I shall not interrupt his pleasure. It is not to him, but to the Abbe Sieyes, that I address this chapter. I am already engaged to the latter gentleman to discuss the subject of monarchical government; and as it naturally occurs in comparing the old and new systems, I make this the opportunity of presenting to him my observations. I shall occasionally take Mr. Burke in my way.

Though it might be proved that the system of government now called the NEW, is the most ancient in principle of all that have existed, being founded on the original, inherent Rights of Man: yet, as tyranny and the sword have suspended the exercise of those rights for many centuries past, it serves better the purpose of distinction to call it the new, than to claim the right of calling it the old.

The first general distinction between those two systems, is, that the one now called the old is hereditary, either in whole or in part; and the new is entirely representative. It rejects all hereditary government: First, As being an imposition on mankind. Secondly, As inadequate to the purposes for which government is necessary.

With respect to the first of these heads- It cannot be proved by what right hereditary government could begin; neither does there exist within the compass of mortal power a right to establish it. Man has no authority over posterity in matters of personal right; and, therefore, no man, or body of men, had, or can have, a right to set up hereditary government. Were even ourselves to come again into existence, instead of being succeeded by posterity, we have not now the right of taking from ourselves the rights which would then be ours. On what ground, then, do we pretend to take them from others?

All hereditary government is in its nature tyranny. An heritable crown, or an heritable throne, or by what other fanciful name such things may be called, have no other significant explanation than that mankind are heritable property. To inherit a government, is to inherit the people, as if they were flocks and herds.

With respect to the second head, that of being inadequate to the purposes for which government is necessary, we have only to consider what government essentially is, and compare it with the circumstances to which hereditary succession is subject.

Government ought to be a thing always in full maturity. It ought to be so constructed as to be superior to all the accidents to which individual man is subject; and, therefore, hereditary succession, by being subject to them all, is the most irregular and imperfect of all the systems of government.

We have heard the Rights of Man called a levelling system; but the only system to which the word levelling is truly applicable, is the hereditary monarchical system. It is a system of mental levelling. It indiscriminately admits every species of character to the same authority. Vice and virtue, ignorance and wisdom, in short, every quality good or bad, is put on the same level. Kings succeed each other, not as rationals, but as animals. It signifies not what their mental or moral characters are. Can we then be surprised at the abject state of the human mind in monarchical countries, when the government itself is formed on such an abject levelling system?- It has no fixed character. To-day it is one thing; to-morrow it is something else. It changes

with the temper of every succeeding individual, and is subject to all the varieties of each. It is government through the medium of passions and accidents. It appears under all the various characters of childhood, decrepitude, dotage, a thing at nurse, in leading-strings, or in crutches. It reverses the wholesome order of nature. It occasionally puts children over men, and the conceits of nonage over wisdom and experience. In short, we cannot conceive a more ridiculous figure of government, than hereditary succession, in all its cases, presents.

Could it be made a decree in nature, or an edict registered in heaven, and man could know it, that virtue and wisdom should invariably appertain to hereditary succession, the objection to it would be removed; but when we see that nature acts as if she disowned and sported with the hereditary system; that the mental character of successors, in all countries, is below the average of human understanding; that one is a tyrant, another an idiot, a third insane, and some all three together, it is impossible to attach confidence to it, when reason in man has power to act.

It is not to the Abbe Sieyes that I need apply this reasoning; he has already saved me that trouble by giving his own opinion upon the case. "If it be asked," says he, "what is my opinion with respect to hereditary right, I answer without hesitation, That in good theory, an hereditary transmission of any power of office, can never accord with the laws of a true representation. Hereditaryship is, in this sense, as much an attaint upon principle, as an outrage upon society. But let us," continues he, "refer to the history of all elective monarchies and principalities: is there one in which the elective mode is not worse than the hereditary succession?"

As to debating on which is the worst of the two, it is admitting both to be bad; and herein we are agreed. The preference which the Abbe has given, is a condemnation of the thing that he prefers. Such a mode of reasoning on such a subject is inadmissible, because it finally amounts to an accusation upon Providence, as if she had left to man no other choice with respect to government than between two evils, the best of which he admits to be "an attaint upon principle, and an outrage upon society."

Passing over, for the present, all the evils and mischiefs which monarchy has occasioned in the world, nothing can more effectually prove its uselessness in a state of civil government, than making it hereditary. Would we make any office hereditary that required wisdom and abilities to fill it? And where wisdom and abilities are not necessary, such an office, whatever it may be, is superfluous or insignificant.

Hereditary succession is a burlesque upon monarchy. It puts it in the most ridiculous light, by presenting it as an office which any child or idiot may fill. It requires some talents to be a common mechanic; but to be a king requires only the animal figure of man- a sort of breathing automaton. This sort of superstition may last a few years more, but it cannot long resist the awakened reason and interest of man...

But I might go further, and place also foreign wars, of whatever kind, to the same cause. It is by adding the evil of hereditary succession to that of monarchy, that a permanent family interest is created, whose constant objects are dominion and revenue...

I presume that no man in his sober senses will compare the character of any of the kings of Europe with that of General Washington. Yet, in France, and also in England, the expense of the civil list only, for the support of one man, is eight times greater than the whole expense of the federal government in America. To assign a reason for this, appears almost impossible. The generality of people in America, especially the poor, are more able to pay taxes, than the generality of people either in France or England.

But the case is, that the representative system diffuses such a body of knowledge throughout a nation, on the subject of government, as to explode ignorance and preclude imposition. The craft of courts cannot be acted on that ground. There is no place for mystery; nowhere for it to begin. Those who are not in the representation, know as much of the nature of business as those who are. An affectation of mysterious importance would there be scouted. Nations can have no secrets; and the secrets of courts, like those of individuals, are always their defects.

In the representative system, the reason for everything must publicly appear. Every man is a proprietor in government, and considers it a necessary part of his business to understand. It concerns his interest, because it affects his property. He examines the cost, and compares it with the advantages; and above all, he does not adopt the slavish custom of following what in other governments are called LEADERS.

It can only be by blinding the understanding of man, and making him believe that government is some wonderful mysterious thing, that excessive revenues are obtained. Monarchy is well calculated to ensure this end. It is the popery of government; a thing kept up to amuse the ignorant, and quiet them into taxes.

The government of a free country, properly speaking, is not in the persons, but in the laws. The enacting of those requires no great expense; and when they are administered, the whole of civil government is performed- the rest is all court contrivance.

---

**SOURCE**

The text of this document can be found at: http://www.yale.edu/lawweb/avalon/paine/ritestwo.htm.

THE AMERICAN REVOLUTION

# James Otis, *The Rights of the British Colonies Asserted and Proved, Letter Two* (1767)

*Americans in the 1700s generally embraced the ancient teaching that said if human law departs from the law of nature it is, in fact, no longer law but a perversion of the law. This general idea is captured in James Otis'* Rights of British Colonies Asserted and Proved. *Otis's pamphlet uses this logic to defend the rights of the colonists against British encroachment.*

**POLITICAL WRITINGS 308—11**

Let no Man think I am about to commence advocate for *despotism,* because I affirm that government is founded on the necessity of our natures; and that an original supreme Sovereign, absolute, and uncontrollable, *earthly* power *must* exist in and preside over every society; from whose final decisions there can be no appeal but directly to Heaven. It is therefore *originally* and *ultimately* in the people. I say supreme absolute power is *originally* and *ultimately* in the people; and they never did in fact *freely,* nor can they *rightfully* make an absolute, unlimited renunciation of this divine right.[*] It is ever in the nature of the thing given in *trust,* and on a condition, the performance of which no mortal can dispence with; namely, that the person or persons on whom the sovereignty is confer'd by the people, shall *incessantly* consult *their* good. Tyranny of all kinds is to be abhor'd, whether it be in the hands of one, or of the few, or of the many.—And tho'"in the last age a generation of men sprung up that would flatter Princes with an opinion that *they* have a *divine right* to absolute power"; yet "slavery is so vile and miserable an estate of man, and so directly opposite to the generous temper and courage of our nation, that 'tis hard to be conceived that an *englishman,* much less a *gentleman,* should plead for it."[**] Especially at a time when the finest

writers of the most polite nations on the continent of *Europe,* are enraptured with the beauties of the civil constitution of *Great-Britain;* and envy her, no less for the *freedom* of her sons, than for her immense *wealth* and *military* glory.

But let the *origin* of government be placed where it may, the *end* of it is manifestly the good of *the whole. Salus populi supreme lex esto,* is of the law of nature, and part of that grand charter given the human race, (tho' too many of them are afraid to assert it,) by the only monarch in the universe, who has a clear and indisputable right to *absolute* power; because he is the *only* One who is *omniscient* as well as *omnipotent.*

It is evidently contrary to the first principles of reason, that supreme *unlimited* power should be in the hands of *one* man. It is the greatest "idolatry, begotten by *flattery,* on the body of pride", that could induce one to think that a *single mortal* should be able to hold so great a power, if ever so well inclined. Hence the origin of *deifying* princes: It was from the trick of gulling the vulgar into a belief that their tryants were *omniscient,* and that it was therefore right, that they should be considered as *omnipotent.* Hence the *Dii majorum et minorum gentium;* the great, the monarchical, the little Provincial subordinate and subaltern gods, demigods, and semidemi-gods, ancient and modern. Thus deities of all kinds were multiplied and increased in *abundance;* for every devil incarnate, who could enslave a people, acquired a title to *divinity;* and thus the "rabble of the skies" was made up of locusts and caterpillars; lions, tygers and harpies; and other devourers translated from plaguing the earth!***

The *end* of government being the *good* of mankind, points out its great duties: It is above all things to provide for the security, the quiet, and happy enjoyment of life, liberty, and property. There is no one act which a government can have a *right* to make, that does not tend to the advancement of the security, tranquility and prosperity of the people. If life, liberty and property could be enjoyed in as great perfection in *solitude,* as in *society,* there would be no need of government. But the experience of ages has proved that such is the nature of man, a weak, imperfect being; that the valuable ends of live cannot be obtained without the union and assistance of many. Hence 'tis clear that men cannot live apart or independent of each other: In solitude men would perish; and yet they cannot live together without contests. These contests require some arbitrator to determine them. The necessity of a common, indifferent and impartial judge, makes all men seek one; tho' few find him in the *sovereign power,* of their respective states or any where else in *subordination* to it.

Government is founded *immediately* on the necessities of human nature, and *ultimately* on the will of God, the author of nature; who has not left it to men in general to choose, whether they will be members of society or not, but at the hazard of their senses if not of their lives. Yet it is left to every man as he comes of age to chuse *what society* he will continue to belong to. Nay if one has a mind to turn *Hermit,* and after he has been born, nursed, and brought up in the arms of society, and acquired the habits and passions of social life, is willing to run the risque of starving alone, which is generally most unavoidable in a state of hermitage, who shall hinder him? I know

of no human law, founded on the law of *nature,* to restrain him from separating himself from the species, if he can find it in his heart to leave them; unless it should be said, it is against the great law of *self-preservation:* But of this every man will think himself *his own judge.*

The few *Hermits* and *Misanthropes* that have ever existed, show that those states are *unnatural.* If we were to take out from them, those who have made great *worldly* gain of their *godly* hermitage, and those who have been under the madness of *enthusiasm,* or *disappointed* hopes in their *ambitious* projects, for the detriment of mankind; perhaps there might not be left ten from *Adam* to this day.

The form of government is by *nature* and by *right* so far left to the *individuals* of each society, that they may alter it from a simple democracy or government of all over all, to any other form they please. Such alteration may and ought to be made by express compact: But how seldom this right has been asserted, history will abundantly show. For once that it has been fairly settled by compact; *fraud force or accident* have determined it an hundred times. As the people have gained upon tyrants, these have been obliged to relax, *only* till a fairer opportunity has put it in their power to encroach again.

But if every prince since *Nimrod* had been a tyrant, it would not prove a *right* to tyranize. There can be no prescription old enough to supersede the law of nature, and the grant of God almighty; who has given to all men a natural right to be *free,* and they have it ordinarily in their power to make themselves so, if they please.

Government having been proved to be necessary by the law of nature, it makes no difference in the thing to call it from a certain period, *civil.* This term can only relate to form, to additions to, or deviations from, the substance of government: This being founded in nature, the super-structures and the whole administration should be conformed to the law of universal reason. A supreme legislative and supreme executive power, must be placed *somewhere* in every common-wealth: Where there is no other positive provision or compact to the contract, those powers remain in the *whole body of the people.* It is also evident there can be but *one* best way of depositing those powers; but what that way is, mankind have been disputing in peace and in war more than five thousand years. If we could suppose the individuals of a community met to deliberate, whether it were best to keep those powers in *their own* hands, or dispose of them in *trust,* the following questions would occur— Whether those two great powers of *Legislation* and *Execution* should remain united? If so, whether in the hands of the many, or jointly or severally in the hands of a few, or jointly in some one individual? If both those powers are retained in the hands of the many, where nature seems to have placed them originally, the government is a simple *democracy,* or a government of all over all. This can be administered, only by establishing it as a first principle, that the votes of the majority shall be taken as the voice of the whole. If those powers are lodged in the hands of a few, the government is an *Aristocracy* or *Oligarchy.* Here too the first principles of a practicable administration is that the majority rules the whole. If those great powers are both lodged in the hands of one man, the government is a *simple Monarchy,* commonly, though falsly called *absolute,* if by that term is meant a right to do as one pleases.—*Sic volo, sic jubeo, stet pro ratione voluntas,* belongs not of right to any mortal man.

The same law of nature and of reason is equally obligatory on a *democracy,* an *aristocracy,* and a *monarchy:* Whenever the administrators, in any of those forms, deviate from truth, justice and equity, they verge towards tyranny, and are to be opposed; and if they prove incorrigible, they will be *deposed* by the people, if the people are not rendered too abject. Deposing the administrators of a *simple democracy* may sound oddly, but it is done every day, and in almost every vote. A.B. & C. for example, make a *democracy.* Today A & B are for so vile a measure as a standing army. Tomorrow B & C vote it out. This is as really deposing the former administrators, as setting up and making a new king is deposing the old one. *Democracy* in the one case, and *monarchy* in the other, still remain; all that is done is to change the administration.

The first principle and great end of government being to provide for the best good of all the people, this can be done only by a supreme legislative and executive ultimately in the people, or whole community, where God has placed it; but the inconveniencies, not to say impossibility, attending the consultations and operations of a large body of people have made it necessary to transfer the power of the whole to a *few:* This necessity gave rise to deputation, proxy or a right of representation.

---

**NOTES**

\*    The power of GOD almighty is the only power that can properly and strictly be called supreme and absolute. In the order of nature immediately under him, comes the power of a simple *democracy,* or the power of the whole over the whole. Subordinate to both these, are all other political powers, from that of the French Monarque to a petty constable.

\*\*   Mr. Locke.

\*\*\*  Kingcraft and Priestcraft have fell out so often, that 'tis a wonder this grand and ancient alliance is not broken off forever. Happy for mankind will it be, when such a separation shall take place.

---

**SOURCE**

**The Founders' Constitution**
Volume 1, Chapter 2, Document 5
The University of Chicago Press

"Some Political Writings of James Otis." Collected by Charles F. Mullett. *University of Missouri Studies* 4 (1929): 257–432.

The text of this document can be found at:
http://press-pubs.uchicago.edu/founders/documents/v1ch2s5.html.

# Samuel Adams, *The Rights of the British Colonists* (1772)

---

*The Rights of the British Colonists embodies the whole philosophy of human rights applied to the immediate circumstances of an emerging American nation. The report created a powerful sensation, both in America and in England. It considered the rights of the colonists as men, as Christians, and as subjects. The Rights of the Colonists became an important platform upon which many state papers of the Revolution were written.*

---

**THE REPORT OF THE COMMITTEE OF CORRESPONDENCE TO THE BOSTON TOWN MEETING, NOV. 20, 1772**

**I. NATURAL RIGHTS OF THE COLONISTS AS MEN.**

Among the natural rights of the Colonists are these: First, a right to life; Secondly, to liberty; Thirdly, to property; together with the right to support and defend them in the best manner they can. These are evident branches of, rather than deductions from, the duty of self-preservation, commonly called the first law of nature.

All men have a right to remain in a state of nature as long as they please; and in case of intolerable oppression, civil or religious, to leave the society they belong to, and enter into another.

When men enter into society, it is by voluntary consent; and they have a right to demand and insist upon the performance of such conditions and previous limitations as form an equitable original compact.

Every natural right not expressly given up, or, from the nature of a social compact, necessarily ceded, remains.

All positive and civil laws should conform, as far as possible, to the law of natural reason and equity.

As neither reason requires nor religion permits the contrary, every man living in or out of a state of civil society has a right peaceably and quietly to worship God according to the dictates of his conscience.

"Just and true liberty, equal and impartial liberty," in matters spiritual and temporal, is a thing that all men are clearly entitled to by the eternal and immutable laws of God and nature, as well as by the law of nations and all well-grounded municipal laws, which must have their foundation in the former.

In regard to religion, mutual toleration in the different professions thereof is what all good and candid minds in all ages have ever practised, and, both by precept and example, inculcated on mankind. And it is now generally agreed among Christians that this spirit of toleration, in the fullest extent consistent with the being of civil society, is the chief characteristical mark of the Church. Insomuch that Mr. Locke has asserted and proved, beyond the possibility of contradiction on any solid ground, that such toleration ought to be extended to all whose doctrines are not subversive of society. The only sects which he thinks ought to be, and which by all wise laws are excluded from such toleration, are those who teach doctrines subversive of the civil government under which they live. The Roman Catholics or Papists are excluded by reason of such doctrines as these, that princes excommunicated may be deposed, and those that they call heretics may be destroyed without mercy; besides their recognizing the Pope in so absolute a manner, in subversion of government, by introducing, as far as possible into the states under whose protection they enjoy life, liberty, and property, that solecism in politics, imperium in imperio, leading directly to the worst anarchy and confusion, civil discord, war, and bloodshed.

The natural liberty of man, by entering into society, is abridged or restrained, so far only as is necessary for the great end of society, the best good of the whole.

In the state of nature every man is, under God, judge and sole judge of his own rights and of the injuries done him. By entering into society he agrees to an arbiter or indifferent judge between him and his neighbors; but he no more renounces his original right than by taking a cause out of the ordinary course of law, and leaving the decision to referees or indifferent arbitrators.

In the last case, he must pay the referees for time and trouble. He should also be willing to pay his just quota for the support of government, the law, and the constitution; the end of which is to furnish indifferent and impartial judges in all cases that may happen, whether civil, ecclesiastical, marine, or military.

The natural liberty of man is to be free from any superior power on earth, and not to be under the will or legislative authority of man, but only to have the law of nature for his rule.

In the state of nature men may, as the patriarchs did, employ hired servants for the defence of their lives, liberties, and property; and they should pay them reasonable wages. Government was instituted for the purposes of common defence, and those who hold the reins of government have an equitable, natural right to an honorable support from the same principle that " the laborer is worthy of his hire." But then the same community which they serve ought to be the assessors of their pay. Governors have no right to seek and take what they please; by this, instead of being content with the station assigned them, that of honorable servants of the society, they would soon become absolute masters, despots, and tyrants. Hence, as a private man has a right to say what wages he will give in his private affairs, so has a community to determine what they will give and grant of their substance for the administration of public affairs. And, in both cases, more are ready to offer their service at the proposed and stipulated price than are able and willing to perform their duty.

In short, it is the greatest absurdity to suppose it in the power of one, or any number of men, at the entering into society, to renounce their essential natural rights, or the means of preserving those rights; when the grand end of civil government, from the very nature of its institution, is for the support, protection, and defence of those very rights; the principal of which, as is before observed, are Life, Liberty, and Property. If men, through fear, fraud, or mistake, should in terms renounce or give up any essential natural right, the eternal law of reason and the grand end of society would absolutely vacate such renunciation. The right to freedom being the gift of God Almighty, it is not in the power of man to alienate this gift and voluntarily become a slave.

---

**SOURCE**

The text of this document can be found at:
http://history.hanover.edu/texts/adamss.html.

# Joseph Galloway, *Plan of the Union* (1774)

*Joseph Galloway wrote his "Plan of the Union" to help bring a peaceful resolution to the conflict with Britain. The plan was considered very attractive to many, as it proposed a popularly elected Grand Council which would represent the interests of the colonies as a whole, and would be a continental equivalent to the English Parliament. After a sincere debate, it was rejected by a vote of six-to- five.*

**CHAPTER 7**

28 Sept. 1774 *Journals 1:49–51*

Resolution submitted by Joseph Galloway:

*Resolved,* That the Congress will apply to his Majesty for a redress of grievances under which his faithful subjects in America labour; and assure him, that the Colonies hold in abhorrence the idea of being considered independent communities on the British government, and most ardently desire the establishment of a Political Union, not only among themselves, but with the Mother State, upon those principles of safety and freedom which are essential in the constitution of all free governments, and particularly that of the British Legislature; and as the Colonies from their local circumstances, cannot be represented in the Parliament of Great-Britain, they will humbly propose to his Majesty and his two Houses of Parliament, the following plan, under which the strength of the whole Empire may be drawn together on any emergency, the interest of both countries advanced, and the rights and liberties of America secured.

*A Plan of a proposed Union between Great Britain and the Colonies.*

That a British and American legislature, for regulating the administration of the general affairs of America, be proposed and established in America, including all the said colonies; within, and under which government, each colony shall retain its present constitution, and powers of regulating and governing its own internal police, in all cases whatsoever.

That the said government be administered by a President General, to be appointed by the King, and a grand Council, to be chosen by the Representatives of the people of the several colonies, in their respective assemblies, once in every three years.

That the several assemblies shall choose members for the grand council in the following proportions, viz.

New Hampshire.

Massachusetts-Bay.

Rhode Island.

Connecticut.

New-York.

New-Jersey.

Pennsylvania.

Delaware Counties.

Maryland.

Virginia.

North Carolina.

South-Carolina.

Georgia.

Who shall meet at the city of for the first time, being called by the President-General, as soon as conveniently may be after his appointment.

That there shall be a new election of members

for the Grand Council every three years; and on the death, removal or resignation of any member, his place shall be supplied by a new choice, at the next sitting of Assembly of the Colony he represented.

That the Grand Council shall meet once in every year, if they shall think it necessary, and oftener, if occasions shall require, at such time and place as they shall adjourn to, at the last preceding meeting, or as they shall be called to meet at, by the President-General, on any emergency.

That the grand Council shall have power to choose their Speaker, and shall hold and exercise all the like rights, liberties and privileges, as are held and exercised by and in the House of Commons of Great-Britain.

That the President-General shall hold his office during the pleasure of the King, and his assent shall be requisite to all acts of the Grand Council, and it shall be his office and duty to cause them to be carried into execution.

That the President-General, by and with the advice and consent of the Grand-Council, hold and exercise all the legislative rights, powers, and authorities, necessary for regulating and administering all the general police and affairs of the colonies, in which Great-Britain and the colonies, or any of them, the colonies in general, or more than one colony, are in any manner concerned, as well civil and criminal as commercial.

That the said President-General and the Grand Council, be an inferior and distinct branch of the British legislature, united and incorporated with it, for the aforesaid general purposes; and that any of the said general regulations may originate and be formed and digested, either in the Parliament of Great Britain, or in the said Grand Council, and being prepared, transmitted to the other for their approbation or dissent; and that the assent of both shall be requisite to the validity of all such general acts or statutes.

That in time of war, all bills for granting aid to the crown, prepared by the Grand Council, and approved by the President General, shall be valid and passed into a law, without the assent of the British Parliament.

---

SOURCE

**The Founders' Constitution**
Volume 1, Chapter 7, Document 3
http://press-pubs.uchicago.edu/founders/documents/
v1ch7s3.html.

**The University of Chicago Press**
Journals of the Continental Congress, 1774–1789. Edited by Worthington C. Ford et al. 34 vols. Washington, D.C.: Government Printing Office, 1904–37.

The text of this document can be found at:
http://press-pubs.uchicago.edu/founders/.

# John Adams, *Declaration and Resolves of the First Continental Congress* (1774)

*On October 14, 1774, the Congress, chaired by President Peyton Randolph of Williamsburg, announced a set of Declarations and Resolves. The delegates adopted the detailed articles on October 22, 1774.*

Whereas, since the close of the last war, the British parliament, claiming a power, of right, to bind the people of America by statutes in all cases whatsoever, hath, in some acts, expressly imposed taxes on them, and in others, under various presences, but in fact for the purpose of raising a revenue, hath imposed rates and duties payable in these colonies, established a board of commissioners, with unconstitutional powers, and extended the jurisdiction of courts of admiralty, not only for collecting the said duties, but for the trial of causes merely arising within the body of a county:

And whereas, in consequence of other statutes, judges, who before held only estates at will in their offices, have been made dependant on the crown alone for their salaries, and standing armies kept in times of peace: And whereas it has lately been resolved in parliament, that by force of a statute, made in the thirty-fifth year of the reign of King Henry the Eighth, colonists may be transported to England, and tried there upon accusations for treasons and misprisions, or concealments of treasons committed in the colonies, and by a late statute, such trials have been directed in cases therein mentioned:

And whereas, in the last session of parliament, three statutes were made; one entitled, ":An act to discontinue, in such manner and for such time as are therein mentioned, the landing and discharging, lading, or shipping of goods, wares and merchandise, at the town, and within the harbour of Boston, in the province of Massachusetts-Bay in New England;": another entitled, ":An act for the better regulating the government of the province of Massachusetts-Bay in New England;": and another entitled, ":An act for the impartial administration of justice, in the cases of persons questioned for any act done by them in the execution of the law, or for the suppression of riots and tumults, in the province of the Massachusetts-Bay in New England;": and another statute was then made, ":for making more effectual provision for the government of the province of Quebec, etc.": All which statutes are impolitic, unjust, and cruel, as well as unconstitutional, and most dangerous and destructive of American rights:

And whereas, assemblies have been frequently dissolved, contrary to the rights of the people, when they attempted to deliberate on grievances; and their dutiful, humble, loyal, and reasonable petitions to the crown for redress, have been repeatedly treated with contempt, by his Majesty's ministers of state:

The good people of the several colonies of New-Hampshire, Massachusetts-Bay, Rhode Island and Providence Plantations, Connecticut, New-York, New-Jersey, Pennsylvania, Newcastle, Kent, and Sussex on Delaware, Maryland, Virginia, North- Carolina and South-Carolina, justly alarmed at these arbitrary proceedings of parliament and administration, have severally elected, constituted, and appointed deputies to meet, and sit in general Congress, in the city of Philadelphia, in order to obtain such establishment, as that their religion, laws, and liberties, may not be subverted: Whereupon the deputies so appointed being now assembled, in a full and free representation of these colonies, taking into their most serious consideration, the best means of attaining the ends aforesaid, do, in the first place, as Englishmen, their ancestors in like cases have usually done, for asserting and vindicating their rights and liberties, DECLARE,

That the inhabitants of the English colonies in North-America, by the immutable laws of nature, the principles of the English constitution, and the several charters or compacts, have the following RIGHTS:

Resolved, N.C.D. 1. That they are entitled to life, liberty and property: and they have never ceded to any foreign power whatever, a right to dispose of either without their consent.

Resolved, N.C.D. 2. That our ancestors, who first settled these colonies, were at the time of their emigration from the mother country, entitled to all the rights, liberties, and immunities of free and natural- born subjects, within the realm of England.

Resolved, N.C.D. 3. That by such emigration they by no means forfeited, surrendered, or lost any of those rights, but that they were, and their descendants now are, entitled to the exercise and enjoyment of all such of them, as their local and other circumstances enable them to exercise and enjoy.

Resolved, 4. That the foundation of English liberty, and of all free government, is a right in the people to participate in their legislative council: and as the English colonists are not represented, and from their local and other circumstances, cannot properly be represented in the British parliament, they are entitled to a free and exclusive power of legislation in their several provincial legislatures, where their right of representation can alone be preserved, in all cases of taxation and internal polity, subject only to the negative of their sovereign, in such manner as has been heretofore used and accustomed: But, from the necessity of the case, and a regard to the mutual interest of both countries, we cheerfully consent to the operation of such acts of the British parliament, as are bonfide, restrained to the regulation of our external commerce, for the purpose of securing the commercial advantages of the whole empire to the mother country, and the commercial benefits of its respective members; excluding every idea of taxation internal or external, for raising a revenue on the subjects, in America, without their consent.

Resolved, N.C.D. 5. That the respective colonies are entitled to the common law of England, and more especially to the great and inestimable privilege of being tried by their peers of the vicinage, according to the course of that law.

Resolved, N.C.D. 6. That they are entitled to the benefit of such of the English statutes, as existed at the time of their colonization; and which they have, by experience, respectively found to be applicable to their several local and other circumstances.

Resolved, N.C.D. 7. That these, his Majesty's colonies, are likewise entitled to all the immunities and privileges granted and confirmed to them by royal charters, or secured by their several codes of provincial laws.

Resolved, N.C.D. 8. That they have a right peaceably to assemble, consider of their grievances, and petition the king; and that all prosecutions, prohibitory proclamations, and commitments for the same, are illegal.

Resolved, N.C.D. 9. That the keeping a standing army in these colonies, in times of peace, without the consent of the legislature of that colony, in which such army is kept, is against law.

Resolved, N.C.D. 10. It is indispensably necessary to good government, and rendered essential by the English constitution, that the constituent branches of the legislature be independent of each

---

**SOURCE**

The text of this document can be found at:
http://www.history.org/almanack/life/politics/resolves.cfm.

# Thomas Paine, *Common Sense* (1776)

*Thomas Paine was not a great fan of the British monarchy. In fact, he became an articulate spokesperson for the American independence movement. Paine's pro-independence pamphlet* Common Sense, *published on January 19, 1776, quickly became well known to every literate colonist. It is claimed that as many as half a million copies may have been distributed in a country with only a few million inhabitants.*

In the following pages I offer nothing more than simple facts, plain arguments, and common sense; and have no other preliminaries to settle with the reader, than that he will divest himself of prejudice and prepossession, and suffer his reason and his feelings to determine for themselves; that he will put on, or rather that he will not put off, the true character of a man, and generously enlarge his views beyond the present day.

Volumes have been written on the subject of the struggle between England and America. Men of all ranks have embarked in the controversy, from different motives, and with various designs; but all have been ineffectual, and the period of debate is closed. Arms, as the last resource, decide the contest; the appeal was the choice of the king, and the continent hath accepted the challenge.

It hath been reported of the late Mr. Pelham (who tho' an able minister was not without his faults) that on his being attacked in the house of commons, on the score, that his measures were only of a temporary kind, replied, 'they will fast my time.' Should a thought so fatal and unmanly possess the colonies in the present contest, the name of ancestors will be remembered by future generations with detestation.

The sun never shined on a cause of greater worth. 'Tis not the affair of a city, a country, a province, or a kingdom, but of a continent of at least one eighth part of the habitable globe. 'Tis not the concern of a day, a year, or an age; posterity are virtually involved in the contest, and will be more or less affected, even to the end of time, by the proceedings now. Now is the seed time of continental union, faith and honor. The least fracture now will be like a name engraved with the point of a pin on the tender rind of a young oak; The wound will enlarge with the tree, and posterity read it in full grown characters.

By referring the matter from argument to arms, a new area for politics is struck; a new method of thinking hath arisen. All plans, proposals, &c. prior to the nineteenth of April, i. e. to the commencement of hostilities, are like the almanacs of the last year; which, though proper then, are superseded and useless now. Whatever was advanced by the advocates on either side of the question then, terminated in one and the same point, viz. a union with Great Britain; the only difference between the parties was the method of effecting it; the one proposing force, the other friendship; but it hath so far happened that the first hath failed, and the second hath withdrawn her influence.

As much hath been said of the advantages of reconciliation, which, like an agreeable dream, hath passed away and left us as we were, it is but right, that we should examine the contrary side of the argument, and inquire into some of the many material injuries which these colonies sustain, and always will sustain, by being connected with, and dependant on Great Britain. To examine that connection and dependance, on the principles of nature and common sense, to see what we have to trust to, if separated, and what we are to expect, if dependant.

I have heard it asserted by some, that as America hath flourished under her former connection with Great Britain, that the same connection is necessary towards her future happiness, and will always have the same effect. Nothing can be more fallacious than this kind of argument. We may as well assert, that because a child has thrived upon milk, that it is never to have meat; or that the first twenty years of our lives is to become a precedent for the next twenty. But even this is admitting more than is true, for I answer roundly, that America would have flourished as much, and probably much more, had no European power had any thing to do with her. The commerce by which she hath enriched herself are the necessaries of life, and will always have a market while eating is the custom of Europe.

But she has protected us, say some. That she hath engrossed us is true, and defended the continent at our expense as well as her own is admitted, and she would have defended Turkey from the same motive, viz. the sake of trade and dominion.

Alas, we have been long led away by ancient prejudices and made large sacrifices to superstition. We have boasted the protection of Great Britain, without considering, that her motive was interest not attachment; that she did not protect us from our enemies on our account, but from her enemies on her own account, from those who had no quarrel with us on any other account, and who will always be our enemies on the same account. Let Britain wave her pretensions to the continent, or the continent throw off

the dependance, and we should be at peace with France and Spain were they at war with Britain. The miseries of Hanover last war Ought to warn us against connections .

It hath lately been asserted in parliament, that the colonies have no relation to each other but through the parent country, i.e. that Pennsylvania and the Jerseys, and so on for the rest, are sister colonies by the way of England; this is certainly a very roundabout way of proving relation ship, but it is the nearest and only true way of proving enemyship, if I may so call it. France and Spain never were, nor perhaps ever will be our enemies as Americans, but as our being the subjects of Great Britain.

But Britain is the parent country, say some. Then the more shame upon her conduct. Even brutes do not devour their young; nor savages make war upon their families; wherefore the assertion, if true, turns to her reproach; but it happens not to be true, or only partly so, and the phrase Parent or mother country hath been jesuitically adopted by the king and his parasites, with a low papistical design of gaining an unfair bias on the credulous weakness of our minds. Europe, and not England, is the parent country of America. This new world hath been the asylum for the persecuted lovers off civil and religious liberty from every Part of Europe. Hither have they fled, not from the tender embraces of the mother, but from the cruelty of the monster; and it is so far true of England, that the same tyranny which drove the first emigrants from home pursues their descendants still.

In this extensive quarter of the globe, we forget the narrow limits of three hundred and sixty miles (the extent of England) and carry our friendship on a larger scale; we claim brotherhood with every European christian, and triumph in the generosity of the sentiment.

It is pleasant to observe by what regular gradations we surmount the force of local prejudice, as we enlarge our acquaintance with the world. A man born in any town in England divided into parishes, will naturally associate most with his fellow parishioners (because their interests in many cases will be common) and distinguish him by the name of neighbor; if he meet him but a few miles from home, he drops the narrow idea of a street, and salutes him by the name of townsman; if he travels out of the county, and meet him in any other, he forgets the minor divisions of street and town, and calls him countryman; i. e. countyman; but if in their foreign excursions they should associate in France or any other part of Europe, their local remembrance would be enlarged into that of Englishmen. And by a just parity of reasoning, all Europeans meeting in America, or any other quarter of the globe, are countrymen; for England, Holland, Germany, or Sweden, when compared with the whole, stand in the same places on the larger scale, which the divisions of street, town, and county do on the smaller ones; distinctions too limited for continental minds. Not one third of the inhabitants, even of this province, are of English descent. Therefore I reprobate the phrase of parent or mother country applied to England only, as being false, selfish, narrow and ungenerous.

But admitting that we were all of English descent, what does it amount to? Nothing. Britain, being now an open enemy, extinguishes every other name and title: And to say that reconciliation is our duty, is truly farcical. The first king of England, of the present line (William the Conqueror) was a Frenchman, and half the peers of England are descendants from the same country; wherefore by the same method of reasoning, England ought to be governed by France.

Much hath been said of the united strength of Britain and the colonies, that in conjunction they might bid defiance to the world. But this is mere presumption; the fate of war is uncertain, neither do the expressions mean anything; for this continent would never suffer itself to be drained of inhabitants to support the British arms in either Asia, Africa, or Europe.

Besides, what have we to do with setting the world at defiance? Our plan is commerce, and that, well attended to, will secure us the peace and friendship of all Europe; because it is the interest of all Europe to have America a free port. Her trade will always be a protection, and her barrenness of gold and silver secure her from invaders.

I challenge the warmest advocate for reconciliation, to show, a single advantage that this continent can reap, by being connected with Great Britain. I repeat the challenge, not a single advantage is derived. Our corn will fetch its price in any market in Europe, and our imported goods must be paid for buy them where we will.

But the injuries and disadvantages we sustain by that connection, are without number; and our duty to mankind I at large, as well as to ourselves, instruct us to renounce the alliance: Because, any submission to, or dependance on Great Britain, tends directly to involve this continent in European wars and quarrels; and sets us at variance with nations, who would otherwise seek our friendship, and against whom, we have neither anger nor complaint As Europe is our market for trade, we ought to form no partial connection with any part of it. It is the true interest of America to steer clear of European contentions, which she never can do, while by her dependance on Britain, she is made the makeweight in the scale of British politics.

Europe is too thickly planted with kingdoms to be long at peace, and whenever a war breaks out between England and any foreign power, the trade of America goes to ruin, because of her connection with Britain. The next war may not turn out like the Past, and should it not, the advocates for reconciliation now will be wishing for separation then, because, neutrality in that case, would be a safer convoy than a man of war. Every thing that is right or natural pleads for separation. The blood of the slain, the weeping voice of nature cries, 'TIS TIME TO PART...

A government of our own is our natural right: And when a man seriously reflects on the precariousness of human affairs, he will become convinced, that it is in finitely wiser and safer, to form a constitution of our own in a cool deliberate manner, while we have it in our power, than to trust such an interesting event to time and chance. If we omit it now, some Massenello (note-CmnSns-1) may hereafter arise, who laying hold of popular disquietudes, may collect together the desperate and the discontented, and by assuming to themselves the powers of government, may sweep away the liberties of the continent like a deluge. Should the government of America return again into the hands of Britain, the tottering situation of things, will be a temptation for some desperate adventurer to try his fortune; and in such a case, what relief can Britain give? Ere she could hear the news the fatal business might be done, and ourselves suffering like the wretched Britons under the oppression of the Conqueror. Ye that oppose independence now, ye know not what ye do; ye are opening a door to eternal tyranny, by keeping vacant the seat of government. There are thousands and tens of thousands; who would think it glorious to expel from the continent, that barbarous and hellish power, which hath stirred up the Indians and Negroes to destroy us; the cruelty hath a double guilt, it is dealing brutally by us, and treacherously by them.

To talk of friendship with those in whom our reason forbids us to have faith, and our affections wounded through a thousand pores instruct us to detest, is madness and folly. Every day wears out the little remains of kindred between us and them, and can there be any reason to hope, that as the relationship expires, the affection will increase, or that we shall agree better, when we have ten times more and greater concerns to quarrel over than ever?

Ye that tell us of harmony and reconciliation, can ye restore to us the time that is past? Can ye give to prostitution its former innocence? Neither can ye reconcile Britain and America. The last cord now is broken, the people of England are presenting addresses against us. There are injuries which nature cannot forgive; she would cease to be nature if she did. As well can the lover forgive the ravisher of his mistress, as the continent forgive the murders of Britain. The Almighty hath implanted in us these inextinguishable feelings for good and wise purposes. They are the guardians of his image in our hearts. They distinguish us from the herd of common animals. The social compact would dissolve, and justice be extirpated the earth, of have only a casual existence were we callous to the touches of affection. The robber and the murderer, would often escape unpunished, did not the injuries which our tempers sustain, provoke us into justice.

O ye that love mankind! Ye that dare oppose, not only the tyranny, but the tyrant, stand forth! Every spot of the old world is overrun with oppression. Freedom hath been hunted round the globe. Asia, and Africa, have long expelled her. Europe regards her like a stranger, and England hath given her warning to depart. O! receive the fugitive, and prepare in time an asylum for mind.

I have never met with a man, either in England or America, who hath not confessed his opinion, that a separation between the countries, would take place one time or other. And there is no instance in which we have shown less judgment, than in endeavoring to describe, what we call, the ripeness or fitness of the Continent for independence.

---

**SOURCE**

The text of this document can be found at:
http://www.fordham.edu/halsall/mod/paine-common.html.

# Thomas Jefferson, *The Declaration of Independence of the Thirteen Colonies* (1776)

*The Declaration of Independence was ratified by the Continental Congress on July 4, 1776. This anniversary is celebrated as Independence Day in the United States. A copy of the Declaration of Independence is on display to the public in the National Archives in Washington, D.C. The independence of the American colonies was recognized by Great Britain on September 3, 1783, by the Treaty of Paris.*

When in the Course of human events, it becomes necessary for one people to dissolve the political bands which have connected them with another, and to assume among the powers of the earth, the separate and equal station to which the Laws of Nature and of Nature's God entitle them, a decent respect to the opinions of mankind requires that they should declare the causes which impel them to the separation.

We hold these truths to be self-evident, that all men are created equal, that they are endowed by their Creator with certain unalienable Rights, that among these are Life, Liberty and the pursuit of Happiness. —That to secure these rights, Governments are instituted among Men, deriving their just powers from the consent of the governed, —That whenever any Form of Government becomes destructive of these ends, it is the Right of the People to alter or to abolish it, and to institute new Government, laying its foundation on such principles and organizing its powers in such form, as to them shall seem most likely to effect their Safety and Happiness. Prudence, indeed, will dictate that Governments long established should not be changed for light and transient causes; and accordingly all experience hath shewn, that mankind are more disposed to suffer, while evils are sufferable, than to right themselves by abolishing the forms to which they are accustomed. But when a long train of abuses and usurpations, pursuing invariably the same Object evinces a design to reduce them under absolute Despotism, it is their right, it is their duty, to throw off such Government, and to provide new Guards for their future security. —Such has been the patient sufferance of these Colonies; and such is now the necessity which constrains them to alter their former Systems of Government. The history of the present King of Great Britain [George III] is a history of repeated injuries and usurpations, all having in direct object the establishment of an absolute Tyranny over these States. To prove this, let Facts be submitted to a candid world.

He has refused his Assent to Laws, the most wholesome and necessary for the public good.

He has forbidden his Governors to pass Laws of immediate and pressing importance, unless suspended in their operation till his Assent should be obtained; and when so suspended, he has utterly neglected to attend to them.

He has refused to pass other Laws for the accommodation of large districts of people, unless those people would relinquish the right of Representation in the Legislature, a right inestimable to them and formidable to tyrants only.

He has called together legislative bodies at places unusual, uncomfortable, and distant from the depository of their public Records, for the sole purpose of fatiguing them into compliance with his measures.

He has dissolved Representative Houses repeatedly, for opposing with manly firmness his invasions on the rights of the people.

He has refused for a long time, after such dissolutions, to cause others to be elected; whereby the Legislative powers, incapable of Annihilation, have returned to the People at large for their exercise; the State remaining in the mean time exposed to all the dangers of invasion from without, and convulsions within.

He has endeavoured to prevent the population of these States; for that purpose obstructing the Laws for Naturalization of Foreigners; refusing to pass others to encourage their migrations hither, and raising the conditions of new Appropriations of Lands.

He has obstructed the Administration of Justice, by refusing his Assent to Laws for establishing Judiciary powers.

He has made Judges dependent on his Will alone, for the tenure of their offices, and the amount and payment of their salaries.

He has erected a multitude of New Offices, and sent hither swarms of Officers to harass our people, and eat out their substance.

He has kept among us, in times of peace, Standing Armies without the consent of our legislatures.

He has affected to render the Military independent of and superior to the Civil power.

He has combined with others to subject us to a jurisdiction foreign to our constitution and unacknowledged by our laws; giving his Assent to their Acts of pretended Legislation:

For Quartering large bodies of armed troops among us:

For protecting them, by a mock Trial, from punishment for any Murders which they should commit on the Inhabitants of these States:

For cutting off our Trade with all parts of the world:

For imposing Taxes on us without our Consent:

For depriving us, in many cases, of the benefits of Trial by Jury:

For transporting us beyond Seas to be tried for pretended offences:

For abolishing the free System of English Laws in a neighbouring Province, establishing therein an Arbitrary government, and enlarging its Boundaries so as to render it at once an example and fit instrument for introducing the same absolute rule into these Colonies:

For taking away our Charters, abolishing our most valuable Laws, and altering fundamentally the Forms of our Governments:

For suspending our own Legislatures, and declaring themselves invested with power to legislate for us in all cases whatsoever.

He has abdicated Government here, by declaring us out of his Protection and waging War against us.

He has plundered our seas, ravaged our Coasts, burnt our towns, and destroyed the lives of our people.

He is at this time transporting large Armies of foreign Mercenaries to compleat the works of death, desolation and tyranny, already begun with circumstances of Cruelty and perfidy scarcely paralleled in the most barbarous ages, and totally unworthy the Head of a civilized nation.

He has constrained our fellow Citizens taken Captive on the high Seas to bear Arms against their Country, to become the executioners of their friends and Brethren, or to fall themselves by their Hands.

He has excited domestic insurrections amongst us, and has endeavoured to bring on the inhabitants of our frontiers, the merciless Indian Savages, whose known rule of warfare, is an undistinguished destruction of all ages, sexes and conditions.

In every stage of these Oppressions We have Petitioned for Redress in the most humble terms: Our repeated Petitions have been answered only by repeated injury. A Prince whose character is thus marked by every act which may define a Tyrant, is unfit to be the ruler of a free people.

Nor have We been wanting in attentions to our British brethren. We have warned them from time to time of attempts by their legislature to extend an unwarrantable jurisdiction over us. We have reminded them of the circumstances of our emigration and settlement here. We have appealed to their native justice and magnanimity, and we have conjured them by the ties of our common kindred to disavow these usurpations, which, would inevitably interrupt our connections and correspondence. They too have been deaf to the voice of justice and of consanguinity. We must, therefore, acquiesce in the necessity, which denounces our Separation, and hold them, as we hold the rest of mankind, Enemies in War, in Peace Friends.

We, therefore, the Representatives of the united States of America, in General Congress, Assembled, appealing to the Supreme Judge of the world for the rectitude of our intentions, do, in the Name, and by the Authority of the good People of these Colonies, solemnly publish and declare, That these United Colonies are, and of Right ought to be Free and Independent States; that they are Absolved from all Allegiance to the British Crown, and that all political connection between them and the State of Great Britain, is and ought to be totally dissolved; and that as Free and Independent States, they have full Power to levy War, conclude Peace, contract Alliances, establish Commerce, and to do all other Acts and Things which Independent States may of right do. And for the support of this Declaration, with a firm reliance on the protection of divine Providence, we mutually pledge to each other our Lives, our Fortunes and our sacred Honor.

## THE SIGNERS OF THE DECLARATION REPRESENTED THE NEW STATES AS FOLLOWS:

**New Hampshire:**
Josiah Bartlett, William Whipple, Matthew Thornton

**Massachusetts:**
John Hancock, Samual Adams, John Adams, Robert Treat Paine, Elbridge Gerry

**Rhode Island:**
Stephen Hopkins, William Ellery

**Connecticut:**
Roger Sherman, Samuel Huntington, William Williams, Oliver Wolcott

**New York:**
William Floyd, Philip Livingston, Francis Lewis, Lewis Morris

**New Jersey:**
Richard Stockton, John Witherspoon, Francis Hopkinson, John Hart, Abraham Clark

**Pennsylvania:**
Robert Morris, Benjamin Rush, Benjamin Franklin, John Morton, George Clymer, James Smith, George Taylor, James Wilson, George Ross

**Delaware:**
Caesar Rodney, George Read, Thomas McKean

**Maryland:**
Samuel Chase, William Paca, Thomas Stone, Charles Carroll of Carrollton

**Virginia:**
George Wythe, Richard Henry Lee, Thomas Jefferson, Benjamin Harrison, Thomas Nelson, Jr., Francis Lightfoot Lee, Carter Braxton

**North Carolina:**
William Hooper, Joseph Hewes, John Penn

**South Carolina:**
Edward Rutledge, Thomas Heyward, Jr., Thomas Lynch, Jr., Arthur Middleton

**Georgia:**
Button Gwinnett, Lyman Hall, George Walton

---

SOURCE

The text of this document can be found at:
http://www.law.indiana.edu/uslawdocs/declaration.html.

# Abbé Emmanuel Sieyès, *What is the Third Estate?* (1789)

*In France during the time of the French Revolution, the term "Third Estate" was used to refer to people who were not part of the clergy (also referred to as the First Estate) nor of the nobility (also referred to as the Second Estate). The Third Estate included peasants, working people, and the bourgeoisie. In 1789, the Third Estate made up 98 percent of the population in France.*

What is necessary that a nation should subsist and prosper?

Individual effort and public functions.

*Individual Efforts*

All individual efforts may be included in for classes:

1. Since the earth and the waters furnish crude products for the needs of man, the first class, in logical sequence, will be that of all families which devote themselves to agricultural labor.

2. Between the first sale of products and their consumption or use, a new manipulation, more or less repeated, adds to these products a second value more or less composite. In this manner human industry succeeds in perfecting the gifts of nature, and the crude product increases two-fold, ten-fold, one hundred-fold in value. Such are the efforts of the second class.

3. Between production and consumption, as well as between the various stages of production, a group of intermediary agents establish themselves, useful both to producers and consumer; these are the merchants and brokers: the brokers who, comparing incessantly the demands of time and place, speculate upon the profit of retention and transportation; merchants who are charged with distribution, in the last analysis, either at wholesale or at retail. This species of utility characterizes the third class.

4. Outside of these three classes of productive and useful citizens, who are occupied with real objects of consumption and use, there is also need in a society of a series of efforts and pains, whose objects are directly useful or agreeable to the individual. This fourth class embraces all those who stand between the most distinguished and liberal professions and the less esteemed services of domestics.

Such are the efforts which sustain society. Who puts them forth? The Third Estate.

*Public Functions*

Public functions may be classified equally well, in the present state of affairs, under four recognized heads; the sword, the robe, the church and the administration. It would be superfluous to take them up one by one, for the purpose of showing that everywhere the Third Estate attends to nineteen-twentieths of them, with this distinction; that it is laden with all that which is really painful, with all the burdens which the privileged classes refuse to carry. Do we give the Third Estate credit for this? That this might come about, it would be necessary that the Third Estate should refuse to fill these places, or that it should be less ready to exercise their functions. The facts are well known. Meanwhile they have dared to impose a prohibition upon the order of the Third Estate. They have said to it: "Whatever may be your services, whatever may be your abilities, you shall go thus far; you may not pass beyond!" Certain rare exceptions, properly regarded, are but a mockery, and the terms which are indulged in on such occasions, one insult the more.

If this exclusion is a social crime against the Third Estate; if it is a veritable act of hostility, could it perhaps be said that it is useful to the public weal? Alas! who is ignorant of the effects of monopoly? If it discourages those whom it rejects, is it not well known that it tends to render less able those whom it favors? Is it not understood that every employment from which free competition is removed, becomes dear and less effective?

In setting aside any function whatsoever to serve as an appanage for a distinct class among citizens, is it not to be observed that it is no longer the man alone who does the work that it is necessary to reward, but all the unemployed members of that same caste, and also the entire families of those whoa re employed as well as those who are not? Its it not to be remarked that since the government has become the patrimony of a particular class, it has been distended beyond all measure; places have been created not on account of the necessities of the governed, but in the interests of the governing, etc., etc.? Has not attention been called to the fact that this order of things, which is basely and—I even presume to say—beastly respectable with us, when we find it in reading the History of Ancient Egypt or the accounts of Voyages to the Indies, is despicable, monstrous, destructive of all industry, the enemy of social progress; above all degrading to the human race in general, and particularly intolerable to Europeans, etc., etc? But I must leave these considerations, which, if they increase the importance of the subject and throw light upon it, perhaps, along with the new light, slacken our progress.

It suffices here to have made it clear that the pretended utility of a privileged order for the public service is nothing more than a chimera; that with it all that which is burdensome in this service is performed by the Third Estate; that without it the superior places would be infinitely better filled; that they naturally ought to be the lot and the recompense of ability and recognized services, and that if privileged persons have come to usurp all the lucrative and honorable posts, it is a hateful injustice to the rank and file of citizens and at the same a treason to the public.

Who then shall dare to say that the Third Estate has not within itself all that is necessary for the formation of a complete nation? It is the strong and robust man who has one arm still shackled. If the privileged order should be abolished, the nation would be nothing less, but something more. Therefore, what is the Third Estate? Everything; but an everything shackled and oppressed. What would it be without the privileged order? Everything, but an everything free and flourishing. Nothing can succeed without it, everything would be infinitely better without the others.

It is not sufficient to show that privileged persons, far from being useful to the nation, cannot but enfeeble and injure it; it is necessary to prove further that the noble order does not enter at all into the social organization; that it may indeed be a burden upon the nation, but that it cannot of itself constitute a nation.

In the first place, it is not possible in the number of all the elementary parts of a nation to find a place for the caste of nobles. I know that there are individuals in great number whom infirmities, incapacity, incurable laziness, or the weight of bad habits render strangers tot eh labors of society. The exception and the abuse are everywhere found beside the rule. But it will be admitted that he less there are of these abuses, the better it will be for the State. The worst possible arrangement of all would be where not alone isolated individuals, but a whole class of citizens should take pride in remaining motionless in the midst of the general movement, and should consume the best part of the product without bearing any part in its production. Such a class is surely estranged to the nation by its indolence.

The noble order is not less estranged from the generality of us by its civil and political prerogatives.

What is a nation? A body of associates, living under a common law, and represented by the same legislature, etc.

Is it not evident that the noble order has privileges and expenditures which it dares to call its rights, but which are apart from the rights of the great body of citizens? It departs there from the common law. So its civil rights make of it an isolated people in the midst of the great nation. This is truly *imperium in imperia*.

In regard to its political rights, these also it exercises apart. It has its special representatives, which are not charged with securing the interests of the people. The body of its deputies sit apart; and when it is assembled in the same hall with the deputies of simple citizens, it is none the less true that its representation is essentially distinct and separate: it is a stranger to the nation, in the first place, by its origin, since its commission is not derived from the people; then by its object, which consists of defending not the general, but the particular interest.

The Third Estate embraces then all that which belongs to the nation; and all that which is not the Third Estate, cannot be regarded as being of the nation.

What is the Third Estate?

It is the whole.

---

**SOURCE**

The text of this document can be found at:
http://www.fordham.edu/halsall/mod/sieyes.html.

# The Tennis Court Oath (1789)

*The Tennis Court Oath was an early decisive step in starting the French Revolution. It was a revolutionary act and an assertion that political authority derived from the people and their representatives rather than from the monarch. The Tennis Court Oath is often considered the moment of the birth of the French Revolution.*

**JUNE 20, 1789**

The National Assembly, considering that it has been summoned to establish the constitution of the kingdom, to effect the regeneration of the public order, and to maintain the true principles of monarchy; that nothing can prevent it from continuing its deliberations in whatever place it may be forced to establish itself; and, finally, that wheresoever its members are assembled, there is the National Assembly;

Decrees that all members of this Assembly shall immediately take a solemn oath not to separate, and to reassemble wherever circumstances require, until the constitution of the kingdom is established and consolidated upon firm foundations; and that, the said oath taken, all members and each one of them individually shall ratify this steadfast resolution by signature.

**SOURCE**

The text of this document can be found at:
http//:www.historywiz.org.

THE FRENCH REVOLUTION

# The Decree Abolishing the Feudal System (1789)

*The abolition of the feudal system took place during a night session of the Assembly in August 1789. It was caused by the reading of a report on the misery and disorder that prevailed in the provinces of France. With the hope of pacifying and encouraging the people, the Assembly abolished many of the ancient abuses. The document seen here is the revised decree, completed a week later.*

**AUGUST 11, 1789**

**ARTICLE I.** The National Assembly hereby completely abolishes the feudal system. It decrees that, among the existing rights and dues, both feudal and *censuel*,* all those originating in or representing real or personal serfdom shall be abolished without indemnification. All other dues are declared redeemable, the terms and mode of redemption to be fixed by the National Assembly. Those of the said dues which are not extinguished by this decree shall continue to be collected until indemnification shall take place.

**II.** The exclusive right to maintain pigeon houses and dovecotes is abolished. The pigeons shall be confined during the seasons fixed by the community. During such periods they shall be looked upon as game, and every one shall have the right to kill them upon his own land.

**III.** The exclusive right to hunt and to maintain unenclosed warrens is likewise abolished, and every landowner shall have the right to kill, or to have destroyed on his own land, all kinds of game, observing, however, such police regulations as may be established with a view to the safety of the public.

All hunting *capitaineries*, including the royal forests, and all hunting rights under whatever denomination, are likewise abolished. Provision shall be made, however, in a manner compatible with the regard due to property and liberty, for maintaining the personal pleasures of the king.

The president of the Assemby shall be commissioned to ask of the king the recall of those sent to the galleys or exiled, simply for violations of the hunting regulations, as well as for the release of those at present imprisoned for offenses of this kind, and the dismissal of such cases as are now pending.

**IV.** All manorial courts are hereby suppressed without indemnification. But the magistrates of these courts shall continue to perform their functions until such time as the National Assembly shall provide for the establishment of a new judicial system.

**V.** Tithes of every description, as well as the dues which have been substituted for them, under whatever denomination they are known or collected (even when compounded for), possessed by secular or regular congregations, by holders of benefices, members of corporations (including the Order of Malta and other religious and military orders), as well as those devoted to the maintenance of churches, those impropriated to lay persons, and those substituted for the *portion congrue*,** are abolished, on condition, however, that some other method be devised to provide for the expenses of divine worship, the support of the officiating clergy, for the assistance of the poor, for repairs and rebuilding of churches and parsonages, and for the maintenance of all institutions, seminaries, schools, academies, asylums, and organizations to which the present funds are devoted. Until such provision shall be made and the former possessors shall enter upon the enjoyment of an income on the new system, the National Assembly decrees that the said tithes shall continue to be collected according to law and in the customary manner.

Other tithes, of whatever nature they may be, shall be redeemable in such manner as the Assembly shall determine. Until this matter is adjusted, the National Assembly decrees that these, too, shall continue to be collected.

**VI.** All perpetual ground rents, payable either in money or in kind, of whatever nature they may be, whatever their origin and to whomsoever they may be due, . . . shall be redeemable at a rate fixed by the Assembly. No due shall in the future be created which is not redeemable.

**VII.** The sale of judicial and municipal offices shall be abolished forthwith. Justice shall be dispensed *gratis*. Nevertheless the magistrates at present holding such offices shall continue to exercise their functions and to receive their emoluments until the Assembly shall have made provision for indemnifying them.

**VIII.** The fees of the country priests are abolished, and shall be discontinued so soon as provision shall be made for increasing the minimum salary [*portion congrue*] of the parish priests and the payment to the curates. A regulation shall be drawn up to determine the status of the priests in the towns.

**IX.** Pecuniary privileges, personal or real, in the payment of taxes are abolished forever. Taxes shall be collected from all the citizens, and from all property, in the same manner and in the same form. Plans shall be considered by which the taxes shall be paid proportionally by all, even for the last six months of the current year.

**X.** Inasmuch as a national constitution and public liberty are of more advantage to the provinces than the privileges which some of these enjoy, and inasmuch as the surrender of such privileges is essential to the intimate union of all parts of the realm, it is decreed that all the peculiar privileges, pecuniary or otherwise, of the provinces, principalities, districts, cantons, cities, and communes, are once for all abolished and are absorbed into the law common to all Frenchmen.

**XI.** All citizens, without distinction of birth, are eligible to any office or dignity, whether ecclesiastical, civil, or military; and no profession shall imply any derogation.

**XII.** Hereafter no remittances shall be made for annates or for any other purpose to the court of Rome, the vice legation at Avignon, or to the nunciature at Lucerne. The of the diocese shall apply to their bishops in regard to the filling of benefices and dispensations, the which shall be granted *gratis* without regard to reservations, expectancies, and papal months, all the churches of France enjoying the same freedom.

**XIII.** [This article abolishes various ecclesiastical dues.]

**XIV.** Pluralities shall not be permitted hereafter in cases where the revenue from the benefice or benefices held shall exceed the sum of three thousand livres. Nor shall any individual be allowed to enjoy several pensions from benefices, or a pension and a benefice, if the revenue which he already enjoys from such sources exceeds the same sum of three thousand livres.

**XV.** The National Assembly shall consider, in conjunction with the king, the report which is to be submitted to it relating to pensions, favors, and salaries, with a view to suppressing all such as are not deserved, and reducing those which shall prove excessive; and the amount shall be fixed which the king may in the future disburse for this purpose.

**XVI.** The National Assembly decrees that a medal shall be struck in memory of the recent grave and important deliberations for the welfare of France, and that a Te Deum shall be chanted in gratitude in all the parishes and the churches of France.

**XVII.** The National Assembly solemnly proclaims the king, Louis XVI, the *Restorer of French Liberty*.

**XVIII.** The National Assembly shall present itself in a body before the king, in order to submit to him the decrees which have just been passed, to tender to him the tokens of its most respectful gratitude, and to pray him to permit the Te Deum to be chanted in his chapel, and to be present himself at this service.

**XIX.** The National Assembly shall consider, immediately after the constitution, the drawing up of the laws necessary for the development of the principles which it has laid down in the present decree. The latter shall be transmitted by the deputies without delay to all the provinces, together with the decree of the 10th of this month, in order that it may be printed, published, read from the parish pulpits, and posted up wherever it shall be deemed necessary.

---

**NOTES**

* This refers to the *cens*, a perpetual due similar to the payments made by English copyholders.

** This expression refers to the minimum remuneration fixed for the priests.

---

**SOURCE**

The text of this document can be found at: http://history.hanover.edu/texts/abolfeud.htm.

## THE FRENCH REVOLUTION

# *Declaration of the Rights of Man and of the Citizen* (1789)

*The Declaration of the Rights of Man and of the Citizen was one of the fundamental documents of the French Revolution, defining a set of individual rights and the collective rights of the people. It was adopted on August 26, 1789, by the National Constituent Assembly as the first step toward writing a constitution.*

Approved by the National Assembly of France, August 26, 1789

The representatives of the French people, organized as a National Assembly, believing that the ignorance, neglect, or contempt of the rights of man are the sole cause of public calamities and of the corruption of governments, have determined to set forth in a solemn declaration the natural, unalienable, and sacred rights of man, in order that this declaration, being constantly before all the members of the Social body, shall remind them continually of their rights and duties; in order that the acts of the legislative power, as well as those of the executive power, may be compared at any moment with the objects and purposes of all political institutions and may thus be more respected, and, lastly, in order that the grievances of the citizens, based hereafter upon simple and incontestable principles, shall tend to the maintenance of the constitution and redound to the happiness of all. Therefore the National Assembly recognizes and proclaims, in the presence and under the auspices of the Supreme Being, the following rights of man and of the citizen:

**ARTICLES:**

1. Men are born and remain free and equal in rights. Social distinctions may be founded only upon the general good.

2. The aim of all political association is the preservation of the natural and imprescriptible rights of man. These rights are liberty, property, security, and resistance to oppression.

3. The principle of all sovereignty resides essentially in the nation. No body nor individual may exercise any authority which does not proceed directly from the nation.

4. Liberty consists in the freedom to do everything which injures no one else; hence the exercise of the natural rights of each man has no limits except those which assure to the other members of the society the enjoyment of the same rights. These limits can only be determined by law.

5. Law can only prohibit such actions as are hurtful to society. Nothing may be prevented which is not forbidden by law, and no one may be forced to do anything not provided for by law.

6. Law is the expression of the general will. Every citizen has a right to participate personally, or through his representative, in its foundation. It must be the same for all, whether it protects or punishes. All citizens, being equal in the eyes of the law, are equally eligible to all dignities and to all public positions and occupations, according to their abilities, and without distinction except that of their virtues and talents.

7. No person shall be accused, arrested, or imprisoned except in the cases and according to the forms prescribed by law. Any one soliciting, transmitting, executing, or causing to be executed, any arbitrary order, shall be punished. But any citizen summoned or arrested in virtue of the law shall submit without delay, as resistance constitutes an offense.

8. The law shall provide for such punishments only as are strictly and obviously necessary, and no one shall suffer punishment except it be legally inflicted in virtue of a law passed and promulgated before the commission of the offense.

9. As all persons are held innocent until they shall have been declared guilty, if arrest shall be deemed indispensable, all harshness not essential to the securing of the prisoner's person shall be severely repressed by law.

10. No one shall be disquieted on account of his opinions, including his religious views, provided their manifestation does not disturb the public order established by law.

11. The free communication of ideas and opinions is one of the most precious of the rights of man. Every citizen may, accordingly, speak, write, and print with freedom, but shall be responsible for such abuses of this freedom as shall be defined by law.

12. The security of the rights of man and of the citizen requires public military forces. These forces are, therefore, established for the good of all and not for the personal advantage of those to whom they shall be intrusted.

13. A common contribution is essential for the maintenance of the public forces and for the cost of administration. This should be equitably distributed among all the citizens in proportion to their means.

14. All the citizens have a right to decide, either personally or by their representatives, as to the necessity of the public contribution; to grant this freely; to know to what uses it is put; and to fix the proportion, the mode of assessment and of collection and the duration of the taxes.

15. Society has the right to require of every public agent an account of his administration.

16. A society in which the observance of the law is not assured, nor the separation of powers defined, has no constitution at all.

17. Since property is an inviolable and sacred right, no one shall be deprived thereof except where public necessity, legally determined, shall clearly demand it, and then only on condition that the owner shall have been previously and equitably indemnified.

---

**SOURCE**

The text of this document can be found at:
http://www.yale.edu/lawweb/avalon/rightsof.htm.

THE FRENCH REVOLUTION

# Declaration of Pillnitz (1791)

*When they signed the Declaration of Pillnitz in 1791, the Austrian and Prussian monarchs intended it to serve as a warning to the French revolutionaries not to infringe further on the rights of Louis XVI. The inflammatory language of the Declaration was used by the radical Brissotin faction as proof of Austrian and Prussian intentions to crush the Revolution and reinstate the Ancien Regime. (The Brissotins hoped that a war would lead to a radicalization of the Revolution and a lessening of the King's powers.) The Brissotins engineered a declaration of war by the National Assembly against Austria on April 20, 1792. Ironically, if the French had known the content of the secret provisions of the declaration, there would have been no need for concern, since they are concerned mostly with matters not related to France (such as the Polish succession). Since the contracting parties agreed to act only in concert, (or if France were to nullify her treaties) an invasion of France was unlikely. Furthermore, the parties hoped to reduce their armies with France focused on internal affairs.*

**27 AUGUST 1791**

His Majesty the Emperor and His Majesty the King of Prussia having understood the desires and the representations of Monsieur (Their Brother, the King of France) and of the Count of Artois, declare conjointly that they regard the situation in which His Majesty the King of France is actually found is an object of common interest to all the sovereigns of Europe. They hope that this interest cannot fail to be recognized by the powers for which the assistance is demanded; and that in consequence they will not refuse to employ, conjointly with their Majesties, the most effective means, relative to their forces, in order to put the King of France in a position to affirm in the most perfect liberty, the basis of a monarchial government equally suitable to the rights of sovereigns and to the well-being of the French nation. Then in this case, their Majesties the Emperor and the King of Prussia are resolved to act promptly in a mutual agreement with the necessary forces in order to obtain the proposed and common goal.

Meanwhile, they will give to their troops suitable orders so that they had carried to activate it [the agreement].

At Pillnitz, the 27th of August 1791.

Leopold. Frederick William.

Additional secret articles to the preceding declaration

1. The High Contracting Powers will take in concert the most effective measures in general, as much for the maintenance of the treaties which remain with France, as particularly for the representations made to this nation, and will invite all of the Empire to work towards [the common good], in the case that the friendly representations prove fruitless.

2. The two parties will try to agree as much as possible with the court of Petersburg in favor of the Electoral Court of Saxony for the succession to the throne of Poland.

3. They reserve for themselves respectively the power to exchange for their benefit, several of their present and future acquisitions, for which they will observe a perfect equality of

revenues as well as to the prescribed order of the constitution of the Germanic Corps. In consequence of which the two parties will agree amicably as much between themselves as in the other interests that this exchange will be concerned with.

4. They will concert themselves on the diminution of their respective armies, as soon as their connections with the other powers will permit it.

5. His Prussian Majesty promises to the Archduke Francis his vote for Francis' election as King of the Romans, as long as none oppose what is provided for the establishment of one or the other of the Archdukes, and provided that it is done in a manner which accords with the Germanic Constitution.

6. On the one hand the Emperor will employ willingly his good offices towards the Court of Petersburg and the Republic of Poland in order to obtain the cities of Thorn and Danzig [for Prussia]; But on the other hand His Imperial Majesty intends that His Prussian Majesty will employ the same [offices] towards England and the Estates General of the United Provinces, [i.e., the Netherlands] relative to the desired modifications to the convention concluded at la Haye on the subject of the Belgian affairs.

---

### SOURCE

The text of this document can be found at:
http//:www.NapoleonSeries.org.

# *Levée en Masse* (1793)

*In response to the dangers of foreign war, France's Committee of Public Safety established a mass conscription (Levée en Masse) and succeeded in training an army of about 800,000 soldiers in less than a year. This was a much larger army than any of those in other European states, and it laid the basis for Napoleon's domination of Europe. The Levée en Masse represents a turning point in the history of warfare. From that point on, war was to become a total effort, involving all elements of the population and all the reserves of the state.*

**AUGUST 23, 1793**

1. From this moment until that in which the enemy shall have been driven from the soil of the Republic, all Frenchmen are in permanent requisition for the service of the armies. The young men shall go to battle; the married men shall forge arms and transport provisions; the women shall make tents and clothing and shall serve in the hospitals; the children shall turn old linen into lint; the aged shall betake themselves to the public places in order to arouse the courage of the warriors and preach the hatred of kings and the unity of the Republic.

2. The national buildings shall be converted into barracks, the public places into workshops for arms, the soil of the cellars shall be washed in order to extract therefrom the saltpeter.

3. The arms of the regulation caliber shall be reserved exclusively for those who shall march against the enemy; the service of the interior shall be performed with hunting pieces and side arms.

4. The saddle horses are put into requisition to complete the cavalry corps the draft horses, other than those employed in agriculture, shall convey the artillery and the provisions.

5. The Committee of Public Safety is charged to take all necessary measures to set up without delay an extraordinary manufacture of arms of every sort which corresponds with the ardor and energy of the French people. It is, accordingly, authorized to form all the establishments, factories, workshops, and mills which shall be deemed necessary for the carrying on of these works, as well as to put in requisition, within the entire extent of the Republic, the artists and workingmen who can contribute to their success.

6. The representatives of the people sent out for the execution of the present law shall have the same authority in their respective districts, acting in concert with the Committee of Public Safety; they are invested with the unlimited powers assigned to the representatives of the people to the armies.

7. Nobody can get himself replaced in the service for which he shall have been requisitioned. The public functionaries shall remain at their posts.

**SOURCE**

F. M. Anderson, ed., *The Constitutions and Other Select Documents Illustrative of the History of France*, 1789–1907, 2d Ed. (Minneapolis: H. W. Wilson Co., 1908), 184–185. Scanned by Jerome S. Arkenberg, Department of History, California State University, Fullerton.

The text of this document can be found at: http://www.fordham.edu/halsall/mod/1793levee.html.

# Maximilien Robespierre, *Justification of the Use of Terror* (1794)

*As leader of the Committee of Public Safety, which effectively governed France at the height of the French Revolution, Maximilien Robespierre directed its energies against counter-revolutionary uprisings, especially in the south and west of France. In doing so, the Reign of Terror was unleashed. The figures behind this speech indicate that in the five months from September, 1793, to February 5, 1794, the revolutionary tribunal in Paris convicted and executed 238 men and 31 women and acquitted 190 people, and that on February 5 there were 5,434 people in the prisons in Paris awaiting trial.*

But, to found and consolidate democracy, to achieve the peaceable reign of the constitutional laws, we must end the war of liberty against tyranny and pass safely across the storms of the revolution: such is the aim of the revolutionary system that you have enacted. Your conduct, then, ought also to be regulated by the stormy circumstances in which the republic is placed; and the plan of your administration must result from the spirit of the revolutionary government combined with the general principles of democracy.

Now, what is the fundamental principle of the democratic or popular government-that is, the essential spring which makes it move? It is virtue; I am speaking of the public virtue which effected so many prodigies in Greece and Rome and which ought to produce much more surprising ones in republican France; of that virtue which is nothing other than the love of country and of its laws.

But as the essence of the republic or of democracy is equality, it follows that the love of country necessarily includes the love of equality.

It is also true that this sublime sentiment assumes a preference for the public interest over every particular interest; hence the love of country presupposes or produces all the virtues: for what are they other than that spiritual strength which renders one capable of those sacrifices? And how could the slave of avarice or ambition, for example, sacrifice his idol to his country?

Not only is virtue the soul of democracy; it can exist only in that government....

. . .

Republican virtue can be considered in relation to the people and in relation to the government; it is necessary in both. When only the government lacks virtue, there remains a resource in the people's virtue; but when the people itself is corrupted, liberty is already lost.

Fortunately virtue is natural to the people, notwithstanding aristocratic prejudices. A nation is truly corrupted when, having by degrees lost its character and its liberty, it passes from democracy to aristocracy or to monarchy; that is the decrepitude and death of the body politic....

But when, by prodigious efforts of courage and reason, a people breaks the chains of despotism to make them into trophies of liberty; when by the force of its moral temperament it comes, as it were, out of the arms of the death, to recapture all the vigor of youth; when by turns it is sensitive and proud, intrepid and docile, and can be stopped neither by impregnable ramparts nor by the innumerable ammies of the tyrants armed against it, but stops of itself upon confronting the law's image; then if it does not climb rapidly to the summit of its destinies, this can only be the fault of those who govern it.

…

From all this let us deduce a great truth: the characteristic of popular government is confidence in the people and severity towards itself.

The whole development of our theory would end here if you had only to pilot the vessel of the Republic through calm waters; but the tempest roars, and the revolution imposes on you another task.

This great purity of the French revolution's basis, the very sublimity of its objective, is precisely what causes both our strength and our weakness. Our strength, because it gives to us truth's ascendancy over imposture, and the rights of the public interest over private interests; our weakness, because it rallies all vicious men against us, all those who in their hearts contemplated despoiling the people and all those who intend to let it be despoiled with impunity, both those who have rejected freedom as a personal calamity and those who have embraced the revolution as a career and the Republic as prey. Hence the defection of so many ambitious or greedy men who since the point of departure have abandoned us along the way because they did not begin the journey with the same destination in view. The two opposing spirits that have been represented in a struggle to rule nature might be said to be fighting in this great period of human history to fix irrevocably the world's destinies, and France is the scene of this fearful combat. Without, all the tyrants encircle you; within, all tyranny's friends conspire; they will conspire until hope is wrested from crime. We must smother the internal and external enemies of the Republic or perish with it; now in this situation, the first maxim of your policy ought to be to lead the people by reason and the people's enemies by terror.

If the spring of popular government in time of peace is virtue, the springs of popular government in revolution are at once *virtue and terror:* virtue, without which terror is fatal; terror, without which virtue is powerless. Terror is nothing other than justice, prompt, severe, inflexible; it is therefore an emanation of virtue; it is not so much a special principle as it is a consequence of the general principle of democracy applied to our country's most urgent needs.

It has been said that terror is the principle of despotic government. Does your government therefore resemble despotism? Yes, as the sword that gleams in the hands of the heroes of liberty resembles that with which the henchmen of tyranny are armed. Let the despot govern by terror his brutalized subjects; he is right, as a despot. Subdue by terror the enemies of liberty, and you will be right, as founders of the Republic. The government of the revolution is liberty's despotism against tyranny. Is force made only to protect crime? And is the thunderbolt not destined to strike the heads of the proud?

…

… Indulgence for the royalists, cry certain men, mercy for the villains! No! mercy for the innocent, mercy for the weak, mercy for the unfortunate, mercy for humanity.

Society owes protection only to peaceable citizens; the only citizens in the Republic are the republicans. For it, the royalists, the conspirators are only strangers or, rather, enemies. This terrible war waged by liberty against tyranny- is it not indivisible? Are the enemies within not the allies of the enemies without? The assassins who tear our country apart, the intriguers who buy the consciences that hold the people's mandate; the traitors who sell them; the mercenary pamphleteers hired to dishonor the people's cause, to kill public virtue, to stir up the fire of civil discord, and to prepare political counter-revolution by moral counterrevolution-are all those men less guilty or less dangerous than the tyrants whom they serve?

**SOURCE**

Robespierre: *On the Moral and Political Principles of Domestic Policy.*

The text of this document can be found at: http://www.fordham.edu/halsall/mod/robespierre-terror.html.

**THE FRENCH REVOLUTION**

# Maximilien Robespierre, *On the Principles of Political Morality* (1794)

*In the midst of the Reign of Terror, Robespierre delivered this speech to the Convention in early February 1794. In the speech, Robespierre sought to justify the actions taken in the name of the Terror. By this time, the threat of Austrian, British, and Prussian invasion had declined dramatically, yet Robespierre emphasized that only a combination of virtue (a commitment to republican ideals) and terror (coercion against those who failed to demonstrate such a commitment) could assure the survival of the Republic, since it would always be faced with the potential for subversion from within, even if its warring, external enemies were defeated. The speech was delivered in the name of the Committee of Public Safety.*

**CITIZENS, REPRESENTATIVES OF THE PEOPLE:**
Some time since we laid before you the principles of our exterior political system, we now come to develop the principles of political morality which are to govern the interior. After having long pursued the path which chance pointed out, carried away in a manner by the efforts of contending factions, the Representatives of the People at length acquired a character and produced a form of government. A sudden change in the success of the nation announced to Europe the regeneration which was operated in the national representation. But to this point of time, even now that I address you, it must be allowed that we have been impelled thro' the tempest of a revolution, rather by a love of right and a feeling of the wants of our country, than by an exact theory, and precise rules of conduct, which we had not even leisure to sketch.

It is time to designate clearly the purposes of the revolution and the point which we wish to attain: It is time we should examine ourselves the obstacles which yet are between us and our wishes, and the means most proper to realize them: A consideration simple and important which appears not yet to have been contemplated. Indeed, how could a base and corrupt government have dared to view themselves in the mirror of political rectitude? A king, a proud senate, a Caesar, a Cromwell; of these the first care was to cover their dark designs under the cloak of religion, to covenant with every vice, caress every party, destroy men of probity, oppress and deceive the people in order to attain the end of their perfidious ambition. If we had not had a task of the first magnitude to accomplish; if all our concern had been to raise a party or create a new aristocracy, we might have believed, as certain writers more ignorant than wicked asserted, that the plan of the French revolution was to be found written in the works of Tacitus and of Machiavel; we might have sought the duties of the representatives of the people in the history of Augustus, of Tiberius, or of Vespasian, or even in that of certain French legislators; for tyrants are substantially alike and only differ by trifling shades of perfidy and cruelty.

For our part we now come to make the whole world partake in your political secrets, in order that all friends of their country may rally at the voice of reason and public interest, and that the French nation and her representatives be respected in all countries which may attain a knowledge of their true principles; and that intriguers who always seek to supplant other intriguers may be judged by public opinion upon settled and plain principles.

Every precaution must early be used to place the interests of freedom in the hands of truth, which is eternal, rather than in those of men who change; so that if the government forgets the interests of the people or falls into the hands of men corrupted, according to the natural course of things, the light of acknowledged principles should unmask their treasons, and that every new faction may read its death in the very thought of a crime.

Happy the people that attains this end; for, whatever new machinations are plotted against their liberty, what resources does not public reason present when guaranteeing freedom!

What is the end of our revolution? The tranquil enjoyment of liberty and equality; the reign of that eternal justice, the laws of which are graven, not on marble or stone, but in the hearts of men, even in the heart of the slave who has forgotten them, and in that of the tyrant who disowns them.

We wish that order of things where all the low and cruel passions are enchained, all the beneficent and generous passions awakened by the laws; where ambition subsists in a desire to deserve glory and serve the country: where distinctions grow out of the system of equality, where the citizen submits to the authority of the magistrate, the magistrate obeys that of the people, and the people are governed by a love of justice; where the country secures the comfort of each individual, and where each individual prides himself on the prosperity and glory of his country; where every soul expands by a free communication of republican sentiments, and by

the necessity of deserving the esteem of a great people: where the arts serve to embellish that liberty which gives them value and support, and commerce is a source of public wealth and not merely of immense riches to a few individuals.

We wish in our country that morality may be substituted for egotism, probity for false honour, principles for usages, duties for good manners, the empire of reason for the tyranny of fashion, a contempt of vice for a contempt of misfortune, pride for insolence, magnanimity for vanity, the love of glory for the love of money, good people for good company, merit for intrigue, genius for wit, truth for tinsel show, the attractions of happiness for the ennui of sensuality, the grandeur of man for the littleness of the great, a people magnanimous, powerful, happy, for a people amiable, frivolous and miserable; in a word, all the virtues and miracles of a Republic instead of all the vices and absurdities of a Monarchy.

We wish, in a word, to fulfill the intentions of nature and the destiny of man, realize the promises of philosophy, and acquit providence of a long reign of crime and tyranny. That France, once illustrious among enslaved nations, may, by eclipsing the glory of all free countries that ever existed, become a model to nations, a terror to oppressors, a consolation to the oppressed, an ornament of the universe and that, by sealing the work with our blood, we may at least witness the dawn of the bright day of universal happiness. This is our ambition, - this is the end of our efforts....

Since virtue and equality are the soul of the republic, and that your aim is to found, to consolidate the republic, it follows, that the first rule of your political conduct should be, to let all your measures tend to maintain equality and encourage virtue, for the first care of the legislator should be to strengthen the principles on which the government rests. Hence all that tends to excite a love of country, to purify manners, to exalt the mind, to direct the passions of the human heart towards the public good, you should adopt and establish. All that tends to concenter and debase them into selfish egotism, to awaken an infatuation for littlenesses, and a disregard for greatness, you should reject or repress. In the system of the French revolution that which is immoral is impolitic, and what tends to corrupt is counter-revolutionary. Weaknesses, vices, prejudices are the road to monarchy. Carried away, too often perhaps, by the force of ancient habits, as well as by the innate imperfection of human nature, to false ideas and pusillanimous sentiments, we have more to fear from the excesses of weakness, than from excesses of energy. The warmth of zeal is not perhaps the most dangerous rock that we have to avoid; but rather that languour which ease produces and a distrust of our own courage. Therefore continually wind up the sacred spring of republican government, instead of letting it run down. I need not say that I am not here justifying any excess. Principles the most sacred may be abused: the wisdom of government should guide its operations according to circumstances, it should time its measures, choose its means; for the manner of bringing about great things is an essential part of the talent of producing them, just as wisdom is an essential attribute of virtue....

It is not necessary to detail the natural consequences of the principle of democracy, it is the principle itself, simple yet copious, which deserves to be developed.

Republican virtue may be considered as it respects the people and as it respects the government. It is necessary in both. When however, the government alone want it, there exists a resource in that of the people; but when the people themselves are corrupted liberty is already lost.

Happily virtue is natural in the people, [despite] aristocratical prejudices. A nation is truly corrupt, when, after having, by degrees lost its character and liberty, it slides from democracy into aristocracy or monarchy; this is the death of the political body by decrepitude....

But, when, by prodigious effects of courage and of reason, a whole people break asunder the fetters of despotism to make of the fragments trophies to liberty; when, by their innate vigor, they rise in a manner from the arms of death, to resume all the strength of youth when, in turns forgiving and inexorable, intrepid and docile, they can neither be checked by impregnable ramparts, nor by innumerable armies of tyrants leagued against them, and yet of themselves stop at the voice of the law; if then they do not reach the heights of their destiny it can only be the fault of those who govern.

Again, it may be said, that to love justice and equality the people need no great effort of virtue; it is sufficient that they love themselves....

If virtue be the spring of a popular government in times of peace, the spring of that government during a revolution is virtue combined with terror: virtue, without which terror is destructive; terror, without which virtue is impotent. Terror is only justice prompt, severe and inflexible; it is then an emanation of virtue; it is less a distinct principle than a natural consequence of the general principle of democracy, applied to the most pressing wants of the country.

It has been said that terror is the spring of despotic government. Does yours then resemble despotism? Yes, as the steel that glistens in the hands of the heroes of liberty resembles the sword with which the satellites of tyranny are armed. Let the despot govern by terror his debased subjects; he is right as a despot: conquer by terror the enemies of liberty and you will be right as founders of the republic. The government in a revolution is the despotism of liberty against tyranny. Is force only intended to protect crime? Is not the lightning of heaven made to blast vice exalted?

The law of self-preservation, with every being whether physical or moral, is the first law of nature. Crime butchers innocence to secure a throne, and innocence struggles with all its might against the attempts of crime. If tyranny reigned one single day not a patriot would survive it. How long yet will the madness of despots be called justice, and the justice of the people barbarity or rebellion? - How tenderly oppressors and how severely the oppressed are treated! Nothing more natural: whoever does not abhor crime cannot love virtue. Yet one or the other must be crushed. Let mercy be shown the royalists exclaim some men. Pardon the villains! No: be merciful to innocence, pardon the unfortunate, show compassion for human weakness.

The protection of government is only due to peaceable citizens; and all citizens in the republic are republicans. The royalists, the conspirators, are strangers, or rather enemies. Is not this dreadful contest, which liberty maintains against tyranny, indivisible? Are not the internal enemies the allies of those in the exterior? The assassins who lay waste the interior; the intriguers who purchase the consciences of the delegates of the people: the traitors who sell them; the mercenary libellists paid to dishonor the cause of the people, to smother public virtue, to fan the flame of civil discord, and bring about a political counter revolution by means of a moral one; all these men, are they less culpable or less dangerous than the tyrants whom they serve? ...

To punish the oppressors of humanity is clemency; to forgive them is cruelty. The severity of tyrants has barbarity for its principle; that of a republican government is founded on beneficence. Therefore let him beware who should dare to influence the people by that terror which is made only for their enemies! Let him beware, who, regarding the inevitable errors of civism in the same light, with the premeditated crimes of perfidiousness, or the attempts of conspirators, suffers the dangerous intriguer to escape and pursues the peaceable citizen! Death to the villain who dares abuse the sacred name of liberty or the powerful arms intended for her defence, to carry mourning or death to the patriotic heart....

SOURCE

From M. Robespierre, *Report upon the Principles of Political Morality Which Are to Form the Basis of the Administration of the Interior Concerns of the Republic* (Philadelphia, 1794).

The text of this document can be found at:
http://www.fordham.edu/halsall/mod/1794robespierre.html.

# Thomas Babington Macaulay, *Speech On The Reform Bill of 1832* (1831)

*Lord Macaulay was an active supporter of reform of the British Parliament. Until the Reform Bill, the House of Commons had been elected in almost completely non-democratic ways. The 1832 bill did not create a democracy, but it did enfranchise the British middle class. The process of extending the franchise continued for almost one hundred years, until women were given equal access to the vote.*

*On Lord John Russell's motion for leave to bring in a Bill to amend the Representation of the People of England and Wales.*

It is a circumstance, sir, of happy augury for the measure before the House, that almost all those who have opposed it have declared themselves altogether hostile to the principle of Reform. Two members, I think, have professed, that though they disapprove of the plan now submitted to us, they yet conceive some alteration of the representative system to be advisable. Yet even those gentlemen have used, so far as I have observed, no arguments which would not apply as strongly to the most moderate change as to that which has been proposed by his Majesty's Government. I say, sir, that I consider this as a circumstance of happy augury. For what I feared was, not the opposition of those who shrink from all reform, but the disunion of reformers. I knew that during three months every reformer had been employed in conjecturing what the plan of the Government would be. I knew that every reformer had imagined in his own mind a scheme differing, doubtless, in some points from that which my noble friend the Paymaster of the Forces (Lord John Russell) has developed. I felt, therefore, great apprehension that one person would be dissatisfied with one part of the Bill, that another person would

be dissatisfied with another part, and that thus our whole strength would be wasted in internal dissensions. That apprehension is now at an end. I have seen with delight the perfect concord which prevails among all who deserve the name of reformers in this House, and I trust that I may consider it as an omen of the concord which will prevail among reformers throughout the country.

I will not, sir, at present express any opinion as to the details of the Bill; but having during the last twenty-four hours given the most diligent consideration to its general principles, I have no hesitation in pronouncing it a wise, noble, and comprehensive measure, skilfully framed for the healing of great distempers, for the securing at once of the public liberties and of the public repose, and for the reconciling and knitting together of all the orders of the State. The hon. baronet (Sir John Walsh) who has just sat down has told us that the Ministers have attempted to unite two inconsistent principles in one abortive measure. He thinks, if I understand him rightly, that they ought either to leave the representative system such as it is, or to make it symmetrical. I think, sir, that they would have acted unwisely if they had taken either of these courses. Their principle is plain, rational, and consistent. It is this-to admit the middle class to a large and direct share in the representation, without any violent shock to the institutions of our country....

… I praise the Ministers for not attempting, under existing circumstances, to make the representation uniform - I praise them for not effacing the old distinction between the towns and the counties-for not assigning members to districts, according to the American practice, by the rule of three. They have done all that was necessary for the removing of a great practical evil, and no more than was necessary....

… I believe that there are societies in which every man may safely be admitted to vote.... I say, sir, that there are countries in which the condition of the labouring-classes is such that they may safely be intrusted with the right of electing members of the Legislature. If the labourers of England were in that state in which I, from my soul, wish to see them-if employment were always plentiful, wages always high, food always cheap - If a large family were considered not as an incumbrance but as a blessing-the principal objections to universal suffrage would, I think, be removed. Universal suffrage exists in the United States without producing any very frightful consequences; and I do not believe that the people of those States, or of any part of the world, are in any good quality naturally superior to our own countrymen. But, unhappily, the lower orders in England, and in all old countries, are occasionally in a state of great distress....

For the sake, therefore, of the whole society, for the sake of the labouring-classes themselves, I hold it to be clearly expedient that, in a country like this, the right of suffrage should depend on a pecuniary qualification. Every argument, sir, which would induce me to oppose universal suffrage, induces me to support the measure which is now before us. I oppose universal suffrage, because I think that it would produce a destructive revolution. I support this measure, because I am sure that it is our best security against a revolution....

… I support this measure as a measure of reform; but I support it still more as a measure of conservation. That we may exclude those whom it is necessary to exclude, we must admit those whom it may be safe to admit....

My hon. friend the member of the University of Oxford tells us that, if we pass this law, England will soon be a Republic. The reformed House of Commons will, according to him, before it has sat ten years, depose the King, and expel the Lords from their House. Sir, if my hon. friend could prove this, he would have succeeded in bringing an argument for democracy infinitely stronger than any that is to be found in the works of Paine. His proposition is, in fact, this-that our monarchical and aristocratical institutions have no hold on the public mind of England; that these institutions are regarded with aversion by a decided majority of the middle class.... Now, sir, if I were convinced that the great body of the middle class in England look with aversion on monarchy and aristocracy, I should be forced, much against my will, to come to this conclusion, that monarchical and artstocratical institutions are unsuited to this country. Monarchy and aristocracy, valuable and useful as I think them, are still valuable and useful as means, and not as ends. The end of government is the happiness of the people; and I do not conceive that, in a country like this, the happiness of the people can be promoted by a form of government in which the middle classes place no confidence, and which exists only because the middle classes have no organ by which to make their sentiments known. But, sir, I am fully convinced that the middle classes sincerely wish to uphold the royal prerogatives, and the constitutional rights of the Peers....

… Is it possible that gentlemen long versed in high political affairs cannot read these signs? Is it possible that they can really believe that the representative system of England, such as it now is, will last till the year 1860? If not, for what would they have us wait? Would they have us wait merely that we may show to all the world how little we have profited by our own recent experience? Would they have us wait that we may once again hit the exact point where we can neither refuse with authority nor concede with grace? Would they have us wait that the numbers of the discontented party may become larger, its demands higher, its feelings more acrimonious, its organisation more complete? Would they have us wait till the whole tragi-comedy of 1827 has been acted over again-till they have been brought into office by a cry of "No Reform!" to be reformers, as they were once before brought into office by a cry of "No Popery!" to be emancipators? Have they obliterated from their minds-gladly, perhaps, would some among them obliterate from their minds-the transactions of that year? And have they forgotten all the transactions of the succeeding year? Have they forgotten how the spirit of liberty in Ireland, debarred from its natural outlet, found a vent by forbidden passages? Have they forgotten how we were forced to indulge the Catholics in all the license of rebels, merely because we chose to withhold from them the liberties of subjects? Do they wait for associations more formidable than that of the Corn Exchange, for contributions larger than the rent-for agitators more violent than those who, three years ago, divided, with the King and the Parliament, the sovereignty of Ireland? Do they wait for that last and most dreadful paroxysm of popular rage-for that last and most cruel test of military fidelity? Let them wait, if their past experience shall induce them to think that any high honour or any exquisite pleasure is to be obtained by a policy like this. Let them wait, if this strange and fearful infatuation be indeed upon them, that they should not see with their eyes, or hear with their ears, or understand with their heart.

But let us know our interest and our duty better. Turn where we may-within, around-the voice of great events is proclaiming to us, "Reform, that you may preserve." Now, therefore, while everything at home and abroad forebodes ruin to those who persist in a hopeless struggle against the spirit of the age; now, while the crash of the proudest throne of the Continent is still resounding in our cars; ... now, while the heart of England is still sound; now, while the old feelings and the old associations retain a power and a charm which may too soon pass away; now, in this your accepted time; now, in this your day of salvation, take counsel, not of prejudice, not of party spirit, not of the ignominious pride of a fatal consistency, but of history, of reason, of the ages which are past, of the signs of this most portentous time. Pronounce in a manner worthy of the expectation with which this great debate has been anticipated, and of the long remembrance which it will leave behind. Renew the youth of' the State. Save property divided against itself. Save the multitude, endangered by their own ungovernable passions. Save the aristocracy, endangered by its own unpopular power. Save the greatest, and fairest, and most highly, civilised community that ever existed, from calamities which may lit a few days sweep away all the rich heritage of so many ages of wisdom and glory. The danger is terrible. The time is short. If this Bill should be rejected, I pray to God that none of' those who concur in rejecting it may ever remember their votes with unavailing regret, amidst the wreck of laws, the confusion of ranks, the spoliation of property, and the dissolution of social order.

**SOURCE**

From Thomas Babington Macaulay, *Speeches, Parliamentary and Miscellaneous* (London: H. Vizetelly, 1853), Vol. 1, pp. 11–14, 20–21, 25–26.

The text of this document can be found at: http://www.fordham.edu/halsall/mod/ 1832macaulay-reform.html.

# The Great Reform Act of 1832

*The British Reform Act of 1832 introduced the first changes to voting rights in almost one hundred fifty years. The Act extended the right to vote into the middle classes, increasing the electorate from 435,000 to 652,000 (1 in 7 males) and giving greater political influence to urban centers in the north while leaving the rural areas under aristocratic control.*

### DISENFRANCHISEMENT CLAUSES

56 nomination or rotten boroughs returning 111 MPs lost their representation

30 boroughs with less than 4,000 inhabitants lost one MP each

Weymouth and Melcombe Regis gave up two of their four MPs

### ENFRANCHISEMENT

65 seats were awarded to the counties

44 seats were distributed to 22 larger towns including Birmingham, Manchester, Leeds, Sheffield and the new London metropolitan districts

21 smaller towns were given one MP each

Scotland was awarded 8 extra seats

Ireland was given 5 extra seats

### FRANCHISE QUALIFICATION

**THE BOROUGH FRANCHISE** was regularised. The right of voting was vested in all householders paying a yearly rental of £10 and, subject to one year residence qualification £10 lodgers (if they were sharing a house and the landlord was not in occupation).

**IN THE COUNTIES,** the franchise was granted to:

40 shilling freeholders

£10 copyholders

£50 tenants

£10 long lease holders

£50 medium lease holders

Borough freeholders could vote in the counties if their freehold was between 40 shillings and £10, or if it was over £10 and occupied by a tenant.

### SOURCE

The text of this document can be found at: http://www.cyberartsweb.org/victorian/history/reform2.html.

## THE MEXICAN REVOLUTION

# *The Constitution of 1857*

---

*The Mexican Constitution of 1857 retained most of the Roman Catholic Church's Colonial-era privileges and revenues, but unlike the earlier constitution did not mandate that the Catholic Church be the nation's exclusive religion. Such reforms were unacceptable to the leadership of the clergy and the Conservatives, and a revolt was declared.*

---

ICNACIO COMONFORT, Temporary President of the Mexican Republic, to the inhabitants of her, may it be known: That the constituent extraordinary Congress has decreed the following: In the name of God and with the authority of... the representatives of the different States, of the District and Territories that compose the Republic of Mexico, it is called by the plan proclaimed...on the 1st of March of 1854, reformed in Acapulco that I gave the 11th of the same month...and by the assembly delivered October 17th of 1855, to constitute to the Nation under the form of a democratic, popular and representative republic, putting in exercise the power in which they are invested and comply with their high assignment, decreeing the following:

POLITICAL CONSTITUTION OF THE MEXICAN REPUBLIC
THE INDESTRUCTIBLE BASE OF THEIR LEGITIMATE INDEPENDENCE, PROCLAIMED

SEPTEMBER 16, 1810 AND CONSUMMATE SEPTEMBER 27, 1821

**ART. 27.** The property of the persons cannot be occupied without their consent, except for public utility and subject to compensation.

The law determines the authority that should do the expropriation and the requirements with which this should be verified. No corporation, whether civil or ecclesiastic or any that be its character, denomination or object, will have legal capacity to acquire in property or to administer such, the only exception being the buildings immediate and directly destined to the service or object of the institution.

---

### SOURCE

Spanish-language text of this document can be found at: http://www.constitution.org/cons/mex1857.txt.

Excerpt translated by Kara McNeese, 2004.

# *Lerdo's Law* (1857)

*Lerdo's Law, named for Miguel Lerdo de Tejada, was a law that was incorporated into the Mexican constitution of 1857 stating that the Church could not own real estate that was not being used for religion.*

June 25, 1856—Decree of the government— About the disentailment of rural and urban properties that serve as civil corporate landowners or ecclesiastics of the Republic.

Secretary of State and the Office of Estate and Public Credit—The excellent Mr. Vice President of the Republic has been served to direct me the following decree:

Ignacio Comonfort, Vice President of the Mexican Republic, to the inhabitants of her (Mexico), be known:

That considering that one of the major obstacles of the prosperity and growth of the nation is the lack of movement or free circulation of a great part of the property, the fundamental base of the public wealth; and in the use of the faculties that the proclaimed plan gives me in Ayutla and reformed in Acapulco have been well decreed as the following:

**ARTICLE 1.** All the rural and urban property that today have or serve as civil corporations or ecclesiastics of the Republic as landholders will appoint in ownership to those who lease it by the value corresponding to the rent that they actually pay, calculated at the rate of six percent annually.

**ARTICLE 2.** The same adjudgment will be done to the ones that today have a emphyteutic agreement on rural or urban corporation property, the fee that they pay is capitalized at six percent in order to determine the value.

**ARTICLE 3.** Under the names of corporations is understood to include all religious communities of both sexes, confraternities and privileged confraternities, congregations, brotherhoods, parishes, town halls, schools and in general all establishments or foundations that have the character of perpetual or indefinite duration.

**ARTICLE 4.** The urban properties leased directly by the corporation to various tenants, will be adjudged, capitalizing the sum of the leasing to that of the present renters who pay the higher rent, and in the case of equality, the former applies. In respect to the rural (properties) that find themselves in the same case, one will adjudge to each renter the part that they have rented.

**ARTICLE 5.** As much as the urban as the rural that is not leased by the date of this publication of this law, they will be adjudged to the highest bidder at auction that will take place before the authority of the first Party.

**ARTICLE 6.** Having judgment already executed on the same date as the release of some property, they will be considered not rented, although in fact they still occupy them, but these will conserve the rights that the present law gives them if they were pending judgment on the release. Also they will be considered as tenants or renters for the effects of this law, all those that have already formally contracted leasing of some rural or urban property, even though they may not be, in fact, in possession of it.

**ARTICLE 7.** In all the adjudgments under this law, the price of the taxes will remain at six percent annually and to the redeemable agreement about the same properties, when they want the new owners to redeem them or a part that is not less than 1,000 pesos in respect of the properties who value exceeds 2,250 in which they lower the said price.

**ARTICLE 8.** The only exception of the transferring of property that remains advised, the assigned buildings immediately and directly assigned to the service of the object of the institute or corporation, although one rents some part not separated from them, such as, the convents, the Episcopal or municipal palaces, schools, hospitals, markets, correction houses, and charities. As part of each one of the said buildings, it could be understood in this exception a house that is linked to them and one inhabits it because of an office that they serve to the object of the institution, such as the house of the parish priests or religious chaplain. Of the properties belonging to the town halls, also being exempt, the buildings, egidos, and lands destined exclusively for the public service of the towns to which they belong.

**ARTICLE 9.** The adjudgments and auction sales should be made within three months counted from the publication of this law in each Party.

**ARTICLE 10.** Passing the three months without having formalized the adjudgment, the renting tenant will lose this right to it, substituting in his place with equal right the sublet of some other person that in his default presents the accusations before the first political authority of the Party, provided that the one puts in for, on this behalf, the adjudgment within the next fifteen days of the date of the accusations. On the contrary case, failing this, the expressed authority will adjudge the land at auction to the highest bidder.

**ARTICLE 11.** Not promoting some corporation before the same authority within the term of three months, the sale of the unrented property, if one would accuse them, an eighth part of the price will apply in order that the result should exhibit the amount that fingered in the closure, remaining to acknowledge the remainder of the corporation.

**ARTICLE 12.** When the awarding of property is done on behalf of the tenant, it will not be able to discount the price any quantity of Guantes, transfers or improvements, and when one does so on behalf of the sublet of his place, he will pay cash to the renter in only the amount of the guantes, transfer or improvements that the corporation have recognized precisely in writing before the publication of this law leaving both cases on behalf of the whole price, capitalized the actual rent at six percent. En the case of sale to the highest bidder, one will discount the price that has been set as the tax of the land that be paid to the renter by being recognized in the aforesaid form.

---

**SOURCE**

Translated from Spanish by Kara McNeese, 2004.

# The Plan of San Luis Potosi (1910)

*The Mexican presidential election of 1910 was stolen when Porfirio Diaz, the longtime dicta-
tor, had his opponent, Madero, arrested and imprisoned. Madero later issued the Plan of San
Luis Potosi. The plan called for the nullification of the elections and called upon Mexicans to
take up arms against the government. The date of its issue, November 20, 1910, marks the
beginning of the Mexican Revolution*

Peoples, in their constant efforts for the triumph of the ideal of liberty and justice, are forced, at precise historical moments, to make their greatest sacrifices.

Our beloved country has reached one of those moments. A force of tyranny which we Mexicans were not accustomed to suffer after we won our independence oppresses us in such a manner that it has become intolerable. In exchange for that tyranny we are offered peace, but peace full of shame for the Mexican nation, because its basis is not law, but force; because its object is not the aggrandizement and prosperity of the country, but to enrich a small group who, abusing their influence, have converted the public charges into fountains of exclusively personal benefit, unscrupulously exploiting the manner of lucrative concessions and contracts.

The legislative and judicial powers are completely subordinated to the executive; the division of powers, the sovereignty of the States, the liberty of the common councils, and the rights of the citizens exist only in writing in our great charter; but, as a fact, it may almost be said that martial law constantly exists in Mexico; the administration of justice, instead of imparting protection to the weak, merely serves to legalize the plunderings committed by the strong; the judges instead of being the representatives of justice, are the agents of the executive, whose

interests they faithfully serve; the chambers of the union have no other will than that of the dictator; the governors of the States are designated by him and they in their turn designate and impose in like manner the municipal authorities.

From this it results that the whole administrative, judicial, and legislative machinery obeys a single will, the caprice of General Porfirio Diaz, who during his long administration has shown that the principal motive that guides him is to maintain himself in power and at any cost.

For many years profound discontent has been felt throughout the Republic, due to such a system of government, but General Diaz with great cunning and perseverance, has succeeded in annihilating all independent elements, so that it was not possible to organize any sort of movement to take from him the power of which he made such bad use. The evil constantly became worse, and the decided eagerness of General Diaz to impose a successor upon the nations in the person of Mr. Ramon Corral carried that evil to its limit and caused many of us Mexicans, although lacking recognized political standing, since it had been impossible to acquire it during the 36 years of dictatorship, to throw ourselves into the struggle to recover the sovereignty of the people and their rights on purely democratic grounds....

In Mexico, as a democratic Republic, the

public power can have no other origin nor other basis than the will of the people, and the latter can not be subordinated to formulas to be executed in a fraudulent manner... ,

For this reason the Mexican people have protested against the illegality of the last election and, desiring to use successively all the recourses offered by the laws of the Republic, in due form asked for the nullification of the election by the Chamber of Deputies, notwithstanding they recognized no legal origin in said body and knew beforehand that, as its members were not the representatives of the people, they would carry out the will of General Diaz, to whom exclusively they owe their investiture.

In such a state of affairs the people, who are the only sovereign, also protested energetically against the election in imposing manifestations in different parts of the Republic; and if the latter were not general throughout the national territory, It was due to the terrible pressure exercised by the Government, which always quenches in blood any democratic manifestation, as happened in Puebla, Vera Cruz, Tlaxcala, and in other places.

But this violent and illegal system can no longer subsist.

I have very well realized that if the people have designated me as their candidate. for the Presidency it is not because they have had an opportunity to discover in me the qualities of a statesman or of a ruler, but the virility of the patriot determined to sacrifice himself, if need be, to obtain liberty and to help the people free themselves from the odious tyranny that oppresses them.

From the moment I threw myself into the democratic struggle I very well knew that General Diaz would not bow to the will of the nation, and the noble Mexican people, in following me to the polls, also knew perfectly the outrage that awaited them; but in spite of it, the people gave the cause of liberty a numerous contingent of martyrs when they were necessary and with wonderful stoicism went to the polls and received every sort of molestation.

But such conduct was indispensable to show to the whole world that the Mexican people are fit for democracy, that they are thirsty for liberty, and that their present rulers do not measure up to their aspirations.

Besides, the attitude of the people before and during the election, as well as afterwards, shows clearly that they reject with energy the Government of General Diaz and that, if those electoral rights had been respected, I would have been elected for President of the Republic.

Therefore, and in echo of the national will, I declare the late election illegal and, the Republic being accordingly without rulers, provisionally assume the Presidency of the Republic until the people designate their rulers pursuant to the law. In order to attain this end, it is necessary to eject from power the audacious usurpers whose only title of legality involves a scandalous and immoral fraud.

With all honesty I declare that it would be a weakness on my part and treason to the people, who have placed their confidence in me, not to put myself at the front of my fellow citizens, who anxiously call me from all parts of the country, to compel General Diaz by force of arms, to respect the national will.

### SOURCE

From United States Congress, Senate Subcommittee on Foreign Relations, *Revolutions in Mexico*, 62nd Congress, 2nd Session (Washington, D.C.: Government Printing Office, 1913), pp. 730–736, passim.

The text of this document can be found at: http://www.fordham.edu/halsall/mod/1910potosi.html.

# The Constitution of 1917

**TITLE ONE**

**CHAPTER I INDIVIDUAL GUARANTEES**

**ARTICLE 27.** Ownership of the lands and waters within the boundaries of the national territory is vested originally in the Nation, which has had, and has, the right to transmit title thereof to private persons, thereby constituting private property.

Private property shall not be expropriated except for reasons of public use and subject to payment of indemnity.

The Nation shall at all times have the right to impose on private property such limitations as the public interest may demand, as well as the right to regulate the utilization of natural resources which are susceptible of appropriation, in order to conserve them and to ensure a more equitable distribution of public wealth. With this end in view, necessary measures shall be taken to divide up large landed estates; to develop small landed holdings in operation; to create new agricultural centers, with necessary lands and waters; to encourage agriculture in general and to prevent the destruction of natural resources, and to protect property from damage to the detriment of society. Centers of population which at present either have no lands or water or which do not possess them in sufficient quantities for the needs of their inhabitants, shall be entitled to grants thereof, which shall be taken from adjacent properties, the rights of small landed holdings in operation being respected at all times.

In the Nation is vested the direct ownership of all natural resources of the continental shelf and the submarine shelf of the islands; of all minerals or substances, which in veins, ledges, masses or ore pockets, form deposits of a nature distinct from the components of the earth itself, such as the minerals from which industrial metals and metalloids are extracted; deposits of precious stones, rock-salt and the deposits of salt formed by sea water; products derived from the decomposition of rocks, when subterranean works are required for their extraction; mineral or organic deposits of materials susceptible of utilization as fertilizers; solid mineral fuels; petroleum and all solid, liquid, and gaseous hydrocarbons; and the space above the national territory to the extent and within the terms fixed by international law.(6)

In the Nation is likewise vested the ownership of the waters of the territorial seas, within the limits and terms fixed by international law; inland marine waters; those of lagoons and estuaries permanently or intermittently connected with the sea; those of natural, inland lakes which are directly connected with streams having a constant flow; those of rivers and their direct or indirect tributaries from the point in their source where the first permanent, intermittent, or torrential waters begin, to their mouth in the sea, or a lake, lagoon, or estuary forming a part of the public domain; those of constant or intermittent streams and their direct or indirect tributaries, whenever the bed of the stream, throughout the whole or a part of its length, serves as a boundary of the national territory or of two federal divisions, or if it flows from one federal division to another or crosses the boundary line of the Republic; those of lakes, lagoons, or estuaries whose basins, zones, or shores are crossed by the boundary lines of two or more divisions or by the boundary line of the Republic and a neighboring country or when the shoreline serves as the boundary between two federal divisions or of the Republic and a neighboring country; those of springs that issue from beaches, maritime areas, the beds, basins, or shores of lakes, lagoons, or estuaries in the national domain; and waters extracted from mines and the channels, beds, or shores of interior lakes and streams in an area fixed by law. Underground waters may be brought to the surface by artificial works and utilized by the surface owner, but if the public interest so requires or use by others is affected, the Federal Executive may regulate its extraction and utilization, and even establish prohibited areas, the same as may be done with other waters in the public domain. Any other waters not included in the foregoing enumeration shall be considered an integral part of the property through which they flow or in which they are deposited, but if they are located in two or more properties, their utilization shall bedeemed a matter of public use, and shall be subject to laws enacted by the States.(7)

In those cases to which the two preceding paragraphs refer, ownership by the Nation is inalienable and imprescriptible, and the exploitation, use, or appropriation of the resources concerned, by private persons or by companies organized according to Mexican laws, may not be undertaken except through concessions granted by the Federal Executive, in accordance with rules and conditions established by law. The legal rules relating to the working or exploitation of the minerals and substances referred to in the fourth paragraph shall govern the execution and proofs of what is carried out or should be carried out after they go into effect, independent of the date of granting the concessions, and their nonobservance will be grounds for cancellation thereof. The Federal Government has the power to establish national reserves and to abolish

them. The declarations pertaining thereto shall be made by the Executive in those cases and conditions prescribed by law. In the case of petroleum, and solid, liquid, or gaseous hydrocarbons no concessions or contracts will be granted nor may those that have been granted continue, and the Nation shall carry out the exploitation of these products, in accordance with the provisions indicated in the respective regulatory law.(8)

It is exclusively a function of the general Nation to conduct, transform, distribute, and supply electric power which is to be used for public service. No concessions for this purpose will be granted to private persons and the Nation will make use of the property and natural resources which are required for these ends.(9) (Note: A transitory provision of the amendment adding the foregoing paragraph to Article 27 states:

"A regulatory law shall establish the rules to which concessions granted prior to the enactment of the present law (amendment) shall be subject".)

Legal capacity to acquire ownership of lands and waters of the Nation shall be governed by the following provisions:

I. Only Mexicans by birth or naturalization and Mexican companies have the right to acquire ownership of lands, waters, and their appurtenances, or to obtain concessions for the exploitation of mines or waters. The State may grant the same right to foreigners, provided they agree before the Ministry of Foreign Relations to consider themselves as nationals in respect to such property, and bind themselves not to invoke the protection of their governments in matters relating thereto; under penalty, in case of noncompliance with this agreement, of forfeiture of the property acquired to the Nation. Under no circumstances may foreigners acquire direct ownership of lands or waters within a zone of one hundred kilometers along the frontiers and of fifty kilometers along the shores of the country.

The State, in accordance with its internal public interests and with principles of reciprocity, may in the discretion of the Secretariat of Foreign Affairs authorize foreign states to acquire, at the permanent sites of the Federal Powers, private ownership of real property necessary for the direct services of their embassies or legations.(10)

**II.** Religious institutions known as churches, regardless of creed, may in no case acquire, hold, or administer real property or hold mortgages thereon; such property held at present either directly or through an intermediary shall revert to the Nation, any person whosoever being authorized to denounce any property so held. Presumptive evidence shall be sufficient to declare the denunciation well founded. Places of public worship are the property of the Nation, as represented by the Federal Government, which shall determine which of them may continue to be devoted to their present purposes. Bishoprics, rectories, seminaries, asylums, and schools belonging to religious orders, convents, or any other buildings built or intended for the administration, propagation, or teaching of a religious creed shall at once become the property of the Nation by inherent right, to be used exclusively for the public services of the Federal or State Governments, within their respective jurisdictions. All places of public worship hereafter erected shall be the property of the Nation.

**III.** Public or private charitable institutions for the rendering of assistance to the needy, for scientific research, the diffusion of knowledge, mutual aid to members, or for any other lawful purpose, may not acquire more real property than actually needed for their purpose and immediately and directly devoted thereto; but they may acquire, hold, or administer mortgages on real property provided the term thereof does not exceed ten years. Under no circumstances

may institutions of this kind be under the patronage, direction, administration, charge, or supervision of religious orders or institutions, or of ministers of any religious sect or of their followers, even though the former or the latter may not be in active service.

**IV.** Commercial stock companies may not acquire, hold, or administer rural properties. Companies of this kind that are organized to operate any manufacturing, mining, or petroleum industry or for any other purpose that is not agricultural, may acquire, hold, or administer lands only of an area that is strictly necessary for their buildings or services, and this area shall be fixed in each particular case by the Federal or State Executive.

**V.** Banks duly authorized to operate in accordance with the laws on credit institutions may hold mortgages on urban and rural property in conformity with the provisions of such laws but they may not own or administer more real property than is actually necessary for their direct purpose.

**VI.** With the exception of the corporate entities referred to in clauses III, IV, and V hereof, and the centers of population which by law or in fact possess a communal status or centers that have received grants or restitutions or have been organized as centers of agricultural population, no other civil corporate entity may hold or administer real property or hold mortgages thereon, with the sole exception of the buildings intended immediately and directly for the purposes of the institution. The States, the Federal District, and the Territories, and all Municipalities in the Republic, shall have full legal capacity to acquire and hold all the real property needed to render public services.

The federal and state laws, within their respective jurisdictions, shall determine in what cases the occupation of private property shall be considered to be of public utility; and in accordance with such laws, the administrative authorities shall issue the respective declaration. The amount fixed as compensation for the expropriated property shall be based on the value recorded in assessment or tax offices for tax purposes, whether this value had been declared by the owner or tacitly accepted by him by having paid taxes on that basis. The increased or decreased value of such private property due to improvements or depreciation which occurred after such assessment is the only portion of the value that shall be subject to the decision of experts and judicial proceedings. This same procedure shall be followed in the case of property whose value is not recorded in the tax offices.

The exercise of actions pertaining to the Nation by virtue of the provisions of this article shall be made effective by judicial procedure, but during these proceedings and by order of the proper courts, which must render a decision within a maximum of one month, the administrative authorities shall proceed without delay to occupy, administer, auction, or sell the lands and waters in question and all their appurtenances, and in no case may the acts of such authorities be set aside until a final decision has been rendered.

**VII.** (11) The centers of population which, by law or in fact, possess a communal status shall have legal capacity to enjoy common possession of the lands, forests, and waters belonging to them or which have been or may be restored to them.

All questions, regardless of their origin, concerning the boundaries of communal lands, which are now pending or that may arise hereafter between two or more centers of population, are matters of federal jurisdiction. The Federal Executive shall take cognizance of such controversies and propose a solution to the interested parties. If the latter agree thereto, the proposal of the Executive shall take full effect as a final decision and shall be irrevocable; should

they not be in conformity, the party or parties may appeal to the Supreme Court of Justice of the Nation, without prejudice to immediate enforcement of the presidential proposal.

The law shall specify the brief procedure to which the settling of such controversies shall conform.

**VIII.** The following are declared null and void:

a. All transfers of the lands, waters, and forests of villages, rancherías, groups, or communities made by local officials (jefes políticos), state governors, or other local authorities in violation of the provisions of the Law of June 25, 1856, and other related laws and rulings.

b. All concessions, deals or sales of lands, waters, and forests made by the Secretariat of Development, the Secretariat of Finance, or any other federal authority from December 1, 1876 to date, which encroach upon or illegally occupy communal lands (ejidos), lands allotted in common, or lands of any other kind belonging to villages, rancherias, groups or communities, and centers of population.

c. All survey or demarcation-of-boundary proceedings, transfers, alienations, or auction sales effected during the period of time referred to in the preceding sub-clause, by companies, judges, or other federal or state authorities entailing encroachments on or illegal occupation of the lands, waters, or forests of communal holdings (ejidos), lands held in common, or other holdings belonging to centers of population.

The sole exception to the aforesaid nullification shall be the lands to which title has been granted in allotments made in conformity with the Law of June 25, 1856, held by persons in their own name for more than ten years and having an area of not more than fifty hectares.

**IX.** Divisions or allotments of land among the inhabitants of a given center of population which, although apparently legitimate are not so, due to a mistake or defect, may be annulled at the request of three fourths of the residents holding one fourth so divided, or one fourth of such residents holding three fourths of the lands.

**X.** Centers of population which lack communal lands (ejidos) or which are unable to have them restored to them due to lack of titles, impossibility of identification, or because they had been legally transferred, shall be granted sufficient lands and waters to constitute them, in accordance with the needs of the population; but in no case shall they fail to be granted the area needed, and for this purpose the land needed shall be expropriated, at the expense of the Federal Government, to be taken from lands adjoining the villages in question.

The area or individual unit of the grant shall hereafter be not less than ten hectares of moist or irrigated land, or in default of such land its equivalent in other types of land in accordance with the third paragraph of section XV of this article.(12)

**XI.** For the purpose of carrying out the provisions of this article and of regulating laws that may be enacted, the following are established:

a. A direct agency of the Federal Executive entrusted with the application and enforcement of the agrarian laws;

b. An advisory board composed of five persons to be appointed by the President of the Republic and who shall perform the functions specified in the organic laws;

c. A mixed commission composed of an equal number of representatives of the Federal Government, the local governments, and a representative of the peasants, to be appointed in the manner set forth in the respective regulating law, to function in each State, Territory, and the Federal District, with the powers and duties set forth in the organic and regulatory laws;

d. Private executive committees for each of the centers of population that are concerned with agrarian cases;

e. A communal office (comisariado ejidal) for each of the centers of population that possess communal lands (ejidos).

**XII.** Petitions for a restitution or grant of lands or waters shall be submitted directly to the state and territorial governors.

The governors shall refer the petitions to the mixed commissions, which shall study the cases during a fixed period of time and render a report; the State governors shall approve or modify the report of the mixed commission and issue orders that immediate possession be given to areas which they deem proper. The case shall then be turned over to the Federal Executive for decision.

Whenever the governors fail to comply with the provisions of the preceding paragraph, within the peremptory period of time fixed by law, the report of the mixed commission shall be deemed rejected and the case shall be referred immediately to the Federal Executive. Inversely, whenever a mixed commission fails to render a report during the peremptory time limit, the Governor shall be empowered to grant possession of the area of land he deems appropriate.

**XIII.** The agency of the Executive and the Agrarian Advisory Board shall report on the approval, rectification, or modification of the reports submitted by the mixed commissions, containing the changes made therein by the local governments, and so notify the President of the Republic, who as the supreme agrarian authority will render a decision.

**XIV.** Landowners affected by decisions granting or restoring communal lands and waters to villages, or who may be affected by future decisions, shall have no ordinary legal right or recourse and cannot institute amparo proceedings.

Persons affected by such decisions shall have solely the right to apply to the Federal

Government for payment of the corresponding indemnity. This right must be exercised by the interested parties within one year counting from the date of publication of the respective resolution in the Diario Oficial. After this period has elapsed, no claim is admissible.

Owners or occupants of agricultural or stockraising properties in operation who have been issued or to whom there may be issued in the future certificates of non-affectability may institute amparo proceedings against any illegal deprivation or agrarian claims on their lands or water.(13)

**XV.** The mixed commissions, the local governments and any other authorities charged with agrarian proceedings cannot in any case affect small agricultural or livestock properties in operation and they shall incur liability for violations of the Constitution if they make grants which affect them. Small agricultural property is that which does not exceed one hundred hectares of first-class moist or irrigated land or its equivalent in other classes of land, under cultivation.

To determine this equivalence one hectare of irrigated land shall be computed as two hectares of seasonal land; as four of good quality pasturage (agostadero) and as eight as monte (scrub land) or arid pasturage.

Also to be considered as small holdings are areas not exceeding two hundred hectares of seasonal lands or pasturage susceptible of cultivation; or one hundred fifty hectares of land used for cotton growing if irrigated from fluvial canals or by pumping; or three hundred, under cultivation, when used for growing bananas, sugar cane, coffee, henequen, rubber, coconuts, grapes, olives, quinine, vanilla, cacao, or fruit trees.

Small holdings for stockraising are lands not exceeding the area necessary to maintain up to five hundred head of cattle (ganado mayor) or their equivalent in smaller animals (ganado menor - sheep, goats, pigs) under provisions of law, in accordance with the forage capacity of the lands.

Whenever, due to irrigation or drainage works or any other works executed by the owners or occupants of a small holding to whom a certificate of non-affectability has been issued, the quality of the land is improved for agricultural or stockraising operations, such holding shall not be subject to agrarian appropriation even if, by virtue of the improvements made, the maximums indicated in this section are lowered, provided that the requirements fixed by law are met.

**XVI.** Lands which are subject to individual adjudication must be partitioned precisely at the time the presidential order is executed, according to regulatory laws.

**XVII.** The Federal Congress and the State Legislature, within their respective jurisdictions, shall enact laws to fix the maximum area of rural property, and to carry out the subdivision of the excess lands, in accordance with the following bases:

a. In each State, Territory, or the Federal District, there shall be fixed a maximum area of land of which a single individual or legally constituted society may be the owner.

b. The excess over the fixed area shall be subdivided by the owner within the time fixed by the local law, and these parcels shall be offered for sale under terms approved by the governments, in accordance with the aforementioned laws.

c. If the owner should oppose the subdivision, it shall be carried out by the local government, by expropriation.

d. The value of the parcels shall be paid by annual installments which will amortize principal and interest, at an interest rate not exceeding 3% per annum.

e. Owners shall be required to receive bonds of the local Agrarian Debt to guarantee payment for the property expropriated. For this purpose, the Federal

Congress shall enact a law empowering the States to create their Agrarian Debt.

f. No subdivision can be sanctioned which fails to satisfy the agrarian needs of neighboring settlements (poblados inmediatos). Whenever subdivision projects are to be executed, the agrarian claims must be settled within a fixed period.

g. Local laws shall organize the family patrimony, determining what property shall constitute it, on the basis that it shall be inalienable and shall not be subject to attachment or encumbrance of any kind.

**XVIII.** All contracts and concessions made by former Governments since the year 1876, which have resulted in the monopolization of lands, waters, and natural resources of the Nation, by a single person or company, are declared subject to revision, and the Executive of the Union is empowered to declare them void whenever they involve serious prejudice to the public interest.

**SOURCE**

The text of this document can be found at: http://www.latinamericanstudies.org/mexico/1917-Constitution.htm.

# The Constitution of 1917
# TITLE VI, Labor and Social Security

**ARTICLE 123.(50)** The Congress of the Union, without contravening the following basic principles, shall formulate labor laws which shall apply to:

A.Workers, day laborers, domestic servants, artisans (obreros, jornaleros, empleados domésticos, artesanos) and in a general way to all labor contracts:

**I.** The maximum duration of work for one day shall be eight hours.

**II.**(51) The maximum duration of nightwork shall be seven hours. The following are prohibited: unhealthful or dangerous work by women and byminors under sixteen years of age; industrial nightwork by either of these classes; work by women in commercial establishments after ten o'clockat night and work (of any kind) by persons under sixteen after ten o'clock at night.

**III.** The use of labor of minors under fourteen years of age is prohibited. Persons above that age and less than sixteen shall have a maximum workday of six hours.

**IV.**For every six days of work a worker must have at least one day of rest.

**V.** During the three months prior to childbirth, women shall not perform physical labor that requires excessive material effort. In the month followingchildbirth they shall necessarily enjoy the benefit of rest and shall receive their full wages and retain their employment and the rights acquiredunder their labor contract. During the nursing period they shall have two special rest periods each day, of a half hour each, for nursing theirinfants.

**VI.** The minimum wage to be received by a worker shall be general or according to occupation. The former shall govern in one or more economiczones; the latter shall be applicable to specified branches of industry or commerce or to special occupations, trades, or labor.

The general minimum wage must be sufficient to satisfy the normal material, social, and cultural needs of the head of a family and to provide forthe compulsory education of his children. The occupational minimum wage shall be fixed by also taking into consideration the conditions ofdifferent industrial and commercial activities

Farm workers shall be entitled to a minimum wage adequate to their needs.

The minimum wage is to be fixed by regional committees, composed of representatives of the workers, employers, and the Government, and willbe subject to approval by a national committee, organized in the same manner as the regional committees.

**VII.** Equal wages shall be paid for equal work, regardless of sex or nationality.

**VIII.** The minimum wage shall be exempt from attachment, compensation, or deduction.

**IX.** (52) Workers shall be entitled to a participation in the profits of enterprises, regulated in conformity with the following rules:

a. A national committee, composed of representatives of workers, employers, and the Government, shall fix the percentage of profits to bedistributed among workers.

b. The national committee shall undertake research and make necessary and appropriate studies in order to become acquainted with thegeneral conditions of the national economy.

It shall also take into consideration the need to promote the industrial development of thecountry, the reasonable return that should be obtained by capital, and the necessary reinvestment of capital.

c. The committee may revise the fixed percentage whenever new studies and research so justify. d. The law may exempt newly established enterprises from the obligation of sharing profits for a specified and limited number of years forexploration work and other activities so justified by their nature or peculiar conditions. e. To determine the amount of the profits of each enterprise the basis to be taken is the taxable income according to the provisions of theincome tax law. Workers may submit to the appropriate office of the Secretariat of Finance and Public Credit any objections they maydeem pertinent, in accordance with procedure indicated in the law. f. The right of workers to participate in profits does not imply the power to intervene in the direction or administration of an enterprise.

**X.** Wages must necessarily be paid in money of legal tender and cannot be paid in goods, promissory notes, or any other token intended as asubstitute for money.

**XI.** Whenever, due to extraordinary circumstances, the regular working hours of a day must be increased, one hundred percent shall be added to theamount for normal hours of work as remuneration for the overtime. Overtime work may never exceed three hours a day nor three timesconsecutively. Persons under sixteen years of age and women of any age may not be admitted to this kind of labor.

**XII.** In any agricultural, industrial, or mining enterprise or in any other kind of work, employers shall be obliged to furnish workmen comfortable andhygienic living quarters for which they may collect rent that shall not exceed one half percent monthly of the assessed valuation of the property. They also must establish schools, hospitals, and any other services necessary to the community. If the enterprise is situated within a town andemploys more than one hundred workers, it shall be responsible for the first of the above obligations.

**XIII.** In addition, in these same work centers, when the population exceeds 200 inhabitants, a tract of land of not less than five thousand square metersmust be reserved for the establishment of public markets, the erection of buildings destined for municipal services, and recreation centers. Establishments for the sale of intoxicating liquors and houses for games of chance are prohibited in all work centers.

**XIV.** Employers shall be responsible for labor accidents and for occupational diseases of workers, contracted because of or in the performance oftheir work or occupation; therefore, employers shall pay the corresponding indemnification whether death or only temporary or permanentincapacity to work has resulted, in accordance with what the law prescribes. This responsibility shall exist even if the employer contracts for thework through an intermediary.

**XV.** An employer shall be required to observe, in the installation of his establishments, the legal regulations on hygiene and health, and to adoptadequate measures for the prevention of accidents in the use of machines, instruments, and materials of labor, as well as to organize the same insuch a way as to ensure the greatest possible guarantee for the health and safety of workers as is compatible with the nature of the work, underthe penalties established by law in this respect.

**XVI.** Both employers and workers shall have the right to organize for the defense of their respective interests, by forming unions, professionalassociations, etc.

**XVII.** The laws shall recognize strikes and lockouts as rights of workmen and employers.

**XVIII.** Strikes shall be legal when they have as their purpose the attaining of an equilibrium among the various factors of production, by harmonizing therights of labor with those of capital. In public services it shall be obligatory for workers to give notice ten days in advance to the Board ofConciliation and Arbitration as to the date agreed upon for the suspension of work. Strikes shall be considered illegal only when the majority ofstrikers engage in acts of violence against persons or property, or in the event of war, when the workers belong to establishments or services ofthe Government.

**XIX.** Lockout shall be legal only when an excess of production makes it necessary to suspend work to maintain prices at a level with costs, and withprior approval of the Board of Conciliation and Arbitration.

**XX.** Differences or disputes between capital and labor shall be subject to the decisions of a Board of Conciliation and Arbitration, consisting of anequal number of workmen and employers, with one from the Government.

**XXI.** (53) If an employer refuses to submit his differences to arbitration or to accept the decision rendered by the Board, the labor contract shall beconsidered terminated and he shall be obliged to indemnify the worker to the amount of three months' wages and shall incur any liability resultingfrom the dispute. This provision shall not be applicable in the case of actions covered in the following section. If the refusal is made by workers,the labor contract shall be considered terminated.

**XXII.** (54) An employer who dismisses a worker without justifiable cause or because he has entered an association or union, or for having taken part ina lawful strike, shall be required, at the election of the worker, either to fulfill the contract or to indemnify him to the amount of three months'wages. The law shall specify those cases in which the employer may be exempted from the obligation of fulfilling the contract by payment of anindemnity. He shall also have the obligation to indemnify a worker to the amount of three months' wages, if the worker leaves his

employment dueto lack of honesty on the part of the employer or because of ill treatment from him, either to himself or to his wife, parents, children, or brothersand sisters. An employer may not relieve himself of this responsibility when the ill treatment is attributable to his subordinates or members of hisfamily acting with his consent or tolerance.

**XXIII.** Credits in favor of workers for wages or salary earned within the last year, and for indemnity compensation, shall have priority over all otherobligations in the event of receivership or bankruptcy.

**XXIV.** A worker alone shall be responsible for debts contracted by himself and payable to his employer, his associates, members of his family, ordependents, and in no case and for no purpose may payment be exacted from members of the worker's family, nor are these debts demandablefor an amount exceeding the wages of the worker for one month.

**XXV.** Services of employment placement for workers shall be gratuitous, whether such service is performed by a municipal office, labor exchange, orany other official or private institution.

**XXVI.** Every labor contract made between a Mexican and a foreign employer must be notarized by a competent municipal authority and countersignedby the consul of the nation to which the worker intends to go, because, in addition to the ordinary stipulations, it shall be clearly specified that theexpenses of repatriation shall be borne by the contracting employer.

**XXVII.** The following conditions shall be considered null and void and not binding on the contracting parties, even if expressed in the contract:

a. Those that stipulate a day's work that is inhuman because it is obviously excessive, considering the kind of work;

b. Those that fix wages that are not

remunerative, in the judgment of Boards of Conciliation and Arbitration;

c. Those stipulating a period of more than one week before payment of a day's wages;

d. Those indicating as the place of payment of wages a place of recreation, an inn, café, tavern, bar, or store, except for the payment ofemployees of such establishments;

e. Those that include the direct or indirect obligation of acquiring consumer goods in specified stores or places;

f. Those that permit the retention of wages as a fine;

g. Those that constitute a waiver by the worker of indemnification to which he is entitled due to labor accidents or occupational diseases,damages occasioned by the nonfulfillment of the contract, or by being discharged;

h. All other stipulations that imply waiver of any right designed to favor the worker in the laws of protection and assistance for workmen;

**XXVIII.** The laws shall determine what property constitutes the family patrimony, property that shall be inalienable, not subject to encumbrances ofattachment, and that shall be transmissible by inheritance with simplification of the formalities of succession.

**XXIX.** Enactment of a social security law shall be considered of public interest and it shall include insurance against disability, on life, against involuntarywork stoppage, against sickness and accidents, and other forms for similar purposes;

**XXX.** Likewise, cooperative societies established for the construction of low-cost and hygienic houses to be purchased on installments by workers,shall be considered of social utility;

**XXXI.** (55) Enforcement of the labor laws belongs to the authorities of the States, in their respective jurisdictions, but it is the exclusive jurisdiction of thefederal authorities in matters relating to the textile, electrical, motion picture, rubber, sugar, mining, petrochemical, metallurgical, and steelindustries, including the exploitation of basic minerals, their processing and smeltering, as well as the production of iron and steel in all their formsand alloys and rolled products, hydrocarbons, cement, railroads, and enterprises that are administered directly or in decentralized form by thefederal Government; enterprises that operate by virtue of a federal contract or concession, and connected industries; enterprises that carry onwork in federal zones and territorial waters; disputes that affect two or more federal entities; collective contracts that have been declaredobligatory in more than one federal entity, and finally, obligations that in educational matters belong to employers in the manner and form fixed bythe respective law. B. (56) The branches of the Union, the governments of the Federal District and of the federal Territories and their workers:

**I.** The maximum working day for day and nightwork shall be eight and seven hours respectively. Those in excess will be overtime and will be paidby a one hundred percent addition to the remuneration fixed for regular service. In no case may overtime exceed three hours a day or threeconsecutive times.

**II.** For every six days of work a worker shall be entitled to one day of rest, at least, with full wages.

**III.** Workers shall be entitled to vacations of not less than twenty days a year.

**IV.** (57) Wages shall be fixed in the respective budgets, and their amount may not be decreased while a given budget is in effect.

In no case may wages be lower than the minimum for workers in general in the Federal District and in agencies of the Republic.

**V.** Equal wages shall be paid for equal work, without regard to sex.

**VI.** Withholdings, discounts, deductions, or attachments from wages may be made only in those cases provided by law. VII. The appointment of personnel shall be made by systems which permit a determination of the skills and aptitudes of applicants. The State shallorganize schools of public administration. VIII. Workers shall be entitled to the rights of a classification scale so that promotions may be made on the basis of skills, aptitudes, and seniority.

**IX.** Workers may be suspended or discharged only on justifiable grounds, for reasons prescribed by law.

In the event of unjustifiable discharge, a worker has the right to choose between reinstatement in his work or to appropriate indemnity,determined by legal proceedings. In case of abolishment of positions, the affected workers shall have the right to another position equivalent tothe one abolished or to an indemnity.

**X.** Workers shall have the right to associate together for the protection of their common interests. They may also make use of the right to strike afterfirst complying with requirements prescribed by law, with respect to one or more offices of the public powers, whenever the rights affirmed bythis article are generally and systematically violated.

**XI.** Social security shall be organized on the following minimum bases:

a. It shall cover work accidents and occupational diseases, nonoccupational illness and maternity; and retirement, disability, old age, anddeath.

b. In case of accident or illness, the right to work shall be retained for the time specified by law.

c. Women shall be entitled to one month's leave prior to the approximate date indicated for childbirth and to two months' leave after suchdate. During the nursing period, they shall have two extra rest periods a day, of a half hour each, for nursing their children. In addition, theyare entitled to medical and obstetrical attention' medicines, nursing aid, and infant care services.

d. Members of a worker's family shall be entitled to medical attention and medicines, in those cases and in the proportions specified by law.

e. Centers are to be established for vacations and convalescence, as well as economy stores for the benefit of workers and their families.

f. Workers will be allotted low-cost housing for rent or sale, in accordance with previously approved programs.

**XII.** Individual, collective, and interunion disputes shall be submitted to a federal tribunal of conciliation and arbitration to be organized as provided inthe regulatory law.

Disputes between the federal judicial branch and its employees shall be settled by the plenary Supreme Court of Justice of the Nation.

**XIII.** Military and naval personnel and members of the public security corps, and personnel of the foreign service, shall be governed by their own laws.

**XIV.** The law shall determine what positions are to be regarded as those of personal trust (de confianza). Persons who hold such positions shall beentitled to the benefits of measures for the protection of wages and social security. (Note: A transitory article of the amendment states that untilthe respective regulatory law is enacted, the Statute for Workers in the Service of the Powers of the Union shall remain in effect insofar as it is notcontrary to the present amendment.)

---

**SOURCE**

The text of this document can be found at:
http://www. latinamericanstudies. org/mexico/
1917-Constitution. htm.

# Lenin, *What is to be Done?* (1902)

*With "What is to be Done?," Lenin makes his argument for a coherent, strictly controlled party of dedicated revolutionaries as a basic necessity for a revolution. Some have seen an analogy with the Jesuit Order in his proposals for an elite corps to lead the masses. It is also possible to see in Lenin's proposals a deep insight into the necessary requisites for a revolution, or a deep contempt for the working classes.*

The history of all countries shows that the working class, exclusively by its own effort, is able to develop only trade union consciousness, *i. e,* it may itself realise the necessity for combining in unions, for fighting against the employers and for striving to compel the government to pass necessary labour legislation, etc. The theory of socialism, however, grew out of the philosophic, historical and economic theories that were elaborated by the educated representatives of the propertied classes, the intellectuals. According to their social status, the founders of modern scientific socialism, Marx and Engels, themselves belonged to the bourgeois intelligentsia. Similarly, in Russia, the theoretical doctrine of Social Democracy [*Note: By "social democracy" Lenin means revolutionary political Marxism, not the later concept of "moderate" socialism*] arose quite independently of the spontaneous growth of the labour movement; it arose as a natural and inevitable outcome of the development of ideas among the revolutionary socialist intelligentsia. At the time of which we are speaking, *i. e.*, the middle of the nineties, this doctrine not only represented the completely formulated programme of the Emancipation of Labour group, but had already won the adherence of the majority of the revolutionary youth in Russia.

\*\*\*

It is only natural that a Social Democrat, who conceives the political struggle as being identical with the "economic struggle against the employers and the government," should conceive of an "organisation of revolutionaries" as being more or less identical with an "organisation of workers." And this, in fact, is what actually happens; so that when we talk about organisation, we literally talk in different tongues. I recall a conversation I once had with a fairly consistent Economist, with whom I had not been previously acquainted. We were discussing the pamphlet *Who Will Make the Political Revolution?* and we were very soon agreed that the principal defect in that brochure was that it ignored the question of organisation. We were beginning to think that we were in complete agreement with each other-but as the conversation proceeded, it became clear that we were talking of different things. My interlocutor accused the author of the brochure just mentioned of ignoring strike funds, mutual aid societies, etc.; whereas I had in mind an organisation of revolutionaries as an essential factor in "making" the political revolution. After that became clear, I hardly remember a single question of importance upon which I was in agreement with that Economist!

What was the source of our disagreement? The fact that on questions of organisation and politics the Economists are forever lapsing from Social Democracy into trade unionism. The political struggle carried on by the Social Democrats is far more extensive and complex than the economic struggle the workers carry on against the employers and the government. Similarly (and indeed for that reason), the organisation of a revolutionary SocialDemocratic Party must inevitably *differ* from the organisations of the workers designed for the latter struggle. A workers' organisation must in the first place be a trade organisation; secondly, it must be as wide as possible; and thirdly, it must be as public as conditions will allow (here, and further on, of course, I have only autocratic Russia in mind). On the other hand, the organisations of revolutionaries must consist first and foremost of people whose profession is that of a revolutionary (that is why I speak of organisations of *revolutionaries,* meaning revolutionary Social Democrats). In view of this common feature of the members of such an organisation, *all distinctions as between workers and intellectuals,* and certainly distinctions of trade and profession, must be obliterated. Such an organisation must of necessity be not too extensive and as secret as possible.

***

I assert:

1. that no movement can be durable without a stable organisation of leaders to maintain continuity;

2. that the more widely the masses are spontaneously drawn into the struggle and form the basis of the movement and participate in it, the more necessary is it to have such an organisation, and the more stable must it be (for it is much easier for demogogues to sidetrack the more backward sections of the masses);

3. that the organisation must consist chiefly of persons engaged in revolutionary activities as a profession;

4. that in a country with an autocratic government, the more we *restrict* the membership of this organisation to persons who are engaged in revolutionary activities as a profession and who have been professionally trained in the art of combating the political police, the more difficult will it be to catch the organisation, and

5. the *wider* will be the circle of men and women of the working class or of other classes of society able to join the movement and perform active work in it....

The active and widespread participation of the masses will not suffer; on the contrary, it will benefit by the fact that a "dozen" experienced revolutionaries, no less professionally trained than the police, will centralise all the secret side of the work-prepare leaflets, work out approximate plans and appoint bodies of leaders for each urban district, for each factory district and to each educational institution, etc. (I know that exception will be taken to my "undemocratic" views, but I shall reply to this altogether unintelligent objection later on. ) The centralisation of the more secret functions in an organisation of revolutionaries will not diminish, but rather increase the extent and the quality of the activity of a large number of other organisations intended for wide membership and which, therefore, can be as loose and as public as possible, for example, trade unions, workers' circles for self-education and the reading of illegal literature, and socialist and also democratic circles for *all other sections of the population.* etc, etc We must have *as large a number as possible* of such organisations having the widest possible variety of functions, but it is absurd and dangerous to *confuse those with organisations of revolutionaries,* to erase the line of demarcation between them, to dim still more the masses already incredibly hazy appreciation of the fact that in order to "serve" the mass movement we must have people who will devote themselves exclusively to Social Democratic activities, and that such people must *train* themselves patiently and steadfastly to be professional revolutionaries.

Aye, this appreciation has become incredibly dim. The most grievous sin we have committed in regard to organisation is that *by our primitiveness we have lowered the prestige o revolutionaries in Russia.* A man who is weak and vacillating on theoretical questions, who has a narrow outlook who makes excuses for his own slackness on the ground that the masses are awakening spontaneously; who resembles a trade union secretary more than a people's tribune, who is unable to conceive of a broad and bold plan, who is incapable of inspiring even his opponents with respect for himself, and who is inexperienced and clumsy in his own professional art-the art of combating the political police-such a man is not a revolutionary but a wretched amateur!

Let no active worker take offense at these frank remarks, for as far as insufficient training is concerned, I apply them first and foremost to myself. I used to work in a circle that set itself great and allembracing tasks; and every member of that circle suffered to the point of torture from the realisation that we were proving ourselves to be amateurs at a moment in history when we might have been able to say, paraphrasing a wellknown epigram: "Give us an organisation of revolutionaries, and we shall overturn the whole of Russia!"

SOURCE

From, V. I. Lenin: "What is to Be Done?", *Lenin: Collected Works* Vol. V, pp. 375–76, 451–53, 464–67.

The text of this document can be found at: http://www.fordham.edu/halsall/mod/1902lenin.html.

# Father Gapon, *Petition to Czar Nicholas II* (1905)

*On January 9, 1905, a massive procession of workers led by Father Georgi Gapon, an Orthodox priest loyal to Czar Nicholas, carried a petition to present to the czar at his imperial palace in St. Petersburg. The czar was not there, but government officials ordered troops to fire on the crowd that had assembled. "Bloody Sunday," as it was called, precipitated the Revolution of 1905.*

Sovereign! We the workers and the inhabitants of various social strata of the city of St. Petersburg, our wives, children, and helpless old parents, have come to you, Sovereign, to seek justice and protection. We are impoverished; our employers oppress us, overburden us with work, insult us, consider us inhuman, and treat us as slaves who must suffer a bitter fate in silence. Though we have suffered, they push us deeper and deeper into a gulf of misery, disenfranchisement, and ignorance. Despotism and arbitrariness strangle us and we are gasping for breath. Sovereign, we have no strength left. We have reached the limit of endurance. We have reached that terrible moment when death is preferable to the continuance of unbearable sufferings.

And so we left our work and informed our employers that we shall not resume work until they meet our demands. We do not demand much; we only want what is indispensable to life and without which life is nothing but hard labor and eternal suffering. Our first request was that our employers discuss our needs jointly with us. But they refused to do this; they even denied us the right to speak about our needs, saying that the law does not give us such a right. Also unlawful were our requests to reduce the working day to eight hours, to set wages jointly with us; to examine our disputes with lower echelons of factory administration; to increase the wages of unskilled workers and women to one ruble [about $1.00] per day; to abolish overtime work; to provide medical care without insult….

Sovereign, there are thousands of us here; outwardly we resemble human beings, but in reality neither we nor the Russian people as a whole enjoy any human right, have any right to speak, to think, to assemble, to discuss our needs, or to take measures to improve our conditions. They have enslaved us and they did it under the protection of your officials, with their aid and with their cooperation. They imprison and send into exile any one of us who has the courage to speak on behalf of the interests of the working class and of the people…. All the workers and peasants are at the mercy of bureaucratic administrators consisting of embezzlers of public funds and thieves who not only disregard the interests of the people but also scorn these interest…. The people are deprived of the opportunity to express their wishes and their demands and to participate in determining taxes and expenditures. The workers are deprived of the opportunity to organize themselves in unions to protect their interest.

Sovereign! Is all this compatible with God's laws, by the grace of which you reign? And is it possible to live under such laws? Wouldn't it be better for all of us if we, the toiling people of all Russia died? … Sovereign, these are the problems that we face and these are the reasons that we have gathered before the walls of your palace. Here we seek our last salvation. Do not refuse to come to the aid of your people.

---

**SOURCE**

The text of this document can be found at: http://teachers. sduhsd. net/mmontgomery/world_history/ russsian_rev/gapon. htm.

# Manifesto of October 17, 1905

*The October Manifesto was issued by Emperor Nicholas II of Russia as a response to the Russian Revolution of 1905. The document pledged to grant certain concessions to the Russian people, including freedom of conscience, speech, assembly, and association; a system of government consisting of two legislative chambers; broad participation in the Duma (the Russian Parliament); and a decree that no law should come into force without the consent of the state Duma.*

*We, Nicholas II, By the Grace of God Emperor and Autocrat of all Russia, King of Poland, Grand Duke of Finland, etc., proclaim to all Our loyal subjects:*

Rioting and disturbances in the capitals [i.e., St. Petersburg and the old capital, Moscow] and in many localities of Our Empire fill Our heart with great and heavy grief. The well-being of the Russian Sovereign is inseparable from the well-being of the nation, and the nation's sorrow is his sorrow. The disturbances that have taken place may cause grave tension in the nation and may threaten the integrity and unity of Our state.

By the great vow of service as tsar We are obliged to use every resource of wisdom and of Our authority to bring a speedy end to unrest that is dangerous to Our state. We have ordered the responsible authorities to take measures to terminate direct manifestations of disorder, lawlessness, and violence and to protect peaceful people who quietly seek to fulfill their duties. To carry out successfully the general measures that we have conceived to restore peace to the life of the state, We believe that it is essential to coordinate activities at the highest level of government.

We require the government dutifully to execute our unshakeable will:

(1.) To grant to the population the essential foundations of civil freedom, based on the principles of genuine inviolability of the person, freedom of conscience, speech, assembly and association.

(2.) Without postponing the scheduled elections to the State Duma, to admit to participation in the duma (insofar as possible in the short time that remains before it is scheduled to convene) of all those classes of the population that now are completely deprived of voting rights; and to leave the further development of a general statute on elections to the future legislative order.

(3.) To establish as an unbreakable rule that no law shall take effect without confirmation by the State Duma and that the elected representatives of the people shall be guaranteed the opportunity to participate in the supervision of the legality of the actions of Our appointed officials.

We summon all loyal sons of Russia to remember their duties toward their country, to assist in terminating the unprecedented unrest now prevailing, and together with Us to make every effort to restore peace and tranquility to Our native land.

Given at Peterhof the 17th of October in the 1905th year of Our Lord and of Our reign the eleventh.

Nicholas

SOURCE

The text of this document can be found at:
http://artsci.shu.edu/reesp/documents/october%20manifesto.htm].

# The Russian Fundamental Law of 23 April 1906

*In April 1906 the Russian government issued the Fundamental Law, setting the limits of the workings of the government. The czar was confirmed as absolute leader, with complete control of the executive, foreign policy, Church, and the armed forces. The Duma, the Russian Parliament, was moved to become the lower chamber below the czar-appointed State Council. Legislation had to be approved by the Duma, the Council, and the czar to become law and in "exceptional conditions" the government could bypass the Duma.*

1.  The Russian State is one and indivisible....

2.  The Grand Duchy of Finland, while comprising an inseparable part of the Russian state, is governed in its internal affairs by special decrees based on special legislation.

3.  The Russian language is the general language of the state, and its use is compulsory in the army, the navy and state and public institutions....

## CHAPTER I. THE ESSENCE OF THE SUPREME AUTOCRATIC POWER

4.  The All-Russian Emperor possesses the supreme autocratic power. Not only fear and conscience, but God himself, commands obedience to his authority.

5.  The person of the Sovereign Emperor is sacred and inviolable.

6.  The same supreme autocratic power belongs to the Sovereign Empress, should the order of succession to the throne pass to a female line; her husband, however, is not considered a sovereign; except for the title, he enjoys the same honours and privileges reserved for the spouses of all other sovereigns.

7.  The sovereign emperor exercises power in conjunction with the State Council and the State Duma.

8.  The sovereign emperor possesses the initiative in all legislative matters. The Fundamental Laws may be subject to revision in the State Council and State Duma only on His initiative. The sovereign emperor ratifies the laws. No law can come into force without his approval....

9.  The Sovereign Emperor approves laws; and without his approval no legislative measure can become law.

10.  The Sovereign Emperor possesses the administrative power in its totality throughout the entire Russian state. On the highest level of administration his authority is direct; on subordinate levels of administration, in conformity with the law, he determines the degree of authority of subordinate branches and officials who act in his name and in accordance with his orders.

11.  As supreme administrator, the Sovereign Emperor, in conformity with the existing laws, issues decrees for the organization and functioning of diverse branches of state administration as well as directives essential for the execution of the laws.

12.  The sovereign emperor takes charge of all the external relations of the Russian State. He determines the direction of Russia's foreign policy ...

13.  The Sovereign Emperor alone declares war, concludes peace, and negotiates treaties with foreign states.

14.  The sovereign emperor is the Commander-in-Chief of the Russian army and navy.

15. The sovereign emperor appoints and dismisses the Chairman the Council of Ministers and individual Ministers....

16. The Sovereign Emperor has the right to coin money and to determine its physical appearance.

17. The Sovereign Emperor appoints and dismisses the Chairman of the Council of Ministers, Ministers, and Chief Administrators of various departmerits, as well as other officials whose appointment or dismissal has not been determined by law.

18. As supreme administrator the Sovereign Emperor determines the scope of activity of all state officials in accordance with the needs of the state.

19. The Sovereign Emperor grants titles, medals and other state distinctions as well as property rights. He also determines conditions and procedures for gaining titles, medals, and distinctions.

20. The Sovereign Emperor directly issues decrees and instructions on matters of property that belongs to him as well as on those properties that bear his name and which have traditionally belonged to the ruling Emperor. The latter cannot be bequeathed or divided and are subject to a different form of alienation. These as well as other properties are not subject to a different form of alienation. These as well as other properties are not subject to levy or collection of taxes.

21. As head of the Imperial Household, the Sovereign Emperor, in accordance with Regulations on the Imperial Family, has the right to issue regulations affecting princely properties. He also determines the composition of the personnel of the Ministry of the Imperial Household, its organization and regulation, as well as the procedure of its administration.

22. Justice is administered in the name of the Sovereign Emperor in courts legally constituted, and its execution is also carried out in the name of His Imperial Majesty.

23. The Sovereign Emperor has the right to pardon the accused, to mitigate the sentence, and even to completely forgive transgressions, including the right to terminate court,actions against the guilty and to free them from trial and punishment. Stemming from royal mercy, he also has the right to commute the official penalty and to generally pardon all exceptional cases that are not sub'ect to general laws, provided such actions do not infringe upon civil rights or the legally protected interests of others.

24. Statutes of the *Svod Zakonov* (Vol. 1, part i, 1892 edition) on the order of succession to the throne (Articles 3-17), on the coming of age of the Sovereign Emperor, on government and guardianship (Articles 18-30), on the ascension to the throne and on the oath of allegiance (Articles 31-34 and Appendix V), on the sacred crowning and anointing (Articles 35 and 36), and on the title of His Imperial Majesty and on the State Emblem (Articles 37-39 and Appendix 1), and on the faith (Articles 40-46), retain the force of the Fundamental Laws.

25. The Regulation on the Imperial Family (*Svod zakonov*, Vol. 1, part i, 1892 edition, Articles 82-179 and Appendices II-IV and VI), while retaining the force of the Fundamental Laws, can be changed or amended only by the Sovereign Emperor personally in accordance with the procedure established by him, provided these changes or amendments of these regulations do not infringe general laws or provided they do not call for new expenditures from the treasury.

26. Decrees and commands that are issued directly or indirectly by the Sovereign Emperor as supreme administrator are implemented either by the Chairman of the Council of Ministers, or a subordinate minister, or a department head, and are published by the Governing Senate.

## CHAPTER II. RIGHTS AND OBLIGATIONS OF RUSSIAN SUBJECTS

27. Conditions for acquiring rights of

Russian citizenship, as well as its loss, are determined by law.

28. The defence of the Throne and of the Fatherland is a sacred obligation of every Russian subject. The male population, irrespective of social status, is subject to military service determined by law.

29. Russian subjects are obliged to pay legally instituted taxes and dues and also to perform other obligations determined by law.

30. No one shall be subjected to persecution for a violation of the law except as prescribed by the law.

3I. No one can be detained for investigation otherwise than prescribed by law.

32. No one can be tried and punished other than for criminal acts considered under the existing criminal laws, in force during the perpetration of these acts, provided newly enacted laws do not exclude the perpetrated criminal acts from the list of crimes.

33. The dwelling of every individual is inviolable. Breaking into a dwelling without the consent of the owner and search and seizure are allowed only in accordance with legally instituted procedures.

34. Every Russian subject has the right to freely select his place of dwelling and profession, to accumulate and dispose of property, and to travel abroad without any hindrance. Limits on these rights are determined by special laws.

35. Private property is inviolable. Forcible seizure of immovable property, should state or public need demand such action, is permissible only upon just and decent compensation.

36. Russian subjects have the right to organize meetings that are peaceful, unarmed, and not contrary to the law. The law determines the conditions of meetings, rules governing their termination, as well as limitations on places of meetings.

37. Within the limits determined by law everyone can express his thoughts orally or in writing, as well as distribute these thoughts through publication or other means.

38. Russian subjects have the right to organize societies and unions for purposes not contrary to the law. Conditions for organization of societies and unions, their activity, terms and rules for acquiring legal rights as well as dosing of societies and unions, is determined by law.

39. Russian subjects enjoy freedom of religion. Terms of enjoyment of this freedom are determined by law.

40. Foreigners living in Russia enjoy the rights of Russian subjects, within limitations established by law.

4I. Exceptions to the rules outlined in this chapter include localities where martial law is declared or where there exist exceptional conditions that are determined by special laws.

**CHAPTER III. LAWS**

42. The Russian Empire is governed by firmly established laws that have been properly enacted.

43. Laws are obligatory, without exception, for all Russian subjects and foreigners living within the Russian state.

44. No new law can be enacted without the approval of the State Council and the State Duma, and it shall not be legally binding without the approval of the Sovereign Emperor.

45. Should extraordinary circumstances demand, when the State Duma is not in session, and the introduction of a measure requires a properly constituted legal procedure, the Council of Ministers will submit such a measure directly to the Sovereign Emperor. Such a measure cannot, however, introduce any changes into the Fundamental Laws, or to the organization of the State Council or the State Duma, or to the rules governing elections to the Council or to the Duma. The validity of such a measure is terminated if the responsible minister or the head of a special department fails to introduce appropriate legislation in the State Duma during

the first two months of its session upon recon-vening, or if the State Duma or the State Council should refuse to enact it into law.

46. Laws issued especially for certain local-ities or segments of the population are not made void by a new law unless such a voiding is specifically intended.

47. Every law is valid for the future, except in those cases where the law itself stipulates that its force is retroactive or where it states that its intent is to reaffirm or explain the meaning of a previous law.

48. The Governing Senate is the general depository of laws. Consequently, all laws should be deposited in the Governing Senate in the original or in duly authorized lists.

49. Laws are published for general knowl-edge by the Governing Senate according to established rules and are not legally binding before their publication.

50. Legal decrees are not subject to publi-cation if they were issued in accordance with the rules of the Fundamental Laws.

51. Upon publication, the law is legally binding from the time stipulated by the law itself, or, in the case that such a time is omitted, from the day on which the Senate publication containing the published law is received locally. The law itself may stipulate that telegraph or other media of communication be used to trans-mit it for execution before its publication.

52. The law cannot be repealed otherwise than by another law. Consequently, until a new law repeals the existing law, the old law retains fully its force.

53. No one can be excused for ignorance of the law once it is duly published.

54. Regulations governing combat, techni-cal, and supply branches of the Armed Forces, as well as rules and orders to institutions and authorized personnel of the military and naval establishments are, as a rule, submitted directly to the Sovereign Emperor upon review by the Military and Admiralty Councils, provided that these regulations, rules, and orders affect pri-marily the above mentioned establishments, do not touch on matters of general laws, and do not call for new expenditures from the treasury; or, if they call for new expenditure, are covered by expected savings by the Military or Naval Ministries. In cases where the expected saving is insufficient to cover the projected expenditure, submission of such regulations, rules, and orders for the Emperor's approval is permitted only upon first requesting, in a prescribed manner, the necessary appropriation.

55. Regulations governing military and naval courts are issued in accordance with Regulations on Military and Naval Codes.

**CHAPTER IV. THE STATE COUNCIL, STATE DUMA, AND THE SCOPE OF THEIR ACTIVITY**

56. The Sovereign Emperor, by a decree, annually convenes the session of the State Council and of the State Duma.

57. The Sovereign Emperor determines by a decree the length of the annual session of the State Council and of the State Duma, as well as the interval between the sessions.

58. The State Council is composed of members appointed by His Majesty and of elected members. The total number of appointed members of the Council called by the Emperor to deliberate in the Council's proceed-ings cannot exceed the total number of the elected members of the Council.

59. The State Duma consists of members elected by the population of the Russian Empire for a period of five years, on the basis of rules governing elections to the Duma.

60. The State Council examines the cre-dentials of its members. Equally, the State Duma examines the credentials of its members.

61. The same person cannot serve simulta-neously as a member of the State Council and as a member of the State Duma.

62. The Sovereign Emperor, by a decree,

can replace the elected membership of the State Council with new members before its tenure expires. The same decree sets new elections of members of the State Council.

63.  The emperor who holds the throne of all Russia cannot profess any religion save the Orthodox....

64.  The State Council and the State Duma have equal rights in legislative matters.

65.  In the administration of the church, the autocratic power act through the intermediary of the Holy Governing Synod which it has instituted.

66.  All subjects of the Russian state who do not belong to the established church ... as well as foreigners ... residing in Russia, shall everywhere be free to profess their religion, and to worship in accordance with its ritual.

67.  Freedom of religion is accorded, not only to Christians of foreign denominations, but also to Jews, Muslims and heathens....

68.  Those legislative measures that are considered and approved by the State Duma are then submitted to the State Council for its approval. Those legislative measures that have been initiated by the State Council are reviewed by the Council and, upon approval, are submitted to the Duma.

69.  Legislative measures that have been rejected either by the State Council or by the State Duma are considered defeated.

70.  Those legislative measures that have been initiated either by the State Council or by the State Duma [and approved by both], but which have failed to gain Imperial approval, cannot be resubmitted for legislative consideration during the same session. Those legislative measures that have been initiated by either the State Council or by the State Duma and are rejected by either one of the Chambers, can be resubmitted for legislative consideration during the same session, provided the Emperor agrees to it.

71.  Legislative measures that have been initiated in and approved by the State Duma and then by the State Council, and likewise legislative measures initiated and approved by the State Council and then by the State Duma, are submitted by the Chairman of the State Council to the Sovereign Emperor.

72.  No one can be prosecuted for criminal offences except in the manner prescribed by law.

73.  No one can be held under arrest except in cases prescribed by law....

74.  If the state budget is not appropriated before the appropriation deadline, the budget that had been duly approved in the preceding year will remain in force with only such changes as have resulted from those legislative measures that became laws after the budget was approved. Prior to publication of the new budget, on the decision of the Council of Ministers and rulings of Ministries and Special Departments, necessary funds will be gradually released. These funds will not exceed in their totality during any month, however, one-twelfth of the entire budgetary expenditures.

75.  All dwellings are inviolable. No search or seizure may take place in a dwelling without the consent of the head of the household, except in cases and in a manner prescribed by law.

76.  Every Russian subject has the right freely to choose his place of residence and occupation, to acquire and dispose of property, and to travel abroad without hindrance. Limitations of these rights are regulated by special laws.

77.  Property is inviolable. Compulsory alienation of property, when such is necessary for the welfare of the state or the public, is permissible only on the basis of just and adequate compensation.

78.  Russian subjects have the right to organize meetings for purposes that are not contrary to the laws, peacefully, and without weapons....

79.  Everyone may, within the limits of the

law, express his ideas orally and in writing and may also disseminate them by means of the press or by other methods.

80. Russian subjects have the right to form societies and associations for purposes that are not in contravention of the laws....

81. The Chairman of the Council of Ministers, Ministers, and Heads of various departments, are responsible to the Sovereign Emperor for State administration. Each individual member is responsible for his actions and decisions.

82. For official misconducts in office, the Chairman of the Council of Ministers, Ministers and Heads of various departments are sub')ect to civil and criminal punishment established by law.

86. No new law can come into force without the approval of the State Council and State Duma and the ratification of the sovereign emperor.

87. If extraordinary circumstances require legislative action whilst the State Duma is in recess, the Council of Ministers may make recommendations direct to the sovereign emperor. Such a measure may not, however, introduce changes in the Fundamental Laws, in the statutes of the State Council and State Duma or in the regulations governing elections to the Council and the Duma. Should such a measure not be introduced into the Duma as a bill within two months from the date of its next meeting ... it loses force....

98. The State Council and State Duma are summoned annually by edict of the sovereign emperor....

106. The State Council and the State Duma possess equal legislative powers...

108. The State Council and State Duma may ... interpellate ministers ... concerning actions taken by them, or by persons or agencies under their jurisdiction that are held to be illegal.....

123. The Chairman of the Council of Ministers and the Ministers..... are responsible to the sovereign emperor for the general operation of the state administration. Each of them is individually responsible for his own actions and orders.

SOURCE

Svod *Zakonov Rossiiskoi Imperii*, 3rd series, vol. 1, pt. 1. St. Petersburg, 1912, pp. 5–26.

The text of this document can be found at: http://www. dur. ac. uk/~dml0www/fundlaws. html.

# *Abdication of Nikolai II*, March 15, 1917

*The second Russian revolution, also referred to by historians as the "February Revolution," forced the abdication of Czar Nicholas. It stopped short, however, of overthrowing the ruling capitalist class and the establishment of a social and economic dictatorship of the working class.*

By the Grace of God, We, Nikolai II, Emperor of All the Russias, Tsar of Poland, Grand Duke of Finland, and so forth, to all our faithful subjects be it known:

In the days of a great struggle against a foreign enemy who has been endeavouring for three years to enslave our country, it pleased God to send Russia a further painful trial.

Internal troubles threatened to have a fatal effect on the further progress of this obstinate war. The destinies of Russia, the honour of her heroic Army, the happiness of the people, and the whole future of our beloved country demand that the war should be conducted at all costs to a victorious end.

The cruel enemy is making his last efforts and the moment is near when our valiant Army, in concert with our glorious Allies, will finally overthrow the enemy.

In these decisive days in the life of Russia we have thought that we owed to our people the close union and organisation of all its forces for the realisation of a rapid victory; for which reason, in agreement with the Imperial Duma, we have recognized that it is for the good of the country that we should abdicate the Crown of the Russian State and lay down the Supreme Power.

Not wishing to separate ourselves from our beloved son, we bequeath our heritage to our brother, the Grand Duke Mikhail Alexandrovich, with our blessing for the future of the Throne of the Russian State.

We bequeath it our brother to govern in full union with the national representatives sitting in the Legislative Institutions, and to take his inviolable oath to them in the name of our well-beloved country.

We call upon all faithful sons of our native land to fulfil their sacred and patriotic duty of obeying the Tsar at the painful moment of national trial and to aid them, together with the representatives of the nation, to conduct the Russian State in the way of prosperity and glory.

May God help Russia.

Declaration from the Throne by Grand Duke Mikhail, March 16, 1917

A heavy task has been entrusted to me by the will of my brother, who has given me the Imperial Throne at a time of unprecedented war and domestic strife.

Animated by the same feelings as the entire nation - namely, that the welfare of the country overshadows all other interests - I am firmly resolved to accept the Supreme Power only if this should be the desire of our great people, which must, by means of a plebiscite, through their representatives in the Constituent Assembly, establish the form of government and the new fundamental law of the Russian State.

Invoking God's blessing, I therefore request all citizens of Russia to obey the Provisional Government, set up on the initiative of the Duma and invested with plenary powers, until, within as short a time as possible, the

Constituent Assembly, elected on a basis of universal, equal, and secret suffrage, shall express the will of the nation regarding the form of government to be adopted

SOURCE

*Svod Zakonov Rossiiskoi Imperii*, 3rd series, vol. 1, pt. 1. St. Petersburg, 1912, pp. 5–26.

The text of this document can be found at: http://www. dur. ac. uk/~dml0www/abdicatn. html.

# Lenin, *Decree on Land* (1917)

*The "Decree On Land," written by Lenin, was passed by the Second Congress of the Soviet of Workers', Soldiers', and Peasants' Deputies on October 26, 1917, following the success of the October Revolution. It proposed an abolition of private property, and the redistribution of the landed estates among the peasant class..*

All private ownership of land is abolished immediately without compensation. (2) All landowners' estates and all lands belonging to the Crown, to monasteries, church lands with all their live stock and inventoried property, buildings and appurtenances, are transferred to the disposition of the township Land Committees and the district Soviets of Peasants' Deputies until the Constituent Assembly meets.

### SOURCE

The text of this document can be found at:
http://www. spartacus. schoolnet. co. uk/RUSlenin. htm.

## THE RUSSIAN REVOLUTION

# *The Peace Treaty of Brest-Litovsk*, March 3, 1918

---

*The Treaty of Brest-Litovsk brought to an end Russia's involvement in World War I. The treaty was practically obsolete before the end of the year but is significant as a chief contributor, although unintentionally, to the independence of Finland, Estonia, Latvia, Lithuania, and Poland. Civil war and foreign intervention delayed Communist control of all of Russia until 1920.*

---

**ARTICLE I.** Germany, Austria-Hungary, Bulgaria, and Turkey, for the one part, and Russia, for the other part, declare that the state of war between them has ceased. They are resolved to live henceforth in peace and amity with one another.

**ARTICLE II.** The contracting parties will refrain from any agitation or propaganda against the Government or the public and military institutions of the other party. In so far as this obligation devolves upon Russia, it holds good also for the territories occupied by the Powers of the Quadruple Alliance.

**ARTICLE III.** The territories lying to the west of the line agreed upon by the contracting parties which formerly belonged to Russia, will no longer be subject to Russian sovereignty; the line agreed upon is traced on the map submitted as an essential part of this treaty of peace. The exact fixation of the line will be established by a Russo-German commission.

No obligations whatever toward Russia shall devolve upon the territories referred to, arising from the fact that they formerly belonged to Russia.

Russia refrains from all interference in the internal relations of these territories. Germany and Austria-Hungary purpose to determine the future status of these territories in agreement with their population.

**ARTICLE IV.** As soon as a general peace is concluded and Russian demobilization is carried out completely Germany will evacuate the territory lying to the east of the line designated in paragraph 1 of Article III, in so far as Article IV does not determine otherwise.

Russia will do all within her power to insure the immediate evacuation of the provinces of eastern Anatolia and their lawful return to Turkey.

The districts of Erdehan, Kars, and Batum will likewise and without delay be cleared of the russian troops. Russia will not interfere in the reorganization of the national and international relations of these districts, but leave it to the population of these districts, to carry out this reorganization in agreement with the neighboring States, especially with Turkey.

**ARTICLE V.** Russia will, without delay, carry out the full demobilization of her army inclusive of those units recently organized by the present Government. Furthermore, Russia will either bring her warships into russian ports and there detain them until the day of the conclusion of a general peace, or disarm them forthwith. Warships of the States which continue in the state of war with the Powers of the Quadruple Alliance, in so far as they are within Russian sovereignty, will be treated as Russian warships.

The barred zone in the Arctic Ocean

continues as such until the conclusion of a general peace. In the Baltic sea, and, as far as Russian power extends within the Black sea, removal of the mines will be proceeded with at once. Merchant navigation within these maritime regions is free and will be resumed at once. Mixed commissions will be organized to formulate the more detailed regulations, especially to inform merchant ships with regard to restricted lanes. The navigation lanes are always to be kept free from floating mines.

**ARTICLE VI.** Russia obligates herself to conclude peace at once with the Ukrainian People's Republic and to recognize the treaty of peace between that State and the Powers of the Quadruple Alliance. The Ukrainian territory will, without delay, be cleared of Russian troops and the Russian Red Guard. Russia is to put an end to all agitation or propaganda against the Government or the public institutions of the Ukrainian People's Republic.

Esthonia and Livonia will likewise, without delay, be cleared of Russian troops and the Russian Red Guard. The eastern boundary of Esthonia runs, in general along the river Narwa. The eastern boundary of Livonia crosses, in general, lakes Peipus and Pskow, to the southwestern corner of the latter, then across Lake Luban in the direction of Livenhof on the Dvina. Esthonia and Livonia will be occupied by a German police force until security is insured by proper national institutions and until public order has been established. Russia will liberate at once all arrested or deported inhabitants of Esthonia and Livonia, and insures the safe return of all deported Esthonians and Livonians.

Finland and the Aaland Islands will immediately be cleared of Russian troops and the Russian Red Guard, and the Finnish ports of the Russian fleet and of the Russian naval forces. So long as the ice prevents the transfer of warships into Russian ports, only limited forces will remain on board the warships. Russia is to put an end to all agitation or propaganda against the Government or the public institutions of Finland.

The fortresses built on the Aaland Islands are to be removed as soon as possible. As regards the permanent non- fortification of these islands as well as their further treatment in respect to military technical navigation matters, a special agreement is to be concluded between Germany, Finland, Russia, and Sweden; there exists an understanding to the effect that, upon Germany's desire, still other countries bordering upon the Baltic Sea would be consulted in this matter.

**ARTICLE VII.** In view of the fact that Persia and Afghanistan are free and independent States, the contracting parties obligate themselves to respect the political and economic independence and the territorial integrity of these states.

**ARTICLE VIII.** The prisoners of war of both parties will be released to return to their homeland. The settlement of the questions connected therewith will be effected through the special treaties provided for in Article XII.

**ARTICLE IX.** The contracting parties mutually renounce compensation for their war expenses, i. e. , of the public expenditures for the conduct of the war, as well as compensation for war losses, i. e. , such losses as were caused [by] them and their nationals within the war zones by military measures, inclusive of all requisitions effected in enemy country.

**ARTICLE X.** Diplomatic and consular relations between the contracting parties will be resumed immediately upon the ratification of the treaty of peace. As regards the reciprocal admission of consuls, separate agreements are reserved.

**ARTICLE XI.** As regards the economic relations between the Powers of the Quadruple Alliance and Russia the regulations contained in Appendices II-V are determinative....

**ARTICLE XII.** The reestablishment of public and private legal relations, the exchange of war prisoners and interned citizens, the question of amnesty as well as the question anent the treatment of merchant ships which have come into the power of the opponent, will be regulated in separate treaties with Russia which form an essential part of the general treaty of peace, and, as far as possible, go into force simultaneously with the latter.

**ARTICLE XIII.** In the interpretation of this treaty, the German and Russian texts are authoritative for the relations between Germany and Russia; the German, the Hungarian, and Russian texts for the relations between Austria-Hungry and Russia; the Bulgarian and Russian texts for the relations between Bulgaria and Russia; and the Turkish and Russian texts for the relations between Turkey and Russia.

**ARTICLE XIV.** The present treaty of peace will be ratified. The documents of ratification shall, as soon as possible, be exchanged in Berlin. The Russian Government obligates itself, upon the desire of one of the powers of the Quadruple Alliance, to execute the exchange of the documents of ratification within a period of two weeks. Unless otherwise provided for in its articles, in its annexes, or in the additional treaties, the treaty of peace enters into force at the moment of its ratification.

In testimony whereof the Plenipotentiaries have signed this treaty with their own hand.

Executed in quintuplicate at Brest-Litovsk, 3 March, 1918.

---

**SOURCE**

The text of this document can be found at:
http://www. lib. byu. edu/~rdh/wwi/1918/brestlitovsk. html.

# Lenin, *New Economic Policy* (1921)

*The Bolshevik revolutionary takeover in October 1917 was followed by over two years of civil war in Russia between the new Communist regime and its enemies. The struggle saw much brutality and excesses on both sides with the peasants suffering most. The sailors at the Kronstadt naval base rebelled in March 1921. Though the rebellion was crushed, the regime was forced to moderate its ruthlessness. The New Economic Policy (NEP) was the result, a small concession to the capitalist and free-market instincts of peasant and petty bourgeois alike.*

... The most urgent thing at the present time is to take measures that will immediately increase the productive forces of peasant farming. Only in this way will it be possible to improve the conditions of the workers and strengthen the alliance between the workers and peasants, to strengthen the dictatorship of the proletariat.....

This cannot be done without a serious modification of our food policy. Such a modification [effected by NEP] was the substitution of the surplus-appropriation system [a euphemism for forcible acquisition of grain production above what is needed for subsistence] by the tax in kind [i. e. , handing over of grain in amounts to satisfy tax due], which implies free trade ... The tax in kind is one of the forms of transition from that peculiar "War Communism," which we were forced to resort to by extreme want, ruin and war, to the proper socialist exchange of products. The latter, in its turn, is one of the forms of transition from Socialism, with the peculiar features created by the predominance of the small peasantry among the population, to Communism.

The essence of the peculiar "War Communism" was that we actually took from the peasant, all the surplus grain—and sometimes even not only surplus grain, but part of the grain the peasant required for food—to meet the requirements of the army and sustain the workers ..It was a temporary measure. The correct policy of the proletariat which is exercising its dictatorship in a small-peasant country is to obtain grain in exchange for the manufactured goods the peasant requires.... only such a policy can strengthen the foundations of Socialism and lead to its complete victory ...

The effect will be the revival of the petty bourgeoisie and of capitalism on the basis of a certain amount of free trade (if only local). This is beyond doubt. It would be ridiculous to shut our eyes to it.

The question arises: Is it necessary? Can it be justified? Is it dangerous? ...

What is to be done? Either to try to prohibit entirely ... all development of private, non-state exchange, i. e. , trade, i. e. , capitalism, which is inevitable amidst millions of small producers. But such a policy would be foolish because such a policy is economically impossible. It would be suicidal because the party that tried to apply such a policy would meet with inevitable disaster. We need not conceal from ourselves the fact that some Communists sinned.... in this respect ... We shall try to rectify these mistakes ... otherwise things will come to a very sorry state. A wise Communist will not be afraid of learning from a capitalist (no matter whether that capitalist is a big capitalist ... or a little capitalist cooperator). Did we not in the Red Army [which was partly created from officers and men of the old tsarist army]learn to catch treacherous military experts, to single out the honest and conscientious, and on the whole, to utilize ... tens of thousands of military experts? ... We shall learn to do the same ... with the commission agents, with the buyers who are working for the state, with the little-cooperator capitalists, with the entrepreneur concessionaires, etc....

---

### SOURCE

(Ref.: Robert V. Daniels, *A Documentary History of Communism*, Vol. 1, pp. 213–16).

The text of this document can be found at:
http://web. jjay. cuny. edu/~jobrien/reference/ob40. html.

THE CHINESE REVOLUTION

# Sun Yat-sen's "Three Principles of the People" (1924)

*The "Three Principles of the People" is a political philosophy developed by Sun Yat-sen in 1924 as part of a program to make China a free, prosperous, and powerful nation. Its legacy of implementation is most apparent in the governmental organization of the Republic of China.*

1.   Nationalism—finding evidence of proto-nationalism throughout Chinese history, Sun believed that he had enlarged and modernized the principle to include opposition to foreign imperialism and a firm sense of China as an equal among the nations of the world. He also addressed the need for self-determination for China's minorities.

2.   Democracy—finding important Chinese precedents for the notion of the voice of the people, Sun introduced the new notions of a republican government and a constitution as the best way to articulate and protect people's rights. Sun advocated popular elections, initiative, recall and referendum, but he felt that China was not yet ready for full democracy, requiring instead a preparatory period of political tutelage.

3.   Livelihood—Sun believed in both economic egalitarianism and economic development. He sketched out a complicated plan to equalize land holdings and ensure that taxation was both widely and fairly implemented. Dedicated to industrialization but concerned about China's difficulty in securing investment capital and also about social unrest, Sun advocated nationalization of key industries as the best way to ensure both economic development and political stability.

SOURCE

The text of this document can be found at:
http://afe. easia. columbia. edu/china/modern/rd_bck. htm#Sun%20Yatsen.

**THE CHINESE REVOLUTION**

# Mao Tse-Tung, *On New Democracy*, January 1940

### I. WHITHER CHINA?

A lively atmosphere has prevailed throughout the country ever since the War of Resistance began, there is a general feeling that a way out of the impasse has been found, and people no longer knit their brows in despair. Of late, however, the dust and din of compromise and anti-communism have once again filled the air, and once again the people are thrown into bewilderment. Most susceptible, and the first to be affected, are the intellectuals and the young students. The question once again arises: What is to be done? Whither China? On the occasion of the publication of *Chinese Culture,*\* it may therefore be profitable to clarify the political and cultural trends in the country. I am a layman in matters of culture; I would like to study them, but have only just begun to do so. Fortunately, there are many comrades in Yenan who have written at length in this field, so that my rough and ready words may serve the same purpose as the beating of the gongs before a theatrical performance. Our observations may contain a grain of truth for the nation's advanced cultural workers and may serve as a modest spur to induce them to come forward with valuable contributions of their own, and we hope that they will join in the discussion to reach correct conclusions which will meet our national needs. To "seek truth from facts" is the scientific approach, and presumptuously to claim infallibility and lecture people will never settle anything. The troubles that have befallen our nation are extremely serious, and only a scientific approach and a spirit of responsibility can lead it on to the road of liberation. There is but one truth, and the question of whether or not one has arrived at it depends not on subjective boasting but on objective practice. The only yardstick of truth is the revolutionary practice of millions of people. This, I think, can be regarded as the attitude of *Chinese Culture.*

### II. WE WANT TO BUILD A NEW CHINA

For many years we Communists have struggled for a cultural revolution as well as for a political and economic revolution, and our aim is to build a new society and a new state for the Chinese nation. That new society and new state will have not only a new politics and a new economy but a new culture. In other words, not only do we want to change a China that is politically oppressed and economically exploited into a China that is politically free and economically prosperous, we also want to change the China which is being kept ignorant and backward under the sway of the old culture into an enlightened and progressive China under the sway of a new culture. In short, we want to build a new China. Our aim in the cultural sphere is to build a new Chinese national culture.

### III. CHINA'S HISTORICAL CHARACTERISTICS

We want to build a new national culture, but what kind of culture should it be?

Any given culture (as an ideological form) is a reflection of the politics and economics of a given society, and the former in turn has a tremendous influence and effect upon the latter; economics is the base and politics the concentrated expression of economics. \*\* This is our fundamental view of the relation of culture to politics and economics and of the relation of politics to economics. It follows that the form of culture is first determined by the political and economic form, and only then does it operate on and influence the given political and economic form. Marx says, "It is not the consciousness of men that determines their being, but, on the contrary, their social being that determines their consciousness."*** He also says, "The philosophers have only *interpreted* the world, in various ways; the point, however, is to *change* it."+ For the first time in human history, these scientific formulations correctly solved the problem of the relationship between consciousness and existence, and they are the basic concepts underlying the dynamic revolutionary theory of knowledge as the reflection of reality which was later elaborated so profoundly by Lenin. These basic concepts must be kept in mind in our discussion of China's cultural problems.

Thus it is quite clear that the reactionary elements of the old national culture we want to eliminate are inseparable from the old national politics and economics, while the new national culture which we want to build up is inseparable from the new national politics and economics. The old politics and economics of the Chinese nation form the basis of its old culture, just as its new politics and economics will form the basis of its new culture.

What are China's old politics and economics? And what is her old culture?

From the Chou and Chin Dynasties onwards, Chinese society was feudal, as were its politics and its economy. And the dominant culture, reflecting the politics and economy, was feudal culture.

Since the invasion of foreign capitalism and the gradual growth of capitalist elements in Chinese society, the country has changed by degrees into a colonial, semi-colonial and semi-feudal society. China today is colonial in the Japanese-occupied areas and basically semi-colonial in the Kuomintang areas, and it is pre-dominantly feudal or semi-feudal in both. Such, then, is the character of present-day Chinese society and the state of affairs in our country. The politics and the economy of this society are predominantly colonial, semi-colonial and semi-feudal, and the predominant culture, reflecting the politics and economy, is also colonial, semi-colonial and semi-feudal.

It is precisely against these predominant political, economic and cultural forms that our revolution is directed. What we want to get rid of is the old colonial, semi-colonial and semi-feudal politics and economy and the old culture in their service. And what we want to build up is their direct opposite, *i. e.*, the new politics, the new economy and the new culture of the Chinese nation.

What, then, are the new politics and the new economy of the Chinese nation, and what is its new culture?

In the course of its history the Chinese revolution must go through two stages, first, the democratic revolution, and second, the socialist revolution, and by their very nature they are two different revolutionary processes. Here democracy does not belong to the old category— it is not the old democracy, but belongs to the new category—it is New Democracy.

It can thus be affirmed that China's new politics are the politics of New Democracy, that China's new economy is the economy of New Democracy and that China's new culture is the culture of New Democracy.

Such are the historical characteristics of the Chinese revolution at the present time. Any political party, group or person taking part in the Chinese revolution that fails to understand this will not be able to direct the revolution and lead it to victory, but will be cast aside by the people and left to grieve out in the cold.

**IV. THE CHINESE REVOLUTION IS PART OF THE WORLD REVOLUTION**

The historical characteristic of the Chinese revolution lies in its division into the two stages, democracy and socialism, the first being no longer democracy in general, but democracy of the Chinese type, a new and special type, namely, New Democracy. How, then, has this historical characteristic come into being? Has it been in existence for the past hundred years, or is it of recent origin?

A brief study of the historical development of China and of the world shows that this characteristic did not emerge immediately after the Opium War, but took shape later, after the first imperialist world war and the October Revolution in Russia. Let us now examine the process of its formation.

Clearly, it follows from the colonial, semi-colonial and semi-feudal character of present-day Chinese society that the Chinese revolution must be divided into two stages. The first step is to change the colonial, semi-colonial and semi-feudal form of society into an independent, democratic society. The second is to carry the revolution forward and build a socialist society. At present the Chinese revolution is taking the first step.

The preparatory period for the first step began with the opium War in 1840, *i. e.*, when China's feudal society started changing into a semi-colonial and semi-feudal one. Then came the Movement of the Taiping Heavenly Kingdom, the Sino-French War, the Sino-Japanese war, the Reform Movement of 1898, the Revolution of 1911, the May 4th Movement, the Northern Expedition, the War of the Agrarian Revolution and the present War of Resistance Against Japan. Together these have taken up a whole century and in a sense they represent that first step, being struggles waged by the Chinese people, on different occasions and in varying degrees, against imperialism and the feudal forces in order to build up an independent, democratic society and complete the first revolution. The Revolution of 1911 was in a fuller

sense the beginning of that revolution. In its social character, this revolution is a bourgeois-democratic and not a proletarian-socialist revolution. It is still unfinished and still demands great efforts, because to this day its enemies are still very strong. When Dr. Sun Yat-sen said, "The revolution is not yet completed, all my comrades must struggle on", he was referring to the bourgeois-democratic revolution.

A change, however, occurred in China's bourgeois-democratic revolution after the outbreak of the first imperialist world war in 1914 and the founding of a socialist state on one-sixth of the globe as a result of the Russian October Revolution of 1917.

Before these events, the Chinese bourgeois-democratic revolution came within the old category of the bourgeois-democratic world revolution, of which it was a part.

Since these events, the Chinese bourgeois-democratic revolution has changed, it has come within the new category of bourgeois-democratic revolutions and, as far as the alignment of revolutionary forces is concerned, forms part of the proletarian-socialist world revolution.

Why? Because the first imperialist world war and the first victorious socialist revolution, the October Revolution, have changed the whole course of world history and ushered in a new era.

It is an era in which the world capitalist front has collapsed in one part of the globe (one-sixth of the world) and has fully revealed its decadence everywhere else, in which the remaining capitalist parts cannot survive without relying more than ever on the colonies and Semi-colonies, in which a socialist state has been established and has proclaimed its readiness to give active support to the liberation movement of all colonies and semi-colonies, and in which the proletariat of the capitalist countries is steadily freeing itself from the social-imperialist influence of the social-democratic parties and has proclaimed its support for the liberation movement in the colonies and semi-colonies. In this era, any revolution in a colony or semi-colony that is directed against imperialism, *i. e.*, against the international bourgeoisie or international capitalism, no longer comes within the old category of the bourgeois-democratic world revolution, but within the new category. It is no longer part of the old bourgeois, or capitalist, world revolution, but is part of the new world revolution, the proletarian-socialist world revolution. Such revolutionary colonies and semi-colonies can no longer be regarded as allies of the counter revolutionary front of world capitalism; they have become allies of the revolutionary front of world socialism.

Although such a revolution in a colonial and semi-colonial country is still fundamentally bourgeois-democratic in its social character during its first stage or first step, and although its objective mission is to clear the path for the development of capitalism, it is no longer a revolution of the old type led by the bourgeoisie with the aim of establishing a capitalist society and a state under bourgeois dictatorship. It belongs to the new type of revolution led by the proletariat with the aim, in the first stage, of establishing a new-democratic society and a state under the joint dictatorship of all the revolutionary classes. Thus this revolution actually serves the purpose of clearing a still wider path for the development of socialism. In the course of its progress, there may be a number of further sub-stages, because of changes on the enemy's side and within the ranks of our allies, but the fundamental character of the revolution remains unchanged.

Such a revolution attacks imperialism at its very roots, and is therefore not tolerated but opposed by imperialism. However, it is favoured by socialism and supported by the land of socialism and the socialist international proletariat.

Therefore, such a revolution inevitably becomes part of the proletarian-socialist world revolution.

The correct thesis that "the Chinese revolution is part of the world revolution" was put forward as early as 1924-27 during the period of China's First Great Revolution. It was put forward by the Chinese Communists and endorsed by all those taking part in the anti-imperialist and anti-feudal struggle of the time. However, the significance of this thesis was not fully expounded in those days, and consequently it was only vaguely understood.

The "world revolution" no longer refers to the old world revolution, for the old bourgeois world revolution has long been a thing of the past, it refers to the new world revolution, the socialist world revolution. Similarly, to form "part of" means to form part not of the old bourgeois but of the new socialist revolution. This is a tremendous change unparalleled in the history of China and of the world.

This correct thesis advanced by the Chinese Communists is based on Stalin's theory.

As early as 1918, in an article commemorating the first anniversary of the October Revolution, Stalin wrote:

The great world-wide significance of the October Revolution chiefly consists in the fact that:

1) It has widened the scope of the national question and converted it from the particular question of combating national oppression in Europe into the general question of emancipating the oppressed peoples, colonies and semi-colonies from imperialism;

2) It has opened up wide possibilities for their emancipation and the right paths towards it, has thereby greatly facilitated the cause of the emancipation of the oppressed peoples of the West and the East, and has drawn them into the common current of the victorious struggle against imperialism;

3) *It has thereby erected a bridge between the socialist West and the enslaved East,* having created a new front of revolutions *against* world imperialism, extending from the proletarians of the West, through the Russian Revolution, to the oppressed peoples of the East. [++]

Since writing this article, Stalin has again and again expounded the theory that revolutions in the colonies and semi-colonies have broken away from the old category and become part of the proletarian-socialist revolution. The clearest and most precise explanation is given in an article published on June 3o, 1925, in which Stalin carried on a controversy with the Yugoslav nationalists of the time. Entitled "The National Question Once Again", it is included in a book translated by Chang Chung-shih and published under the title *Stalin on the National Question.* It contains the following passage:

Semich refers to a passage in Stalin's pamphlet *Marxism and the National Question,* written at the end of 1912. There it says that "the national struggle under the conditions of *rising* capitalism is a struggle of the bourgeois classes among themselves". Evidently, by this Semich is trying to suggest that his formula defining the social significance of the national movement under the present historical conditions is correct. But Stalin's pamphlet was written before the imperialist war, when the national question was not yet regarded by Marxists as a question of world significance, when the Marxists' fundamental demand for the right to self-determination was regarded not as part of the proletarian revolution, but as part of the bourgeois-democratic revolution. It would be ridiculous not to see that since then the international situation has radically changed, that the war, on the one hand, and the October Revolution in Russia, on the other, transformed the national question from a part of the bourgeois-democratic revolution into a part of the proletarian-socialist revolution. As far back as October 1916, in his article, "The

Discussion on Self-Determination Summed Up", Lenin said that the main point of the national question, the right to self-determination, had ceased to be a part of the general democratic movement, that it had already become a component part of the general proletarian, socialist revolution. I do not even mention subsequent works on the national question by Lenin and by other representatives of Russian communism. After all this, what significance can Semich's reference to the passage in Stalin's pamphlet, written in the period of the *bourgeois*-democratic revolution in Russia, have at the present time, when, as a consequence of the new historical situation, we have entered a new epoch, the epoch of *proletarian* revolution? It can only signify that Semich quotes outside of space and time, without reference to the living historical situation, and thereby violates the most elementary requirements of dialectics, and ignores the fact that what is right for one historical situation may prove to be wrong in another historical situation. [+++]

From this it can be seen that there are two kinds of world revolution, the first belonging to the bourgeois or capitalist category. The era of this kind of world revolution is long past, having come to an end as far back as 1914 when the first imperialist world war broke out, and more particularly in 1917 when the October Revolution took place. The second kind, namely, the proletarian-socialist world revolution, thereupon began. This revolution has the proletariat of the capitalist countries as its main force and the oppressed peoples of the colonies and semi-colonies as its allies. No matter what classes, parties or individuals in an oppressed nation join the revolution, and no matter whether they themselves are conscious of the point or understand it, so long as they oppose imperialism, their revolution becomes part of the proletarian-socialist world revolution and they become its allies.

Today, the Chinese revolution has taken on still greater significance. This is a time when the economic and political crises of capitalism are dragging the world more and more deeply into the Second World War, when the Soviet Union has reached the period of transition from socialism to communism and is capable of leading and helping the proletariat and oppressed nations of the whole world in their fight against imperialist war and capitalist reaction, when the proletariat of the capitalist countries is preparing to overthrow capitalism and establish socialism, and when the proletariat, the peasantry, the intelligentsia and other sections of the petty bourgeoisie in China have become a mighty independent political force under the leadership of the Chinese Communist Party. Situated as we are in this day and age, should we not make the appraisal that the Chinese revolution has taken on still greater world significance? I think we should. The Chinese revolution has become a very important part of the world revolution.

Although the Chinese revolution in this first stage (with its many sub-stages) is a new type of bourgeois-democratic revolution and is not yet itself a proletarian-socialist revolution in its social character, it has long become a part of the proletarian-socialist world revolution and is now even a very important part and a great ally of this world revolution. The first step or stage in our revolution is definitely not, and cannot be, the establishment of a capitalist society under the dictatorship of the Chinese bourgeoisie, but will result in the establishment of a new-democratic society under the joint dictatorship of all the revolutionary classes of China headed by the Chinese proletariat The revolution will then be carried forward to the second stage, in which a socialist society will be established in China.

This is the fundamental characteristic of the Chinese revolution of today, of the new revolutionary process of the past twenty years (counting from the May 4th Movement of 1919), and its concrete living essence.

NOTES

* Chinese Culture was a magazine founded in January 1940 in Yenan; the present article appeared in the first number.

** See V. I. Lenin, "Once Again on the Trade Unions, the Present Situation and the Mistakes of Trotsky and Bukharin", Selected Works, Eng. ed. , International Publishers, New York, 1943, Vol. IX, p. S4.

*** Karl Marx, "Preface to A Contribution to the Critique of Political Economy", Selected Works of Marx and Engels, Eng. ed. , FLPH, Moscow, 1958, Vol. I, p. 363.

+ Karl Marx, "Theses on Feuerbach", Selected Works of Marx and Engels, Eng. ed. , FLPH, Moscow, 1958, Vol. II, p. 405.

++ J. V. Stalin, "The October Revolution and the National Question", Works, Eng. ed. , FLPH, Moscow, 1953, Vol. IV, pp. 169–70.

+++ J. V. Stalin, "The National Question Once Again", Works, Eng. ed. , FLPH Moscow, 1954, Vol. VII, pp. 225–27.

SOURCE

The text of this document can be found at:
http://www. etext. org/Politics/MIM/classics/mao/sw2/mswv2_26. html.

# *Quotations from Chairman Mao Tse-Tung (1939–1957)*

*For a short period in the late 1960s the thoughts of Chinese Communist Party Chairman Mao were some of the most intensively-studied ideas in the world. They were intended as a guide for those involved in the Cultural Revolution of 1966–1969. Mao argued that the Chinese Revolution had become rigid and betrayed its basic principles. To reinvigorate it, he invited young people to join the Red Guards and attack "bourgeois" elements in society. Everyone in China was forced to gather in study groups to spend hours discussing every line of his quotations and applying them to their lives.*

## "TO BE ATTACKED BY THE ENEMY IS NOT A BAD THING BUT A GOOD THING," (MAY 26, 1939)

*How does Mao turn criticism into an advantage?*

I hold that it is bad as far as we are concerned if a person, a political party, an army or a school is not attacked by the enemy, for in that case it would definitely mean that we have sunk to the level of the enemy. It is good if we are attacked by the enemy, since it proves that we have drawn a clear line of demarcation between the enemy and ourselves. It is still better if the enemy attacks us wildly and paints us as utterly black and without a single virtue; it demonstrates that we have not only drawn a clear line of demarcation between the enemy and ourselves but achieved a great deal in our work.

## SPEECH AT THE CHINESE COMMUNIST PARTY'S NATIONAL CONFERENCE ON PROPAGANDA WORK (MARCH 12, 1957)

*This passage was used to justify the intensive "reeducation" sessions which tried to bring all Chinese people into line. The final qualifying phrases were usually ignored.*

In our country bourgeois and petty-bourgeois ideology, anti-Marxist ideology, will continue to exist for a long time. Basically, the socialist system has been established in our country. We have won the basic victory in transforming the ownership of the means of production, but we have not yet won complete victory on the political and ideological fronts. In the ideological field, the question of who will win in the struggle between the proletariat and the bourgeoisie has not been really settled yet. We still have to wage a protracted struggle against bourgeois and petty-bourgeois ideology. It is wrong not to understand this and to give up ideological struggle. All erroneous ideas, all poisonous weeds, all ghosts and monsters, must be subjected to criticism; in no circumstance should they be allowed to spread unchecked. However, the criticism should be fully reasoned, analytical and convincing, and not rough, bureaucratic, metaphysical or dogmatic.

## "ON THE PEOPLE'S DEMOCRATIC DICTATORSHIP" (JUNE 30, 1949)

*The ultimate goal of Marxists was not unlike that of anarchists: the complete abolition of state power and the establishment of direct democracy among the people. However both Marx and Lenin* had argued that a period of transition called *"socialism" was necessary, in which the state would organize the conditions necessary for its own abolition. But the only Communist states which abolished themselves, like that of the Soviet Union, did so in order to transform themselves into conventional states.*

*What reasons does Mao give for not abolishing state power right away? (This speech was given immediately after the triumph of the Communists.)*

"Don't you want to abolish state power?" Yes, we do, but not right now; we cannot do it yet. Why? Because imperialism still exists, because domestic reaction still exists, because classes still exist in our country. Our present task is to strengthen the people's state apparatus—mainly the people's army, the people's police and the people's courts—in order to consolidate national defense and protect the people's interests.

### "PROBLEMS OF WAR AND STRATEGY" (NOVEMBER 6, 1938)

*In its original context this saying meant that the Communists would never be allowed to come to power in China without a successful violent revolution. In the context of the Cultural Revolution it meant that the Chinese People's Army had to play a leading role in sustaining, purifying, and spreading Communism. And abroad it was often used to justify revolutionary terrorism.*

Every Communist must grasp the truth, "Political power grows out of the barrel of a gun."

### SPEECH AT THE MOSCOW MEETING OF COMMUNIST AND WORKERS' PARTIES (NOVEMBER 18, 1957)

*Mao was widely ridiculed abroad for stating that the U.S. and its nuclear arsenal were "paper tigers." Many supposed that Mao would have willingly plunged the world into a nuclear war out of sheer ignorance. But it seems more probable that, lacking such arms himself, he used his most power-*

*ful weapon: the bluff. The bomb was not a very effective tool of diplomacy because the threat it posed was only as credible as the willingness of any nation to plunge the world into a holocaust, very probably destroying itself in the process. Mao had every reason to let the world think he was not afraid of the bomb no matter what his private thoughts might have been.*

I have said that all the reputedly powerful reactionaries are merely paper tigers. The reason is that they are divorced from the people. Look! Was not Hitler a paper tiger? Was Hitler not overthrown? I also said that the tsar of Russia, the emperor of China and Japanese imperialism were all paper tigers. As we know, they were all overthrown. U. S. imperialism has not yet been overthrown and it has the atom bomb. I believe it also will be overthrown. It, too, is a paper tiger.

### "SOME QUESTIONS CONCERNING METHODS OF LEADERSHIP" (JUNE 1, 1943)

*This is the core of the ideology that made the Cultural Revolution so appealing to many young idealists; but in the end learning from the people turned out to mean learning only from Chairman Mao and his allies.*

In all the practical work of our Party, all correct leadership is necessarily "from the masses, to the masses." This means: take the ideas of the masses (scattered and unsystematic ideas) and concentrate them (through study turn them into concentrated and systematic ideas), then go to the masses and propagate and explain these ideas until the masses embrace them as their own, hold fast to them and translate them into action, and test the correctness of these ideas in such action. Then once again concentrate ideas from the masses and once again go the masses so that the ideas are persevered in and carried through. And so on, over and over again in an endless spiral, with the ideas becoming more correct, more vital and richer each time. Such is the Marxist theory of knowledge.

**INTRODUCTORY NOTE TO "WOMEN HAVE GONE TO THE LABOR FRONT" (1955)**

*Women had been oppressed in China as much as anywhere on earth, and Mao often spoke of the important role they would play in building Communism. Many concrete advances were made for women; however, except for his wife Jian Qing, who was very influential during the Cultural Revolution, women were generally relegated to subordinate positions in the party leadership.*

In order to build a great socialist society, it is of the utmost importance to arouse the broad masses of women to join in productive activity. Men and women must receive equal pay for equal work in production. Genuine equality between the sexes can only be realized in the process of the socialist transformation of society as a whole.

**ON THE CORRECT HANDLING OF CONTRADICTIONS AMONG THE PEOPLE (FEBRUARY 27, 1957)**

*Of all the quotations in the "Little Red Book" none is more inspiring or chilling than this. It comes from a brief period of reform in the fifties known as the "Hundred Flowers Campaign" during which Mao encouraged complete freedom of thought, including criticism of the Party. The result was much more vigorous debate than Mao had expected and the period ended with an abrupt crackdown against those who had raised their voices in opposition. It could stand as a critique of the failures of the Cultural Revolution itself, which tried to settle ideological questions by force under the guise of debate.*

Letting a hundred flowers blossom and a hundred schools of thought contend is the policy for promoting the progress of the arts and the sciences and a flourishing socialist culture in our land. Different forms and styles in art should develop freely and contend freely. We think that it is harmful to the growth of art and science if administrative measures are used to impose one particular style of art or school of thought and to ban another. Questions of right and wrong in the arts and sciences should be settled through free discussion in artistic and scientific circles and through practical work in these fields. They should not be settled in summary fashion.

**SOURCE**

The text of this document can be found at:
http://www.wsu.edu/~wldciv/world_civ_reader/world_civ_reader_2/mao.html.

# The Speeches of Ayatollah Khomeini

*Ayatollah Khomeini's speeches talked of his overthrow of the previous government, of the important role of the military in governing the people, and of the need for revolt in the case of foreign intervention in Iran.*

**CHAPTER ONE: 1ST SPEECH.**

"I must tell you that Mohammad Reza Pahlavi, that evil traitor, has gone. He fled and plundered everything. He destroyed our country and filled our cemeteries. He ruined our country's economy. Even the projects he carried out in the name of progress, pushed the country towards decadence. He suppressed our culture, annihilated people and destroyed all our manpower resources. We are saying this man, his government, his Majlis are all illegal. If they were to continue to stay in power, we would treat them as criminals and would try them as criminals. I shall appoint my own government. I shall slap this government in the mouth. I shall determine the government with the backing of this nation, because this nation accepts me."

**CHAPTER TWO: 1ST SPEECH.**

"This government represents a regime, whose leader and his father were illegally in power. This government is therefore illegal. The deputies appointed to work in the Majlis are there illegally. The Majlis itself and the Senate are illegal. How can anyone appointed by the Shah be legal? We are telling all of them that they are illegal and they should go. We hereby announce that this government, which has presented itself as a legal government is in fact illegal. Even the members of this government before accepting to be ministers, were considering the whole establishment to be illegal. What has happened now, that they are claiming to be legitimate?

This gentleman, Dr Bakhtiar, does not accept himself, and his friends do not accept him either. The nation does not accept him and the army does not accept him. Only America is backing him and has ordered the army to support him. Britain has backed him too and had said that he must be supported. If one were to search among the nation, one would not find a single person among all strata of the nation, who accepts this man, but he is saying that one country cannot have two governments. Well of course, it is clear that this country does not have two governments and in any case, the illegal government should go. You are illegal. The government of our choice relies on the nation's backing and enjoys the backing of God. If you claim that your government is legal, you must necessarily be denying God and the will of the nation. Someone must put this man in his place."

**CHAPTER THREE: 1ST SPEECH.**

"We want our army to be independent. You army commanders, you generals and major generals, do you not wish to be independent? What is our reward for saying that we would like our army to be independent? Is it right to punish us by killing our young men in the street just because we wish you to be your own master rather than taking orders from foreign powers? At this point I would like to thank those units of the army, which have joined the ranks of the nation. We praise the NCOs, the air force, and officers of the air force, who are already with us and call upon the rest of you to join. Abandon your foreign masters and do not fear that if you abandon them , we will come and hang you. Such rumours are spread by your enemies. Can you not see your other comrades, the officers, the NCOs and the pilots, who have joined us? We love them, we respect them and we want to keep our strong army intact. We want to have a powerful country. We want to preserve the structure of the army, but for the service of the nation."

**CHAPTER FOUR: 1ST SPEECH.**

"Now that the armed forces have stepped back, have declared their neutrality in the face of political affairs and have expressed support for the nation, the dear and courageous nation is expected to maintain law and order when the troops return to barracks. You should stop saboteurs, who may try to create catastrophe and instruct them of their religious and humanitarian obligations. Do not allow anyone to attack foreign embassies. If, God forbid, the army were to enter the arena again, you must defend yourselves with all your might. I hereby inform senior army officers that if they were to stop the army's aggression, and instruct them to join the nation and its legal Islamic government, we would regard the army as part of the nation and vice versa.

---

### SOURCE

The text of this document can be found at:
http://www. bbc. co. uk/persian/revolution/khomeini. shtml.

# INDEX

## PICTURE CREDITS

page:

xiv: Courtesy Lena Kozlova-Pates
4: Library of Congress, LC-USZC4-7647
8: © Getty Images
12: Library of Congress, LC-USZC4-2542
16: © Getty Images
21: © Bettmann/CORBIS
28: © Wally McNamee/CORBIS
36: © CORBIS
48: © Getty Images
54: © Getty Images
61: © Getty Images
62: Library of Congress
66: Library of Congress, LC-USZ62-17110
70: © Peter Lamb
74: Library of Congress, LC-USZ62-10599
76: Library of Congress
81: Library of Congress, LC-USZC2-3156
84: © Peter Lamb
94: © Bettmann/CORBIS
98: © Peter Lamb
101: © Getty Images
109: © Bettmann/CORBIS
112: © Ali Meyer/CORBIS
114: © Peter Lamb
119: © Getty Images
131: © Leonard de Selva/CORBIS
144: © Getty Images
150: © Peter Lamb
152: © Getty Images
161: Library of Congress, LC-DIG-ppmsca-02334
178: © Getty Images

180: © Peter Lamb
188: Library of Congress, LC-USZ62-98851
194: © Getty Images
205: © Bettmann/CORBIS
212: © Bettmann/CORBIS
219: © Bettmann/CORBIS
224: © Peter Lamb
235: © Peter Lamb
242: © Bettmann/CORBIS
249: © Getty Images
258: © Peter Lamb
264: © Getty Images
267: © Hulton-Deutsch Collection/CORBIS
270: © CORBIS
276: Library of Congress, LC-USW33-019081-C
280: © Peter Lamb
291: © Bettmann/CORBIS
298: Library of Congress
300: Associated Press
305: © Peter Lamb
312: © Getty Images
328: © Bettmann/CORBIS
338: © Peter Lamb
350: © Getty Images
355: © Bettmann/CORBIS
356: © Bettmann/CORBIS
368: © SETBOUN/CORBIS
378: © Getty Images
391: Associated Press, AP
394: Associated Press, AP/Leslie Mazoch
400: Associated Press, AP/Jaime Puebla

Frontis  © Gianni Dagli Orti/CORBIS
Cover:  Associated Press

## ABOUT THE AUTHORS

**Tim McNeese** is an associate professor of history at York College in York, Nebraska, where he has been teaching for 13 years. Professor McNeese earned an Associate of Arts degree from York College, a Bachelor of Arts degree in history and political science from Harding University, and a Master of Arts degree from Southwest Missouri State University.

McNeese has published more than 70 books and a variety of other educational materials over the past 20 years. He has written on a wide range of topics for elementary, middle school, and high school readers. He has been an author and series consulting editor on several Chelsea House series. His work has earned him a citation in *Something About the Author*, a library reference work. Readers are encouraged to contact Professor McNeese at *tdmcneese@york.edu.*

**Samuel Willard Crompton** lives in the Berkshire Hills of western Massachusetts. Professor Crompton teaches American history and Western civilization at Holyoke Community College. He is a major contributor to *American National Biography*, published in 1999 by Oxford University Press. He has written a number of other books for Chelsea House on topics ranging from religious figures to modern and ancient world leaders.

## American Revolution

**1765** Parliament passes the revenue-generating Stamp Act

**1766** Parliament repeals the Stamp Act in March, after months of colonial protest

**1767** Parliament passes the Townshend Duties on listed trade items, including tea

**1770** Rioting in Boston results in "The Boston Massacre"

**1773** The "Boston Tea Party"

**1774** Twelve colonies send 56 delegates to the First Continental Congress.

**1775** British and American troops fire on one another at Lexington and Concord

**1776** Congress votes to accept the Declaration of Independence

**1781** Washington defeats Gener army near Yorktown

**1765····1781**

## eteenth-Century olutions

**1814–1815** Congress of Vienna reestablishes traditional power following Napoleon

**1821–1827** Greeks revolt against the Ottoman Empire

**1830** French king Louis XVIII establishes the "July Ordinances" independence

**1832** Great Reform Bill passed in Great Britain

**1833** The word *socialist* is first coined

**1838–1839** Chartist reform movement takes Britain

*lism* is created

June Days"

1848

O circ

10/31/06

— 1750

1850 —

## French Revolution

meet at Versailles

**June 17** Third Estate forms the National Assembly

**July 14** Riots across Paris target the Bastille

**August 4–5** National Assembly enacts sweeping changes, including end to serfdom

**August 26** National Assembly adopts Declaration of the Rights of Man

**October 5–6** "March of the Women to Versailles"

**1792 January 21** King Louis is executed on the guillotine

**October 16** Marie Antoinette is condemned and executed by guillotine

**1793 Summer–Summer 1794** Reign of Terror results in the executions of 40,000

**1794 July 26–27** Robespierre is executed on the guillotine